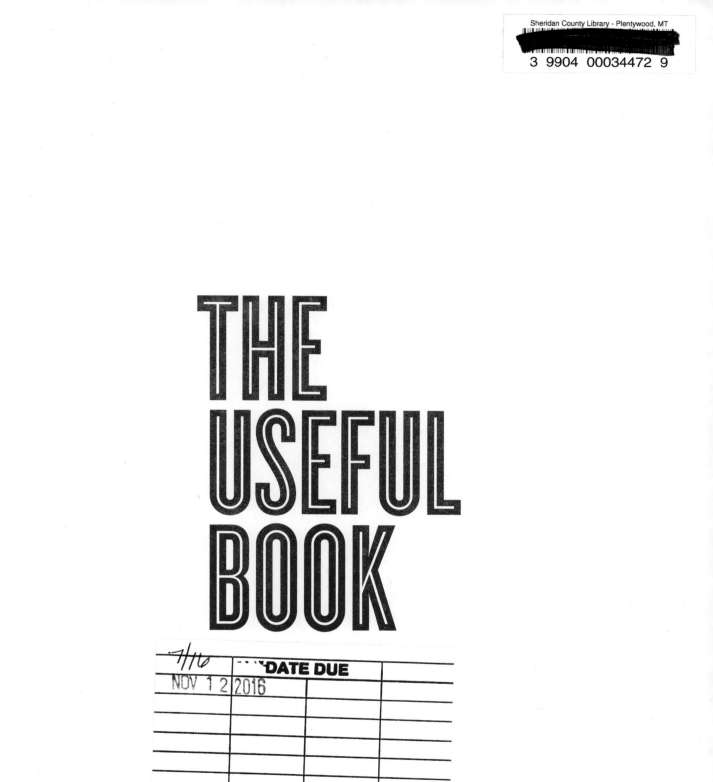

# THE USEFUL BOOK

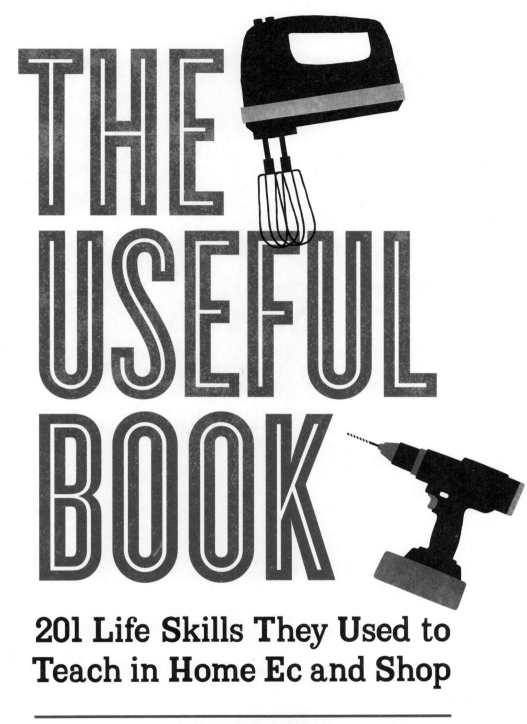

# THE USEFUL BOOK

## 201 Life Skills They Used to Teach in Home Ec and Shop

**SHARON AND DAVID BOWERS**

Illustrated by Sophia Nicolay

**WORKMAN PUBLISHING | NEW YORK**

# FOR HUGH AND PEARSE

Library of Congress Cataloging-in-Publication Data is available.

ISBN 978-0-7611-7173-7

Design by Ariana Abud
Cover design by John Passineau

Workman books are available at special discounts when purchased in bulk for premiums and sales promotions as well as for fund-raising or educational use. Special editions or book excerpts can also be created to specification. For details, contact the special sales director at the address below or send an email to specialmarkets@workman.com.

Workman Publishing Co., Inc.
225 Varick Street
New York, NY 10014-4381
workman.com

WORKMAN is a registered trademark of Workman Publishing Co., Inc.

Printed in the United States of America

First printing May 2016

10 9 8 7 6 5 4 3 2 1

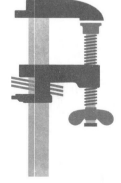

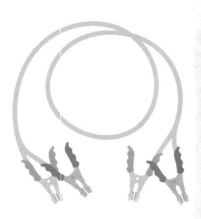

# ACKNOWLEDGMENTS

There's no way that this book would have emerged as actually "useful" without the help of a whole lot of people!

Above all, warmest thanks to Lynn Cohen on the *Home Ec* side and Garth Sundem in *Shop* for making it all possible. Without your incredibly talented and brilliant help, coming as it did at a difficult time, this book would simply never have been completed. The words "thank you" do not even begin to express our sincere gratitude for all your hard work and kindness.

To Jennifer Griffin and Angela Miller, endless thanks for your calm and steady guiding hands, and all the backup, pickup, and support along the way.

Any author who's been published by Workman knows what a pleasure and a privilege it is to work with this houseful of consummate professionals. "Team Useful" was most ably captained by the terrific Megan Nicolay, and the MVP is Liz Davis! Thanks to both of you for your patience and attention to detail and smart fixes—it was all noticed and much appreciated throughout the process. This book stemmed from a great idea by Raquel Jaramillo, and while it has undergone some changes since then, it is at its core much the same as the original concept, and we're proud to be part of it. Special thanks also to Jane Treuhaft, Ariana Abud, Kate Karol, Claire McKean, Annie O'Donnell, Barbara Peragine, Califia Suntree, Janet Vicario, Jen Keenan, James Williamson, and everyone else who influenced this book along the way. And finally, the lovely illustrations by Sophia Nicolay made the whole thing spring to life—many thanks for making it all clear.

# CONTENTS

# HOME EC

## COOKING | 2

**Learning how
to feed yourself
starts here**

## SEWING | 111

**Simple tasks like sewing a
button are impressive when
done the right way**

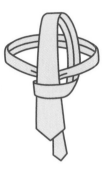

# LIFE SKILLS
# 191

**A few grace notes for the finishing touches of pleasant living**

# DOMESTIC ARTS
# 172

**The life-changing magic of keeping a clean home**

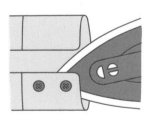

# LAUNDRY & CLOTHING
# 149

**From laundry labels to shrunken sweater care**

# SHOP

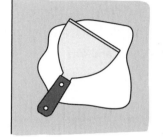

## DOMESTIC REPAIR
## 214

**Your home tool kit and how to use it**

## WOODWORKING & METALWORKING
## 273

**The fine art of measuring, cutting, soldering, and making with your hands**

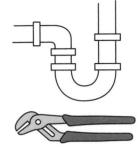

# PLUMBING
# 317

Learn to unplug, seal up, and troubleshoot to make all your "pipe dreams" come true.

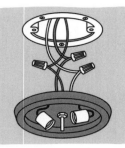

# ELECTRICAL
# 343

Wires, circuits, fixtures, and switches

# MECHANICAL
# 361

Keep those wheels and gears turning

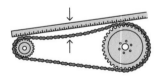

# INTRODUCTION

Remember when computers were going to make offices "paperless"? Around that same time, the powers that be decided America would henceforth specialize in producing "information workers." Nobody would need to dirty their hands with machinery and grease when *technology* was the name of the game. What's more, fast food was cheaper than ever, so presumably we'd all just order takeout while sitting in our cubicles working diligently at our computers. Throughout the 1990s, school systems, faced with budget cuts and with an eye on this promised future, dismissed their home ec teachers and dismantled wood and metal shops. (Shouldn't someone have checked first to see how paperless our offices became? Mine sure isn't!)

Of course, life (even in the twenty-first century) is not a sci-fi movie. Even in space, someone's got to fix a busted rover and feed hungry astronauts! That careless eradication of classes that taught essential how-tos and shared practical knowledge has had serious consequences: a whole generation of people who never learned to cook, do basic mending, or change the oil in their cars. They can't fix a broken hinge on their own front doors or stop a toilet from leaking. They don't know how to bake cookies or iron their shirts or figure out why their brakes are squeaking. If a lamp breaks, they're more inclined to throw it in the trash than to rewire it. Encouraged by cheap imports and our utter lack of know-how, we've accelerated our "disposable" culture into something that's plainly unsustainable.

Becoming more self-sufficient is not only easier than many people imagine, it's also extremely satisfying. Work that you do with your own hands is work held to a single standard: Did I fix it? And if the answer is yes, you're finished. It's a feeling of accomplishment that a day spent poring over spreadsheets can't approach. By the same token, a delicious homemade meal—made with attention and care and not ordered from a drive-through or reheated from a box—is well within the reach of anyone who takes a few minutes to learn the kitchen basics.

Whether you aspire to brew the perfect cup of coffee, make fluffy scrambled eggs, hem your own pants, or change the oil in your car, those skills are now literally within your grasp. Read on, then get busy!

# HOME EC

# COOKING

**A**re you going to spend the rest of your life calling for takeout when you're hungry? The fascinating little secret about being able to cook is being able to make what you want, and make it taste the way you want it to, at any time you like. The other interesting thing to know is that it's not that hard. Learn some basics and pretty soon you can improvise like a pro.

# DRY, CANNED, FRESH, FROZEN...
# A FULL PANTRY

## IN THE PANTRY

Baking powder

Baking soda

Bouillon cubes (beef, chicken, vegetable)

Bread

Canned beans (black, cannellini, kidney, pinto)

Canned tomatoes

Canned soups

Chocolate chips

Cocoa

Coffee

Cooking oil

Cornmeal

Cornstarch

Flour

Honey

Hot sauce

Nuts

Olive oil

Pasta

Peanut butter

Raisins

Rice

Rolled oats

Soy sauce

Spices and dried herbs

Sugar (brown and white)

Tea

Tomato paste

Tuna

Vanilla extract

Vinegar

Worcestershire sauce

## IN THE REFRIGERATOR

Butter or margarine

Cheeses

Cottage or ricotta cheese

Cucumber

Eggs

Fresh herbs (basil, parsley, rosemary)

Jam or jelly

Ketchup

Lettuce

Mayonnaise

Mustard

Orange (or other fruit) juice

Plain yogurt

Sour cream

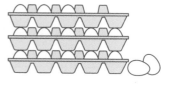

## IN THE VEGETABLE BASKET & IN THE FRUIT BOWL

Apples

Bananas

Cabbage

Carrots

Celery

Garlic

Ginger

Grapefruit

Jam or jelly

Lemons

Onions

Oranges

Potatoes

Sweet Potatoes

## IN THE FREEZER

Bread

Chicken breasts and fillets

Fish fillets

Frozen vegetables (corn, peas, spinach)

Hamburger (in 1 or ½ pound packs)

Ice

Steak or pork chops

# COOKING TOOL KIT

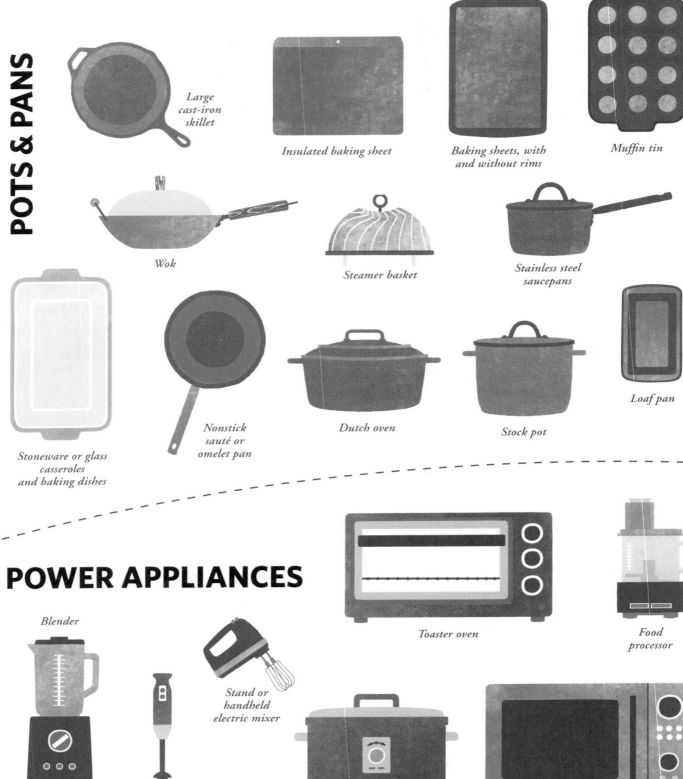

## POTS & PANS

Large cast-iron skillet

Insulated baking sheet

Baking sheets, with and without rims

Muffin tin

Wok

Steamer basket

Stainless steel saucepans

Stoneware or glass casseroles and baking dishes

Nonstick sauté or omelet pan

Dutch oven

Stock pot

Loaf pan

## POWER APPLIANCES

Blender

Stand or handheld electric mixer

Toaster oven

Food processor

Hand or stick blender

Slow cooker

Microwave

# KNIVES & UTENSILS

Pastry brush

Corkscrew

Vegetable peeler

Garlic press

Slotted spoon

Large chef's knife

Midsize utility knife

Paring knife

Serrated bread knife

Meat cleaver

Kitchen shears

Grater

Small grater/ zester for citrus, nutmeg, or Parmesan (Microplane)

Potato masher

Standard spatula

Can opener

Whisk

Ladle

Extra-large serving spoons

Wooden spoons

Rubber or silicone spatula

Frosting spatula

Tongs

## MISC. EQUIPMENT

Measuring cup

Plastic cutting board

Wooden cutting board

Salad spinner

Magnetic knife rack

Salt and pepper mills

Cup and spoon measures

Colander

Large and small mixing bowls

Juicer

# #1
# HOW TO BOIL WATER
## (The First Step to Cooking at Home)

There are fancier culinary techniques, but I can't think of many foods that can't be cooked in (or over) a pot of boiling water. Simple, straightforward, accessible. If you're ever stumped about what to make for a meal, put a pot of water on the stove, open your refrigerator and pantry, and start grabbing what looks good. Within minutes, you could be heading down the road toward chicken salad, spaghetti and meatballs, vegetable soup, or deviled eggs.

**1 PICK YOUR POT.** Always use one bigger than you think you'll need in order to accommodate the displacement of the water by the food you'll be adding. (If you bring your water to a boil and then add, say, a bunch of potatoes, once the water reaches the boiling point again, it'll spill over onto your stovetop.)

**2 FILL YOUR POT WITH COLD** water. (But don't fill it all the way to the top!) It feels counterintuitive to use cold water, but hot water has been sitting in your taps longer, possibly pulling unwanted residue from your pipes.

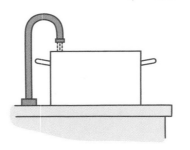

**3 PUT THE POT ON A BURNER SET** to high heat. You can always reduce the heat later if you are after a simmer or a gentle poach.

**4 COVER YOUR POT WITH A** close-fitting lid. This prevents steam from escaping and speeds up the process.

ⵝ ⵝ ⵝ ⵝ ⵝ ⵝ ⵝ ⵝ ⵝ ⵝ ⵝ ⵝ ⵝ ⵝ ⵝ ⵝ

## TRY AN ELECTRIC KETTLE

The fastest and *most* efficient way to boil water is in an electric kettle, which can bring two quarts to 212 degrees Fahrenheit in less than two minutes. It's an inexpensive gadget that can make your life a lot easier. Boil the kettle, pour it in the pot, and speed up dinner.

## What's the Point?

The boiling point is the temperature at which a liquid becomes a gas. Water's boiling point is 212 degrees Fahrenheit (100 degrees Celsius) at sea level. A higher elevation will change the equation: The lower the air pressure (that is, at higher altitudes), the easier it is for water molecules to push out of their liquid prison. In a nutshell, water will boil at the top of a mountain at 185 degrees Fahrenheit. That means, if you're trying to boil an egg, you'll have to leave it in the pot longer. So cooking times will vary from Albuquerque to Aspen, and if your dish must reach a specific temperature to be safe to eat, it's smart to have an instant-read thermometer at the ready.

## Top Ten Reasons to Cook

To nourish your body, mind, and soul, nothing beats the fruits of your own labor, in your own kitchen. Here are ten reasons why:

**1. It's cheaper.** Dining out means paying a mark-up on your meals to cover the restaurant's operating costs, plus tipping the staff (not to mention the cost of getting there and back). If you outline your menus in advance, stock your pantry, use coupons, buy in bulk, and prepare batches to freeze, you can really stretch your food dollar.

**2. It's healthier.** American restaurants often plate portions that are 30 to 50 percent larger than the recommended size. And diners often view meals out as a splurge or treat, which can translate to fried food, dishes drenched in melted cheese, or big hunks of red meat, as well as sugary drinks and desserts. In short, lots of what's bad for you. At home, you control the freshness (therefore peak nutritional content) of foods, as well as choose the fat, salt, and sugar content of sauces and condiments. Plating your own food gives you control over portion sizes and helps prevent unwanted weight gain.

*Recommended portion*

*Restaurant portion*

## WORTH YOUR SALT?

**A**dding anything to water—salt included—elevates its boiling point, increasing the time it takes the water to bubble. The difference in temperature between unsalted and salted water—based on a ratio of 1 teaspoon of salt per quart of water—is 1 or 2 degrees Fahrenheit, a difference that can matter for foods that cook quickly and in recipes that require precision. (The same principle applies to so-called hard water, which has a high mineral content.)

Some recipes call for salt in the water because it makes for a hotter boil, which cooks foods faster and more thoroughly. Mostly, though, salting simply adds flavor. For pasta, you'll want to salt the water in the cooking pot just as it comes to a boil. The salt dissolves in the water, and the pasta absorbs some of it as it cooks, so it gets salted from the inside out. If you salt already cooked pasta, it can't permeate the toothsome noodles. For a 4-quart pot, add about 1 tablespoon of salt to the water.

**3. You get what you want.** Hate mushrooms? Don't put them in the sauce. Love black pepper? Grind away without the embarrassment of having to signal for more . . . more . . . just a little more. If you're gluten free, you don't have to wonder if the chef *really* used rice flour in that batter—because *you're* the chef.

**4. It saves you time.** By the time you decide on a restaurant, walk or drive yourself there, wait for your food, and eat it or bring it home and serve it, you could have easily made a salad, omelet, pasta dish, burger, or stir-fry from scratch. If you've cooked ahead and stored individual portions, it takes just a quick reheat and some garnishing before you are ready to sit down to a wholesome meal in a matter of minutes.

**5. You can balance your diet.** At home, you're not limited to "one from column A and one from column B." By serving yourself appropriate combinations of foods from the Food and Drug Administration's recommended guidelines—once a pyramid, now a plate—you can ensure you are getting the proper daily balance of fat, protein, carbohydrates, and fiber.

6. **You're less likely to get food poisoning.** The Centers for Disease Control and Prevention estimate that about 75 million people per year in the United States experience food poisoning. Food-borne pathogens such as bacteria, viruses, and parasites can sicken or even kill. Improper cooking temperatures, cross-contamination between raw and cooked foods, and poor sanitation are risk factors. At home, you can control cooking temperatures, sanitize surfaces and hands, and properly wash raw produce—steps often overlooked or skipped by inexperienced or rushed employees in fast-food kitchens.

7. **It promotes friendship and family.** Planning meals, cooking side by side, laying the table with special touches, and relaxing over good food and conversation bond people together. For humans, eating means survival. Sharing food is like a primal signal for "I've got your back."

8. **Practice makes perfect.** Or at the very least, practice assures progress. If you think you can't cook, there's no better cure for that than getting in the kitchen. If you start by following step-by-step recipes, with repetition, you'll begin to identify basic techniques such as searing, thickening sauces, and caramelizing vegetables, and they'll become muscle memory. Soon, you'll be able to grab ingredients from the fridge and cook a meal without cracking a book.

9. **It's good for the planet.** Restaurant dining leaves a pretty huge carbon footprint: Driving there requires fuel, sit-down restaurants generate lots of food waste (think of the uneaten breadbaskets that must be dumped), and takeout restaurants require a veritable mountain of wrappers, containers, and disposable cutlery.

10. **It gives you a sense of pride.** Whether it's building bookshelves, knitting a scarf, or preparing a nourishing and delicious dinner, we feel a sense of accomplishment when we create something from nothing and embellish it with unique personal touches.

## A Boil by Any Other Name

**Scald.** A moist-heat cooking technique using liquid or steam to help dissolve solids such as salt, sugar, chocolate, or flour. Think hot cocoa: scalded milk with sugar and cocoa powder dissolved into it.

× × × × × × × × × × × × × × × × × × × × × × × × ×

# NUKE IT! BOILING LIQUIDS IN THE MICROWAVE

**Y**ou can use your microwave to boil, but be extremely cautious of "superheating." This occurs when water heats past the boiling point without forming bubbles to release air, then erupts in a dangerous, scalding volcano. Here are some tips for safer microwaving:

• **Before heating, stir the liquid thoroughly to add air.**

• **Before heating, place a nonmetal object in your bowl or cup to encourage the formation of bubbles. A wooden chopstick works well.**

• **Heat in short stints, carefully stirring at intervals.**

• **Heat in a vessel with an irregular interior. Ridges and bumps offer what scientists call a "nucleation site," serving as a starting point for bubbling.**

**Poach.** The gentlest boil. Use this technique for foods that can fall apart, dry out, or overcook easily. Poaching preserves the flavor of delicate foods. Think fish, eggs (out of the shell), pears, and chicken breasts.

**Blanch.** A French cooking technique whereby you plunge food briefly into rapidly boiling water to cook it but maintain its color and crispness. Think haricots verts (green beans) and asparagus. Also used to loosen the skins on soft fruits such as tomatoes and peaches, so they can be easily slid off.

**Simmer.** Stopping just short of a boil, with liquid cooking at 180 to 205 degrees Fahrenheit so that the flavor isn't cooked away and the amount of liquid isn't reduced. Think stocks and soups.

**Rolling boil.** The most vigorous boil, often called for when a food isn't introduced until the liquid is as hot as possible. Think pasta.

**Reduce, aka "making a reduction."** Used to thicken and intensify the flavor of a liquid by boiling off the water. Often done in a wide, shallow pan with no lid in order to enable evaporation. Think glazes and sauces.

# #2
# HOW TO BOIL AN EGG

Just drop an egg in boiling water, right? Sure, you'll wind up with something technically edible that way, but to avoid pitfalls like funky green yolks and rubbery whites, read on. Just a little care is all that's needed for boiled eggs that are tender, creamy, and fresh tasting.

**1 START WITH COLD EGGS FROM** the refrigerator, and place them in a single layer in a heavy-bottomed saucepan or pot with a tightly fitting lid.

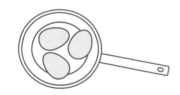

**2 COVER WITH COLD WATER, TO** at least 1 inch above the top of the eggs.

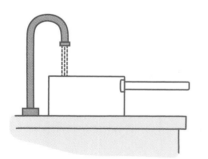

**3 PLACE THE POT OVER MEDIUM** heat, uncovered, and bring to a rolling boil.

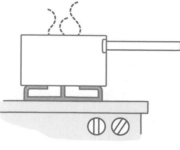

**4 REMOVE THE POT FROM THE** heat, cover it, and let it stand for 12 minutes to hard-boil and 6 minutes to soft-boil.

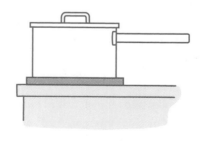

**5 USING A HEATPROOF SLOTTED** spoon, scoop out the eggs and place them in a bowl of ice water. Let stand for 10 minutes.

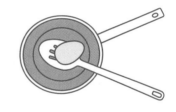

**6 PEEL AND SERVE RIGHT AWAY** (see How to Peel a Boiled Egg, page 10) or refrigerate the unpeeled eggs for up to a week.

**TIP:** If you notice the white seeping out of a cracked egg during boiling, add a little vinegar to the water. This helps the proteins in the egg white coagulate faster, sealing the crack.

# #3 HOW TO PEEL A BOILED EGG

Nothing dampens enthusiasm for this tasty, high-protein snack like the struggle to free it from its natural wrapper. Here's how to peel eggs with ease and keep the whites smooth and even.

**1 START WITH OLDER EGGS.** The higher pH of older eggs strengthens the membrane, making it easier to separate from the white. Eggs less than 3 days old are harder to peel. I like to keep eggs in the fridge for up to 2 weeks before boiling them, for easier peeling. Don't know how old your eggs are? Put them in a bowl of water. If they stand on their ends, they're old enough. (Older eggs have bigger air cells, the concave part at the flat end of a hard-boiled egg.)

**2 BEFORE BOILING YOUR EGGS,** do one of the following: Make a crack or pinhole in the large end of the uncooked eggs. (This allows carbon dioxide to escape.) Add a teaspoon of salt to each quart of egg-boiling water. (When salt permeates the egg, its proteins coagulate and firm up, making the white easier to pull from the shell.)

**3 AFTER REMOVING THE COOKED** eggs from the hot water (see How to Boil an Egg, page 9), gently crack the shells before plunging them into ice water.

**TIP:** You can avoid the peeling issue completely by slicing the whole, boiled egg, shell on, in half with a very sharp knife, then scooping out the good stuff with a fine-edged spoon.

ⵝ ⵝ ⵝ ⵝ ⵝ ⵝ ⵝ ⵝ ⵝ ⵝ ⵝ ⵝ ⵝ ⵝ ⵝ ⵝ ⵝ ⵝ ⵝ ⵝ ⵝ ⵝ ⵝ ⵝ ⵝ ⵝ ⵝ ⵝ ⵝ ⵝ ⵝ ⵝ ⵝ ⵝ ⵝ ⵝ ⵝ

# WHAT TO DO WITH HARD-BOILED EGGS

If a box of eggs has been sitting in your fridge for two to three weeks, hard-boil them all. Not only will they last another week or so, but you can make...

- *Egg Salad:* Dice or mash the whole peeled eggs with a fork and add mayonnaise, salt, pepper, diced celery, chopped scallions, chives, parsley, or any other aromatic that catches your fancy.

- *Deviled Eggs:* Split lengthwise and spoon the yolks into a bowl. Stir in mayo (or a little softened butter) and a bit of mustard or cider vinegar. Add salt and pepper to taste, along with a little hot sauce if desired. Spoon back into the halved whites and top with a dash of paprika or some crumbled bacon or finely sliced scallions.

- *Niçoise Salad:* Crumble them over a green salad, dice and toss into tuna, cube them up and add to your favorite potato salad, or lay slices over a dish of hummus drizzled with olive oil.

## Boiled Eggs: Troubleshooting

*Ick! My yolk is green. Can I still eat it?*
Green yolk is simply a formation of ferrous sulfide where the yolk meets the white. This normal, harmless, chemical reaction occurs when the yolk's iron touches the white's hydrogen sulfide. Yolks and whites cook at different temperatures, and overcooking contributes to this unsightly coloration. To prevent it, start with cold eggs in cold water, and once the eggs are cooked, plunge them into an ice-water bath to stop the cooking process.

*Why are my egg whites rubbery?*
Simply put: overcooking. Egg whites are largely protein, and like meat, when overcooked, they become tough. Start with cold water and cold eggs in order to gently raise the temperature of the whites while ensuring that heat permeates to the center in order to fully cook the yolk.

*All of my boiled eggs are cracked. Help!*
Never stack eggs—cook them in a single layer. This will reduce jostling. Also, as eggs cook, the gases inside them expand, forming hairline cracks and holes in the shell. Bringing an egg to high heat rapidly causes an internal explosion. Start cold and heat gradually.

# #4
# HOW TO CRACK AN EGG

**E**ggs are a basic building block for cooks, with properties that can seem almost magical. They add lift, fluffiness, and silkiness; they serve as a binder (the "glue" in a meatloaf or veggie burger!); and they make for a quick snack or meal at any time of day.

**1** **HOLDING THE EGG IN ONE HAND,** rap it sharply on the side of the bowl you're breaking it into. Always crack with conviction! If you rap hesitantly, you're more likely to get a messy break and egg all over your fingers.

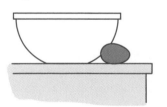

**2** **HOLDING THE EGG WITH BOTH** hands, with the cracked side facing down into the bowl, put the tips of your thumbs into the broken spot and pull.

**3** **WASH YOUR HANDS** with soap when you're done; don't just wipe them on a towel!

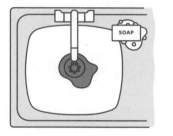

**4** **IF A BIT OF SHELL HAS** dropped into the bowl, use the tip of a spoon or your washed fingertips to pull out any broken bits. (Resist the urge to use one half of the shell to scoop it out—there are bacteria on the outside of the shell.)

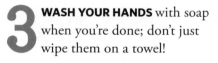

## SKILLET SAVVY

**U**se a cast-iron skillet for cooking nearly everything—except scrambled eggs. It can leave tiny bits of black from the iron pan visible on the eggs' surface; scrambled eggs also adhere so strongly to the pan that they can ruin its finish. An enamel-coated or nonstick skillet will make eggs fluffier and cleanup easier.

## RECIPE: PERFECT SCRAMBLED EGGS

One of the most trusted recipes in your arsenal should be the perfect scramble. The trick is not to touch them too much.

**Serves 2 to 4**

4 large eggs
2 tablespoons unsalted butter
1 tablespoon milk
Salt and freshly ground pepper

**1.** Crack the eggs into a medium-size bowl and discard the shells.

**2.** Put a medium-size (8- or 10-inch) skillet on a burner over medium heat. Place the butter in the pan to melt.

**3.** While the butter melts, use a fork or a whisk to beat the eggs vigorously. If using a fork, hold the tines of the fork parallel to the bottom of the bowl and whip the eggs over and over in a circular motion, to break the yolks and incorporate them into the whites.

**4.** Beat in the milk (it helps make the eggs creamier) and a pinch of salt and pepper. As the butter starts to sizzle, tip the eggs into the pan.

**5.** Use a wooden spoon or a heatproof silicone spatula to turn the eggs over gently as they cook (infrequently, so you're not touching them too much), pulling a track through the eggs as they set so that more uncooked egg touches the pan.

**6.** After a minute or two, when there is still a little runny egg visible, turn the scrambled eggs into a serving bowl or onto plates. The residual heat will continue cooking the eggs so that they're perfect by the time they reach the table.

## The Freshness Test

Eggs can be stored in the refrigerator for several weeks without much quality loss, but the shells are permeable to air. As an egg ages, the white shrinks and an air pocket grows; until, eventually, the egg turns. To tell if an egg is fresh, fill a cup with cold water and set the egg into it. A fresh egg will lie on the bottom of the cup. An older egg, with a larger air pocket will stand on its end.

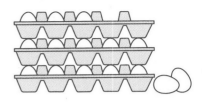

A super-fresh egg is perfect for scrambling. But for poaching or boiling, a slightly older egg is best. When you boil a fresh egg, the white is still closely bound to the shell, so it will also peel off in raggedy chunks; the shell will peel smoothly from an egg that's a week or so old. Similarly, an older egg forms a neater oval shape when poached, without lots of trailing threads of white.

## Size It Up

Eggs at the grocery store are available in a dizzying range of sizes and "grades": small, medium, large, extra-large, jumbo, and AA. The letter grades identify quality, as determined by the USDA; the highest grade is AA. Size is determined by weight per dozen, and most recipes assume you are using large eggs, unless a different size is specifically called for. Any size egg that you have in your refrigerator will work just fine. In small amounts, the volume difference is not so great that it will have a massive impact.

## Organic—Worth the Price?

A certified organic egg comes from a hen that eats organic feed, is grown without pesticides, and is not fed antibiotics. That chicken, however, might live in a "battery" farm, where chickens are subjected to inhumane treatment and exceedingly crowded conditions. The best eggs—in terms of flavor as well as animal welfare—are organic and "free range," meaning the chickens have constant or daily access to the outdoors, to roam freely and peck at insects and plants.

The best eggs are from a farmers' market, where the vendor can probably tell you personally about the chickens' living conditions. In summertime, a farm egg has a deep orange yolk that's particularly thick and rich, and this is the benchmark for the best eggs. In a supermarket, you can't always be sure from the box.

## Are Brown Eggs Better?

Only if you prefer the color. Otherwise, brown eggs and white eggs are eggs-actly the same. They are no more natural or farm-fresh than white eggs; they're just from a breed of chicken that lays brown eggs, just as some birds lay pale green or blue eggs. If you want an egg to taste different, you have to switch birds: Try duck, goose, or quail eggs for a different flavor.

## Red Alert

That red dot on the yolk does *not* mean that the egg was fertilized. It is simply a tiny bit of blood that got into the egg as it formed in the hen. It won't hurt you at all, but it's a little unappetizing. Use the tip of a spoon to dip it out and discard it.

# #5
# HOW TO WHIP CREAM

**W**alk right past those containers of "whipped topping" in the freezer section of the supermarket—they are an unappetizing concoction of sugar, vegetable oils, thickeners, and emulsifiers, often containing no dairy at all—and skip those cans of prewhipped cream, which also contain stabilizers and emulsifiers. All you need is heavy cream (not "whipping cream"), usually sold in ½ pint (8-ounce) containers. One container will yield 1 cup of cream that will whip into 2 cups. For peaky, airy whipped cream, I have just two words for you: cold and fast.

**1** **PUT A LARGE METAL MIXING** bowl and a whisk in the freezer for at least 1 hour before you make your whipped cream.

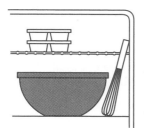

**2** **POUR 1 CUP OF VERY COLD** heavy cream into the bowl. To keep the bowl steady on the counter, dampen a kitchen towel and coil it around the base of the bowl.

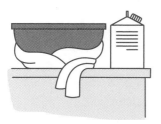

**3** **TIP THE BOWL SLIGHTLY** toward you with one hand and use the whisk in the other hand to beat the cream with broad oval strokes. Don't beat in a small circle, or it will take longer. If you beat in a large circle, you're more likely to splash the cream everywhere.

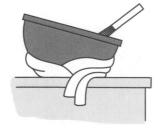

**4** **BEAT THE CREAM UNTIL** soft peaks form, 3 to 5 minutes, depending on room temperature. If you beat past the

soft peak stage, the cream will stiffen perceptibly and may turn into butter.

*Soft Peak*    *Stiff Peak*

**5** **USE THE WHIPPED CREAM** immediately. Store any leftover cream tightly covered in the refrigerator and use within a few days, beating it with a whisk again to reincorporate some air, if needed.

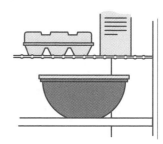

## The Lowdown on Dairy

Discover a day or two later that your milk product has gone off? It may have been because low-fat and nonfat dairy products don't stay fresh nearly as long as their creamier counterparts. Fat retains not only flavor, but also freshness. Understanding the various products offered in the dairy case can help you wisely choose—and use—your milk products.

### Whole, skim, or in between?

Depends on what you need it for. Nutritionists usually recommend whole milk for children to drink until the age of two, then low-fat versions for all ages after that, but lower-fat milks typically have more sugar. In the end, you might be just as well to go with your personal preference.

### What about the creamy stuff?

Half-and-half is a mixture of equal parts heavy cream and whole milk, with a butterfat content of about 15 percent. Light cream ranges from 15 to 30 percent butterfat. Heavy cream can be 36 to 40 percent butterfat. Half-and-half and light cream will not whip, but they're ideal for coffee or cooking, allowing you to add some richness with less fat.

### How much fat is in yogurt? And what makes yogurt "Greek"?

It depends on what you start with. All yogurt can be made with whole or skim milk, or any of the percentages in between. Greek-style yogurt can be nonfat if it's made with skim milk, or it can taste as rich as heavy cream if made with whole milk. That's because the milk is treated with a yogurt culture to slightly sour and thicken it. Greek-style yogurt is strained to remove excess liquid, resulting in a much thicker product. Whatever you prefer, consider buying yogurt without added sweeteners, and then add fruit or sweeten it yourself. Flavored yogurts are far more likely to contain chemical flavors, colors, and stabilizers than plain yogurt, and typically cost more, too.

### Is there butter in buttermilk?

Real buttermilk is the by-product of the butter-making process. When fresh cow's milk, with the cream still in it, is churned, the butterfat separates into a lump of butter, and the remaining liquid is buttermilk. Most of what you find in the supermarket, however, is cultured buttermilk—a low-fat milk that has been treated with a culture to give it the tangy flavor and acidity of real buttermilk.

× × × × × × × × × × × × × × × × × × × × × × × × × × × × × ×

# SWEETENED WHIPPED CREAM

**P**lain whipped cream is ideal for topping sweet and rich desserts. If you prefer sweetened whipped cream, add 2 tablespoons granulated sugar (or more or less to taste) and ½ teaspoon vanilla extract before beating.

### How long will it keep?

Stored in the refrigerator at 38 degrees Fahrenheit, whole milk will easily stay fresh for a week or more, a bit longer than low-fat. Half-and-half or light cream will last longer than whole milk, and heavy cream can sit in your refrigerator for nearly a month with no loss in quality.

The date on the label is the date after which the store must not *sell* the product, in the interest of public health. But if your milk, cream, buttermilk, or yogurt is only a day or two past its date, has been kept at 38 degrees or colder, and, most important, has not been opened, it may still be fresh enough to drink. Opening a container allows oxygen to contact the product, making it degrade more quickly. An unopened carton of milk (particularly whole milk) may still be good a few days past the sell-by date, and yogurt almost always is. Just give it the sniff test: If it smells fine, it's probably fine to drink. But if there's any question, throw it out.

× × × × × × × × × × × × × × × × × × × × × × × × × × × × × ×

# SWEET OR SALTY?

**M**ost cooks prefer unsalted butter, also called "sweet cream" butter, in part because it's believed to be fresher (salt acts as a preservative) but mostly because it won't add unwanted extra salt to a recipe. Salted butter, though best for buttering toast or baked potatoes, can be tricky to work with, especially in baking, because different butter-makers use different amounts of salt in their product. If you add salted butter to a recipe that calls for unsalted butter, always decrease the amount of table salt called for by ¼ teaspoon (per stick).

# #6

# HOW TO STOCK UP

## (Weekly Shopping and Long-Term Planning)

Planning grocery purchases in advance helps save you money, minimizes trips to the store, and guarantees that you will always have staples on hand. Shop with menus in mind, and you'll never find yourself desperate for fresh cilantro in the middle of chopping tomatoes for your famous salsa.

**1 SET THE STANDARD.** Taking the time for this step will pay off again and again. Head to your favorite supermarkets and big-box stores—wherever you like to shop—with a pen and paper. Starting at one end of the store (I suggest the dairy case), write down the prices for the items you usually buy or are likely to buy. Don't skip any aisles—this list is your shopping bible, and you want it to be comprehensive. At home, write a multipage checklist for each store, grouping the items by type (produce, meat, etc.) or by aisle number. If you do this in your regular stores, you'll quickly figure out that some places are ideal to stock up on, say, olive oil, flour, and sugar, whereas others are less expensive if you're just running in for a gallon of milk and some eggs.

**2 COLLECT COUPONS.** Keep a manila envelope tacked to a bulletin board or a divided folder in a drawer. Before hitting the supermarket, go through your coupon stash and compare it with your list. Saving a few pennies on items you don't need or won't eat isn't smart, but reducing the bill on shelf-stable staples or needed weekly menu ingredients makes sense (and cents!).

**3 HIT THE BOOKS.** Before your weekly shopping trip, look through your cookbooks and recipes, and plan what meals you'd like that week, along with big-batch freezables such as chili, soups, stews, and casseroles like lasagna. This curbs impulse buying and helps prevent overbuying and waste.

**4 CROSS-REFERENCE.** If you know you need fresh parsley for chicken soup, and bunches are twice as big as you'll need, plan to also make tabbouleh or chimichurri sauce. Then check those recipes and list their ingredients so you're not caught short.

**5 CHECK YOUR SUPPLY OF** perishables**.** With fresh staples such as milk, eggs, bread, and cheese and the addition of pantry items such as olive oil, dried pasta, canned tomatoes, canned fish, jarred olives, and jams on hand, you'll be able to make a quick, hearty meal, any time of day.

**Coca-Cola inventor John Pemberton is considered by many to be the godfather of coupons. In 1887, he offered certificates for a free drink to entice customers.**

# #7 HOW TO BE A THRIFTY SHOPPER

Remember: A penny saved is a penny earned. And coupons aren't the only way to save at the grocery store. Here's how to shop on a budget.

**1 THE BIGGER, THE BETTER.** Buy nonperishable items in bulk and large sizes. Prices are better per unit, and you can repackage at home to make storage more convenient.

**2 EXTRA! EXTRA!** Read supermarket circulars in the Sunday papers, or check out advertised sales as you enter the store and adjust your list accordingly. Be flexible: Ground turkey can replace ground beef in your recipes if it's being offered at a better price.

**3 GO GENERIC.** In many cases, the food inside the ho-hum packaging of generics and store brands is the same, produced by the same manufacturer, differing only in label and price. My family likes only a certain brand of mayonnaise, so I splurge or use coupons. With frozen peas, however, one brand (or nonbrand) is as good as another.

**4 KEEP IT SIMPLE.** Less processing usually means lower costs. A whole chicken (which you can cut up at home) is typically cheaper than a chicken cut into parts. Similarly, dried beans and peas are cheaper than canned, and cooking them isn't labor-intensive. Pop your own corn and save big compared to microwave style (bonus: no nasty chemical "flavorings").

**5 PUT IT ON ICE.** Buy meat and produce when it's cheap, then clean it (in the case of meat) or cook it (in the case of vegetables) and freeze it in individual portions.

# #8

# HOW TO FREEZE HAMBURGER MEAT

## (or Anything Else)

The invention of the freezer was a godsend for thrifty cooks. When our forebears slaughtered a cow or chicken, they had to eat it in short order to prevent spoilage and, therefore, illness. Freezing meat gives us access to safe, quality, high-protein meals on demand. In the United States, ground beef plays a starring role in most kitchens as a versatile and economical staple. Understanding how to buy, store, and freeze it is key to learning best practices in shopping, storing, and cooking all manner of meats and prepared dishes.

**1 AT THE STORE, LOOK FOR TEARS** in the packaging and check the expiration date. The meat should look bright red—browning indicates age or unsafe storage—and have uniform fat marbling.

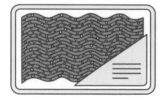

**2 AT HOME, REMOVE THE MEAT** from its packaging and divide it into recipe-size portions (½ pound, 1 pound, 2 pounds, etc.) or form it into burger patties. Using freezer paper, with the shiny side in, tightly wrap each portion of meat, forcing out as much air as possible, and tape it tightly shut. Do this twice, for an additional protective layer. Patties must be wrapped individually, or they'll freeze in a single block. If you don't have freezer paper, wrap in plastic wrap or foil, then place them inside gallon-size freezer bags, forcing out the air before sealing. Label and date all frozen parcels. The USDA suggests freezing for no more than 4 months. If you will be using the meat within 2 days, no need to freeze it—stash it immediately in the coldest part of the refrigerator.

**3 WHEN YOU ARE READY TO USE** the ground beef, you have a few options for thawing.

⚜ To thaw it in the refrigerator, simply place the package on a plate to catch any juices that might leak; allow 24 hours to fully thaw.

⚜ For a quicker thaw, unwrap the ground beef and seal it in a zip-top bag (if it's not already in one). Stopper the sink, fill it with cold water, and fully immerse the meat in the water. Change the water every half hour until the meat is thawed. Do not use hot water because bacteria can form under warm conditions.

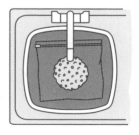

⚜ To thaw it in the microwave, remove all wrapping and place the ground beef on a microwave-safe plate. Thaw it on the lowest defrost setting, checking frequently so that it doesn't begin to cook. Once the meat is thawed, cook it immediately and do not refreeze or re-refrigerate it.

## RECIPE: PERFECT MEAT LOAF

**M**eat loaf is a favorite everywhere, loved for its economy, ease, and flexibility. Go basic with mashed potatoes and gravy, fancy with grilled vegetables and capellini (angel hair pasta), or enjoy it cold on a next-day sandwich! This is the way my mother made it, but once you master this recipe, improvise and customize to your heart's content. Wrap it in bacon, glaze it with sweet and sour sauce, top it with ketchup and hot sauce, or spice it with garam masala and serve it with basmati rice.

### Serves 8

1 large yellow onion, diced

2 pounds ground beef (I prefer ground chuck)

½ cup ketchup

½ cup Dijon mustard

2 eggs, beaten

1¼ cups bread crumbs

Salt and freshly ground black pepper

**1.** Preheat the oven to 350°F. Line a baking sheet with foil.

**2.** In a large mixing bowl, combine all ingredients and mix with slightly wet hands until evenly combined.

**3.** Scoop the mixture onto the prepared baking sheet and form it into 1 large loaf or 2 small loaves. Bake a large loaf for 1 hour or smaller loaves for 45 minutes.

**4.** Let the meat loaf stand for 15 minutes before slicing so it doesn't fall apart.

**TIP:** Bread crumbs can be store-bought or you can whir chunks of bread in a blender or food processor. In a pinch, slice bread thinly with a bread knife and then chop.

## How Much Should I Buy?

If ground beef (or any other freezer staple) is on deep sale, buy as much as you can reasonably store. Familiarize yourself with standard prices by reading store circulars, talking with butchers, and reading the cost-per-pound breakdowns at the meat counter. Bulk is usually cheaper than prepackaged. Four ounces (about ½ cup) of cooked ground beef is considered one serving, and 1 pound of raw beef will equal 2 cups of cooked ground beef.

## A Cut Above

Types and grades of ground beef differ depending on which part of the cow they came from and the percentage of fat they contain. Use this basic guide when shopping.

**Ground beef (aka hamburger meat).** For this classification, there is no assurance about which part of the cow is used. Scraps from other butchered beef cuts are included, but no innards are permitted. USDA standards allow up to 30 percent fat in ground beef, though some labels indicate the amount of fat and say "75 percent lean." It is good for stretching your food dollar by adding flavor to pasta sauces, chili, and soups, and it makes for juicy burgers.

**Ground chuck.** This comes from the "chuck," or shoulder, of the cow. Generally, these cuts are more expensive because of the popularity of chuck roasts and chuck steak. They feature a lot of connective tissue and benefit from long, slow cooking. When ground, chuck offers drier, leaner meat that is good for meatballs or meat loaves, goulashes that stand up to noodles and gravy, or any recipe that benefits from a firm texture.

**Ground sirloin.** Sirloin comes from the hip region of the cow. It's also more expensive than hamburger. The fat content of ground sirloin varies between 7 and 10 percent. Tender, with a pronounced beef flavor, it enjoys cult status among health-conscious cooks. Use it in heavily spiced chilis or for burgers piled high with add-ons such as mushrooms, peppers, and onions.

**Ground round.** The round comes from the rump area of a cow. Leaner than chuck, round's fat content hovers between 10 and 15 percent. The resulting burgers may be more steaklike, so they are tastiest when cooked medium or medium-rare and topped with juicy condiments. Ground round is a good choice for thick, meaty pasta sauces, lasagna, and tacos.

## Make It Last

Here's a quick guide to storing common grocery items:

**Meat.** Ground meat and fresh poultry will store safely in the refrigerator for one to three days, and chops, roasts, and steaks for three to four days. If sealed properly and stored in the freezer, uncooked meat can last for four to twelve months. Buy meat in bulk for economy, and once home, divide it immediately among zip-top bags, forcing out as much air as possible when you seal the bag. If you're planning to freeze meat for several months, it's worth it to buy heavy-duty freezer bags.

**Fruit.** In general, fruit stays fresh longer left unpeeled and uncut. Seal whole fruit such as apples, peaches, and pears in plastic bags and keep them in the crisper drawer. Don't put any fruits on the top shelf because many refrigerators freeze food at this level. Berries and grapes are better left in the vented plastic store packaging; before refrigerating, slide the whole package into a brown paper bag to protect them from light and humidity. Bananas keep longer in the fridge, but the peel will brown. Pineapples and mangoes should be peeled, sliced, and stored in an airtight, lidded bowl. To discourage browning, toss cut fruit with a few teaspoons of lemon juice.

**Nuts.** Shelled nuts, if not used quickly, get rancid and soggy faster than you'd think. Store them in a zip-top bag with the air pushed out, inside of a sealed container in the refrigerator for up to three months or stashed in the freezer for up to a year. Always do a taste test with older nuts before using them in brownies or on salad.

**Cheese.** The first thing to know is that cheese is a living, breathing thing. The most common mistake is wrapping it in plastic, suffocating the flavor. For cheese that comes in plastic, unwrap it immediately at home, and then repackage it by wrapping it tightly in parchment, waxed paper, or paper towels. Then put it in a partially sealed zip-top bag. Rub the outer layer of firm cheeses (not blue or Stilton!) with olive oil. If mold begins to form, you can then wipe and rinse it away, or cut off the outermost layer, preserving the bulk of it.

**Bread.** Moist breads last longer in the fridge or freezer (where they will keep for three to six months), but I abhor cold bread. When I'm forced to prolong the shelf life of bread by chilling it, I designate those loaves for toast, bread pudding, or stuffing. Storing home-baked or artisanal breads made without preservatives can be tricky; don't use plastic wrap nor plastic bags. The bread will turn gummy and quickly grow mold. My grandmother had the right idea with her ceramic bread box—it kept out air (and critters!) but allowed for breathing. No room for a bread box? Wrap your bread in a clean dishtowel and put it in a paper bag.

BREAD BOX

**Vegetables.** Onions and potatoes can be stored at room temperature, preferably in a cool, dry place. But most veggies—including carrots, cabbage, and cauliflower—do better in the fridge. In fact, you can also store onions in the refrigerator to reduce tears when chopping. If you have a "vegetable" setting on your fridge drawers, use it—the purpose is to reduce humidity, which most veggies prefer.

✕✕✕✕✕✕✕✕✕✕✕✕✕✕✕✕✕✕✕✕✕✕✕✕✕✕✕✕✕✕✕✕✕✕✕✕✕✕✕

# WHAT IS FREEZER BURN?

Those leathery, brownish patches and wrinkled, crystallized spots on frozen foods are caused by a combination of dehydration and oxidization. Freezer burn isn't harmful; it just doesn't taste good. Airtight packaging helps stave it off, and some experts recommend freezing water in open, plastic containers in your freezer to maintain humidity.

# #9
# HOW TO BUY AN APPLE
## (or, How to Shop for Produce)

Fresh, ripe natural foods nourish the body and delight the senses. If you shop smart, they also offer excellent mileage for your food dollar. Choosing the best the market has to offer isn't rocket science, but it takes some know-how and a little common sense.

**1 THERE ARE NO STUPID** questions. Don't know the difference between a mutsu and a winesap? Ask the seller. Whether it's the produce manager at your grocery store or the stall-keeper at the farmers' market, they should know the answer or can at least find out for you.

**2 INSPECT FOR "YUCK" FACTORS.** You know what you don't like to eat: bugs, rotten spots, bruised flesh, weird bumps. If it's not appetizing, pick another one off the pile.

**3 USE YOUR FIVE SENSES.** If a peach doesn't smell like a peach, don't buy it. If it's green when it's supposed to be red, keep searching. If there are samples, taste them. If you shake a melon or squash and it sounds like a baby's rattle, it's dried out—and shouldn't go in your cart.

**4 LOOK FOR AVERAGE SIZES AND** shapes. Comically large produce (like strawberries) often means it's either old or has been bred for something other than flavor.

**5 BUY LOCAL, WHEN POSSIBLE.** Generally, the less it has traveled, the fresher, riper, and least chemically treated it is.

**6 BUY WHAT YOU'LL** realistically eat. Don't buy spinach if you hate it, and buy only as much produce as you will eat in a few days, or up to a week. More than that, and it loses precious nutrients or, worse, goes bad.

**7 TRY TO BUY WHAT'S IN SEASON.** If you don't know, ask. Usually, in-season produce is at its peak of flavor and (bonus!) at its cheapest because it's abundant.

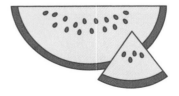

## Is Organic Really Better?

Ideally, *organic produce* would be defined as produce grown without pesticides or chemicals, from seeds that weren't genetically engineered, in a way that doesn't harm the soil or the water table. In truth, the standards vary. Even though the USDA has a certification for organic foods, the edges are fuzzy. For example, organic soup need contain only 95  percent organic ingredients, and the standards don't apply at all to growers who sell less than $5,000 worth of goods yearly.

The USDA and the government set allowable pesticide residue limits deemed safe for humans to eat, and groceries must meet those standards. Doctors, nutritionists, and even pro-organic activist groups say that the benefits of eating fresh fruits and vegetables outweigh the known risks of consuming pesticide residue. Your body and brain thrive on the vitamins, minerals, and fiber from fresh foods. Make the best choices you can, given your budget and options.

Note that conventional (nonorganic) produce such as bananas, grapefruits, onions, cantaloupe, and avocados are fine choices because we don't eat the peels; other items are best bought organic because they are pesticide-heavy and we eat the peels or the whole food. Go organic if you can for apples, bell peppers, blueberries, celery, grapes, kale, lettuce, peaches, spinach, and strawberries.

Organic or not, all produce should be carefully washed before eating, with special attention given to produce with edible peels. Using warm water, either place your produce in a colander and rinse, or for sandy or extra-dirty vegetables like spinach or potatoes, soak in a stoppered sink. If using a brush, make sure the bristles aren't too stiff, or you'll tear delicate skins and peels. The FDA doesn't recommend using soap; however, some health food stores sell food-grade sprays and washes to remove oil-based residues that are not entirely water-soluble, such as  pesticides, waxy preservatives, and oils from the hands of shoppers and handlers.

## Rethink Salad

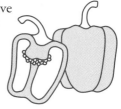

You shopped for a mountain of vegetables, determined to increase your intake. And then, guiltily, you found yourself tossing away soft cucumbers and unhappy-looking lettuce, deflated radishes, and eggplant that's withered and brown. It's disheartening, when your intentions were so good! But when you open the vegetable drawer and it all seems like too much trouble, think again. *What* would make those vegetables be tempting to you?

Roasting is always good: You can toss practically anything with olive oil, salt and pepper, and roast it on a baking sheet at 375° F until it's brown and crisp-edged, tender and delicious: cauliflower florets, broccoli stems, onion half-moons, green beans, asparagus, eggplant matchsticks, even wedges of cabbage or whole sections of romaine. Don't be stingy with the oil, shake the pan (or flip the veggies with  a big spoon) now and then, and do consider lining your baking sheet with foil, baking paper, or a nonstick mat. It makes cleanup so much easier.

But there is something else you can do: Rethink your definition of "salad." Salad doesn't have to be just a pile of lettuce. Any cooked vegetable, dressed with vinegar and olive oil, becomes "salad," as does any raw vegetable cut thin or small enough to eat with ease. Think thinly sliced fennel with hazelnuts and vinaigrette. Shredded carrots with Greek yogurt, raisins, cumin, and a dash of honey. It doesn't even have to be a vegetable: Diced plums and apricots with almonds, red wine vinegar, olive oil, chopped parsley, and a sprinkle of smoked paprika is a fantastic side dish for roast chicken. Or, dice up melon and cucumbers, toss with soy sauce, sesame oil, cilantro, and mint, and top with roasted peanuts.

A new approach to salad (along with a little help from the Internet when you're feeling stuck) can help transform your vegetable drawer from a place where good intentions go to die into a place where a hearty, healthful dinner can be harvested any night of the week.

# #10
# CARE AND HANDLING OF LETTUCE

## (or, How to Avoid Waste)

**A**mericans throw out food so often that we barely stop to consider what a waste of money it is. In economics, "slippage" means the difference between the estimated cost of a transaction and what you actually pay. Restaurant managers and chefs have borrowed the term and applied it to food: Slippage is when you buy five tomatoes, eat three, and throw away two because they rotted. In any kitchen, waste not want not is the goal.

### Is That Radioactive Waste in My Crisper Drawer?

It's happened to the best of us. After a week of eating out, vows to eat fresh, healthful food are renewed. With green salad in mind, the fridge door is flung open only to find a wilted green puddle where lettuce once was.

This may be a discouraging sight, but don't give up on salads made at home! If you're willing to invest twenty minutes once every two weeks, you'll have a ready supply of crisp lettuce (or spinach or parsley or collards . . . any leafy greens!).

Before we start: Get a salad spinner. In general, I don't tout specific gadgets, but in this case, the right tool for the job is essential. Wetness is the enemy of crisp lettuce. Centrifugal force removes water. Enough said.

## TYPES OF LETTUCE

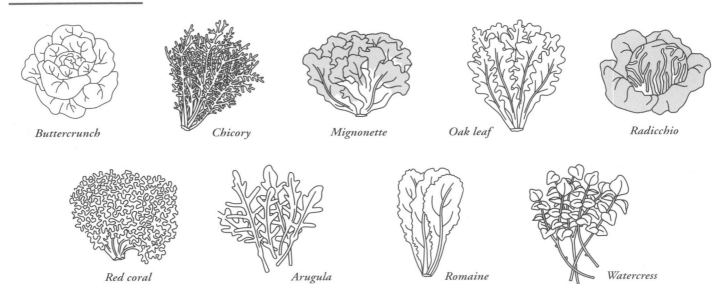

*Buttercrunch*     *Chicory*     *Mignonette*     *Oak leaf*     *Radicchio*

*Red coral*     *Arugula*     *Romaine*     *Watercress*

**1** **FILL A CLEAN SINK WITH VERY** cold water. Separate the leaves of lettuce, put them in the water, and swish them around. For limp leaves, break off the bottom to create a fresh edge, soak them for 30 minutes, and they will miraculously rejuvenate.

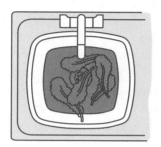

**2** **DRAIN THE WATER.** If the leaves were particularly sandy or dirty, fill the sink again, let soak for 15 minutes, then drain again. Next, rinse each individual leaf under cold running water, and then

place the leaves in the basket of your salad spinner. (Give each leaf a quick once-over to check for clinging bugs!) For large leaves, as with romaine, you can tear them in halves or quarters before placing them in the basket.

**3** **WHEN THE SPINNER IS FULL,** but not too tightly packed, spin the lettuce until dry.

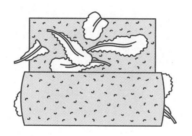

**4** **ROLL OUT SEVERAL PAPER** towels on a countertop and stack the dry leaves in the center. Wrap the lettuce loosely with the paper towels.

**5** **PLACE THE WRAPPED LETTUCE** in a gallon-size zip-top bag, gently press out the air, and close the bag. Store in the refrigerator and use as needed. When the bag is empty, simply rinse, air-dry, and reuse it.

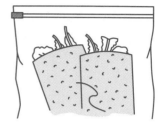

## More About Salad Spinners

Some salad spinners have holes in the bottom of the outer container so that the water can drain directly into the sink. Which is great if you don't mind leaning down into your sink to turn the handle or crank the knob or pull the cord.

However, what's great about the spinners with a solid exterior bowl is that they can serve first as a lettuce refresher. If your lettuce is not looking as crisp as you might wish, fill the bowl with cold water and let the lettuce soak in it for 10 or 15 minutes while you get dinner ready. Then lift the wet leaves into the inner sieve. If any dirt has soaked off, it will fall to the bottom, and you want to lift the greens off the grit, not pour it back over. Spin vigorously, then pour off any water and spin again.

### Up the Creek Without a Spinner

If you find yourself without a salad spinner—such as in a vacation kitchen—you can use an old French trick for the most effective spinning ever. Wash the lettuce under running water, and tear up the leaves into serving pieces directly onto a clean dishtowel. Gather up the four edges of the towel, go outdoors, and swing your arm in a big circle, like a baseball pitcher winding up. Family and friends may want to line up in the doorway to watch but tell them to stay back. Water flies out in a massive arc around you! The lettuce will be perfectly dry and crisp, even if the bottom of the towel is soaked. It's a great way to dry a salad, and a terrific party trick.

# #11 HOW TO CARE FOR ICEBERG LETTUCE

A head of iceberg lettuce requires slightly different handling than other less densely packed varieties.

**1 REMOVE THE CORE BY SHARPLY** knocking the head, stem down, against a countertop or cutting board until it's loose.

**2 TWIST THE STEM UNTIL IT PULLS** out easily. Discard the core, along with the outer layer of leaves.

**3 RINSE THE WHOLE HEAD OF** lettuce well under very cold, running water and shake it dry over the sink.

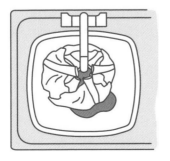

**4 WIPE OFF THE EXCESS WATER WITH** a clean dish towel or paper towels.

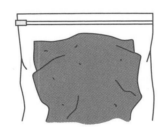

**5 WRAP THE WHOLE HEAD IN PAPER** towels, place it in a zip-top bag, press out the air, seal it, and store it in the fridge.

**6 KEEP IT UP TO A WEEK, MAYBE** even a few days longer, ready to pull off a few leaves for sandwiches, shred finely to top tacos or nachos, or cut off a wedge to eat with blue cheese dressing.

# #12 HOW TO MAKE VINAIGRETTE

The simplest salad dressing of them all is also perhaps the most delicious—classic vinaigrette is tangy and light, with just enough flavor to make any salad sing. I like a lot of mustard, which acts as an emulsifier, meaning it makes it possible for the vinegar and oil to mix. The salt counters the blandness of the oil, the vinegar adds tanginess, and the pepper offers bite. It's remarkably versatile; dress any pile of greens or veggies (or even pasta) with it. You can halve this recipe, but it stores well for a couple days.

**Makes 1 cup**

3 tablespoons red wine vinegar
1 clove garlic, minced
Pinch of kosher salt
2 tablespoons Dijon mustard
¾ cup extra-virgin olive oil
Freshly ground black pepper

**1.** Put the vinegar, garlic, and salt in a small glass jar and let sit for 2 minutes. (This lessens the garlic's bite and dissolves the salt.)

**2.** Add the mustard, olive oil, and pepper to taste. Cap the jar tightly and shake vigorously.

**Variations:** Chopped fresh herbs are nice. Use grainy or mild mustard. Try balsamic vinegar for a robust fragrance; apple cider vinegar for a fruity finish; or lemon juice for extra tartness. Experiment with different oils, including nut oils and infused oils.

# #13
# HOW TO MAKE CAESAR SALAD
## (or, How to Construct a Salad and Make Dressing)

Tossed tableside at supper clubs by tuxedoed waiters, the Caesar salad is arguably the most sophisticated and romantic of all lettuce-based dishes. Once a mere starter, the Caesar salad has become a favorite entrée with the addition of extras such as grilled chicken, shrimp, or steak.

The original recipe, attributed to chef and restaurateur Caesar Cardini, was said to have included olive oil, coddled eggs, and whole romaine lettuce leaves, meant to be plucked from the plate by the stem and nibbled by hand. (The lore goes that Caesar Cardini invented the Caesar salad out of desperation one summer's night when his kitchen was running out of staple menu ingredients.) Chopping it makes for tidier eating, but eating salad with your hands is a fun change of pace.

**1 SELECT A SALAD BOWL.** I have a favorite, large wooden bowl that's functional and beautiful. For a classic Caesar, use romaine lettuce, torn into large chunks. As with all green salads, it's imperative to make sure the leaves are dry (see Care and Handling of Lettuce, page 22). Use a salad spinner and allow the lettuce to air dry. If needed, pat with a clean dish towel.

**2 MAKE THE DRESSING.** (See Classic Caesar Dressing, page 26.)

**3 POUR ON THE DRESSING, AND** then toss with your salad spoons or a pair of tongs. How much dressing to use is a matter of taste—some people like their salad really wet, some like it really dry— but a rough estimate is 1 tablespoon of dressing for every 2 cups of leaves. Start with that and add more as

needed. First, be sure to toss well so each leaf is coated in a very thin layer of dressing. Once tossed, top with homemade croutons (see How to Make Croutons page 46), a final grind of pepper, and some big, flat shavings of Parmesan cheese.

*(continued)*

**4** **SERVE THE SALAD RIGHT AWAY.** As with all lettuces, the romaine will start to wilt immediately upon being dressed.

**5** **ONCE YOU'VE MASTERED THE** basic Caesar, improvise! Try: lime juice, balsamic vinegar, red onion, Boston or butter lettuce, mesclun mix, spinach, capers, crumbled bacon, and scallions.

✕ ✕ ✕ ✕ ✕ ✕ ✕ ✕ ✕ ✕ ✕ ✕ ✕ ✕ ✕ ✕ ✕ ✕ ✕ ✕ ✕ ✕ ✕ ✕ ✕ ✕ ✕ ✕ ✕ ✕ ✕ ✕ ✕ ✕ ✕ ✕ ✕ ✕ ✕

## RAW EGGS: ARE THEY SAFE TO EAT?

The dressing for a Classic Ceasar salad is traditionally made with raw egg. According to the FDA, raw eggs can carry a risk of salmonella contamination. In 2009, they did a study that showed the risk to be lower than originally thought: About 1 in 30,000 eggs was found to be contaminated, and even then, the bacteria may not have penetrated the shell. Since 2010, all commercially produced eggs have been treated to kill the bacteria, but there is no 100 percent guarantee that salmonella won't be present.

My family and I eat raw eggs. My children are past the vulnerable infant and toddler stages; we're all healthy and we get our eggs from reputable sources. I also make sure that the shells are washed and that the eggs stay refrigerated. I hard-boil all of my eggs that float (instead of sink) in water, which indicates advanced age.

If you want to use raw eggs but have concerns, consider using those that are pasteurized in-shell or coddle them by slipping whole eggs into boiling water for one minute, then immediately plunging them into an ice-water bath to halt cooking. Then you can separate the white from the yolk, if called for.

Juice of 1 lemon (see "How to Juice a Lemon," page 28)

**Anchovies—small saltwater fish rich in Omega-3 fatty acids—are a secret key ingredient in dressings, and pastas, adding "umami," the savory depth our tongues crave.**

## RECIPE: CLASSIC CAESAR DRESSING

Ideas about the salad vary, but the real marker of a good Caesar salad is the dressing. I often use my blender to make salad dressings. For vinaigrettes, I simply add all the ingredients to a tightly sealed jar and shake it. But a blender helps make this dressing creamy. If you don't want to use one, simply whisk everything but the olive oil in a medium-size bowl, then drizzle in the oil while whisking.

### Makes ½ cup, to dress enough salad for 3 or 4 people

3 anchovy fillets (or 1 tablespoon anchovy paste)

1 clove garlic, chopped finely or pressed

1 large egg yolk

Juice of 1 lemon (see "How to Juice a Lemon," page 28)

¼ cup freshly grated Parmesan cheese

¼ teaspoon kosher salt

¼ teaspoon freshly ground black pepper

½ cup extra-virgin olive oil

**1.** Put the anchovy, garlic, egg, and lemon juice in a blender. Pulse to combine.

**2.** Add the Parmesan cheese, salt, pepper, and ¼ cup of the olive oil. Pulse to make a smooth paste.

**3.** With the blender on medium speed, slowly drizzle in the remaining ¼ cup olive oil to make a creamy dressing. If the dressing seems too thick, add a little more olive oil, taste it for balance, and add a little salt, if needed. Use it right away; this dressing does not store well.

# #14
## HOW TO ZEST A LEMON

**M**ost citrus-accented recipes (lemon bars, orange chocolate chip cookies, Meyer lemon vinagrette, chicken a l'orange) will call for "zest." This simply means the colored part of the rind, minus the white part (called pith), which is unpleasantly bitter. Here's how to properly remove the zest and leave the pith.

**1** **WASH THE LEMON IN RUNNING** water or soak the lemon in a bowl of water and then rinse.

**2** **GRIP THE LEMON IN YOUR PALM** from end to end, so that the pointier end touches your little finger and the other end touches your thumb.

**3** **PROP A MICROPLANE GRATER** against a clean cutting board, angling it at 45 degrees. Twist your wrist while scraping the fruit against the grater in a long stroke, from one end of the lemon to the other. Don't press too hard, or you'll scrape the pith.

**4** **ROTATE THE LEMON.** Repeat the zesting motion one strip at a time, until the whole fruit—or as much as you need—is scraped clean of the yellow part.

**5** **IF YOU DON'T HAVE A** Microplane, you can use a lemon zester—a specialized peeler that pulls off 3 or 4 tiny strips at a time—or a vegetable peeler to pull off super-thin strips. If you use a peeler, you'll likely need to scrape off the pith and chop the zest finely with a knife. You can also put wide strips of zest in a food processor and process it finely.

## If Life Gives You Lemons. . .

If you need lemon zest for a recipe, but not the juice, you'll be left with a naked lemon. What to do? Waste not, want not! Why not?

⚜ Stuff it into the cavity of a chicken before roasting, along with aromatics like rosemary and sage. This lends a tangy citrus flavor and keeps the meat moist.

⚜ Chop it into chunks, put them in a bowl, and cover liberally with granulated sugar. Scoop ½ cup of the lemon-sugar mixture into the bottom of a tall glass, add ice, and top with cranberry juice for a bracing summer cocktail.

⚜ Cut it into wedges and freeze for later use. Add the frozen wedges to a pot of homemade chicken soup or a pitcher of water to brighten the flavor.

⚜ Make lemon syrup by combining equal amounts lemon juice and sugar, heating the lemon juice gently in the microwave or on the stovetop to help the sugar melt. Add ice and gin for a cocktail, seltzer or water for lemonade.

⚜ Bleach a stain out of cotton by rubbing lemon juice and salt into it. Lemon juice is especially good for removing food stains.

## RECIPE: ZESTY LEMON SEASONING

Fragrant, oily lemon rind enhances the flavor of both sweet and savory foods. For a seasoning that packs a punch, lemon pepper is the way to go on fish, fowl, fresh salads, and more. I love it sprinkled on cantaloupe chunks, or speared with slices of prosciutto or thin-cut ham, and it's the ideal flavoring for roasted chicken.

**Makes about ½ cup**

6 lemons
⅓ cup crushed black peppercorns
¼ cup kosher salt

1. Preheat the oven to 200°F and line a baking sheet with parchment paper.

2. Zest the lemons and set the zest aside.

3. Grind the peppercorns coarsely, either in a pepper mill, a clean coffee grinder, or with a mortar and pestle.

4. Mix the lemon zest and peppercorns together in a bowl, and then spread the mixture out on the prepared baking sheet. Bake until the zest is completely dried, about 25 to 30 minutes.

5. Transfer the dried lemon-pepper mixture to a spice grinder, clean coffee grinder, or mortar and pestle, and grind until blended and finer in texture.

6. Transfer the mixture to a small bowl, add the salt, and stir until well combined. Store in an airtight container for up to a month.

# #15 HOW TO JUICE A LEMON

The thickest, fattest, prettiest lemons often have the least juice, oddly enough. For the juiciest squeeze, look for thin-skinned lemons. You can tell because the exterior is actually smoother, almost a little translucent, not knobby and bumpy as it is with thick skins.

A lemon will yield, roughly, 3 to 4 tablespoons of juice, so if a recipe calls for "juice of 1 lemon," you can feel safe squeezing whatever size you have at hand. A tablespoon more or less in a recipe is mainly about your own taste and it won't do any harm.

**1 START WITH A LEMON AT ROOM-** temperature. If you're taking a lemon straight from the fridge, soak it in hot tap water for 2 minutes or microwave it for 20 seconds.

**2 WASH THE LEMON IN CLEAR** running water or soak it in a bowl of water and rinse.

**3 USING THE PALM OF YOUR** hand, roll the lemon on a clean countertop or cutting board, pressing down as firmly as you can without popping the fruit. This bursts the individual cells, releasing the juices inside.

**4 WITH A SHARP CHEF'S KNIFE, CUT** the lemon in half widthwise.

**5 USING A CITRUS REAMER, IF YOU** have one, or a fork if you don't, hold the lemon half over a bowl and twist the tool and the lemon half in opposite directions while squeezing.

**6 ONCE MOST OF THE JUICE IS OUT,** fold the lemon like a sandwich and squeeze with your hands. Insert the tool and scrape left to right inside the peel to get the last remaining juice.

**7 STRAIN THE JUICE TO REMOVE** seeds and any bits of fruit pulp that may have fallen into the bowl.

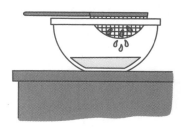

# #16
# HOW TO CUT A LEMON WEDGE GARNISH

For everything from cocktails to grilled fish, a lemon wedge is a must. Here's how to cut presentation-ready lemon garnishes.

**1 HOLDING THE LEMON BROADSIDE** against a cutting board, use a sharp chef's knife to cut off the pointy ends, just enough to leave a clean, flat edge.

**2 PLACE ONE OF THE CUT ENDS** down on the cutting board and slice the lemon lengthwise, leaving two long halves.

**3 LAY ONE OF THE HALVES CUT** side down, peel-side up, on the cutting board, and cut it in half again, lengthwise. Repeat with the other half so that you have 4 long quarters.

**4 CUT EACH OF THE QUARTERS IN** half again, lengthwise, slicing at a beveled angle.

**5 SLICE OFF THE OUTER ⅛ INCH OF** membrane on each wedge. This will allow you to push the seeds out easily with your finger.

**6 TO STORE, SEAL THE WEDGES IN** an airtight container or zip-top bag and put them in the fridge. They can last up to 3 days.

## RECIPE: REAL LEMONADE

Fresh lemonade offers a lot of refreshing flavor in return for very little effort. The secret is simple syrup—a solution of sugar and water that mixes easily into cool drinks and eliminates the problem of undissolved sugar granules sinking to the bottom. You can make this same recipe with limes.

**Serves 4**

¾ cup granulated sugar

¾ cup lemon juice (from 3 to 4 big, juicy lemons)

1 cup ice

**1.** In a small saucepan over medium-high heat, combine the sugar and ¾ cup water to create simple syrup. Stir occasionally until the sugar is dissolved.

**2.** Combine the lemon juice and the simple syrup in a pitcher. Add the ice and 2 cups of cold water, using more or less depending on the strength you desire.

**3.** Serve with lemon wedge garnishes (see How to Cut a Lemon Wedge Garnish, left) or keep in the refrigerator for up to a week.

✕ ✕ ✕ ✕ ✕ ✕ ✕ ✕ ✕ ✕ ✕ ✕ ✕ ✕ ✕ ✕

## ARNOLD WHO?

Down South, the mixture of iced tea with lemonade in equal proportions is called a Half and Half. Legend has it that Arnold Palmer, the famous American golfer, ordered this drink in a bar in Palm Springs circa 1960, and it became forever associated with him—thus the "Arnold Palmer." Some people say an Arnold Palmer is actually a Half and Half with a jigger of vodka, so the nonalcoholic version is a "Virgin Palmer." Replace the vodka with beer and you get a "Hard Palmer."

# #17
# HOW TO CHOP AN ONION

## (or, Basic Knife Skills)

Next to washing dishes and toasting bread, chopping onions may be the most common task in the kitchen. Learn to do this cleanly and swiftly, and you'll have mastered the foundation of many recipes.

Slicing, dicing, and chopping onions (or anything) into uniform pieces isn't just for show, it's the only way to ensure even cooking. Otherwise, the small bits burn, and the big ones are nearly raw. Remember: Never, ever put an onion in the food processor; you'll wind up with an unappetizing mush! To prepare, dampen a dish towel, spread it out on the countertop, and set a cutting board on it. This will prevent slips and cuts to your hands. Make sure your knife blade is very sharp and longer than the onion.

**1** **PLACE THE ONION ON THE** board and slice it down the middle vertically, through the root and stem. Lay each half cut-side down, and cut about ½ inch off of the stem end. Roughly peel both halves. Don't be dainty—onions are cheap, and you don't want peels in your food. Save all the trimmings to simmer for stock if you like.

**2** **WORKING WITH ONE HALF,** still cut-side down, make several small, vertical slices from the cut end toward the root end, but don't cut all the way through. Leaving the end intact holds the onion together.

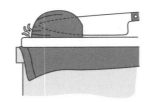

**3** **ROTATE THE ONION HALF 90** degrees and crosscut, stopping just short of the root, making small slices that will result in a dice. Cut to the last ½ inch of the root and discard it.

**TO MINCE:** Use the same technique, but make three horizontal cuts as well, bracing the onion against your curled-under fingers (cutting toward the root) before rotating and crosscutting.

**TO SLICE:** Simply cut the onion halves into half-moons, and don't crosscut.

**TO CHOP COARSELY:** Quarter the onion and use a rocking motion to slice it into large chunks.

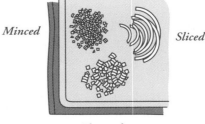

*Minced*          *Sliced*

*Chopped*

## Chemical Warfare

You've no doubt heard scores of old wives' tales and "scientific" advice for slicing onions without tears. The most farfetched include holding a match between your teeth and actually chewing on a raw onion! The real trick is keeping irritants away from your face.

When you slice an onion, you break cells, releasing what's inside and allowing amino acid sulfoxides to form sulfenic acids. Enzymes once kept apart now mix together, producing syn-propanethial-S-oxide, a volatile sulfur compound that reacts with the water in your eyes to form sulfuric acid. The sulfuric acid burns, stimulating your eyes to release tears to wash away the irritant. Cooking renders the compound inactive, but here are some tips that will help with the burn:

⚜ Chill out: Less syn-propanethial-S-oxide evaporates from cold onions. Don't freeze them, though—thawed onions are mushy.

SYN-PROPANETHIAL-S-OXIDE

⚜ Use a knife that's super sharp and at least twice as long as your onion. Long, smooth strokes do less cell-wall damage, releasing fewer gases.

⚜ Once you've handled an onion, don't touch your face. The sulfuric compound will irritate eyes, nose, and throat.

⚜ Keep exposed cuts pointed away from you—the second you cut an onion in half, turn both halves face-down on the cutting board. Don't peel the side you aren't currently chopping.

⚜ Turn on your vent hood or place a small fan on the countertop, directed away from you. Fumes that can't reach your face won't irritate your eyes.

---

# In the Middle Ages, onions were used as wedding gifts.

---

× × × × × × × × × × × × × × × × × × × × × × × × × × × × × × × × × × × × × × × × × × × × × × × × × × × × × × × × × × ×

# HOW DO I GET THIS SMELL OFF MY HANDS?

Second to tears, scented skin is the major drawback of handling onions. Here are some tips for overriding the odor:

• Some swear by rubbing their hands on stainless steel (there are even patented "soaps" made of the metal). The theory goes that the metal's self-restoring layer of chromium oxide, which protects its surface, prompts an oxygen exchange that might neutralize onion odor.

• One tried and true method is to cut a lemon in half and rub it over your hands and nails.

• Rub a handful of coffee beans over the fronts and backs of your hands, allowing the warmth of your skin to release their oils.

• Soak your hands in a bowl of tomato juice for at least five minutes. It works for "deskunking" dogs, and it works with onions, too.

• Rub your hands with baking soda. (Add a little moisture for the full effect.) It absorbs the odor and sloughs off the stinky cells from the skin's surface.

## Knife Basics

Many of us are given, or we buy, a knife set at some point when setting up a kitchen, and it usually contains the basic knives you need:

**Paring knife.** A 3-inch blade for small jobs such as peeling garlic.

**Utility knife.** A slightly longer blade for bigger jobs like cutting up apples or slicing a cucumber into a salad bowl.

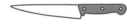

**Serrated knife.** Ideal for cutting bread but is also useful for thinly slicing soft vegetables such as tomatoes.

**Chef's or cook's knife.** A large blade—usually 8 to 10 inches—for big chopping jobs.

Of the basic knives, the chef's knife is the one you might want to buy separately to make sure you get a high-quality blade that suits your hand.

## The Chef's Knife

The workhorse of the kitchen, the chef's knife is typically between 8 and 12 inches long and falls into two categories: German, with a curve at the front allowing for a rocking motion, and French, a straight version that requires an up-and-down slicing motion.

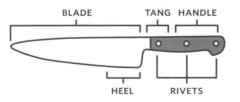

**Blade.** Usually made of high-carbon stainless steel. This strong metal helps maintain sharpness and prevents nicks in the blade.

**Handle.** Usually wooden or plastic, though higher-tech versions are all steel, lowering the possibility of harboring bacteria and increasing durability.

**Heel.** From the (blunt) end of the blade to the beginning of the handle. This is where you bear down with your palm when cutting through thick or hard foods.

**Tang.** Located under the handle, this is the continuation of the blade's steel all the way through the end of the knife.

**Rivets.** The bolts that attach the handle to the tang. In good knives, they are smooth and do not protrude.

## Knife Skills

Although you may teach yourself to chop well while holding your chef's knife like it's a hammer, what's called a "pinch grip" allows for more control over whatever you're hacking into bits with your chef's knife. (It's how the pros do it.) To start, pinch the top of the blade, near the handle, between your index finger and your thumb—use two fingers if it makes you feel better—and then wrap your remaining fingers loosely around the knife handle.

While precise measurements don't matter as much in a home kitchen, the exact dimensions of various cuts are something culinary students are expected to learn—and replicate, over and over again. To cut into the fixed dimensions below, start by making whatever vegetable you're using into a rectangle, and then go from there.

The American Culinary Federation gives exact dimensions for cuts as follows:

Batonnet (long stick): ¼" by ¼" by 2.5"
Large dice: ¾" cube
Medium dice: ½" cube
Small dice: ¼" cube
Brunoise: ⅛" cube
Fine Brunoise: ¹⁄₁₆" cube
Regular Julienne (or matchstick): ⅛" square by 2" strip
Fine Julienne: ¹⁄₁₆" square by 2" strip

Most cookbooks, however, use "chopped" or "diced" simply to mean that you should be cutting your vegetable or meat into uniform pieces. If every piece is exactly the same, you'll have much better luck cooking your food evenly.

# #18
# HOW TO MEASURE FLOUR

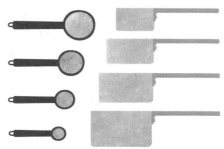

How important is measuring? Depends on what you're making. You can be extremely casual with savory foods, because a few more tomatoes, extra garlic, and a couple added glugs of wine won't break (and might *make*) a dish. Baking is a little different because of the chemical interaction of the wet and dry ingredients and the leavening agents. Pro bakers work solely by weight, but that's too fussy for most home cooks. (Although, if you're into precision, go get yourself a kitchen scale stat.) You can generally get very good results by adhering to the measurements in a baking recipe, using this simple technique.

To get the most accurate quantities, liquid and dry ingredients should be measured using measuring cups designed for each. Here's how to measure flour to ensure best results with all your baking recipes. Note that this technique should also be applied to measuring out all dry ingredients, such as teaspoons of spices, salt, sugar, baking powder, and baking soda.

**1** **DIP A 1-CUP DRY MEASURE INTO** a container of flour and lift out an overflowing cupful.

**2** **HOLDING THE MEASURING CUP** over the flour container, draw the flat (broad side) of a knife across the top of the cup to level it, letting the excess fall back into the container.

**3** **PUT THE MEASURED FLOUR** into your mixing bowl. Don't shake the cup or it will settle the flour and make it denser.

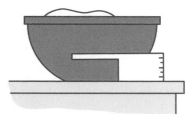

# It takes about 350 ears of wheat to make enough flour for a loaf of bread.

## The Pancake Primer

A big platter heaped high with pancakes, edges crisp and golden, interiors fluffy and light—this is (almost) everyone's fantasy breakfast. If you've resigned yourself to the heavy, slightly off-tasting pancakes you get from packaged mixes, you'll be delighted to learn that tasty pancakes are just as easy to make without a mix! You're rewarded with better flavor, fluffier texture, and the freedom to tweak and customize to your heart's (stomach's?) content.

### Mile-High Cakes

Buttermilk and baking soda are the ingredients responsible for making pancakes puff, but adding a little baking powder as a backup can help ensure a quick rise. The other secret to getting height is a slightly thick batter; runny batter makes delicious thin pancakes, but not thick, tall ones.

### Flour Arrangement

Buckwheat flour imparts an almost sourdough-like flavor and is beloved by many pancake fans. Interestingly enough, buckwheat is not actually wheat, it's a ground seed, and for pancakes it works best when mixed half and half with all-purpose flour. Whole-wheat flour also works best mixed with all-purpose, or the pancakes will be quite heavy and dense. To get more whole grains in your diet, however, there is another option: Whole-wheat pastry flour is so finely milled that it can take the place of all-purpose flour in many baked goods, such as pancakes, piecrusts, cookies, and quick breads (though not most cakes or yeast breads).

✕ ✕ ✕ ✕ ✕ ✕ ✕ ✕ ✕ ✕ ✕ ✕ ✕ ✕ ✕ ✕ ✕ ✕ ✕ ✕ ✕ ✕ ✕ ✕ ✕ ✕ ✕

# WHAT ABOUT WAFFLES?

The biggest difference between pancake and waffle batters is that, for waffles, the eggs must be separated and the whites beaten until soft peaks form. The beaten whites are then folded in at the very end, for a lighter, airier batter.

### Got Buttermilk?

Most people don't keep buttermilk on hand, so impromptu pancake breakfasts might find you scrambling for this key ingredient. Don't panic—there's an easy workaround: In a glass or ceramic cup (not a metal one), combine 1 cup milk and 1 tablespoon fresh lemon juice. Let it sit for ten minutes, and you'll have a slightly thickened, acidic milk that can replace buttermilk in your recipe. You can also whisk ½ cup milk with ½ cup sour cream or plain yogurt to make 1 cup of buttermilk substitute for baking or cooking.

### Hot Hot Heat

Regulating the heat for pancakes is a tricky business, but with experience, you will quickly get the hang of it. Electric griddles and skillets have thermostats that set the ideal temperature, but for stovetop cooking, heat a large cast-iron skillet or griddle over medium-high heat for several minutes. (It's best not to heat a nonstick pan with nothing in it lest the coating be damaged.) The time-honored way to tell when the pan is hot enough is to sprinkle in a few drops of water off your fingertips. If the water bounces once or twice on the surface, the heat is ideal. If it sits and sizzles, it's not hot enough; if it instantly evaporates without bouncing, the pan is too hot. Turn off the heat and cool the pan slightly before proceeding.

### The First Pancake

The very first pancake is rarely perfect. Too much or too little oil or butter, a batter that is too thick or thin (adjust with a little more buttermilk or flour), or a pan that is too hot or too cold will all affect that first cake the most. The second pancake nearly always comes out better, so adjust whatever needs adjusting and eat the first one yourself (or share it with your kitchen helpers).

### Keeping the Cakes Warm

If you're cooking a casual breakfast for just a few loved ones, you might just plate them right from the pan, so family members can eat as you cook. If you prefer to serve them all at once, turn the oven on to its lowest setting, usually 175 or 180 degrees Fahrenheit, and set a large, ovenproof plate in the oven. As each pancake is cooked, transfer it to the plate; they'll hold up well for up to about thirty minutes. The edges won't be quite as crisp this way, but the pancakes will still be practically perfect when they come to the table, and you can't beat the presentation!

### Flip Like a Pro

If you've always admired people who can flip a pancake high and catch it effortlessly in the pan, know that the technique is mainly confidence. Once the first side is cooked, loosen the pancake with a spatula. Grasp the handle of the pan firmly (using a potholder if needed) and shake it back and forth a few times to make sure the pancake is loose. Then flip it upward with a sharp jerk of your wrist. Try to throw it high, a good 12 to 18 inches up. If you throw too low, you will end up with a pancake only half-flipped, folded back on itself, or caught on the edge of the pan.

## Baking Basics: Biscuits and Quick Breads

Quick breads, unlike yeast breads, are simply mixed and baked, relying on the rising action of baking powder or baking soda combined with an acidic element such as buttermilk, yogurt, or sour cream. Quick breads can be savory, such as biscuits, or sweet, like a loaf of banana bread. Experienced cooks can make a batch of biscuits, start to finish, in about seventeen minutes, so they truly are quick.

### On the Rise

Most quick breads get their lift from baking powder, a combination of baking soda and an acidic salt, such as cream of tartar or monocalcium phosphate, usually mixed into a base such as cornstarch. The liquid in the batter causes the chemicals in the baking powder to combine and release carbon dioxide gas bubbles. "Double-acting" baking powders have a second acid salt, such as sodium aluminum sulfate, which releases gas upon being heated, giving the bread a second, later lift when the batter goes into the hot oven.

Baking soda, meanwhile, works like that familiar childhood science experiment, when baking soda and vinegar combine with a rush to shoot off a bottle rocket or gush out of a papier-mâché "volcano." The soda and an acidic component are combined just before the dough or batter goes in the oven; the chemical reaction gives off carbon dioxide, and those tiny bubbles of gas raise the bread. This is why quick breads are usually baked in a very hot oven, typically anywhere from 375 to 425 degrees Fahrenheit: The high temperature helps "set" the structure of the bread as the bubbles rise, trapping them inside so that the finished product is fluffy and tender.

### Don't Wait to Bake

This leavening action also explains why quick bread batters cannot be mixed in advance and stored. As soon as the wet ingredients go into the dry ones, the batter should be poured directly into the prepared pan and popped in the preheated oven. If quick bread batters hang around waiting to be baked, all the carbon dioxide will bubble out, and the resulting bread will be flat and tough. Nearly all savory quick breads are best the day they're made; keeping them overnight tends to make them tough and dry. Quick breads that contain sugar, eggs, and butter, however, will last longer.

### Good Fat

Aside from Irish soda bread—which contains only flour, baking soda, salt, and buttermilk—most quick breads have a high proportion of fat to flour compared to yeast breads, which may have no fat at all. Whether it's butter, oil, lard, or vegetable shortening, the fat coats the molecules of the flour and helps prevent gluten from developing as the bread rises in the oven. When the gluten doesn't develop, the crumbs don't have as much elasticity, so instead of the chewy texture of a yeast bread, a quick bread will remain tender, coming apart easily when you tear or cut it.

⤬ ⤬ ⤬ ⤬ ⤬ ⤬ ⤬ ⤬ ⤬ ⤬ ⤬ ⤬ ⤬ ⤬ ⤬ ⤬ ⤬ ⤬ ⤬ ⤬ ⤬ ⤬ ⤬ ⤬ ⤬ ⤬ ⤬

## CAKE VS. QUICK BREAD

Though cakes also depend on baking powder or soda to rise, they get additional lightness from eggs and from the air that is whipped in as the sugar and butter are beaten together. A quick bread also has a coarser texture—called the "crumb" in baking parlance—than a cake.

# RECIPE: BUTTERMILK BISCUITS

A standard Home Ec class recipe, buttermilk biscuits may seem intimidating, but once you learn how to make them, the effort pays off in the form of buttery, heavenly goodness.

**Makes 8 to 12 biscuits**

2 cups all-purpose flour (plus 2 to 3 tablespoons for shaping)

1 teaspoon salt

1 teaspoon baking soda

½ cup (1 stick) cold, salted butter

½ cup well-shaken buttermilk

2 tablespoons milk (optional)

**1.** Preheat the oven to 425°F and set out a baking sheet.

**2.** In a large mixing bowl, stir the flour, salt, and baking soda together with a wooden spoon.

**3.** Cut the butter into 8 pieces and drop them into the bowl. Use a fork or your fingers to "cut" or "rub" the butter into the dough, breaking it up into smaller and smaller bits as you combine it with the flour. (You can also use a pastry cutter for this job.) Stop when the flour mixture looks like a mass of crumbs, with no large lumps of butter visible.

**4.** Make a well in the center of the dough. Pour the buttermilk into the well.

**5.** Combine with the spoon, stirring just until the dough comes together into a clump.

**6.** Sprinkle 2 to 3 tablespoons of flour in a circle about 10 inches wide on a clean countertop or work surface, and then turn the dough out onto the flour along with any remaining dry bits left in the bowl.

**7.** Knead the dough briefly, folding and pressing it gently with the flat of your palms 3 or 4 times so that the shaggy mass becomes a smooth(ish) whole. Pat it gently into a sort of rectangle about ¾ inch thick.

**8.** Use a sharp knife to divide the dough into 8 to 12 squares. Lift the squares onto the baking sheet, gently rounding the edges—without overworking the dough.

**9.** If you like, use a pastry brush to lightly brush the surface of each biscuit with the milk. This helps make an evenly golden crust. Bake them for 10 to 12 minutes, until they are puffed and golden. Remove from the oven and serve immediately.

✕ ✕ ✕ ✕ ✕ ✕ ✕ ✕ ✕ ✕ ✕ ✕ ✕ ✕ ✕ ✕ ✕ ✕ ✕ ✕ ✕ ✕ ✕ ✕ ✕ ✕ ✕ ✕ ✕ ✕ ✕ ✕ ✕ ✕

# BISCUIT VARIATIONS

Biscuits are ideal for add-ins. Before adding the buttermilk, you can stir in 2 to 3 tablespoons of chopped fresh herbs such as chives, parsley, or rosemary. Or reduce the butter by half and add 1 cup grated Cheddar or Parmesan cheese. Or go in another direction entirely and add 2 tablespoons sugar and a large egg to make scones, best served warm with butter and jam.

# RECIPE: FLUFFY PANCAKES

Short stack or silver dollar, blueberry or banana, pancakes are the classic and beloved weekend breakfast of champions.

**Serves 6**

2¼ cups all-purpose flour

2 tablespoons granulated sugar

1½ teaspoons baking powder

1 teaspoon baking soda

Pinch of salt

6 tablespoons unsalted butter, melted

1½ cups buttermilk

2 large eggs

Vegetable oil or butter, for cooking

**1.** Preheat the oven to 185°F and put a heatproof platter in the oven.

**2.** In a large bowl, whisk together the flour, sugar, baking powder, baking soda, and salt.

**3.** In a separate large bowl, whisk the butter with the buttermilk and eggs.

**4.** Heat a griddle or large frying pan over medium-high heat, and add 1 tablespoon of vegetable oil or butter to grease it. When the pan is hot (see Hot Hot Heat, page 34), pour the dry ingredients into the wet and stir to combine.

**5.** Ladle about ½ cup batter into the pan to make 1 large pancake or 4 dollops of 2 to 3 tablespoons each to make silver-dollar pancakes. Cook until the edges start to look dry and a few bubbles begin to rise to the top, 2 to 4 minutes, depending on the size of the pancake. The cooked side should be just golden and not too brown.

**6.** Flip the pancake—you should then see it swell and rise as the gas bubbles released are trapped against the underside of the cooked surface. Cook 1 to 2 minutes more until just cooked through and golden on the second side. Transfer to the platter in the oven. Repeat with the remaining batter. Use caution when removing the platter from the oven because it will be hot!

## Beginner's Bread: The Magic of Yeast

Do you dream of fragrant loaves of freshly baked bread, light in the middle and toothsome at the crust, warm from the oven, and slathered with creamy butter? Do you instead settle for spongy, gummy, plastic-wrapped store-bought bread? If your answer is "Yes, because baking bread is too complicated," you'll be pleasantly surprised to learn that a basic bread recipe has just four ingredients: flour, water, yeast, and salt. That's it. And once you understand how bread works, you can confidently master any bread recipe.

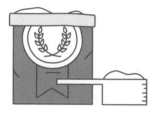

**Flour.** There are myriad types of flour, made from many grains from around the globe, but in the US, the most common is wheat flour. That category can be further broken down into enriched, blended, whole grain, bread, graham, bolted, cake, bleached and unbleached, and so on. Overwhelmed? Start with all-purpose flour, sold inexpensively at any supermarket in variously sized bags. And there you have your cornerstone.

**Water.** Water serves two functions in bread making: It activates the yeast and dissolves the ingredients into a uniform dough. More water means you get a stickier dough, which results in irregular holes, as in baguette or ciabatta. Skimp on the water, and you'll wind up with a dense, dry loaf.

**Yeast.** Yeast makes dough rise by "exhaling" carbon dioxide bubbles. The gluten in the flour stretches to accommodate them, like miniballoons, making the dough ball expand. Instant or rapid-rise yeast, sold in packets at the supermarket, is inexpensive and easy to get your hands on. It quickens the process and minimizes steps, but some complain that flavor is sacrificed. Another option for the beginning baker is active dry yeast, which is a yeast that is dormant until you add water. Active dry yeast performs best if you "proof" it first—that is, combine it with slightly warm water and a bit of sweetener (to feed the yeast) until it turns bubbly and creamy. Artisanal bakers and pastry chefs use fresh yeast, mostly because of its flavor, but dried yeast produces excellent homemade loaves.

**Salt.** Salt adds flavor but also controls the yeast by slowing the fermentation process, keeping the bread matrix from overstretching and subsequently deflating. For a proper rise, you have to get the salt-to-yeast ratio right. Plain table salt will do, though some prefer the flavor of sea salt.

### It's Alive!

Yeast are living organisms, in the kingdom Fungi (which also includes mushrooms). Here's how we know:

**1.** Yeast respires, a form of breathing. It takes in oxygen in the form of glucose, a simple sugar.

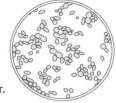

**2.** It eats and produces waste. After eating the sugar, it releases carbon dioxide gas, and, in anaerobic (air-free) environments, ethanol alcohol. Enzymes in the yeast turn starch into maltose, another sugar. This fermentation process is used in brewing beer, which is why certain breads have a beery taste, and accounts for why bread doesn't taste like flour-and-water paste!

**3.** And yeast reproduces. A single-celled organism, yeast reproduces through budding. This process happens when a smaller cell splits off from the edge of another cell.

×××××××××××××××××××××××××××××××××××××××××××

# ON SPOON SELECTION

**W**ooden spoons are ideal for stirring dough because they have a large surface area for mixing, they won't bend under pressure, and they feel good in your hand when moving around heavy dough and batters—they don't cut uncomfortably into your palm the way a metal spoon might.

# #19
## HOW TO KNEAD BREAD DOUGH

Kneading is the process of combining water and flour (and any other ingredients) in a way that will result in springy, elastic dough and airy, nicely chewy bread. Many bakers use mixers equipped with dough hooks to combine the ingredients and stretch the resulting dough, but kneading by hand is the traditional way and is remarkably easy. (Of course, you don't *have* to knead to make bread—see the Four-Ingredient No-Knead Bread recipe that follows.)

**1 PUT YOUR DOUGH ON A LIGHTLY** floured surface. To avoid adding too much flour to your recipe, use as little flour as is effective to keep the dough from sticking.

**2 WASH AND DRY YOUR HANDS** and remove any rings or dangling bracelets. Lightly flour your hands.

**3 GATHER THE DOUGH INTO A** ball and start working it with the heel of your hand, pressing and stretching it until it has a little spring to it.

**4 FOLD THE DOUGH IN HALF,** rotate it 90 degrees, and repeat, continuing until the dough is smooth and stretchy, typically about 10 minutes (though this depends on the recipe).

## RECIPE: FOUR-INGREDIENT NO-KNEAD BREAD

This bread relies on fermentation from a very long rise, rather than kneading, to break down the proteins and form the strands of gluten that structure the loaf. Make it in the morning and let it rise all day, or make it before bed and let it rise all night. If you like, use half whole-wheat flour here instead, but increase the water to 2 cups.

**Makes one (8-inch) loaf**

3½ cups all-purpose flour

2 teaspoons kosher salt

¼ teaspoon instant yeast (see Note)

1¾ cups lukewarm water

**1.** Combine all of the ingredients in a large mixing bowl and mix thoroughly with a wooden spoon, stirring the dough about 20 times.

**2.** Once mixed, cover the bowl tightly with plastic wrap and keep covered for 12 hours at room temperature. Generously grease an 8-inch loaf pan.

**3.** Once the dough has risen, turn it into the loaf pan. It will be soft. Let rise again, covered with plastic wrap until it has doubled in size, about 2 hours.

**4.** Preheat the oven to 375°F.

**5.** Bake until it smells fragrant and has a golden-brown crust, 30 to 40 minutes.

**NOTE:** You can substitute ½ teaspoon active dry yeast for the instant. Proof it according to package directions before adding to the other ingredients.

## RECIPE: THE VERY BEST SANDWICH BREAD

Making bread is something of a project, so make sure you have a few hours to spare. Of course, most of that time is needed for the dough to rise.

**Makes two (8-inch) loaves**

2 cups warm water

2 tablespoons active dry yeast

2 teaspoons salt

2 tablespoons plus 2 teaspoons vegetable oil

⅓ cup granulated sugar

5½ cups bread flour, plus more for kneading

**1.** In a large bowl, combine the warm water, yeast, salt, oil, sugar, and half the flour. Mix thoroughly with a wooden spoon, and let rise in a warm place until it doubles in size, about 2 hours.

**2.** Turn the dough out onto a floured surface and gradually knead in the rest of the flour; continue kneading until smooth.

**3.** Put the dough ball into a large, lightly oiled bowl, and turn it several times to coat. Cover with a damp dish towel and leave it in a warm place until the dough doubles in size, about an hour.

**4.** Punch down the dough with your fist (this releases air bubbles), then let it rest for a few minutes. Meanwhile, lightly oil two 8-inch loaf pans.

**5.** Divide the dough into two equal parts. Pat each piece into an oval shape on a lightly floured work surface, and then fold the top and bottom over the middle like folding a letter. Put each loaf seam-side down into the prepared pans and cover lightly with plastic wrap. Let rise in a warm place until it's almost doubled, about an hour.

**6.** Preheat the oven to 350°F.

**7.** Bake for 35 to 45 minutes, until the crust is lightly browned and the loaves sound hollow when tapped.

## RECIPE: WHOLE-WHEAT SANDWICH BREAD

If you are looking to get more whole grains in your diet or simply prefer the toasty flavor of whole-wheat bread, this honey-sweetened loaf is the one to try.

**Makes two (8-inch) loaves**

2¾ cups warm water

2¼ teaspoons (1 envelope) active dry yeast

⅓ cup honey

¼ cup olive oil

3 teaspoons salt

4 cups whole-wheat flour

3 cups all-purpose flour, plus more for kneading

Non-stick cooking spray

**1.** Stir the warm water and yeast together in a large bowl. Let stand for 5 minutes.

**2.** Gently stir in the honey, olive oil, and salt.

**3.** Gradually add both types of flour while you stir. Mix until the ingredients are thoroughly combined and the dough begins to pull away from the sides of the bowl.

**4.** On a lightly floured surface, knead the dough until it is smooth and elastic (see "How to Knead Bread Dough," opposite). If the dough is sticky, add a bit more flour.

**5.** Put the dough ball into a large, lightly oiled bowl. Spray a sheet of plastic wrap with cooking spray, cover the bowl, and allow the bread to rise for about an hour or until doubled in size. Lightly grease two 8-inch loaf pans.

**6.** Punch the dough down and divide it in half, using a sharp knife. On a clean work surface, lightly sprinkled with flour, shape each piece into an oval, and fold the top and bottom over the middle like folding a letter. Put each loaf seam-side down in the prepared pans, and cover with the oiled plastic wrap. Let rise again, until doubled in size, 30 minutes to 1 hour.

**7.** Preheat the oven to 375°F.

**8.** Remove the plastic wrap, and bake the loaves until the crust is lightly browned and the loaves sound hollow when lightly tapped, about 30 minutes.

**When paired with salt, bread is a traditional offering of welcome in many cultures. In fact, the phrase "Bread and salt!" is a greeting in Russia, often uttered by a guest as an expression of gratitude and good wishes to a host.**

# #20
# HOW TO MAKE A SANDWICH

**P**ortable and tidy, with rich layers of meat, vegetables, and condiments tucked between slices of bread, the beloved sandwich allows the hungry to eat a quick and tasty, nutritious meal-in-one without the fuss of cutlery—anytime, anyplace.

## What Makes It a Sandwich?

A Boston court, when confronted with the question in a case regarding a zoning law for "sandwich shops," ruled that it is commonly understood that a "sandwich" includes at least two slices of bread. As a fan of the open-faced sandwich, featuring items stacked atop a single slice, I beg to differ. But the ruling did get to the heart of the matter—a sandwich must involve bread, which serves as an edible container for fillings (meat, vegetables, cheeses—the possibilities are endless) and spreads (mayo, mustard, jellies, hot sauce, and so on), which add flavor and moisten the bread to prevent dryness.

## A World of Bread Awaits

**Sliced white or wheat bread.** A perfectly acceptable choice as a foundation for your sandwiches, but there's a big world beyond Wonder. Explore and taste—you'll likely discover a new favorite.

**Baguette.** Long, narrow French bread loaves. Cut it into lengths, then split lengthwise and layer with slices of Brie cheese (no need to slice off the white rind, it's delicious!) and roasted red peppers from a jar. Or slather it with chocolate-hazelnut paste (such as Nutella), dot with sliced banana, and serve open-faced with coffee for a sweet breakfast.

**Hard rolls.** Also called bulkies, Vienna rolls, Kaiser rolls, and crusty rolls. Ideal for fried egg and cheese, with a little ketchup; pulled pork with pickles; or tuna salad with lettuce and a light layer of mayo.

**Rye and pumpernickel.** These flavorful old-world breads are made with rye flour as well as wheat, and are deli favorites for pastrami and corned beef, whitefish or lox, and toppings such as sauerkraut, Dijon mustard, and dill relish.

**Flavored breads.** Olive, onion, garlic, jalapeño, and so forth. These serve their purpose in a sandwich, plus bring intense taste to the table. Although you can certainly double-down with strong-tasting fillings such as fragrant cheeses, smoked or canned fish, and spicy or pungent condiments, these breads do a lot of the heavy lifting flavorwise and are delicious with just a simple schmear of goat cheese or mild deli meats such as honey-roasted or smoked turkey.

**English muffins.** These round, crusty flat rolls aren't just for breakfast! The nooks and crannies are excellent conveyors of spreadable fillings such as cream cheese or pimento cheese, and the sourdough flavor works well with milder items such as ham, Cheddar, or American cheese.

**Flatbreads.** Generally lower in calories than thicker breads, these chewy wraps are ideal with hummus, topped with sliced olives, or filled with cream cheese and cucumber. For a nutritious and delicious sandwich, fill a flatbread with grilled vegetables sprinkled with olive oil.

## TYPES OF BREADS

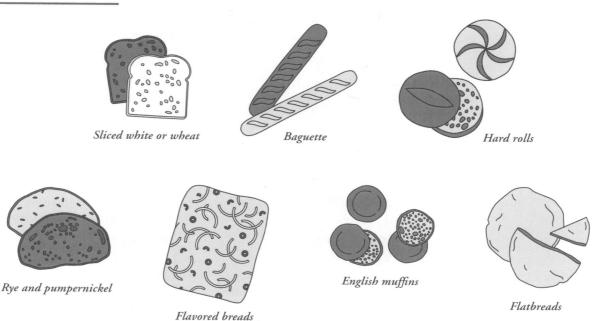

Sliced white or wheat

Baguette

Hard rolls

Rye and pumpernickel

Flavored breads

English muffins

Flatbreads

**1 CHOOSE YOUR BREAD.** In general, consider sturdier or toasted breads for wet or saucy fillings, and softer breads when the contents are sturdy and harder to chew. For example, never put a Sloppy Joe on thin, white sandwich bread—it will soak through and get *too* sloppy. Conversely, for thick slices of roast beef, piled high with lettuce, tomato, and Russian dressing, a softer bread such as packaged sliced rye or white makes the sandwich easier to bite into.

**2 IF YOU WANT TO, LIGHTLY** toast the bread. For a wetter sandwich with juicy fillings such as tomatoes or dressing, or a very moist tuna salad, toasting keeps the finished sandwich from falling apart.

**3 SPREAD SOMETHING TASTY** on the bread. Down South, practically every sandwich gets spread with an ultrathin layer of butter. This delicious coating of fat serves as a barrier to lock in juicy fillings and kept the bread from drying out during hot summer picnics. I still love butter on a ham sandwich, but I've spread the love to other toppings, too.

**4 FILL YOUR SANDWICH.** The range is almost overwhelmingly broad here—practically anything you can slap on bread fits the bill. See "Types of Fillings" (page 43) to get you started.

**5 ENJOY YOUR SANDWICH.** Open-faced, triple-decker, cut into triangles, hot or cold— layer up and customize however you like. Creativity is most definitely rewarded.

**Mayonnaise.** Creamy, eggy, and salty, much like butter it moistens and adds subtle flavor. I especially love it mixed with diced egg, canned tuna, or lunchmeats. (See recipe at right to make your own.)

**Mustard.** Low in calories, piquant, and available in a wide variety of styles. On a burger, I'll take American yellow mustard, but on a cheese sandwich, give me seedy English mustard or German mustard accented with a burst of horseradish.

**Ketchup.** Sweet and vinegary, ketchup also brings the tang of tomatoes and salt to a sandwich. Best on hot sandwiches.

**Barbecue sauce.** Like ketchup, with smoke. Perfect for roasted pork and grilled chicken breast.

**Avocado.** Smash avocado onto bread with a fork and sprinkle with a little salt, and you have a moist, flavor-rich, nutritious spread full of healthy fats.

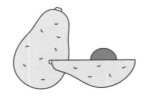

**Secret sandwich sauce.** One of my best-kept secrets is just mayonnaise and anything tangy. Try mayonnaise and a little ketchup, or mayonnaise and Dijon, or mayonnaise and steak sauce blended. The proportions are entirely up to you, but the blend is always delicious. For a little spiciness, try mayonnaise and a spoonful of chipotle in adobo.

## RECIPE: HOMEMADE MAYO

Most people don't even know what's in mayonnaise, that bewitching sauce originating in Mahon, Spain, let alone how easy it is to make from scratch. At its most basic, mayo has just four ingredients—though you should feel free to doctor it up with white pepper, paprika, mustard, hot sauce, or a minced garlic clove. (Before you start, see "Raw Eggs: Are They Safe to Eat?" page 26.) You can skip the whisking and make this in the blender, if you like, drizzling in the oil in a thin stream as the machine runs at a medium speed.

### Makes 1 cup

2 large egg yolks

Juice of 1 lemon

½ teaspoon salt

1 cup mild-flavored oil, such as vegetable or canola

**1.** In a large mixing bowl, whisk together the egg yolks, lemon juice, and salt.

**2.** Continue to whisk while you pour the oil into the mix in a very slow stream. If you stop whisking or add the oil too quickly, it will separate and not thicken into an emulsion.

**3.** Keep whisking for 2 to 3 minutes until the mixture is creamy and thick. Taste and add a bit of salt or more lemon juice if you feel you need it. Serve at once and store extra tightly covered, in the refrigerator, for up to 5 days.

## TYPES OF FILLINGS

**Meats.** Thinly sliced generally is best. Roasted meats such as turkey, ham, and beef are favorites, as are cured meats such as salami and mortadella. Try grilled steak, pork chops, or chicken breast, sliced horizontally with a sharp knife, for a variation. (A sandwich is an excellent use for leftovers.)

**Vegetables.** Hot or cold, veggie sandwiches rule. Try roasted vegetables such as peppers, onions, eggplant, or summer squash, and melt cheese on them if you like. Stack thinly sliced raw vegetables with bean sprouts or watercress, and then moisten with plenty of spread.

**Eggs.** Boil them for egg salad, dice them into tuna salad, fry and top with grated Cheddar—eggy sandwich possibilities abound. An excellent source of protein, you'll walk away satisfied.

## RECIPE: THE CLASSIC BLT

Ubiquitous in American culture, from the lunch counters of the 1940s to the trendy gastropubs of today, the BLT may be the single most popular sandwich after the hamburger. In a bacon, lettuce, and tomato sandwich, three ingredients vie to be top dog. I like them all equally. But I can't help thinking it should be called a BLTM because it wouldn't be the same without the mayo.

**Makes 1 sandwich**

3 slices thick-cut bacon

2 slices sturdy white bread, lightly toasted

1 to 2 tablespoons mayonnaise (preferably homemade, see "Homemade Mayo," facing page)

2 to 4 leaves romaine lettuce

2 to 3 slices ripe tomato (preferably beefsteak)

Salt and freshly ground black pepper

**1.** In a medium-size skillet, fry the bacon until just crisp. Once cooked, transfer it to 2 layers of paper towels to drain. Lay another layer of paper towels on top and set aside.

**2.** Slather the lightly toasted bread with mayonnaise. On one slice, lay 1 or 2 leaves of lettuce, depending on their size, covering the bread completely.

**3.** Break the drained bacon strips in half and layer on top of the lettuce. Top with 2 to 3 slices of tomato, completely covering the bacon. Season the tomato with salt and pepper to taste.

**4.** Add another layer of lettuce, then top with the remaining slice of bread, mayo-side down.

**5.** Put the sandwich on a plate and slice in half diagonally. Flank with a pickle and potato chips, and serve.

# #21
# HOW TO REFRESH STALE BREAD

Cutting costs on groceries is one of the surest ways to slash household expenses. And the first step to spending less on food is to not waste what you buy. This is obviously a big issue to tackle all at once, so let's start with the basics: bread. A backbone of the Western diet, bread unfortunately doesn't stay fresh long. Because stale bread is practically a given, a little culinary creativity is called for to make sure it doesn't end up in the trash. Here are some ideas to give new life to the staff of life.

**Toast it.** If your bagel, boule, or baguette is starting to harden, slice it and make toast. (Who doesn't love toast?) Bump this bread to the front of the meal-planning line and make grilled cheese sandwiches, BLTs on toast, tea with cinnamon toast, toasty garlic bread drizzled with olive oil, or mini-pizzas made with a slather of jarred marinara and grated cheese. You can make big batches of toast in the broiler on a cookie sheet.

**Transform it.** Make that stale bread into bread crumbs or croutons and give it a whole new life. Get started with recipes for French Toast Casserole, Panzanella (Bread Salad), and Meatballs, on pages 45–46.

**Make it dessert.** Bread pudding is a time-honored way to use up stale bread (see Banana–Chocolate Chip Bread Pudding, facing page), but there are simpler routes to dessert: Top sliced bread (try a baguette, an English muffin, or a bagel) with chopped bittersweet chocolate or a sprinkling of chocolate chips, and then toast until the bread is golden brown and the chocolate is melted. Spread the chocolate smooth and drizzle with extra-virgin olive oil and sea salt. For dessert crostini, thinly slice Italian or French bread, brush with oil, and toast under the broiler until lightly browned, about five minutes. Top with ricotta or goat cheese mixed with honey, mashed berries, or even caramel sauce.

If your loaf is a bit past its prime, don't despair. Here's how to soften bread that has hardened.

**1** PREHEAT THE OVEN TO 325°F.

**2** PUT THE STALE BREAD IN A clean paper bag and twist the end shut tightly.

**3** SPRINKLE THE BAG LIGHTLY and evenly with cool water, but don't soak it.

**4** HEAT THE ENTIRE PACKAGE IN the oven (keeping it far away from the heating element or flame), allowing 5 minutes for small rolls and 20 minutes for full loaves. If needed, rewet the bag and repeat.

**5** SERVE THE BREAD WITHIN 10 minutes, or it will harden again.

## RECIPE: BANANA–CHOCOLATE CHIP BREAD PUDDING

**A**ny kind of bread pudding works for me, but banana and melted chocolate take this dish from homey to fabulous. Serve it topped with freshly whipped cream (see Sweetened Whipped Cream, page 14) and shaved chocolate.

**Serves 4 to 6**

8 large slices stale white bread

3 tablespoons butter, melted

¾ cup chocolate chips

2 bananas, sliced

6 large eggs, beaten

2½ cups whole milk

1 cup granulated sugar

1 teaspoon ground cinnamon

2 teaspoons vanilla extract

**1.** Preheat the oven to 350°F.

**2.** Break the bread into small pieces and place them into an 8-inch square baking pan. Drizzle the melted butter over the bread. Sprinkle with the chocolate chips and banana slices.

**3.** In a medium-size mixing bowl, beat together the eggs, milk, sugar, cinnamon, and vanilla.

**4.** Pour the egg mixture over the bread, and lightly push down with your fingertips. Let the pudding stand for 10 minutes until the bread has soaked into the liquid.

**5.** Bake for 45 minutes, until puffy and golden, and the top springs back when lightly pressed.

## RECIPE: BAKED MEATBALLS IN TOMATO SAUCE

**H**earty, flavorful meatballs deploy the frugal cook's secret weapon to stretching ground meat: cubes of stale bread soaked in milk. In fact, meatballs made without bread are heavy, dense, and dry, so it's an excellent way to use up stale bread and make a good dinner at the same time. Baking meatballs is much easier than frying them in batches, and they taste just as good.

**Makes 2 dozen meatballs; serves 4**

1 can (28 ounces) diced tomatoes

1 large onion

4 tablespoons butter

4 slices white bread, torn into large chunks

1 cup whole milk

1 large egg, beaten

1½ pounds ground chuck

½ cup freshly grated Parmesan cheese, plus more for serving

1 clove garlic, minced

1 teaspoon whole dried oregano

1 teaspoon salt

Hot cooked pasta (see page 50)

**1.** Put the diced tomatoes in a medium-size saucepan over medium heat. Peel the onion, slice it in half, and add one entire half to the pan along with the butter. Bring to a simmer, then reduce the heat to medium-low, and let the sauce simmer gently, stirring now and then, while you make the meatballs. Dice the rest of the onion finely and put it in a large mixing bowl.

**2.** Preheat the oven to 350°F. Line a rimmed baking pan with foil (for easier cleanup).

**3.** Add the bread, milk, and egg to the onion in the mixing bowl. Stir and let sit for 3 minutes so the bread absorbs the moisture. Add the meat, Parmesan cheese, garlic, oregano, and salt, and mix thoroughly, ideally using slightly wet hands.

**4.** Form the mixture into 24 meatballs and place them on the baking sheet. Bake for 30 to 40 minutes, until browned and cooked through. (Break one open to check.)

**5.** Remove and discard the onion half from the tomato sauce. Add the baked meatballs to the sauce and toss to coat. Serve over hot pasta with additional Parmesan cheese.

# #22 HOW TO MAKE BREAD CRUMBS

**M**ake old bread the foundation of new dishes with easy, multipurpose fresh bread crumbs.

**1 TEAR THE BREAD INTO CHUNKS** and pulse them in the blender or food processor to the desired consistency.

**2 IF YOU WANT DRY BREAD CRUMBS,** such as for coating chops or chicken breasts before frying or baking, first toast the bread chunks in a 375°F oven until dried out, about 10 or 15 minutes.

**3 SEASON THE CRUMBS WITH FRESH** or dried herbs, ground pepper, or powdered garlic.

**4 STORE THE FRESH BREAD CRUMBS** in the refrigerator in an airtight container for up to a week or freeze for up to 6 months.

# #23
## HOW TO MAKE CROUTONS

Give your soups and salads extra crunch, flavor, and substance with a sprinkling of homemade croutons.

**1** PREHEAT THE OVEN TO 350°F.

**2** DICE BREAD INTO LARGE CUBES, then toss them with enough extra-virgin olive oil to coat but not saturate.

**3** TOAST THE CUBES UNTIL DRIED and lightly golden, 20 to 25 minutes.

**4** AS SOON AS THEY COME OUT OF the oven, toss the croutons with salt and ground black pepper, or fancy them up with pesto, cayenne, onion salt, or lemon pepper.

**5** SERVE IMMEDIATELY OR STORE in an airtight container for up to a week.

## RECIPE: PANZANELLA (BREAD SALAD)

Old-world Italian home cooks thought it was a sin to waste food, especially bread. This salad is my go-to when tomatoes are falling off the vine and I've got bread to repurpose. This salad becomes a full meal if you serve cooked sliced steak or chicken breast over the top.

### Serves 4

2 pounds ripe tomatoes, cored and cubed

1 pound crusty bakery bread, such as a sourdough boule, torn into small pieces and lightly toasted for a few minutes in the oven

1 cup arugula leaves

12 fresh basil leaves, torn into large pieces

½ medium-size red onion, thinly sliced

¾ cup whole pitted olives

½ cup extra-virgin olive oil

4 tablespoons red wine vinegar

2 large or 3 small cloves garlic, minced

Salt and freshly ground black pepper

**1.** In a large bowl, combine the tomatoes, bread, arugula, basil, onion, and olives.

**2.** In a small bowl, whisk together the oil, vinegar, and garlic, and drizzle it over the salad.

**3.** Season the salad generously with salt and pepper, toss, and let stand for 15 minutes before serving.

## RECIPE: FRENCH TOAST CASSEROLE

This French toast improves on the beloved classic by having the stale bread soak overnight in its egg batter. In the morning, all you have to do is pop the pan in the preheated oven and you have a sweet breakfast for the whole family.

### Serves 4 to 6

½ cup dark or light brown sugar

½ cup (1 stick) unsalted butter, melted

3 teaspoons ground cinnamon

8 slices stale bread

½ cup raisins

6 eggs

1½ cups milk

1 tablespoon vanilla extract

**1.** In a small mixing bowl, stir together the brown sugar, butter, and 1 teaspoon of the cinnamon. Pour the mixture into the bottom of a buttered 13-by-9-inch baking pan.

**2.** Arrange the bread slices on top, and dot with the raisins.

**3.** In a large mixing bowl, beat the eggs, milk, vanilla, and the remaining 2 teaspoons cinnamon. Pour the mixture over the bread. Cover the pan with foil and refrigerate for 4 to 8 hours or overnight.

**4.** Preheat the oven to 375°F.

**5.** Bake the casserole, covered with the foil, for 40 minutes. Uncover the pan, and bake for 5 minutes, or until the top is browned. Let stand for 10 minutes before serving.

# #24
## HOW TO MAKE PIZZA

**W**hy go for delivery or frozen pizza when you can make bubbly, cheesy, completely customized pizza at home for a fraction of the cost? Premade dough is typically available for purchase at your local pizzeria, as well as at some supermarkets. Or make your own dough (see Foolproof Pizza Dough, page 48) for the ultimate treat. Homemade pizza can be a healthy, low-fat, high-nutrient supper, topped with tomato sauce, fresh vegetables, low-fat cheeses (such as a sprinkling of salty feta), or greens. Top your pizza with sausage, pepperoni, and extra cheese, and it becomes more of a "sometimes" food. Either way, it's a dinner that's sure to please.

**1** **PREHEAT THE OVEN.** A hot oven is the key to good pizza at home. Turn it up to 450°F or 500°F if your oven goes that high.

**2** **SPRINKLE CORNMEAL ON YOUR** baking sheet. Pat out your dough on a floured work surface to a pizza shape, stretching and pulling it gently to be as thin as possible. If you're having a lot of trouble, use a rolling pin, but wield it gently. Pizza won't roll out like piecrust. Just work slow and steady and it will gradually take shape.

**3** **ADD THE TOMATO SAUCE, NOT** too much (about 1 cup for a 12-inch pizza, 1½ cups for a 16-inch), and put the pizza in the oven. Bake it until the edges are puffed a bit and the sauce looks slightly dry, 7 to 9 minutes.

**4** **REMOVE THE PIZZA AND LAYER** on your toppings. Put the cheese on last so it can melt down over the toppings. And don't put on heaps of cheese (unless that's all you're using). Too much can bury the other flavors.

**5** **IF YOU WANT TO GILD THE LILY,** once you've added the toppings, brush olive oil and very lightly sprinkle salt or sesame seeds or fresh herbs on the outer rim of the crust. It will taste like a breadstick.

**6** **RETURN THE PIZZA TO THE HOT** oven and bake until bubbling. Once you have par-baked the crust with the sauce on it, the final baking time should be about 10 more minutes. Keep an eye on it. Times will vary depending on the toppings.

## Do I Need a Pizza Stone?

A pizza stone is a round stoneware, terra-cotta, or ceramic platter that sits under the pizza while it bakes. The microscopic pores in the pizza stone absorb steamy moisture from the baking dough while distributing heat evenly under the entire crust. The result is a perfectly cooked crust that won't burn before the toppings have cooked through. It's nice to have if you like a very crisp crust, but, like the pizza peel, it's not necessary. You can get excellent results using a baking sheet.

## RECIPE: FOOLPROOF PIZZA DOUGH

### Makes two (12-inch) crusts

1 cup warm water (about 110°F)

2 tablespoons sugar

2¼ tablespoons active dry yeast
   (1 [¼-ounce] envelope)

2 teaspoons extra-virgin olive oil, plus
   more for brushing

3 cups all-purpose flour, plus more for
   kneading

2 teaspoons kosher salt

Cornmeal, for sprinkling

**1.** In a large bowl, combine the water, sugar, yeast, and oil. Let stand for 5 minutes.

**2.** Add half the flour and the salt and mix well to thoroughly combine. Add 1 additional cup of flour, reserving ½ cup, and mix with your hands until combined.

**3.** Turn the dough out onto a floured surface and knead it for 5 minutes, adding the remaining flour as necessary to form a smooth and elastic dough.

**4.** Transfer the dough to a large, lightly oiled bowl and turn it to coat. Cover with a damp towel and let rise in a warm place until it doubles in size, about an hour.

**5.** Punch down the dough and divide it in half. (If you like, you can store the dough for up to a week in a tightly sealed zip-top bag in the refrigerator or freeze it for up to 3 months.) Shape the halves into balls, place them on a cornmeal-coated baking sheet, lightly brush them with olive oil, and cover them with a clean, damp towel.

**6.** Let the dough rest for an hour. Working slowly, use your fingers and the heel of your hand to gently push and stretch it into a circle 12 to 16 inches wide. If you push and tug at it gently, it will gradually give way. But if you pull at it too firmly, it will tear. If it does tear, pinch it firmly back together.

## RECIPE: QUICK NAAN PIZZA

India meets Italy with these simple and healthful entrées. Look for naan (Indian flatbread) in your grocery's Asian or ethnic sections, or in the gourmet deli and cheese section. These light, puffy breads make perfect quick crusts. If you have a jar of store-bought marinara or pizza sauce, it's even faster. If you don't have sauce, use canned tomato sauce (the smooth kind) or puree drained whole tomatoes in the blender with dried oregano.

### Serves 2 to 4

1 cup bottled marinara or pizza sauce

2 large naan breads

8 ounces fresh small mozzarella balls

1 (14-ounce) jar roasted red peppers, cut
   into strips

Other toppings, such as cooked chicken
   cubes or crumbled cooked sausage

Fresh or dried basil, optional

**1.** Preheat the oven to 450°F.

**2.** Spread a thin layer of sauce on each naan bread. Dot with drained fresh mozzarella balls. Fill in the remaining space with pepper strips or other toppings as you like. If you have fresh basil, use your kitchen shears to cut strips from the leaves and sprinkle on top, or shake on some dried basil.

**3.** Bake on a pizza stone or directly on the oven rack, until the cheese is melted and bubbly, 8 to 10 minutes.

## RECIPE: BAGUETTE WHITE PIZZA

White pizza tastes gourmet, yet it requires minimal effort to make. Serve this cut into small squares as a starter, as a side dish with steak, or with an entrée salad as a substitute for garlic bread. You can make this with stale baguette if you need to use it up.

### Serves 6

1 baguette, cut in half lengthwise

½ cup (1 stick) butter, softened

Extra-virgin olive oil

Crushed garlic or garlic salt

16 ounces shredded mozzarella (about
   4 cups)

1 cup ricotta cheese

Freshly ground black pepper

Minced fresh or dried oregano

**1.** Preheat the oven to 400°F and line a baking sheet with foil.

**2.** Take two halves of baguette and cover the cut side completely with a thin layer of soft butter. Pour on some high-quality olive oil, spreading it around with your fingers and sliding it over the butter.

**3.** Dot the bread with fresh, crushed garlic or sprinkle with garlic salt. Cover with shredded mozzarella cheese and dot with teaspoon-size dollops of ricotta cheese. Sprinkle with pepper and oregano to taste.

**4.** Bake for 10 minutes on the foil-lined baking sheet, or until the cheese bubbles and browns.

✕ ✕ ✕ ✕ ✕ ✕ ✕ ✕ ✕ ✕ ✕ ✕ ✕ ✕ ✕ ✕ ✕ ✕ ✕ ✕ ✕ ✕ ✕ ✕ ✕ ✕ ✕ ✕ ✕ ✕ ✕ ✕ ✕ ✕ ✕ ✕ ✕

# CREATIVE CRUSTS AND PIZZA SHORTCUTS

Pizza recipes are really just suggested starting points—the proportions are up to you, and ingredients can be swapped in and out, or omitted as you like. Thinking creatively will help you make a meal in minutes from items you probably already have in your fridge or pantry.

# #25
# HOW TO HAVE DINNER READY IN THIRTY MINUTES

## (or, Meal Planning and Nutrition)

A nutritionally sound meal is made up of macronutrients (fat, protein, and carbohydrates), plus a variety of micronutrients (vitamins and minerals). In other words, dinner should include a nice balance of fruits and vegetables, grains, proteins, dairy, and fats. Variety is the way to go—for health—because it keeps mealtime interesting.

The USDA recommends that 45 to 65 percent of daily calories come from carbohydrates, 10 to 35 percent from protein, and 20 to 35 percent from fats. No need to bring your calculator into the kitchen—just eyeball the plate, filling half with low-starch, low-fat fruits and vegetables (go easy on plantains and avocados) and the remaining half with a combination of lean meat or plant protein and healthful carbohydrates. Follow these steps and you are ready to make dinner in a flash, any night of the week.

**1 MAP IT OUT.** Planning meals helps you avoid the pitfalls of fast food and overspending. Think about it: When you're starved and need to grab something quick, you wind up ordering a pizza or buying premium-priced prepared foods at the store. If you've planned your meals for the week and shopped accordingly, you won't be caught empty-handed and hungry.

**2 PREP YOUR FRESH FOOD IN** advance. Spend 30 minutes preparing a week's worth of produce. Peel and slice carrots, core strawberries, wash and store lettuce (see "Care and Handling of Lettuce," page 22), and cut heads of broccoli and cauliflower into florets. Store in airtight, lidded bowls in the fridge. Ready to be eaten raw in salads or with dips such as hummus and salsa, or sautéed or steamed in the space of 5 minutes, these foods are right for your budget and your health.

**3 MAKE A ROAST.** It can serve as a foundation for a week's meals. Bake a turkey or two chickens, pop a brisket in the slow cooker, or make a pork roast in a Dutch oven. Eat it right away for dinner, then refrigerate or freeze the leftovers for future sandwiches, stir-fries, salads, and soups.

*(continued)*

✕ ✕ ✕ ✕ ✕ ✕ ✕ ✕ ✕ ✕ ✕ ✕ ✕ ✕ ✕ ✕ ✕ ✕ ✕ ✕ ✕ ✕ ✕ ✕ ✕ ✕ ✕ ✕ ✕ ✕ ✕ ✕ ✕ ✕ ✕ ✕

## AREN'T CARBS BAD FOR ME?

Carbohydrates, made up of starches, sugars, and fiber, provide us with the fuel we burn daily. Without them, our bodies can feel sluggish and our brains fuzzy. The higher the fiber and the lower the sugar, the better the carb.

**4** **KEEP QUICK PROTEIN SOURCES** on hand. Eggs are cheap and nutritious, and they are easy to cook. Boil them and slice them over salads, stuff an omelet with veggies and a sprinkle of cheese for a hot dinner, or make quiche, if you are feeling ambitious. Canned beans, packed with protein, fiber, and vitamins, are cooked and ready; toss with onions, chives, peppers, and tomatoes, and dress with oil, vinegar, and salt and pepper, for a 10-minute salad.

**5** **KEEP THE FREEZER STOCKED.** Leftovers, soups and casseroles, meat and fish all keep well for months in the freezer. Flash-frozen vegetables from the store—picked and frozen at their peak—can actually be more nutritious than fresh! Plus, they're cheap and long-lasting. With a full freezer, you are ready for anything.

## RECIPE: LINGUINE PRIMAVERA

Pasta primavera (or "spring pasta"), a vegetable-heavy Italian classic, is an easy, economical, meatless dish that's quick to prepare. Use as a main course, served with green salad and garlic bread (an excellent use for a slightly past its prime baguette or French bread!), or as a side dish for a meat or fish entrée.

### Serves 4 to 6

1 pound linguine (for extra nutrition, use spinach linguine or whole-wheat linguine)

3 tablespoons butter

½ large onion, diced

2 cloves garlic, minced

2 cups chopped broccoli or cauliflower, or a mix (frozen is fine)

1 cup thinly sliced carrots

¾ cup sliced black olives

2 teaspoons Italian seasoning (or substitute 1 teaspoon dried basil and 1 teaspoon dried oregano)

¼ teaspoon freshly ground black pepper

⅓ cup dry white wine, cooking sherry, or chicken broth

1 large tomato, diced

1 cup freshly shaved Parmesan cheese

**1.** Cook the pasta according to package directions. (This should take about 10 minutes.)

**2.** While the pasta boils, melt the butter in a large skillet over medium heat. Add the onions, garlic, broccoli or cauliflower, carrots, olives, Italian seasoning, and black pepper, and sauté for about 5 minutes, until the onions start to soften.

**3.** Pour in the wine, sherry, or chicken broth, and continue to stir. Add the tomato and cook for a minute or two.

**4.** Drain the pasta and transfer it to a large serving bowl. Add the sautéed vegetables and toss well with the pasta. Sprinkle the Parmesan cheese over the top.

### Variations

⊹ For extra protein, add strips of cooked chicken, turkey, drained ground beef, or cannellini (white) beans when you add the tomato.

⊹ For a rich tomato broth, skip the wine, sherry, or broth and substitute jarred marinara.

×××××××××××××××××××××××××××××××××××××××××××××××××××××××××××××××××

# PROCEDURES FOR PERFECT PASTA

Since you learned to boil water on page 6, you should be a real pro at making pasta. All a box of dried pasta requires is a large pot of boiling water and a timer. Here are some tips to refine your pasta-boiling process:

• Fill a large stock pot with water and set it on the stove over high heat, until it comes to a boil. Before you put in the pasta, add generous amounts of salt to the water—this will ensure that the pasta is adequately salted.

• Follow the package instructions to determine how long to cook the pasta. Typically, pastas cook in 8 to 12 minutes. If you prefer your pasta slightly firmer—that is, *al dente*—remove it a minute or two before the package instructions indicate.

• When it's done to your liking, drain the pasta in a colander, then toss with sauce and any other additions, and serve. To fully infuse the pasta with its sauce, dump the drained pasta into the pot with the sauce and cook together for a couple of minutes.

# #26
# HOW TO MAKE SOUP

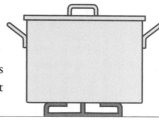

Soup is as old as cooking itself. With the invention of fire, the idea of combining foods, herbs, and flavorings in a pot to transform them into a filling, nutritious, and easily digestible comestible was inevitable, and it has endured. Our word *soup* likely hearkens back to the Latin word *suppa*, meaning "bread soaked in broth." The old ways are often the best ways, and for ease, economy, and variety, soup is a star player at my family's table.

**1 IT ALL STARTS WITH STOCK.** Make stock (a full-flavored broth), the basis for all soups, out of anything edible that imparts flavor and won't disintegrate. Use bones, woody vegetable trimmings, onion and garlic skins, whole herbs, lobster shells, fish parts, or limp vegetables. All you need is a large pot and enough water to cover your components. Bring to a boil, reduce to a simmer, and cook until you have flavorful liquid. (This can take as much time as you have—even a 20-minute simmer makes for a more flavorful base.) Skim the scum from the top and strain, reserving the broth. For added flavor, before adding stock to the pot, roast any bones or meat you are using until fragrant and sizzling or pour olive oil into your stockpot and fry the uncooked meat or bones until browned. (Remove the bone before puréeing, serving, or storing.) If you are using onions and garlic, chop and sauté them in the stockpot until transparent, then add the other ingredients.

**2 ADD YOUR MAIN INGREDIENTS** to your broth. More refined soups will require a recipe, but soup's beauty is that it can be made with whatever you have in the pantry and fridge—leftovers, grains and pastas, veggies past their prime, almost any cut or variety of meat. If you're on a budget, buy whatever's on sale. Anything goes (almost) when you're making soup.

**3 IF YOU'RE USING ALL** vegetables and you like a creamy soup, puree it. This is easiest with a handheld stick blender (beware splashing hot soup!). If you're using a standing blender, blend the soup in small batches and hold the lid on with a dish towel to prevent any splashing. (Transfer each batch of the pureed soup to a clean saucepan.) After pureeing, enrich the soup with a little cream, Greek yogurt, sour cream, milk, or nondairy milk such as rice or almond. Start with a small amount, such as ¼ cup, and taste before adding more. A little bit of creaminess can go a long way; you want to enrich the flavor of the soup, not dilute it.

**4 FINALLY, THE FINISHING** touches. Don't skip out on fresh herbs because they work wonders by brightening a soup's flavors. Depending on your other ingredients, try dill, parsley, oregano, basil, cilantro, or even mint for chilled soups. Chop them finely and add a tablespoon or two to the whole pot, or sprinkle a little on top of each serving. Other good toppings are a dollop of sour cream or yogurt or some shredded cheese. Cook a few slices of bacon to crispness and crumble them. And never underestimate the power of croutons to make a bowl of soup into a meal: You don't need packaged croutons if you've got a toaster (or an oven: See How to Make Croutons, page 46). Toast thick-sliced bread to a golden hue, brush with olive oil, and rub the surface lightly with a garlic clove. Cut into cubes and sprinkle on top.

## A Soup by Any Other Name . . .

Thick or thin, smooth or chunky, hot or cold, soup comes in as many varieties as there are names for it. Here's an overview of common types:

**Stock or broth.** Thin, strained liquid in which meat or vegetables—sometimes with herbs and spices—have been simmered to extract their flavor. Most commonly used as a base for other soups.

**Consommé.** Clarified broth, which has been strained, cooked with egg white and some eggshell to attract solids floating in the broth, then strained again.

**Bisque.** Thick, rich, and smooth. Usually includes chunks of shellfish or vegetables, as in lobster bisque or tomato bisque.

**Chowder.** Thick and chunky, almost stewlike, with a cream or milk base. Traditionally made with seafood but could feature poultry, vegetables, or cheese.

**Chilled.** Made from vegetables, such as gazpacho and borscht, or fruit, as in cold watermelon or sour cherry soup.

**Purees.** Made by blending cooked ingredients into a velvety liquid, as in acorn squash soup or potato-leek soup.

**Stews.** Chili, burgoo, gumbo, and more. Purists may not call these thick concoctions—rich with beans, meat, and vegetables—soup, but depending on how much liquid the cook includes, they are spoon foods served from bowls, like soup.

⨯ ⨯ ⨯ ⨯ ⨯ ⨯ ⨯ ⨯ ⨯ ⨯ ⨯ ⨯ ⨯ ⨯ ⨯ ⨯ ⨯ ⨯ ⨯ ⨯ ⨯ ⨯ ⨯ ⨯ ⨯ ⨯ ⨯ ⨯ ⨯ ⨯ ⨯ ⨯ ⨯ ⨯ ⨯ ⨯ ⨯ ⨯ ⨯ ⨯

# DOES ALCOHOL BURN OFF DURING COOKING?

**M**ostly . . . high temperatures evaporate most alcohol, leaving only the flavor behind. Test results vary regarding how much and how fast it is burned off, depending on whether you're flaming it in a skillet, baking, or simmering. No matter the method, however, the amount of actual alcohol that remains in a dish is usually quite insignificant. If you're very concerned, just leave it out.

## RECIPE: CHORIZO AND BEAN SOUP

**T**his warming sausage soup straddles the middle ground between soup and stew. Try it when time is limited but appetites aren't.

**Serves 4 to 6**

1 tablespoon olive oil

12 ounces dried chorizo sausage, diced

1 large onion, diced

4 stalks celery, chopped

5 large cloves garlic, minced

1 can (14 ounces) garbanzo beans, drained and rinsed

1 can (14 ounces) white beans (such as cannellini), drained and rinsed

4 cups chicken broth (preferably homemade)

½ cup white wine, cooking sherry, or beef broth

1 teaspoon dried thyme

1 teaspoon dried parsley

¼ cup fresh basil or Italian parsley, chopped

½ teaspoon dried chile flakes

**1.** In a large, heavy-bottomed stockpot over high heat, warm half the olive oil, then add the sausage. Cook until browned, about 5 minutes, then transfer to a dish and set aside.

**2.** Set the same pot back over medium heat and warm the rest of the olive oil. Add the onion and celery, and cook until softened, about 10 minutes. Add the garlic and cook until it's golden, another minute.

**3.** Reduce the heat to medium-low and add the cooked sausage, and the garbanzo and white beans. Stir together to combine, until the beans are coated with the onions and oil.

**4.** Add the broth and white wine or sherry, and bring to a boil. Reduce the heat to a simmer and add the dried and fresh herbs and the chile flakes. Simmer until slightly thickened, about 30 minutes.

## RECIPE: THE BEST CHICKEN SOUP

What makes a chicken soup the best? It might sound obvious, but: It's the chicken. My top choice is a free-range, organic kosher pullet. A pullet is a female too young to lay eggs; they generally weigh about 6 pounds at slaughter. Free-range chickens dine on insects and vegetation, adding to their flavor, and if they are organic, they haven't ingested hormones and pesticides. Any chicken, however, will make delicious soup—a whole broiler or even parts, if they are on sale.

### Serves 6

**FOR THE STOCK**

3½- to 4-pound chicken

1 large yellow onion, quartered (unpeeled)

2 large carrots, cut into chunks (unpeeled)

2 stalks celery with leaves, cut into chunks

4 sprigs fresh parsley

4 sprigs fresh thyme

6 cloves garlic (unpeeled)

2 teaspoons salt

½ teaspoon freshly ground black pepper

**FOR THE SOUP**

1 cup finely diced carrots

1 cup thinly sliced celery

1 medium-size yellow onion, minced

**1.** To make the stock, put all the stock ingredients in a large soup pot. Add 2 quarts water, and bring the ingredients to a boil over high heat. Reduce the heat to medium-low, and simmer uncovered for 1 hour.

**2.** Remove the chicken and allow it to cool slightly. Remove all the breast meat and set aside. Return the carcass to the pot and continue to simmer, uncovered, for 2 to 3 hours (you can cook it for less time, but this makes a richer stock).

**3.** Strain the contents of the pot and discard all the solids—their flavor should have all transferred into the broth.

**4.** To make the soup, add the diced carrots, celery, and onions to the chicken stock. Simmer until the vegetables are tender, about 15 minutes.

**5.** Chop the reserved chicken breast meat into bite-size pieces, add it to the pot, and heat through.

**Variations:** There are as many styles of chicken soup as there are cultures on earth. Here are some suggestions:

⌗ Chicken noodle or rice. Add raw or cooked noodles or rice to the boiling soup and simmer until the starch is cooked or heated through as necessary.

⌗ Chicken-vegetable. Zucchini, turnips, parsnips, potatoes, or green peas are all excellent additions. For ease, use frozen mixed vegetables.

⌗ Egg drop. Use a ratio of 1 beaten egg to every 2 cups pure chicken broth. Whisk the egg into the hot broth, top with sliced scallions, and serve.

⌗ Chicken-barley. A filling and nutritious whole grain, barley requires extra salt and pairs well with fresh mushrooms. Add ½ cup medium-size pearl barley with the vegetables and cook until tender, 15 to 20 minutes.

⌗ Matzoh ball. These are dumplings made with unleavened matzoh meal; packaged mixes make them super simple. As with pasta, boil the matzoh balls separately and introduce them to the broth upon serving.

✕ ✕ ✕ ✕ ✕ ✕ ✕ ✕ ✕ ✕ ✕ ✕ ✕ ✕ ✕ ✕ ✕

## DOES CHICKEN SOUP CURE COLDS?

Nothing cures the common cold, but chicken soup can help the symptoms. Old-world moms knew this, which is why it's called Jewish penicillin. Researchers say that chicken soup acts as an anti-inflammatory by slowing the movement of white blood cells, which cause congestion. The steam also temporarily clears a stuffy nose and offers liquid and salt to combat dehydration; in addition, because it's easy to eat and digest, soup provides calories for energy when you're weak.

American families throw away about 14 percent of their food per year, adding up to about $600 per family in wasted groceries. Soup is the perfect recipe to absorb any extra produce left over at the end of the week.

# #27
# HOW TO GRILL VEGETABLES

**D**on't use that grill just for burgers and steaks. Grilling is a quick way to cook a lot of veggies, and it brings out an abundance of flavor. Try spring and summer veggies such as asparagus, eggplant, zucchini, and corn, or even cool-weather produce such as yams, leeks, and fennel.

## A Guide to Cooking Methods

Vegetables are the most health-promoting foods of all. Skip the veg, and you'll miss the benefits of their fiber, antioxidants, and good-for-you phytochemicals. Many adults don't eat nearly enough vegetables, and although many profess to dislike them—I suspect a childhood experience with overcooked, mushy, or canned vegetables that hardly resemble their original form is to blame—even veggie fans often don't cook them because they never learned how. The good news is: There are many ways to cook veggies to their best advantage, and all of them are simple enough for novice cooks.

**1 MAKE SURE YOUR VEGETABLES** are clean and thoroughly dry. Dampness will cause sticking.

**2 CHOP, SEASON, AND MARINATE** your vegetables. A light coating of oil and spices does the trick, or use bottled, oil-based salad dressing in a pinch.

**3 FOR DENSE VEGETABLES, LIKE** potatoes, yams, and winter squash, cube and parboil them for 5 minutes first, then skewer or slice and finish them on the grill.

**4 FOR SMALLER OR SKINNY** pieces, like asparagus stalks, string beans, or broccoli florets, line the grill with foil first or thread them onto kebab sticks.

**TIP:** When making kebabs, skewer vegetables of similar thickness and density together to ensure uniform doneness.

**5 PREHEAT A GAS GRILL ON HIGH** heat with the lid closed for 10 minutes.

**6 LIGHTLY OIL THE RACK.** Arrange the pieces on the grill and cook for 3 to 5 minutes, turning the vegetables until browned and softened. Don't overcook or char when grilling vegetables. Move the pieces around often to avoid blackening. If you're cooking small pieces, you can also use a vegetable grill pan to keep the pieces from falling through.

×××××××××××××××××××××××××××××××××××××××××××

## MELLOW OUT

**I**n general, the longer you cook strong-tasting vegetables, the stronger the resulting flavor and odor becomes. Here are some guidelines to mellow assertive flavors, which should help get vegetable skeptics on board. With all of these cooking methods, start with cleaned and trimmed vegetables, torn or chopped into uniform pieces for even cooking.

- **Cook only until tender; don't boil or stew.**

- **Add salty toppings such as Parmesan cheese or soy sauce.**

- **Make it tangy with lemon, which works with any butter or olive oil on the vegetables to make a sauce.**

- **Add a touch of sweetness with a squeeze of honey when dressing or cooking vegetables with butter.**

---

# #28 HOW TO SAUTÉ VEGETABLES

**F**or this preparation, you'll need a large, heavy-bottomed skillet. Use nonstick if you are shooting for a low-fat meal because you'll need less oil.

**1 USE ENOUGH OIL OR BUTTER TO** coat the pan. For heart-healthy sautéing, use olive, canola, or coconut oil, which hold up well under high temperatures.

**2 BEFORE ADDING THE VEGETABLES,** heat the pan over medium-high heat until it is sizzling hot. You want the shortest cook time possible, and a preheated pan allows your vegetables to slide around without sticking.

**3 LET THE VEGETABLES BROWN** lightly in the hot pan for a moment or two, then add a couple of tablespoons of water or broth. As the liquid evaporates, the vegetables will cook through more evenly.

**4 FOR EXTRA FLAVOR, ADD MINCED** garlic or grated fresh ginger during the last 30 seconds to 1 minute of the sauté. Season with salt and pepper, maybe a touch more butter or olive oil and some soy sauce or chili flakes, and serve at once.

# HOW TO STEAM VEGETABLES

**F**or this method, you will need a steamer basket. These are inexpensive and available at any home goods or grocery store.

**1 PUT A STEAMER BASKET INTO A** saucepan with a lid, and add an inch or two of water. (The water should just reach the bottom of the basket, but not quite touch it.)

**2 PUT THE VEGETABLE PIECES** into the basket, cover the pan, and bring the water to a boil over high heat.

**3 ONCE BOILING, REDUCE THE HEAT** to medium. Throughout cooking, check to make sure the pan doesn't boil dry. Add more water as needed, but make sure whatever you add is hot.

**4 COOK UNTIL VIBRANT IN COLOR** and just tender when pierced with a fork, anywhere from 3 to 30 minutes, depending on the vegetable.

**5 REMOVE THE VEGETABLES** from heat, season, and serve immediately to prevent additional softening.

# #30 HOW TO ROAST VEGETABLES

Caramelized and intensely flavorful, roasted vegetables are an easy and delicious crowd-pleaser. Keep in mind that roasting makes veggies shrink. A pound of vegetables may feed four when steamed, but you'll need half again as much if you're roasting them.

**1 PREHEAT YOUR OVEN TO 425°F.** (You may need to adjust the heat, depending on your vegetable's size and density. Quick-cooking veggies like asparagus can take the higher heat; firmer stuff like potato chunks and squash cubes may need a lower oven, such as 350°F or 375°F, so they cook through.)

**2 LINE A ROASTING PAN WITH FOIL** coated with cooking spray (to ensure easy cleanup).

**3 TOSS THE CHOPPED VEGETABLES** with oil or an oil-based salad dressing before putting them in the pan. Leave space in between to allow hot air to circulate, so they'll cook evenly on all sides. If the vegetables look crowded, use a second pan.

**4 DON'T UNDERCOOK!** Roasting can take a while. Cauliflower florets or butternut squash chunks may need as long as 40 minutes to get nicely browned and tender, whereas asparagus stalks or green beans may be ready in 10 minutes. Shake the pan occasionally to shift the vegetables around and let them brown. Vegetables are done when they're browned and a little shriveled on all sides and tender inside.

× × × × × × × × × × × × × × × × × × × × × × × × × × × × × × × × × ×

## MAKING MEATLESS MEALS

There are many good reasons to be a vegetarian or a vegan: health, thrift, the environment, ethics. Many people who choose not to eat meat or other animal products cite a combination of these motivators. Because American tradition has long defined a square meal as one with meat as its cornerstone, the question becomes: "How do I get the nutrition I need on a plant-based diet?"

Well-planned vegetarian and vegan diets are nutritionally adequate for all people in all stages of life, so long as care is taken to include adequate protein, iron, vitamin B$_{12}$, omega-3 fatty acids, iodine, calcium, iron, and zinc—nutrients sometimes lacking in animal-free diets.

# #31 HOW TO BLANCH VEGETABLES

Cooking vegetables in hot water got a bad name for many people who were subjected to mushy, overboiled cauliflower or tasteless green beans in their youth. But cooking vegetables in salty hot water can bring out the flavor beautifully, if you don't overcook. Blanching lets vegetables have a brief dip in boiling water, then they are rinsed in cold water so the cooking stops before the mushiness starts. This is a great method for green veggies such as string beans and broccoli because it keeps the color bright.

**1 BRING A LARGE POT OF WATER TO** a rolling boil. Add a tablespoon of salt; some chefs say the best cooking water tastes "salty like the sea."

**2 PREP THE VEGETABLE INTO** serving pieces: top and tail green beans, break cauliflower or broccoli into florets, shell the peas.

**3 PUT THE VEGETABLE PIECES INTO** the boiling water and cook for 2 to 3 minutes. Take out a piece with a fork and run it under the cold tap and sample it. When the vegetable is crunchy-tender, pour it into a colander and rinse under cold water to stop the cooking.

**4 DRESS IMMEDIATELY WITH OLIVE** oil or a little melted butter, salt and pepper, and maybe a squeeze of lemon.

# #32
## HOW TO CHOP BROCCOLI

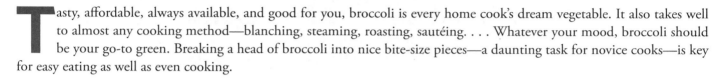

**T**asty, affordable, always available, and good for you, broccoli is every home cook's dream vegetable. It also takes well to almost any cooking method—blanching, steaming, roasting, sautéing. . . . Whatever your mood, broccoli should be your go-to green. Breaking a head of broccoli into nice bite-size pieces—a daunting task for novice cooks—is key for easy eating as well as even cooking.

## Heads Up

Choose broccoli heads with firm, compact clusters of small florets. The individual flowers that make up the florets should be dark green or have a purple cast to them. Reject heads on which the florets are yellowish-green, enlarged, or opened, or if the stalks are rubbery, limp, or wilted.

## Storing and Freezing

For best results, plan to use or freeze fresh broccoli soon after buying it. To store, mist the heads with water, wrap loosely in damp paper towels, slide the bundle into a zip-top bag, and don't seal it. (Fresh broccoli requires air circulation.) It will keep for up to a week.

To freeze, cut washed, raw broccoli into florets and chop the peeled stalks (see instructions, following). Steam or blanch the broccoli for one minute to parboil it (this improves its quality after freezing), then plunge it into ice water, drain, and seal in airtight containers or closed zip-top bags with all the air pressed out. This cooked frozen broccoli can be added to soups or stir-fries at the last minute, or it can be thawed and heated in the microwave for a quick supper side dish.

## Cooking Fresh Broccoli

Cook only what you'll eat right away. Given that fresh broccoli cooks up in just a few minutes, there is no point in making enough for leftovers, which get mushy and are not as flavorful. If you need to save time, wash and cut it in advance. If you do have leftovers, cooked broccoli should be sealed in an airtight container or closed zip-top bag and kept in the refrigerator for no more than two days.

**1** **RINSE, DON'T SOAK, BROCCOLI IN** cool water just before preparing. Remove any leaves attached to the stalk.

**2** **TRIM THE STALKS OFF EACH** head, leaving about an inch of stalk below the florets.

**3** **PEEL OFF THE WOODY, OUTER** layer of the stalks with a paring knife or vegetable peeler.

**4** **SLICE THE HEAD OF THE** broccoli in half lengthwise.

**5** **HOLD THE HALVES TOGETHER** and slice the head crosswise to the desired size.

**6** **FINISH CHOPPING BY CUTTING** each floret off the head in a downward motion, leaving a little stalk on each cluster. If the individual florets are bigger than you'd like, slice them in half lengthwise.

# #33
## HOW TO MAKE MASHED POTATOES
### (or, How to Do Anything with a Spud)

A pillar of the world's cuisine, potatoes come in about five thousand varieties with anywhere from five to ten types available at most American supermarkets. For the best results when cooking with potatoes, the right tuber is key. Potatoes for mashing should be fluffy and somewhat dry, and never gluey, whereas salad potatoes need to be firm enough to hold their own against dressings without dissolving. Potatoes for scalloping can't fall apart during slicing and need heft to convey luscious, creamy sauce.

## The Right Spud for the Job

Practically speaking, potatoes fall into two categories: starchy and waxy. A third, middle-ground type—the all-purpose—offers versatility when storage space is a factor.

**Starchy.** Oblong in shape, with a rough, corklike skin, these are the top choice for baking, mashing, and french fries. Also called floury potatoes, their high starch content makes them less dense, so they break down more during cooking, resulting in a smoother texture. Mashed potatoes will be smoother, baked potatoes fluffier, and fried potatoes will steam from the inside, offering light interiors with crispy exteriors. When pierced with your fingernail, or sliced, this type excretes a milky liquid (that's the starch). Look for these names in your produce section (depending on where you live): baking potatoes, Idaho potatoes, russets, Norgolds, Goldrushes, Cal Whites, German Butterballs, baking whites, and Norkotahs.

**Waxy.** Also called boiling potatoes, these can be round or oval in shape, with a thin, smooth, and waxy skin. These potatoes are best for casseroles, soups, roasting, and salads. If you can scrape off the skin with your fingernail, your potato is waxy. High in sugar and moisture, but low in starch, they are firm and toothsome, holding their shape when sliced and cooked. Look for these names in your produce section: yellow potatoes, salad potatoes, Yellow Finns, fingerlings, new reds, La Sodas, and Australian Crescents.

**All-purpose.** These potatoes fall in the middle, combining dryness and firmness, and can work in most recipes in a pinch. Slightly fluffy when baked, they will also hold their shape when boiled and can be used for mashed potatoes, though they offer a less silky texture. Look for these names in your produce section: Yukon Golds, Katahdins, Kennebecs, Superiors, and Peruvian Blues.

## Yes, They Are a Vegetable

The belief among my Irish husband's people is that humans can survive eating only potatoes, supplemented by dairy for vitamins A and D. True, they contain vitamins, minerals, phenols, and lots of fiber, when the jacket is eaten. Although humans need carbohydrates to survive, high-starch diets alongside sedentary lifestyles are linked to diabetes and heart disease. Preparation method makes a difference, too. Fried or mixed with high-fat dairy, potatoes are more of a treat than a vegetable.

## Freshness Matters

When buying potatoes, look for spuds that are firm to the touch, with no give when squeezed. Reject any with sprouts or "eyes" because this means they have begun to go to seed, and those with green patches, which are a sign of prolonged exposure to light or extreme temperatures. When handling potatoes, take care not to bruise them or it will lead to rot. Store in a cool, dark, and dry place for a long shelf life.

## Green Under the Skin?

That's chlorophyll, which alerts us to the presence of solanine, a natural but poisonous glycoalkaloid found in plants in the nightshade family. This substance defends potatoes against insects and biological disease, and it is toxic to humans. It tastes bitter and can cause nausea, diarrhea, and if eaten in very large quantities, nerve damage or paralysis. Bottom line: If all of the green can be peeled away and discarded, the rest of the potato can be eaten. When in doubt, however, toss the offending spud.

**1 CHOOSE YOUR POTATO.** Pick a type from the starchy or all-purpose categories, avoiding the waxy category. Any will do, but a Yukon Gold has the added bonus of that golden-yellow color, reminiscent of the potato's best friend—butter.

**2 PREPARE THE POTATOES FOR** boiling. Peel them with a vegetable peeler. Quarter them, place them in a very large bowl, and rinse them with cold water to remove excess starch. Transfer the potatoes to a large pot.

**3 BOIL THE POTATOES.** Cover the potatoes with cold water, salt them to your taste (1 teaspoon of salt for every 2 quarts of water is the way my family likes it), and set over medium-high heat to bring them to a boil. Starting in cold water helps your potatoes cook more evenly because the temperature rise is slow. If you throw your tubers into hot water, the outsides will cook first, while the interior will still be raw. Once the water comes to a boil, reduce the heat to a simmer. The potatoes are ready when they are tender when pierced with a fork. Cooking time depends on the size of the potato chunks and the size of your pot, so check on your potatoes every 5 to 10 minutes or so.

**4 DRY THE POTATOES.** Once they are cooked, carefully pour the water out of the pot, cover it, and set it back over the lowest heat setting on your stove for about 5 minutes. This will cook off the excess water, ensuring lighter mashed potatoes.

**5 BRING ON THE FLAVOR!** This is where you choose your mashing tool and use it to combine with your favorite seasonings, creamy ingredients, or broth. Make sure anything cold, like milk or butter, is warmed before adding and that your potatoes travel from stovetop to tabletop pronto.

## Besides rice and wheat, potatoes are the third most important food crop in the world. The tuber was first domesticated in the Andes mountains of South America.

## The Best Tool for the Job

There's more than one way to mash a potato. Here are the options:

**Fork.** In a pinch, crushing cooked potatoes with a fork will do. Use a pressing motion, rather than a stirring motion, for the fluffiest texture and be careful not to overwork the potatoes or they will turn gluey.

**Wire masher.** Looks something like an electric coil. The mashing surface is relatively small, so the potatoes will stay light in texture because it doesn't destroy all the delicate starch granules. Best for those who like small chunks in their mash.

**Flat masher.** A flat disk with holes punched out. Same principle as a fork, but less labor-intensive. The results will be more uniform, but slightly heavier in texture than with a wire masher.

**Potato ricer.** This gadget looks like a giant garlic press, with a lever and small holes through which a cooked potato is forced. Silky-smooth in texture, riced potatoes will be heavier because no air is incorporated as it is with the up-and-down motions of the other methods.

**Whisk.** After crushing the cooked potatoes using one of the gadgets above, you can whisk the mash (with additions like butter and cream) for a minute or two in order to incorporate some air and fluff them up.

**Electric mixer.** Beat crushed potatoes (along with butter and cream) with a hand mixer and your result will be whipped potatoes—light, fluffy, and filled with air. Restaurants use this method for economy: More air means less potato per serving. This style holds up well in a chafing dish, at a steam table, or piped out of a pastry bag if you're being fancy.

**Food processor.** STOP! This appliance (as well as the blender) strikes fear in the heart of starchy vegetables everywhere. The rapidly spinning blade smashes every last starch granule, leaving you with a gluey mess.

## RECIPE: THE BEST MASHED POTATOES

Now that you know the ropes, here's a foolproof recipe for a rich, fluffy mash that elevates any dinner to special-occasion status.

**Serves 4**

1½ pounds Yukon Gold potatoes, peeled and quartered

1 teaspoon salt

¼ cup heavy cream

3 tablespoons butter, at room temperature

Milk, for mashing

**1.** Wash, peel, and quarter the potatoes, as per Step 2 in How to Make Mashed Potatoes (see page 58) and then soak them. After a long soak, as long as overnight, discard the cloudy water and transfer the potatoes to a large pot. Cover them completely with cold water, then add the salt.

**2.** Bring the potatoes slowly to a boil, over medium heat, then reduce the heat and let them simmer, uncovered, until they're fork-tender. Carefully pour off the water, then dry them in the pot as per Step 4 in How to Make Mashed Potatoes, being careful not to let them scorch.

**3.** In a small saucepan over low heat, warm the cream and butter together until the butter melts. Do not allow the mixture to boil. Pour the cream and butter over the potatoes and mash them using your tool of choice. If desired, whip the mashed potatoes with a whisk or hand mixer, adding milk a tablespoon at a time, if needed, for the consistency you like. Do not overbeat, or your potatoes will turn gummy.

# #34
## HOW TO COOK A STEAK

S eems simple enough, but because it involves so many variables—the cut, timing, temperature, and seasoning—cooking a steak takes practice. Quality meat isn't cheap, so the stakes are high, so to speak. Here's how to make sure you'll never have to serve (or eat!) chewy, tasteless, or dry steak again.

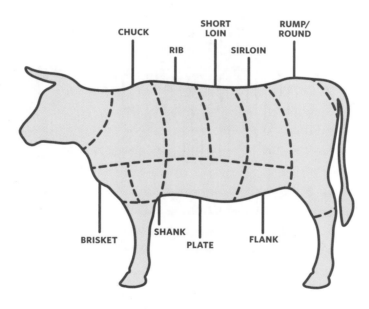

## Start with Good Meat

Consult your butchers. They're experts and will steer you to the best cuts at the best price. Always buy the best grade you can afford (prime, choice, and select, in that order) and inspect the meat closely: Look for pinky-red. Avoid deep red and never buy gray or greenish meat, or steaks that are spongy or slimy, in ripped packages, or have old sell-by dates. Choose steak that's firm to the touch, with a fine texture, and look for marbling—the thin threads of white fat running through the meat.

## What's in a Name?

The most tender meat comes from the least-exercised parts of the cow. Connective tissue is tough, so instead buy cuts from the short loin, tenderloin, or rib sections. Top choices: New York strip, T-bone, porterhouse, rib eye, and tenderloin or filet mignon. Flank steak provides great value and beefy flavor, though it tends to be less tender.

**1** **MARINATE.** Take your steak out of the fridge, place it in a flat, wide bowl and brush it with olive oil or clarified butter. This adds moisture and flavor, and prevents it from sticking to the grill or pan. Sprinkle with salt (ideally kosher)—use a heavy hand, you're seasoning the whole steak, inside and out—plus freshly ground black pepper. If possible, plan ahead and allow it to come to room temperature for about 1 hour (cold steaks take longer to cook, and the longer the cook time, the tougher the steak). If you like, marinate the seasoned steak in a zip-top bag with a couple of tablespoons of olive oil, the juice of a lemon, and a minced garlic clove.

**2** **PREPARE THE FLAME.** The goal is to cook your steak at a high temperature for not much time. Therefore, a grill is best. Before you set meat to flame, heat the grill on high for 20 to 30 minutes.

*If you don't have a grill, use your broiler.* Position your rack about 5 inches from the flame and preheat the broiler to high. Meanwhile, heat a large, empty cast-iron skillet or grill pan over high heat on the stovetop for about 5 minutes. (Open a window or turn on the hood fan—your kitchen is going to get smoky!)

**3** **LAY YOUR PREPPED STEAK ON** the grill. For a ½-inch-thick steak, let it lie for 3 minutes, then flip it with tongs. (For a 1-inch-thick steak, 4 to 5 minutes is good.) Don't poke at it! Piercing a steak releases juices. Once you've flipped the steak, grill it for another 1 or 2 minutes for medium-rare.

*If using a broiler,* coat the bottom of the heated cast-iron skillet with a little oil, lay in the steak, then slide it under the broiler. Cook for 3 minutes, then using tongs, flip it and cook it for another 3 minutes—this timing will work well for a steak about ½ to ¾ inch thick. Test for your preferred timing and try not to overcook.

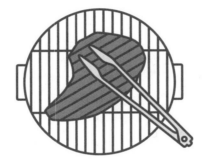

**4** **TEST FOR DONENESS.** The amount of time to cook a steak is partly a learned art, but don't overcook it or even the best meat can taste like shoe leather.

Go for just a few minutes and check it; you can always throw a steak back in the pan but you can't uncook it. Press the middle of the steak with your finger (quickly—it's hot!). If it feels jelly-like, it's too rare. If it just springs back when you press it, it's medium-rare. If it's firm or hard, it's well done (and probably dry). If you're nervous, make a small cut in the center to see if the steak is done the way you like it. You'll let some of the juice escape, but losing some juice is better than overcooking a good steak "just to be safe." If it's not done enough, return it to the grill or broiler for another 1 to 2 minutes. Keep in mind that the steak continues cooking for a minute or two after being removed from the heat.

**5** **LET IT REST FOR FIVE TO TEN** minutes. The temperatures of the center and edges will begin to equalize, allowing the juices to distribute evenly. If you cut it right away, all the juices will pour out the edge and onto the plate, resulting in a less flavorful steak.

✕✕✕✕✕✕✕✕✕✕✕✕✕✕✕✕✕✕✕✕✕✕✕✕✕✕✕✕✕✕✕✕✕✕✕✕✕✕✕✕✕✕✕✕✕✕✕✕✕✕✕✕✕✕✕✕✕✕✕

# PROTEIN PRIMER

**P**roteins are a combination of amino acids that are essential to our bodily functions—like muscle development and repair, and metabolism—and must be obtained through food because they aren't manufactured by our bodies. For healthy individuals eating a balanced diet, 10 to 15 percent of our calories should come from protein. There is no danger from consuming too much protein, except for those with kidney or liver disease who should be planning their meals under the care of doctors and nutritionists.

# #35
# HOW TO COOK LAMB CHOPS

**T**hink lamb chops are fancy and only for gourmet cooks? Think again. This super-simple frying-pan method always yields juicy chops. Choose rib chops, about 1 inch thick, for this method. They're the ones with the long bone "handle" and a circle of meat at the end. Perfect finger food! You'll need two to three chops per person.

**1** **SPRINKLE BOTH SIDES OF THE** chops with salt and freshly ground black pepper.

**2** **PUT 2 TABLESPOONS OF OIL IN A** large, heavy-bottomed skillet and set it over high heat. You want it very hot. To test, add a teaspoon of water to the pan—it should evaporate almost immediately.

**3** **LAY IN THE CHOPS—IF THEY** don't sizzle, the pan's not hot enough. Cook them for 4 minutes per side. Don't touch them or disturb them while they cook, or you won't get a nice crust. When done, they should still be pink in the middle.

**4** **REMOVE THE CHOPS FROM** the pan and serve.

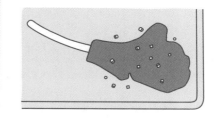

## RECIPE: SMOTHERED PORK CHOPS

**Y**ou can fry a pork chop in a similar way to a lamb chop (adding a minute or two per side), but pork chops particularly like gravy. Thick chops especially are inclined to be dry because most pork is pretty lean these days, so chops take well to being cooked in sauce.

### Serves 4

½ cup all-purpose flour

1 teaspoon salt

½ teaspoon freshly ground pepper

4 boneless pork loin chops, ¾ to 1 inch thick

2 tablespoons vegetable oil, or more as needed

2 cups milk

1 unsalted chicken bouillon cube, optional

**1.** Preheat the oven to 350°F. Put the flour, salt, and pepper in a zip-top bag, and then toss the chops in it. Shake well to coat the chops.

**2.** Heat the vegetable oil over medium-high heat in a Dutch oven or heavy ovenproof pot with a lid. Brown the chops well, about 2 minutes per side, adding a little more oil if needed.

**3.** Sprinkle 2 tablespoons of the seasoned flour over the chops and add the milk and a half cup of water, stirring gently to combine. If desired, crumble the bouillon cube into the milk and stir to combine.

**4.** Cover the pot and bake until the gravy is thickened and the chops are cooked through, 45 to 60 minutes. Alternatively, you can cook it over medium heat, covered, on the stovetop, but check it occasionally and add a little more liquid, if needed—it tends to boil a bit harder on the stovetop.

# #36
# HOW TO COOK CHICKEN BREASTS

Boneless, skinless chicken breasts are excellent meal starters, but many shy away after having eaten one too many that were rubbery and tasteless. The method here finishes them moist and just cooked through, avoiding that stringy dryness that gives chicken a bad name. Serve with a vegetable side, add slices to a salad, or toss with pasta.

**1 POUND EACH BREAST LIGHTLY** (sandwich it in plastic wrap or waxed paper) with a rolling pin or can of beans until it is an even thickness throughout. (Wash the pin or can well with hot soapy water.)

**2 PUT ⅓ CUP FLOUR IN A LARGE** mixing bowl, and then stir in a teaspoon each of salt and pepper. Lightly dredge the chicken breasts in the seasoned flour until just lightly dusted.

**3 HEAT A LARGE, HEAVY-** bottomed skillet that has a tight-fitting lid over medium-high heat. Once hot, add a tablespoon each of olive oil and butter.

**4 WHEN THE BUTTER IS SIZZLING,** reduce the heat to medium, then add chicken breasts in a single layer. Cook for 2 minutes, allowing one side to lightly brown.

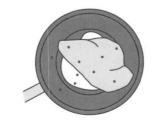

**5 FLIP THE CHICKEN, REDUCE THE** heat to low, and cover the pan. Set a timer for 12 minutes.

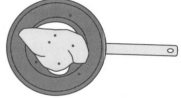

**6 AFTER 12 MINUTES, TURN OFF** the heat, but don't uncover the pan. Set the timer for 8 minutes.

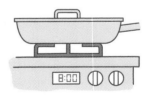

**7 UNCOVER AND SERVE.**

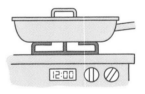

# #37
## HOW TO ROAST A CHICKEN

Roasting a chicken is actually far simpler than the succulent, crispy-skinned, dramatic end result might lead your guests to believe. In fact, a roast chicken is such a thrifty, delicious, and satisfying cornerstone to a meal that you shouldn't save it for only special occasions. Serve it sliced as a main course, then use the leftovers as an ingredient in other dishes such as curried chicken salad, wrap sandwiches, and white pizza. I often roast two or more whole six-pound birds weekly. This technique using a hot skillet in a very hot oven cuts the cooking time and makes a very crisp skin.

**1** PREHEAT THE OVEN TO 425°F.

**2** CHECK THE CAVITY FOR ANY giblets or other parts—often housed in a plastic bag. Using your hands, rub 1 stick of butter, softened to room temperature, all over the chicken, making sure to get it into every crack and crevice. Tuck rosemary sprigs—8 to 10 whole ones—under the breast skin and into the cavity. Halve two lemons and push them into the cavity. Sprinkle the whole chicken liberally with salt and freshly ground black pepper, and also sprinkle salt into the cavity with the lemons and rosemary.

**3** PUT A LARGE, DRY, EMPTY CAST-iron skillet on the stovetop and heat it over high heat for 5 minutes. When it's hot, put the prepped chicken carefully into the hot skillet. It will sizzle loudly! With a potholder or oven mitt, carefully lift the skillet into the oven. Bake the chicken for 1 hour, until the thickest part of the thigh reads 180°F on an instant-read thermometer and the skin is crisp and browned.

**4** REMOVE THE CHICKEN FROM the oven, and tent it with foil. Allow it to rest for 15 minutes, then slice and serve.

TIP: Peel and wash vegetables such as carrots, onions, celery, potatoes, yams, parsnips, and turnips, and cut them into like-size chunks. Toss with olive oil and put them on a baking sheet, in a single layer. Sprinkle with salt and pepper. Roast the vegetables on a different rack while your chicken roasts, and you'll have a complete meal when it's done.

Bake stuffing (or dressing) in a casserole dish, not inside the bird. In order for stuffing to be safe to eat, it needs to reach 165 degrees Fahrenheit. To achieve that, you'd have to overcook the poultry.

## To Baste or Not to Baste?

In a word, not. Basting only flavors the skin; it doesn't penetrate to the meat, so the old myth that it moistens the bird isn't true. Remember the roasting rule: The longer the cook time, the drier the meat. Each time you open the oven to baste, it cools down, and then you have to leave the bird in longer. Skip it.

✕ ✕ ✕ ✕ ✕ ✕ ✕ ✕ ✕ ✕ ✕ ✕ ✕ ✕ ✕ ✕

# HOW DO I CHOOSE A CHICKEN TO ROAST?

**O**nce you learn to roast a whole bird, it can really change your game in the kitchen—it's more economical, often more flavorful, and definitely impressive.

- **Look for Grade A chickens—they have the highest meat-to-bone ratio.**

- **Pass on chicken with torn packaging, old sell-by dates, "off" odors, or grayish skin.**

- **Skin and flesh color should range from pinkish to white to yellow.**

- **Top choice: pullet or roaster. These have a lot of fat under the skin. Look for a 5- or 6-pounder.**

- **Other good choices include: broiler/fryer—these are younger, smaller birds, usually 2½ to 3 pounds, with more flavorful albeit a smaller amount of meat. Cornish game hens, usually 1½ to 2 pounds, are similar to roasters, but a smaller breed (typically, a serving is a whole bird). Moist and meaty.**

# #38 HOW TO BRINE A BIRD
## (or, the Chef's Secret)

**B**rining, or soaking in heavily salted water prior to cooking, is a way of increasing the moisture-holding capacity of poultry, resulting in tender cooked meat. Salt changes the structure of the muscle tissue, allowing it to swell and absorb water along with any flavorings dissolved or infused in the water. Brining is especially beneficial for turkey, but you can also soak chicken, game hens, or any poultry, to delicious effect.

## Keep It Cold

Because brining doesn't preserve meat, the poultry and the brine must be kept cold to inhibit bacteria growth. Both meat and its soaking liquid must remain colder than 40 degrees Fahrenheit, so you'll need a cooler large enough to hold bird and brine or a container that will keep the bird submerged and will also fit into a refrigerator. Plan ahead and clear space if needed.

If using a cooler, it is important to thoroughly clean and sanitize it before and after use. A solution of 1 tablespoon of chlorine bleach to 1 gallon of water will do. Rinse thoroughly with clean water after sanitizing. Next, you must keep the poultry and brine cold without diluting the mixture: Put the bird and brine directly into the cooler, then add zip-top bags filled with ice or reusable gel packs to keep it cool. Monitor the temperature using an instant-read thermometer.

**1 MAKE YOUR BRINE.** Start with ½ cup table salt (or 1 cup kosher salt) per gallon of water. Stir the salt so it dissolves. You need enough brine to fully submerge your bird.

**2 ADD AROMATICS AS DESIRED.** You can squeeze in lemon juice and also toss in the rinds; add 1 tablespoon black peppercorns or ¼ cup hot sauce or a handful of potent dried herbs such as rosemary or oregano leaves. Heat any aromatics in a bit of brine ahead of time to release their flavor.

**3 LET THE BIRD SOAK IN ITS BATH.** The real purpose of brining is to let the salty moisture penetrate the meat, and that takes a long time.

### BRINE SOAKING TIME TABLE

| Whole chicken (6 pounds) | 6 to 12 hours |
|---|---|
| Chicken or turkey parts | 2 hours |
| Whole turkey | 24 hours |
| Turkey breast | 8 hours |
| Cornish game hens | 2 hours |

✕ ✕ ✕ ✕ ✕ ✕ ✕ ✕ ✕ ✕ ✕ ✕ ✕ ✕ ✕ ✕ ✕ ✕ ✕ ✕ ✕ ✕ ✕ ✕ ✕ ✕ ✕ ✕ ✕ ✕ ✕ ✕ ✕ ✕ ✕ ✕ ✕ ✕

# BRINE WARNING!

**D**o not salt brined meat before cooking. As with commercially packaged kosher chicken, the meat is already salty. If your recipe advises sprinkling with salt and freshly ground black pepper, pepper alone will do.

# #39
# HOW TO BRAISE BEEF

Filling and comforting, slow-cooked beef offers the ultimate satisfaction to meat-and-potatoes lovers. A pot roast or stew warms the kitchen on cold or rainy days, and it fills the house with a fragrance that whispers wholesome abundance. A one-dish dinner with the components of a square meal, braises are simple, nutritious, and budget friendly crowd pleasers.

## Tough to Tender

Braising is simply a method of cooking foods over low heat, for a long time, partially submerged in liquid. Cooked incorrectly, pot roast or stew cuts are so tough and dry they are practically inedible, but braised, these meats yield fork-tender, juicy morsels. The cheaper, less tender cuts contain a lot of collagen, the connective tissue that holds muscle fibers together. When cooked slowly in the presence of moisture, collagen dissolves into gelatin, allowing meat fibers to separate. This is the essence of tenderizing tough cuts of meat. The gelatin will set as it cools.

## Go Dutch

To braise meat, you'll need a slow cooker, Dutch oven (a large, heavy cast-iron pot), or other heavy pot with a tight-fitting lid. If using the oven (with the heat set at 325 degrees Fahrenheit), make sure your pot is ovenproof. You'll still need to use the stove for the searing step (see following). Either way, the lid is key because the steam in the pot helps cook and tenderize the meat.

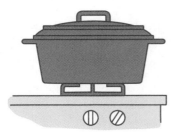

### Advanced Braising

Once you've mastered the basic concepts of braising, and long, slow cooking, branch out and experiment.

**Change up your meat:** Beef with bone (like short ribs) will yield extra flavor from the marrow.

| | |
|---|---|
| Chicken breast or bone-in chicken parts | Pork, with or without bones |
| Game, such as bone-in rabbit or venison | Sturdy seafood such as monkfish, shrimp, lobster, eel, octopus, or squid |
| Lamb or mutton | |

**Play around with veggies:** Anything goes (almost), but firm, hearty ones work best.

| | | | |
|---|---|---|---|
| Beets | Leeks | Tomatoes | Yams |
| Endive | Parsnips | Turnips | |

**Liquid gold:** Water will work, but why not add flavor?

| | |
|---|---|
| Beer or stout | Stock or broth (shortcut: |
| Tomato or vegetable juice | dissolve bouillon cubes |
| Wine—red or white | in hot water) |

**Herbs and spices:** Season to taste.

| | | |
|---|---|---|
| Basil | Garam masala | Rosemary |
| Bay leaves | Oregano | Sage |
| Cilantro | Parsley | Thyme |

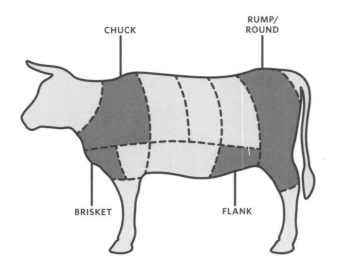

CHUCK

RUMP/ROUND

BRISKET

FLANK

**1** **CHOOSE YOUR CUT.** Tough cuts of beef such as round, brisket, rump, chuck, and flank are often economical, and they hold up the best to long braises. For the best bargains, tell your butcher you want pot roast or stew meat, and he'll point you to what's best and cheapest that day. Because they come from ends of cuts, their availability and price change regularly.

**2** **SEAR THE MEAT.** It's a myth that searing locks in juices, but you should still do it. Browning the meat in oil produces new and complex flavor compounds as the sugars and proteins in the meat react under high temperatures and the surface color deepens. Your braise will have richer flavor, and the meat will have an appealingly brown (rather than gray) hue.

**3** **ADD LIQUID.** Whether you use water, wine, broth, or anything else (see Advanced Braising, page 67), the meat must be mostly submerged to attain a proper braise, but not drowned or you won't get a nice, thick sauce.

**4** **COOK IT LOW AND SLOW.** Collagen softens in low, moist heat, but muscle fiber firms under high heat because proteins unfold and form new linkages. The higher the cooking temperature, the tougher the muscle fibers become, shrinking in length and width, becoming tight. Whether braising on the stovetop or in the oven, don't let it boil—reduce the heat to a gentle simmer and cook it for a long time.

**5** **ADD VEGGIES.** To make your roast or stew into a one-pot supper, add veggies to the braise in the last 45 minutes or hour of cooking. Chop them into uniform pieces so that they'll cook evenly.

**6** **FINALLY, DON'T LEAVE YOUR** braise cooking for *too* long. Check it during the last hour of cooking—going past the fork-tender stage can yield dry, stringy meat.

## RECIPE: BASIC BEEF STEW

Beef stew usually falls into one of three categories: with brown gravy, broth or wine, or a tomato-based sauce. Here's an old-fashioned brown version.

### Serves 6

⅓ cup all-purpose flour

1 teaspoon salt

¼ teaspoon freshly ground black pepper

2 pounds stewing beef, cut into cubes

¼ cup olive oil

½ cup beef broth, wine, or beer

4 cups boiling water

1 tablespoon red wine vinegar

1 tablespoon Worcestershire sauce

1 teaspoon brown sugar

2 large onions, sliced

6 stalks celery, destringed and cut into chunks

3 bay leaves

6 medium-size carrots, peeled and cut into chunks

10 small red potatoes, peeled and halved

**1.** In a shallow dish, mix together the flour, salt, and pepper. Roll the beef cubes in the mixture to coat, shaking off excess.

**2.** Pour the oil into a medium-size Dutch oven and heat on the stovetop over high heat. Working in batches, carefully cook the meat until each piece is browned.

**3.** Once all of the beef is cooked, pour in the broth. With a wooden spoon, scrape the sides and bottom of the Dutch oven to loosen any cooked-on bits.

**4.** Layer the beef cubes back in the Dutch oven and add the boiling water. Stir, then add the vinegar, Worcestershire sauce, brown sugar, onions, celery, and bay leaves. Reduce the heat to low, cover, and simmer until the meat is fork-tender, about 3 hours.

**5.** Add the carrots and potatoes, and simmer until all vegetables are fork-tender, about an hour.

# #40
# HOW TO MAKE A POT OF CHILI

One of those rare comfort foods that is packed with good-for-you ingredients, chili can be a soup or a stew, with as many personalities as there are cooks. Purists insist that chili shouldn't contain beans, tomatoes, or grains because they didn't appear in the original recipes prepared by chuck wagon cooks for settlers in the West and Southwest. Modern cooks and vegetarians, however, like to lighten things up with all manner of legumes and veggies, as well as grains such as bulgur or quinoa. The good-natured debate over what goes into a pot of chili—everything from ground beef and shredded pork to cinnamon and chocolate powder to beans and hot peppers—rages on. I say make it your own, using these tips, tricks, and shortcuts. First, learn the basic guidelines, listed below, and then you'll be able to improvise as you see fit.

**1** ALWAYS BROWN MEATS BEFORE adding liquid to the pot for richer flavor.

**2** IF YOUR RECIPE CALLS FOR chopped fresh chiles, but you like it less spicy, pierce a whole fresh chile pepper several times with a knife tip and let it simmer whole in the sauce, instead of adding it chopped at the beginning. Fish it out and discard before eating.

**3** LET THE FLAVORS MINGLE. Make chili in advance, refrigerate it, and reheat it again later.

**4** WHEN POSSIBLE, USE FRESH herbs. If you must use dried, make sure they haven't been sitting in the back of your pantry for more than a year.

**5** USE BROTH INSTEAD OF WATER in your chili or when cooking dried beans.

✕ ✕ ✕ ✕ ✕ ✕ ✕ ✕ ✕ ✕ ✕ ✕ ✕ ✕ ✕ ✕

## WHAT MAKES WHITE CHILI WHITE?

The absence of tomatoes, red peppers, and red meat. As with regular chili, there are as many styles as you can dream up, but most white chilis include chicken or other poultry, green chiles, and white beans, and some are thickened with masa or cornmeal.

**TYPES OF CHILI MEAT**

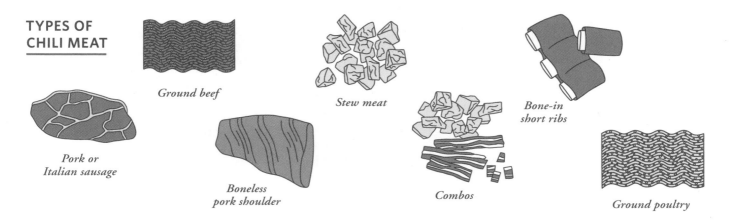

*Ground beef*

*Stew meat*

*Bone-in short ribs*

*Pork or Italian sausage*

*Boneless pork shoulder*

*Combos*

*Ground poultry*

## The Meat of the Matter

You can make a pot of chili from familiar to fancy, with any meat that gets better with a slow simmer.

⚜ **Ground beef.** Use ground beef for fattier, more flavorful chili or ground sirloin or chuck for chili that tastes more like steak.

⚜ **Stew meat.** You can also use brisket or other economy roasts, and cut them into cubes yourself. Remember, low and slow makes these cuts tender. Don't boil them. (See How to Braise Beef, page 67.)

⚜ **Bone-in short ribs.** You'll have to eat around the bone, but the marrow and connective tissue add depth to the flavor.

⚜ **Ground pork or Italian sausage.** Pork is delicious and goes well with classic chili spices. Italian sausage is pre-spiced, so you can cut down on some of the ingredients and steps.

⚜ **Boneless pork shoulder.** Richly flavored and perfect for simmering. Cook it like cubed beef.

⚜ **Venison.** Use it because you love the gamy flavor or because your uncle who hunts has a freezer full of it. Balanced with beans, it's great for chili.

⚜ **Combos.** You don't have to use only ground beef. Try cubed beef and pork, or lamb and beef. You can also add some smoky flavor with chopped, smoked bacon cooked along with the cubed or ground meat. Experiment!

⚜ **Poultry.** Use any you have on hand, from chicken parts to turkey breast to whole stewing chicken. Usually used in white chilis, but it's a great option when you're looking to fortify with lean protein.

✕✕✕✕✕✕✕✕✕✕✕✕✕✕✕✕✕✕✕✕✕✕✕✕✕✕✕✕✕✕✕✕✕✕✕✕✕✕✕✕✕✕✕✕✕✕✕✕✕✕✕✕✕✕✕✕✕✕✕✕✕✕✕✕

# NEVER SALT BEANS UNTIL THEY'RE COOKED—SCIENCE FACT OR SCIENCE FICTION?

Science fiction. Salt them early and often! The old saw says that salt will keep tough skins from softening. In fact, the skins of unsalted beans absorb so much water that the interior puffs up and breaks the skins. Salted bean skins will remain intact. What makes beans hard is age. Really old beans can simmer for hours and never get soft.

Why? Because calcium and magnesium in the skins act as barriers, supporting the structure and keeping them firm. By soaking beans overnight in salted water, you allow sodium ions to switch places with some of the calcium and magnesium ions, which makes the skins and interiors soften at the same rate.

## NEXT-LEVEL CHILI

Once you can master the basics, consider painting outside the lines.

• Add a teaspoon of unsweetened cocoa powder to the pot.

• Use strong coffee instead of water or broth.

• Add a cinnamon stick to the chili (remove before serving).

• Stir in 1 tablespoon peanut butter, for a deep, rich broth that calls to mind Thai sauces.

• Add ½ cup barbecue sauce for a smoky flavor, or add ½ cup red wine vinegar and ½ cup brown sugar to tomato-based chilis for a North Carolina barbecue flavor.

• Bring on the umami! That's the meaty-savory flavor that makes people's mouths water. Add ½ cup soy sauce, 1 tablespoon chopped anchovies, or even a scoop of jarred Marmite (a British condiment made of brewer's yeast) to a pot.

Don't mix up the meat dish and the vegetable—chili with an *i* is the spicy meat stew, while chile with an e refers to the pepper. The powder, because of its use in the stew, is spelled with an *i*.

## RECIPE: BEGINNER'S CHILI

Chili is a great dish for beginning cooks. The mix and balance of ingredients is very forgiving, so it's hard to ruin a pot of chili! For a square meal, ladle it over pasta or rice, and serve with a green salad, or spoon into large tortillas, adding shredded lettuce, cheese, and salsa to make burritos. For a game-day favorite, layer corn chips into pasta bowls with chili, cheese, chopped onion, and hot sauce.

### Serves 6

2 tablespoons vegetable oil

1 pound ground sirloin or chuck

1 cup chopped onion

2 large cloves garlic, finely chopped

1 (14½-ounce) can diced tomatoes, undrained

1 (8-ounce) can tomato sauce

1 tablespoon dried chili powder

¾ teaspoon ground cumin

¼ teaspoon salt

¼ teaspoon freshly ground black pepper

2 cups cooked kidney beans (or 1 [16-ounce] can), rinsed and drained

**1.** Set a large (at least 3-quart), heavy-bottomed pot over high heat and pour in the oil. Add the ground sirloin and, stirring constantly, cook until it begins to brown and crisp at the edges, about 7 to 10 minutes.

**2.** Add the onions and garlic, and cook until they are transparent, but not browned, about 10 minutes.

**3.** Add all of the remaining ingredients, except for the beans. Allow the mixture to come to a boil, then reduce the heat to medium low and simmer for 20 minutes.

**4.** Add the beans, and simmer, uncovered, for an additional 20 to 30 minutes, stirring occasionally, allowing the chili to reduce to your desired consistency.

# #41
# HOW TO FRY CHICKEN
## (or, How to Pan-Fry Anything)

O f all the possible foods that can be fried (shrimp, potatoes, candy bars) chicken is the star. If you've ever gone to the trouble of battering and frying chicken—or any food, for that matter—only to watch breading or batter fall off in the oil, or suffer soggy coating that should have been crisp, then you understand that it takes know-how. Fried food isn't the healthiest, so in my family, we view it as a "sometimes" treat. If I'm going to splurge, I want my fried food to shine, with juicy interiors and golden, crunchy outsides. Here's how to make that happen.

## Pan-Frying Facts

Pan-frying is a dry-heat cooking technique in which food is partially submerged in oil in a pan, on a stovetop, with the aim of a crisp crust and a moist interior. The food is cooked both by contact with the pan and by the hot oil. In deep-frying, food is fully suspended in hot fat and cooked simultaneously on all sides.

### Won't It Be Greasy?

Not if you do it right, which is to use very hot oil. Frying at too low a temperature is what makes fried food greasy. A good rule of thumb is 350 degrees Fahrenheit for deep-frying. Use a deep-fry thermometer, one of the most useful, least-expensive frying and roasting tools, and also try dropping in a cube of bread before you add the food you're actually frying. The bread should sizzle and brown quickly in the oil, not lie limply, soaking up grease.

### Beat the Crowds

Crowding is the biggest no-no when frying. Putting food in hot oil causes the temperature of the oil to drop. Adding too much at once can drastically reduce the temperature, and it can't recover quickly enough to build up sufficient steam to push back against the oil and keep it from infiltrating the food. Leaving space between pieces also allows hot, dry air to circulate, forming crisp crusts. So fry in small batches. It is worth the extra time, so you're not left with a pile of soggy, greasy food.

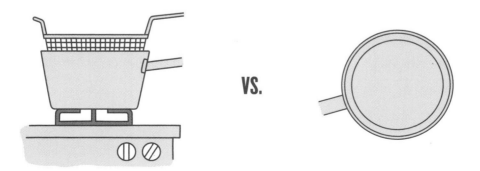

VS.

**1** WHEN BATTERING OR BREADING food to fry in hot oil, the most important thing is to eliminate moisture. Before frying chicken, some soak it in beer, some in buttermilk, and some in brine. To get rid of residual droplets, allow the marinated chicken to dry on a baking rack for up to 10 minutes, and if it's still not dry, dab the chicken with a paper towel or clean dish towel.

**2** THERE ARE THREE STEPS TO breading food for pan-frying:

**a.** Dredge it in flour.

**b.** Dunk it in beaten egg.

**c.** Coat it with breading, such as panko, cracker crumbs or toasted bread crumbs (see "How to Make Bread Crumbs," page 45).

**3** THE FLOUR BONDS THE EGG TO the food, and then breading clings to the egg during frying. Although you always want to shake off any excess egg or crumbs, you want to make sure not to miss a spot. If you fail to coat a small area with egg, hot oil uses that as a gateway, seeping under the crumb layer, causing it to peel away during frying.

**4** CRISP PAN-FRIED FOOD requires sizzling hot fat. Use a frying thermometer and about an inch of oil per pan. The oil's depth should be no more than half the food's height. Too little oil, and the cook time will be too long, resulting in tough meat. Too much oil, and it could boil over or result in greasy food. Heat the oil to 350°F.

**5** USE A LARGE, HEAVY-BOTTOMED and deep saucepan. Avoid nonstick pans because they do not withstand high temperatures. Try a test run; it's a rule of thumb among experienced cooks that the "first" of some fried foods, such as the first fritter, won't be perfect. Put one item in first and see if the oil is hot enough, or too hot, and how long it takes to brown one side before flipping (usually 2 to 4 minutes, depending on the food). If it's perfect, well, that's a little treat for the chef before you continue frying the rest. Timing will vary greatly depending on what you're cooking. Keep a close eye and flip when the first side is golden brown. Pierce the first piece with a knife and be sure it's cooked through. If so, continue with that timing. If not, you may need to lower the heat slightly to prevent excessive browning and cook for a little longer.

**6** BE PREPARED TO TURN UP THE heat after adding the food. The oil might be at the perfect temperature, but adding a batch of food may lower it significantly. Counter this by turning up the flame to high just as you add the food, then lower it again moments later as you continue cooking.

**7** HAVE A PAPER TOWEL–LINED platter ready to receive the cooked food. Put down 3 or 4 layers for best grease absorption.

## RECIPE: BUTTERMILK FRIED CHICKEN

Now that you've got the technique in hand, here's a classic recipe for buttermilk-marinated, down-home-style fried chicken.

### Serves 6 to 8

4 chicken legs, halved into drumsticks and thighs

4 whole chicken breasts, halved

2 cups buttermilk

2 tablespoons salt

2 teaspoons freshly ground black pepper

2 cups all-purpose flour

1 teaspoon paprika

Safflower, sunflower, or peanut oil

**1.** In a large zip-top bag, combine the chicken parts, the buttermilk, and half the salt and pepper, and marinate in the refrigerator for 6 to 8 hours.

**2.** Combine the flour and remaining salt, pepper, and paprika in a large brown paper grocery bag (not a lunch bag) or a plastic shopping bag (be sure there are no holes in the bottom).

**3.** One piece at a time, lift the chicken parts from the buttermilk, drop into the bag containing the flour mixture, and toss until coated. Set each piece aside.

**4.** Prepare two skillets by adding oil to a depth of ½ inch and heat over medium-high heat. When the oil is sizzling hot (350°F), use tongs to lay breast pieces in one skillet, and legs in the other, working in small batches to avoid crowding.

**5.** Fry on the first side for about 10 minutes, then turn the pieces over and fry for another 20 to 25 minutes. Turn the chicken occasionally so it browns on all sides. It's done when the crust is golden and the juices run clear when pricked with the tip of a knife. Remove to a paper towel–lined platter and eat hot or at room temperature. (Once refrigerated, the crust won't be the same.)

# #42
# HOW TO COOK A FRENCH FRY

## (or, How to Deep-Fry Anything)

French fries, doughnuts, onion rings, mozzarella sticks, chicken legs, and cod fillets. . . . Most of us enjoy these crispy morsels at burger joints, state fairs, and chain restaurants, but we rarely cook them at home. It's no wonder—deep-frying works best when you have a special appliance for the task; it can be messy, and there are safety issues to consider. Done right, however, deep-frying can yield surprisingly greaseless, delectably piping-hot morsels made just the way you like them.

## The French Fry—An International Favorite

The French call them *pommes frites,* the Dutch call them *frieten,* and the English call them *chips.* Beloved from Belgium (where they were actually invented) to Australia to Canada, fry lovers coat them in ketchup, drench them in gravy, pair them with fish fillets, douse them in vinegar, shake on garlic salt, and dip them in mayonnaise. From planklike steak fries to whip-thin shoestrings, fries are a treat almost everyone enjoys.

## Pick Your Potato

For frying, you need a starchy potato such as a russet, Long White, Norkotah, or Gold Rush. You can also use all-purpose types such as Kennebec or Yukon Gold. In hot oil, the texture of starchy potatoes stays mealy and dry, making sure the inside of the fry stays fluffy and light.

## Can Your Oil Take the Heat?

To deep-fry any food—be it potatoes, chicken, zucchini, or Oreos—you'll need fat with a very high smoke point, which means it can be heated to high temperatures. If the oil isn't hot enough, breading disintegrates and food acts like a sponge, absorbing the surrounding oil. And greasy deep-fried food tastes awful! Heat a low-smoke-point oil to a high temperature, and it will break down, causing fishy and "off" flavors, doubly ruining your food. There are many choices of high-smoke-point fats (see "Fats for Deep-Frying," below), so pick the right flavor for your dish.

## Deep-Fryer—Fun, but Optional

Deep-fryers are very handy, but not crucial. There are electric fryers that look like big stockpots with a plug, restaurant-style fryers for countertop use, and stovetop deep-fryers fitted with a lift-out basket. These can be good investments if you plan on doing a lot of frying, but to avoid the expense, you can simply use a large pot or Dutch oven and scoop out fried foods with a slotted spoon.

✕ ✕ ✕ ✕ ✕ ✕ ✕ ✕ ✕ ✕ ✕ ✕ ✕ ✕ ✕ ✕ ✕ ✕ ✕ ✕ ✕ ✕ ✕ ✕ ✕ ✕ ✕ ✕

## FATS FOR DEEP-FRYING

In general, the lighter in color and the more refined an oil is, the higher the smoke point. The most popular fat for deep-frying is vegetable or canola oil, which has a mild flavor and is inexpensive—good if you're using a quart of it for frying. You can filter the cooled oil through a paper towel–lined strainer and pour it back into the bottle to save for deep-frying later, but let your nose be your guide: If the oil smells at all funny when you reopen the bottle, the food will taste the same way. Discard it and start fresh.

## Safety First!

The key to deep-frying at home is safety. Boiling hot oil is dangerous, reaching temperatures of more than 400 degrees Fahrenheit. It can boil over, starting a fire or burning you. Set deep-fryers on flat surfaces, far from the edge of countertops, and follow manufacturers' instructions. Use back burners on the stove. Don't fry while wearing loose-fitting clothing or floppy sleeves. And remember, *never* douse a grease fire with water. Always have a fire extinguisher nearby, or smother a fire with a lid, flour, or cornmeal.

**1 CUT THE POTATOES WITH A** large, very sharp knife in order to create smooth surfaces. Jagged cuts allow oil to seep into crevices instead of forming a seal against the oil, resulting in spongy, greasy fries. Cut them into uniform pieces to ensure equal browning. Too thin, and the whole fry will be crispy and lacking a fluffy interior. Too thick, and the crust will be overcooked, leaving the inside raw. Aim for ¼- to ½-inch strips.

**2 IF YOU LIKE, RINSE THE** potatoes in cold water before cooking. Some people feel this washes off the excess starch and makes a crisper fry; others think it's fussy and unnecessary. Try it and see if you care either way!

**3 WHETHER RINSED OR NOT,** potatoes should be quite dry before you fry, for both safety and optimal cooking. Pat the surface with several clean paper towels to dab up any excess moisture.

**4 WORKING IN SMALL BATCHES,** so each fry can be surrounded on all sides by hot oil, parcook the potatoes in the hot fat at a temperature of 325°F. Use the temperature setting on your fryer or set up your pot with a frying thermometer. Cook them until they're blond and limp (3 to 5 minutes), then remove them with a slotted spoon or skimmer.

**5 PUT THE PAR-COOKED FRIES** in a bowl lined with paper towels and let them rest for 15 minutes to 2 hours.

**6 WHEN READY TO SERVE,** reheat your oil to 375°F. Again, working in small batches, repeat the frying process, allowing each batch to fry until golden brown and crispy (4 to 7 minutes), then drain on fresh paper towels. Salt, and then serve very hot. No matter how well cooked, a cold fry is not what you want.

**Charles Dickens references fries in *A Tale of Two Cities* as "husky chips of potato, fried with some reluctant drops of oil."**

# #43
## HOW TO COOK A POT OF BEANS

It's true, you can always use canned beans, which are not so different in flavor when they are used in cooked dishes. But in salads and sandwiches, canned are far inferior to home-cooked dried beans—and they cost more to boot. The main barrier, for the time-starved, is the soaking step. Not only is this effortless, but also, there's a shortcut that gets beans on the table same-day. Here's how to make perfect beans and leave the cans in the pantry.

## Why We Soak

Many think the soaking step is just to reduce the gas that beans cause in poor chili-lovers like me and my family. That's partly true—it may help eliminate indigestible complex sugars, though some food scientists disagree!—but that's not the only reason. Mainly, beans are dirty! During commercial packaging, beans aren't washed because residual moisture causes them to sprout (they're seeds) or to mold and ferment. Rinsing and soaking clears the beans of dirt, pebbles, insects, pesticides, and chemical fertilizer.

**1** **RINSE THE BEANS IN A COLANDER** and pick them over for pebbles, sticks, and debris.

**2** **SOAK THE BEANS.** The larger the bean, the longer the soak. (Small beans and legumes, like lentils, don't require soaking.) And the longer the soak, the shorter the cooking time. Soak beans in roughly three times their volume of cool water for 6 to 8 hours before cooking. Dried beans can be soaked too long, which can cause them to ferment, changing their flavor, and making them less easily digestible.

For a quicker soak, put them in a pot with cold water to cover by 2 to 3 inches. Bring them to a boil, and then, with the pan off the heat, allow them to remain in the water for 1 to 2 hours. They are now ready to cook.

**3** **DRAIN THE BEANS, OR,** preferably, lift them out of the soaking water with a slotted spoon, leaving any grit in the bottom of the bowl. Then, put them in a pot with enough water to cover.

**4** **LOOSELY COVER THE POT, WITH** the lid set slightly askew, and simmer gently over low heat until the beans are creamy and tender, 1 to 2 hours. One pound of dried beans, which is about 2 cups, will yield 6 to 8 cups of cooked beans, depending on the type. Taste them occasionally to test for doneness.

# #44
# HOW TO COOK RICE

If you eat a lot of rice in your home, a rice cooker is well worth a spot on your countertop. In as little as 20 minutes or up to 12 hours or more later, you lift the cover to find hot, perfectly cooked rice, tender but with separate grains. It's a little kitchen miracle. If rice is only an occasional food, however, cook it on the stovetop using the absorption method, which means you put in just as much water as the rice needs to absorb.

Whatever rice you choose, do not use "converted" rice, which is parboiled and dried to cook faster, robbing it of flavor.

## Rice in Season

A stock cube is an easy way to add flavor to a pot of rice. But you can add other flavors as well. Try replacing the water with homemade chicken stock or coconut milk. Cook a minced onion in the rice pot in a little butter until the onion is tender but not brown, and then add the rice and liquid. Add spices or dried herbs along with the water and salt. Rice is very forgiving, so let your taste buds be your guide.

**1 CHOOSE YOUR RICE: WHITE,** brown, jasmine, basmati, and so on, as well as long, medium, or short grain. The only ones to avoid for cooking rice this way are risotto rice, such as Arborio or Carnaroli, which is grown to have the excess starch that makes a risotto creamy, and wild rice, which is technically a seed and needs to be boiled in a lot of water and drained, as if it was pasta.

**2 DECIDE HOW MUCH YOU NEED.** One cup of rice will yield 2 to 3 cups of cooked rice, depending on the type of rice. Brown rice will give you about 2 cups. Basmati will fluff right up into 3 cups. Long-grain white rice will give you about 2½ cups. If you're cooking to serve 4 people, 1½ cups uncooked of rice is reasonable.

**3 MEASURE THE RICE AND WATER** into a pot with a lid. The basic rule of thumb is 1 part rice to 2 parts water, with slight modifications, so 1 cup of long-grain white rice and 2 cups of water. Brown rice needs a little more water—1 cup rice to 2¼ or 2½ cups water, and short grain needs a little less, perhaps 1 cup rice to 1¾ cups water. Try your preferred rice with the 1:2 proportion with water and see if it cooks up the way you prefer.

**4 ADD SALT, ABOUT ½ TEASPOON** per cup of rice. Rice without salt is bland. If the bouillon cube package says that 1 cube makes 2 cups broth, then 1 cube should be okay for 2 cups water and 1 cup rice. Some cooks add a tablespoon of butter or olive oil to enrich the rice, but it's not necessary.

**5 BRING THE POT TO A BOIL OVER** high heat. If you used a bouillon cube, stir it into the boiling water so it doesn't sit there intact as your rice cooks. If you're just using salt, no need to stir.

**6 DECREASE THE HEAT TO LOW** and cover the pan. And now don't touch it. It should not be boiling hard; the lid should not jiggle. Don't stir it; don't take the lid off. Leave it to cook for 15 minutes. Then remove the pan from the heat and let it sit until any steam is absorbed and the rice is tender without being mushy, 8 to 10 minutes.

**7 TAKE OFF THE LID AND FLUFF THE** rice with a fork to separate the grains. Serve at once.

# #45
## HOW TO ROLL A BURRITO
### (or a Wrap)

The burrito is a cousin to the taco—both involve folded-up tortillas stuffed with fillings. In fact, in Mexico, some call burritos *tacos de harina,* or "flour tacos." Literally translated, *burrito* means "little donkey," probably because burritos resemble the rolled-up bundles they transport. American burritos typically hold some combination of beans, rice, meat, lettuce, salsa, guacamole, cheese, and sour cream. But a burrito can be made with whatever's on hand to meet any diet or taste. They're so easy to prepare—consider them your go-to for quick weekday lunches and dinners.

## The Wrap-Up

Burrito's wrapper—the tortilla—is an unleavened bread, usually made with flour, salt, water, and fat. (Some of the puffier, Tex-Mex-style tortillas are leavened with baking powder.) For the health-conscious, they now come in fiber-rich whole wheat, along with rice, quinoa, and other gluten-free flours. For a flavor boost, try the spinach, sundried tomato, chipotle, and jalapeño varieties. Read the label for ingredients and look for wrappers without added preservatives for best flavor.

## All Rolled-Up: Burritos, Wraps, Sushi Rolls, and Egg Rolls

The Earl of Sandwich knew that stuffing tasty fillings into an edible container was a brilliant way to prepare a low-mess, portable meal. Joining, and I'd say surpassing, the beloved sandwich in the annals of smart culinary design are the burrito, the summer roll, sushi rolls, and the wrap.

These delectable rolled meals offer the upgrade of a completely sealed envelope for the meats, vegetables, and condiments inside, making them even more suitable for lunches and meals on the go.

The humble sandwich—cousin to the wrap—was born under curious circumstances: The fourth Earl of Sandwich, John Montagu, was a gambler who famously ate a piece of beef between two slices of toasted bread so he didn't have to leave his game.

**1 PREPARE YOUR FILLINGS.** (This step can be done in advance.) Wash and chop lettuce and tomatoes or other veggies. Cook or warm up some rice. Prepare whole beans seasoned with spicy sauces, or warm refried beans. Fry or sauté ground beef, strips of chicken breast or steak, or fish such as tilapia or monkfish. Grate cheese. The key is to have all ingredients ready for stuffing when the tortillas are warm.

**2 GO BIG!** I recommend 12-inch tortillas or larger to allow a good stuffing of ample fillings for a full meal; this also helps to prevent leakage.

**3 SPRAY A LARGE, HEAVY-** bottomed skillet with cooking spray and set it over high heat to warm. Lay in tortillas one at a time, heating for 30 to 45 seconds per side. Don't overbrown or dry them out. You want them to be slightly puffy and pliable. Lay them flat on a plate to be filled.

**4 SPOON RICE ON FIRST TO FORM** an absorbent layer. Make a rectangle, leaving about 3 inches of space around the perimeter. Don't pile it too thick, or you won't be able to roll it.

**5 ADD LAYERS OF BEANS AND** meat on top of the rice rectangle.

**6 LOCK IT DOWN.** If you're using sour cream or guacamole, layer those in next. They'll act like glue to secure loose ingredients such as shredded cheese, lettuce, jalapeños, and chopped cilantro.

**7 DRESS IT UP.** Add diced and shredded toppings along with saucy condiments for the finishing touch.

**8 SECURE THE PERIMETER.** With the rectangle of layered ingredients oriented vertically, fold the tortilla's left side just over the ingredients, leaving uncovered tortilla to the right. Then fold the bottom up about 1 to 2 inches. (If you're wrapping it up and transporting it to lunch or a picnic, fold in each end to help keep the fillings sealed tight.) Finally, finish rolling the burrito tightly from left to right. It'll look something like a sleeping bag. If done properly, your hands (and shirt!) should stay clean while munching.

×××××××××××××××××××××××××××××××××××××××××××××××××××××××××××××××××

# OTHER FILLING IDEAS

Pretty much anything can go into a wrap—when you're bored with the standard rice and bean base, don't forget these other combinations! Simplicity can be good, but the bigger the wrap, the more you can stuff in, so experimentation is key.

- **Caesar salad with grilled chicken**
- **Baba ganoush spread, hard-boiled egg, cucumber, tomato, tahini, parsley**
- **Spinach salad with honey mustard, dried cranberries, red onions, and chickpeas or turkey**
- **Falafel with hummus, olives, pickled cabbage, and harissa**
- **Prosciutto and arugula with fig spread and goat cheese**
- **Tuna salad with lettuce, celery, tomatoes, and capers**
- **Curried chicken salad or cauliflower with golden raisins and romaine lettuce**

- **Kale with sausage and feta**
- **Roasted red peppers with white bean spread and spinach**
- **Mushrooms, caramelized onions, and polenta**
- **Muffaletta: olive spread, cold cuts, lettuce, and tomato**
- **Tomato, mozzarella, basil, and chicken**
- **Lemon Greek yogurt spread, asparagus, and pancetta**
- **Black beans, corn, and zucchini with salsa and smashed avocado**
- **Pulled pork with BBQ sauce and cole slaw**

# #46
## HOW TO MAKE MAKI
### (or, Making Sense of Sushi)

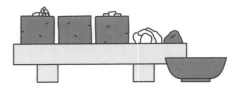

A maki roll is the sushi you're probably most familiar with—those neatly cut rolls sold in Japanese restaurants, deli salad bars, and now, even supermarket cold cases. They're usually made with toasted nori (the green seaweed wrapper that holds them together), rice, and filling.

## Don't I Need Special Equipment?

Not really! I recommend a bamboo sushi mat, known as a makisu mat, which is very inexpensive and easily found in Asian markets. A makisu mat holds the ingredients together while rolling and makes the sushi roll tight and firm so it holds together when you cut it into rounds. If you don't have a mat, you can roll sushi using a clean dish towel.

**1 LAY A TATAMI MAT**
(or whatever you are using to roll) on a clean work surface. Lightly toast a sheet of nori over a gas flame, holding it over the heat for a few seconds using a pair of tongs, or put the nori sheet in a toaster oven for 15 to 20 seconds. This softens it enough to roll without breaking, and toasting improves the flavor.

**2 PLACE THE SHEET OF TOASTED**
nori on top, shiny-side down, rough-side up. The rice will stick to the rough side.

**3 USING A WET WOODEN PADDLE**
or spoon or a rubber spatula, apply a very thin layer of rice (no more than a ¼ inch thick) to the entire sheet, leaving a 1-inch strip bare at the top, for sealing the roll shut. Work around the remaining three sides and edges, then move to the middle. Wet the paddle again, as needed, working slowly and gently. If you tear the nori, the roll will fall apart during cutting.

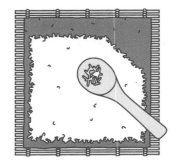

**4** **PLACE A THIN LINE OF** ingredients, about one third of the way up from the bottom.

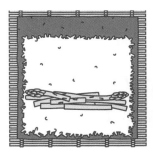

**5** **BEFORE ROLLING, USE YOUR** fingers to gently moisten the exposed strip at the top of the nori. Then dot several grains of rice about ½ inch apart across the strip to glue the roll shut.

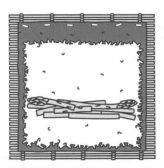

**6** **HOLDING THE BOTTOM EDGE OF** the mat or dish towel with your thumbs, lift the nori and roll it away from you, keeping the ingredients together and pushing to press the rice into place.

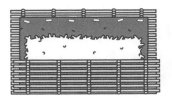

**7** **ALLOW THE SUSHI ROLL TO REST** for 3 or 4 minutes before cutting so that moisture can seep into the nori, softening it so that it's less likely to tear. Using a very sharp knife dipped in water, cut the roll into six pieces.

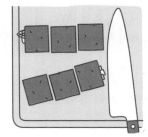

**8** **SERVE WITH SOY SAUCE,** wasabi, and pickled ginger.

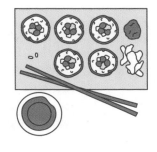

To minimize damage to the fish as it is cut, Japanese knives have a thin carbon steel blade that is sharper than stainless steel knives.

## Am I a Vegetarian If I Eat Fish?

Labels aside, any path toward mindful, healthful eating deserves kudos. But here are the most commonly accepted parameters and definitions of vegetarianism:

**Pescatarian.** Abstains from red meat and poultry but eats dairy products and seafood.

**Flexitarian.** Generally abstains from meat and animal flesh, eats dairy products, and may or may not eat seafood. Occasionally eats meat and poultry in a conscious way.

**Ovo-lacto vegetarian.** Eats eggs and dairy products, and may or may not eat seafood. Does not eat red meat or poultry. *Ovo-vegetarians* eat eggs, but not dairy and eschew meat and poultry. *Lacto-vegetarians* eat dairy but not eggs, and eschew meat and poultry.

**Vegan.** Eats only plant-based products. Does not eat animal flesh, dairy, eggs, seafood, or any product made from animals, including broth or gelatin. Because it is made by bees, honey is a topic of debate.

**Raw vegan.** Eats only an unprocessed diet of vegan food, none of which has been heated to more than 115 degrees Fahrenheit, the belief being that high temperatures affect nutritional value and render some compounds in foods harmful to the body.

**Macrobiotic.** Eats unprocessed vegan foods, such as whole grains, fruits, and vegetables. Emphasis on the vegetables.

# #47
# HOW TO COOK WITH TOFU

In many ways, tofu is a perfect food: low in fat, high in protein, derived from plant sources so it's heart healthy and cholesterol free. It can add creaminess to smoothies, turn a stir-fry into a meal, and stand in, marinated and grilled, as a steak. Time and time again, I hear "I like tofu when I eat it in restaurants, but I don't know how to make it." These basics will set you on the right road.

## Types of Tofu

❖ **Silken tofu.** Usually called for in soup, sauce, and dip recipes. It won't hold its shape, so it's not ideal for stir-fries or grilling. More often than not, you'll find it in a brick pack, unrefrigerated.

❖ **Regular tofu.** This is the most common type and is divided into different firmness levels, including: soft, medium, firm, and extra-firm. It typically comes packed in water and is found in the refrigerator case. Even when extra-firm, this tofu is somewhat soft and benefits from pressing. This is the type to use for stir-fries, casseroles, and stews.

❖ **Brick tofu.** As you'd expect, the package looks like a brick. Because the goal is to offer the firmest tofu possible, it's packed with very little water and comes in a plastic wrapper that almost looks vacuum-packed and is sold in the refrigerator case. This style is best used when a recipe calls for clean slices or cubes that won't fall apart.

It's easy to make most styles of tofu firmer if you want drier tofu to ensure crispy edges when frying, or solid chunks or "steaks" for an entrée.

**1** PLACE A BLOCK OF MEDIUM or firm tofu at the end of a cutting board.

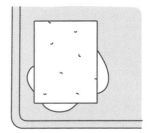

**2** PLACE A SECOND CUTTING board or a heavy, flat plate on top, sandwiching the tofu in a makeshift press. Position the tofu near the edge of the kitchen sink, so that the liquid will run down the drain.

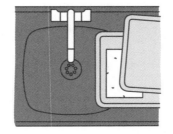

**3** PROP THE BACK END OF THE bottom cutting board up a few inches, using a stable baking tray or casserole dish to angle it.

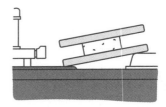

**4 PLACE SOMETHING HEAVY, LIKE** a book, on the top cutting board or plate.

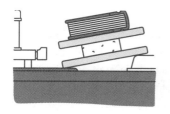

**5 ALLOW THE WEIGHT TO PRESS** the liquid from the tofu over the course of an hour or two.

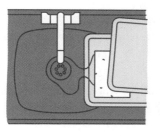

**6 ONCE THE TOFU HAS DRAINED,** it will be quite firm and easy to slice into cubes, or steaks. Marinate the chopped tofu in a mixture of your choice (wet or dry), refrigerated, for several hours. Drain the marinated tofu before cooking.

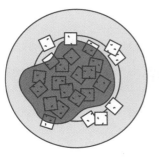

**7 IF FRYING THE TOFU, TO ENSURE** a golden, crispy crust, dredge the cubes in cornstarch before cooking in very hot oil.

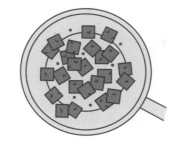

**8 BE PATIENT—ALLOW YOUR** tofu to cook on all sides until nicely browned. It will be flavorful and crunchy on the outside, with a piping hot, creamy interior.

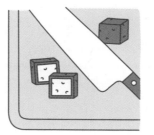

## Protein Sources for Nonmeat Eaters

Whether or not you follow a plant-based diet, there are many sources of protein beyond meat.

Artichokes
Asparagus
Avocados
Beans
Beet greens
Broccoli
Coconut milk
Eggs
Greek-style yogurt (higher in protein than regular yogurt)
Hummus
Kale
Lentils
Low-fat cottage cheese
Low-fat, part-skim cheeses like mozzarella, Cheddar, and Swiss
Nut milks
Nuts and nut butters
Peas
Powdered whey protein (for shakes and smoothies)
Quinoa
Seeds (such as sunflower and pumpkin)
Seitan (dough made from seasoned wheat gluten)
Skim milk
Soy products (including soy nuts, soy butter, soy milk, and tofu)
Spinach
Veggie burgers

## RECIPE: IMPOSSIBLE-NOT-TO-LIKE TOFU STIR-FRY

The tofu in this recipe is firm and crisp, and it absorbs the flavors of the marinade and the vegetables with which it's cooked. The beauty of the recipe is that you can choose whatever vegetables you and your family prefer—it's quite accommodating, as is tofu itself. Serve on top of brown, white, or jasmine rice, or on top of buckwheat soba or white or whole-wheat pasta. Flank with a salad of lettuce, radish, and cucumber, topped with peanut dressing, for extra nutrition and flair.

**Serves about 4**

1 (16-ounce) package extra-firm water-packed tofu

½ cup lemon juice

½ cup soy sauce

½ cup brown sugar

2 teaspoons crushed garlic

1 teaspoon minced fresh ginger

½ teaspoon freshly ground black pepper

1 teaspoon toasted sesame oil

½ cup plus 1 tablespoon cornstarch

½ cup vegetable stock

2 tablespoons peanut oil

2 cups chopped vegetables (broccoli, onions, snow peas, bell peppers, carrots, celery)

**1.** Drain and press the tofu (see "How to Cook with Tofu," page 82). Once firm and dry, cut it into large, uniform cubes.

**2.** In a medium-size saucepan, combine the lemon juice, soy sauce, brown sugar, garlic, ginger, pepper, and sesame oil, and cook over low heat until the sugar is dissolved. This mixture will be your marinade.

**3.** Combine the tofu cubes and one third of the marinade in a zip-top bag, and refrigerate for 4 to 6 hours.

**4.** When ready to cook, pour the marinated tofu cubes into a colander and let drain. Once drained, combine the tofu in a clean zip-top bag with ½ cup cornstarch. Seal the bag and shake to coat.

**5.** In a saucepan, combine the remaining marinade with the vegetable stock. Bring the mixture to a rolling boil, then reduce the heat to medium and cook, stirring, for 4 minutes.

**6.** In a small mixing bowl, whisk 1 tablespoon of the cornstarch with 1 to 1½ tablespoons cold water until there are no lumps.

**7.** Slowly add the cornstarch slurry to the sauce, whisking continuously until it begins to thicken, then reduce the heat to low.

**8.** Heat the peanut oil in a large heavy-bottomed sauté pan over high heat. Add the tofu to the hot oil, working in batches to allow ample space between cubes. Resist the urge to touch your tofu cubes until the edges are brown and crisp on one side, about 6 minutes—then use tongs to flip. Once browned on all sides, set the tofu aside.

**9.** Using the same pan, sauté the vegetables, adding more oil if needed. The vegetables are done when they are bright in color and fork-tender.

**10.** Return the tofu cubes to the pan with the cooked vegetables. Top with the reserved sauce and serve.

XXXXXXXXXXXXXXXXX

## SMOKE POINTS AND OIL TYPES

Some oils withstand high temperatures better than others. The *smoke point* of oils and fats refers to the temperature at which they break down and start to fail as lubricants. When oil breaks down, it will fill your kitchen with smoke, and foods will start to stick to the pan and absorb an "off" taste.

Extra-virgin olive oil tastes great in vinaigrette, but it has a low smoke point. Some better choices for high-temperature frying are safflower oil, sunflower oil, peanut oil, refined canola oil, and coconut oil. Lard and beef fat are what our grandmothers might have recommended.

First developed in China around 200 BC, tofu is a nutritional powerhouse, with all 8 essential amino acids, 10 grams of protein per half cup, and loads of calcium, potassium, and magnesium.

# #48
# HOW TO REPURPOSE COMMON LEFTOVERS

## (or, Giving Meals a Second Career)

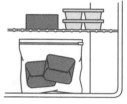

I'd almost feel sorry for the uneaten portions of my meals, if I didn't know they were headed for greatness in Round Two of their culinary lives. To cope with leftovers in a creative way, and to avoid eating the same meal many nights in a row, repurpose the main ingredients into new dishes that are exciting in their own right. Here's how to use up the leftovers most Americans are confronted with on a regular basis.

## Roast Chicken

⸻ Chop it up and make your favorite chicken salad.

⸻ Sandwich it between tortillas with Cheddar cheese for quesadillas.

⸻ Bake it on a pizza crust with mozzarella and ricotta for white pizza.

⸻ Buy a ready-made piecrust and some jarred gravy and mix it with crisp-cooked chopped veggies for chicken pot pie.

## Roast Turkey

⸻ Layer it on a sandwich using cranberry sauce and mashed potatoes as a condiment.

⸻ Simmer it with potatoes and peas in store-bought curry sauce.

⸻ Chop it into canned cream of mushroom or cream of broccoli soup, and then serve over wide egg noodles.

⸻ Mince it and stir it into chili (see Beginner's Chili, page 71).

## Hamburger Meat

⸻ Make a cottage pie. Sauté leftover meat with butter and onions. Add some cooked peas and carrots, and throw in some leftover gravy or beef stock to moisten. Spoon into a casserole dish, top with mashed potatoes, and bake.

⸻ Mix it into macaroni and cheese for a one-dish meal.

⸻ Make a taco salad. Line a bowl with tortilla chips and layer on cooked ground beef, lettuce, onions, tomatoes, sweet corn, jalapeño peppers, Cheddar cheese, and salsa.

⸻ Sauté tomatoes, onions, garlic, and bell peppers. Add cooked rice and cooked ground beef. Layer into bowls and top with shredded cheese.

## Mashed Potatoes

⸻ Mix 1 cup mashed potatoes with a beaten egg, some olive oil, some finely chopped onion, and some fresh herbs. Mold into pancakes and fry.

⸻ Make mashed potato soup. Sauté mushrooms and onions in butter. Add leftover mashed potatoes and chicken stock until it's a chowderlike consistency. Stir in some shredded cheese. Top with sour cream and scallions.

## Spaghetti Sauce

⧈ Use as a pizza sauce on a store-bought or homemade crust (see "Foolproof Pizza Dough," page 48).

⧈ Make pizza burgers by using garlic bread as the bun and spreading spaghetti sauce over the meat patty. Melt mozzarella cheese on top under the broiler.

⧈ Make stuffed peppers by topping and coring green bell peppers and stuffing them with a combination of cooked ground beef, cooked rice, and spaghetti sauce. Put them in a casserole dish, cover them with foil, and bake at 350°F until the peppers are soft, about 30 minutes. Uncover, top with mozzarella cheese, and bake until melted.

⧈ Make a quick minestrone soup. Sauté onions and celery in a large pot with a little olive oil. Add the leftover spaghetti sauce, then pour in beef stock, cooked vegetables, and canned beans.

## Cooked Vegetables

⧈ Use them to top a homemade or store-bought cheese pizza.

⧈ Make a no-crust quiche (see No-Crust Vegetable Quiche, below).

⧈ Make quick vegetable soup. Sauté onions and garlic in olive oil in a soup pot, then pour in beef, chicken, or vegetable stock. Add lots of chopped cooked or frozen veggies, plus chicken or turkey, if you have it.

⧈ Make a stir-fry. Fry strips of chicken or steak in vegetable oil with desired seasonings, then throw in your cooked vegetables for the last minute of cooking.

## RECIPE: NO-CRUST VEGETABLE QUICHE

Take away the crust, and a quiche is an exceedingly easy entrée that comes together in minutes. It's also one of the tastiest ways around to use up leftover cooked vegetables. Broccoli and Cheddar is a classic combo, but this recipe works just as well with extra mushrooms, peppers, wilted greens, and even potatoes!

### Serves 4 to 6

6 large eggs

1 cup milk

¼ cup finely chopped onion

2 tablespoons unsalted butter, melted, plus more for greasing the pan

½ teaspoon salt

Freshly ground black pepper

1 cup chopped cooked vegetables

½ cup shredded Cheddar cheese

½ cup shredded mozzarella cheese

1. Preheat the oven to 400°F. Butter a 9-inch pie plate, and set it aside.

2. In a medium-size mixing bowl, whisk together the eggs, milk, onion, melted butter, salt, and a generous grind of black pepper. Gently fold in the chopped vegetables.

3. Pour the mixture into the pie plate and sprinkle the cheeses evenly over the top.

4. Bake until set and golden brown on top, about 20 minutes.

## RECIPE: FRIED SPAGHETTI OMELET

Oh, the delicious comfort of a fried spaghetti omelet. In a way it's a pasta dish, in another it's a quiche, and in still another it's an Italian egg foo yung! This dish is a brilliant way to put leftover pasta to work, of course, but I sometimes make fresh pasta just to make this recipe. Don't be shy about layering on your favorite toppings!

### Serves 3 to 4

6 tablespoons butter

4 cups cooked spaghetti (or other pasta)

3 large eggs

⅔ cup milk

⅔ cup freshly shredded Parmesan or Pecorino Romano cheese

3 tablespoons chopped fresh flat-leaf parsley

Freshly ground black pepper

Salt

1. In a large, heavy-bottomed skillet, melt the butter over medium heat. Add the pasta and fry it gently in the butter, tossing a couple of times to coat.

2. In a medium-size mixing bowl, whisk together the eggs and milk. Stir in the cheese, parsley, and freshly ground black pepper to taste. (I use a lot.) Pour over the fried pasta.

3. Cook the omelet over medium heat until a golden crust forms on the bottom. Flip it over, and cook the other side until it forms a golden crust (a few more minutes). Slide the omelet out onto a platter.

4. Salt to your taste, cut into wedges, and serve hot with more cheese for sprinkling, if you like.

# #49
# HOW TO START CANNING

**T**hrifty homemakers and practitioners of traditional arts know that canning, or "putting up," food is an excellent way to capitalize on what's fresh and abundant during rotating harvest cycles and to stock a fridge or pantry with delicious treats made by hand. In canning, food is preserved by being processed and then sealed in airtight containers (at home, they are typically jars). A broad range of methods can be deployed when preserving foods this way: pasteurization, boiling, steaming, refrigeration, and freezing among them. Any shelf-stable preserve such as jam, jelly, marmalade, or curd has been temperature-treated in some way to kill microorganisms and render inactive enzymes that could cause spoilage. Food is then vacuum-sealed to prevent air, and the microorganisms that come with it, from entering the container and recontaminating food.

Learning to can—like learning to sew, knit, cook, clean, build shelves, or paint a room—is a valuable skill that offers great rewards. Safe canning practices can get rather involved, so before you get started, visit instructional websites like those of the National Center for Home Food Preservation (nchfp.uga.edu), the Centers for Disease Control and Prevention (cdc.gov), and the Federal Food Safety blog (foodsafety.gov). Your local library will have books describing what you need to buy and do in order to preserve foods you've grown or found at rock-bottom prices at the height of freshness at your grocery or farmers' market.

## Botox's Evil Twin

*Clostridium botulinum.* This potentially deadly microorganism can cause a disease called botulism that can affect the central nervous system. The bacteria is anaerobic, meaning it can grow in low-oxygen conditions, such as in an improperly sealed can or jar, and particularly in low-acid foods, such as canned green beans. Botulism can cause nerve and brain damage, paralysis, and even death in those with weakened or compromised immune systems.

## Why Risk It?

Done properly, canning is a fun and cost-effective way to store foods—and homemade jams and salsas make excellent gifts. With meticulous sterilization practices and the proper equipment, home canning poses almost zero danger, particularly when canning high-acid foods like tomatoes or pickles. Proper canning techniques include choosing only fresh foods to process, washing them thoroughly, adding acids such as lemon juice or vinegar to naturally low-acid foods, using noncompromised jars and brand-new lids, and

## ✕ ✕ ✕ ✕ ✕ ✕ ✕ ✕ ✕ ✕ ✕ ✕ ✕ ✕ ✕ ✕ ✕ ✕ ✕ ✕ ✕ ✕ ✕ ✕ ✕ ✕ ✕ ✕ ✕ ✕
## WHAT'S NONREACTIVE COOKWARE?

**N**onreactive cookware allows you to cook foods that are acidic (citrus, tomato sauce, wine) or alkaline (eggs, dairy, asparagus) without reactivity between the food and the cookware. Problems with reactive cookware include breakdown and discoloration of food (eggs can develop a grayish tinge), metallic or "off" flavors, the leaching of ions from the cookware into the food, and staining or pockmarking of the pan.

Nonreactive materials include glass, stainless steel, ceramic, enamel, and hard anodized aluminum. Reactive materials include (non-stainless) steel, cast-iron, copper, and aluminum. These materials conduct heat evenly and are excellent for boiling water, frying burgers, or making stock. But if you're working with acidic or alkaline ingredients, stick to nonreactive cookware.

vacuum-sealing them in a boiling-water or pressure canner at the right temperature and for the correct period of time.

## The Freezer: An Easier Way to Homemade Jam

You can make preserves to be stored in your refrigerator or freezer. Although they don't last as long as the shelf-stable variety, the cold, and the use of acids like lemon juice, extend the life of your food, keeping bacteria and microorganisms at bay. So, if you have an embarrassment of fruit after a spree at the U-pick farm or a gift from your green-thumb uncle, these shortcut methods are perfect as a simple first stab at home food preservation.

✕ ✕ ✕ ✕ ✕ ✕ ✕ ✕ ✕ ✕ ✕ ✕ ✕ ✕ ✕ ✕ ✕ ✕ ✕ ✕ ✕ ✕ ✕ ✕ ✕ ✕ ✕ ✕

# PECTIN: JAM'S SECRET INGREDIENT

**P**ectin is a natural compound found in all fruits; it causes jams, jellies, and preserves to "set," or gel. Most commercial pectins are extracted from citrus fruit and contain no artificial substances. With cooked preserves, pectin shortens the cooking time, allowing fruits and vegetables to retain more freshness and brighter color.

Pectin requirements differ from fruit to fruit, and in commercially packaged pectin, there are differences between brands and forms, so use the type your recipe specifies. Because pectin reacts with sugar, don't omit or substitute sugar without substituting "light" or "low-sugar" pectin to go with it, or the set of the jam will be off.

---

# RECIPE: STRAWBERRY FRIDGE PRESERVES

**O**ne perk of refrigerator jam is that, because it doesn't get canned, the fruit stays close to its natural state, so it tastes fresh. Try this recipe with fresh strawberries (not frozen)—it will stay delicious for up to 3 weeks. I particularly like this one because it's fruitier than it is sweet. Add a spoonful to oatmeal or yogurt, or spread it on toast.

**Makes about 2 cups**

1 quart (4 cups) strawberries

1½ cups granulated sugar

Juice of 1 lemon

**1.** Wash, hull, and halve the strawberries.

**2.** In a very deep, nonreactive pot, bring the berries and sugar to a boil over high heat, and let cook for 5 minutes. Using a large, flat spoon, skim any foam from the top.

**3.** Reduce the heat to a simmer and add the lemon juice. Allow the mixture to cook for 10 minutes, stirring frequently.

**4.** Remove the pot from the heat, and use a slotted spoon to remove the solid berries to one or more clean lidded jars, filling about halfway. Return the pot to the burner and simmer over low heat until the liquid is reduced by half; depending on the heat, this can take between 10 and 15 minutes. Once reduced, use a ladle to distribute it evenly among the jars.

**5.** Allow the jars to cool completely, cover them securely, and refrigerate.

# RECIPE: NO-COOK PEACH AND RASPBERRY FREEZER JAM

**F**or long-term preservation without the effort of vacuum-sealing, rely on your freezer. The freezer method of jam making is exceptionally easy because it doesn't even require turning on the stove. The secret is "jam sugar," which is available wherever you buy canning supplies in the autumn. It contains enough pectin to break down the structure of the fruit without the need for heat.

**Makes about five (8-ounce) jars**

2 cups (about 6) washed, peeled, and thinly sliced peaches

2 cups washed and hulled raspberries

1½ cups granulated jam sugar

3 tablespoons lemon juice

**1.** In a large mixing bowl, stir the peaches, raspberries, sugar, and lemon juice together until well blended. Let stand for 10 minutes, then crush the mixture lightly using a potato masher to release the juices.

**2.** Ladle the jam into clean jars and let set uncovered for an hour.

**3.** Cover tightly and freeze. The jam should last about 1 year in the freezer.

**TIP:** To peel peaches easily, dunk them in boiling water for a minute, then remove and rinse them in cold water. You should be able to slough off the peel by hand.

# #50
# HOW TO MAKE PERFECT PIECRUST

S omeone who makes a good piecrust is said to have a good "hand" with pastry. And how people adore (and envy) the person with a good pastry hand! In fact, perfect piecrust is within everyone's grasp, once you learn its secrets (see Double-Crust Apple Pie, page 91).

## Get Your Chill On

Cold fat, cold water, cold hands. The flakiness that we so admire in a piecrust happens when the cold fat, be it butter, shortening, or lard, coats the individual flour grains without melting and soaking into them. Many pastry pros use a marble work surface to roll out the dough, because marble is naturally 8 degrees Fahrenheit colder than the surrounding environment, helping keep the pastry chilled. Cool hands have the same effect.

## Fat for Flavor

A crust made with lard or shortening is decidedly the most flaky, but not quite as tasty as an all-butter crust. Many bakers like to use half butter, half lard or shortening in their crusts to get the best of both worlds.

**1** MEASURE THE BUTTER, LARD, OR shortening, cut it into pieces, and put the pieces in the freezer for 30 minutes while you gather your other ingredients.

**2** FILL A CUP WITH COLD WATER and drop in a few ice cubes. Measure the water you need for the pastry directly from this cup (avoiding the cubes).

**3** "CUT" THE CHILLED BUTTER into the dry ingredients. Grasp a butter knife in each hand, then pull them vigorously in opposite directions until the butter disappears into the flour. Sprinkle ice water into the flour mixture until the dough begins to clump.

*(continued)*

**4** **AFTER THE PIECRUST DOUGH** has come together, quickly gather it into a ball, wrap it in plastic wrap, and chill it in the refrigerator for 30 minutes to an hour before rolling. (Too much longer and you'll have to let it warm up a bit at room temperature before you can roll it.)

**5** **SPRINKLE YOUR WORK SURFACE** with a couple tablespoons of flour. Place the pastry ball in the center, pat it into a disc, and start rolling it out gently with a rolling pin lightly dusted with flour. Start in the middle of the disc, and use short, firm strokes. For a professional-looking crust, roll forward only, rotating the crust a quarter turn between each stroke to make a smooth, even circle about 12 inches across and about ¼ inch thick.

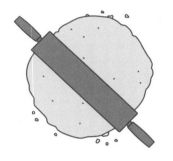

✕ ✕ ✕ ✕ ✕ ✕ ✕ ✕ ✕ ✕ ✕ ✕ ✕ ✕ ✕ ✕

## THE BEST APPLES FOR PIE

The trick is to find an apple that won't dissolve into mushiness but isn't so crisp that it won't soften much at all. Super-crispy varieties such as SweeTango and Honeycrisp are bred to be eating apples, so don't cook with them. Look for deeply flavorful apples that aren't too watery (avoid Red or Golden Delicious for baking) and make sure they have a pronounced tartness. Best choices include Granny Smith, McIntosh, Macoun, and Northern Spy.

## Baking's Heavenly Triumvirate

Any good baker knows that baking is as much about science as it is intuition—chemistry is key. Here are a few truths about baking's big three.

### Butter

✛ Butter, shortening, lard, and margarine can be substituted in equal parts. The difference? Taste. Butter adds a richer flavor than margarine, and shortening doesn't have any flavor at all. Commercial lard tends to be flavorless, but home-rendered lard can have a more meaty flavor. Caution: Don't attempt to substitute "light" butter spreads because they will ruin the texture of your finished product.

✛ Don't swap in liquid fats, like canola oil or peanut oil, when butter (or another hard fat) is required for creaming.

✛ In croissants, piecrust, and puff pastry, the flakiness comes from the butter being chilled. In these applications, the butter is "cut" in rather than being creamed.

✛ If a cake sinks in the center, you might have used too much butter, preventing it from rising properly.

### Sugar

✛ Sugar not only sweetens baked goods but also adds tenderness to delicious cakes, piecrusts, and cookies.

✛ You can generally swap out one granulated sugar for another. Replace white sugar with palm sugar, cane sugar, turbinado sugar, or coconut sugar. You can even substitute brown sugar, but it will darken the color of your baked good.

✛ Sugar helps baked goods brown. If you have a too-pale yellow cake, or straw-colored blondies, lack of sugar could be the culprit. Too brown or burnt? Too much sugar.

### Eggs

✛ Eggs bind, add texture, leaven, and help pastries achieve a golden-brown color. Egg yolks lend moisture and richness. The protein in egg whites forms a fluffy structure that traps air. When whipped, they add lightness and volume.

✛ The more you beat egg whites, the stiffer the protein strands become and the more structure they provide. Caution: No fat can touch beaten egg whites or the structure will break down and they won't stiffen. Use clean tools.

## RECIPE: DOUBLE-CRUST APPLE PIE

There are few desserts that go right to the heart like a freshly baked pie, and apple pie is the queen of American pastries. The classic piecrust in this recipe makes one double-crust pie or two open-top pies. You can also use it for quiches or savory tarts.

### Makes one (9-inch) pie

**FOR THE CRUST:**

2 cups all-purpose flour

1 teaspoon salt

11 tablespoons unsalted butter, cold

⅓ cup ice water

**FOR THE FILLING:**

6 to 8 medium-size apples (see "The Best Apples for Pie," opposite page), peeled, cored, and thinly sliced

½ cup granulated sugar

2 tablespoons all-purpose flour, plus more for rolling

1 teaspoon ground cinnamon

2 tablespoons lemon juice

**1.** Make the crust. In a large mixing bowl, combine the flour and salt. Cut in the butter until the mixture resembles fine crumbs.

**2.** Sprinkle the water over the flour and stir with a wooden spoon just to combine.

**3.** Turn the pastry (and any remaining flour in the bowl) out onto a clean work surface and gather it together into a ball. Divide it in half, pat each half into a thick disc, and wrap each in plastic wrap. Chill in the refrigerator for at least an hour.

**4.** When ready to bake, preheat the oven to 400°F.

**5.** Lightly flour a clean countertop and rolling pin. Roll out one of the pastry discs to a circle 12 inches wide and about ⅛ inch thick. Roll it very loosely around the rolling pin and transfer the pastry to a deep 9-inch pie pan.

**6.** Sprinkle more flour on the work surface and roll out the other pastry disc slightly thicker, to a circle 10 inches wide. Set aside.

**7.** To make the filling, put the sliced apples on the piecrust in the pan and sprinkle evenly with the sugar, flour, cinnamon, and lemon juice. Gently transfer the remaining piecrust to top the pie, and use a fork to press down all around the edges. Use a paring knife to trim off any excess crust around the edges, and then use the tip of the knife or a fork to poke air holes all over the top of the pie.

**8.** Bake for 50 minutes, or until the crust is golden brown and the apples are tender. To test, poke a paring knife into the center of the pie to make sure the apples offer no resistance. If the pie needs a few more minutes, you can cover the crust with foil to keep it from browning too much. Cool slightly before slicing to allow the juices to set.

# #51
## HOW TO PEEL AN APPLE

If you have well-honed knife skills (and a well-honed knife), a paring knife is the old-time way to do it. But for most of us, a knife takes off too much apple along with the skin. Instead, use a sharp vegetable peeler.

**1** START NEAR THE STEM END OF THE apple.

**2** PULL THE PEELER TOWARD YOU AS you rotate the apple away. Ideally, you'll take the skin off in one or two long peels, turning the apple as you work toward the blossom end.

✕ ✕ ✕ ✕ ✕ ✕ ✕ ✕ ✕ ✕ ✕ ✕ ✕ ✕ ✕ ✕

## PIE TOPPING OPTIONS

Pies don't have to be topped with pastry. Make a crumb or streusel topping by combining 1 cup all-purpose flour, ¾ cup light brown sugar, 1 teaspoon cinnamon (if you like), and 6 tablespoons salted butter, melted. The mixture will look like wet sand. Use your fingers to mix it, pinch it into big crumbs, and sprinkle it all over the surface of the pie before baking. To make an oatmeal crumble topping, reduce the flour to ¾ cup and add ½ cup rolled oats to the mixture.

# #52
## HOW TO CREAM BUTTER, SUGAR, AND EGGS

Once you've got this step down, all you need is some flour to make a basic, down-home cake. There's a technique to wedding this trio, though. The secret to perfect creaming—the first step of so many baked goods—is to take your time and whip lots and lots and lots of air into the butter. Air is nature's leavening agent; the more air, the lighter the pastry.

**1 BRING YOUR INGREDIENTS TO** room temperature to allow everything to blend well and to prevent uneven baking.

**2 MEASURE OUT THE BUTTER,** according to your recipe, and put it in the bowl of your stand mixer or in a stable mixing bowl to be used with your hand mixer.

**3 MEASURE OUT THE SUGAR** according to your recipe, and set it aside.

**4 READY YOUR BEATER AND WHIP** the butter on a high speed. Do this for a long time, then do it some more. I say 15 minutes is not too long. You want tiny air pockets to form—the more the better.

**5 REDUCE THE SPEED TO LOW** and add the sugar to the butter a little at a time, until they're combined.

**6 INCREASE THE SPEED, AND** whip the butter and sugar until thoroughly creamed, lightly fluffy with no visible sugar crystals in the mixture.

**7 REDUCE THE SPEED TO LOW** and add the eggs one at a time. Beat the eggs into the creamed butter and sugar until they are thoroughly combined and the mixture turns pale yellow.

**8 NOW THAT THESE THREE** ingredients are creamed, you can add in your remaining ingredients, a little at a time.

---

**Pound cake is so called because the original ingredients required were a pound each of butter, sugar, eggs, and flour.**

---

# RECIPE: RICHEST BROWNIES

There are many types and styles of brownies, all of which I'll eat and enjoy: fudgy brownies; chewy brownies; cakelike brownies; flavored brownies featuring espresso, cinnamon, or chili powder, or add-ins such as walnuts or white chocolate chips; frosted brownies or bare brownies.

But these are my favorite. Rich and dark, they're like a hybrid of brownies and fudge. These are super easy to make, but quality cocoa makes all the difference.

## Makes 24 brownies

1 cup (2 sticks) unsalted butter, melted, plus more for greasing the pan

½ cup all-purpose flour, plus more for dusting the pan

1 cup granulated sugar

1 cup light brown sugar

1 cup cocoa powder

½ teaspoon salt

4 large eggs

2 teaspoons vanilla extract

**1.** Preheat the oven to 350°F. Butter and flour (or use cocoa) an 11-by-7-inch baking pan.

**2.** In a medium-size bowl, combine the flour, granulated sugar, brown sugar, cocoa, and salt.

**3.** In a separate large mixing bowl, beat the eggs with a whisk or hand mixer until they are pale yellow and fluffy. Beat in the melted butter, a little at a time. When combined, add the vanilla, and mix until smooth.

**4.** Add the dry mix to the wet mix, mixing just until combined. Do not overwork the batter.

**5.** Pour the batter into the prepared pan and smooth it out with a rubber spatula dipped in water.

**6.** Bake for 40 to 50 minutes. Check for doneness by inserting a toothpick into the center of the pan. If it comes out clean, they're done. The top should have a crispy, crusty layer.

**7.** Remove the pan to a baking rack and let cool before cutting into 24 bars (otherwise the brownies will tear and crumble). Frost with Cream Cheese Frosting, (below) if desired.

## CREAM CHEESE FROSTING

### Makes about 2 cups

½ cup (1 stick) unsalted butter, at room temperature

4 ounces cream cheese, at room temperature

1 teaspoon vanilla extract

2 cups confectioner's sugar

**1.** With a hand or a stand mixer, beat the softened butter until fluffy and smooth, about 2 minutes.

**2.** Add the cream cheese and beat for 2 more minutes, until fluffy. Beat in the vanilla.

**3.** Working slowly, add the confectioner's sugar to the butter mixture, beating at a medium speed, until the frosting is smooth.

# RECIPE: VERY BEST BLONDIES

Blondies are sometimes described as "brownies without cocoa," but I think of them more as a love child of the brownie and the chocolate chip cookie. They are always super popular, so I suggest making these your signature dish for potlucks, parties, and bake sales. Using a healthy dose of vanilla puts these over the top.

## Makes 24 blondies

½ cup (1 stick) salted unbutter, melted, plus more for greasing the pan

1 cup all-purpose flour, plus more for dusting the buttered pan

1 cup brown sugar, firmly packed

1 egg

2 teaspoons vanilla extract

½ teaspoon salt

½ teaspoon baking powder

⅛ teaspoon baking soda

⅓ cup of butterscotch or chocolate chips, optional

**1.** Preheat the oven to 350°F. Butter and flour an 11-by-7-inch baking pan.

**2.** In a large mixing bowl, whisk together the melted butter and brown sugar, then beat in the egg and vanilla.

**3.** In another bowl, combine the flour, salt, baking powder, and baking soda. Add the dry ingredients to the creamed butter and sugar mixture, stirring just until no streaks show. Add the chips, if using, and mix lightly to combine.

**4.** Pour the batter into the prepared pan, and spread it evenly, using a rubber spatula dipped in water. Bake for 30 to 40 minutes, or until a toothpick inserted into the center comes out clean. The top should have a crispy, crusty layer.

**5.** Remove the pan to a baking rack and let cool completely before cutting into squares (otherwise the blondies will tear and crumble).

# #53
## HOW TO MAKE COOKIES

Cookies are America's most popular dessert, and with thousands of possible variations—from white chocolate raspberry to banana-espresso-chocolate chunk—there's truly something for everyone to appreciate.

Baking is essentially chemistry, but with information and practice, anyone can master it. In days of yore, we learned how to make cookies at the elbow of sensible aunts and grandmothers who tried until they got it right. Nowadays, the secrets are more commonly learned from books, so here's my advice for how to make mouthwatering cookies that would make those aunts and grandmothers proud.

**1** PRECISE RATIOS OF WET AND dry ingredients are important—if you add too much flour to the dough, you'll get tough cookies.

**2** DON'T OVERWORK THE DOUGH (another recipe for toughness), but make sure it's thoroughly mixed or the finished product will be too crumbly. (If you mixed the dough properly and the cookies still crumble, your recipe might need more eggs for binding.)

**3** ALWAYS PREHEAT THE OVEN, as directed. (You will end up with a doughy mess otherwise!) Position racks and baking sheets near the middle of the oven, not too close to the top or bottom.

**4** WHETHER ROLLING, MOLDING, or just dropping the dough from a soupspoon, make all of your cookies the same size to ensure uniform baking.

**5** IF YOUR COOKIES DON'T brown properly, you may not have used enough sugar.

**6** IF THEY BROWN TOO MUCH, it might be your cookie sheet: Avoid dark and shiny baking sheets. Opt instead for dull-finished, heavy-gauge aluminum sheets. If your cookies always seem to burn, your oven might run hot. Check often and adjust cooking time and temperature according to your experience.

**7** IF MAKING BATCHES, AND reusing baking sheets, allow them to cool in between, running the bottoms under cold water as needed.

**8** UNLESS YOUR RECIPE SAYS otherwise, transfer smaller cookies from the baking sheet to a wire rack immediately because the heat of the sheet continues to cook them.

**9** IF YOUR COOKIES GET HARD or too crisp soon after cooling, store them in an airtight container with a slice of bread to soften them.

**10** USE YOUR NOSE! It's as valuable as your timer when baking. As soon as the cookies start to smell done, check them. They probably are. If you like them chewy, take them out immediately so long as they look set and not wet in the center. They'll firm up as they cool.

## RECIPE: SUPREME CHOCOLATE CHIP COOKIES

**P**erfect chocolate chip cookies are a delicious medley of contradictions. There's the thrill of crispy edges giving way to the gooey interiors. There's the contrast of salty and sweet. The cakiness of the cookie dough flanking the chocolaty candy of the chips. This recipe delivers on all fronts, and the cookies are dangerously addictive thanks to an unexpected finishing touch: a sprinkling of kosher salt on top. The real secret is letting the dough sit overnight, so the butter permeates the flour: It's an old bakery trick that will make your cookies taste like a pro baked them.

**Makes 2 dozen large cookies**

3½ cups all-purpose flour

1¼ teaspoons baking soda

1¼ teaspoons baking powder

1½ teaspoons salt

1¼ cups (2½ sticks) unsalted butter, room temperature

1¼ cups light brown sugar, firmly packed

1¼ cups granulated sugar

2 large eggs

2½ teaspoons vanilla extract

16 ounces chocolate chips

Nonstick cooking spray

Kosher salt, for topping (optional)

**1.** Mix the flour, baking soda, baking powder, and salt together into a large mixing bowl.

**2.** In a separate large mixing bowl, using a hand or stand mixer, beat the butter for 1 minute. Add the sugars and cream them with the butter (see "How to Cream Butter, Sugar, and Eggs," page 92) until light and fluffy.

**3.** Add the eggs and vanilla and beat on high until fully combined, 1 to 2 minutes.

**4.** Add the dry ingredients to the wet ingredients, beating on low for the shortest amount of time required to fully combine. Remove the bowl from the stand mixer, if using one, and stir in the chocolate chips using a rubber spatula dipped in hot water.

**5.** Cover the dough tightly with plastic wrap, and refrigerate it for at least 8 hours and up to 24 hours.

**6.** When you're ready to bake the cookies, preheat the oven to 350°F and prepare several large baking sheets by spraying them with nonstick cooking spray. Using a tablespoon, ladle out 6 large dough balls—a generous ⅓ cup each—per sheet. If you like the salty-sweet thing, sprinkle the dough very, very lightly with a few crystals of kosher salt.

**7.** Bake the cookies until golden brown and just set in the center, 16 to 18 minutes, watching carefully so as not to overbrown them. Once done, remove the baking sheet from the oven, place it on a wire rack, and cool about 15 minutes. Then, transfer the cookies directly onto wire racks to continue cooling (although they're excellent when warm). Make sure the baking sheets cool between batches.

**Variations:** Mix in any of the following (at the same time as you add the chocolate chips) for an indulgent treat:

⚜ ½ cup chopped toasted walnuts

⚜ ½ cup M&Ms

⚜ 1 cup mini-marshmallows

⚜ ½ cup mini–Reese's peanut butter cups

⚜ ½ cup peanut butter chips

⚜ 1 cup finely chopped pecans

⚜ ½ cup mashed banana

⚜ ½ cup coarsely chopped Junior Mints

╳ ╳ ╳ ╳ ╳ ╳ ╳ ╳ ╳ ╳ ╳ ╳ ╳ ╳ ╳ ╳ ╳ ╳ ╳ ╳ ╳ ╳ ╳ ╳ ╳ ╳ ╳ ╳ ╳ ╳ ╳ ╳ ╳ ╳ ╳ ╳ ╳ ╳ ╳

## NEWFANGLED COOKIES

**W**ho says a cookie has to be a disc? For parties or special treats, try these shapes:

• *Pat the dough into muffin tins.* They come out thick, a bit cakelike, and require a longer bake time. Top these rounds with a scoop of ice cream.

• *Make cookie "bowls."* Chill cookie dough, then roll cold dough out to a ⅛-inch thickness, as you would pie dough. Flip over a muffin tray, spray the "bumps" with cooking spray, drape circles of dough over each one, and bake. Let them cool on the pan for 15 minutes, then loosen them with a butter knife, carefully flip them over onto wire cooling racks, and let stand for half an hour.

• *Make chocolate chip cookie brownies.* Line a muffin tin with cupcake papers. Fill them one-third full with brownie batter, then fill the next third with chocolate chip cookie dough. (Leave the top third empty.) Bake and remove wrappers for double-layer decadence.

# #54
# HOW TO FROST A BIRTHDAY CAKE

Y ou can celebrate a birthday without balloons and streamers. One can even imagine a birthday without a party. If hard-pressed, a birthday could even survive the absence of the "Happy Birthday" song. But if it's my birthday, there'd better be a cake. And I mean a good one. That's why, in my house, I make all the birthday cakes, including my own (see Yellow Birthday Cake with Chocolate Frosting, page 98).

Let's be honest here, though—as important as flavor is, and it is *very* important, a birthday cake needs "wow" factor. Towering height, gorgeous swirls of frosting, and those dramatic, colorful layers of cake and filling. Although folks often outsource birthday cakes to a bakery, thinking such a creation is beyond their reach, you can make celebration-worthy cakes at home.

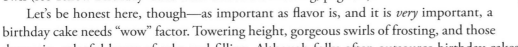

**1** **TO ACHIEVE A BAKERY-STYLE** look and to increase the height of a cake, you can split each cake layer and fill the space between with frosting, jam, or custard.

**2** **USING A LARGE SERRATED** bread knife, slice through the middle of the layer using a sawing motion.

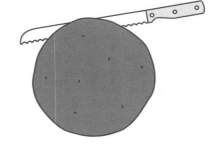

**3** **USING YOUR HANDS, GENTLY** lift the top of the layer off, slipping a rimless baking sheet between the layers. Repeat if you have more than one layer. If your layers aren't quite flat on top, trim a bit more.

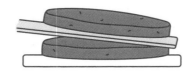

**4** **NOW, FROST THE LAYERS.** Put a dab of frosting in the middle of your cake plate to anchor the bottom layer to it.

**5** **SCOOP ABOUT ½ CUP OF** frosting onto the middle of the bottom layer, and using a rubber spatula or a small offset spatula, spread it outward,

extending beyond the edges. Add more frosting as you go, as needed for a generous filling layer.

**6** STACK ON THE OTHER CAKE layer, cut-side down. Press the layer with your palms to make it level. Either repeat the previous step, if making multiple layers, or prepare to frost the cake.

**7** FIRST CREATE A "CRUMB COAT," a preliminary layer of frosting that seals in crumbs and makes the cake easier to frost. Spread a thin layer of frosting, about 1 cup, over the sides of the cake, working in sections. Incorporate the frosting squeezing out from between the layers. It doesn't have to look perfect—this is just a first coat to hold down the crumbs. Smooth a thin layer of frosting over the top. For a more finished professional look, refrigerate the cake for a half hour. (If

it looks fine and you're not bothered, simply proceed.)

**8** SMOOTH ANOTHER 2 CUPS OF frosting onto the cake, starting on the sides and finishing with the top. If you like, dip the spatula in warm water to prevent streaks in the frosting and achieve a polished look.

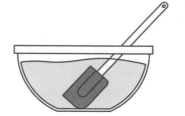

**9** FOR A SUPER-POLISHED LOOK, refrigerate the cake again, then add a third layer of frosting. (If you don't want to, use all the remaining frosting in Step 8.) If you

like swirls, swirl the top with the back of a teaspoon, twisting your wrist to make a little wave in the frosting. For a flat look, use a bench scraper (also called a dough scraper or bowl scraper) and slowly turn the cake on a cake stand as you hold the scraper still against the frosting, pulling it smooth as you turn.

**The largest birthday cake ever made weighed more than 128,000 pounds! It was made in Alabama.**

✕✕✕✕✕✕✕✕✕✕✕✕✕✕✕✕✕✕✕✕✕✕✕✕✕✕✕✕✕✕✕✕✕✕✕✕✕✕

## CAKE FROSTING TIPS

- **Allow your cake layers to fully cool before frosting, or the frosting will melt.**

- **Before frosting, edge the cake plate with strips of waxed paper. Once the frosting sets, peel them away carefully for a neat, clean presentation.**

- **Allow 4 cups of frosting for one 8- to 10-inch two-layer cake.**

- **All frostings aside from whipped cream should be at room temperature before spreading.**

# RECIPE: YELLOW BIRTHDAY CAKE WITH CHOCOLATE FROSTING

Here's my strongest recommendation for this or any layer cake recipe: Beat the living daylights out of the butter and sugar. Cream it for no less than 12 minutes with a hand or a stand mixer. It'll seem like forever, but trust me, it gives the cake a velvety texture that will make everyone think a pro baked it.

For this yellow cake, the buttermilk and vanilla extract really brighten up the flavor. If you don't have buttermilk, stir 2 tablespoons of lemon juice into 2 cups of whole milk, and let it stand while you're creaming the butter. This is already a very big three-layer cake, so I don't split and fill these layers; it's not necessary with this super-moist, dramatically tall confection.

## Makes one (8-inch) three-layer cake

### FOR THE CAKE:
1 cup (2 sticks) unsalted butter, at room temperature, plus more for greasing the pans

4 cups cake (or all-purpose) flour, plus more for dusting the pans

1½ teaspoons baking powder

1 teaspoon baking soda

1 teaspoon salt

2 cups granulated sugar

1 tablespoon vanilla extract

4 large eggs, at room temperature

2 cups buttermilk, room temperature

### FOR THE FROSTING:
1 cup (2 sticks) unsalted butter, softened

1 pound (about 4 cups) confectioner's sugar

⅓ cup cocoa powder

1 teaspoon vanilla extract

1 to 2 tablespoons heavy cream or milk, or more if needed

Sprinkles, or other decoration, optional

**1.** Preheat the oven to 350°F. Butter three 8-inch round cake pans and sprinkle lightly with a little flour, shaking to coat.

**2.** Make the cake: In a medium-size bowl, sift together the flour, baking powder, baking soda, and salt.

**3.** Put the sugar and 1 cup of the butter in a mixing bowl or bowl of a stand mixer and beat at medium-low speed for 3 to 4 minutes, scraping down the bowl several times to incorporate all the sugar. Then turn the mixer to medium and keep beating until the butter and sugar have tripled or quadrupled in volume and are light and impressively fluffy, about 12 minutes. Don't lose heart. Let your mixer do its work.

**4.** Beat in the vanilla, then add the eggs, one at a time, letting each one incorporate well before adding the next. You may need to give each egg a minute or two.

**5.** Add one third of the buttermilk to the butter and sugar mixture, letting it incorporate well, then add one third of the flour mixture. Repeat until the buttermilk and flour mixture are incorporated fully.

**6.** Divide the batter among the prepared cake pans and smooth with a rubber spatula. Bake until golden and fragrant, 20 to 22 minutes, testing with a skewer at the 20-minute mark. You don't want the skewer totally dry—that means the cake is overcooked. As soon as you get a few moist crumbs stuck to the skewer but no wet batter, take the cake out of the oven.

**7.** Cool for 10 minutes in the pans, then run a knife around the edges and flip the rounds carefully onto cooling racks and cool completely.

**8.** Make the frosting: In a large, clean mixing bowl, beat the remaining cup of butter on medium speed until smooth, then gradually add in the confectioner's sugar.

**9.** Beat in the cocoa and vanilla, then add a tablespoon or two of cream or milk and continue beating until the frosting is smooth and fluffy, 3 to 4 minutes. If you feel the mixture is too thick, add another tablespoon of cream or milk, but beat well after each addition to fully combine so you don't overly thin it.

**10.** Assemble and frost the cake (see How to Frost a Birthday Cake, page 96) with a generous amount of frosting between each layer. Chocolate sprinkles on top may be optional at your house, but not at mine.

**TIP:** The point of slowly adding the wet and dry alternately in Step 5 is to keep the volume high. Too much wet or dry all at once would break down all the beautiful air bubbles you've beaten into the butter, sugar, and egg, deflating the mixture.

# #55
## HOW TO MAKE ICE CREAM
### (Without a Machine)

The response I get when I serve ice cream and sorbet to guests, and casually mention it's homemade, is deeply gratifying and worth the minimal effort it takes to pull it off. I also like the control I have over the balance of flavors, ingredients, and add-ins. Because they're all-natural with quality ingredients and lower sugar, I feel good about serving my icy desserts to my family.

For most people, making ice cream at home is an occasional event. Investing in specialized equipment might not be worth the money, particularly if storage space is at a premium. But almost every kitchen has a hand mixer or stand mixer—and that's all you need to make this super simple and perfectly sweet, creamy frozen treat.

**1** **TO MAKE A QUART OF ICE CREAM,** start with 2 cups heavy cream. Using a hand mixer and a large mixing bowl or a stand mixer, whip the cream to heavy, stiff peaks (see "How to Whip Cream," page 13).

**2** **IN ANOTHER LARGE MIXING** bowl, combine 1 can (14 ounces) of sweetened, condensed milk with your desired flavors and add-ins, and mix thoroughly with a rubber spatula.

You can flavor the ice cream with anything you like, but here are some ideas to get you started.

*Butter pecan:* 3 tablespoons melted butter, 1 cup toasted pecans

*Rocky road:* ¾ cup (or more) chopped almonds or walnuts, 1 cup mini-marshmallows, ½ cup chocolate syrup

*Hazelnut and chocolate:* ½ cup chocolate chips, ½ cup toasted hazelnuts, ½ cup Nutella

*Fresh peach:* 3 ripe peaches, peeled, chopped, and tossed with 1 teaspoon lemon juice and 2 tablespoons granulated sugar

**3** **FOLD THE WHIPPED CREAM** into the condensed milk mixture, working slowly, adding a little at a time. Don't overmix or you'll push the air out of the whipped cream.

**4** **POUR INTO A 1-QUART PLASTIC** container, such as a food storage or takeout container, and freeze for at least 8 hours, ideally stirring a few times to break up any ice crystals.

# #56 HOW TO MAKE SORBET IN A BAG

This method relies on the same science as the ice cream ball (see "Machine-Made: The World of Ice Cream Makers," facing page), that is, the chemical reaction between rock salt and ice that quickly freezes the ingredients. This method is so simple that kids can do it, and the time involved from start to finish is about 10 minutes.

Sorbet made this way tends to be icier, rather than smooth, and features more crunchy crystals, like an Italian ice. Go super simple with bottled fruit juice, or amp it up by pureeing and straining fresh fruit and adding special touches like citrus zest or finely chopped herbs. To make 1¼ cups of sorbet, try this technique.

**1 POUR 1 CUP FRUIT JUICE OR** puree into a sturdy, quart-size zip-top bag and seal tightly. Don't completely fill the bag; you need room for expansion. (Note: Adding alcohol changes the freezing point so it will result in a softer, less dense texture; this is a recipe that works best without any add-ins.)

**2 COMBINE 2 CUPS ICE, 1 CUP ROCK** salt, and 1 cup water in a sturdy, gallon-size zip-top bag.

**3 INSERT THE SMALLER BAG INTO** the larger bag, taking care not to spill the water mixture. Shake the bags vigorously, then lightly massage the juice inside the ice-water mixture. Repeat until the juice's consistency becomes sorbetlike, 8 to 10 minutes. Do this step outside or in a space

that's easy to clean up, such as in a deep sink or over a tile floor. Mishaps are not unheard of! It's perhaps not the most practical way to make a frozen dessert, but kids love it; it's like an edible science project for them.

**4 CAREFULLY REMOVE THE SMALLER** bag, scoop out the frozen dessert, and either serve immediately or transfer to an airtight container and freeze for use within a month.

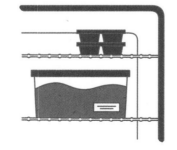

Ice cream's sophisticated cousin, sorbet is elegant in its simplicity. It's a concentration of one or a few flavors, offered in a cold, refreshing form. Generally low- or nonfat, and made without dairy, sorbet is a healthful way to indulge guests—or yourself. You can make it in an ice cream machine, but a food processor works just fine.

### Serves 6

1½ cups granulated sugar

2 quarts fresh strawberries, washed, hulled, and halved

Juice of 1 small or ½ large lemon

**1.** In a medium-size saucepan, combine the sugar with 1½ cups water and bring it to a boil. Reduce the heat and simmer until the sugar completely dissolves, then remove it from the heat and let cool.

**2.** In a food processor, combine the strawberries, sugar syrup, and lemon juice, and blend it until smooth.

**3.** Using a wire-mesh sieve, or cheesecloth laid into a colander, strain the mixture to remove lumps and seeds if you like an ultrasmooth sorbet. You can skip this step if you like texture.

**4.** Line a 9-by-13-inch metal or Pyrex baking dish with plastic wrap, leaving some overhang on each side, and pour the mixture on top. Place the tray in the freezer and freeze until firm, anywhere from 2 to 8 hours.

**5.** Lift out the frozen fruit puree using the rim of plastic wrap. Break the frozen fruit puree into pieces, using a kitchen mallet, meat tenderizer, or the heavy handle of a knife. Working in small batches, process the frozen pieces in the food processor to smooth and blend.

**6.** Serve immediately or freeze the sorbet in an airtight container for up to a month.

## Machine-Made: Ice Cream Makers

Laundry can be done by hand, but a washing machine makes the process faster and less laborious. It's the same with ice cream. A gadget or machine is nice to have, though not strictly necessary. Let's break them down by type.

### Ice Cream Ball

Looks like a soccer ball, and it's meant for playing and roughhousing. Fun on picnics, since it allows you to combine two summer activities—playing ball and making ice cream. Spoon fruit, milk, and other ingredients into a metal chamber, then put ice and rock salt into a chamber surrounding them to bring down the temperature to freezing. The motion of the ball mixes the ingredients and churns in air. Makes a quart or a pint at a time, depending on which model you choose.

### Freezer Bowl

Works like the ice cream ball, with an ice cream chamber surrounded by another chamber filled with a saltwater solution designed to reach and hold low temperatures. Fill it, put it in the freezer for half a day to overnight, then insert the bowl into the electric part of the maker, in which the mixing is done. Most designs make a quart of ice cream, just right for the average family. This is the go-to model at our house. (Essentially, this is a small modern version of the old-fashioned ice cream makers of my youth that made a gallon of ice cream by electrically turning the paddle inside a large metal container surrounded by ice and salt.)

### Hand-Crank Machine

Similar to the freezer bowl, ingredients go in an inner chamber, with ice and salt in a surrounding chamber. As with all old-fashioned household machines, elbow grease gets the job done. A hand crank is attached to an interior paddle that aerates the ice cream, dissolves ice crystals, and ensures smooth and even freezing.

### Self-Contained Compressor Freezer (aka Automatic Ice Cream Machine)

If you make a lot of ice cream and have the counter space, this may be your best bet. Double the size of a bread box, this houses a built-in freezer, allowing it to run continuously at a consistent, freezing temperature. No need to cool ingredients, exert physical labor, or add salt and ice.

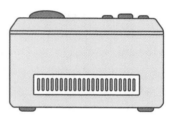

## THE ROCK IN ROCKY ROAD

**M**any ice cream makers rely on rock salt, a very coarse, inedible variety of unrefined salt. (It's the same kind that is sprinkled on icy roads and sidewalks, but it's usually available at a food-grade level in the salt section of your supermarket, labeled "rock salt.") The rock salt slurry that surrounds the freezing cylinder allows the contents to freeze at a lower temperature, speeding up the process.

# #57
# HOW TO MAKE A POT OF COFFEE

The best way to make coffee is a surprisingly controversial subject. Aficionados have lots of advanced ideas from farming to brew methods. But can you make a good cup of coffee with an everyday drip pot? Most definitely. It may not be the top choice of coffee snobs, but there's no denying that drip is the most common way Americans get their fix. You can set it and forget it, and if you do it right, you end up with an excellent cup of joe.

**1 GET A CLEAN START.** If you use your coffeemaker every day, you'll need to clean the unit weekly and the carafe daily to avoid the bitter taste of old coffee (see "How to Clean a Coffeemaker," below).

**2 USE FRESH, COLD, FILTERED** water and freshly ground beans that have been stored (not for too long!) in an airtight container.

**3 CHOOSE THE RIGHT GRIND FOR** your filter. For flat-bottomed paper filters, use a medium-size grind (close to the texture of fine sand). For conical filters, go with medium-fine (a little finer than salt). Plastic or metal reusable filters do best with a medium-coarse grind (similar to sea salt).

**4 PAY ATTENTION TO THE RATIO.** A good place to start is 2 tablespoons ground coffee per 6 ounces water (1 cup on a typical coffeemaker). Experiment to find your preferred ratio.

**5 DECANT IT WHILE IT'S HOT.** If your drip coffeemaker has a glass carafe atop a hotplate-style heating element, don't let it just sit there and scorch. As soon as the cycle is complete, pour the coffee into an airtight thermal carafe. Leaving it on the burner, exposed to air, makes it bitter and burnt-tasting in very short order.

**6 IF YOU LIKE MILK IN YOUR** coffee, warm it first. Cold milk will make your brew's temperature plummet on contact, and who wants lukewarm joe?

# #58
# HOW TO CLEAN A COFFEEMAKER

All you need is the all-natural miracle cleaner: distilled white vinegar.

**1 POUR A MIXTURE OF HALF WHITE** vinegar and half cold water into the tank.

**2 WITH NO COFFEE IN THE BASKET,** run the coffeemaker through a regular cycle.

**3 AFTER ONE CYCLE, COOL THE** vinegar and water mixture and run it through a second time.

**4 DISCARD THE VINEGAR WATER** and clean the carafe with dish soap and water, rinsing very thoroughly.

**5 FILL THE CARAFE WITH COLD** water, and, again with no coffee in the basket, run the plain water through a cycle to rinse out traces of vinegar or soap. Repeat until you no longer smell the scent of vinegar.

## The Buzz on Caffeine

Caffeine levels vary by varietal, and blends will include a combination of beans with lower and higher concentrations. Keep in mind that milk displaces coffee, so a 20-ounce black coffee will typically have more caffeine than a 20-ounce latte. How long the grounds come into contact with the water also has an impact on caffeine levels: Espresso typically has less caffeine per ounce than drip coffee.

## It's in the Water

If your coffee tastes flat, your chlorinated or fluoridated tap water may be to blame. Or if your well water is too hard or soft or slightly sulfurous, the coffee won't be as good as it could be. Always use filtered water for best results.

## Proportion Is Key

The ratio of coffee to water is to some degree a matter of personal taste. My mother prefers her coffee a pale clear brown (my Irish husband calls it "bogwater"), whereas I like mine almost muddy dark, to be tempered with a lot of hot milk. But a good standard brewing proportion is 8 cups of water (as measured on the coffeemaker's carafe, usually 48 ounces) to a level ½ cup of ground coffee.

## Bring on the Beans: Arabica vs. Robusta

The type of beans you buy does matter. The two main species grown are arabica and robusta. How they are classified depends on the region, climate, and elevation at which they grew. Those factors determine quality. Arabica coffee, which contains less caffeine, is more highly regarded than robusta coffee. Robusta is more bitter with less coffee flavor, but has better body than arabica. Cheaper and more abundant, robusta is used in instant coffee blends.

## Regional Accents

The climates of the many coffee-growing countries and regions vary. The impact of this difference on coffee beans is unquestionable and affects signature traits such as body, acidity, and flavor. There are too many varieties to list, but it's worth trying a range of them to see what you like best. For example, Hawaiian Kona tends to be full-bodied, with a mild acidity and a sweet, winelike, mellow flavor. It's also generally among the most pricy. On a tight budget? Try Colombian beans, which boast a medium-full body, medium acidity, and a rich, caramel flavor.

## The Roast

High-quality coffee beans from well-regarded regions are usually roasted lightly so as to maintain the signature flavors of the beans. As beans darken, their flavors are eclipsed by the flavors created by the roasting process itself. In darker roasts, the "roast flavor" is so dominant that it can be difficult to distinguish the origin of the beans, so lesser-quality beans are often used. As with all things coffee, it's a matter of personal taste.

## ✕ ✕ ✕ ✕ ✕ ✕ ✕ ✕ ✕ ✕ ✕ ✕ ✕ ✕ ✕ ✕ ✕ ✕ ✕ ✕ ✕ ✕ ✕ ✕ ✕ ✕ ✕
# BARISTAS SHARE THEIR (COFFEE) TIPS

- **Grind your own beans, fresh. The flavor is worth the extra effort.**

- **Keep beans and grounds in airtight containers in cool, dry, dark places. Don't freeze or refrigerate them! The beans will pick up odors.**

- **Use cold water to brew, regardless of the style of coffeemaker. For a French press or pour-over, fill your kettle with cold water for best flavor.**

- **If you like the scent and taste of cinnamon, vanilla, or cocoa, blend them with the beans and store in a sealed container. For subtle aromatics, use whole spices such as cinnamon sticks, vanilla beans, and cardamom pods instead of extracts and powders.**

- **Before pouring in the java, warm the mug with a few inches of boiling water. Wait a moment, then toss it. This helps maintain the temperature of your drink.**

- **Use an instant-read thermometer to test a pot of coffee the second it's finished brewing. If the temperature isn't between 195 and 205 degrees Fahrenheit, your brew will be bitter. Invest in a new unit.**

# #59
## HOW TO BREW A CUP OF TEA

Yes, it's a simple four-step process: Boil water. Tea bags in. Pause. Tea bags out. But these tips will help you make a perfect, full-flavored cup each time. So many little things can go wrong, however. Was the water at a full rolling boil? Did you "scald" the teapot by pouring in some boiling water to take the chill off for a moment or two? Is your tea fresh, or has it been sitting in a cupboard for a year or two?

### Don't Be Bitter

Tannins are compounds that occur naturally in tea, as well as in nuts, wine, cheeses, cranberries, and chocolate, and they are responsible for dark coloration, bitterness, and astringency. The bitterness of tea also depends on whether it's been fermented—the process through which leaves are crushed, exposing the cells to oxygen and causing them to oxidize and darken—and on brew time. In short, less fermentation means a milder cup, and longer brewing means more tannins are released, resulting in more bitter of a flavor. Therefore, lighter teas and less steep time mean less bitter tea. I prefer black tea, steeped for ages, so I temper my brew with plenty of milk and sugar. If you add milk to your tea, the tannins target the proteins in the milk rather than those in your mouth, resulting in a much less astringent taste.

### Stash It

No health-related concerns govern the storage of tea, but preserving flavor is a concern. Invest in airtight, light-proof containers for storing your tea and label them with the type of tea and the date you purchased it. Tea leaves keep a long time, but not indefinitely. A good rule of thumb is one year for loose tea and six months for tea bags. Store them sealed in a zip-top bag in the freezer and they'll keep twice as long.

In the British Isles, there's a little running joke that whoever pours the tea for a group is called "Mother," regardless of gender. The volunteer reaching for the teapot might say, "I'll be Mother."

## A Gentle Pick-Me-Up

By dry weight, tea in fact contains more caffeine than coffee, but it requires less tea to brew a cup, so a cup of tea has less caffeine than a cup of coffee. When boiling water is poured over tea leaves, most of the caffeine is released in the first 30 to 90 seconds. At this point, the tea is at its most stimulating. Allow it to steep longer, and more tannins and L-theanine (an amino acid linked to relaxation of the nervous system) are extracted. These help cancel the effects of the caffeine, turning the beverage from stimulating to soothing. One study in the United Kingdom found black tea drinkers were able to de-stress faster than those who drank a fake tea substitute because their blood contained lower levels of the stress hormone cortisol.

## Here's to Your Health

Tea contains flavonoids, antioxidants that are found in many fruits and vegetables as well as beverages such as tea, wine, and beer. Flavonoids may help combat the cancer-causing effects of free radicals, or damaged cells, and research suggests that people who drink two cups of tea or more a day have less heart disease, lower risk of stroke, and lower levels of "bad" cholesterol. Polyphenols and other compounds in the tea plant are also natural antimicrobials, promoting dental hygiene by killing harmful bacteria in the mouth.

**1** **HEAT THE WATER.** The better the water, the better the tea. If your tap or well water is hard (has a high mineral content), use filtered, spring, or bottled water. Bring the water to a rolling boil for every type of tea except pure white—for this delicate flower, heat just to the point of boiling.

**2** **HEAT YOUR TEAPOT AND YOUR** cups by pouring in a few inches of boiling water, swirling it around, then pouring it out.

**3** **MEASURE YOUR TEA.** For each 6 ounces of water, use 1 teaspoon of loose tea in a tea ball or sachet, or one tea bag. In the British Isles, most people add another "one for the pot" to make the flavor a little stronger.

**4** **POUR THE BOILING WATER** over the tea and let it steep. How long you let it sit depends on variety and personal taste, but here are "ideal" steeping times.

*White:* Tea bag—1 minute, loose tea—3 minutes

*Green:* Tea bag—2 minutes, loose tea—4 minutes

*Oolong:* Tea bag—3 minutes, loose tea—5 minutes

*Black:* Tea bag—4 minutes, loose tea—6 to 7 minutes

**5** **TO SERVE, REMOVE THE TEA** bag, tea ball, or sachet, and allow the tea to stand and cool for a minute or so. It's most common to offer lemon slices, milk, and sugar to guests, but there's no law on the books forbidding maple syrup, stevia, orange slices, cinnamon sticks, or even peppermint candies!

✕ ✕ ✕ ✕ ✕ ✕ ✕ ✕ ✕ ✕ ✕ ✕ ✕ ✕ ✕ ✕ ✕ ✕ ✕ ✕ ✕ ✕ ✕ ✕ ✕ ✕ ✕ ✕ ✕ ✕ ✕ ✕ ✕ ✕ ✕ ✕ ✕

## JUST THE ONE

**S**uppose you don't want to make a pot and only want one perfect delicious cup of tea for yourself? It does help to "scald" the mug or cup by swishing it out with boiling water for a moment or two, before you pour that water down the drain and start fresh. For best results, be sure to let your mug of tea brew for 4 to 5 minutes before adding milk or sugar.

## Your Cup of Tea: A Guide to Types and Varieties

All tea comes from the exact same species of plant, *Camellia sinensis,* a bush whose leaves are turned into a seemingly endless variety of tea—black, green, and white. The range of types and styles is determined by where the bush is grown, the level of maturity at which the leaves are picked, and how the leaves are processed after harvesting. For instance, some varieties of tea leaves are left in a climate-controlled room to oxidize—a process called fermentation—in order to darken them and draw out specific flavors. Note that herbal teas, also called tisanes or infusions, are a totally different matter and can be made from any herb, fruit, or spice.

**Black tea.** Fully fermented. The most common type, the tea is reddish in hue with a fruity and flowery aroma. Varieties include Darjeeling and Ceylon, or blends such as English Breakfast.

**Oolong tea.** Semi-fermented. The name translates to "black dragon," but the brew is in fact a golden-brown because the fermentation process is stopped when the leaves are merely yellowed, and not fully darkened. This tea has a unique, delicate flavor, and you're likely to be offered it in Chinese restaurants.

**Green tea.** Unfermented. Green tea leaves are heated as soon after harvesting as possible to prevent fermentation. This process preserves the highest level of vitamins, minerals, and antioxidants. Yellowish-green in color, the flavor is herbal and grassy.

**White tea.** Unfermented. Preserved using the same process as green tea, but only the buds of the plant, not the leaves, are used. White tea is more delicate in flavor than green, and it lacks the grassy tones.

# #60
# HOW TO (MOSTLY) DECAFFEINATE YOUR TEA

It's impossible to remove 100 percent of the caffeine from tea or coffee—even commercially decaffeinated varieties still contain some caffeine—but this neat trick will remove up to 80 percent of the caffeine in your cup. If you have sensitivities, though, stick to herbal.

**1** PUT A TEA BAG OR SACHET OR tea ball filled with tea leaves into a mug or tea pot.

**2** POUR IN BOILING WATER.

**3** STEEP FOR 30 TO 90 SECONDS— no more than that! Pour off the steeped tea.

**4** REFILL THE CUP OR POT WITH fresh boiling water and steep to your taste.

# # 61
# HOW TO MAKE ICED TEA

Leaving tea and water to brew in the sun, though picturesque, is unfortunately not a safe practice. Water heated only by the sun won't top 130 degrees Fahrenheit, and to kill harmful water-borne bacteria, it must reach 195 degrees Fahrenheit and stay there for 3 to 5 minutes. Instead, make it in the fridge, cold-brew style.

**1** **COMBINE 8 CUPS COLD WATER** with 6 tablespoons loose-leaf tea or 12 standard-size tea bags in a covered pitcher.

**2** **REFRIGERATE FOR 24 TO 36** hours, until it's ruby red in color.

**3** **STRAIN OUT THE TEA LEAVES** with a fine-mesh sieve or remove the tea bags, and serve.

## CLOUDY TO CLEAR

Cloudiness in iced tea won't affect the taste or harm you, but it's not as pretty. To keep your tea from clouding, never stick hot tea in the refrigerator—bring it to room temperature first. Hard water (water that naturally has a lot of dissolved minerals in it) will interact with the tea's natural tannins and cloud it. Use bottled water if your tap water is hard. If your iced tea does cloud, pour in some boiling water and let it rest. This should clear it up.

## RECIPE: SOUTHERN-STYLE SWEET ICED TEA

It seems so simple, yet there are so many things that can go wrong with iced tea, including it turning cloudy or tasting bitter. Here's how to brew true-flavored, crystal-clear, Southern-style sweet tea. If you love a glass full of clanking ice cubes, brew your tea stronger than recommended to compensate for the dilution ice will cause as it melts.

**Makes 2 quarts**

6 black tea bags

⅛ teaspoon baking soda

1 cup granulated sugar

**1.** Put the tea bags and baking soda (my mom would say "a big ol' pinch") into a large heat proof glass measuring cup or ceramic pitcher, and pour in 2 cups boiling water. Cover and let steep for 20 minutes.

**2.** Remove the tea bags, taking care not to squeeze them because bruising the leaves and using these very concentrated drops of liquid will make the whole pitcher bitter.

**3.** Add the sugar to the still-warm tea, then pour this concentrate into a 2-quart pitcher and add 6 cups cold water. Let cool before refrigerating.

# #62
# HOW TO CLEAN YOUR KITCHEN
## (Without Chemicals)

Learning the basics of cleaning and sanitizing in the kitchen keeps family and guests safe and healthy, and it keeps your kitchen free of dirt, odors, and food-borne contamination. Disease-causing bacteria hide out in more places than just cutting boards. Kitchen sponges, dishtowels, frequently touched surfaces such as the faucet or the inside of the sink, and even your own hands can harbor germs. Fortunately, you don't have to shell out for pricey, gimmicky, name-brand cleansers and gadgets, or depend on harsh chemicals, to keep your kitchen clean and safe. All you need is a little knowledge.

**1 CLEAN WOODEN AND PLASTIC** cutting boards, countertops, and the inside of the sink by scrubbing them with a paste made from equal parts baking soda, salt, and water. Rinse with hot water.

**2 RINSE AND WRING KITCHEN** sponges, and then microwave them on high for 2 minutes to kill bacteria. Zap barely damp dish towels on high for 1 minute.

**3 TO DEODORIZE AND SANITIZE** cutting boards, rub with the cut side of half a lemon or wipe with undiluted lemon juice straight from the bottle.

**4 FOOD PARTICLES CLING TO** damp pipes in your drain, a perfect breeding ground for germs, not to mention clogs. Pour boiling water down your sink daily to keep pipes clean and odor-free.

**5 FOR A NATURAL ABRASIVE** cleanser, use a damp rag and a handful of kosher or rock salt to scrub anything from wooden cutting boards to cast-iron skillets to the tea kettle.

**6 SPRAY UNDILUTED WHITE** vinegar on stainless steel and chrome faucets, aluminum sinks, and on silver and copper items in the kitchen to clean and disinfect, then polish with a soft, damp cloth.

**7 BLEACH'S "GREEN-NESS" IS** hotly debated. Chlorine is natural and found in the human body, but overuse causes buildup in water tables, harming the earth. For home use, just a little bleach is needed to do the job. Use it in a ratio of 1 part bleach to 10 parts water to disinfect and kill germs. (Efficacy wanes with time and exposure to light.) If you prefer, substitute hydrogen peroxide, which also kills germs and removes stains.

## Choosing and Using Your Cutting Board

Every type of board has pros and cons, so, if possible, keep several on hand and dedicate them to specific tasks to avoid cross-contamination. I recommend buying multiply sizes and thickness of wooden boards. As your cooking skills advance and you get a handle on your storage limitations, expand from there.

**Thick plastic.** Affordable, colorful, and dishwasher safe, thick plastic boards can double as trivets. Biggest pro: easy to bleach and dishwash. Biggest con: will nick and stain over time.

**Flexible plastic.** These are cheap and easy to store, clean, and sanitize. Biggest pro: bendable and rollable for easy food transfer. Biggest con: Sharp knives will eventually cut through them.

**Corian.** Tough like a countertop, these come in a variety of sizes and colors. Marks from use can be repaired. Biggest pro: The nonporous surface is virtually stainproof and resists bacterial growth. Biggest con: Heat will damage the surface.

**Tempered glass.** Stylish and complementary to kitchen décor, these durable boards are heavier than most but protect surfaces from extremely hot cookware. Biggest pros: the most resistant to bacteria; won't stain. Biggest con: The sound of the knife hitting the surface can be like nails on a chalkboard. And it's not very good for the sharpness of your knives, either.

**Bamboo.** Objects of beauty, these eco-friendly boards are water-resistant and durable. Harder than maple but lighter than oak, this material requires more care than some cutting boards. Before the first use, treat it with a food-grade oil. Biggest pro: won't shrink or swell like wooden boards, giving them a long lifespan. Biggest cons: Cost and care.

Bamboo tends to be more expensive, and you have to season it regularly.

**Wood.** Affordable hardwood boards, usually made from maple, are great for fruits and vegetables. Good ones can be sanded or replaned when the surface wears. I love the sound of a knife chopping on wood! Biggest pros: easy on knife edges; long-lasting; shown to be more sanitary than plastic. Biggest con: see "Bamboo" at left.

**When in doubt, throw it out.** If your board's cracked, or too deeply nicked to sanitize or resurface properly, toss it. Yes, even if it was expensive! Safety first—if you can't afford another pricey one at toss time, buy some thin plastic ones and save up your pennies for a good one.

## Bacteria Basics

Kitchens are notorious for hosting bacterial nasties and gruesome germs. Worst of all, these lurking monsters are invisible to the naked eye, which means vigilance is required.

***Salmonella.*** Foods contaminated by animal feces transmit this bacteria, which can cause fever, intestinal cramping and diarrhea, nausea and vomiting, and chills. Symptoms appear within eight to seventy-two hours of contact. The most frequently reported bacterial infection according to the CDC, *Salmonella* poisoning often occurs when raw meat mingles with other foods through contaminated dishes, knives, countertops, and cutting surfaces.

***Campylobacter jejuni.*** This bacteria travels in raw and undercooked meat and poultry, and infection targets the digestive tract, causing stomach pain, nausea, vomiting, and diarrhea. Unpasteurized milk often harbors it as do unpasteurized cheeses. The CDC estimates that 47 percent of raw commercial chicken breasts contain *Campylobacter*. When handling poultry at home, meticulous care must be taken to sanitize surfaces (including the sink), and hands must be washed before touching other foods or serving utensils. Even a single drop of liquid from contaminated meat can cause infection.

***Staphylococcus.*** The bacteria *Staphylococcus aureus*, found in animal products, produces a toxin when those foods are stored at the wrong temperature. When present in poultry and other meats, there is danger of cross-contamination of other foods such as in mayonnaise-based salads, poultry and egg dishes, and casseroles. Symptom, including nausea, vomiting, diarrhea, mild fever, and severe abdominal cramps, appear quickly, sometimes within six hours. Dehydration is a major danger.

**E. coli.** Many strains of *E. coli* (*Escherichia coli*) don't cause illness, but the most harmful can damage the small intestine, causing bloody diarrhea and death. Found in seafood, ground beef, unpasteurized milk, and raw vegetables, *E. coli* is easily transmitted human to human after improper hand-washing, and is perhaps the most difficult to ward against. Best practices include storing fish and meats at proper temperatures, thoroughly washing vegetables and fruits, and frequent washing of hands.

## What's In My Cleaning Products?

The obvious solution to all this potentially dangerous bacteria in the kitchen is to clean it. But be aware of the possible harm lurking in commercial cleaning products as well. Science has continued to uncover possible negative effects from the stuff we've long been squirting and spraying all over our cooking surfaces. Parabens and phenols, and bacteria-killers such as triclosan, even the strong fragrances that used to signal "clean," may be doing harm to our bodies long-term, and to our environment.

Increasingly, there are many widely available commercial cleaning products made with all-natural ingredients that are extremely effective. When our grandmothers used to scrub with baking soda and vinegar, turns out they may have known best! So even if you want to scrub your dirty floor with the heavy-duty cleaners, you might want to consider keeping industrial cleaning chemicals off your cooking surfaces, cutting boards, stovetop, counters and pots.

×××××××××××××××××××××××××××××

# ENVIRONMENTALLY FRIENDLY ALL-PURPOSE CLEANER

Using a funnel, combine 1 teaspoon baking soda, ½ teaspoon dish soap, and 2 tablespoons distilled white vinegar in a spray bottle. Cap the bottle, shake gently, and let stand for 5 minutes. Fill the bottle about three-quarters of the way with warm water and shake again. For a nice scent, add 3 drops essential oil. For the kitchen, I like bergamot or eucalyptus.

# SEWING

**A**t one time, everyone but the very wealthy made their own clothes. With the advent of inexpensive machine-made clothing, sewing became a lost art for most people. Some sewing, such as hemming, repairing tears, and replacing buttons, can save you a lot of time and money if you do it yourself. Some of it is practical, such as making a pillow of an exact size. And some of it is not strictly necessary but easy and immensely satisfying: "See these curtains? I *made* them."

# SEWING TOOL KIT

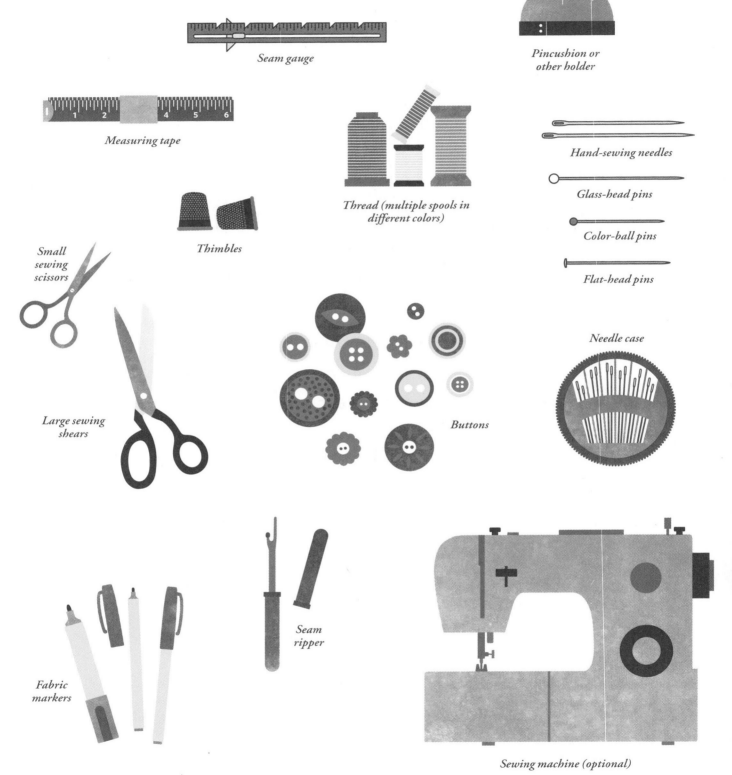

Seam gauge

Pincushion or other holder

Measuring tape

Thread (multiple spools in different colors)

Hand-sewing needles

Glass-head pins

Color-ball pins

Flat-head pins

Thimbles

Small sewing scissors

Buttons

Needle case

Large sewing shears

Fabric markers

Seam ripper

Sewing machine (optional)

# #63
# HOW TO THREAD A NEEDLE

**M**any people may think *I can thread a needle*. They're probably right. But with some tasks, such as cutting an onion (see page 30), there may be a better way than the one you were taught. I don't have much advice about getting a rich man into heaven, but I can tell you how to reduce the pain of threading a needle.

## Learning to Sew

You don't *have* to know how to sew in the same way that you should know how to cook at least the very basics. Sewing is not a daily task—the way eating is—and, yet, you *do* wear clothes every day and they *are* going to need some minor repairs. Being able to sew on a button is an incredibly valuable skill. There's something very satisfying, in our machine-made, store-bought world of clothing, about doing a peaceful, old-fashioned task like stitching up a tear with an invisible seam. And knowing how to hem your own pants is an economic skill, too—tailoring has become an extremely pricey proposition these days: perhaps because so few of us know how.

A sewing machine is not strictly necessary if all you want to do is make minor repairs. But very effective and efficient sewing machines have become seriously inexpensive and are widely available at big-box stores, so as you learn the joys of stitching fabric together, it makes sense to acquire one. It makes jobs such as stitching up a long torn seam, as in a bedsheet, into a breeze, and soon you may find that running up an easy set of curtains is well worth your time. Whether you ever make an item of clothing is up to you, but at least you'll be able to keep the clothing that you have in good shape with very little effort.

Here's the very core of what you need to know (and to have on hand) to start sewing.

## Shopping for Thread

Don't be intimidated by the myriad brands and weights of thread available at fabric stores and in the notions departments of drugstores. They each have a different application, so it's good to have an assortment on hand if you plan to sew with various fabrics. Almost any project done by a beginner can be sewn with these five threads:

**Polyester/cotton.** Sometimes labeled "all-purpose," it's actually polyester thread wrapped in cotton. The best choice to have at home for hand or machine sewing, for use with cotton and cotton blends, polyester/cotton thread is also good for sewing on buttons because it combines flexibility with added strength.

**100 percent polyester.** A smart, basic choice for most hand or machine sewing, this thread is most suitable for synthetic fabrics or stretchy knits. If used on flat cotton, the stitches might look waxy and stand out.

**100 percent cotton.** Best for light- to medium-weight fabrics without much "give" or stretch to them. Cotton thread will not stretch, and the stitches can break if used on a stretchy knit fabric.

**Fine cotton or silk.** For use on sheer fabric and delicate goods such as light scarves or lingerie. For ultralight fabrics with lots of "give," choose silk.

**Heavy-duty or T-40 weight.** The best bets for upholstery fabric, pillows made of heavy fabric, thick woolen coats, and denim.

## Shopping for Needles

It's a good idea to have a multipack of needles on hand. Most packaged kits come with everything a beginner needs for simple hand-sewing projects, from mending to buttons. Here are the five essential needles to start out with:

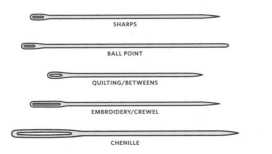

SHARPS

BALL POINT

QUILTING/BETWEENS

EMBROIDERY/CREWEL

CHENILLE

**Sharps.** The most common and useful type. They are of medium length, standard thickness, and of course, very sharp. Sharps are good for pretty much all cotton and synthetic fabrics.

**Ball point.** The second-most-common basic needle. Use with knits, as well as some laces and lingerie fabrics. The rounded point glides between the threads of the weave, and the narrow shaft makes it useful for fine work.

**Quilting/betweens.** Short needles with small, rounded eyes. The short length allows for faster, more accurate stitching. For detailed handiwork and appliqués but with heavier weight thread, quilting/betweens are also useful for heavy fabrics such as denim and canvas.

**Embroidery/crewel.** Same length and thickness as sharps, but with a longer eye to accommodate heavier threads.

**Chenille.** Very thick, very sharp, and with a long eye. Ideal for very thick thread, ribbon, or multiple strands of thread and for stitching through coarse fabrics.

**1** CUT THE THREAD WITH VERY sharp scissors, at an angle. A 45-degree angle is ideal for pushing thread through a small needle's eye, and a sharp cut reduces fuzz at the thread's end.

**2** HOLD THE NEEDLE AND THREAD over a white background. It'll make them easier to see. Keep an index card in your sewing kit, or pierce one with a hole punch, thread a loop of yarn through it, and pin it to your pincushion.

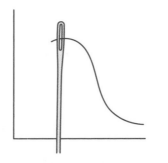

**3** STIFFEN THE THREAD. A small tin of beeswax from a sewing or craft store is a great item to keep on hand. It's cheap, and it lasts forever. In a pinch, use saliva.

**4** BUY A NEEDLE THREADER. This small gadget consists of a thin, flat disc of aluminum and a diamond-shaped, very thin wire. To use it, hold the disc and insert the wire through the eye of the needle. Poke the thread through the "giant" eye. As you draw the needle threader's wire backward through the eye, the thread follows.

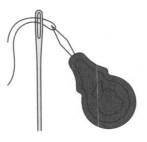

**5 STOP THE SHAKES.** If your hand isn't steady, use a pair of tweezers to hold the thread.

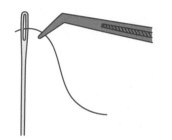

**6 MAKE IT A MATCH.** Your thread size and eye size should be compatible. Don't even try to stuff thick embroidery thread through the tiny eye of a sharp.

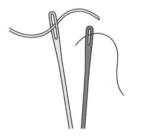

**7 TURN IT AROUND.** Often, due to manufacturing, the eye of a needle will be larger on one side than the other.

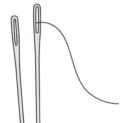

**8 CLOSE ONE EYE.** This balances your close-up vision—human eyes are bifocal and threading needles is done at immediate range.

# #64 HOW TO CARE FOR YOUR NEEDLES

It's true that sewing needles aren't prohibitively costly, nor are they hard to come by. But why not use them to their best advantage, in the interest of economy and sustainability? With frequent use, the nonstick coatings wear off, the points dull, the eyes wear out, and the shafts weaken. Here's how to make 'em last.

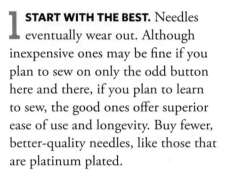

**1 START WITH THE BEST.** Needles eventually wear out. Although inexpensive ones may be fine if you plan to sew on only the odd button here and there, if you plan to learn to sew, the good ones offer superior ease of use and longevity. Buy fewer, better-quality needles, like those that are platinum plated.

**2 USE THE RIGHT TOOL.** Pulling a too-thick needle through fine fabric or jamming a soft tip through tough material will wear out your needles more quickly. If in doubt, test a needle on a patch of fabric that won't be seen, such as inside a hem seam: Thread it and run it through in a few loose stitches (that you can pull out) and make sure there aren't visible holes left behind.

**3 SAFE AND DRY.** Store your needles in a good pincushion—emphasis on "good." Ideally, it should be covered with wool felt and stuffed with something like sawdust that will keep the needle dry and polish it each time it's inserted.

**4 OUT WITH THE BAD.** A small nick or even a bit of debris on a needle may not be visible, but if you feel any sort of a pull in the fabric, or a faint catch as you try to push the needle through, start fresh. Otherwise, you may damage your fabric and you're less likely to get a smooth, flat seam.

# #65
# HOW TO SEW ON A BUTTON

We've all had the experience of preparing for a date or a big meeting at work, or being late for a class only to find we've popped a button. I've resorted to stapling my blouse together or trying to hold the top of my jeans together with a paper clip. But now I play it smart. I don't go anywhere without my compact emergency sewing kit. With just three basic tools from your kit, you can sew on that button by following a few easy steps.

## The Basic Tools

**Two needles.** In your kit, you should have a sharp needle. This is your go-to and will work for almost any job. It's a thinnish, medium-length needle with a sharp point. For the second needle, choose a quilting needle (aka "between") for heavier fabrics such as denim or canvas. You'll need one of these needles to sew and the other to anchor the button. If you have only one needle, use a straightened paper clip, toothpick, or safety pin for the anchor.

**Thread.** Start with at least 12 inches of thread. I like to double my thread so it's stronger and easier to knot at the end—I suggest using 24 inches if you have enough to spare. You can

match the color of either the garment or the button. If that's not possible, use black, white, or tan—whatever color is the most neutral.

**A button.** It's best to use the one that popped off. If that's not possible, check your garment for spare buttons. Sometimes extra buttons are sewn directly onto the inside placket of a shirt or into the waistband of pants.

**Scissors (optional).** If you can't lay your hands on a pair, use a nail clipper or saw the thread on the sharp edge of a table.

**1 THREAD THE NEEDLE AND MAKE** a knot. If you cut 24 inches of thread, double it over by threading the needle and hold the two ends together. Pull the needle until the thread is taut, leaving two equal lengths of thread on either side. Tie a knot at the end of the thread by making a circle, pushing the ends of the thread through, and pulling tight. If the knot seems so small that it will pull through the fabric, repeat this procedure, layering the knots until it's thick enough to catch the fabric.

If you have less than 24 inches

of thread, don't double it over. Thread the needle and make sure that the "short end" is about 3 to 4 inches long. This end will remain unknotted. Holding the other end of the thread between your thumb and forefinger, loosely wrap the short end around your forefinger two or three times while keeping the thread in place with your thumb.

Slide your forefinger down toward the base of your thumb, twisting the threads together until the thread forms a loop and pushes off the forefinger end. Grasp the loop

between your thumb and forefinger at the point where the loop joins the rest of the thread. Pull the loop until a knot is formed. You'll be left with two lengths of thread: a short one with no knot and a long one with a knot at the end.

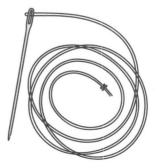

## 2 FIND THE TARGET POINT.

Insert your needle from the back side of the fabric to the front, where the button used to sit. Then insert the needle through the front, so that it comes out the back again. As you go through both sides of the fabric, make a small X where the button will be fastened. This X serves two purposes: It's the target you want to hit when sewing on the button, and it reinforces the spot, ensuring that future stress won't pull the button off again.

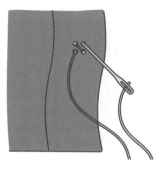

## 3 POSITION AND ANCHOR THE

button. Lay your button on the X and begin sewing it on. Insert the needle behind where the button sits and push it from the back to the front through one of the holes in the button. As you loop through one of the four holes (depending on the button), lay a needle, toothpick, or paper clip on top. This is your anchor: You'll loop the thread over it.

Pull the thread all the way through until the knot presses against the back side of the fabric. Use your finger to keep the button in its place.

From the front side, insert the needle through the hole opposite the one you came up through. Push it through until the thread is taut. You'll now see a small line of thread across the button, connecting two of the four holes (or the two holes, if it's a two-hole button). Repeat

this pattern three or four times for every set of two holes. The needle, toothpick, or paper clip you are using as an anchor will look like a silent movie damsel tied to a railroad track!

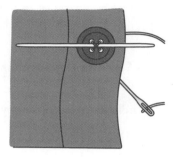

## 4 CREATE THE SHANK. On the

final pass of the needle, sew from back to front of the fabric, but don't push the needle through the button's hole. Pierce the fabric in the same position, turn the needle to the side, and pull it up next to the button, stretching the thread taut.

Next, wrap the length of thread behind the button, so that it encircles the threads you've already stitched. Do this five or six times, effectively creating a tied bundle of thread.

When finished, pull the thread until it's taut, pierce the fabric behind the button, and pull it through to the back side. Now, you're ready to tie off the thread.

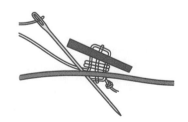

## 5 SECURE THE KNOT AND FREE

the needle. Create a knot on the back side of the fabric by inserting your needle to make a shallow dive into the fabric and, before pulling it taut, push it through the loop. Regardless of whether you tie the knot using your fingers or the needle, position it firmly against the back side of the fabric. Repeat this process three or four times.

Finally, pull out the anchor and voilà! Your button will likely be more secure than it was the first time it was sewn on.

---

# King Francis I of France once wore a court costume with 13,600 gold buttons.

---

# #66 HOW TO MAKE YOUR OWN SEWING KIT

Pack this handy emergency sewing kit in your purse, backpack, or suitcase, and you'll never be caught unprepared—it contains just the basics, all in one place, for simple repairs. Here's what you'll need to include:

⚜ A small, sturdy, puncture-proof container with a tight-fitting lid (think mint tin or lozenge box)

⚜ A rectangle of medium-weight cardboard (cut from a cracker box, 3 by 4 inches)

⚜ Safety pins (three different sizes)

⚜ A needle threader

⚜ Needles (sharps and ball points)

⚜ All-purpose threads in basic colors:

⚜ Several buttons of different sizes and weights

⚜ A tiny pair of scissors (available in craft stores and the notions section of dry goods stores)

**1 USING SHARP SCISSORS, CUT VERY** shallow slits up one of the long sides of the cardboard rectangle at regular intervals. Turn it around and do the same on the other long side, exactly across from each cut you've already made.

**2 WIND BLACK THREAD AROUND** the topmost part of the cardboard, inserting it into the slits to hold it in place and create a kind of a "skein." Don't pull too tight or the cardboard will buckle. After winding the thread around five or six times, tuck in the end so that you can easily find it again later.

**3 DO THE SAME WITH YOUR OTHER** thread colors until the slots on the card are filled. It's useful to have white or off-white, navy, brown, green, and red.

**4 TUCK THE NEEDLES INSIDE THE** thread, piercing the cardboard to hold them in place. You can also fasten your safety pins around a loop of thread so they're easy to find.

✕✕✕✕✕✕✕✕✕✕✕✕✕✕✕✕✕✕

## SOME HELPFUL GLOSSARY TERMS

*Pinking shears.* Scissors with a zigzag cutting edge that looks like a long row of little teeth

*Tailor's chalk.* A thin flat piece of hard chalk or soapstone used by tailors and seamstresses for making temporary marks on cloth

*Seam ripper.* A specialty notion with no moving parts that features a sharp, curved blade ending in a sharp point on one side and a small ball on the other edge that glides over fabric and helps protect it

*Inseam.* The seam of a trouser leg that runs from the crotch down to the bottom of the hem, alongside the inner thigh and calf

*Rayon.* Originally named artificial silk or wood silk, rayon is a transparent fiber made of processed cellulose. Cellulose fibers from wood or cotton are dissolved in alkali to make a solution called viscose, which is then extruded through a spinneret into an acid bath to reconvert the viscose into cellulose. Unlike nylon and polyester, rayon wicks water, so it's ideal for use as a clothing textile.

# #67
## HOW TO BASTE

**B**asting! It's not just for turkeys. Basting, also called tacking, means to sew easily removable stitches to temporarily hold fabric together. Why do double the work? Basting can help you save time in the long run and is often worth the extra step. It is possible to baste with a sewing machine set to big loose stitches, but hand-basting is more common. To hand-baste, you'll use a running stitch.

## In Praise of Basting

⚜ Basting stitches on seams let you test the fitting (side seams) or placement (darts) before final stitches.

⚜ Basting can hold slippery fabric in place while you sew regular stitches.

⚜ Basting allows you to hold together two layers of fabric in order to work them as one layer.

⚜ Basting lets you hold trim or bric-a-brac in place until you firmly sew it on.

**1** **USE STRAIGHT PINS TO PIN** together the layers or pieces the way you'd like them sewn.

**2** **THREAD A NEEDLE AND KNOT** the end.

**3** **DO NOT BASTE EXACTLY WHERE** you will sew the permanent stitches. If you sew over the basting stitches, it will be difficult to remove them.

**4** **STARTING ON THE BACK SIDE OF** the fabric, insert the needle through to the other side, through both layers of fabric, allowing the knot to stop the thread. Then push it back through in the opposite direction. Move on to repeat this process everywhere you intend to sew a final seam. This is called a running stitch. You can choose the size of the stitches: long or short. (Long stitches take less time.)

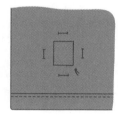

**5** **ONCE YOU HAVE BASTED THE** layers of fabric you want to attach, cut the thread at the needle and tie a simple knot to secure the stitching.

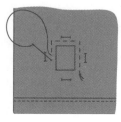

# #68
## HOW TO ATTACH A SNAP

**W**hen the fabric around a button seems worn and you want to secure it in a new way, consider a snap. The easiest way to install a snap doesn't involve sewing, but rather using one of two tools that not everyone has handy: a hammer tool or a plier tool.

There are two sides to a snap: male and female. They both consist of two parts: the male (the stud and the ring prong) and the female (the socket and the ring prong). The stud "snaps" into the socket, which is the hollowed-out side; the prongs are what fasten both the stud and the socket to the fabric.

## Tools and Hardware

If using a hammer tool, position it so that when struck by a hammer (which you'll also need), the prongs bend around the stud or socket. If using a plier tool, fit the head of the pliers around the stud or socket opposite the prongs and squeeze in order to bend the prongs.

If you don't want to invest in the hammer or plier tools, or if you don't want the metal rings to show, a sew-on snap is the best option. This snap is best used in a place on a garment that won't be subjected to too much stress or strain. A snap is the best choice when one garment edge overlaps another, hiding the snap from view. What you see on the outside of the garment is smooth fabric with an edge.

Unlike the first snap defined in this section, the sew-on snap has two parts instead of four: the ball side (aka the stud side) and the socket side. Here's how to fasten a snap to your garments.

**1** DETERMINE AND MARK THE placement of your snap.

**2** THREAD AND KNOT A NEEDLE (follow Step 1 in How to Sew on a Button, page 116).

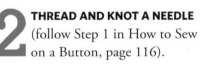

**3** LAY THE BALL SIDE OF THE SNAP on the inside hemmed edge of the layer of material that will overlap the other layer of material.

**4** **HOLDING THE BALL SIDE OF THE** snap in place, work from the back side of the material. Plunge the threaded needle through the fabric and one of the holes on the outer edge of the snap.

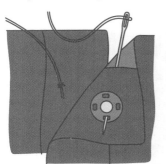

**5** **SINK THE NEEDLE IN AT THE** outer rim of the snap. Keep the needle in between the outer layer of fabric and the layer to which the snap is being attached. This will hide the stitching from the right side.

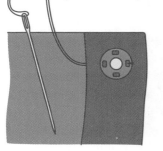

**6** **WORKING WITH ONLY ONE** hole at a time, bring the needle up again along the outer edge of the snap next to the same hole your first stitch went through. Next, take the needle down again through the same hole. Repeat this process four or five times.

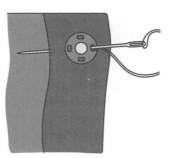

**7** **REPEAT STEPS 4 THROUGH 6** for every hole in the ball side of the snap. Move from one hole to the next by slipping your needle through the two layers of material.

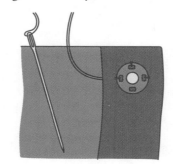

**8** **SECURE THE STITCHES BY** making tiny knots close to the first series of stitches.

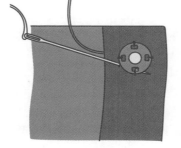

**9** **RUB TAILOR'S CHALK ALONG** the ball of the snap and overlap the edges of the garment the way they will lay when the garment is finished.

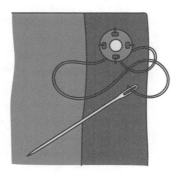

**10** **PRESS DOWN ON THE BALL** firmly so that a chalk mark is transferred to the underlying layer of material to mark where the stud or socket half of the snap will be sewn on.

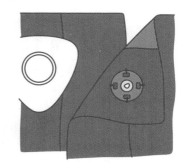

**11** **CENTER THE STUD OR** socket half over the chalk mark and hold it in place.

**12** **REPEAT STEPS 4 THROUGH 8,** attaching the other side of the snap to the material.

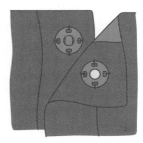

# #69
# HOW TO FIX A RIP IN YOUR JEANS

Fixing a pair of blue jeans is the right project for a beginning mender. Let's just assume your jeans are more in the Levi or Lee class than the top-tier Joe's Jeans or 7 for All Mankind class. Unlike with a filmy nightgown, or silk shirt, repairs in jeans are fairly forgiving. Even if they're not perfect, they'll still be wearable. There are many types of tears: tri-corner tears, holes, frays, punctures, and rips. And these bad things happen to good fabrics. There's no "one size fits all" way to tackle these heartaches, but here's some advice to help you deal with common denim boo-boos:

## Fusible Tricot Reinforcement

To repair a heavy fabric like jeans, an iron-on patch coupled with stitching may be your best bet. This works especially well with a three-corner (L-shaped) tear. Fusible tricot interfacing works best on 100 percent cotton fabrics like denim. You can purchase fusible tricot by the yard at sewing and craft stores, but beware! It must be preshrunk before you use it, or it will later buckle and bunch when you wash your jeans. To preshrink, simply soak the whole piece in warm water, then hang it to dry before using it. There is also tricot marked "preshrunk" available, so buy that if possible.

**1** ONCE THE TRICOT IS DRY, TURN your jeans inside out, and cut a piece of tricot about twice as large as the tear or the hole so that there will be a solid square or rectangle over the ripped area. Preheat the iron to the highest setting.

**2** PLACE A PRESS CLOTH OVER THE tricot, lightly spray it with water, and then hold the iron down firmly for about 15 seconds. Lift the iron, move it to the next area, slightly overlapping where you have already fused the interfacing (like mowing a lawn), and repeat, until the whole sheet of tricot has been fused.

**3** NEXT, TURN THE JEANS RIGHT side out, keeping the press cloth in place, and repeat the process. Use a stamping motion with the iron, instead of a gliding motion, when applying the fusible tricot.

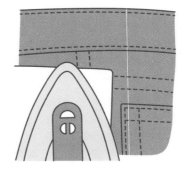

**4** **LET THE WHOLE PROJECT COOL** completely before taking the jeans off your ironing board. This will take only a few moments, but the freshly ironed synthetic material is very hot, so be careful.

**5** **ONCE THE TRICOT IS COOL,** thread a needle with dark thread. Working from the inside to the outside of the fabric, pull the thread until the knot is firmly in place on the inside of your jeans. Make evenly spaced X stitches all around the perimeter of the tear. True, this won't be as dainty as a machine-sewn repair, but for work jeans, it will do the job and also make sure the torn section isn't vulnerable or weak.

## Simple and Secure Hand Stitching

If you don't have access to an iron-on patch for reinforcement, hand sewing is a fine alternative. The doubled-over thread will hold up well, and hand stitching allows for freedom of movement as you work.

**1** **TAKE 24 INCHES OF THREAD AND** double it by bringing the ends together. Push the ends through a quilting needle, so that you have a double string of thread for extra reinforcement.

**2** **WORKING FROM THE INSIDE OF** the jeans, push the needle through the fabric at one end of the tear. Using your finger, hold about an inch of the thread on the underside of the fabric. Go back through the fabric with the needle, making sure to pass it through the loop of thread you're holding secure on the inside of the jeans. This will secure the thread without a knot.

**3** **HOLDING THE TORN FABRIC IN** place, stitch along the edges of the tear by passing the needle up and down through the fabric, in a looping motion.

**4** **IF YOU START TO RUN OUT OF** thread, tie a knot on one of your "down" passes. To do this, pass the needle under a couple of stitches four or five times, then tie off the thread and cut it with scissors.

**5** **THREAD THE NEEDLE AND** repeat the process until you've stitched around the entire tear.

# #70
## HOW TO FIX A HOLE IN YOUR SHIRT

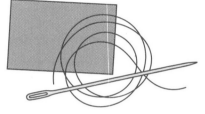

For finer fabrics, in places that show, you'll want to take extra care when mending a wardrobe mishap. Try this technique with a basic cotton or cotton-polyester blend shirt. Make sure your iron is ready to go on the appropriate setting for the fabric.

**1 START SMART.** With sharp fabric scissors, cut around the hole, making a neat square. Trim any loose threads or frayed edges. At each corner of the square hole, cut a ¼-inch notch at a 45-degree angle. Turn your garment inside out, then fold the narrow flaps formed by your cuts onto the material's inside, aka "wrong" side, and iron flat.

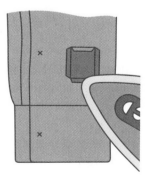

**2 MATCH AND MARK.** Find a matching piece of fabric. If the hole is small, you can sometimes use part of the shirttail. For broadcloth oxford shirts, it's sometimes possible to find a near match at the local thrift store. Barring all those, try your local fabric store. (Don't forget to bring the garment you want to match!) Mark and measure a square of the size you'll need from the matching fabric, and cut it a ½ inch bigger than the square hole you've cut in your shirt.

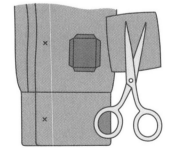

**3 LINE IT UP.** Turn your shirt inside out and line up the patch on top of the square hole. Make sure the right side of the fabric is turned up and the grains are going in the same direction. Turn your shirt right side out and use straight pins to secure the patch. Baste all around the patch (see How to Baste, page 119). Remove the pins.

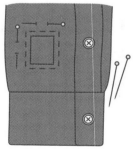

**4 SEW IT TOGETHER.** Turn your shirt inside out. Fold back the ½ inch of excess fabric so it's flush with the folded edge of the hole, folding the corners over each other. Insert the needle through the folded edge of the replacement fabric patch, just catching the very edge. Next, stitch up diagonally through the folded edge of the original shirt, securing the two fabrics together. Do this around the entire square. When you've sewn the whole square, remove the basting thread by snipping the knot off with scissors and gently pulling it out.

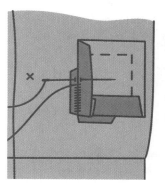

**5 ADD A FINISHING TOUCH, OR** "create a clean edge." Use a catch-stitch to finish the edges of the patch inside the shirt. Catch-stitches hold fabrics against each other, as in hems or seam allowances. To make one, you need to "catch" a few threads from the underside of the top layer of fabric. Insert the needle, and then gently pick up a few threads from the very surface of the top fabric layer, without pushing the needle all the way through. It's a delicate procedure, and you have to kind of feel your way to it, so try a few sample stitches to get the hang of it. You may need to unstitch some initially. This style of stitching is referred to as "blind" stitching because it is invisible from the outside. It has some give, but it holds well. Using this technique will ensure that the patch stays in place.

**6 TACK THE PATCH.** Cut off the tips of the patch's corners at 45-degree angles. Fold back each edge ¼ inch. Cross-stitch the

edges to the shirt, picking up only one or two threads with each stitch. Inserting the needle from right to left, create a series of tiny Xs.

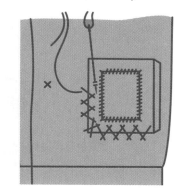

**7 PRESS IT AND GO.** When you're finished with the sewing, iron the patch in place with the shirt inside out. Allow the area to cool, then iron the shirt from the front, starting with the patch.

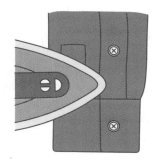

Over 2 billion T-shirts are sold every year, worldwide. A single T-shirt can require up to 700 gallons of water to produce (so learning to mend them is helpful to the environment)!

# #71
# HOW TO HEM PANTS
## (Measuring, Pinning, and the Invisible Hand Stitch)

Hemming a pair of pants is a great beginner project. Great results are easy to achieve, and the effort is rewarded in spades. Standard pant lengths for off-the-rack clothes simply do not flatter everyone. People's bodies vary: This man needs a large waist, so the pants are cut long. This woman has a long torso, but short legs. That kid grew 6 inches in a year, and his ankles are sticking out like a baby giraffe's. The correct pant length goes a long way toward cutting a fine figure.

Don't suffer pants that don't fit, and don't go broke over pricey trips to the tailor and dry cleaner. Follow these steps, and you'll be walking tall in no time.

## Glossary of Hemming Accessories

**Sewing pins.** Used to temporarily hold fabric together prior to sewing and when attaching or cutting patterns. The shaft of the pin is typically made of brass, nickel, steel, or a combination of those metals. When used for machine sewing, you can quickly and easily remove them as you stitch. Sold in a variety of lengths and thicknesses, as well as with different types of pinheads.

⚬ *Glass-head pins.* Straight pins topped with large, colored balls made of glass, making them easier to see and grasp, and allowing them to withstand heat from irons and dryers.

⚬ *Color-ball pins.* Like glass heads, but less expensive, and topped with plastic heads. Not suitable for use with heat.

⚬ *Flat-head pins.* The most common type of straight pin, they feature blunt-nubbed "heads" of the same metal as the pin shaft.

**Seam gauge.** A sewing gauge is a small ruler used in sewing. Generally 6 inches in length, it has a sliding marker, or flange, that is set to a specific measurement and is especially useful when measuring the same length repeatedly.

**1 WASH IT.** Check the fabric care label on your pants. If your pants are made of cotton, rayon, or a blend of both, preshrink them by following the manufacturer's washing and drying directions. Iron the pants before you start to stretch and smooth the material. A warm wash also gets rid of any stiffener, which would make it more difficult to get an even hem.

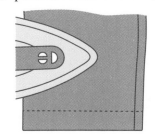

**2 RIP IT.** Using a seam ripper, take out the stitches of the original hem. If the fabric doesn't hang downward, iron it down.

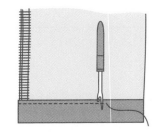

**3 MARK IT.** If possible, enlist a friend to help you with this. Try on the pants and stand on a chair. Have your friend fold the fabric at the bottom of the pants upward and inward, until the fold hits about three quarters of the way down the back of your heel, and, using one straight pin at the back, mark the spot.

If you're on your own, do this in front of a full-length mirror. Be aware, though, that bending and standing will change the length, so you may have to try a few times to get it right.

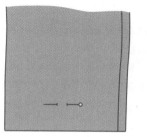

**4 MEASURE, FOLD, AND PRESS.** Take off the pants you're hemming and turn them inside out. Measure the inseam, which is the seam that runs from the crotch down the inside of the leg, all the way to the bottom of the hem. Then measure the inseam on a pair of pants you already wear. Compare the two to make sure your measurements are correct.

Starting at the pin on one leg, use a tape measure to measure the length from the edge of the fabric to the bottom fold. Use that measurement to fold and pin the hem around the bottom of the leg with five or six straight pins. Repeat the process on the other leg. Iron the hems where you want them to be, making a crease. With the pants still inside out, use your tape measure to measure 2 inches of fabric from the ironed

hemline. Mark the pants with tailor's chalk, making a dotted line around the entire leg.

**5 CUT.** Take out the pins and cut the fabric on the dotted line (use pinking shears if you have them; the jagged scissor edge prevents fraying).

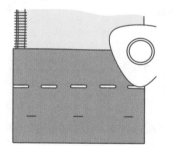

**6 PIN THE HEM BACK INTO PLACE** using the five or six pins. Thread a sharp with the right thread for the pants (see How to Thread a Needle, page 113). Don't double the thread over. Instead, pull about an inch of thread through the needle and knot the opposite end. With the pants inside out, sew a blind hem stitch (see How to Fix a Hole in Your Shirt, page 124) beginning at the side seam. Knot the thread on the inside of the pants when you've sewn the entire leg. Repeat for the other leg. When finished, iron the hems flat. Then iron the pants and hang them in the closet.

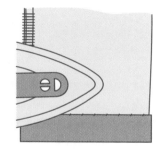

× × × × × × × × × × × × × × × × × × × × × × × × × × × × × × × × × × × × × × ×

# HEMMING ADVICE FROM MY MOM

- Check your hemline against a pair of your pants in your closet by laying the pants flat, one pair over the other, on an ironing board. Take the measurements from the inseam, not the waistband.

- If you like the way the original hem was sewn, examine it and take notes about it before you start sewing the new hem. There may be something about the style you'd like to copy.

- Just like a carpenter does: Measure twice, cut once.

- If you've no one to help you pin your pants, you can tape a fabric marker to a chair leg, put on your pants, and spin yourself in a circle.

- Compare your thread color to your pants both in natural sunlight and under harsh bathroom lights.

- Wear shoes with the same heel that you're likely to wear with your pants as you measure.

- Stand on a chair or hard floor as you measure. (Avoid shag rugs or flooring with padding!)

- Measure both legs. All of us have one shorter and one longer leg, which may not be apparent to the naked eye.

# #72 HOW TO HEM THE NO-SEW WAY

**F**usible fabric tape isn't the best permanent solution for hemming pants, but if you can iron, you can skip the sewing steps. The tape is great for times when you're traveling (many hotels have irons) or when the hem on your favorite pants falls and you're in a rush to get to a meeting or an appointment. Ready? Roll tape!

**1 MEASURE YOUR HEM AND IRON** the new hem in place as you would following the steps outlined in How to Hem Pants, Step 4, page 127.

**2 CUT THE TAPE TO FIT BETWEEN** the layers of the fabric. Make sure it doesn't stick out too far: Once you iron it, the tape melts onto the surrounding area.

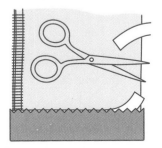

**3 LAY A DAMP PRESS CLOTH OVER** the area to be hemmed.

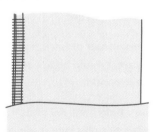

**4 PRESS IT WITH A HOT IRON TO** melt the fibers in the tape, taking care not to scorch your pants.

**5 REMOVE THE CLOTH AND PRESS** the pants directly, melting the fibers of the tape.

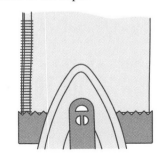

**6 LEAVE YOUR PANTS ON THE** ironing board until you are sure they are cool. Don't touch the newly fused part if you can help it. This is like letting glue dry between two sheets of paper.

✕ ✕ ✕ ✕ ✕ ✕ ✕ ✕ ✕ ✕ ✕ ✕ ✕ ✕ ✕
## FUSE WITH CARE

• **It doesn't last forever.** I don't tumble-dry garments with fusible fabric tape in them because the heat of the dryer can weaken or dislodge the tape.

• **Use fusible fabric tape only on stiff, heavy fabrics** because the tape itself becomes stiff and heavy after it's ironed into your garment.

• **It's best for use on cottons and canvas.** Fusible fabric tape doesn't stretch, so it will look odd if ironed into flowy or stretchy garments.

# #73
# HOW TO THREAD A SEWING MACHINE

Threading a sewing machine is like riding a bike: easy once you've done it successfully once or twice. Sewing machines vary, of course, but the basic principle is the same. They create stitches by interlocking the upper thread (from a spool that winds through the needle) with the lower thread (that comes up through the bobbin).

**1 USING THE HANDWHEEL (OR THE** "needle up" button), raise the needle to its highest position.

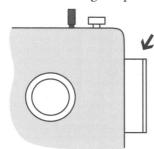

**2 RAISE THE PRESSER FOOT TO** disengage the tension discs. This will ensure that the needle doesn't "unthread" when you turn on the machine and begin stitching.

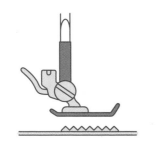

**3 PLACE A SPOOL OF THREAD ON** the spool pin on the top of the machine. If your machine's pin is horizontal, add the cap to firmly secure the spool.

**4 TAKE THE THREAD BETWEEN** your thumb and forefinger and pull it across the top of the machine and through the first thread guide. The thread should unwind easily from the spool. If it doesn't, check the spool to find where the tension or snag is occurring.

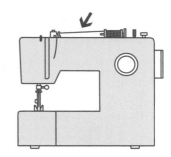

**5 PULL THE THREAD TO THE** front of the machine, down through the tension assembly, and around the next thread guide. Make sure the thread has passed between two tension discs as well as the hook that may be attached to the left side of the tension dial.

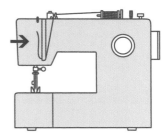

**6** PULL THE THREAD UP AND through the hole or slot in the take-up lever.

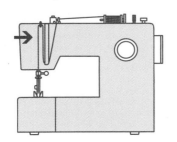

**7** PULL THE THREAD BACK DOWN through any remaining thread guides and place the thread from the front through the back of the needle eye. Some machines have built-in needle threaders that make quick work of threading the needle. To thread a machine needle manually, follow the groove in the needle shaft to determine from which direction (left to right or front to back) to thread the needle. Raise the presser foot so that you'll feel slight resistance when pulling the thread through the machine.

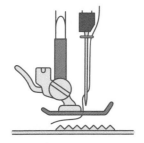

**8** LOWER THE PRESSER FOOT AND gently pull the thread to check and ensure that the tension discs are engaged.

**9** INSERT A WOUND, FULL BOBBIN, taking care that its rotational direction is correct and that the bobbin tension spring is engaged. If applicable, close the throat plate.

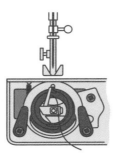

**10** RAISE THE PRESSER FOOT and hold the upper thread (needle thread) while lowering and raising the needle one time to loop the upper thread around the lower thread (bobbin thread).

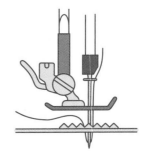

**11** GENTLY PULL THE END OF the upper thread to bring the lower thread up through the needle hole in the throat plate. Pull several inches of both the upper-thread and lower-thread ends under the presser foot together, toward the back of the machine.

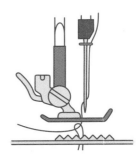

## Although he violated Elias Howe's patent (and later paid for it), American inventor Isaac Singer improved upon the design of the two-thread sewing machine and was responsible for popularizing it.

## Quick Reference: The Parts of a Sewing Machine

1. **Spool pin.** Holds a spool of thread that feeds the upper thread
2. **Bobbin winder spindle.** Small pole to hold bobbin during the winding procedure
3. **Bobbin winder stop.** Stops the loading process once the bobbin is full
4. **Stitch-width dial.** Allows you to control the size of zigzag stitches
5. **Stitch-length dial.** Allows you to control the length of the stitch
6. **Handwheel.** Allows you to raise and lower the needle manually (useful for jams and for inserting or releasing projects from the machine)
7. **Pattern-selector dial.** Allows you to choose the stitch pattern by symbol
8. **Reverse-stitch lever (or button).** Allows you to run the fabric through the machine backward
9. **Power button or switch.** Controls on/off mechanism
10. **Bobbin-winder thread guide.** Directs the thread while the bobbin is being loaded
11. **Thread-tension dial.** Allows you to control the tension on the upper thread
12. **Thread take-up lever.** Moves up and down; it's where the upper thread is guided through
13. **Needle-clamp screw.** Locks sewing machine needle in place
14. **Presser foot.** Holds the fabric firmly in place and is controlled with a lever at the back of the machine
15. **Bobbin cover.** Holds the bobbin in place and keeps dust and debris off the thread
16. **Bobbin-cover release button.** Allows you to open the cover and gain access to the bobbin
17. **Feed dogs.** Pull fabric away from you during the sewing process
18. **Needle.** Pushes and pulls thread through the fabric to create stitches
19. **Needle plate, or throat plate.** A metal plate located underneath the needle and presser foot; its openings allow the needle and feed dogs to make contact with the fabric

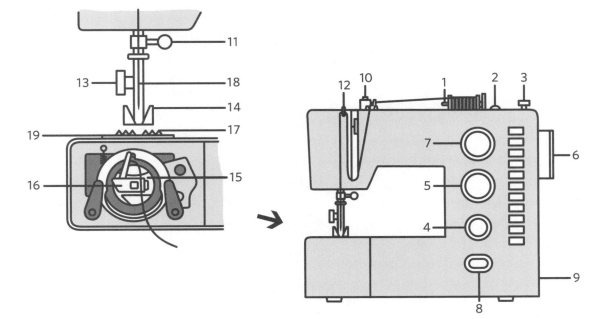

# Troubleshooting Common Sewing Machine Problems

The good news is this: Many of your problems will be related to poor maintenance or neglect of your machine. Needless to say, the amount of maintenance needed depends on how much use your machine gets. As with any appliance, you should carefully read the owner's manual and follow recommendations for care and maintenance. If you don't have it, go online to download or order a copy, or check directly with a local dealer.

As with most equipment, the best measure you can take to prevent your machine from malfunctioning is to keep it clean. Cover your machine when not in use. Dust, lint, and pet hair are enemies of a smooth-running sewing machine. Use compressed air to blast away dust particles, especially dust and lint from fabric as you sew (never blow because the moisture from breath can gum up the machine). Have a store of pipe cleaners, muslin squares, and sewing machine oil. Use the pipe cleaners for swabbing out crevices. Slide squares of clean muslin between tension discs (be sure to raise the presser foot). For more specific problems, try the following tips before spending money at the repair shop.

*Breaking needles?*

⁜ Use the right size needle and thread for your fabric.

⁜ Center the presser foot and make sure it's secure.

⁜ Never pull the fabric through the machine. Let the machine feed it.

⁜ Make sure your needle is securely fastened.

⁜ Remove straight pins before sewing or position them so they don't run under the needle.

*Noisy machine?*

⁜ Try cleaning and oiling, as oil may have dried and gummed up the machine.

⁜ Check to see if thread is caught or is too tight in the bobbin case.

⁜ Check the belt, and tighten or loosen as needed.

*Seams puckering?*

⁜ Check to see if the tension is too tight.

⁜ Check your stitches; if they are too long, the fabric can pinch and gather.

⁜ Try a new or sharper needle.

⁜ Make sure the upper thread size and bobbin thread size are the same weight and made of the same fiber.

⁜ Avoid pressing down too hard on the foot while using lightweight fabric; a slower pace keeps light fabric from bunching.

*Upper thread breaking?*

⁜ Make sure the tension isn't too tight.

⁜ Check to see if your needle is dull or bent.

⁜ Use the right size needle for the thread. Too small a needle will cause bunching as the thread slides through.

⁜ Your thread could be old or of poor quality, causing knotting, stripping, and lint deposits in the machine.

*Lower thread breaking?*

⁜ Make sure the tension isn't too tight.

⁜ Use the right size needle for the thread. Too small a needle will cause bunching as the thread slides through.

⁜ Check to see if the thread in the bobbin case is stuck or tangled.

⁜ Take care not to pull the thread too tightly while winding the bobbin.

⁜ Check for a possible sharp edge, or burr, on the throat plate that could be cutting the thread.

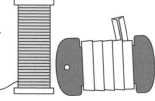
# #74
## HOW TO HEM A SKIRT

**A**lthough it's certainly possible to hem any skirt by hand, using a machine yields a more professional look—once you get the hang of it. And once you've mastered the techniques, hemming skirts on a machine takes very little time. You'll be richly rewarded if you take patience and care in measuring, pinning, and pressing the hems as you go. As with most sewing projects, the devil is in the details. Use these three basic techniques for hemming most A-line, dirndl, full, pencil, or tube skirts.

### "Double Turn-Back" and "Topstitched" Hem

This is the most common hem. It simply involves turning the unfinished edge of the fabric under.

**1** **USING A SEAM GAUGE, DIVIDE** the total hem allowance in half. For example, if working with a 1-inch hem, turn the garment inside out and iron the hem up a ½ inch on the wrong side. It's easiest to use glass-head pins to pin the fabric to the ironing board. Press the hem flat.

**2** **TURN THE HEM UP ANOTHER** ½ inch, and then press the new fold flat. Some pros are able to skip this step, but its worth the extra few moments of ironing to get a really smooth, flat hem.

**3** **WORKING FROM THE OUTSIDE** of the fabric, so you can't see the raw edge, line up the fold against the left edge of the presser foot. You can feel the edge of the hem with your fingers even if you cannot see the "bump" through the fabric. Adjust the sewing machine needle to the left position, if your machine has a needle-right position. Topstitch the hem into place.

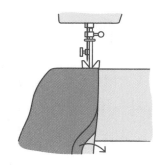

## "Faced" Hem

Use this technique if you don't have much fabric to invest in the hem. It generally can be done with only a ¾-inch fabric loss. The bias tape used here will bend around curved edges, providing a polished, finished look.

**1** **PRESS THE RIGHT SIDE OF THE** bias tape's fold open. Take care not to iron it completely flat. You need to be able to see the crease.

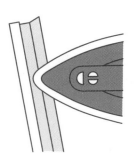

**2** **LAY THE BIAS TAPE FACE-DOWN** on top of the right side of the fabric. Line up the raw edge of the tape with the raw edge of the fabric. Secure it with pins. Using your sewing machine, stitch in the crease.

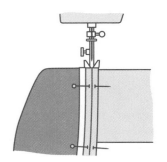

**3** **USING A WARM IRON, PRESS** the seam flat.

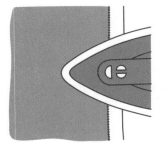

**4** **PRESS THE TAPE ON THE** wrong side of the fabric and pin.

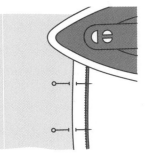

**5** **USING AN EDGE STITCH,** machine-sew the tape in place, and then remove any pins.

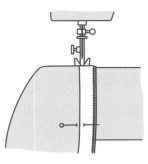

## "Blind" Hem

This technique makes a nearly invisible stitch. You can also use it on dressier fabrics where it's important not to see the stitching. Try to match the color and weight of the thread exactly with the fabric.

**1** **INSTALL THE BLIND-HEM FOOT** onto your machine.

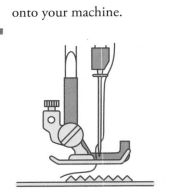

**2** **TURN THE SKIRT INSIDE OUT** and press 1 inch of fabric up on the wrong side.

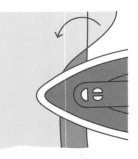

**3** **OPEN THE CREASE** temporarily to fold ¼ inch of the raw edge into the hem and press. Then refold the crease from Step 2.

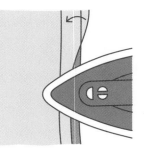

**4** **SET THE MACHINE TO THE** blind-edge stitch. Nearly every modern machine has this setting, but if you're working on a really old machine, set it on the smallest stitch you can work with easily.

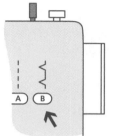

**5** **USE THE HANDWHEEL TO** "walk" the machine. Do this until the needle swings to the far-left zigzag. Allow the needle to just barely catch the fold. Use the hand screw to adjust the bar on the foot so that it butts directly up against the fold. This will ensure even stitches.

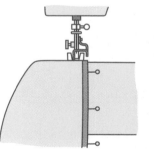

**6** **THE BIG ZIGZAG OF THE STITCH** will catch just a thread of the fold, and the little zigzags will finish the raw edge, guarding against future fraying.

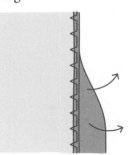

**7** **UNFOLD THE HEM AND USE AN** iron to press it flat.

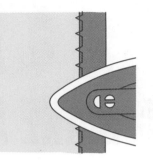

**8** **FROM THE OUTSIDE, YOU'LL SEE** a tiny stitch that looks like a dot about every ½ inch around the bottom of the skirt. If you see big stitches, it's an indication that you've stitched too much onto the fold. Carefully rip out the stitches with a seam ripper and begin again.

The skirt is thought to be the second oldest form of clothing, preceded only by the loincloth. But—flashing forward many centuries—Christian Dior is credited with inventing the pencil skirt and the A-line skirt.

# #75
# HOW TO MAKE A PILLOW

**M**aking and stuffing a pillow by hand is an excellent (and useful!) project for beginner DIY folk. That said, no seamstress should ever view herself as too grand for the task. Homemade pillows are cheap and quick to make, and they instantly transform the décor of a room. Once you learn how, there'll be little need to purchase accent pillows ever again!

**1 FIGURE OUT WHAT SIZE PILLOW** you'd like to make. Add ½ to 1 inch for a seam allowance. If you aren't exactly sure of the size, I suggest purchasing about a yard of fabric. If you'd like the front and the back to be different patterns, you may want to start with a ½ yard of each.

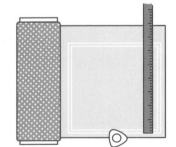

**2 CUT THE FABRIC TO THE** desired dimensions.

**3 LAY THE FABRIC ONE PIECE ON** top of the other, right sides in.

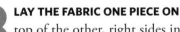

**4 SITTING AT YOUR SEWING** machine, use a straight stitch to sew up three edges of the pillow.

**5 WHEN YOU GET TO SIDE FOUR,** sew until you have about 5 inches unsewn, making, essentially, a hole in a pouch.

**6 TURN THE "BAG" INSIDE OUT BY** pulling it through the hole. Now the right side (or out-facing side) of the fabric will be showing.

**7** **STUFF POLYFILL OR OTHER** filling, as desired, through the hole until the pillow is as plump as you'd like.

**8** **TUCK THE UNSTITCHED FABRIC** edges into the hole and pin them in place so the folded-over edge lines up with the outer seam. Pin the fabric edge to itself, but don't pin the hole closed.

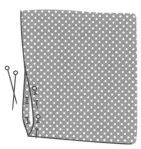

**9** **THREAD A SHARP NEEDLE WITH** a single knotted thread that best matches your pillow in color and weight.

**10** **YOU DON'T WANT A** hand-sewn whip stitch or a machine stitch that will show on the outside of the pillow. Use the following invisible stitch to keep the fabric closed and hidden beneath the folds of the fabric: Pierce the edge of the fabric on the inside of the pillow, so the knot remains unseen on the inside layer.

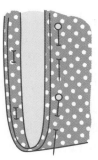

**11** **TAKE THE NEEDLE AND** bring it through the seam crease right across from where the thread is coming out on the other side.

**12** **KEEP THE NEEDLE INSIDE** the fabric under the fold for about ¼ to ½ inch, and then poke it out a little.

**13** **BRING THE POINT OF THE** needle toward you and pick up some fabric (not too much) from the fold of the other side.

**14** **PULL THE THREAD UNTIL** it's taut, and then repeat the same action all across the opening.

**15** **PIERCE THE FABRIC ACROSS** from where the thread is coming out, then travel under the fold and come out toward your body, grabbing a small amount of fabric from the other fold. Tie off the end by knotting inside the folds of the seam.

Very different from their Western equivalent, pillows made in ancient China were often crafted from porcelain. The material was thought to have health benefits in this form—and may have been thought to inspire dreams.

## Pillow-Making FAQs

*How much fabric do I need?*

You'll need to use your math skills on this one because it's all about geometry. The amount of fabric depends on the width of the fabric and on the size of the pillow you desire. My advice? Stick with squares as you learn, then progress to rectangles. As you gain skill, you can branch out.

Every basic pillow has two sides. You need to add about an inch to each edge for the seams. Think of it this way: A 12-inch square pillow requires two 14-inch squares. One square in front, one in back, and extra fabric to sew the seams.

*How do I buy it?*

Fabric is sold by the yard (which is, as you know, 36 inches). In a fabric store, you'll see that most yardage is between 36 and 60 inches wide. The exception to this is upholstery fabrics, which are commonly 54 inches wide. A square of 54-inch fabric is 1½ yards long. That'll get you two 16-inch square pillows, plus a length of fabric left over.

*How do I trim it?*

Add fringed trim to pillows by pinning the trim between the two layers of fabric with the fringed portion facing the center of the pillow. You'll sew it inside out. When you turn the pillow right-side out, you'll have trim on the outside.

*What fabric should I use?*

The only rule is that you should use durable fabric for outdoor pillows. I suggest cotton canvas, duck cloth, vinyl, olefin, or use a shower curtain! (Hint: Make sure your fillings are 100 percent waterproof, too.) I like to make pillows out of blankets or bedspreads that have suffered a stain that I can cut out or sew around.

*What fabric should I avoid?*

Pillows can be a real art form for the inspired designer. But for everyday home use, consider avoiding silks or brocades that will show stains easily and that require dry-cleaning or special care.

# #76 HOW TO MAKE A COMFY NO-SEW FLEECE PILLOW

All you need to make this cozy pillow is a pillow or pillow form, two pieces of fleece (or other no-fray fabric such as felt), a pair of scissors, ruler, and your own two hands.

**1 START WITH A SQUARE PILLOW TO** cover. Then select your fleece and wash it to remove any manufacturer's sizing.

**2 MEASURE THE PILLOW FROM SEAM** to seam. Allow for the thickness of the pillow and the knotted closures by adding 8 inches to the width and length of your measurements. This is the size your fabric should be. Measure twice, cut once.

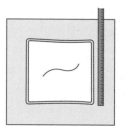

**3 LAY THE TWO SQUARES OF FLEECE** on top of each other, right-sides together.

**4 PLACE A RULER ABOUT 3 INCHES** from the edge and cut into the fabric at 1-inch intervals. Cut out a 3-inch square from each corner.

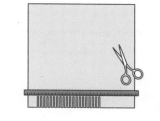

**5 YOU'LL BE LEFT WITH 1-INCH-** wide, 3-inch-long fringe strips. Flip the pieces over, right-sides out, one on top of the other.

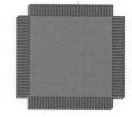

**6 TIE DOUBLE OVERHAND KNOTS** using one fringe piece from each fleece layer.

**7 TIE THESE KNOTS AROUND THREE** sides, leaving one end open.

**8 INSERT YOUR PILLOW INTO THE** open end.

**9 TIE THE FRINGES ON THE** remaining side.

**10 CHECK ALL THE KNOTS.**

# #77 HOW TO MAKE A SUPER-EASY NO-SEW KNOT PILLOW

**N**o scissors? No ruler? No problem! All you need is a large square of fabric and a pillow or pillow form to make this very chic, knotted, decorator pillow. You need a piece of fabric three times as wide (plus a couple of more inches) and twice as long (plus a few more inches) as the pillow or pillow form.

**1 IRON THE FABRIC FLAT TO STRETCH** it out and to remove any wrinkles or bunches.

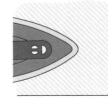

**2 LAY OUT THE FABRIC WRONG-SIDE** up and center the pillow or pillow form in the middle.

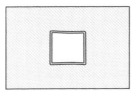

**3 FOLD THE TOP HALF OF THE FABRIC** to the center dividing line of the pillow.

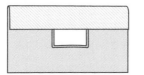

**4 FOLD THE BOTTOM HALF UP SO** that it just extends past the edge of the first folded piece of fabric. It'll look like your pillow or pillow form is in a tube or like the beginnings of a wrapped piece of candy.

**5 TAKE THE SQUARED-OFF CORNERS** of one end and fold them in one time each, as if you are wrapping a present, bringing the tube ends to triangle points. Repeat on the other side.

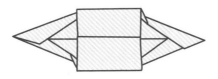

**6 FOLD THE RIGHT TRIANGLE IN** across the top of the pillow. Then cover it with the other triangle end once you fold that across.

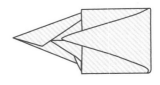

**7 TIE THE ENDS TOGETHER IN A** square knot, by taking the fabric over-under, then under-over.

**8 TUCK THE ENDS SECURELY** behind the knot.

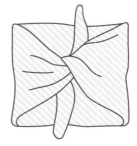

## One old superstition suggests a key should be slipped into a child's pillowcase to ward off evil spirits.

# #78

## HOW TO MAKE AN APRON

**G**athering fabric is exactly what it sounds like: "gathering" or bunching fabric together along one edge so that a ruffle effect is created. This technique is used in many sewing projects, such as puffed sleeves, can-can skirts, tote bags, and . . . aprons!

## MATERIALS:

- **1⅓ yards of 45-inch-wide light cotton fabric**
- **Thread that closely matches the fabric in color and weight. Use 100 percent cotton thread.**

## Cutting the Fabric

**1** **CUT ONE PIECE OF FABRIC 36** inches wide by 45 inches long to form the body of the apron.

**2** **CUT FOUR PIECES OF FABRIC** 3 inches wide by 45 inches long each to make the ties of the apron.

## Making the Body

**1** **TURN THE TOP EDGE OF THE** body fabric down ¼ inch to the inside (you'll attach this edge to the ties). Using an iron, press the seam allowance. Turn again, and using your sewing machine, sew a running stitch close to the pressed edge.

**2** **FOLLOW STEP 1 FOR THE HEM,** working from the bottom of the fabric, opposite the part you just sewed.

**3** **FOLLOW STEP 1 AGAIN FOR** each side of the apron body. You now have, essentially, an edged rectangle.

## Making the Apron Ties

**1** **LINE UP TWO OF THE FOUR** already-cut pieces, right sides together.

**2** **WITH THE RIGHT SIDES STILL** together, use the sewing machine to sew the 3-inch width, making a ⅜-inch seam.

**3** REPEAT STEPS 1 AND 2 WITH the other two pieces. You now have two 90-inch-long ties.

**4** ON EACH OF THE TWO APRON ties, use a warm iron to press the long edges under ¼ inch to the inside.

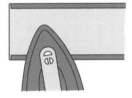

**5** REPEAT STEP 4 TO PRESS UNDER the short ends of the apron ties.

**6** LAY OUT THE PIECES, WRONG-sides together. Pin them in place, and use the sewing machine to sew close to the edge for the entire length.

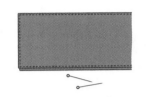

**7** PIN AND SEW ALONG THE short ends of each of the apron ties. Use a small stitch and proceed slowly to keep the narrow ties as flat and smooth as possible, since long, narrow seams like this are inclined to pucker.

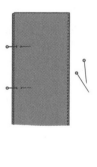

## Sewing the Gather Stitch

**1** USING THE SEWING MACHINE, sew a gather stitch all along the top end of the fabric. (Choose the longest length possible on your stitch-length selector so the fabric gathers more quickly.) Place the presser foot about ⅛ inch or ¼ inch in from the edge of the fabric. Don't forward or backstitch at the beginning of the stitch (as you normally would). Keep a long tail of thread and sew a straight line parallel to the edge of your fabric. Grasp the thread with one hand and push the fabric over with the other hand. You'll see the fabric easily gather over the thread.

**2** CONTINUE GATHERING, pushing, and shifting the fabric until you have evenly spaced gathers and the top edge of the apron body measures about 20 inches.

In 16th and 17th century England, the color and pattern of your apron indicated your trade. Barbers wore a checked pattern, while butchers and porters wore green.

## Attaching the Apron Tie

**1 FOLD THE GATHERED APRON** body in half to locate the center, and then mark it with a pin.

**2 FOLD THE APRON TIE IN HALF** to locate its center, and mark it with a pin.

**3 LAY THE CENTER OF THE TIE** over the pin in the center of the apron body.

**4 KEEP THE TIE AT THE VERY TOP** edge of the body piece. Smooth the gathers at the inside of the apron body.

**5 DOUBLE-CHECK YOUR** measurement to ensure that you are maintaining the 20 inches at the top of the apron.

**6 DOUBLE-CHECK TO ENSURE** that you will have the same apron tie length on both ends by checking the center of the tie.

**7 PIN THE TIE IN PLACE AND SEW** along the top edge.

**8 REPEAT STEP 7 FOR THE** bottom of the tie.

**9 PRESS.**

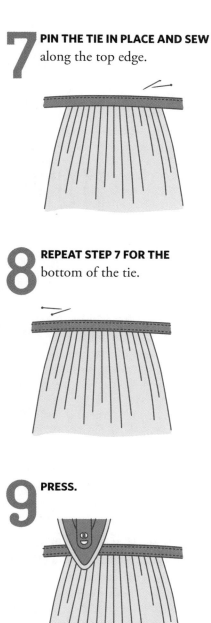

# #79
# HOW TO INSTALL A ZIPPER

Zippers are nothing short of miraculous when they function properly. When they jam or break in public, however, our love affair generally cools. But don't default to snaps, Velcro, or hook-and-eye closures simply because you're intimidated by zippers. It's not rocket science. It just takes a little practice. For your first-time zipper projects, try to choose a zipper with a slider on the smallish side. They're easier to deal with because they're less bulky. Also, do your best to match the length of the zipper with the length of the opening in your project.

Zippers are sewn into seams, for the most part. Rarely does a zipper run down the entire length of a garment's side. For most projects, like sewing a zipper into a pillow, you'll need to sew a regular seam before and after you sew in a zipper. Here's what to do.

## Sew It Together

**1** **TAKE THE TWO PANELS OF** fabric that will flank your zipper and finish the edges with a serger or a zigzag seam. Then sew the two right-hand sides using a ⅝-inch seam allowance and a long stitch length (basting stitch). If you have a pattern or instructions with a different seam allowance, use that.

**2** **TURN OUT THE WRONG SIDE OF** the sewn-together fabric and iron the new seams open flat.

## Line It Up

**1** **PLACE THE ZIPPER SO THE TEETH** fall in the ditch of the seam you just made, with the right side of the zipper face-down. Now you'll need to figure out the exact placement.

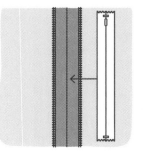

**2** **YOU'LL HAVE A STARTING AND** stopping point for the zipper on the fabric. It could be the top edge of the fabric or ½ inch down. Wherever it is, place the end of the zipper where it needs to begin, with your zipper still face-down. Line up the center of the zipper teeth along the center of that open seam. Now it's time to pin the zipper in place.

## Pin It

**1** **PIN THE ZIPPER INTO THE SEAM** face-down with the pins running parallel to the sides of the zipper.

**2** **NEXT, THINK ABOUT THE WAY** you will be sewing the zipper. You'll start on one side of the zipper, sew along it, then turn and sew the opposite direction. Position the heads of the pins so they face toward you as you sew; this makes them very easy to remove. In other words: The heads of the pins on the right side of the zipper will face one way while the heads of the pins on the left side will face the opposite.

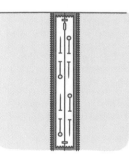

## Prepare to Sew

**1** **TURN THE FABRIC OVER AND** mark it with a pin just above where the bottom of the zipper lays. This will show you where to stop sewing because you don't want to sew over the metal or thick plastic piece at the end of the zipper.

**2** **ATTACH A ZIPPER FOOT TO** your sewing machine. Use thread that matches both the zipper and the fabric. Make sure the same thread is loaded for the upper and lower stitches. Many zipper feet have two locations where they can be attached to the machine to enable you to start stitching on either side of a zipper. In this case, attach the zipper foot on the left side.

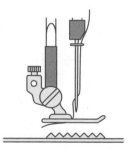

✕ ✕ ✕ ✕ ✕ ✕ ✕ ✕ ✕ ✕ ✕ ✕ ✕ ✕ ✕ ✕

# THE PARTS OF A ZIPPER

*Chain.* The continuous piece that is formed when both halves of a zipper are meshed together

*Teeth.* The individual elements that make up the chain

*Slider.* The device that moves up and down the chain to open and close the zipper

*Pull tab.* The part of the slider that you grasp to move it up or down

*Tape.* The fabric behind the zipper mechanism

*Tape ends.* The fabric that extends past the teeth at the top and bottom of the chain

*Top stop.* Two devices at the top end of the zipper that halt the slider from going off the chain

*Bottom stop.* A device attached to the bottom end of the zipper to halt further movement of that half of the zipper

*Bridge stop.* Similar to a bottom stop, this device is used at the top end of a zipper to prevent each half of the zipper from separating

*Pin.* A device used on a separating zipper that encourages the joining of the two zipper halves

*Box.* A device used on a separating zipper that helps correctly align the pin, so that the joining of the two zipper halves can begin

## Stitching It In

**1 STITCH AROUND ALL FOUR SIDES** of the zipper with a zigzag stitch, keeping the side of the zipper foot as close to the zipper as possible.

**2 STITCH DOWN THE RIGHT SIDE** of the zipper, stopping just a few stitches past the end of the zipper with the needle in the down position.

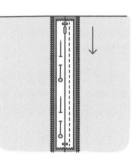

**3 ROTATE THE ZIPPER AND FABRIC** 90 degrees, then stitch just a few stitches beyond the edge of the zipper. Stop with the needle in the down position.

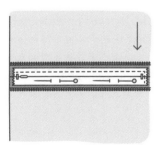

**4 ROTATE THE ZIPPER AND FABRIC** 90 degrees, then stitch up the left side of the zipper and a few stitches beyond the edge of the zipper. Stop with the needle in the down position.

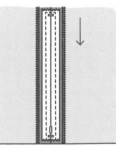

**5 ROTATE THE ZIPPER AND FABRIC** 90 degrees. Stitch until you are about 2 inches from your starting point. Leave your needle down in the fabric to hold it in place.

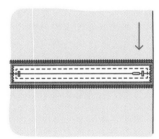

## Unpick, Unzip, Flip, Finish

**1 WITH THE NEEDLE STILL IN THE** fabric, carefully begin to unpick the original center seam (the zipper is now underneath it, and you should be able to feel the closed teeth under the fabric) until just beyond the back of the zipper foot.

**2 UNZIP THE ZIPPER SO THAT THE** pull is out of the way and just behind the zipper foot. Move the edge of the fabric a little to the right to give extra room for the zipper pull.

**3 CONTINUE SEWING THE** additional 2 inches to the very end, and backstitch.

**4 FLIP THE PROJECT OVER AND** unpick the entire center seam, exposing the zipper. Check to see that the zipper opens and closes correctly.

# #80 HOW TO FIX A BROKEN PULL

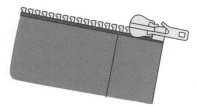

For a super-quick, on-the-go repair, use a safety pin to replace a missing or broken zipper pull tab. To permanently replace it, try this.

**1 REMOVE THE PULL TAB FROM** the slider.

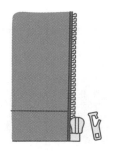

**2 TEST TO ENSURE THAT THE SLIDER** can functionally slide up and down the chain (you might have to use a safety pin).

**3 USING A MAGNIFYING GLASS,** inspect the break in the pull tab.

**4 USING A PAIR OF PLIERS, BEND THE** broken sections of the pull tab so there is ample space between them to allow the tab to fit back into the slider.

**5 USING A METAL FILE, FILE DOWN** any burred or sharp spots on the break point, taking care not to file off an excessive amount.

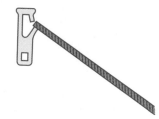

**6 INSERT THE PULL TAB BACK INTO** the slider, and then use the pliers to gently squeeze the broken sections back together. If possible, overlap the broken pieces slightly.

## Unsticking a Zipper

**If the teeth are sticking.** Zip the zipper all the way to the top, if possible. Then, rub the teeth with a graphite pencil. Inch the zipper down a little at a time.

**If the fabric is caught in the teeth.** Use white vinegar or glass cleaner as a lubricant. These are not oil based and generally won't ruin fabric, but test an unseen or small patch before going all-in with this technique. Soak the fabric around the zipper with the white vinegar or glass cleaner.

Really douse it. Don't be afraid because you are going to wash the garment as soon as you get the zipper free.

Very, very slowly (a millimeter at a time) pull the zipper in the direction you would to unzip the garment. Go a bump past the point at which you think it won't slide anymore, then relax your grip and rest for a second or two. Repeat. Each time the zipper should move a little tiny bit farther. If you see any fabric bunching, give it a hard tug while pulling opposite that bunch with the zipper.

# #81 HOW TO FIX A SEPARATED ZIPPER

Of all the frustrating zipper mishaps, a set of teeth that refuse to keep closed are some of the most aggravating. Luckily—if you can locate needle-nose pliers, and a needle and thread—there's an easy fix.

**1 USING A SMALL PAIR OF NEEDLE-** nose pliers, pry off the zipper's metal stop.

**2 MOVE THE SLIDER ALL THE WAY** to the bottom of the zipper, going just below the bottom-most teeth.

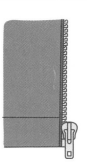

**3 USE YOUR HANDS TO REALIGN** the teeth so that they mesh.

**4 ZIP THE ZIPPER BY SLIDING IT TO** the top.

**5 THREAD A NEEDLE WITH** embroidery or another very strong thread, and knot it off.

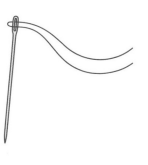

**6 STARTING WITH THE THREAD ON** the back side of the zipper, make six stitches the size of the old stop across the bottom of the zipper where the old stop was.

**7 TIE A KNOT ON THE UNDERSIDE OF** the fabric to secure the "stop."

× × × × × × × × × × × × × × × × × × × × × × × × × × × × × × × × × × × × × × × × × × × ×

## THE HISTORY OF THE ZIPPER

Elias Howe, the inventor of the sewing machine, patented the "automatic, continuous, clothing closure" in 1851 but he never tried seriously to market or publicize the clever gadget. Forty-two years later, Whitcomb Judson marketed the "clasp locker," taking the same technology a bit further, and debuted it at the Chicago World's Fair. Thus, Judson is generally credited with inventing the device. B. F. Goodrich was the first to call it a "zipper," but it didn't enjoy popularity until 1937, when Esquire magazine touted it as the "newest tailoring idea for men."

# LAUNDRY & CLOTHING

**W**hen you first start doing your own laundry, whether you're 12 or 22 or older, it can be a real shock to discover that just throwing things into the washing machine and then the dryer doesn't work! Clothes can look and feel much better if you know the tips and tricks to get them clean, keep them colorfast, and prevent shrinking or stretching. With a little skill and luck, you can cut down on dry-cleaning bills as well. Like dishes, laundry has to be done frequently. And it's too easy to end up with faded colors and graying whites if you don't exercise a little care. But despite the complex hieroglyphics of the modern laundry label, a little care and attention—and a few tricks up your sleeve—will keep your laundry fresh and bright.

# LAUNDRY TOOL KIT

Chalk

Rubbing alcohol

Baking soda

Stain removal spray

Laundry detergent

Bleach

Glycerin

Ammonia

Distilled white vinegar

# #82
## HOW TO READ A LAUNDRY LABEL

"How should I best wash and care for my cute new top or dark-wash jeans?" you may ask. The obvious answer is, "Check the care label," right? Ummm, not necessarily. A dirty little secret about laundry care labels is that they don't always tell you how to best clean the clothes.

Why, you might ask, would the manufacturer bother to include them? Because they're compelled by law. The Federal Trade Commission (FTC) mandates that clothing companies meet federal agency regulatory requirements. Sadly, because sometimes laundry care labels are created with only the letter of the law in mind, they do not always communicate optimal instructions for care.

The mission then becomes how to interpret the secret code on these labels to know what you really can and cannot do to get your clothes clean. In some cases, clothing tags advise us to "dry clean only" or "machine wash, tumble dry." Making it still more confusing to average citizens, these phrases often have a different legal meaning versus practical meaning.

## Practical Advice for Heeding Words on Common Laundry Care Labels

Some directions in the labels are more meaningful than others. You may have to ignore some of the more poorly written labels and use common sense. Still, it's always worth checking, and here's some translation to help you wade through:

⚓ Check the label for important instructions like "wash separately" or "dry-clean only." These instructions are intended to lengthen the life of your clothes and prevent them from being ruined (see When to Dry-Clean, page 168).

⚓ Don't forget to look for drying instructions like "air-dry" or "tumble dry low." The way in which you dry your clothes is just as important as how they are washed, and placing delicate items in a hot dryer can ruin them. When in doubt, dry fragile items on a line or a drying rack.

⚓ Interpret any laundry label symbols. (This can be daunting if you're not a visual person.) The system is intended to be a straightforward guide to give

instructions on washing, bleaching, and drying. If you don't feel you understand what the symbols are trying to tell you, check other laundry care advice in this book such as How to Hand-Wash (page 167) or How to Care for a Sweater (page 160).

## Universal Visual Symbols for Laundry Care

Recently, a new layer of complexity has been introduced to us from European standards and practices, in the form of labels featuring no words, only laundry symbols. These symbols can be confusing. Many clothing labels provide only pictograms and omit written instructions and important details for keeping our garments looking their best. Familiarize yourself with the chart, on pages 152–153, before you attempt to do your first load of laundry. I've included a common-sense translation of the symbols you'll most often find.

# GUIDE TO UNIVERSAL HOME LAUNDRY SYMBOLS

| CARE SYMBOL | DESCRIPTION OF SYMBOL | WHAT CARE SYMBOLS MEAN |
|---|---|---|
| | Washtub. | Indicates where you'll find washing instructions. Accompanying this symbol, you'll find additional directions. |
| | One dot in the washtub. | Machine wash in cold water. |
| | Two dots in the washtub. | Machine wash in warm water. |
| | Three dots in the washtub. | Machine wash in hot water. |
| | One line under the washtub. | Use the permanent press setting on the washing machine. |
| | Two lines under the washtub. | Use the delicate or gentle cycle on the washing machine. |
| | A crossed-out washtub. | Do not machine wash. |
| | A hand in the washtub. | Hand-wash only. |
| | Triangle. | Accompanying this symbol, you'll find detailed bleaching instructions. On clothing manufactured in Japan, a chemical flask is used. |
| | Open triangle. | Use bleach as needed. |
| | Two lines in a triangle. | Use nonchlorine bleach as needed. |
| | A crossed-out triangle. | Do not use bleach. |
| | Square. | Accompanying this symbol, you'll find detailed drying instructions. For machine drying, the square will have a large circle inside. |
| | A solid black circle within the square. | Tumble dry with no heat. |
| | A single dot within the square. | Tumble dry with low heat. |
| | Two dots within the square. | Tumble dry with medium heat. |

| CARE SYMBOL | DESCRIPTION OF SYMBOL | WHAT CARE SYMBOLS MEAN |
|---|---|---|
| | Three dots within the square. | Tumble dry with high heat. |
| | A single line underneath the square. | Use the permanent press setting on the dryer. |
| | Two lines underneath the square. | Use the gentle setting on the dryer. |
| | A crossed-out square. | Do not tumble dry. |
| | A horizontal curve inside the square. | Line dry. |
| | Three vertical lines inside the square. | Drip dry. |
| | One horizontal line inside the square. | Dry flat. |
| | Two diagonal lines inside the square. | Dry in shade. |
| | A crossed out twisted garment | Do not wring. |
| | Iron. | Accompanying this symbol, you'll find detailed ironing instructions. |
| | Single dot within the iron. | Iron with low heat. |
| | Two dots within the iron. | Iron with medium heat. |
| | Three dots within the iron. | Iron with high heat. |
| | An iron with crossed-out lines underneath. | Avoid steam while ironing. |
| | A crossed-out iron. | Do not iron. |
| | Circle. | Accompanying this symbol, you'll find detailed dry-cleaning instructions (these are useful only for dry-cleaning professionals). |
| | A crossed-out circle. | Do not dry-clean. |

# #83 HOW TO SORT A HEAP OF DIRTY CLOTHES FOR WASHING
## (Including Fabric Types)

Doing laundry may seem like a mindless, simple chore, but in actuality, it requires high-level thinking. Basic knowledge of fabric types, a design eye to group clothes by color, a rudimentary understanding of the mechanics of the machine, and some smarts about the chemistry around bleach and detergent are necessary. The good news is that all of this can be learned.

As with any task, there is a starting line. With laundry, that line is the sorting of the pile. Here are the basics.

**1** **DUMP YOUR LAUNDRY ONTO AN** expanse of floor so you can see what you're working with.

**2** **PICK OUT ANY OBVIOUS** non–machine washables that may have wound up in the hamper, including wool sweaters; delicate lingerie; fine silks; heavy woolen slacks; skirts, or jackets; and anything dry-clean only. Hand-wash or dry clean these items.

**3** **DO THE FIRST-ROUND SORT.** Put all white items in one pile, and all colored items in a second pile.

**4** **PULL OUT ANY LINT-SHEDDING** items, such as towels and terry-cloth robes, and put them in their own pile.

**5** **SORT BY WEIGHT.** Tumbling heavy denim or canvas items with light cotton nighties or undershorts will wear or possibly damage the light items. Plus, drying times for blankets are vastly different from those for socks.

**6** **GO THROUGH THE COLORED PILES,** and pull out any noncolorfast items, including red garments, denim, and new black, navy, and deep purple items. (Always test brand-new garments for colorfastness *before* washing in loads. The exception to this is when washing like items: Wash new dark-wash jeans with jeans you want to keep dark, and new red items with other red items of the same fabric.)

**7** **SORT OUT HEAVILY SOILED ITEMS** and wash them separately. For example, if someone in the family is a pastry chef with clothing coated in flour and food dye, his or her garments need to be removed from the general mix. Same goes for clothing caked with mud or saturated with automotive grease.

**8** **WHEN IT'S TIME TO MACHINE** wash, follow the instructions on the washing machines and dryers, the garments' care labels, and the laundry detergent packaging to ensure that you use the right water temperature, rinse temperature, and amount of detergent for each pile of laundry. Pay special attention to front-loading washers: You'll need to use high-efficiency (HE) detergent, and less of it.

✕ ✕ ✕ ✕ ✕ ✕ ✕ ✕ ✕ ✕ ✕ ✕ ✕ ✕ ✕ ✕ ✕ ✕ ✕ ✕ ✕ ✕ ✕ ✕ ✕ ✕ ✕ ✕ ✕ ✕ ✕ ✕ ✕ ✕ ✕ ✕

## BEFORE YOU SORT: STAIN SCREENING

Ideally, you should treat stains at the moment of contact. If you spill red wine on your cotton shirt, it's a good idea to blot it with seltzer and a cloth napkin. Sometimes, that's not practical, so here are some tips.

• **Deal with the stain when you undress.** Don't toss the soiled garment in the hamper. If appropriate, presoak it in your washer with the right type of detergent or stain remover.

• If you can't soak the item immediately, spray the stain with an on-the-spot stain remover.

• When you're sorting laundry, if you see a stain that's been left untreated, start the stain-removal process by soaking or treating the stain before washing it with a regular load (see page 156).

• If possible, do similar laundry with similar stains in the same load (i.e., grease stains with grease stains, grass stains with grass stains, and so on).

# #84

## HOW TO REMOVE KETCHUP FROM A WHITE SHIRT

**M**urphy's law says if something can splash, plop, run, or spill, it will happen when you're wearing lucky khakis or your most beloved blazer. Fortunately, once you learn how to handle troublesome stains, you can keep your most valuable clothes from winding up in the rag pile. Removing stains and keeping them from setting permanently takes a little know-how and a bit of elbow grease, but it's worth it to preserve your wardrobe and your budget.

All too common, and notoriously hard to remove: the ketchup stain. If you're like most diners in the Western world, you've overshot a plate of fries more often than you care to admit. Here's how to tackle the aftermath.

**1 REMOVE THE CULPRIT.** Scrape as much ketchup off the fabric as you can, as soon as you can. Use a spoon, butter knife, or credit card. Try not to rub it in further.

**2 FORCE IT INTO A BACK-PEDAL.** Run cold water through the *back* of the stained fabric as soon as possible. This forces the stain back out. (Don't run it through the front because you'll only set it in deeper.)

**3 GET IT IN A LATHER.** Rub a liquid detergent (or shaving cream, if you have it) into the stain, using a gentle, circular motion beginning at the outer edges of the stain and working inward.

**4 LATHER, RINSE, REPEAT.** Keep soaping and rinsing until the stain is fully gone. Hold the fabric up to a bright light. If you see the slightest hint of brown or pink, repeat the previous steps.

**5 USE THE BIG GUNS.** The minute you can get some, apply a stain remover. Use a wipe, stick, gel, or spray. Allow it to saturate and do its job for at least a half hour.

**6 LAUNDER AS USUAL.** Wash the garment as you normally would. Check for the stain by holding the garment up to a bright light before tumble drying. Use caution here: If the stain isn't gone, the heat can set it permanently.

**7 ONE LAST BLAST.** If you still see a shadow of the stain, re-treat with stain remover, and let it sit overnight before laundering again.

**8 USE BLEACH.** If the garment is white or light colored (and you've tested it for colorfastness), use a mild bleaching agent. Try hydrogen peroxide, white vinegar, or lemon juice dabbed on with a damp sponge. Allow it to work for at least an hour, then relaunder.

In the early 1800s, enterprising salesmen like Archibald Miles and Dr. John Cook Bennett sold ketchup in pill form. It was touted as a medicine against certain ailments such as jaundice, diarrhea, and dyspepsia.

## Five More Common Stains (and How to Remove Them)

**1. Blood.** If the stain is new, soak the stained area in cold water with a splash of ammonia for a half hour. If the stain has set, dampen it with warm water, then pour on some unseasoned meat tenderizer, gently dabbing it into the stain. Cover with a lightly dampened, clean washcloth or dish towel and leave it overnight. The next day, rinse with warm water mixed with a few spoonfuls of ammonia, and launder as normal. Do not tumble dry until you check the stain. If the stain persists, carefully apply bleach (test for colorfastness!) or dry-cleaning solvent from the inside of the garment, and allow it to soak for an hour. Wash again as usual.

**2. Coffee.** Soak immediately in lukewarm water. Gently dab the stain with laundry detergent or a vinegar-and-water solution. Launder the garment in the hottest water recommended for the fabric, check to see if the stain is gone, and repeat as needed. Avoid bar soap, which can set the stain permanently.

**3. Ring-around-the-collar.** Rub white chalk over the stain. It will lift out some of the oils in the collar, then you can launder as normal. (It won't remove the stain completely,

like bleach does, but it will improve the look.) If the stain persists, launder again, using a cup of distilled white vinegar in the rinse water. If that doesn't work, launder again adding a cup of baking soda in the main wash. If the stain remains, and the shirt is white or colorfast, use diluted bleach dabbed on with a sponge, then launder as normal.

**4. Ballpoint pen.** For ballpoint pen ink stains on your dress-shirt pockets, rinse the stain with glycerin, not water, at your earliest opportunity. Let the fabric soak for at least 10 minutes, up to an hour, then apply detergent mixed with water and add two or three drops of ammonia. Let the ammonia soak in for an hour, blotting occasionally. Rinse thoroughly. If the stain remains, dab on a solution of bleach and water, but only if the garment is white or colorfast.

**5. Crayon.** Scrape off the excess wax with a spoon, butter knife, or credit card. Lay the stained area face down on a white paper towel and cover the garment with another paper towel. Smooth a warm iron over the top paper towel. The heat will melt the greasy wax, which will be absorbed by the paper. Repeat the process, using fresh paper towels until no more stain transfers to the paper towel.

⤬ ⤬ ⤬ ⤬ ⤬ ⤬ ⤬ ⤬ ⤬ ⤬ ⤬ ⤬ ⤬ ⤬ ⤬ ⤬ ⤬ ⤬ ⤬ ⤬ ⤬ ⤬ ⤬ ⤬ ⤬ ⤬ ⤬

# TESTING FOR COLORFASTNESS

A garment that isn't colorfast may bleed its dye in the wash and stain other clothing. Luckily, it's easy to test colorfastness before washing. Simply soak the fabric in soapy (room temperature) water, and, after a half-hour or so, take it out and check for dye in the water. Set your garment on paper towels to dry. If no dye bleeds into the water or onto the towels, your garment is colorfast.

## A Glossary of Common Household Stain Removers, A to Z

**Ammonia.** Helps fade perspiration stains from light-colored and white shirts (see How to Remove Pit Stains from a White Shirt, page 170).

**Baking soda.** Removes odors and helps remove stains from chrome and stainless steel.

**Bleach.** Probably not your first line of defense, but bleach works well on faint, lingering stains (especially food or dirt marks) on white cotton.

**Cream of tartar.** Excellent on rust stains and food stains; mix it with lemon juice to make a paste.

**Denture-cleaning tablets.** Great for food stains on table-cloths; stretch the fabric over a bowl, dissolve one tablet in ½ cup water, and pour directly on stain or spot.

**Dishwasher detergent (liquid).** Use this for any stain that you might normally bleach (heed fabric-care labels regarding bleaching).

**Dishwashing liquid.** Great spot-treater; use undiluted on tough stains like chocolate.

**Glycerin.** Effective on sticky stains such as tree sap, gum, and tar; also useful for juice and condiment stains (such as those from ketchup and mustard).

**Hydrogen peroxide.** Very effective on blood stains and stains on bathroom tile and grout; excellent for bleaching out stains on white clothes (mix 1 cup hydrogen peroxide with 1 tablespoon ammonia for a great liquid stain-fighter).

**Laundry detergent.** Seems obvious, right? When you cannot launder clothing right away, spot-treat with some detergent rubbed directly onto the spot.

**Lemon juice.** Use this to bleach spots out of white cotton and linen; use as a pre-laundry stain treatment for diaper, baby formula, grass, and tomato sauce stains.

**Meat tenderizer (unseasoned *only*).** Mix with very cold water to treat protein-based stains such as blood, milk, broth, or egg yolk stains.

**Mineral spirits.** An intense treatment for very stubborn greases like asphalt, tar, and motor oil; do not use on fragile or delicate materials; wash clothing thoroughly after treatment and air-dry.

**Rubbing alcohol.** Great for grass stains, shoe polish stains, and plant-based food stains.

**Salt.** Combine salt and lemon juice to tackle mildew stains; sprinkle salt on red wine or grape juice stains to prohibit setting until fabric can be laundered.

**Seltzer.** Safe for any fabric or surface that can be treated with water; prohibits stains from setting and brings staining agents to the surface of fabrics.

**Shampoo.** Use this for dirt and mud stains, cosmetic stains, and ring-around-the-collar.

**Shaving cream.** Shaving cream is basically aerated soap; use it to immediately spot-treat stains by applying it to fabric, then rubbing the area with a wet washcloth.

**Sunlight.** Not only will sunlight naturally bleach and fade stains, but it is germicidal; laying cottons and other fabrics out in direct sunlight can fade scorch marks, blood stains, mildew stains, and diaper stains; if you have the space, consider dragging mattresses out on hot, dry, sunny days to whiten and refresh them.

**WD-40 lubricant.** A great spot-treater for oil-based stains such as lipstick, salad dressing, meaty sauce, or motor oil.

**White vinegar.** Use undiluted as a spot-treater on suede items; on other fabrics, it's great for beer or berry stains.

# #85
# HOW TO WASH A LOAD OF CLOTHES

Learning how to do your own laundry will save you a boatload of money in drop-off fees and dry-cleaning bills. As with cooking, if you are a beginner, this task can seem daunting. My advice: Roll up your sleeves and learn. It's a basic life skill, like cleaning a toilet or shopping for groceries. Mom won't be willing to do it forever, and even if she is, sooner or later every grown-up should take charge of his or her own underwear!

## How Big Is a Load of Laundry?

"But the lid stayed shut!" isn't a good reason to stuff your entire pile of dirties into a washing machine. Industry professionals judge load size by weight. The definition of "a load" of laundry depends on the capacity or size of the machine at hand.

Small-capacity top loaders may hold only 5 to 6 pounds of dirty clothing. Medium-capacity top loaders can usually handle 7 to 8 pounds. Large-capacity top loaders can clean about 12 to 15 pounds per load.

Front-loading washing machines can hold as much as 18 pounds of clothing. To find out how much your loads weigh, first weigh yourself, then weigh yourself holding a load of laundry in a lightweight, collapsible hamper. Subtract your weight from the weight of you *and* the laundry. Some average weights of common laundry items:

⚜ Twin-size quilt: 3 to 5 pounds

⚜ Complete child's outfit: 2 to 4 pounds

⚜ Complete adult's outfit: 3 to 5 pounds

⚜ Traditional square laundry basket (filled): 18 to 25 pounds

⚜ Standing rectangular hamper (filled): 21 to 28 pounds

⚜ Down or synthetic comforter: 2 to 7 pounds

**1 SORT AND SEPARATE INTO PILES.** Divide by weight, level of dirtiness, type of fabric, and color. Categories can include whites, delicates, towels, noncolorfast garments, jeans, and blankets (see How to Sort a Heap of Dirty Clothes for Washing, page 154).

**2 PICK A PILE AND PREPARE.** Scan items for stains and spot-treat them. Empty pockets of coins, papers, and folding money. (Look twice for pens. Ink will ruin the laundry forever.) Turn colorfast items and garments with heavy hardware (like metal buttons) inside out.

**3 ADD THE DETERGENTS.** Carefully follow instructions on both the machine and the product packaging for adding detergent to the machine. For example, if you're using a high-efficiency washer and your local water is soft, you should use the bare minimum of detergent recommended. Use more for standard washers with hard water. Add liquid softener and bleach to the appropriate dispensers, if needed. Dilute bleach with water, using a separate plastic container, and taking extreme care not to splash it on surfaces or the clothes you're wearing. Never pour laundry chemicals directly onto dirty garments.

**4 SELECT THE APPROPRIATE** water temperature. Colors require cold water. Whites, under most circumstances, can be washed in warm water. When bleaching cotton whites, like sheets, use hot. To kill mites, lice, or bedbugs on bed linens (especially pillowcases), use the hottest water available.

**5 HONOR THE CARE LABELS.** Follow the recommendations and set the temperature on the machine.

**6 ADD THE CLOTHING TO THE** machine. Don't overstuff it or the clothes won't get clean.

**7 WHEN THE CYCLE IS COMPLETE,** prepare to dry. After the garments are washed, shake out individual items so they'll dry more quickly, with fewer wrinkles.

**8 BEFORE DRYING, CLEAN AND** empty the lint trap. Do this every time. Dryer lint is responsible for a great number of house fires. Make this a mindless habit and a step you never skip.

**9 DRY LIKE CLOTHES TOGETHER.** Dry heavy towels with other heavy towels. Dry jeans with jeans. Otherwise, your heavy items won't dry and your delicate items will wear out faster.

**10 GET 'EM WHILE THEY'RE** hot. Don't let warm clothing languish in the dryer: Remove it as soon as possible once the cycle is done. Not doing so will leave you with a pile of wrinkled clothes.

**11 FOLD AND HANG.** The same applies here. The sooner you neatly fold or hang your garments, the fewer creases you'll face when you dress.

# #86 HOW TO WASH A DOWN COMFORTER

Recommendations say to wash your down comforter every two years. Good-quality comforters are expensive, and they can last a lifetime when well cared for. Follow these tips before tossing yours in the washer.

**1 DON'T USE YOUR TOP-LOADING** machine. With a capacity of around 12 to 15 pounds, it usually can't handle a queen- or king-size comforter. Often, the agitator will be in the way. For better results, use a high-efficiency front loader with no agitator. Take it to a laundromat if necessary.

**2 TREAT IT GENTLY.** Use cold water and set the machine to the gentle or delicate cycle. Down feathers are fragile, so use a mild soap without enzymes, such as Ivory Snow or Woolite. Do not use fabric softener in the water, as it will cause feathers to clump and not dry properly, leading to unpleasant odor.

**3 SPINNING AND DAMPNESS.** When the wash cycle is over, check the comforter for wetness. Generally, running it through one or two more spin cycles is a good idea. If it still feels soaking wet, wrap it in beach towels and wring it out to remove excess water. Once it's damp but not soaking wet, it is ready to be dried.

**4 DRY AND DRY AGAIN.** Use a large dryer for comforters: the bigger, the better. Dry on low heat to avoid damaging the feathers. It will take longer, but it will preserve your investment. Once the comforter is halfway dry, throw a clean tennis ball in the dryer to fluff the down.

# #87

# HOW TO CARE FOR A SWEATER

Mating socks and tossing underwear in a drawer are great beginner skills to master along the road to learning proper maintenance of your own wardrobe. Caring for a sweater is a more sophisticated undertaking. Here are my favorite tips and tricks.

**1** **SWEATERS SHOULD BE FOLDED.** Don't hang sweaters on hangers or hooks because the fibers will become misshapen, stretched out, and eventually damaged permanently.

**2** **SWEATERS SHOULD BE** groomed regularly. Use a clean baby hairbrush to remove lint, hair, and dandruff. To get rid of pills, purchase a small shaver or handheld depilling machine. Or, you can pick them off by hand, one at a time.

**3** **SWEATERS REQUIRE TIMELY** repairs. When zippers break, buttons are lost or broken, or holes appear, make the fixes right away. Unchecked holes will only get bigger.

**4** **SWEATERS LAST LONGER WHEN** dry-cleaned or hand-washed. This is especially true of sweaters made from animal fibers.

**5** **SWEATERS REQUIRE CAREFUL** off-season storage. Stow your sweaters in dust-proof bags layered with sachets of lavender, cedar chips, or dried bay leaves to keep them smelling nice. Make sure all sweaters are freshly washed and completely dry before storing to keep unseen stains from becoming permanent. These tips will also help to deprive hungry moths of meals.

# #88 HOW TO SAVE A SHRUNKEN SWEATER

If you pull a suddenly shrunken sweater out of the wash, don't panic. You may have to chalk it up to a laundry learning experience, but don't give up hope immediately. With emergency care, there's a chance of saving it.

**1** **FIRST, WHEN YOU SPOT THE** horrifyingly transformed garment after the wash cycle, *never* put it in the dryer. That will seal the deal. Instead, gently squeeze it in a thick towel to absorb moisture.

**2** **NEXT, FILL YOUR SINK WITH** cold water, and add 1 to 2 tablespoons of baby shampoo and ½ to 1 tablespoon of gentle conditioner. Gently swish the sweater in the water to thoroughly saturate all fibers. Soak for an hour, then remove it without rinsing.

**3** **USING A PIECE OF CORK BOARD** and stainless-steel push pins, gently begin stretching the sweater back into its original shape and size and pinning it into place. Check on it every few hours to reshape as needed.

# #89 HOW TO DRY SWEATERS ON A DRYING RACK

Few people seem to have the patience anymore to care for sweaters, but if you take the time to wash and dry them properly, you will be richly rewarded. By following these basic tenets of sweater care, you'll extend the life of your favorite cotton or woolly wonder exponentially.

**1 ACQUIRE A DRYING RACK.** The ideal racks for drying and reshaping sweaters are stackable, made of plastic mesh, and have the surface area of a card table. They are inexpensive, fold and store easily, and can be found at any housewares store. Airflow is optimal, so allow space for sweaters to be stretched out to their full length and width.

**2 AVOID RACKS WITH BARS.** Racks with bars are great for underwear and socks, cotton items to be ironed later, and synthetics like nylon and polyester. When you lay sweaters across the bars, however, lumps and bumps will form.

**3 ALWAYS LAY FLAT.** First, water and wood don't mix. You run the risk of ruining nice hangers by dampening them. The rule of thumb: *Never* hang a wet sweater on *any* kind of hanger. The weight of the wet fibers will stretch the garment as it dries, leaving the shoulders stretched out. Not only will the sweater look odd on your body, but you will permanently damage the fibers.

✕ ✕ ✕ ✕ ✕ ✕ ✕ ✕ ✕ ✕ ✕ ✕ ✕ ✕ ✕ ✕ ✕ ✕ ✕ ✕ ✕ ✕ ✕ ✕ ✕ ✕ ✕ ✕ ✕ ✕ ✕ ✕ ✕ ✕ ✕

## REJUVENATE SWEATER CUFFS, NECKLINES, OR WAISTBANDS

Don't send your hard-worn, favorite sweater to the charity shop without giving this refresher a try.

1. Attack only one problem at a time. Choose cuffs, neckline, or waistband.

2. Pour boiling water into a large, heatproof bowl set on a secure surface (a heatproof kitchen counter, covered with a damp dish towel to anchor the bowl will do).

3. Dampen the cuffs (or neckline or waistband) of your cotton, alpaca, cashmere, wool, or angora sweater. Use your fingers to pinch together the fibers and to reshape as desired.

4. Use a blow dryer on the cuffs (or neckline or waistband) as you shape them.

# #90 HOW TO RESHAPE A SWEATER

**1 AFTER WASHING, GENTLY REMOVE** excess water by squeezing the sweater in an absorbent towel and laying it out flat on a new, dry towel (or two, if needed, to accommodate your sweater with both arms extended), spread out on a waterproof surface, such as a plastic-topped card table, or net drying rack.

**2 WITH VERY GENTLE STRETCHING** and manipulation, arrange the sweater into its original shape. Gently push the ribbing together at the neckband, wristbands, and waistband. Fasten all zippers or buttons. If there is a tab collar, fold it into place. Dry a removable belt separately and spread out an attached belt to its full length.

**3 ALLOW THE SWEATER TO DRY FOR** a full day and night.

**4 SWITCH OUT THE OLD TOWELS** for new, dry ones. Flip your sweater over and arrange it into shape, and allow it to dry for another 24 hours.

**5 IF THE SWEATER IS STILL DAMP,** replace the towels and shape it again.

**6 ONCE YOUR SWEATER IS BONE** dry, without a hint of dampness, fold and store it.

# #91
# HOW TO FOLD A FITTED SHEET
## (and Storage Tips for Other Items)

Folding fitted sheets neatly, with their rounded, elasticized corners, is hardly intuitive. Don't despair and resign yourself to living with lumpy, balled-up bed sheets in your linen closet. The method for taming them involves tucking the corners into each other to achieve a crisp, flat rectangle. This technique is written for a right-handed person. Lefties: Simply do it in reverse.

**1** **FOR SHEETS WITH THE FEWEST** possible wrinkles, fold them straight from the dryer. Grab a warm, fitted sheet and shake it out.

**2** **STAND HOLDING THE SHEET BY** the two adjacent corners of one of the shorter edges. (The bulk of the sheet will be lying against your body as you fold.) With the sheet inside out, insert one hand into each of these two corner "pockets."

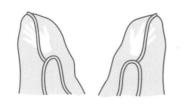

**3** **BRING YOUR RIGHT HAND** across to your left and fold the corner in your right hand over the one in your left, enveloping it.

**4** **NEXT, REACH DOWN AND OVER** and pick up the corner hanging in front (this is the third corner). Bring that corner up and fold it over the two corners you're holding in your left hand. The visible corner will be inside out.

**5** **BRING UP THE FOURTH CORNER** and fold it over the others. It should not be inside out. You want the correct side to be visible. This corner will envelop the three others.

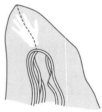

**6** **NEXT, LAY THE FOLDED SHEET** on a clean, flat surface and straighten it out.

**7** FOLD IN THE TWO EDGES IN SO the elastic is hidden.

**8** NOW, FOLD THE SHEET INTO a rectangle.

**9** FOLD THE SHEET INTO AS MANY rectangles as you require until it's the size you prefer.

## How to Safely Store Off-Season Garments

We all know the drill: In the spring, pack up your sweaters, coats, and ski wear and bring out the shorts, bathing suits, and Hawaiian shirts. In the winter, reverse. To preserve your clothing for years to come, it's imperative to store off-season garments with care to avoid damage from insects, mildew, and mold.

Here are a few basic rules about storing any type of clothing:

⊹ Wash and thoroughly dry all fabric items before storing.

⊹ Never store clothes or blankets in plastic bags or airtight containers.

⊹ Wicker hampers or wooden and rattan trunks are best for storing garments and linens because they breathe.

## SAFE STORAGE OF SOME COMMON FABRIC TYPES

*Leather and suede.* **Store in a dry closet. When possible, cover the garments with clean, white cotton sheets. For soft leathers, store garments flat and wrap them in white tissue or sheets.**

*Rayon.* **Store flat, wrapped in white tissue paper or sheets, or hang garments, and cover with sheets.**

*Linen.* **Roll the items, don't fold, and cover with sheets.**

*Silks and knits.* **Store flat, wrapped in tissue paper or sheets.**

*Fur.* **Professional cold storage is the way to go for expensive or valuable garments. If you must store at home, be sure to store in a cool, dark place, and cover with sheets.**

*Wool.* **Lay flat and cover with sheets. Store in a cool, dark place.**

The average person spends one third of his or her life in bed. After a lifespan of 75 years, that amounts to 25 years, or 9,125 days, of sleep.

# #92
# HOW TO IRON A SHIRT

My mother saw the advent of synthetic fabrics as freedom from tyranny. Give her a nice drip-dry blouse and some wrinkle-free bed sheets, and she's one happy camper.

I, on the other hand, relish the feel (and smell!) of a crisp, white dress shirt or Egyptian cotton linens. I don't mind putting in the work now and then because the payoff in luxury can be worth it. Sometimes, I actually like to iron. Repetitive and relaxing, it puts me in a zenlike state enhanced by the heat of the steam and the aroma of the starch.

Most people hate ironing because they simply don't know how. The good news is you can learn quickly and say good-bye to scorching skirts and ironing wrinkles into pillowcases.

**1 PREHEAT YOUR IRON.** Warm the iron using the manufacturer's listed settings. The highest temps are usually for linen and cotton. Start with the collar. Lay the shirt on your ironing board, front facing downward. Spray the collar with water, and with starch, if desired. Next, iron the underside, moving the iron from one point to the other with a pressing motion. Smooth wrinkles to the bottom of the collar as they appear. When finished, flip the shirt and repeat on the top side.

**2 THE CUFFS.** Start by unbuttoning the cuff. Now, iron the inside of the cuff, moving all wrinkles to the edges. Repeat on the outside. Next, carefully iron around the buttons, even on the back side, where the button is sewn on. Ironing over buttons leaves a mark.

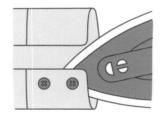

**3 SHIRT FRONT.** Start around the buttons, carefully working the iron point around the buttons on the placket. Move back up to the top of the shoulder and work your way down the front of the shirt, pressing the iron in long, smooth strokes. Repeat on the other side. It's worth spending a bit more time on the front placket and areas near the collar to make them perfect, especially if you're not planning on wearing a jacket over the shirt.

**Completed in 1902, the Flatiron Building in New York City is so named because of its unusual triangular shape that resembles an early clothing iron.**

**4** **SHIRT BACK.** Lay the shirt flat on the ironing board, front facing downward. It works best to position one of the sleeve heads into the square edge of the board. That presents half of the back of the shirt smoothly. After completing the first half, you can neatly slide the shirt over to iron the remaining half. Start at the top by ironing the yoke (back shoulder area), then slowly slide the iron down to the bottom of the shirt with a pressing motion. If your shirt features a center box pleat, iron around it. After the back of the shirt is wrinkle-free, reposition it lengthwise on the board, and take a few seconds to iron the pleat back in so it looks crisp.

**5** **SLEEVES.** I prefer to iron sleeves last. This is the trickiest part of ironing a shirt. The issue here is that you're ironing a double layer of fabric. If one of the layers is bunched, you'll be ironing wrinkles into your shirt. Take the time needed to make sure your fabric is fully flat and aligned before applying heat. Using your fingertips, pick up one sleeve by the seam and lay the whole sleeve (along with the better part of the shirt) flat on the ironing board. If there are visible creases on the top of the sleeve, left over from previous ironing, match them again. This ensures that you'll have a single crease line. Start ironing at the shoulder and armpit area, where the sleeve is sewn onto the shirt, then smooth down with a pressing motion toward the cuff. Next, turn the sleeve over and repeat the motion. Finally, repeat the process with the other sleeve.

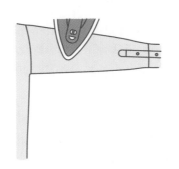

**6** **SPOT CHECK, AND HANG.** When you're finished with a shirt, do a quick check of the key areas. If you see wrinkles, touch up the shirt, and then hang it on a hanger immediately. Make sure the shirt has plenty of space: Pressing hot shirts together causes them to form new wrinkles that will set as they cool.

## Why Iron a Dress Shirt?

No-iron and wrinkle-resistant shirts are widely available at reasonable prices. So, why on earth would anyone iron a dress shirt? There are many reasons.

**Because you hate no-iron shirts.** Many people don't like the feel or smell of no-iron shirts. Manufacturers treat them with a formaldehyde resin bath, which makes the cellulose strands bond to one another at the molecular level. Those chemicals emit an odor when these shirts are new, and the smell can last through several washings. Generally, no-iron shirts are stiff and a bit scratchy instead of being soft and slick. Unlike pure, untreated cotton, these processed fabrics don't breathe well. If you like the feel of cotton, you have to iron because wrinkly cotton shirts are a sartorial no-no.

**Details matter.** Wearing wrinkled clothes sends a signal that you lack discipline and attention. Even in a casual work environment, wrinkles convey sloppiness.

**Customized shirt care.** You know your own clothes best. Wine stain on the placket? Unlike some dry cleaners, you'll work to get it out before you apply heat. Prefer stiff collars and cuffs? You'll starch.

**Cotton shirts at the ready.** Those who use dry cleaners inevitably find themselves stuck without a favorite (or any!) pressed shirt when they need one. Do it at home and take back control.

**Your shirts will last longer.** Hand-washing combined with hang-drying help prevent wear on the fabric as well as shrinkage. Dry cleaners can stretch and abuse shirts, as evidenced by the small tears and missing and broken buttons on the ones I've received back. Wash and press your own shirts, and you can concentrate on the stained portions and heavily soiled areas, like collars and cuffs, and ease off on the less-abused areas.

**It's kind of fun.** Seriously, though—it's easier than you think, and when you do it right, the rhythm can lull you into a calm state. Plus, there's a true sense of pride and accomplishment that comes from turning a large wrinkled pile of shirts into a small, orderly stack.

## Getting Started: Tools of the Trade

**1. A well-built iron.** Irons have come a long way since your great-grandmother had to heat two cast-iron triangles on the woodstove, alternating them to always use the hot one. You don't have to spend a large

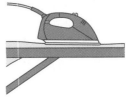

amount to get a high-quality one, but here are some things to look for:

✢ *A smooth, solid soleplate.* This is the flat metal plate that heats up and is pressed onto fabric. Look for aluminum-coated cast iron, solid steel, or titanium-coated metal. Poor-quality irons can heat unevenly or have burrs and nicks, leading to damage.

✢ *High heat.* Some natural fabrics, such as cotton and linen, require high heat to loosen and reform the shape of the fibers. A very hot iron helps slash ironing time in half, so that you're not passing the hot iron over the same spots repeatedly, stretching and wearing the fibers. The heat from the soleplate helps the steam heat up and maintain a high temperature.

✢ *A steaming device.* Hot moisture attacks the toughest wrinkles, smoothing them with minimal work by helping distribute heat throughout fibers.

**2. A good ironing board.** Make sure it has a large surface area, is easy to fold without pinching fingers, and is adjustable to a height that is comfortable for your back. Invest in a good pad and cover, and replace these as they wear or become soiled.

**3. A spray bottle.** Fill this with water, and water only, and dedicate it to your ironing. I advise purchasing a new bottle. When using a spray bottle that previously contained a cleaning product, residues can transfer to garments. Have it at the ready for spot-spraying or in cases when you disable the steam feature.

**4. Spray starch.** Use starch in moderation, if you like crisp-to-stiff shirts. Overdoing it can stifle cotton's breathability and encourage wrinkling. Spray lightly, too, because excessive application can cause visible flaking of the starch. If you don't like aerosol cans, make your own by dissolving 1 tablespoon of cornstarch in 2 cups of hot water, and spraying it from a pump bottle.

# #93
# HOW TO HAND-WASH

In my great-grandmother's day, Monday was Wash Day. Back then, laundry was washed by hand with lye soap, and you were lucky if you had a crank roller to wring out heavy items like sheets and quilts.

Today's hand-washing isn't the backbreaking chore it once was. Generally, we reserve it for pricey and delicate items, to save money on dry cleaning, or occasionally, we find ourselves short of skivvies, so we do it to avoid wearing a bathing suit under our work clothes. Before you (or your delicates!) take the plunge, here's the least of what you need to know.

**1 START WITH A CLEAN SINK OR** bathtub. Scrub off scum, then make sure all cleanser has been washed down the drain. Bleaches and dyes from cleaning products could discolor or weaken your garments.

**2 KEEP YOUR COOL.** Wash in lukewarm water, cooler than bathwater. Never use hot water—colors could bleed, and fibers could shrink.

**3 MILD, NOT WILD.** Choose detergent formulated especially for delicates. It's not harsh enough to fade colors, and it dissolves in cool to warm water.

**4 KEEP IT LIGHT.** Save hand-washing for smaller, lightweight items. Lingerie, silk shirts, scarves, and dress socks are all good candidates. Don't use this method for towels and jeans—for one thing, you'll use gallons of water for a clean rinse, and for another, they require days to line dry.

**5 ASSESS THE RISK.** If a laundry item is marked "dry-clean only," you could ruin it forever by saturating it with water or the wrong soap.

**6 HAND-WASHING DOES NOT** equal the delicate cycle. Agitation causes stress on a garment. Even front-loading machines toss and tumble. For sturdier items, such as synthetic nightgowns or top-quality men's undershirts, washing on delicate with similar colors and fabrics shouldn't cause harm. If you have doubts, wash them in the sink.

**7 RINSE, THEN REPEAT.** This step takes time and effort. You'll need to fully drain the sink or bathtub, and then refill it with water twice—if not several—times. Add ¼ cup distilled white vinegar to a sinkful of rinse water or 1 cup to a bathtub of rinse water to help dissolve detergent residue. Tip: You'll need to rinse at least twice after that to wash away the vinegar so you don't smell like a dyed Easter egg.

**8 SQUEEZE, DON'T WRING.** After the final rinse, use your hands to push and squeeze out the water without twisting your garment. Twisting stretches and pulls fibers, leaving you with saggy clothes. Then lay the garment out on a drying rack or a clean towel (if using a towel, you'll have to switch out damp for dry one or two times).

## When to Dry-Clean

"Do I really have to schlep to the dry cleaner and shell out the big bucks to clean this garment?" you may ask yourself. Maybe not. Many garments labeled "dry-clean only" can be safely washed on the gentle cycle or by hand (see How to Hand-Wash, page 167). Use these steps to help you decide.

**Decipher and interpret the care label.** Manufacturers are required to list only one way to clean a garment. If the label says "dry-clean only," it's smartest to obey it. If it says "dry-clean," that means that is the recommended method, but not necessarily the only method.

**Examine and think about the fabric.** Unless the label says something different, dry-clean silk, acetate, suede, leather, velvet, wool, and taffeta. Cotton, rayon, linen, microfiber, cashmere, polyester, acrylic, and nylon can generally be washed at home on the delicate cycle, or by hand. First check for colorfastness: Moisten a cotton ball with mild detergent and a little water and dab it on a hidden seam or hem to see if any dye comes off. Wash noncolorfast items with like colors always.

**Consider and test the detailing.** Some care instructions are for the fabric only—not the embellishments or hardware, which may be attached at another factory. This is why some labels come with caveats, such as "exclusive of decorative trim." Before attempting to wash items featuring beads, sequins, fringe, or tassels, make sure they are sewn on (not glued) and colorfast.

## Dry-Cleaning Myths Debunked

Dry cleaners may seem like magicians, but once you know the inside scoop, you'll feel more empowered when making the decision "to dry-clean, or not to dry-clean."

**Dry-cleaning is not dry.** Water isn't used, but a toxic cocktail of other wet chemicals is. The most common liquid used is perchlorethylene, and even so-called "green" dry cleaners use liquid carbon dioxide and silicone fluids.

**Men's shirts aren't necessarily dry-cleaned.** The placard outside the cleaners may say, "Men's shirts: $2.50," but that doesn't mean they're being dry-cleaned. They're laundered in a big machine with detergent, starched if requested, then pressed and dried on a shirt form.

**You'll never get reimbursed for ruined clothes.** Not fully, anyway. Legally, the dry cleaner can cite depreciation. In some cases, you'll get the full value if the garment is less than four months old. If your garment is older than two years, expect no more than 20 percent of its original value.

**Say good-bye to lost clothes.** Once gone, they're likely gone forever. In many cases, your garments will be sent home in a bundle with another customer who won't bother to return them. Wash irreplaceable items at home or pay top dollar at a reputable white-glove or French cleaner.

**Some stains are permanent.** Dry cleaners have tricks, but they aren't magic. The key is to rush stained garments in as soon as possible. Natural fabrics like silk, cotton, and wool absorb and retain stains over time.

**Only half of complaints are resolved.** According to the Better Business Bureau, in 2009, only half of consumer complaints to dry cleaners were even addressed. It's a good reason to take more control of your clothing's care.

# #94 HOW TO HAND-WASH CURTAINS

You may want to consider taking very expensive drapes with heavy liners to a dry cleaner. Same goes with antique drapes or with intricate pleating or folds. But for many styles—if the drapes and the liners are both made of washable fabrics like cottons or sturdy synthetics—hand-washing is a perfectly good (and economical) choice. Here's how to do it right.

**1 BEFORE YOU WASH, VACUUM.** Most vacuum cleaners have hoses and brush attachments for cleaning curtains and drapes. Suck out the dust before washing.

**2 REMOVE ANY ORNAMENTS** or trim. If they're tacked on, carefully remove them with a seam ripper and tack them back on after washing the curtains.

**3 USING A STURDY LADDER OR STEP** stool, remove the curtains from their rods.

**4 REMOVE ALL HARDWARE, SUCH** as pins and hooks, and store in a zip-top bag or shoebox.

**5 HAND-WASH THE DRAPES IN** lukewarm water with mild detergent. Sheers and light panels will fit, one at a time, in the sink. Larger panels may require the bathtub.

**6 AFTER SEVERAL RINSES, SQUEEZE** (don't wring) the panels. If your dryer has a no-heat setting, you can tumble the panels one at a time. Do not use heat. Dry panels on a clothesline or stretch them across drying racks.

**7 PRESS PANELS WITH A COOL** iron, using a press cloth to avoid scorching or leaving a "sheen" on the fabric.

**8 REATTACH ANY HARDWARE YOU** removed, and hang the panels while still the slightest bit damp: The weight of the fabric will help pull out the wrinkles and allow the drapes to dry as they are meant to hang.

---

They that wash on
  Monday
Have all the week to dry;
They that wash on
  Tuesday
Are not so much awry;
They that wash on
  Wednesday
Are not so much to
  blame;

They that wash on
  Thursday,
Wash for very shame;
They that wash on Friday,
Must only wash in need;
And they that wash on
  Saturday,
Are lazy folks indeed.

—from *A Book of Nursery Rhymes*
by Charles Welsh

# #95
# HOW TO MAKE A DINGY T-SHIRT WHITE AGAIN

Bright white clothing screams "clean." Even if it's not seen and admired by the public, a fresh, new undershirt, pair of socks, or set of underclothes can make a person feel more confident, adding a little spring to the step. And don't forget the warning handed down by my Mom and mothers like her about clean underwear! Making sure your whites are sparkling falls under the category of "plan for every inevitability." The good news is that you don't have to constantly toss and rebuy basics to maintain your bright whites. With a little know-how, you can keep them shimmering long past their expected expiration date. Here are some tips for keeping your whites bright.

**1 SORTING.** Keep whites separate. Sort whites from colored clothes. Dye molecules will bleed into the water and subtly tint your whites.

**2 TREATING STAINS.** Attack spills and smudges immediately. Use a solid stain stick or spot-treating liquid and carefully follow package directions because all fabrics and all stains are unique.

**3 LOADING THE WASHER.** Pack the washing machine loosely, allowing enough room for the dirt to lift out and float away rather than be redeposited.

**4 BLEACHING.** Don't always reach for the chlorine bleach. Overusing it on pure cotton fabrics can increase yellowing. An oxygen-based bleach will generally do the job and is safer in most cases. Use chlorine bleach every fourth wash and follow package directions carefully.

**5 RECALIBRATING HARD WATER.** Because minerals deposit on whites, leaving them looking dingy, if your local water is hard, invest in a water-softening device or add softener to each load.

**6 LINE DRYING.** When possible, allow whites to dry in the sun. Ultraviolet rays, although undesirable for humans, help whiten already white fabric.

## How to Remove Pit Stains from a White Shirt

It's hard to exude confidence when you're sporting half-moon rings in the underarm region. These unsightly patches can be caused by the aluminum chloride used in many deodorants or from minerals in your perspiration. Try these tips to keep your white shirts brilliant, from collar to hem.

⌗ Wash the shirt with every wear, even if it looks and smells clean. Chemicals from products, and your own body, can get to work over time. In other words, while your shirt languishes in the hamper, the stain will grow.

For newish stains, turn the shirt inside out, rinse the pits, then allow the shirt to soak in cold water.

If soaking doesn't remove a new stain, use a solution of 2 tablespoons ammonia to 1 cup water. Pour the solution onto the stain and let it rest for an hour. Then wash the garment on the hottest setting the care label recommends. Then allow the shirt to air-dry because the heat of the dryer will set the stain. Repeat if necessary.

If ammonia doesn't remove a new stain, try chlorine bleach (use only color-safe bleach on light pastel colors). Use a solution of 1 tablespoon bleach to 1 cup water. Pour the solution onto the stain and let it rest for an hour. Wash the garment on the hottest setting the care label recommends. Allow it to air-dry and repeat if necessary.

For older stains, pour distilled white vinegar onto the stain and let it rest for an hour. Wash the garment on the hottest setting the care label recommends. Allow the shirt to air-dry because the heat of the dryer will set the stain. Repeat if necessary.

## Little Laundry Facts

To keep black clothes black, use an antifade detergent. This keeps the chlorine in the water from fading the dye. When washing, turn the garment inside out and hang or lay it flat to dry.

To reduce odors, add ½ cup baking soda to 1 gallon water and presoak the garments for at least three hours. Then, as you machine wash them, add ½ cup distilled white vinegar to the rinse cycle.

To disinfect your washing machine, pour in ½ cup mouthwash and run it through a regular cycle using hot water.

To dry clothes in a hurry, twirl the load on the spin cycle in the washer an extra time. Then, when putting them in the dryer, throw in a dry towel or two. Finally, as with a pot of rice, don't open the dryer door to keep checking if it's done.

# #96 HOW TO FOLD A T-SHIRT THE RETAIL-STORE WAY

**1 WITH THE SHIRT FACE DOWN IN** front of you, fold the sleeves, one at a time, in to the center. If the sleeves are too long (as they will be on an adult shirt, but not necessarily on a child's shirt), fold each sleeve down toward the bottom hem after they've been folded in to the center.

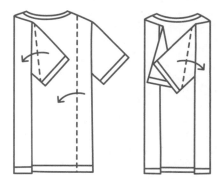

**2 FOLD THE BOTTOM HALF UP** toward the shoulders, making a rectangle.

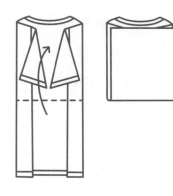

**3 STACK SHIRTS IN LARGE** rectangles or, if you prefer, bring the bottom fold up to the shoulders once more to make a smaller base rectangle. Once you start folding T-shirts in this simple clean line, it's hard to go back to anything more elaborate.

# DOMESTIC ARTS

General housecleaning has to be done at some time or another, or eventually the dust bunnies gather into a herd and start peeping out at you from under the beds and furniture. It's true that these days people seem less inclined to spend a lot of time mopping and polishing than perhaps they once did. As with most things, domestic work is inclined to fill the space allotted to it, so once you start looking, you'll always find more dirt that needs cleaning. How scrupulous you want to be is entirely up to you, but here's how to do the basics and delve into the nooks and crannies.

# DOMESTIC ARTS TOOL KIT

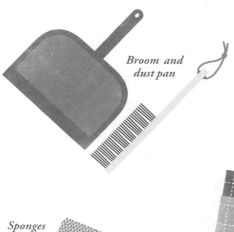

*Broom and dust pan*

*Baking soda*

*All-purpose surface cleaner*

*Paper towels and soft cotton rags*

*Sponges*

*Window cleaner*

*Vinegar*

*Vacuum*

*Mop and bucket*

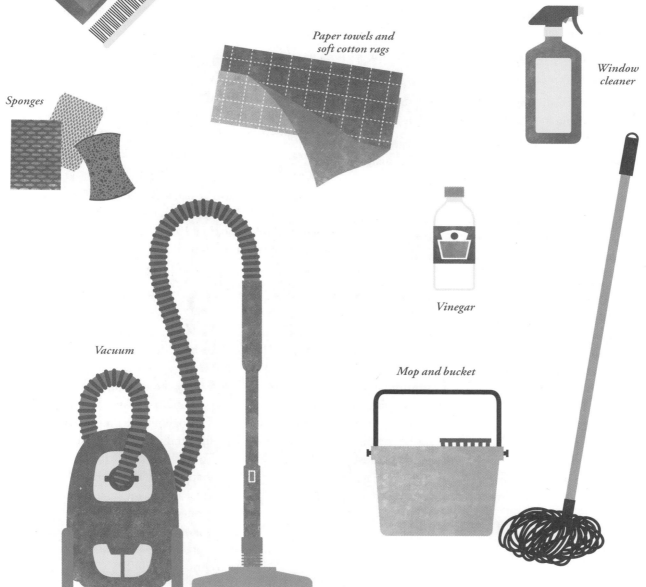

# #97
# HOW TO HAND-WASH A PLATE

Even those who have a dishwasher will occasionally have to wash dishes by hand: After a big Thanksgiving meal, when your dishwasher breaks down, when you run out of dishwasher detergent, or in a vacation cabin or hotel suite.

No one I know enjoys hand-washing dishes, but do it we must for hygienic and aesthetic reasons. Take heart; when done properly, this chore can be accomplished efficiently and effectively with a minimum of dishpan hands and floor puddles. Here's what to remember.

⚜ **Roll up your sleeves.** This is always a good idea, unless, of course, you're already wearing short sleeves.

⚜ **Tie on an apron.** This is optional, but I prefer to wear one because it allows me to work faster without fear of soaking my clothes.

⚜ **Don rubber gloves.** As with an apron, this is optional, but for those with dry skin or other problematic skin conditions, it's a good idea.

⚜ **Set up a dish tub.** If you don't have one, go out and buy a proper plastic dish tub because this inexpensive tool will save you not only time but also water and energy

(and therefore, money). If you don't have a dish tub now, use your largest plastic bowl. Set up a drying rack. Again, if you don't have one, buy one. They're easy to find and cheap. I suggest a metal one with a metal run-off tray; they resist mildew better than rubber or vinyl-covered ones.

⚜ **Scrape first.** Thoroughly scrape plates and dishes into the trash or compost bin before you start.

⚜ **Have hand lotion at the ready.** I keep a large bottle on my windowsill. (Tip: It also encourages good health practices during cooking. Family members are more likely to scrub up when soothing lotion is available.)

**1 SOAK POTS AND PANS.** If dirties include pots, pans, or casserole dishes crusted with baked-on food, fill them individually with hot water, then set them out of the way on the counter to soak about 15 minutes. If you have encrusted spatulas, ladles, or other small items, drop these in the larger vessels to soak. For heatproof pots and casseroles lined with baked-on food, fill with water and set on a low burner to simmer off the matter.

**2 FILL THE SINK WITH WATER.** Use the hottest water possible without burning yourself (rubber gloves help with this) and add one or two squeezes of dishwashing liquid. The hotter the water, the more likely glass and silverware will dry without marks or streaks. Don't fill the tub all the way to the top because dirty dishes will displace water, causing overflow.

**3 WASH IN THE RIGHT ORDER.** Begin with the crystal, then glasses, glass plates, and dessert dishes. Move on to flatware, then servingware, then serving dishes. Empty the soaking water from pots and pans, and wash them last. Throughout the process, empty your sink and refresh the water as needed. To wash, immerse the dishes in the soapy water, then scrub off grease, sauce, and food with a kitchen brush, sponge, or steel wool pad. (Steel wool is abrasive—don't use it on delicate items made of crystal, porcelain, china, or stainless steel.)

**4** **RINSE THE DISHES.** As you finish scrubbing each item, rinse it off under the running tap in groups of six or seven items at a time. Use lukewarm water. Begin with the outsides of glasses, and the backs of plates and bowls. Rinse the eating surfaces last. Alternatively, you can fill the sink with lukewarm water and immerse the items, refreshing the rinse water as needed.

**5** **CHECK THE DISHES.** After you rinse each item, double-check for residue. Any remaining sauce or food will be fairly obvious, but it's a good practice to remove your gloves and check with your fingers to ensure that all grease has been removed. Rewash stubborn soil from unclean pieces. If dairy products or starchy residues (such as flour, cornstarch, or gravy) remain, wash again using cold water because hot water forms a chemical reaction that causes gumminess. For heavily soiled pots, pour in kosher salt and scrub with paper towels before repeating the washing process.

**6** **DRY THE DISHES.** Once you're sure each dish is clean, let it rest on your rack (or dish towels) to air-dry. Stack bowls and glasses upside down so water drains instead of pooling. If you are ready to put dishes away immediately, you can hand dry them with a dish towel, one item at a time. Don't use bath towels or hand towels because they'll leave lint behind. If you can, recruit a friend or family member to help you dry items and to get them neatly put away.

×  ×  ×  ×  ×  ×  ×  ×  ×  ×  ×  ×  ×  ×  ×  ×  ×  ×  ×  ×  ×  ×  ×  ×  ×  ×  ×  ×  ×  ×  ×  ×  ×  ×  ×  ×  ×

## SUPER SECRETS FOR DOING THE DISHES

There are secrets to making any chore seem less daunting. Here are five to keep in mind when you're the one in charge of setting the rules around the kitchen sink.

• **Wash dishes immediately after meals.** Never let dishes pile up or sit in a sink overnight. It isn't going to get any easier or any more fun. Trust me. Just do it!

• **Have every household member stick to one cup or glass.** Rinse it between uses and set it aside. Washing twenty cups and glasses a day is time-consuming and wastes resources.

• **Use good-quality dish soap.** For cutting grease, it really is worth the extra pennies to buy Dawn.

• **Don't throw sharp knives into soapy water.** Soak them in their own bowl or dishpan, or wash them by hand under the tap and put them away immediately. Better safe than sorry.

• **Don't stack heavy casseroles or pots on top of fragile glasses or dishware.** This seems obvious, but it's tempting to take the risk when you're surrounded by dirty dishes after a big party. Work slowly and steadily, and make good choices. Remember the old riddle: How do you eat an elephant? One bite at a time!

**In a 2015 study, Swedish researchers determined that children were 40 percent less likely to develop allergies if their families hand-washed their dishes.**

# #98 HOW TO LOAD A DISHWASHER

I lived many blissful years of married life without a dishwasher, without feeling slighted. Once our family grew to include our two sons, I decided it was time for this labor-saving device. Not counting the days my babies were born, I'd say that the arrival of my dishwasher was one of the happiest days of my life! Of course, that's an exaggeration, but I won't lie—I do love it.

From the get-go, however, my husband hovered over me as I stacked the dishes, telling me what to put where. I'd walk away, and he'd restack the whole load! I decided to get the real skinny on how it should be done. And I'm happy to share.

**1 PROVIDED YOUR DISHWASHER** was made in the last ten years, you don't need to rinse the dishes first. In most cases, scraping should be enough. Water temperatures are higher, spray power is stronger, and rack design and sprayer placement are now very effective.

**2 LOAD IT UP.** Generally the rule is heavy on bottom and light on top. But there are many nuances to the game of dishwasher Tetris. See How to Load a Dishwasher David's Way, opposite.

**3 SELECT A DETERGENT AND RINSE** agent. Use tabs or all-in-one packs. They contain premeasured detergent and add a rinse agent for you so you don't need to remember to fill the reservoir. If you choose not to use a premeasured pack, there's no difference between liquid and powder. You will, however, need to use a rinse agent. This will get food debris off dishes effectively and reduce spotting on glasses.

**4 IF YOU HAVE A DISPOSAL, RUN IT** and make sure it's clear before starting the dishwasher. Dishwashers usually share a drain pipe with the sink, so you don't want anything blocking in there.

**5 MAKE SURE SPINNING ARMS ARE** not blocked and that no small items have fallen into the drain area. Close the door and select a cycle based on what you're washing and the manufacturer's instructions.

Scrape, but don't pre-wash! Your dishes need to be dirty in order for the detergent to clean them properly. (Enzymes in the detergent are made to cling to food particles.) Plus, pre-washing can waste up to 6,000 extra gallons of water per year.

## How to Load a Dishwasher David's Way (aka "The Right Way")

⚜ Scrape first. Use a brush or spatula for stubborn bits.

⚜ Put pots, pans, and heavy-duty casseroles on the bottom rack, open side down.

⚜ Insert plates in the slots in the bottom rack, facing center. If they lean, lean them inward. Make sure there are spaces in between so sprayers can do their job.

⚜ Glasses, crockery, and delicate items go on the top rack—don't position them with the prongs inside the items. Instead, use the prongs to hold them in place like fences. When possible, stack bowls on an incline.

⚜ Yes, even wineglasses, all but the super-thin type, can be dishwashed. Either lower the top rack to make space for the stems or make sure they don't butt up against other dishes. Even crystal can go in, if your dishwasher features a crystal mode or a temperature setting under 149° F.

⚜ Plastic items like storage bowls with lids go on top. Heating elements on the bottom might melt them.

⚜ Don't overpack the cutlery basket. Knife points and fork tines should go heads down for safety. Make sure spoon surfaces are separated so water can flow between them. (Mix different types in the same compartments so they don't nest.) Lay very long pieces in the upper basket, as they can impede the spray arm. Put small teaspoons in the special spoon basket if your model has one.

⚜ Lay long serving utensils, like tongs and spatulas, in the upper basket. Make sure spoons and ladles face down so they don't collect water.

⚜ Put cutting boards or baking trays in the outermost slots of the bottom rack.

✕✕✕✕✕✕✕✕✕✕✕✕✕✕✕✕✕✕✕✕✕✕✕✕✕✕✕✕✕✕✕✕✕✕✕✕✕✕✕✕✕✕✕✕✕✕✕✕✕✕✕✕✕✕✕

# BETCHA DIDN'T KNOW . . .

**Y**ou can put silver flatware in the dishwasher! But there are a few rules to follow if you do:

• Rinse the pieces under the tap before loading them. This removes potentially damaging substances like lemon, vinegar, and salt, which could mar surfaces if the items are left sitting.

• Never put stainless steel with sterling or silverplate in the dishwasher. The two metals react with each other, and you'll do permanent damage to both.

• Hand-wash and dry sterling and silverplate at least three times before putting them through your dishwasher.

• When putting real silver in the dishwasher, use half the normal amount of detergent and make sure it contains no citrus or lemon additives. Don't worry—unless heavily soiled, your dishes will still come out clean.

• Pay special attention to knives. If your knives were made prior to World War II, then hand-wash them. Knives consist of two elements, the hollow, silver handle and the blade. High heat can melt the resin commonly used in antique knives that seals these components together.

• Skip the heated dry cycle when washing silver in the dishwasher. Take out the pieces and dry them by hand.

# #99
## HOW TO MOP A FLOOR

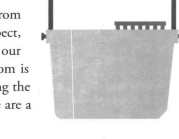

"**D**on't come in here, I just mopped!" is something I heard my mother shouting from inside the kitchen when I was a kid. Even then, I treated that warning with respect, and so did my siblings. We steered clear until drying time was over, leaving our muddy shoes on the mat. There's nothing like a floor you can eat off of to signal that a room is clean. Now that I'm in charge of my own floors, I'm the shouter. But I look forward to passing the mop handle on to my boys, just as soon as they're tall enough to wield it with aplomb. Here are a few lessons I plan to impart.

❖ **Sweep floors daily.** This protects floors from abrasions caused by feet walking across particles of debris. It also reduces your need to mop.

❖ **Some flooring, such as polyurethane-coated wood, can't handle harsh detergents.** When in doubt, consult the professional who installed it or the home-improvement store where you purchased it.

❖ **Old-fashioned hardwood floors shouldn't be mopped with water.** Instead, sweep with a broom and clean with a dust mop. Spot-clean stubborn areas with commercial hardwood cleaner or distilled white vinegar dissolved in a little bit of water, then wring out the mop or sponge until it's almost dry. If the floor is damp after cleaning, dry it with a soft towel.

❖ **When your sponge mop begins to crumble, chuck the head and buy a new one.** For rag or string mops, rinse and wring repeatedly, or throw in the washing machine.

❖ **Start with a clean bucket.** Refilling one that's less than sparkling sets you up to spread germs.

**1** BEFORE YOU START, GIVE THE floor its daily brush or sweep.

**2** CHECK FOR MARKS AND STAINS. If you find any, clean them up using the guide provided in "How to Tackle Stubborn Spills and Stains on Floors," opposite.

**3** FILL YOUR BUCKET WITH HOT water and mix in the quantity of floor cleaner specified on the cleaner's label.

**4** WRING THE MOP SO THAT IT'S not dripping, but barely damp. Wear rubber gloves and squeeze it out with your hands or buy a commercial bucket that includes a sturdy wringer.

**5** WORK THE ROOM STARTING from a corner, working backward rather than forward so you are not stepping on your cleanly mopped floor.

**6** EMPTY AND REFILL YOUR bucket with water and cleaner mixture as soon as the water starts to become dirty.

**7** IF THE ROOM YOU'RE MOPPING is a high-traffic room, dry the floor on your hands and knees with an old towel rather than waiting for it to air-dry.

## How to Tackle Stubborn Spills and Stains on Floors

Before you mop, survey the area for any of these common stains. Or, better, stay ahead of the game and attack these issues as they arise.

**Blood.** Wipe up any excess with paper towels. Then clean with a sponge dampened with very cold water. If the stain persists, sponge it with a solution of half ammonia and half very-cold water, making sure to blot excess water away with a clean towel.

**Crayon or wax.** Put a clean rag over the spot and iron with a warm iron. Next, rub the affected area with mineral spirits applied to a soft cloth. If dye from the candle or crayon persists, put on a pea-size dab of white toothpaste and rub gently with a soft, dry cloth.

**Ink.** If pooled, carefully dab up with a soft cloth (don't use paper towels because they may stick, making the mess worse). Then rub with a cloth dampened with warm water and Dawn dishwashing detergent.

**Oil.** Soak up the majority with lots of paper towels. Then saturate a soft cloth with dry cleaning fluid (you can buy this at a hardware store) and lay the cloth over the spill for 10 minutes. Next, wipe with a cloth barely dampened with distilled white vinegar and a squirt of Dawn dishwashing liquid. Dry the area with a clean cloth.

**Scuff marks.** First, try to erase them with a gum eraser. If stains persist, dab on a small amount of liquid floor wax and rub gently with a fine-gauge sandpaper. Sprinkle on a small amount of baking soda and rub with a sponge, dampened with hot water. Dry excess dampness with a clean cloth.

**Shoe polish.** Using a square of superfine steel wool, rub the area gently. Work very slowly because you are essentially sanding off the top layer. Then wipe with a cloth barely dampened with distilled white vinegar and dry with a clean cloth.

**Tar.** Fill a zip-top bag with ice cubes and lay it on the patch of tar. Then, using a plastic knife or spatula, scrape off the tar. If a fine layer remains, follow the directions for removing oil by using dry cleaning fluid.

**Urine.** Soak up the majority of the puddle with paper towels as soon as possible.

**Wine.** Rub the stain with a sponge barely dampened with warm water and Dawn dishwashing detergent. Then rub with a cloth dampened with denatured alcohol. Repeat the process as necessary, alternating between the two cleaners.

## Sweep First, Mop Later

Guess what happens when you try to mop an unswept floor? You make mud! Even if you think you know how to sweep, using the proper technique makes the job easier.

**Get a good broom.** Invest money in a good one, and when it starts to wear, replace it. For floors with lots of dirt or hunks of debris, consider a broom with a broad end, to cover more surface with fewer strokes. For lightly dirty floors, a dust mop will do the trick.

**Clear your space.** Sounds obvious, but lots of people try to "sweep around it." Trust me, the few minutes you spend decluttering pays off. You can finish the job in broad strokes instead of working around obstacles.

**Close off the area to pedestrians.** This includes pets.

**Start in the far corner and sweep toward the middle of the room, using overlapping strokes.** Pull the broom against the floor (and toward your body) to either the right or left, then lift it back to that edge in the opposite direction.

**Be sure the broom reaches into the angle of each corner.** It's important to be able to access all of the nooks and crannies where dirt accumulates.

**Working around the room, collect debris in small piles.** Leave them!

**When finished, use a dustpan and brush to collect the piles.** When you see a "line" of dirt left, turn the dustpan to the opposite angle and sweep it in the pan. If the lines aren't vanishing, wipe them up with a damp paper towel.

# #100
## HOW TO VACUUM

**V**acuuming. Informal surveys tell me that some people love it and some people loathe it. The lovers talk about the soothing hum that drowns out the noise of the day and the relaxation that comes with the repetitive motion. The haters say it's boring and takes too much time. Love it or hate it, we all have to do it.

**1** **VACUUMING SHOULD BE YOUR** last chore. Dust, clean mirrors, wipe down surfaces, and take down curtains and drapes *before* you vacuum. Any dust rustled up by other tasks will fall to the floor. You don't want to vacuum twice.

**2** **CLEAR THE WAY.** This sounds obvious, but I have stood and watched my sister vacuum around items ranging from a cardigan sweater to a pile of blocks. Pick up the clutter and your job will go faster.

**3** **USE A DETECTIVE'S EYE.** Now that you've cleared shoes and books, think smaller. Use your hands to pick up thumbtacks, balls of hair, gum wrappers, or pebbles. It's easy, and it will extend the life of your vacuum.

**4** **SURROUND THE AREA.** If you plan to vacuum a rug sitting on a wooden or linoleum floor, sweep those areas with a broom before starting the vacuum.

**5** **SCOPE OUT THE OUTLETS.** The less cord you have to let out, the less chance you'll have of knocking something over. Change outlets as you move from area to area.

**6** **START YOUR ENGINE.** Begin by the door and work your way across the room, going back and forth, overlapping each strip by a few inches. Don't push backward and forward, using short, tiny movements; this takes longer and requires more energy. Long, smooth strokes will achieve results.

**7** **CUTTING CORNERS.** If you have wall-to-wall carpet, you need to focus on the corners only every third or fourth vacuuming. You may need to use the wand or nozzle attachment for hard-to-reach parts. If your floor is a hard surface or wood, you may need to do this each time because of dust bunnies. Warning: Vacuums can scratch wood floors. Check and wipe down the vacuum's wheels before you begin to get rid of grit. Switch off the beater bar and work parallel to the planks.

**8** **SLOW DOWN AT THE FRINGES.** Vacuum rug fringes by moving the vacuum from the rug to the ends of the fringes (not the other direction), or the fringes may get sucked up and jam the vacuum's moving parts.

**9** **ACT FAST.** If you hear a loud or unusual noise, or if your self-propelling vacuum stops moving, shut it off immediately. When this happens, it's likely something is caught in your brush bar. Running the motor when there's a blockage is likely to burn it out.

## Vacuum FAQs

*How do I vacuum blinds?*
Use the brush attachment. A plain nozzle will scratch or chip them. Close the blinds so that they're flat. Vacuum across the slats, not up and down. Then reverse the slats and vacuum the other way.

*How do I vacuum curtains?*
Use the lowest suction setting and the upholstery attachment. Begin vacuuming at the top of the curtain and work your way down in overlapping "strips."

*How do I vacuum furniture?*
For upholstered pieces, use the upholstery attachment. Use the crevice tool attachment for corners, edges, and between cushions. Use the brush attachment for vinyl or leather furniture. To do cabinets or bookshelves, use either the dust brush or crevice tool attachment. I don't recommend vacuuming fine wood furniture because it's not worth the risk of scratching it. Do these pieces by hand with a dust cloth and a mild wood soap, if necessary. In general, however, avoid wetting or dampening wooden furniture. A wipe with a microfiber cloth may be all that's required to remove dust.

*Can I vacuum drawers?*
Yes! Especially cutlery drawers, where crumbs tend to collect. Remove the contents and use the wand or crevice tool attachment.

*Can I vacuum dust mites from my pillows?*
You can vacuum pillows with the soft brush attachment. Or you can place a pillow inside a thick plastic bag, and while holding the bag closed around the nozzle, suction all the air from the pillow. Afterward, refluff the pillow.

*Can I use my vacuum as an air freshener?*
To remove airborne dust, allergens, and odors from a room, remove the hose and leave the vacuum on for 15 minutes with the doors shut. This is a great practice after a big spring cleaning or if you've had a smoker in the house. Caution: Don't leave the vacuum on for extended periods, as you risk burning out the motor or starting a fire.

*How about the walls?*
Yes. Vacuuming is a great idea, especially before a thorough washing or painting. Use a brush attachment.

## What's Wrong with My Vacuum?

Here are the top four most likely diagnoses:

**1. Broken or loose belt, or broken brush roll.** The cleaning head of an upright or canister vacuum cleaner is equipped with a spinning brush roll that fluffs and moves the carpet fibers. The belt is connected to the vacuum's drive shaft and to the brush, thus spinning it. The movement of the carpet fibers loosens dirt and dust so the suction can capture it and move it to the dirt collector. A damaged brush roll can't agitate the carpet, and a broken or loosened belt will not spin the brush roll. At this point, the only action left is suction, making the vacuum far less effective.

**2. A clog in the bag or filter.** The bag collects dirt and dust sucked through the vacuum's hose. The bag also functions as a filter that the air passes through. When the bag is overfull, suction decreases. Bagless vacuums rely on filters to force air from the vacuum. Blocked, wet, and clogged bags and filters impede exhausted airflow, thus decreasing suction power.

**3. Clogged hose.** Upright vacuums rely on the hose to suck air from the cleaning head into the dirt collector. Clogged hoses have less air to pull dirt and dust from carpet fibers, upholstery, and other surfaces. Canister vacuum cleaners are particularly tricky because the hoses are often longer. It goes without saying: Air cannot flow through a clogged hose.

**4. Electrical failure.** The electric motor powers the fans used to provide airflow and to power the driveshaft that spins the brush roll. If electrical problems occur in the motor itself, you'll need a new motor or electrical trouble-shooting and repair performed by a qualified technician.

# #101
## HOW TO MAKE A BED

"What's the point of making my bed?" my teenage brother used to reason with my mother. "I'm just going to sleep in it again tonight." This argument did not fly with my father, whose military training included learning to make hospital corners and to pull a sheet taut enough to bounce a quarter.

I, for one, cannot stand to slide into an unmade bed. To my mind, a crisply made bed is a welcoming combination of style and comfort. Cozy comforters and bed linens, properly layered, result in a safe and dreamy refuge. In short, there's a lot more to making a bed than simply slapping on some sheets and blankets.

**1 START WITH YOUR BARE** mattress. Buy the best one you can afford. You'll be spending a lot of time on it. Make sure it's clean and fresh. I advise vacuuming it regularly, turning it (if it's not a pillow top), and occasionally laying it out in bright, direct sunlight if possible (see How to "Spring Clean," page 189).

**2 LAYER ON A MATTRESS COVER** or mattress pad. For one, it will prevent you from ever coming in direct contact with the cold, slippery mattress if your sheets come untucked. It also adds a layer of padding and wicking for comfort. Finally, it extends the life of your mattress by adding a line of defense against spills or stains.

**3 NEXT UP ARE THE SHEETS.** Because sheets directly touch your skin, you want to make sure they're soft and comforting; I

prefer cotton ones, with a high thread count. These are the most expensive option and require the most labor to care for (special washing and ironing), but I think they're worth it. Alternatively, you can seek out some budget-level poly-cotton blends that still feature breathability. Start by stretching the fitted sheet across the mattress, pulling the elastic hem all the way over the bottom edge of the mattress. Tuck in the sides and corners as tightly as possible.

**4 LAY THE FLAT SHEET ON TOP** with the top edge meeting the end of the mattress, and tuck the sides and bottoms under. I suggest making hospital corners (see Perfect Hospital Corners, opposite).

**5 LAYER ON A COZY BLANKET** for color, texture, and warmth. You can tuck this in just like you did with the sheet, or leave it hanging evenly over the sides.

**6 THE CROWNING GLORY IS THE** comforter, duvet, or bedspread. The top layer is your visual statement, so let it reflect your personality. This layer should tie the look of the linens together and complement other visual elements in the room. I suggest switching top covers seasonally. Having three or four of different weights and thicknesses also allows you to rotate them for washing.

**7 PILLOWS COME NEXT.** Choose feather or down for warmth and softness, or firmer synthetics for support. Replace pillows when you notice obvious signs of fraying or wear, and do it pre-emptively every year to discourage proliferation of allergy-causing mites. In addition to comfort and neck support, pillows can be decorative. Consider shams to tie your bed's look together; and square European-style pillows are great for adding a decorative touch that anchors the bedding to the headboard. Round bolster pillows make a grand statement and also serve as back support for reading in bed. Have fun with small, decorative throw pillows and use them as statement pieces.

×××××××××××××××××××××××××××××××××××××××

# PERFECT HOSPITAL CORNERS

**A** neatly made bed is like a gorgeously gift-wrapped box. If you love crawling into a fresh, finished bed, you'll want to learn the art of folding orderly hospital corners. For a fresh feel, and corners that stay tucked in, do this:

**1. Start by putting on the bottom sheet. Tightly secure the first corner, then move to the one diagonal to it. Pull firmly and secure. Repeat, pulling and tucking until you have a flat, taut surface.**

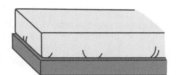

**2. Spread your top sheet (the flat sheet) over the bottom sheet, centering it. Make sure to pull it from the corners, then the sides, until it rests flat.**

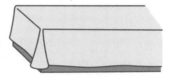

**3. Tuck the bottom edge of the sheet (by your feet) firmly under the bottom of the mattress, letting the sides hang down.**

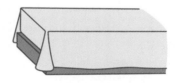

**4. On one hanging side, grasp the edge of the sheet about 12 to 18 inches from the foot of the bed. Pull it straight up to form a triangle. Then just lay it there. Tuck the end that drapes tightly underneath the mattress.**

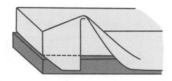

**5. Still leaving the triangle, tuck in the long part that hangs down on the sides.**

**6. Now, pick up the triangle and pull it straight down with a firm force, making a diagonal line.**

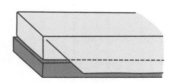

**7. Finally, tuck the triangle tightly under the mattress.**

# #102
## HOW TO START A BEDROOM ROUTINE

**F**or me, the bedroom is a refuge from the noise and chaos of the outside world. In order to relax my mind and body, I need my surroundings to be as free from chaos as possible. For that reason, I tidy daily. Doing a little bit each day keeps the chore from feeling insurmountable.

**1 MAKE THE BED.** (Obviously!)

**2 OPEN THE SHADES AND THE** window(s). Regardless of the season, I leave a window open for a short portion of the day. The fresh air makes the room smell good, and it promotes health.

**3 FOLD AND HANG ALL CLOTHES** (and put away jewelry, belts, and shoes). Dirty clothes go in the hamper.

**4 STRAIGHTEN THE BEDSIDE TABLE.** Put away jewelry, and arrange books or magazines.

**5 GO OVER SURFACES WITH A** microfiber cloth or a feather duster (this will make deep cleaning less frequent).

**6 SPOT-VACUUM THE FLOOR, IF** necessary, using a handheld model (the full vacuuming is done with the rest of the house).

# #103
## HOW TO HANG CURTAINS

So you've decided to dress your window! Congratulations. But get mentally prepared. That first decision just set off a chain of other decisions to consider: What style will you choose? How much coverage is ideal? What measurements are most important?

Curtains and drapes do a lot for a home. They ensure privacy, they keep out furniture-fading sunlight, they put the finishing touch on room décor, they make a room appear larger, and, depending on the season, they can block out or hold in heat and coolness. Here are some hints to help you navigate this unfamiliar terrain.

**1 DECIDE ON THE STYLE OF THE** window dressing. Some choices include floor-length formal drapes, informal tab-top curtains, or whimsical café-style curtains.

**2 FIGURE OUT WHERE YOU'LL** hang the rod. You might choose the customary 4 inches above the top of the window frame. Depending on whether the curtains have tucks, flat tops, tabs, or ruffles, you may choose to hang them higher or lower. For a tall, deep window, you could consider hanging the rod inside the window frame.

**3 DETERMINE THE LEVEL OF** coverage. A good rule of thumb is to extend the top of the curtain 4 inches above the top of the window frame, 2 inches to the sides of the window frame, and 2 inches below the bottom of the window frame. Choose dimensions based on how much privacy you require, how much light you want to block out, and whether you want the window to appear larger than it actually is for aesthetic reasons.

**4 NOW YOU CAN MEASURE!** Use a tape measure to measure from the curtain rod to the desired bottom point and from side to side. Double the side-to-side measurement so that you'll have enough fabric for full, gathered curtains. Now, measure the window. Take three sets of measurements: Measure the inside of the window frame, the outside of the window frame, and the frame itself. You may get to the store and decide to switch from one type of window dressing to another. Having all relevant measurements will save you a trip.

**5 PROCURE YOUR SUPPLIES.** Make sure the person helping you at the fabric or home-improvement store understands the difference between the projected dimensions of the curtains and the actual dimensions of the window. Have the dimensions of the actual frame on hand, too.

**Make windows look larger by hanging curtains above the top of the frame and letting them hang to the floor.**

### The Rod

As I mentioned earlier, the most common mount for a curtain rod is 4 inches higher than the top of the window frame, allowing the curtains to hang 2 inches below the bottom of the window frame. To give the illusion of a taller window, hang the rod 8 inches above the frame. For a very dramatic effect, you could opt to hang it all the way up to the molding by the ceiling. To give the illusion of width, extend the rod farther than the common 2 inches beyond each side, anywhere up to 6 inches. Unless your goal is to make a strong statement and buck convention, having a rod no wider than a third of the window-width makes for nice proportions.

### The Width

Most people like the look of curtains hanging in folds. You want to be generous with the amount of fabric, so the panels should be at least one and a half times the width of the window (or of the rod, if your goal is to give the illusion of a wider window). For a flatter, more modern look, measure your fabric at the width of the window, plus 1 inch on either side. For a luxurious, baroque look, measure the fabric at three times the window width.

ͯ ͯ ͯ ͯ ͯ ͯ ͯ ͯ ͯ ͯ ͯ ͯ ͯ ͯ ͯ ͯ ͯ ͯ ͯ ͯ ͯ ͯ ͯ ͯ ͯ ͯ ͯ ͯ ͯ ͯ ͯ ͯ

# NO-SEW CURTAINS

If you like the homespun look of plain linen, and hate to sew, have I got the curtain solution for you!

If you don't already know, drop cloths are available at hardware and home improvement stores, and they come hemmed on all four sides.

The very first thing you'll want to do is iron the fabric, so that it's crisp, flat, and stretched out. Then re-measure regardless of what the package says.

Drop cloths are commonly 6 feet by 9 feet. It's quite possible to make those dimensions work, especially for floor-length curtains with a bit of romantic, pooling fabric at the floor level. If you need to adjust the length, you can hem them quickly with iron-on hem tape (see How to Hem the No-Sew Way, page 128).

To affix your curtains to the rod, open the sides of the top hem and slide the rod through or purchase snap-on grommets or clip-on rings from any craft or fabric store.

To embellish, I suggest iron-on bric-a-brac that you can find at the same craft or fabric store!

### The Length

For floor-length drapes, measure from the top of the rod all the way to the floor, then subtract to allow for the hanging hardware. When purchasing premeasured drapes and curtains, bear in mind that the length given is from the top of the pocket into which the rod is inserted to the hemmed, bottom edge. When in doubt, round up. Hemming curtains is easier than lengthening them.

## The Care and Maintenance of Your Drapes and Curtains

In addition to the occasional machine washing or trips to the dry cleaner (see How to Hand-Wash Curtains, page 169), your drapes and curtains will last longer and look fresher if you follow these tips:

**Keep 'em dry.** Close the window when it's raining and don't subject curtains and drapes to direct steam, such as from a radiator or humidifier. Water stains can become permanent, as can mildew stains.

**Buddy up with blinds.** Even inexpensive plastic mini-blinds can help protect your curtains. In direct sunlight or under conditions of extreme heat, draw the blinds. This will keep fabric fibers in curtains, drapes from breaking down, and dyes from fading.

**Rotate!** If several of the windows in your room have the same dimensions and have identical curtains, swap them out. Conditions are different from window to window. Or keep several sets of curtains available in your linen closet for any given window. Rotating will not only make your favorites last longer, but it's also a great way to refresh the room's look from season to season.

**Shake 'em down.** Between vacuuming and washing, beat and shake your curtains (while they're still on the rod) to loosen dust and debris, and to rid them of minute mites. Do this with the windows open or with your vacuum set to "suction" with no hose attached (see How to Vacuum, page 180).

# #104
## HOW TO REMOVE GUM FROM A RUG

No matter how vigilant, tidy, or house-proud you might be, there will come a time when a stealthy piece of chewing gum will find a patch on your carpet or rug and take up residence. My advice is to take a deep breath and keep these tricks up your sleeve, not only for the gum, but also for some of the more stubborn staining culprits.

**1 FILL A ZIP-TOP FREEZER BAG** with ice. Lay it on the patch of gum and let it rest there at least 15 minutes.

**2 USING YOUR FINGERS AND** fingernails, pick as much of the freezing cold gum out of the carpet fibers as possible.

**3 REPEAT.** Freeze the gum again and use your hands to remove more gum. Smaller pieces should chip off as you pick through the fibers.

**4 POUR A GENEROUS AMOUNT OF** olive oil onto the corner of an absorbent rag or old dish towel. Dab it onto the gum patch, scrubbing as you do. Keep adding oil, but only by dabbing. Resist the temptation to pour oil directly onto the spot.

**5 USING A SERRATED-EDGED** knife, scrape at the spot to loosen gum particles. Alternate this with scrubbing with your lightly oiled cloth. Repeat until all of the gum is gone.

**6 YOU MIGHT BE THINKING,** *Now I have an oil stain instead of a gum stain!* You would be right. Cover the spot with baking soda and press it into the carpet fibers. Allow it to soak up the oil for at least 15 minutes.

**7 AFTER THE RESTING PERIOD,** use your hand to rub in even more baking soda. Vacuum up the oily baking soda.

**8 FINALLY, CLEAN THE AREA BY** dabbing it with a sponge soaked in a solution of warm water and a few drops of Dawn dishwashing liquid. Rinse and repeat as necessary until all the soap and oil are removed.

**9 DAB DRY WITH A CLEAN TOWEL,** then allow the area to air-dry fully.

×××××××××××××××××××××××××××××××××××××××××

## LIQUID SPILL? DON'T RUB OR SCRUB!

For a liquid spill, the first line of defense is soak and dab. When possible, place a layer of paper towels on top and allow physics to do the work. You want liquid to transfer to the place of least concentration (the clean towels) from the place of most concentration (the spill site). Pressure can force the staining agent deep into the rug's fibers.

# #105 HOW TO ERASE AN INK SPILL FROM CARPET

## Rubbing Alcohol Method

**1** **IMMEDIATELY DAB AT THE LIQUID** with paper towels, absorbing as much as you can without pressing.

**2** **SATURATE A RAG WITH RUBBING** alcohol and dab at the spot. Replace your rag and resaturate with alcohol as needed. You don't want to dab ink back onto the carpet.

**3** **REPEAT UNTIL THE INK HAS BEEN** fully removed.

## Lubricant Method

**1** **IMMEDIATELY DAB AT THE LIQUID** with paper towels, absorbing as much as you can without pressing.

**2** **GRAB A CAN OF SPRAY-ON** lubricant, such as WD-40. Test a small patch of carpet near an edge or under a piece of furniture. Spray it on, sponge with a solution of warm water and Dawn dishwashing detergent, and then rinse with another damp sponge. If it doesn't dry clean, proceed to Step 3.

**3** **SPRAY THE LUBRICANT ON THE** stain, covering it but without forming a pool. Let sit for 15 minutes.

**4** **USING A SPONGE SATURATED WITH** warm water and Dawn, dab at the spot. Change sponges and add more water as needed.

**5** **ONCE THE INK IS GONE, RINSE THE** area with clear, warm water, press a dry towel into the carpet to absorb dampness, and allow it to air-dry.

# #106 HOW TO REMOVE PET STAINS FROM CARPET
## (or, What to Do When You Love Spot, but Not "Spots")

They don't mean to make a mess! Really! Frustrating as pet stains and odors in your carpet may be, most people who love animals consider the cleanup to be a small price to pay in exchange for the cuteness and companionship. Here are three green ways to tackle the accidents.

**1** **DISTILLED WHITE VINEGAR.** Vinegar's acidity helps neutralize odors, making it a great option for dealing with fresh pet urine. Lightly dab and blot with clean paper towels. Remember: Don't rub or scrub! Using a solution of equal parts cold water and distilled white vinegar, sponge the soiled area. Wring and  repeat several times. When you're satisfied that the urine has been removed, blot the carpet with a thick, dry towel and allow it to fully air-dry.

**2** **BAKING SODA.** For old or dried urine spots, baking soda is the answer. Pour a generous pile on the spot and rub it in lightly with your (gloved) fingertips. Let it sit overnight, then vacuum it up. Caution: Pets may be tempted to play with or eat the pile. Overturn a large plastic bowl or a laundry basket over the area and weight it down with thick books.

**3** **SELTZER WATER.** The bubbling action in the seltzer is what makes it an effective stain fighter. Before pouring on a small amount of fizzy water, blot and dab urine stains with paper towels. Once the liquid has stopped fizzing, blot the spot again and repeat as necessary. For a fresh stain, this may be all the treatment you need. For old or set-in stains, consider this a pretreatment. Allow the carpet to dry, then treat with the baking soda method (Step 2).

# #107 THE POOP ON POOP

**H**andling another creature's waste is not at the top of anyone's wish list. Once you become a pet owner (or a parent!), however, duty trumps squeamishness.

**1** **GET YOUR TOOLS.** You will need rubber gloves, a dustpan, a scrub brush, and a paint scraper or spatula.

**2** **PUT ON RUBBER GLOVES.** (For the chemical and the ick factor!)

**3** **USE THE SCRAPER TO SCOOP THE** bulk of the feces into the dustpan.

**4** **DAB UP ANY EXCESS WASTE WITH** damp paper towels, taking care not to grind it into carpet fibers.

**5** **SPRAY THE STAIN WITH A** prewash laundry stain remover. It must be a product that's labeled "oxi-action," "oxygen power," or "oxygenated." Scrub it in with the scrub brush.

**6** **DAB THE AREA WITH A DAMP** sponge saturated with a solution of dishwashing liquid and cold water.

**7** **SPRAY AGAIN WITH LAUNDRY** prewash. Alternate as necessary.

**8** **DO THIS UNTIL THERE IS NO** visible stain. When finished, blot the area with a clean, dry towel and allow it to air-dry.

**9** **ONCE DRY, IF AN ODOR PERSISTS,** treat the area with distilled white vinegar or baking soda.

**10** **SOAK WHATEVER YOU USED** in a sink filled with a gallon of hot water, with 1 cup of bleach poured in. Take great care not to splash the solution on anything: Bleach discolors clothing, hair, and some countertops and flooring. Not to mention—it's really bad for your skin.

---

**Pets—dogs in particular—can provide many health benefits, ranging from reduced blood pressure to elevated seratonin and dopamine. Some studies have shown that dog owners are less likely to experience depression than those without pets.**

---

# #108
## HOW TO "SPRING CLEAN"

In the days before modern conveniences, the first warm weather made it possible to do a sweeping house-cleaning. After a long, hard winter, it must have felt great to throw open the windows and let the dust blow out, to wash walls down with water that didn't freeze, and to toss out your sour mattress ticking.

These days, most of us clean throughout the year, but there's no denying that the brighter sun and the longer days still invigorate us, filling us with the desire for a fresh start. Here are some suggestions for ways to kick off the warmest part of the year with renewed and refreshed surroundings.

## Kitchen

+ **Freezer.** Empty it completely and toss anything with freezer burn (grayish brown and dried-out). Dissolve 3 tablespoons baking soda in a quart of hot water. Using a soft, mesh sponge, wipe down the inside.

+ **Refrigerator.** Repeat the freezer-cleaning process detailed above, but toss anything growing a culture.

+ **Stove and oven.** Remove control knobs, burners, and spill catchers, and soak them in a sink of hot water, Dawn dishwashing detergent, and 1 tablespoon baking soda. Run the oven cleaning cycle or do it manually. Clean the stove top with nonabrasive scouring liquid.

+ **Countertop appliances.** Thoroughly clean the toaster oven, blender, coffeemaker, and food processor. Run removable parts through the dishwasher or soak them in a sink of hot water and dish soap.

+ **Behind the scenes.** Enlist help to pull out the stove and refrigerator. Vacuum, then mop around them. Vacuum out the refrigerator coils.

+ **Sink.** Soak the drain cover in a bowl of hot water and dish soap. Pour a box of baking soda into the drain and let it sit for an hour. Then pour in distilled white vinegar to loosen any clogs, followed by a whole kettle of boiling water down the drain to flush out grease and debris.

## Living Room

+ **Declutter.** Put away items where they belong (shoes to closets, school books to bedroom shelves, quilts to linen closets). Enlist the help of everyone in the household to make this a regular task, weekly, or, even better, daily.

+ **Shelves.** Dust knick-knacks and bookshelves. Remove each item, dust the shelves themselves, and then carefully dust each item before replacing.

+ **Rugs and carpets.** Shampoo or steam-clean the rugs and wall-to-wall carpet. Vacuuming and spot-cleaning are for maintenance. The big clean must be done regularly. Have antique or precious rugs professionally cleaned.

+ **Curtains and drapes.** Throw curtains in the laundry if their care labels indicate that it's safe. Send expensive drapes to the dry cleaner.

+ **Lamps.** Dust the bases and wipe off any greasy areas with a solution of hot water and distilled white vinegar, making sure to dry thoroughly with a clean towel. Dust or vacuum the shades.

+ **TVs and computer monitors.** Clean screens by wiping them down with a microfiber cloth lightly dampened with distilled water. Dust the plastic parts, then wipe down with a vinegar-and-water solution as needed, avoiding electronic components. Use compressed air to dust in crevices.

## Bathroom

+ **Medicine cabinet.** Toss expired medications and deteriorating cosmetics. Take inventory. Wipe down the interiors, then clean the mirrors.

+ **Fans and vents.** Take them apart with a screwdriver and soak individual pieces in a solution of hot water and Dawn dishwashing detergent.

+ **Shower curtain.** Replace the interior liner and machine wash the shower curtain.

+ **Towels and washcloths.** Make rags of the ones with frays or stains, or donate them to an animal shelter, where they'll be used for bedding.

+ **Floor.** Scrub the floor with a brush. A flick with a wet mop is fine for maintenance, but you'll need some elbow grease to really get the scum out of cracks and crevices.

+ **Drain.** Pour a box of baking soda into the drain and let it sit for an hour. Then pour a whole kettle of boiling water down the drain to flush out grease and debris.

+ **Showerhead.** De-scum the showerhead. If you can easily remove the head, soak it in a sink filled with a solution of half distilled white vinegar and half boiling water. Once the water has fully cooled, scrub it with a stiff brush. If you can't remove the showerhead, fill a heavy-duty zip-top freezer bag with vinegar and warm water and tie it to the pipe with kitchen twine or a rubber band. Let it hang there overnight. Remove the bag and scrub the showerhead with a stiff brush, taking care not to scratch the finish.

## Bedroom

+ **Mattress.** Strip the mattress of bedding and lay it in the sun on a clean blanket in the backyard (if you have one!). Mark which side was last facing up; if your mattress is not a pillow top, flip it.

+ **Pillows.** Machine wash them, if possible. Most down- and fiber-filled pillows can go through the wash (check the label). Don't overstuff the machine; run one or two pillows through per cycle, using gentle detergent. Make sure all pillows are completely dry to avoid mildew.

+ **Dressers and armoires.** Remove all items from the interior. Vacuum and dust inside cabinets and drawers.

+ **Bed linens.** Wash pillow shams, the mattress pad, the bed skirt, and the duvet cover. Check labels; send anything not machine washable to the dry cleaner.

+ **Windows.** Use a bucket filled with warm water and a drop of dish soap, and a soft, microfiber cloth. Be sure to do the sills and frames. Finish by washing the panes with a nonstreaking glass cleaner.

+ **Blinds and curtains.** Vacuum blinds using your vacuum's wand attachment and machine wash curtains or send them to the dry cleaner.

## Closets

+ **Take inventory and declutter.** Go through each item in your closet. Decide if you are going to keep, donate, or trash the contents, one piece at a time. For items you are keeping stored away, make a list of the contents and whereabouts.

+ **Seasonal clothing.** Rotate seasonal clothing and store what's not needed.

+ **Boxes and trunks.** Label the contents on all sides, as well as on the top.

+ **Regroup.** Organize your clothes by color, type, or use.

+ **Shelves.** Remove all items and clean as needed, vacuum and dust the shelves, then reshelve the items.

+ **Floor.** Vacuum and mop the floor.

## Around the House

+ **Metal fixtures.** Clean and polish all brass and metal fixtures, including outdoor doorknobs, the door knocker, pot and pan racks, and finials.

+ **Wood.** Using proper wood soap and wax, clean fine woods, including banisters, finials, and art pieces.

+ **Wall hangings.** Remove mirrors, wall art, and photos from the wall. Dust around them, clean the frames, and then clean the glass.

+ **Air-conditioning filters.** If you don't have disposable filters, gently pull out each filter and rinse it with warm water in the bathtub. For spot-cleaning, use a small brush and some dish soap diluted in hot water. Allow them to dry, then pop them back into place.

+ **Light switches.** Fill a bucket with a gallon of hot water, a drop of dishwashing detergent, and ½ cup white vinegar. Wipe down every switch and switch plate in the house.

+ **Doorknobs.** Fill a bucket with hot water and household cleaner, following the instructions on the bottle. Wipe down every doorknob inside the house.

# LIFE SKILLS

**T**here's more to running a home than cooking and cleaning, laundry, and (occasionally) sewing. You may have to write things such as checks and thank-you notes, invite friends or family over for food, set a table, and perhaps even get dressed for a fancy event. Some life skills are simply acquired over time by seeing things happen in the homes of others, but here's a general overview of some of the basics and also a crash course on a few of the little grace notes for the finishing touches of pleasant living.

# #109
## HOW TO MAKE A HOUSEHOLD BUDGET

If the word *budget* makes you want to take to your bed and turn off your phone, you're not alone. "I don't want to be told what I can and cannot do with my money," you might say. But the fact of the matter is that a budget is your key to feeling calm and happy in relation to your money. If you take a deep breath and read on, you'll see that a budget isn't Big Brother or a straitjacket. It's a tool designed to help you live your life with as little stress, fear, and worry as possible. Here are some guidelines to keep in mind:

**Know you're in control.** Repeat: I am the boss of me. If the idea of taking your head out of the sand and creating a budget makes you uncomfortable or scared, remind yourself that you are the final word. You don't *have* to carry through with adhering to it, but information is power. Once you know what there is to know, you are free to ignore the whole idea.

**Keep it simple.** My husband loves the idea of Excel spreadsheets and Quicken. Gadgets and apps excite him. I'm the opposite. I still enjoy my Rolodex and my pen and notebook. If you're a techno-geek, great! Use the tools. If not, don't put the obstacle of learning the program or software in your way. Use an old-fashioned sheet of paper.

**Identify a goal or dream.** Decide what would make you happy. Paying off a student loan? Buying a car? A down payment on a house? Having zero credit card debt? Keeping the prize in mind will help you stick to your budget.

**Commit to a trial period.** For me, the idea of doing something—or anything—forever is overwhelming. It makes me not want to start. As with exercising, eating healthfully, or keeping a clean house, I hold myself accountable for only short periods. Then, if I like what I'm doing, I re-up. Sometimes, a new practice becomes a lifelong habit.

**1** WRITE DOWN YOUR TOTAL monthly income. For freelancers and project workers, this may be trickier, and you may have to estimate. Look at your monthly income over the last six months to gauge best- and worst-case scenarios for the future.

**2** SEPARATE YOUR SPENDING into fixed, variable, and discretionary spending categories.

In one column identify essential fixed expenses, such as rent and mortgage payments, car insurance, medical insurance, cable bills, and student loan payments. These payments will be the exact same amount each billing cycle.

In another, list your monthly essential but variable expenses, such as utilities, phone bills, groceries, gasoline expenditures, credit card payments, clothing costs, car maintenance, household repair, medication, and medical bills. Try to round off numbers to the nearest $10 if possible, or $50 if more breadth is needed. Base your estimations on past bills, if you have them.

✢ In a third column, list reasonable amounts for nonessential expenses. These include gifts for birthdays and holidays, eating out, entertainment, hobbies, personal care, and travel. Check old credit card statements by the month to ground yourself in actual numbers of dollars spent.

**3** **ATTACK DEBT FIRST.** The bottom line is that your money isn't your money if you're in debt. If you're reeling from the weight of credit card bills or other debt, a budget can help you see how to dig your way out. Overbudget so that you are always paying more than the minimum on credit cards. If you have extra money from another category at the end of the month, make extra payments to reduce debt. If you have a serious debt problem, you may need the help of a credit counseling agency. Beware, though: Some purport to be helpful and instead prey on the indebted. Confirm their authenticity through the National Foundation for Credit Counseling or the Association of Independent Consumer Credit Counseling Agencies.

**4** **BUILD IN A BUFFER.** What was the amount of your highest-ever utility bill? Write that number into your monthly budget. Also budget amounts for emergencies and, if you have enough, for "mad money" to be spent without any questions asked or eyebrows raised. With that covered, you're likely to feel more comfortable investing a designated amount monthly. This investment could simply mean putting $10 into a savings account. Do not, however, invest large amounts of money if you are in debt. Look for places to cut without pain. This is personal. For one woman, giving up her latte on the way to the office would make every day feel like torture. She might, however, be fine with eating out less. Another may not be able to fathom buying nonorganic meat but would be happy to give up premium channels on cable. The idea here is to decrease spending without feeling deprived.

**5** **FOLLOW THE PLAN AS CLOSELY** as possible for several months and analyze the outcome. Although "forever" is too long, you will need to give the plan a chance to play out. After a reasonable amount of time, reassess. Are you paying down debt or at least not incurring new debt? Are you paying bills on time without robbing Peter to pay Paul? Have you banked or saved any money? Has it been painful, tolerable, or exhilarating?

The life expectancy of an American one dollar bill is about 18 to 22 months—coins, however, can remain in circulation as long as a quarter century.

## BUDGETING TIPS AND TRICKS

**S**ticking to a budget reduces stress and helps personal relationships. Financial issues can cause families and couples to fight, but being in control and knowing the facts about money and spending can bring peace.

• For each expense, label an envelope in a cardboard box (or use hanging files or a foldover binder). Put the cash for each category in its proper place. There's nothing like a hands-on illustration to bring the cold, hard facts home.

• Pay cash for everything for at least one month. This gives you the real-world sense that your money isn't just an idea.

• Instead of surfing the Internet nightly, or plopping down in front of the tube, go through newspapers and circulars and look for coupons to clip. There are TV shows and websites dedicated to this money-saving practice. Many people get a thrill out of the "game" of couponing.

# #110
## HOW TO SET THE TABLE FOR A FANCY FORMAL DINNER

Special occasions, such as engagement announcements, anniversary and birthday dinners, and holiday feasts call for something fancier than the traditional place setting. Although today's customs allow for more individual creativity than in the past, there are some basic rules. Once you learn them, you can observe them or bend them as you like.

## The Basic Layout

The place setting wasn't devised as a puzzle or a test. It's based on logic and grew out of rhyme and reason. Utensils to be used first are laid on the outside. Diners work their way inward as courses are served and cleared.

The main dinner plate is right in front of the diner. Glasses and stemware are placed above the dinner plate and to the right because the majority of diners are right-handed and glasses are reached for repeatedly. Bread plates are placed above the dinner plate and to the left. The setup makes it easy to eat without much movement, which could lead to spills and breaks.

## Setting the Table

Here is the traditional formula for a basic "cover" or place setting, in order of setup. Remember, you aren't just setting the table, you're setting the tone for the event.

**1 CHARGER AND DINNER PLATE** (or "service plate"). First, put down the charger plate. A charger is a plate larger than the dinner plate and is used to dress up the table. Ideas about when to clear the charger vary. Sometimes, chargers are removed as guests are seated. It is becoming more common for charger plates to remain on the table during the service of soups and first courses, to act as a base on which food-bearing plates and bowls will sit. If the design of the chargers complements the design of the dinner plates, they may remain on the table throughout the courses of the meal. Charger plates are, however, always removed before serving dessert. If your dishware is already formal or pleasing, and you choose not to use chargers, lay out the dinner plate only.

**2 SOUP BOWL.** Center it on top of the charger and/or dinner plate.

**3 BREAD PLATE.** Place this above and to the left of the charger or dinner plate. Lay the bread knife on it, facing the blade tip away from the charger. It should be horizontal, lining up with the edge of the table.

**4 COFFEE CUP.** Place this, on its saucer, slightly below and to the left of the bread plate.

**5 FORKS AND NAPKIN.** To the left of the dinner plate, working from the edge of the plate outward, lay the dinner fork, the fish fork, and then the salad fork (or rearrange to match the order of your courses). Next to the salad fork, lay the rectangular napkin. Note: All flatware should align with the bottom of the plate.

**6** **SPOONS AND KNIFE.** To the right of the dinner plate, working from the edge of the plate outward, lay the dinner knife, fish knife, and salad knife (blades facing the plate), and the teaspoon. If you have a soup course, put a soup spoon on the far right. If your courses move in a different order, rearrange so the last knife used is on the inside.

**7** **GLASSES AND STEMWARE.** Above the spoons and knife, to the right of the plate, set the water glass on the inside (closest to the bread plate) and two wineglasses beside it, grouping the two together. Just above the wineglasses, set a Champagne glass.

**8** **DESSERT SPOON AND FORK.** Place these horizontally above the dinner plate, with the spoon on top with its handle facing to the right; the fork sits below with its handle facing left.

# When electricity was first invented, not all households could afford it. Even if you could, it was considered polite to avoid boasting. To make guests feel comfortable, hosts kept charred candle wicks on the tables so that no one could be singled out as having more affluence.

## A Word on Tablecloths

Like a bedspread, the tablecloth is the icing on the cake. It unifies the table settings and the décor of the room. On a practical level, the tablecloth can protect the table itself and dampen the noise at crowded or lively parties. Here are some points to consider as you choose tablecloths for various occasions:

✧ **Overhang.** For a formal dinner, a deep and dramatic overhang is the order of the day. A drop of 10 to 15 inches will allow it to rest in guests' laps. For a relaxed, casual dinner, a drop of 10 inches is appropriate.

✧ **Silence cloth.** The silence cloth is used underneath the decorative tablecloth to give it a fluffy, drapey, luxurious effect. Silence cloths are commercially available in materials such as felt, foam-backed vinyl, wool, and quilted cotton, but you can easily make them yourself because they simply require cutting and measuring—no hemming.

✧ **The basic tablecloth.** If you buy only one, get it in a solid color that matches or complements your dinnerware and accent pieces. Remember, the more precious the fabric, the more care you'll have to take with spills and splashes. Some very nice tablecloths are sold in poly-cotton blends and are machine washable. For Grandma's heirloom lace or linen, however, you're looking at a trip to the dry cleaner after each event.

## At the Center of It All

Nothing indicates the mood of a festive meal more than the centerpiece. If there's a horn of plenty on the table, you know it's Thanksgiving. With centerpieces, you are limited only by your imagination—and the height of your guests. Don't stack anything on the table that might prevent easy eye contact during conversation.

Although you can buy lovely centerpieces at home goods stores, here are some fun DIY alternatives:

✧ **Floating the idea.** Use fruit in a glass bowl or large vase. Try using lemons for a cheerful spring luncheon or create a tableau of plums, blueberries, and red grapes floating in water for a romantic deep-winter's dinner.

✧ **Falling for flowers and leaves.** Spread apart the leaves of small purple and green cabbages, and plunge stems of flowers into the centers. Or invert various sizes of bowls, drape them with ivy, fall leaves, or bunches of grapes, and place pomegranates or squash on top.

✧ **Stack it.** Use a flat platter or plate with a rim, and pile it high with pinecones, palm fronds, or anything that suits the theme.

✕ ✕ ✕ ✕ ✕ ✕ ✕ ✕ ✕ ✕ ✕ ✕ ✕ ✕ ✕ ✕ ✕ ✕ ✕ ✕ ✕ ✕ ✕ ✕ ✕ ✕ ✕ ✕ ✕ ✕ ✕ ✕ ✕ ✕ ✕ ✕ ✕ ✕ ✕ ✕ ✕ ✕ ✕ ✕ ✕ ✕ ✕ ✕ ✕

# TIPS FOR A SUCCESSFUL DINNER

Hosting can be stressful, but with a few advanced considerations your dinner can be a memorable—and enjoyable—evening. Here are a few tips (keeping in mind of course that, as with all matters of etiquette, your guests' comfort trumps any rule).

• If you're having more than twelve guests, cater, staff, or provide buffet service.

• Have one or two spares of everything on standby in the kitchen, in case something gets broken or dropped.

• Don't crowd your guests. If you need space, don't set out the coffee cup or dessert flatware until the other dishes have been cleared. If it's very crowded, consider seating guests at two tables.

• Formal tables are beautiful and indicate that an occasion is special and should be treated with honor.

# #111
## HOW TO ANSWER A WEDDING INVITATION

Responding promptly to a wedding invitation shows the sender your gratitude for being included. It also shows that you understand our society's customs and are willing to participate in them, therefore ensuring future inclusion and connection. Most of all, though, it really helps the person planning (and paying for) the wedding estimate how many chairs will be needed and what the grand total of the bill might be. Here's a to-do list.

**1** **IF THERE'S A RESPONSE CARD,** fill it out and send it back as soon as possible. Most are preprinted, and you need to check boxes and fill it out. If you see "M_____ will attend _____ will not attend," it means to finish the courtesy title and write in your name. For instance, a single man, might write something like "r. Smith" on the line, a married couple might finish it with "r. and Dr. Smith."

**2** **SOME INVITATIONS INCLUDE** entrée selections. If yours does, and you're responding in the affirmative, check the box or boxes for your desired entrée.

**3** **IF YOUR INVITATION DOESN'T** include a response card, you are often expected to hand-write a response (although sometimes a website where you can RSVP may be provided). Use the plainest, nicest cardstock you can find. Be quite formal. You are elevating the event and giving it the gravitas it deserves. Say something like, "Ms. Flattered Guest accepts with pleasure your wedding invitation for Sunday, the tenth of June, at four o'clock in the afternoon."

✕✕✕✕✕✕✕✕✕✕✕✕✕✕✕✕✕✕✕✕✕✕✕✕✕✕✕✕✕✕✕✕✕✕✕✕✕✕

## THE PLUS ONE

If you are single, unless the invitation specifies "Mr. Happy-to-Attend and Guest," you are *not* invited to bring anyone. Plates at weddings are costly. Don't put the couple in an awkward position by increasing numbers. Also, children are not invited with parents unless their names appear on the envelope. Many couples want weddings to be adults-only affairs.

> Although rumor has it that a wedding guest has an entire year to send a gift, it's considerate to send one before the wedding or shortly (no more than three months) thereafter.

# #112
## HOW TO PACK A SUITCASE

**P**acking a suitcase is an art. Flight attendants, globetrotters, and frequent business travelers can attest. Have you ever suffered the embarrassment of being invited to a fancy restaurant when you've packed only hiking boots and sandals? Or the discomfort of shivering in a tank top, envious of those around you who thought to pack fleeces (even though it rarely snows in Florida in March)?

With ever-increasing baggage fees, and constantly shrinking carry-on space, knowing how to pack your bags efficiently can also save you money when you fly. Whether traveling by train, bus, or car, packing the right items can take the stress (and high cost!) out of travel. Minimizing the number of bags you carry helps make the journey as sweet as the destination.

Most important, you'll be secure in the knowledge that you have what you need when you unpack. It's easy when you plan ahead by following these tips.

## Before You Travel

⚜ **Prepare like an athlete.** See your doctor before you travel to discuss any health complaints or to get refills on medications or prescriptions for anything new you might need. For the week leading up to your departure, maintain your health and fitness: eat well, sleep well, and de-stress. Travel requires stamina. There's luggage to haul, time zones to negotiate, and you'll want to be at your calmest in case of irritations like flight delays or lost bags.

⚜ **Be a good citizen.** For foreign travel, don't assume you know what paperwork or vaccinations (and proof thereof) you'll need. Check individual countries' websites or contact the U.S. State Department. Then make an appointment with your primary care doctor to make sure you're up to date on any required vaccines.

⚜ **Avoid a postage pile-up.** Have a friend pick up your mail or fill out a card (or online form) to have it stopped temporarily while you're away.

⚜ **Pay your bills.** This sounds obvious, but you never know when travel delays could put you behind, racking up costly late fees or harming your credit. If you don't want to pay in advance, call providers and lenders, and arrange for delayed due dates.

⚜ **Alert the bank.** If you're traveling abroad, tell the banks that issue your credit and debit cards. To protect you from fraud, they might shut down your account after recognizing a sudden spate of atypical activity like purchasing several sets of skis in Switzerland, or frequenting a beer garden in Germany. Also, check with your bank to make sure that your credit card will be accepted where you are going. And remember that currency conversion fees may apply to foreign purchases; you may want or need to use particular credit cards to avoid such unnecessary fees. Be aware that you'll likely get the best conversion rates simply by taking cash from a local bank machine with your normal debit card.

⚜ **Let the loved ones know.** Give your itinerary and contact information to loved ones. They may need to reach you in case of an emergency (or to let you know you won the lottery!).

## Planning and Prep

⚜ **Make a list.** And then, check it twice. You can probably wait to decide if you'll take the yellow shirt or the blue, but some items are nonnegotiable. Avoid that sickening feeling of remembering something crucial just as the plane is taxiing down the runway. Eyeglasses, contact lenses, passports and visas, medicines, hostess gifts, and work-related documents top the list of forgotten items.

❧ **Don't wait until the last minute!** If you're furiously throwing things into bags at midnight before your 5:00 a.m. flight, you may wind up in Paris with a camp lantern. Instead, start packing a week in advance. Leave your suitcase open in a corner of the room, and stash items you have multiples of, like socks, underwear, and dental floss. (Keep your packing list and a pen nearby.)

❧ **Check the weather.** Even if we can't fully predict conditions, in this age of advanced technology, you'll be able to gauge likely temperatures. Why drag a winter coat if Amsterdam will be enjoying a warm spring?

❧ **Survival of the fittest.** Plan so you'll always have food and water at hand. It's true that you can't carry more than 3 fluid ounces of liquid through airport security, but you can carry an empty water bottle to refill on the other side. Bring a granola bar, nuts, or other small snack that will keep to help maintain your blood sugar levels.

❧ **Wear it; don't carry it.** Yes, you'll have to take off heavy shoes and jackets going through airport security, but it's a huge space-saver payoff. Once aboard a plane or train, you can stash your heavy coat overhead or under the seat.

❧ **Color coordinate.** Pack clothes that match. Bring coats and jackets in neutral colors, and have every top match every bottom. Save pizzazz for accessories.

## Get Packing: The Hand Luggage

❧ **Keep essentials close.** Carry medicines, a light wrap or jacket, travel documents, make-up, a pair each of clean socks and underwear, credit cards, and money in a large purse or backpack (along with your snacks and water). And don't let it out of your sight!

❧ **When asleep, loop the strap around your feet.** Once you're off the plane, never hand it to a porter or valet. Think of it this way: If all your luggage were lost but this piece, could you get through a week in a strange place?

❧ **Save your screen.** Tuck laptops and tablets into your hand luggage, when possible. You'll have to present these at security, so try not to have to dig deep. If you don't need a laptop on the trip, and you're checking a bag, pack it in the middle of your soft clothing.

## Get Packing: The Big Bag

❧ **Roll 'em!** Roll everything. It's the most efficient way to use space and the best packing method for avoiding wrinkles. You can even roll a suit by actually turning the jacket inside out, folding it in half lengthwise, then folding it in half, top to bottom, and rolling. For pants, lay them out as you would hang them up. Fold dress shirts the way they're boxed at the dry cleaner; place the shirts on the top part of the pants, then fold the pants over the shirts. Another way to keep shirts wrinkle-free is to fold them into thirds from outside to inside, with the sleeves folded in. Next, fold the shirt into roughly 3- to 5-inch sections, working upward, until the collar is on top. Once you've rolled everything, set it aside.

❧ **The shoes fit.** Line sides of the case with shoes, putting each one in a shoe bag or gallon-size zip-top bag. Stuff rolled-up socks, scarves, neckties, and underwear inside them. If your shoes are smelly, try following the instructions in Banish Odors and Keep Shoes Smelling Fresh, page 207.

❧ **Go heavy duty.** Line the bottom with jeans, canvas coats, and other heavy rolls. This will help if the suitcase won't close and compressing is needed.

❧ **Layer it on.** Continue layering on and filling in cracks with medium-heavy items, such as jackets.

❧ **Lighten up.** Move on to lighter items, such as knits, shirts, lingerie, and pajamas.

❧ **Keep it dry.** Pack any nonessential toiletries in side pockets, making sure they're sealed in zip-top bags in case of leaks.

❧ **Cut the cord.** Don't take a hairdryer unless you know your host or hotel doesn't have one to lend. If you need one, invest in a small travel version and tuck it, along with any other appliances such as shavers or curling irons, into cracks between clothes rolls.

❧ **Sheathe your jewelry.** Never travel with expensive jewelry. There's too much value in such small items, and the threat of loss or theft is too real. For the jewelry you do pack, place each item in a separate zip-top bag, lay out a pillowcase, and space the bags out within the pillowcase. Roll the pillowcase and pack it in your pajama and lingerie layer.

# #113
## HOW TO TIE A SCARF

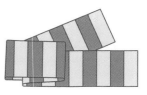

**U**nisex, utilitarian, and fashionable, the right scarf, tied with aplomb, marks the wearer as the kind of thoughtful dresser who goes the extra mile to look perfect and polished. These styles are ridiculously easy to execute; most are complete in three steps or less.

### The Classic Once-Around

For both men and women, this is a classic way to tie a warm winter scarf for a commute to work or an evening out. This style is casual, and with a wool scarf, will help you hold in precious body heat during cold winter days. Drape the scarf around your neck, letting one end drop lower than the other. Take the long end, wind it loosely around your neck, and let it drape over your chest.

### The Parisian Knot

This is likely the most popular knot for both genders. For men, it can be used for a silk or cashmere blend that accents a smart outfit or for a thin wool scarf. For women, it's an all-purpose knot for any scarf. Take a scarf in both hands and fold it lengthwise. Drape it around your neck, then insert both ends through the loop and pull them through.

### The Asymmetrical

A classic woman's look, perfect for adding an accent to a neat, traditional suit, double-breasted coat, or suit jacket. Open the scarf fully and wrap it around your shoulders like a shawl. Now, pull the right side down, so that it's longer than the left side by a third. Toss the right side over your left shoulder and allow the left side to hang down.

### The Bohemian

Best with lightweight cotton or open-weave scarves. This method makes a statement. For men, this look complements an unzipped, short leather jacket or close-cut, trendy blazer. For women, it can pair with any cardigan, jacket, or coat, or it can be worn with blouses and dresses to amp up the style. Drape the scarf around the back of your neck and allow both ends to hang down in the front, one equally as long as the other. Cross the ends over themselves, and tie them together to create one parallel knot. Repeat this three to five times, until you have a braided necktie effect.

# The Big Ten: Items Every Wardrobe Needs

Forget the trends. There are certain agreed-upon classic wardrobe pieces for both men and women. Invest in the top-of-your-budget versions of these staples, and you'll never spend the hours before a big date, interview, or presentation thinking, *I don't have a thing to wear.*

## For Men

**1. Gray wool suit.** Equally at home in the conference room or cocktail lounge. This uniform says, "I belong."

**2. Navy wool jacket.** Easy to throw on over jeans, or the matching trousers it came with when you purchased it as a "four-season suit." It's as indispensable as underwear.

**3. Belted trench coat.** Suitable for nearly all weather, the versatile belted trench can be worn with a suit or jeans. Invest in a good one; it'll never go out of style.

**4. White button-down shirt.** Dress it up or dress it down. Wear it under a sports jacket at dinner or untucked on the beach. This is the number one essential for travel.

**5. French blue dress shirt.** Doubles for work and play. Tuck it in and top it with a tie for the office, or untuck it with black jeans and boots for hanging out.

**6. Brown leather jacket.** Try a classic bomber style. Rugged but sophisticated, it transforms you from casual to polished.

**7. Elegant black/brown belt.** Choose a 1-inch width with a simple buckle and it'll complement any pants or trousers.

**8. Neutral chinos.** Buy flat-front, slim-legged, 100 percent cotton. Try on as many pairs as it takes to find your perfect fit. You'll be wearing these all the time.

**9. Cashmere V-neck.** Go for a dark, neutral color.

**10. Leather, waxed cotton, or other sturdy duffel bag.** This bag will take you anywhere and match anything you wear. Don't get caught on a business trip with your logoed nylon gym bag. This duffel marks you as a grown man.

## For Women

**1. A crisp white shirt.** Look for high-quality cotton and a highly tailored look. Try on lots of styles, find the one that fits you best, and invest in two or three.

**2. Perfect jeans.** You may have to try on a hundred pairs to find the style that flatters you best, but when you find your denim soul mate, you'll be glad you did. Buy them in a dark wash, so they dress up more easily.

**3. Black pencil skirt.** Flatters every figure and looks neat and polished with any top, from a cashmere shell to a silk bow-front blouse to a cotton scoop-neck tee.

**4. Little black dress.** The LBD is a foolproof way to look pulled-together, and it goes from daytime, paired with ballet flats or low pumps, to evening, paired with strappy sandals or peek-toe high heels.

**5. Tailored pantsuit.** Buy the best one you can afford, in a neutral color and an all-season fabric. Spend the money to have it tailored. Mix and match accessories, and you could wear this every day of your working life.

**6. Slim black pants.** Pull them on, and your look is instantly sleek and polished. These can be dressed down for everyday wear, but they'll never stoop to sloppy.

**7. Classic-cut, colorful blazer.** Choose the most basic of cuts, and you'll be able to throw this blazer over every skirt and pair of pants or jeans you own. Buy it in a bright color like red, purple, or royal blue.

**8. A good leather tote bag.** Doubles as a briefcase or computer bag during working hours and a shopping bag or weekender hand luggage during leisure hours.

**9. A cashmere cardigan.** Tuck it into your bag to protect you from winter drafts or summer air conditioning.

**10. The right bra.** It's really worthwhile to be fitted by a professional. The right bra perks you up, makes you look trimmer, and makes all of your clothes look great.

# #114
## HOW TO TIE A TIE

If you've never tied a man's necktie, you may gape in wonder as you watch an experienced business-man whip the ends of his about, without even a glance in the mirror. The art of tying a tie lies simply in practice. Here are instructions for tying the three most popular styles with ease.

## The Four-in-Hand Knot

This asymmetrical method of tying is slightly youthful, jaunty, and casual. Some call it "the schoolboy." Very easy to execute, and a great choice for button-down shirts. This style works best with heavier-weight fabrics and wider cuts.

**1 DRAPE THE NECKTIE AROUND** your neck. The wide end should drop down about a foot below the narrow end of the tie.

**2 NOW, CROSS THE WIDE PART OF** the tie over the narrow end.

**3 TURN THE WIDE END BACK** underneath the narrow end.

**4 CONTINUE BY BRINGING THE** wide end back over in front of the narrow end once again.

**5 PULL THE WIDE END UP AND** through the loop around your neck.

**6 HOLD THE FRONT OF THE KNOT** loosely with your index finger and bring the wide end down and through the front loop.

**7 REMOVE YOUR FINGER AND** tighten the knot carefully to the collar by holding the narrow end and sliding the knot up.

## The Half-Windsor Knot

This is the junior version of the windsor knot. This triangular and symmetrical shape is best used with dress shirts and light- to medium-weight fabrics. For shirts with standard collars, it's a safe and traditional choice.

**1** **DRAPE THE NECKTIE AROUND** your neck. The wide end should drop down about a foot below the narrow end. Cross the wide part of the tie over the narrow end.

**2** **BRING THE WIDE END OF THE** tie around and to the back of the narrow end.

**3** **PUSH THE WIDE END UP AND** pull it down through the hole between your collar and tie.

**4** **BRING THE WIDE END AROUND** the front, over the narrow end, from right to left.

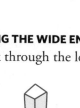

**5** **BRING THE WIDE END UP AND** back through the loop again.

**6** **PULL THE WIDE END DOWN** through the knot in front.

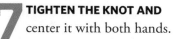

**7** **TIGHTEN THE KNOT AND** center it with both hands.

## The Windsor Knot

A bold, thick, and symmetrical knot, this style has long been associated with confidence and power. This knot pairs best with a wide-spread collar and is appropriate for important events like job interviews and work presentations, as well as formal events like business dinners and awards ceremonies.

**1** **DRAPE THE NECKTIE AROUND** your neck. The wide end should drop down about a foot below the narrow end. Cross the wide part of the tie over the narrow end.

**2** **BRING THE WIDE END OF THE** tie up through the hole between your collar and the tie, then, pull it down toward the front.

**3** **PULL THE WIDE END TO THE** back of the narrow end, and then to the right.

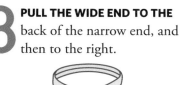

**4** **TAKE THE WIDE END BACK** through the loop one more time. You will have a triangle now, where the necktie's knot will ultimately be.

**6** **BRING THE WIDE END UP** through the loop a third time.

**8** **TIGHTEN THE KNOT AND** center it with both hands.

**5** **WRAP THE WIDE END AROUND** the triangle by pulling that end from right to left.

**7** **PULL THE WIDE END THROUGH** the knot in the front.

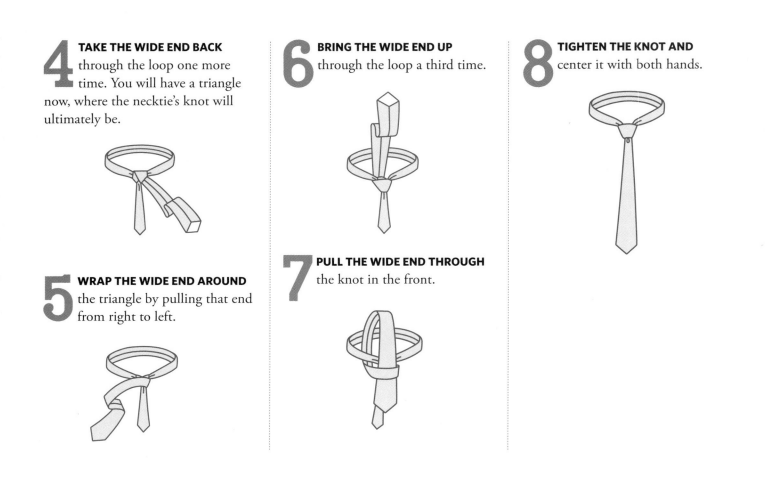

Famous for their perfect dimple, Windsor knots came about in the early 20th century when the fashionable Duke of Windsor (briefly King Edward VIII) inspired their creation.

# #115 HOW TO TIE A NECKTIE ON SOMEONE ELSE

Are you the Katharine Hepburn or Loretta Young type who loves to do all things sophisticated and nostalgic? Helping someone with his necktie will surely elevate you to the status of classy dame!

Or maybe you're a nice guy who wants to help out a haberdashery-loving gal who loves dressing up like Annie Hall but is clumsy with knots.

Or maybe, like me, you've needed merely to quickly dress two little boys for a wedding. Either way, it's a nice skill to have.

If you can tie a tie for someone else, you'll be the hero of the day. Which is the go-to knot to use for doing a tie-wearer a favor, you ask? Why, the half-windsor, of course. Once tied on yourself, it can be loosened and slipped over your head, then transferred to the grateful recipient.

Tie the tie on yourself, following the instructions for the half-windsor knot on page 203, and omit Step 7. Then simply place the loop of the necktie around the neck of the man, woman, or child who will be wearing the necktie and push the knot up to the neck.

But if you'd like to tie the tie directly on the other person, try this.

**1** **FLIP UP THE SHIRT COLLAR AND** drape the necktie around the neck of the recipient, with the wide end on your right. Allow the wide end to drop down about a foot below the narrow end.

**2** **CROSS THE WIDE END OVER THE** narrow end and bring it up through the neck loop and down the front.

**3** **SWING THE WIDE END TO THE** right, passing it under the narrow end.

**4** **CROSS THE WIDE END BACK OVER** the narrow end to the left.

**5** **AFTER THIS, PUSH IT UP THROUGH** the neck hole. Now, tuck it through the knot and let it hang down.

**6** **TIGHTEN THE TIE AND FOLD THE** shirt collar down, and voilà: He (or she) will be dressed to the nines!

# #116
## HOW TO POLISH A PAIR OF SHOES

There's an old saying that goes "If you're wearing good shoes, and carrying a good bag, the rest of the outfit doesn't matter." Good-quality shoes, kept meticulously neat, speak volumes about the wearer. Actor Conrad Cantzen felt so strongly about the impression shoes make that in 1945 he bequeathed his estate to The Actors Fund with the stipulation that it be used to help actors buy shoes so they did not appear "down at the heels" when auditioning for jobs. In short, good-looking shoes can vastly improve your life!

Here are some ways to keep your shoes sweet smelling (or at least *not* smelling), spick and span, and in good repair.

**1** **COVER AN AREA OF THE FLOOR** with sheets of newspaper or an old towel.

**2** **CHECK YOUR SHOES FOR** spatterings of dirt or debris. If they're filthy, wipe them down with a damp rag and let dry.

**3** **TAKE A HORSEHAIR SHOE** polish brush and rub it into your wax shoe polish. Scrub your shoes vigorously. Use plenty of polish so that you leave a film on the outside of the shoe.

**4** **LET THEM ABSORB THE POLISH** for a few minutes, then wipe down the outside of the shoes with a soft, lint-free cloth. Use a circular motion and rub hard to buff them to a high gloss.

In the 1800s, the first commercially available shoe polish—or shine—was made from sugar, vinegar, black dye, and water. Shortly thereafter tallow (an animal by-product) was introduced as an ingredient to prevent the polish from rubbing off on clothes, but it wasn't until 1904, when Kiwi brand introduced a vastly improved formula, that commercial shine began to resemble the modern shoe polish available today

## When Good Shoes Go Bad: Shoe Repair and Maintenance Tips

### Self-Sufficiency: When to Do It at Home

Channel your inner cobbler, and your shoes will last longer and perform better.

✛ **Heels wearing out?** This seems obvious, but I'm going to say it: Alternate the pairs of shoes you wear to preserve the ones you love most.

✛ **Slick bottoms?** Rub the bottom with sandpaper or a wire brush to add traction. Still slick? Spray the bottoms with hairspray and let it dry completely before wearing.

✛ **Waterproof it.** Rub a new pair of leather shoes or boots with mink oil. This neutral-colored oil softens the leather and makes it water resistant. Allow it to dry fully, then treat shoes with spray-on water repellent at the seams and all over the insides.

✛ **Soles or heels coming off?** Glue them on at home with glue specifically designed for shoes (ask for it at a hardware store). Before you start, rub the surfaces to be glued with sandpaper to improve the bond. This works especially well on sneakers.

✛ **Scuffed-up suede?** The best tool to erase surface marks is a dry cleaning bar, usually sold with a stiff-bristle brush. The bar is like a pencil eraser: use it to remove marks from suede. Then use the brush to bring the nap back up. Finish with a deep-cleaning suede spray.

✛ **Mark on nonpatent leather shoes or boots?** Try rubbing the stain off with a gum eraser. If that fails, invest in a small bottle of shoe polish that matches the shoe color precisely and paint over the scuff.

✛ **Crack or nick in leather?** Find a Sharpie marker in the same color as the shoe, and simply draw over the affected area, and then let it dry.

### Shoe Store Support: When to Pay for It

An investment in a trip to the shoe repair store for repairs and maintenance can save you money in the long run. Buy the highest-quality shoes you can afford and keep them in good repair. Here's what to pay for:

✛ **New shoes too tight?** Have them stretched. Some places can even stretch specific parts of the shoe, such as the heels or the "bunion" area. It's an inexpensive service that can make a big difference.

✛ **Uncomfortable standing all day in your new shoes?** Invest in gel insoles. Slide them inside your shoes to absorb shock between your feet and the sidewalk. It's worth the investment because they'll relieve and prevent pain.

✛ **Want to make them last?** Have your shoemaker put on rubber heels and toe taps. It's a great way to keep the bottoms from wearing out. Replace the taps as they wear down or fall off.

✛ **Slippery soles?** Have your shoemaker install sole protectors. They'll add life to a quality pair of shoes and provide traction to help you avoid slips on the ice or slick flooring.

✕ ✕ ✕ ✕ ✕ ✕ ✕ ✕ ✕ ✕ ✕ ✕ ✕ ✕ ✕ ✕ ✕ ✕ ✕ ✕ ✕ ✕ ✕ ✕ ✕ ✕ ✕

# BANISH ODORS AND KEEP SHOES SMELLING FRESH

• *Use a powder.* After taking off your shoes nightly, sprinkle a thin layer of baking soda inside. In the morning, take them outdoors and clap the soles together. The odor will be carried off with the powder.

• *Make room in the freezer.* Put each shoe in its own gallon-size zip-top freezer bag, and put them in the freezer overnight to kill odor-causing fungus and bacteria.

• *Raid the laundry room.* Before bed, crumple up dryer sheets and insert them into shoes.

# #117
# HOW TO WRITE A THANK-YOU NOTE

Polite behavior and good manners in a person are universally appreciated. Why? Because they indicate regard and respect for fellow human beings. Behaving in this way also marks you as a person who not only knows the right way to act, but also cares enough to follow through. My favorite thing about proper etiquette is that participation is open to everyone. One needn't be born into a blue-blood family, or have piles of money in the bank, in order to have lovely behavior. And it's that behavior that marks someone as a quality person, not connections or wealth.

## Thank You FAQS

*How long do I have to send a thank-you note?*
For a regular gift, try to write the note and mail it within two to three days, so it arrives within the week. Notes for wedding gifts should be sent out two weeks after the wedding date.

*Can I type a thank-you note?*
No. Even if your handwriting is terrible, write it by hand.

*Is there a rule about stationery?*
Not really, but have something on hand like postcards of a local landmark or museum art piece, a box of unisex "Thank You" cards, or a pack of neutral-colored stationery. The need to shop for supplies will delay the thank-you! The classic choice is a card with your initials at the top.

**1 WRITE A GREETING.** It need not be more complicated than "Dear Uncle Frank."

**2 NAME THE GIFT.** Never just say: "Thank you for the gift." The giver will wonder if you mixed it up with other gifts and lost the tag. For an added bonus, compliment the gift, as in: "Thank you so much for the beautifully hand-knit wool scarf." However, there are exceptions.

⹋ **Money.** Here's an instance where you do not name the gift. Instead, say, "I'm truly grateful for your generous gift."

⹋ **Intangibles.** If your friend let you borrow her beach house, or if someone did you a favor, define the gift in a flattering way. Don't say, "Thanks for the couch and the grub," but do say, "Thank you for your gracious hospitality." It's okay to be simple.

**3 TELL HOW YOU USE THE GIFT.** If you love a new bathrobe, say, "I've barely taken off my robe since I opened the box." Don't lie, though. Say something that's true, even if you hate the gift. "The practical umbrella hat is such a pretty shade of purple!" Regarding money, it's okay to mention how it will be used. "Your generous gift will help when I buy my new bike," is fine, but don't write, "Your fifty bucks will get me two butter knives and a serving spoon off my registry."

**4 TALK ABOUT THE PAST AND THE** future. This is a time to underscore your connection to the giver. "It was so nice to see you at my graduation party, and I look forward to sharing Thanksgiving with you." If you see the giver often, try "I know we'll talk at work, but I wanted to take a moment to express my gratitude." If it's someone you rarely see, use a phrase like, "I'm thinking of you, and wishing you all the best."

**5 WRAP UP.** Say thanks again with a short, simple phrase. "Thank you again for the present," and then the sign-off. If "Love," or "Yours Truly," work, say that. If not, simply sign your name.

# #118

# HOW TO STOCK A FIRST-AID KIT

How many times have you had a bump, scrape, or burn only to find that your medicine cabinet lacks basic first-aid supplies? There's no better time than the present to put together complete kits and stash them where they'll be needed most. And if you do it the DIY way, buying in bulk for several kits at a time, you'll save some green, too.

## Where Do I Need First-Aid Kits?

- In every bathroom of your home
- In your car
- In the workshop or garage
- In your disaster evacuation backpack
- In the home office
- In your hiking and camping equipment
- In a child's stroller or diaper bag

## What Should a First-Aid Kit Contain?

The basics, as recommended by the American Red Cross:

- 2 absorbent compress dressings (5 by 9 inches)
- 25 adhesive bandages (assorted sizes)
- 1 adhesive cloth tape (10 yards by 1 inch)
- 5 antibiotic ointment packets (approximately 1 gram each)
- 5 antiseptic wipe packets
- 2 packets of aspirin (81 mg each)
- 1 blanket (thermal space blanket)
- 1 breathing barrier (with one-way valve)
- 1 instant cold compress
- 2 pairs of nonlatex gloves (size: large)
- 2 hydrocortisone ointment packets (approximately 1 gram each)
- Scissors
- 1 roller bandage (3 inches wide)
- 1 roller bandage (4 inches wide)
- 5 sterile gauze pads (3 by 3 inches)
- 5 sterile gauze pads (4 by 4 inches)
- Oral thermometer (nonmercury/nonglass)
- 2 triangular bandages
- Tweezers
- First-aid instruction booklet

Clearly, first-aid kits should be tailored to their specific uses. If you live in an urban area, you probably don't need a snake-bite kit in your bathroom. You might, however, need one if you live in or near the woods or to stock your hiking backpack.

## WHAT ABOUT SYRUP OF IPECAC?

**Once a standard in every home first-aid kit, syrup of ipecac does not necessarily help a person who has swallowed poison. Parents are now advised not to use it. Instead, in the case of a suspected poisoning, call Poison Control at 800-222-1222 or call 911.**

## What Specifics Should I Have for a Children's First-Aid Kit?

⚜ Eyedrops

⚜ Anti-itch lotion

⚜ Baby wipes

⚜ A list of emergency phone numbers (doctor, hospital, Poison Control)

⚜ Rectal thermometer

⚜ Mouthpiece for administering CPR (available from your local Red Cross)

⚜ Children's ibuprofen and acetaminophen (but never aspirin, which can cause fatal Reye's syndrome in young children—check with your doctor, even before giving baby aspirin)

⚜ A tooth preservation kit

⚜ Activated charcoal powder (to use only when advised by poison control)

## How Can I Personalize My First-Aid Kit?

⚜ Be sure to include your prescription or over-the-counter medications when you're traveling. Make sure to check expiration dates every so often and replace as needed.

⚜ If you wear eyeglasses or contact lenses, have extra lenses as well as extra cleaning and storage solutions in first-aid kits in your car or camping gear.

⚜ If you are allergic to nuts, bee stings, shellfish, or any other potentially anaphylaxis-inducing substance, have an EpiPen in every kit.

⚜ If you have sensitive skin, consider packing emollients for dry skin or cornstarch-based body powder (avoid talc, as it's harmful when breathed into the lungs).

The concept of the first-aid kit has been around for quite some time—aviator Charles Lindbergh carried one across the Atlantic on his first successful ocean crossing in 1927.

# TWENTY SAFETY TIPS FOR EVERY HOME

**1. *Keep car keys and cell phone on your nightstand.*** If you hear suspicious noises in the night, press the panic button to set off the car alarm. Given the commotion, an intruder is likely to flee the scene. Landlines can be cut; having a cell phone near at night secures the opportunity to call 911 if necessary.

**2. *Keep shrubbery trimmed.*** Heavy dark shrubbery growing high close to a house can give someone a place to hide when you're coming home at night.

**3. *Enlist a neighbor to check for leaflets.*** When you're away from home for an extended period of time, even if you stop the mail and the newspaper, marketers could still leave fliers, brochures, or pamphlets stuck in the door crack or lying on the porch. Don't broadcast that household members are away.

**4. *Install smoke detectors.*** Smoke detectors should be on every floor and carbon monoxide detectors near bedrooms. Test them regularly and replace the batteries every daylight savings time change.

**5. *Secure tall bookshelves to the wall.*** This is especially important in households with young children. Climbing on them can cause them to topple over and injure someone.

**6. *Cover all unused outlets.*** Plastic outlet covers are cheap and readily available. Even if no kids or pets live in your home, you never know when you might have visitors.

**7. *Don't pile firewood along the outside of your house.*** Intruders can climb aboard, gaining access to windows. It can also fuel house fires. Instead, pile it next to a fence or shed, at least 20 feet away from the dwelling.

**8. *Put up a security-system decal.*** Even if you don't really have a system in place, this could discourage inexperienced burglars.

**9. *Take care with extension cords.*** Never place them under rugs or heavy furniture. Wear and fraying could lead to fires.

**10. *Create a plan in case of fire.*** Practice a fire escape plan with your family. Identify two exits for every room and assign jobs for rescuing small children or pets.

**11. *Avoid burns in the shower and bath.*** Set your water heater below 120 degrees Fahrenheit to avoid potential burns (and to save energy).

**12. *Invest in fire extinguishers.*** Place all-purpose fire extinguishers in key locations in your home: the kitchen, bedrooms, and the basement. Check expiration dates regularly.

**13. *Skid-proof your tub or shower.*** Use rubber mats, adhesive decals, or strips to help prevent falls.

**14. *Store heavy items properly.*** They should be organized in cabinets at waist level or below.

**15. *Don't overload outlets.*** Be certain that you have no more than one high-wattage appliance plugged in to any given power point.

**16. *Spring for a chimney sweep.*** If you burn wood in a fireplace, be sure to have the flues and chimneys professionally cleaned and swept annually.

**17. *Be strict and unfailing about firearms.*** If there are guns in the house, make sure they are locked up, unloaded, and stored separately from ammunition.

**18. *Fence in the pool.*** All pools by law require a four-sided fence and a child-proof gate. If you have a temporary pool—even a small wading pool—empty it when it's not being supervised.

**19. *Make sure your house number is visible.*** Visitors should be able to read the number from the street. This will lead emergency workers directly to your door when needed.

**20. *Paint the bottom steps of the stairs white.*** This will help reduce tripping and falls.

# SHOP

# DOMESTIC REPAIR

One Sunday's to-do list might include anything from fixing a leak, to painting a shelf, to banging down stray deck boards, to putting a new blade on the lawn mower, to hanging a picture. How can you predict what you'll need next Sunday? You can't, which is why your home tool kit needs to be flexible, complete—and organized! A trip to the hardware store for a screw or tool that you know is hiding somewhere in the garage can turn a two-minute fix into a two-hour job. Having the right tool on hand can also be the difference between an easy DIY job and a costly call to the handyman. Spending $200 on tools now can save you many times that amount later.

# DOMESTIC REPAIR TOOL KIT

Cordless drill

Pry bar

Wire cutter/stripper

Utility knife

Slip-joint or channel lock pliers

Locking pliers

Needle-nose pliers

Saw

Tape measure

Phillips-head screwdrivers

Flathead screwdrivers

Voltage detector

Staple gun

Carpenter's square

Stud finder

Electrical tape

Chisel

Hammer

Level

Screws

Duct tape

Sandpaper

Nails

Bolts

Glue

(continued)

**Hammer.** You can't go wrong with a lightweight framing hammer—such as a 20-ounce, smooth-faced model with a straight claw.

**Screwdrivers.** A medium and a large Phillips ( + ) and flathead ( – ) is a great place to start.

**Tape measure.** A 1-inch-wide, 25-foot-long tape measure is indispensable. Make sure it's high enough quality to assure a working lock and well-made retrieval spring.

**Pry bar.** A short cat's paw pry bar will do just fine to pull nails and lift floorboards.

**Locking pliers.** Why burn your own grip strength to hold pliers closed? Instead, a pair of versatile, locking Vise-Grips are essential for keeping most things pinched around the house. Consider a pair of Irwin 10-inch curve pliers.

**Needle-nose pliers.** These are meant for electrical work—to bend and cut wires—but you'll use them for everything from pinching tiny screws to pulling large splinters.

**Slip-joint pliers.** The most common pliers are two-position, slip-joint pliers, which allow you to close tight in one position and grip large objects in the other. Plastic-coated or otherwise, padded handles are a plus.

**Wire cutter/stripper.** Go with a multi-size wire cutter/stripper, which you'll use when rewiring lamps and hanging light fixtures.

**Voltage detector.** You'll need a voltage detector to help locate the source of the trouble in light fixtures, circuit breakers, wires, and cables.

**Cordless drill.** Look for a variable speed, reversible, twist-lock model with a good set of bits. In addition to a kit of standard bits in a range of sizes, you might want a couple of spade bits, a masonry bit, a hole cutter, and bits used for driving screws (Phillips and flathead).

**Chisel.** Get a wood chisel, and try to keep it for shaving wood off a loose door jamb instead of opening paint cans.

**Saw.** A straight handsaw will cut boards quickly and even trim the odd tree branch in a pinch.

**Level.** You can get a pen-sized laser level for about the same price as a four-foot bubble level, and you will find pros who swear by each. Pick one or the other.

**Stud finder.** Yes, you can knock on the wall until the hollow sound goes solid, but while you hone your 2 × 4 divination skills, get a stud finder.

**Utility knife.** A retractable-blade utility knife will do everything from cutting carpet to opening boxes.

**Carpenter's square.** Carpenters use an L-shaped or triangular steel or aluminum square when building with 2 × 4s. You'll want one around to double-check the angles of the broken picture frame you tacked back together.

**Staple gun.** A well-made, hand-powered staple gun is essential for hanging holiday lights and tacking upholstered furniture. Make sure the gun you buy accepts staples up to ⅝" and ask a salesperson if you can give the staple gun a few test squeezes before buying. Buy a range of staples—½" and ⅜" are the most useful.

**Electrical tape.** There are some jobs that require exactly the right gear, and rewiring is one of them. For splicing even the smallest wires, you need vinyl electrical tape, which stretches, adheres to, and insulates wires.

**Duct tape.** It binds the world together.

**Sandpaper.** Common aluminum oxide sandpaper runs from the coarse grit of P12 to the fine grit of P220 (and even higher for finish papers). Usually you'll use a coarse paper first and finish with a finer grit, so it's worth buying a set.

**Nails, screws, and bolts.** Even the most basic home repair tool kit should include a range of nails—ranging from 4d (1½") to 16d (3½")—and screws. Wood and drywall screws have coarse threads, whereas metal screws have finer threads. Get a range of both. It's also worth having a couple of carriage bolts, eye bolts, and screw eyes on hand.

**Glue.** Super glue, wood glue, Elmer's glue, maybe an epoxy for special projects. Along with duct tape, glue will hold everything together.

# #119
## HOW TO HANG A PICTURE

Humans follow a consistent picture-hanging progression. You start putting art on the wall by taping the first concert poster to your childhood bedroom. Then maybe you move on to thumbtacks. In your early twenties you might graduate to a single nail driven into the wall, then you'd hang with wire across the back of the frame. You reach picture-hanging maturity once you deploy the bracket. This section details this method of grown-up picture hanging.

### Where to Place a Picture on the Wall

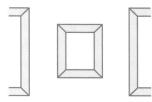

Lay out your pictures on the floor as if it were the wall and play with your options. (Alternatively, make poster board templates the same size as your pictures and then temporarily tack them to the walls with removable adhesive.) Start with the art you imagine as your centerpiece—not necessarily the biggest picture, but the one you most want people to notice—and then add remaining pieces around it. Successfully decorating a wall is about balance. You want neither a tiny piece of art on a vast wall, nor pictures claiming every square inch of wall space. Pictures should be hung so that their center point is at eye level—typically about five feet from the floor—but needn't be hung in frames of matching size. If art is obviously part of the same series, or if displaying a number of photographs, consider using complementary frames—perhaps made of the same material in different colors. The more eclectic your choice of frames, the more your home will look like a gallery; the more standardized your frames, the cleaner it will look.

Keep the following design guidelines in mind: When hanging art above a couch, don't go any higher than six inches from the top of the backrest—any more and the eye goes to the wall, not the art. Unframed, abstract, or "challenging" modern art requires more negative space around it than do portraits, framed pieces, landscapes, and representative art. The darker the room, the more space the art needs (or install accent lights; see page 358). If you have two pictures of the same size, consider breaking up the flow of this art by placing a smaller picture between. Of course, these rules are frequently broken—trust your eye or solicit the opinion of someone whose taste you do trust.

### Selecting Hanging Hardware

Hanging art by a wire stretched across its back is easy—you drive a nail, balance the art on its wire, and then slide it until the art hangs level. However, wire is imprecise and prone to slippage, and is therefore not the first choice of most professional decorators. Instead, consider brackets in which one side mounts to the wall and the other mounts to the picture. They take a little more care going up, but assuming you did your homework before putting holes in the wall, you've got the hang you want for good (or until your taste in art changes). Resist the temptation to hook the back of a picture's frame onto a bare nail head. It's not a secure way of hanging a picture and could cause damage to the wall (and the picture!) if the nail pulls out, as it may. At the very least attach a hoop or tooth-style hanger on the back of the frame, which grabs on to a matched hook on the wall.

## TOOLS:

**Measuring tape** ▪ **Pencil** ▪ **Stud finder** ▪ **4-foot level**

## MATERIALS:

- **Nails**
- **Hooks, brackets, or wire-mounts**

**1** **DOUBLE-CHECK PLACEMENT.** Before you start banging holes in the wall, consider the weight of your art—heavy art should be hung to a stud and not held only by drywall. Art over 50 pounds, such as a large mirror, is best hung on two studs. (See page 220 for how to locate studs.) Does this change your design? Consider the position of your heaviest piece and shift the overall placement of pieces as needed.

**2** **MEASURE AND MARK.** Once you're confident in your design, measure up the wall 5 feet and make a light mark with a pencil in a location that will be covered by a picture. We'll call this "eye level." Alternatively, place sticky notes on the wall at the proper height to indicate positions (these are nice because you can also write measurement notes on them). Measure the height of your picture and divide by two—that's the height above your eye-level mark that you want the top of the picture. Measure up from your 5-foot eye-level mark and make a light line with pencil or hang a sticky note.

TOP OF THE PICTURE

EYE LEVEL

**3** **IF YOU'RE USING A HANGING** wire, measure the distance from the wire to the top of the frame, and subtract this measurement from the above-eye-level height. Mark this spot lightly on the wall, use nails to mount a picture hook over the mark, and hang the picture.

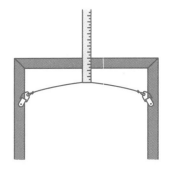

**4** **TO HANG WITH BRACKETS OR** hooks, you'll need to be a little more precise. Hold the picture up to the wall and lay a 4-foot carpenter's level across the top of the frame. Work to perfectly position the piece and then use a pencil to draw a light line along the top where it should hang.

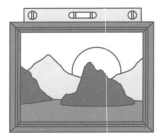

× × × × × × × × × × × × × × × × × × × × × × × × × × × × × × × × × × × × × × × × ×

## OFF THE WALL

**H**anging art flat on the wall isn't your only presentation option. Instead, consider building or installing a small shelf and setting framed art on it. And plates aren't the only items that can go in a wall-mounted plate display rack. Or turn art into a floor-piece by mounting it on a decorative easel. With a couple of eye screws and some wire, twine, or even yarn, art can be hung from the ceiling, too.

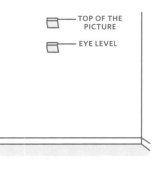

WALL-MOUNTED DISPLAY

CEILING-MOUNTED DISPLAY

**5** **DETERMINE YOUR HARDWARE** location. On the back of the frame, measure the distance from the hanging point or points to the top of the frame. Note that if a frame includes two hooks on the back, there is no guarantee these two hooks are equal distance from the top. Measure each separately, as even a ⅛" error in hook height can make a world of difference in how level your art looks. Note also the distance these mounting hooks are from each other (unless there is only one hook).

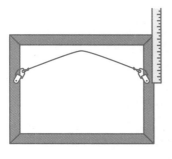

**6** **MOUNT THE HARDWARE.** Measure down from the top-of-frame line you drew on the wall to precisely mark the locations of the hanging hardware.

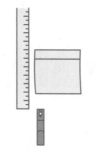

Mark these locations on the wall and mount the hanging hardware.

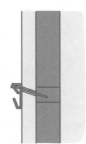

**7** **HANG YOUR ART.** If you're using a hanging wire, make sure that the wire catches on the hook(s) of the hanging hardware before you remove your hands from the frame.

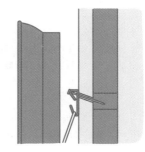

Although a frame may seem to be an arbitrary or replaceable border for a piece of fine art, it's deeply connected to the work itself and intertwined with its history. Changing the frame can de-value a piece of art, so make sure to properly box and store your art *and* its frame to best preserve the original work.

# #120
## HOW TO HANG A SHELF

Some projects—such as advanced joinery—might as well be rocket science. Others, like building a table, are surprisingly simple. Then there's hanging shelves, which seems like it would be easy, but if you want the job done right, turns out to be fairly tricky. How you go about it depends on where you want it hung and what material you'll be drilling into. Here's how to hang shelves that stay put.

### What a Stud!

Drywall anchors tend to pull out if they're loaded with more than about 25 pounds, and so when you're hanging a shelf in drywall, you'll almost always want to attach the shelf brackets to the wooden studs behind the wall. There are two types of stud finders—magnetic and electronic—and many models can be switched between the two. As the name implies, a magnetic stud finder contains a magnet and the finder beeps when it discovers the steel nails used to hook drywall to the studs. An electronic stud finder measures wall density by electrostatic fields and will sound when the density switches from just drywall to drywall backed by a stud. Because studs are not the only things in your walls that might make a finder beep, it's worth confirming by checking for studs on either side. The construction norm is to set studs at 16" centers (rarely at 24" centers), meaning that every 16" along your wall you should find the dead center of a stud. Once you discover one stud with your finder, check for additional studs 16" in either direction. Mark the studs lightly with a pencil.

If you don't have a stud finder, look for existing screw or nail holes or for slightly raised nail heads covered in paint. Or look for electrical outlets, which are frequently attached to the studs. Tap with your knuckle as you move across the wall, listening for a solid rather than hollow sound, or push on the wall to check for give. Once you're moderately confident in your clues—from a stud finder or from exploration—probe with a thin drill bit to see if your hunch leads

to solid wood. Be ready to close any holes you make with putty and paint.

### Finding Studs in a Plaster Wall

The walls of most newer homes are made of sheets of drywall mounted with nails to studs, sometimes finished with a thin layer of plaster. Until the late 1950s, however, many builders in the United States and Canada used a technique called lath and plaster, in which narrow wooden strips (laths) were tacked to studs and then covered in thick plaster. A stud finder is completely or almost completely useless in a lath and plaster wall, so instead use the tapping method described above to sleuth your way to stud locations. Once you have educated guesses, drill small exploratory holes, being sure to vary the heights of these holes so as not to weaken large sections of plaster. Older homes with lath and plaster walls may also suffer from imprecise stud spacing, meaning they might vary from 16" centers. In these plaster walls, it's even more important to drill exploratory holes to locate exact stud position before hanging shelves or anything heavy. Mark the edges of studs lightly with a pencil to ensure that you hit the center.

### If Your Wall Is Masonry . . .

The good news is there are no studs in a brick or concrete wall. You can hang a shelf or heavy mirror wherever you like. The bad news is, you need specialized tools and a little extra hardware to do it. First, you'll need masonry anchors. Most common are expansion anchors, either nails or screws. If your wall is made of multiple layers of masonry with air between the layers, you can also use masonry toggle bolts, which will push through the first layer and then swivel flat against the layer's back edge (like a drywall butterfly bolt). To hang a shelf, you'll need a bracket at each end and spaced about every 24" in between. Choose anchors that are rated to hold about four times what you expect them to carry—estimate the weight of your loaded shelf, divide it by the number of anchors you plan to use, then multiply this number by four. Because masonry anchors exert force on the wall, they can't be clustered too close to each other for fear of cracking the concrete or brick. The rule of thumb is that masonry anchors should be placed no closer than 10 times the diameter of the anchor—so ¼" masonry anchors should be spaced at least 2½" apart. You'll also need either a hammer drill (rent one from your local home improvement store) or a masonry bit for your electric drill. Make sure the size of your drill bit is appropriate for your anchors. Drill the holes and insert the anchors as specified by the package directions or by hardware store experts.

## TOOLS:

**Stud finder (optional; see What a Stud!, opposite) • Measuring tape • Pencil • 4-foot level • Power drill • Screwdriver bit**

## MATERIALS:

- **Shelf**
- **Bracket or mounting hardware**
- **Wood screws**

**1** DETERMINE THE MATERIAL OF your wall. If your walls are plaster or drywall, locate the studs (see What a Stud!, opposite).

**2** INSTALL THE BRACKETS ON THE shelf (the specific procedure will depend on your shelf and brackets—check the instructions that came with your bracket).

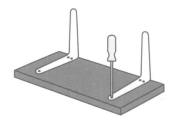

**3** PLAN THE POSITION OF YOUR screw holes. The best template for these holes is the shelf itself. With the mounting brackets installed on the shelf, lay a 4-foot level across the shelf and position it against the wall where you want it to hang. For drywall or plaster, make sure your mounting brackets are placed every 16" and aligned with studs. In masonry walls, brackets can be 24" apart. With a pencil, mark the wall through the screw holes in the shelf brackets. Remove the shelf and use a thin drill bit to double-check that each hole hits a stud.

**4** ATTACH THE SHELVES TO THE wall. Using your drill and screws appropriate to your wall material, attach the bracketed shelf to the wall. Depending on your mounting hardware, you may be able to drive the screws and then hang the shelf directly on them, or you may need to hold the shelf in place while you drive screws through the mounting brackets.

**Before they were used to stack books spine-out, shelves held piles of scrolls, and later, books with the spine facing *in*.**

# #121
# HOW TO INSTALL A CLOSET ROD

The specifics of hanging a closet rod may vary, but there is one consistent absolute: Hang it strong. Not only are your clothes heavy and the distance the bar spans likely to be wide, but this bar is likely to see abuse as you yank free a shirt on the way to work or pull pants straight off the hanger. So don't skimp on the mounting hardware, and never try to hang a rod directly from drywall. The instructions here are for hanging the traditional 1¼" wooden dowel closet rod.

## Too Clever by Half

There is a fine line dividing genius from gimmick. And that line is practicality. Yes, there are systems that hang from the back of a closet door that allow you to organize 50 pairs of shoes, but if that hanging is going to bang around every time you open the door, making a ruckus and preventing you from closing it, it's not your best option. Likewise, there are hooks that mount to walls, allowing you to hang many items from one attachment, but then you can't see what's in the back. There are battery-powered tie racks and push-button shoe racks—the list goes on. If your stuff is, in fact, overflowing your closet and there is no hope of organizing it neatly in a traditional bar-and-shelf system, you may have to explore other options. First try getting rid of stuff—thrift and consignment stores will gladly accept gently used items. But if your storage needs aren't extreme, bars and shelves are likely your cleanest, easiest option.

## TOOLS:

**Measuring tape** ▪ **Pencil** ▪ **Handsaw (optional)** ▪ **Drill screwdriver bit**

## MATERIALS:

- **1 × 4 piece of lumber**
- **2½" wood screws (or closet rod manufacturer's hardware)**
- **Hanging brackets (buy premade or use about 6" chunks of 2 × 4)**
- **1¼" wooden dowel**

**1 LOOK FOR STUDS.** Locate the studs in the sidewalls of your closet and mark their location. (See page 220 for instructions on locating studs.) Ideally, you will find them located between 12" and 14" in from the back wall—enough space to properly hang clothes. If you do find such studs, skip to Step 3.

**2 FORGET THE STUDS.** The chances of finding appropriately placed studs on either side of the closet are about the same as winning the lottery. Instead, it's very likely you'll have to hang the rod from strips of 1 × 4 lumber mounted to the studs. Start by cutting two strips of wood to match the depth of the closet's sidewalls (or have them cut at the lumber store).

**3 MOUNT THE BRACE.** Most closet rods are hung at eye level. Either eyeball the height and mark it on the walls, or make a mark on the wall about 5 feet up from the floor. (Be double sure that your measurements match at every point, or you will have a frustratingly slanted closet rod.) Hold a wood strip at this height, level it, and mark the location of the stud(s) on the strip. Screw or nail the wood strip through the side wall into the stud(s). Repeat with the other side. If there is no stud or wood whatsoever behind the closet drywall, use appropriate drywall mounting hardware for the wood strips. Then you'll have to reinforce the rod with supports that reach out from the wall studs along the back of the closet.

**4 ATTACH THE BRACKETS.** It's easiest to use commercial rod-hanging brackets, though you can certainly make your own—a chunk of 2 × 4 with a 1¼" hole drilled in the middle makes a fine bracket. One bracket should be closed all the way around and the other should be open at the top. If you're using premade brackets, follow the manufacturer's mounting instructions. If you're using chunks of 2 × 4, use 2½" screws to screw through the 2 × 4 and into the wood strips mounted to the wall.

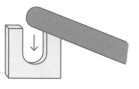

**5 HANG THE ROD.** Once you've mounted the brackets to the wood strips, push the dowel into the closed side and set it into the open bracket.

---

# CLOSET OVERHAUL

An organized closet is the first step toward good feng shui and a harmonious life. But don't plunge directly into screwing things to your walls or assembling a one-size-fits-all wire rack system. That's because one size certainly does not fit all when it comes to organizing a closet. Spend ample time planning and figuring out your particular organizational needs before you begin.

Start by evaluating the large items like shirts, pants, and other clothes that need to be hung—this will help define the broad strokes of how your space will be divided. Generally, there are two ways to deal with these clothes: a single horizontal bar or layers of bars. A single bar is easiest—see How to Install a Closet Rod, opposite, for instructions. But if that long expanse is too long for your needs, you're inviting dead space. Imagine other possibilities. Assume you don't want to hang clothes at ceiling height and instead anything above about head level will be home to a shelf of boxes, bins, baskets, or purses.

To "stack" the bars, you'll be dividing the space vertically. Say shirts claim half the available height, and pants and dresses take two thirds. You can either make the shirts double-decker or longer straight across. Decide whether you prefer the usable space to be above or below the pants and dresses—space above can hold shelves for folded clothes and space below can hold bins, drawers, or shelves to hold socks, shoes, and undergarments. If you like, draw a picture of your closet and then fill it in with lines to split this space in various ways. (If you really want to do it right, use graph paper and plot out the precise dimensions.) Then evaluate your construction skills—can you build your vision yourself, do you need to hire a contractor, or can you approximate it with a some-assembly-required closet organization system?

# #122
## HOW TO PATCH A HOLE IN DRYWALL

There's a distinctive sound drywall makes when it gets punched with a stray furniture leg or burdened to the breaking point with an improperly secured shelf—a sickening crunch followed by an agonizing cracking noise. If you haven't heard this, you will someday, and when that day comes you'll want to know how to patch a hole in drywall. Depending on the size of your puncture (from nail hole to gaping abyss), there are different techniques to fix it. Pick your poison from the instructions below.

### Patch a Tiny Hole

Nail and screw holes, along with other small punctures, can be covered over directly with drywall joint compound, aka putty, patching compound, or mud. (In a move-out pinch, you can use toothpaste on white walls to plug tiny holes. Just don't tell your landlord.)

### TOOLS:

**Fine sandpaper • Rags • Flexible 4" putty knife**

### MATERIALS:

• **Drywall compound**

**1 SAND AROUND THE HOLE TO** flatten any rough spots. Wipe away any sanding dust with a wet rag and let the area dry.

**2 USE A PUTTY KNIFE TO APPLY** drywall compound. Place a small amount directly into the small hole and then smooth it flat to the wall with the wide blade of the putty knife. Let it dry for about 2 hours and then apply a second layer if needed.

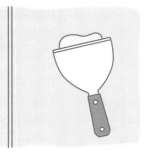

**3 SAND THE PUTTY SMOOTH, IF** needed. Dab the patch with paint to match the wall.

**Drywall panels are made from a compressed rock known as gypsum. Since gypsum contains water (bound in crystalline form) the material is considered to provide some protection against fire.**

## Patch Small Holes

If it's bigger than the size of a quarter but smaller than 8" × 8", you'll need to repair the hole with an adhesive wall patch as well as drywall compound.

## TOOLS:

**Rough sandpaper** ▪ **Medium sandpaper block** ▪ **Utility knife** ▪ **Putty knife** ▪ **Rags**

## MATERIALS:

- **Adhesive wall patch**
- **Drywall compound**
- **Texture spray (optional)**
- **Paint**

**1 REMOVE ANY LOOSE DRYWALL** in or around the hole. Use a utility knife to free any dangling pieces and to trim the edges of the hole until smooth. Finish cleaning the hole with coarse sandpaper.

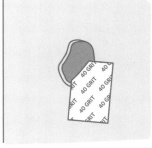

**2 COVER THE HOLE.** Fit an adhesive wall patch over the hole, extending around it several inches in each direction. It should look like you've covered the hole with cheesecloth. This is the backing against which you will apply drywall compound. A slightly larger hole, around 8" × 8", would require a galvanized metal patch, also available at your local hardware store.

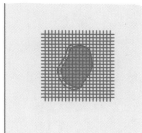

**3 SMOOTH OUT THE PATCH.** Use a putty knife to apply drywall compound over the wall patch. Starting out past the edges and moving toward the center, smooth the compound to completely cover the patch. You may need to let the edges of the patching compound dry for 15 or 20 minutes so that it can support the putty in the center of the wall patch. Don't worry about making the putty exactly smooth now—you'll sand it in the next step. Let the patching compound dry overnight.

**4 SMOOTH AGAIN.** Use fine sandpaper stapled to a wood block or a similar sanding tool to smooth the patching compound. Be aware that a somewhat flimsy adhesive patch is the only thing backing your hole, so pushing firmly into it while sanding is likely to crack the compound. Wipe away any sanding dust with a wet rag and let dry.

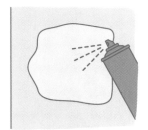

**5 PAINT THE PATCH.** Cover the patching compound with paint that matches the surrounding wall. If the wall is textured, spray it with wall texture spray to match, let dry overnight, and then paint.

## Patch Medium Holes

If your hole is greater than 8 inches square, you'll need to repair it with a Sheetrock plug. Common drywall (aka Sheetrock) is gypsum paste poured and hardened between sheets of paper. It can be cut to shape and used to plug large holes for a sturdier fix.

## TOOLS:

**Utility knife** ▪ **Measuring tape** ▪ **Pencil** ▪ **Medium sandpaper block** ▪ **4" putty knife**

## MATERIALS:

- **Square piece of drywall**
- **Drywall compound**
- **Texture spray (optional)**
- **Paint**

**1 REMOVE ANY LOOSE DRYWALL** and smooth out the hole as described in Step 1 on page 225.

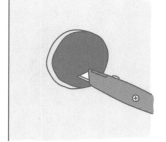

**2 MAKE THE PLUG.** On a square of drywall at least 2 inches wider than the hole on all sides, draw the shape of the cleaned and prepped hole. (Trace it first if it's too irregular to freehand.) Use a utility knife to cut out the shape of the plug

through the first layer of paper and also through the gypsum core, but leave the second layer of paper intact. It's better to cut the plug a little too big rather than too small, so cut around the outline to be safe.

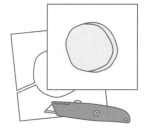

**3 FIT THE PLUG.** Shave the edges of the Sheetrock plug with a utility knife until it fits snugly in the wall hole.

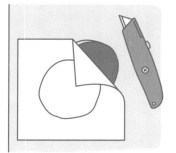

**4 SLOT THE PLUG INTO THE HOLE.** Position it with the intact layer of Sheetrock paper on the outside. If needed, trim the drywall paper so that it overlaps the dimensions of the hole by about an inch on all sides.

**5 ATTACH THE PLUG.** Spread a thin layer of drywall patching compound on the side of the paper that lies flush against the wall and press the paper firmly to the drywall around the hole to stick the plug in place.

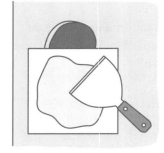

**6 FINISH THE PLUG.** Use a putty knife to patch the plug with drywall compound so that it's smooth and flush with the wall. Sand, texture-spray, and paint as described in Step 5 on page 225.

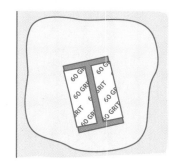

## Patch Large Holes

A hole of more than about a square foot in area requires something more than an adhesive patch or a drywall plug to properly fill it. In this case, you'll need to frame the back of the hole with a 2 × 4, and then attach a larger drywall patch to the frame.

## TOOLS:

**Utility knife** ▪ **Measuring tape** ▪ **Handsaw** ▪ **4" putty knife** ▪ **Medium sandpaper block**

## MATERIALS:

▪ **Scrap 14½" 2 × 4**
▪ **Framing nails or wood screws**
▪ **Drywall**
▪ **Drywall screws**
▪ **Drywall compound**
▪ **Texture spray (optional)**
▪ **Paint**

**1** **SQUARE UP YOUR HOLE.** Use a utility knife to cut the hole to a good approximation of a clean rectangle, extending toward the vertical wall studs on either side of the hole.

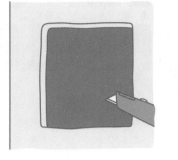

**2** **FRAME THE HOLE.** Cut one or more sections of scrap 2 × 4 to 14¼" lengths. These 2 × 4s will span between framing studs;

use enough 2 × 4s to reduce the size of any hole to less than a foot per side. Place these sections in the hole horizontally between the wall studs. Nail or screw the backing wood in place by reaching into the wall and nailing the 2 × 4s diagonally (see Toe-nailing box, below) through the backing wood and into the studs.

**3** **PLUG THE HOLE.** Draw the dimensions of the hole onto a piece of drywall and cut out the plug with a utility knife. Use drywall screws to attach the plug to the 2 × 4 backing and to any exposed vertical studs.

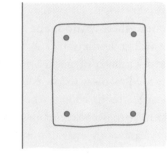

**4** **FINISH THE PATCH.** Use a putty knife to patch the plug with drywall compound so that it's smooth and flush with the wall. Sand, texture-spray, and paint as described on page 225.

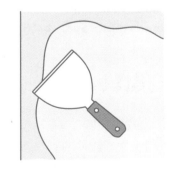

✕ ✕ ✕ ✕ ✕ ✕ ✕ ✕ ✕ ✕ ✕ ✕ ✕ ✕ ✕ ✕ ✕ ✕ ✕ ✕ ✕ ✕ ✕ ✕ ✕ ✕ ✕ ✕ ✕ ✕ ✕ ✕ ✕ ✕ ✕ ✕ ✕ ✕ ✕

# TOE-NAILING: IT HAS NOTHING TO DO WITH PEDICURES

**D**riving a nail into the end of a board at an angle can help you anchor it to another board. This procedure is called toe-nailing. Although it seems straightforward, it can be tricky, so here are a few tips:

• It's best to visualize where the nail will be going—you can do this by holding the nail up next to the boards at an angle.

• Start by tapping the nail in straight on to make the first hole. Then readjust your angle after you've made a small indent.

• If you can drive the nail at an angle through the first board and *then* position it on the other board, that's ideal.

• If you're at a loss for space, try drilling a pilot hole first.

# #123
## HOW TO PLASTER A WALL

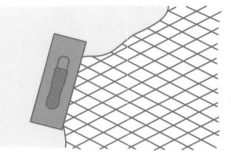

Lath and plaster—a technique for building walls that involves nailing narrow strips of wood (lath) across vertical studs to serve as a foundations for spreading plaster—was the dominant method of interior wall finishing in the US and Canada until the 1950s. As was typical of prewar construction, precision in lath-and-plaster work wasn't necessarily of utmost importance. So the laths that span horizontally across a plaster wall are likely to be somewhere around, but not exactly, 2" wide by ¾" thick, leaving about a ⅜" gap between courses. After the laths were laid, builders covered them with a thick layer of plaster, followed by a thinner second coat. The plaster was allowed to push through the gaps in the laths to the back, where it hooked around the boards which, when dry, held the plaster in place.

You may have historic plaster walls in your house, or you might have faux-finish plaster meant to replicate the feel of these walls. Whatever the case, it's useful to know how to repair it. The techniques in this section apply to stucco (usually an exterior finish) as well as to lime plaster (calcium hydroxide mixed with sand and water), though you'll need to add Portland cement to the mix for exterior stucco surfaces (the experts at your local home improvement store should be able to help).

## TOOLS:

**Bucket** • **Drill with stirring attachment** • **Trowel** • **Spot board** • **Joint spackling knife** • **Comb or plasterer's rake** • **Spray bottle of water**

## MATERIALS:

• **Plaster powder**
• **Sand**

**1 MIX THE PLASTER.** See How to Mix Plaster, page 230. Apply the rough coat. Use the flat edge of a joint knife to apply the first coat of plaster. Lay it on about ¼" thick (more than that and the plaster will take forever to dry and can be prone to cracking). Force this coat through the laths (or into the bricks) so that when the plaster dries, the hardened pieces that pushed through form "keys" that hold it firmly to the backing. Once you start a layer, work quickly to finish applying plaster to the wall before it dries, otherwise you're likely to be left with start and stop lines.

**2 RAKE THE PLASTER.** Before the rough coat dries completely, use a sturdy comb or plasterer's rake to score the surface into ridges that will help the next layer bond. Let the layer dry at least 24 hours or, ideally, 36 hours. Use a spray bottle to gently dampen the surface a couple of times to allow the plaster to dry slowly—this will make it stronger.

**3 APPLY THE SECOND LAYER.** This next coat is called the brown coat and goes on exactly like the first, ¼" thick, mixed with sand, but this time you don't rake the surface.

**4 APPLY THE FINAL LAYER.** For the third layer, leave the sand out of your plaster and, if you like, choose from a range of commercial colors and textures. (Follow manufacturer's instructions to add to the plaster.) Before the brown coat is completely dry, mix the plaster and apply it directly on top. While you apply the finish coat, it's very helpful to keep a spray bottle on hand to lightly mist the area where you're working. That will help this final layer go on smoother rather than having patches dry as you work (although the plaster won't be fully dry for 36 hours or more).

## Go Metal

If you're starting a plaster wall from scratch or if your job requires pulling plaster down to the laths, consider replacing wood laths with new metal ones. As wood laths expand and contract with moisture and temperature changes, they can crack the plaster. Metal laths don't have this problem and are also fitted with additional holes and pockets ("keys") that allow the plaster to hold more tightly. If plastering over brick, rather than laths, consider priming with a bonding agent that will help the plaster stick.

## PATCHING A HOLE IN PLASTER

**U**se a utility knife to clean the edges of the hole and remove any loose or cracked plaster. Then use a screwdriver to dig out the back of the hole (without further chipping the front!). Trimming behind the hole will allow new plaster to grab the laths behind the hole. Use one rough coat and one finishing coat to first fill and then cover the hole.

## Lime plaster is one of the oldest materials used for building—it's traditionally involved mixing horsehair into the water, lime, and sand for reinforcement.

# #124 HOW TO MIX PLASTER

Traditionally, plasterers used putty to create a reservoir on a plastering board. They poured water into this reservoir and then sprinkled it with plaster until it *felt* just right. When the lime in the plaster powder hits water, it creates a chemical reaction that releases heat—so when traditional plasterers felt that the heat was gone, they knew the plaster was ready for use. You can approximate this art in a bucket.

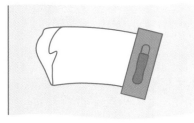

## TOOLS:

**Bucket** ▪ **Drill with mixing paddle attachment** ▪ **Trowel** ▪ **Spot board**

## MATERIALS:

▪ **Patching plaster**

**1 FILL A LARGE BUCKET WITH WATER.** You'll need enough water for a ratio of one part plaster to one part water. Consider starting with less plaster than you think you'll need and then making another batch once you've been through the process. Traditionally, the first coat of plaster was mixed with a bit of horsehair to help the plaster adhere to itself. Today, lime or gypsum plaster is mixed with sand, fiber, and water. Replacing lime with gypsum removes the need for fiber. Consider mixing three parts silica sand to one part gypsum powder for your first, rough coat of plaster.

**2 ADD PLASTER POWDER UNTIL** it starts to accumulate on the surface of the water (about half the total plaster you will be using). Use a stirring attachment on your drill to mix until smooth. Add half the remaining plaster powder and again mix until smooth, being sure to scrape the edge of the bucket free of lumps that can be difficult to blend with the smoother plaster. Continue adding plaster and mixing until it reaches a consistency at which it sits on a flat trowel without running off (make it a little thicker if you are plastering ceilings).

**3 POUR A WORKABLE AMOUNT OF** the mixture onto your plastering spot board. You have about 30 minutes to apply the plaster before it will be too dry to properly mold. See page 228 for best application practices.

# #125 HOW TO REPAIR CRACKED PLASTER

As the foundation settles, shifting can create hairline or larger cracks in plaster walls. It's easier to repair a wide crack than a hairline, which is too thin to allow plaster to form "keys" and adhere. So your first step in repairing a very thin crack is in fact to widen it.

## TOOLS:

**Utility knife** ▪ **Joint (spackling) knife**

## MATERIALS:

▪ **Patching plaster**

**1 USE A UTILITY KNIFE OR THE EDGE** of a trowel to dig into the hairline crack, widening it to about ⅛".

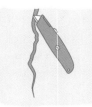

**2 MIX UP A SMALL AMOUNT OF** plaster (see How to Mix Plaster, left). Use a spackling knife to apply a ¼" layer of finish plaster (with color or texture added, as necessary to match), pressing it as deeply as possible into the crack and blending the edges of the new plaster over the existing finish.

# #126
## HOW TO PREPARE A SURFACE FOR PAINTING

Instead of painting a beautiful color on your walls that's doomed to peel or flake off and will require another coat (or two), always prime first. Any surface you paint should be primed, including walls, wood, concrete, or metal. The only time you may be able to skip priming is when you're painting over an already painted surface—that is, as long as the existing paint is in good condition and the new paint you're applying matches the base (oil or water) of the existing paint. If the existing paint is cracking, peeling, or chipped, or if you're applying oil-based paint over latex or vice versa, you must prime.

The tools you choose will depend on how much existing paint you need to rip off before applying new paint. So tools may range from a paint scraper to a wire brush to just a damp washcloth. Gauge the tools you need, and if at first you don't succeed, try something a little more heavy-duty.

## TOOLS:

**Paint scraper, wire brush, or damp washcloth (see headnote)** • **Fine sandpaper**

## MATERIALS:

• **Primer**

**1** IF YOU ARE SWITCHING FROM AN oil-based to a water-based paint (or vice versa) and the paint is intact on the surface, apply primer evenly and move on.

**2** IF THE EXISTING PAINT IS flaking, it's time to get scraping (or see How to Strip Paint, page 240). Scrape until paint stops coming off.

**3** AFTER SCRAPING, YOU'LL WANT to sand. This helps to get those last few chips of old paint off the surface and will also smooth imperfections.

**4** WIPE THE SURFACE WITH A damp washcloth to remove sawdust, dust, spiderwebs, and everything else you prefer not to make a permanent part of the surface.

**5** FINALLY, APPLY PRIMER. Paint it on as you would a regular coat of paint (see How to Paint a Room, page 232), and let dry.

**Pro tip: Tint the primer with a little bit of the final paint color.**

# #127
## HOW TO PAINT A ROOM

**M**aybe your attitude doesn't require, as Jimmy Buffett posited, a change in latitude. Maybe it just requires a new color scheme! If those beige walls are dragging you down, change it up. Painting is one of those DIY jobs that looks like a big deal but really isn't. It should only take one day to repaint a room. As with many projects, preparation turns out to be at least half the battle.

## Picking Your Paint

Paint finishes range in shine from flat to glossy. Flat finish paints are sometimes referred to as wall paint—they're the norm for most interior applications. For trim (baseboards, molding), go shinier—at least satin, if not semi-gloss, or even gloss. The contrast of flat to satin texture adds depth to a room, and glossier paints are formulated to withstand scrubbing—perfect for moldings, kids' rooms, and kitchens.

If you do go glossy, be sure to do your prep work—high-gloss finishes highlight imperfections that a flat paint will hide. One gallon of paint covers about 350 square feet of wall space. To estimate how much paint you'll need, multiply the length and height of your walls and add the surfaces together, subtracting 20 square feet for each door and about 10 square feet for the average window.

## TOOLS:

**Drop cloths • Painter's tape • Screwdriver • Rags • 4" putty knife • Paintbrushes (angled, trim) • 50-grit sandpaper • Paint tray and/or small paint bucket • Paint roller**

## MATERIALS:

- **Putty and/or patching caulk**
- **Soap**
- **Primer (if needed)**
- **Paint**
- **Paint thinner (if using oil-based paint)**

**1** **PREPARE THE SPACE.** Remove pictures and other hanging art and move furniture to the middle of the room or far enough from the walls to provide easy access. Cover the floor and furniture with drop cloths and tape them down with painter's tape to avoid slipping. Remove all electrical switch plates and then cover the sockets with painter's tape.

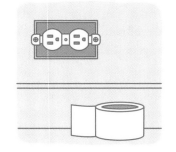

**2** **PUTTY OR OTHERWISE PATCH** all holes. Caulk or otherwise fill all gaps. Wash your old wall with soap and water to remove all oil, dirt, and accumulated grime. Perhaps more than anything else, this step is the difference between a pristine painted surface and a wall full of imperfections and drips.

**3 IF NECESSARY, PRIME THE WALL.**
New paint will stick to old paint (as long as you aren't changing from oil-based to water-based, or vice versa—see page 231), but it won't stick so well to bare drywall or plaster. Even if you have existing paint, if you've puttied large holes or otherwise done significant repair, consider priming to put all of your new paint on equal footing. When in doubt, prime. Primer can take anywhere from 30 minutes to 3 hours to dry, depending on the temperature of the room and how thick you apply it. Make sure you allow it to dry fully before moving to the next step.

**4 SAND.** Whether you are working with a primed wall or an old layer of paint, scuff the surfaces with 50-grit sandpaper to help the new paint adhere. You're not trying to rip away paint with this sanding, so you can do it by stapling your sandpaper to scrap wood and sanding by hand. Wipe down the surfaces with a damp rag to remove accumulated dust.

**5 TAPE—BUT DON'T OVER-TAPE!**
You know that sticking a layer of blue painter's tape to fixtures, baseboards, and crown molding can keep the paint just where you want it. But tape also gives you *permission* to make slips. And inevitably, if you're using tape as your ruler and simply painting over it, paint will sneak underneath and make a mess. If you have hard-to-reach places likely to see significant painting errors or any surfaces that for whatever reason can't be retouched, tape them. But be stingy with the tape and rely instead on angled brushes and a steady hand.

**6 DO YOUR EDGE WORK.** Pour a small reservoir of paint into a paint tray or small paint bucket (so you don't need to cart around the entire can). Then, starting with an angled brush, carefully paint along all edges, including 3 inches in from junctions with walls, corners, and molding. When you use an angled brush, only wet it with paint about a third of the way up the bristles and then tap it instead of wiping it to clear the extra paint. Run a stroke about an inch away from molding or another unpainted surface and then gently press the longer bristles of the brush close to precisely where the wall meets the base of the molding— hold your breath and draw a very straight line. Either hang a damp rag

from your belt or keep one within arm's reach so that you can quickly wipe away mistakes. If you wait until they dry, errors are much more difficult to remove.

Complete the edges of only one wall area and make the switch to rollers. This will help ensure your detail work is still wet when you apply the first rolled coat.

**7 PREPARE YOUR ROLLER.** Fill a paint tray with just enough paint so the top of the puddle reaches the bottom of the ridged grate. Dampen the roller. Use water for latex paint or paint thinner for oils. Smush the roller into the paint and then draw it up the grate to spread it uniformly across the roller. A splotchy roller makes for a splotchy paint job.

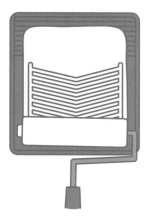

**8 ROLL OUT THE PAINT.** Slop paint onto the wall in large W shapes. Your goal at this stage isn't to cover the wall, merely to generally distribute the paint.

**9 FINISH THE FIRST COAT.** Once the paint starts to run thin on your W patterns, go back over the wall with even, vertical strokes. These strokes should spread the initially slopped paint evenly, and should overlap so the strokes bleed into each other. When the roller starts to make a crackling sound, reload it with paint. Remember: The first layer needn't be perfect.

**10 APPLY A SECOND COAT.** Let this layer dry thoroughly. Latex paints should dry within an hour; give oil-based paints a full 24 hours. If you need to apply a third coat, clean and sand the second (as in Steps 2 and 4) and then start again with the angled brush and roller (as in Step 8). When you've completed all coats on one wall, move on to the next and start over with Step 5.

**11 PAINT THE TRIM.** If you'd like to paint the molding and other trim, do that after the walls are rolled out. Start with a brush that's slightly narrower than the trim. For wide molding this can be a broad, straight brush but for thinner trim, consider a small angled brush. Once you've painted the front of the molding, finish the sides with a very small angled brush. This can take the steadiness of a surgeon and the patience of Mother Teresa. If in doubt, leave the molding to the pros.

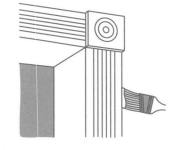

**If you're painting the ceiling, do that first (put down lots of dropcloths or newspaper!) as it will inevitably drip onto everything below. The techniques here apply to both ceilings and walls.**

# #128 HOW TO PAINT A FAUX FINISH

Have you ever wanted to sleep in the Sistine Chapel? How about the Taj Mahal? Or the Vatican? Well, you can't—but you can make your walls *look* like a marble sanctuary. Faux painting can do wonders for a room or piece of furniture, whether you are striving to replicate the look of a more expensive finish or simply adding spice to an otherwise monochromatic space. Here are guidelines for a variety of popular faux finishing techniques. Whenever trying a faux painting technique for the first time, experiment first on scrap board instead of going straight to the walls.

## Bronze

Recreating the look of bronze requires three slightly adjusted degrees of bronze glaze over a base coat.

## TOOLS:

**Paint roller and paint tray (optional)** ▪ **Paintbrushes** ▪ **50-grit sandpaper** ▪ **Rags** ▪ **3 buckets** ▪ **Sea sponge**

## MATERIALS:

- **Dark yellow latex (eggshell) paint**
- **Acrylic clear glaze**
- **Metallic topcoat glaze**

**1 PREP THE PAINTING SURFACE.** See How to Prepare a Surface for Painting, page 231.

**2 PAINT THE SURFACE.** Roll or brush on a latex eggshell base coat in a shade of dark yellow.

**3 PREPARE THE GLAZE.** In three separate buckets, mix the following three solutions: In the first, combine one part yellow base-layer paint with three parts clear glaze; in the second, combine some of the first bucket's mixture with a metallic topcoat glaze to blend. And in the third bucket mix one part of the second bucket's mixture with ½ part water.

**4 ADD THE GLAZE.** Use a roller or brush to apply these three mixtures to the wall, over your base coat. If you have three people painting, start at the same time, one with each mixture; otherwise start painting with any mixture and then switch frequently to the others. Patterns should be random and overlapping. Use a sea sponge to push the three mixtures into each other, covering the entire wall with blended glaze.

**5 FINISH THE GLAZE.** Let the wall dry completely and then use a sea sponge to dab on a metallic topcoat glaze.

1 PART BASE-LAYER PAINT & 3 PARTS CLEAR GLAZE

SOME OF BUCKET 1 MIX & METALLIC TOPCOAT GLAZE

1 PART OF BUCKET 2 MIX & 1/2 PART WATER

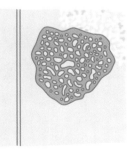

## Marble

Marble is a tricky faux finish, so make sure you practice on a (primed) scrap board. There are many colors of marble, ranging from pink to orange to red to green and blue. Replicating the look of marble is more an art than a craft. When choosing your paint, imagine four colors that come together in your ideal marble. Keep a photo of your model marble on hand to review as you paint.

## TOOLS:

**Paintbrushes** ▪ **50-grit sandpaper** ▪ **4 paint buckets** ▪ **Rags** ▪ **Sea sponge**

## MATERIALS:

- **Primer**
- **Paint (4 shades, including white: see headnote)**
- **Latex glaze**
- **Varnish**

**1 PREP THE SURFACE AS PER STEP 1** in Bronze. Prime, and apply a white base coat. Let it dry and then sand it lightly, brushing free any dust with a damp rag.

**2 PAINT THE BASE COAT.** In four separate buckets, mix one part paint with one part water and one part clear latex glaze. Start with two somewhat similar colors as your base. Brush wavy patterns of these two colors onto the wall or piece of furniture so they bleed into each other in fairly organic patterns. Use a wet painting sponge to soften and blur the lines between them.

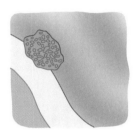

**3 ADD THE MARBLING.** Paint veins with the other two colors. Use a paintbrush or sponge to drip a small ribbon of paint in from the top of the wall and then feather the edges of these veins into the base colors by pulling their edges with a dry brush.

**4 REFINE THE MARBLING.** Review your image of marble—likely there are thinner, crisper veins in addition to the wider, colored swaths you just painted. Use a thin paintbrush to snake appropriately colored veins (likely white) through the multicolored base you laid.

**5 ADD DETAIL.** Marble also frequently includes colored mineral intrusions. Using your best artistic sense, add these intrusions by dabbing on your fourth color of paint with a sea sponge and then feather the edges into the background with a dry brush.

**6 FINISH UP—OR START OVER.** If your marbling simply didn't work, prime over it and try again. Once you're comfortable with its appearance, finish the marbling with a layer of protective varnish.

## Terra Fresco

For that Italian villa look, cover your walls with a faux finish that replicates this classic Mediterranean plastering technique. Mimicking this surface requires plaster and three off-brown colors of latex paint. Think shades of ochre and café au lait—choose according to your preference and decor. As with other finishes, using an image as a guide can be helpful.

## TOOLS:

- Rags ▪ 50-grit sandpaper ▪
- 3 buckets ▪ Plasterer's blade

## MATERIALS:

- **Primer**
- **Drywall compound**
- **3 colors of latex paint in reddish brown, orangish brown, and brick**

**1 PREP THE SURFACE AS PER** Step 1 in Bronze.

**2 MIX THE PAINT WITH DRYWALL** compound. In three separate buckets, add drywall compound to three shades of paint, just until the paint thickens slightly.

**3 APPLY THE BASE COAT.** Choose base color—not necessarily the darkest or lightest color, but the color that is closest to the desired finished color—and use a plasterer's blade to apply a fairly thin layer of the plaster mixture to a section of the wall. Cover the wall completely with this base layer. You can make this a slightly thicker consistency than the top layers.

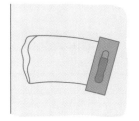

**4 ADD THE LAYERS.** While the base plaster is still wet, use the blade to blend smaller amounts of the other two colors into the wall. Use your aesthetics—this step should make the wall look very close to your image of terra fresco. Apply thin coats, being careful not to overload the surface of the wall with plaster.

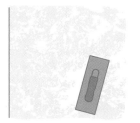

## Stone

From fireplace mantels to tabletops, a stone finish adds texture and warmth. As with terra fresco, you combine plaster with paint to get the desired organic look. Faux stone finishes can range from a deep red sandstone to gray slate. Basically, you'll want to pick a base color and two highlight colors—consider looking online at pictures of the rock you plan to mimic and choosing your colors accordingly.

## TOOLS:

**50-grit sandpaper • Plasterer's blade or trowel • Paintbrush**

## MATERIALS:

- **Primer**
- **Drywall compound**
- **3 colors of latex paint**
- **Clear latex glaze**

**1 PREP THE SURFACE AS PER STEP 1** in Bronze.

**2 PLASTER THE SURFACE.** After prepping the wall, spread a thin (¼") layer of drywall compound over it with a plasterer's blade.

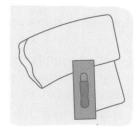

**3 TEXTURE THE SURFACE.** When the compound is tacky but not yet dry, press the blade (or a trowel) flat into the compound and pull it straight out to texture the entire surface. This will take some art—shoot for gentle texture rather than the peaks and valleys of cake frosting. Let the plaster dry fully.

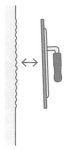

**4 PAINT THE WALL.** Brush on a base coat that matches your desired color of stone. Allow the layer to dry.

**5 APPLY ACCENT COLORS.** Use a painter's sponge to dab on each accent color in patterns that match your desired stone look. If necessary, use a dry rag to blend accent colors into the base color.

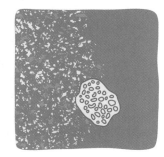

# #129
## HOW TO POLISH FURNITURE

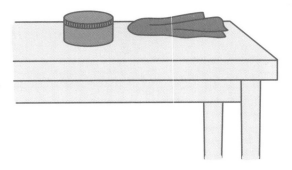

**W**ax finishes have been used for a thousand years, but their modern use has waned (pardon the pun). That's because they're not especially protective, as it turns out. Yes, you can coat a console table in wax, but don't expect it to resist water and wear. Instead, a wax finish alone is best reserved for hands-off wood pieces like art. However, paired with a protective finish like lacquer, shellac, or varnish, wax will fill tiny scratches to restore luster, so polishing finished furniture with wax makes it really shine. Wax-based furniture polishes are common—when your finish loses its glow, simply rub on a new layer.

## Why Wax?

Stain colors wood. Varnish, lacquer, shellac, and other finishes protect wood. And wax shines wood. Because wax locks in oils and keeps a piece from drying and cracking, it's especially useful for finished furniture that sits in a sunny location. No matter how you use it, wax is rarely worth using alone—it provides no barrier against water, heat, or a wine spill. Instead, combine it with stains and protective finishes to achieve the look you want with the durability you need. Though some woodworkers insist otherwise, protective finishes like lacquer, shellac, and varnish shouldn't be applied on top of wax—they simply won't grip. Instead think of wax as the finishing touch.

## Which Wax?

Like oil finishes and varnishes, many wax furniture finishes are derived from natural sources. Chief among these are carnauba wax, derived from the leaves of the carnauba palm, and beeswax, which is derived from, well, bees.

Most waxes are sold in a tin similar to the kind you would expect to hold shoe polish. That's no accident—wax finishes, in fact, work very much like shoe polish, and are applied in the same way. And like shoe polish, you should match the color of the wax to the color of the piece. Wax in a complementary color can make a finish shine; contradictory wax color will cloud it. You can find paint-on wax finishes, but they're traditionally (and still most commonly) sold as pastes.

Be sure that whatever wax you get, it's compatible with the existing finish. Some waxes include a solvent that makes the wax easier to work with and can help create a more uniform finish, but solvent-based wax will eat into a water-based finish. Likewise, make extra sure that your protective finish has dried completely before applying a solvent-based wax, otherwise you risk harming the finish.

## TOOLS:

**Lint-free rags**

## MATERIALS:

- **Oil soap**
- **Furniture wax**

**1 APPLY THE WAX.** Before application, thoroughly wipe the piece clean with a rag dampened with soap and water. Wipe the piece dry with a lint-free cloth to be sure no dust, dirt, or other impurities remain. Start with a small dollop of paste wax on a clean cloth covering your first two fingers. A little wax goes a surprisingly long way and it's easier to apply wax a little at a time than to end up with gobs of wax that must be scrubbed away. Like polishing a shoe, rub the wax onto the wood piece with circular motions. If applying wax directly to bare wood or to stained (but not protected) wood, focus on pushing the wax down into the wood grain. The most forceful stroke should go with the wood grain, but continue to work the polish in a circular pattern. If applying wax over a protective finish like a lacquer, varnish, or shellac, the wood's grain will already be hidden and you can wax the piece just as you would wax a car or shoe. Apply wax until you see it start to build up on the surface of the piece.

**2 BUFF THE FURNITURE.** After applying wax, wait for the wood to turn hazy—this indicates dried wax remaining on the surface, instead of sinking into the pores, which must be wiped from the piece. However, if you wait too long, wax will dry into a fairly impervious shell that can be difficult to remove. Buff when wax is cloudy but not yet firm. Use a clean piece of lint-free, cotton cloth to rub the waxed furniture until it shines. Don't be shy: You should expect to remove the bulk of the wax you just applied. If you accidentally wait too long, consider applying another layer of wax, which can help to significantly loosen the dried first layer.

**Beeswax was so highly coveted in the ancient world that it was considered a valuable form of currency. When the Romans conquered the island of Corsica in 181 BC, the defeated Corsicans were taxed 100,000 pounds of beeswax.**

# #130
## HOW TO STRIP PAINT

You know for a fact that there's a gorgeous oak chair underneath that hideous hot-pink paint, and you need to set it free. Or perhaps you'd like to expose the wood trim in your old farmhouse. There are so many reasons to want to remove paint, and the results are almost always worth the hassle.

### Chemical Warfare

For years, the standby chemical for stripping paint has been methylene chloride; however, it's exceedingly toxic and can even be fatal. Opt instead for benzyl alcohol or soy-based strippers, which are safer for you and the environment. (If you do use a methylene chloride–based paint stripper, you must wear a respirator, chemical-resistant gloves, and protective clothes, and catch all excess chemicals with a drop cloth and rags.)

Some paint strippers are spray-on liquids while others are paint-on gels. Liquids are good for removing one or two coats of paint and for hard-to-reach or irregular surfaces. Gels generally sit on the paint longer and fight gravity better—they can be painted on walls and even overhangs. Because gels sit longer, they work better for tough projects, like removing 15 layers of paint from century-old clapboard.

### The Sanding Option

You can also sand away old paint. But for a large job like the side of a house, sanding is a fairly inefficient method. Likewise, it may not be the right method for a delicate job like fine furniture, because it removes a layer of the underlying wood along with the paint. For those Goldilocks jobs that are neither too big nor too fine, scouring the paint away with coarse-grain sandpaper helps you avoid the use of chemicals.

### Get the Lead Out

In 1978, lead was outlawed as a paint additive. Before that, however, it was used widely. So if you're stripping layers of old paint, be aware that it might contain lead. In that case, stay away from sanding, which can create inhalable lead-tinged dust. While stripping, make sure you catch lead paint flakes on a drop cloth, and bag and dispose of them properly at a hazardous waste collection center.

✕ ✕ ✕ ✕ ✕ ✕ ✕ ✕ ✕ ✕ ✕ ✕ ✕ ✕ ✕ ✕ ✕ ✕ ✕ ✕ ✕ ✕ ✕ ✕ ✕ ✕ ✕ ✕

## SOME LIKE IT HOT

If you want to avoid chemicals, you can also strip paint with a heat gun. Hold the heat gun in one hand and a paint scraper in the other as you heat and then scrape away the paint, one small section at a time. Be sure to keep the heat gun moving constantly so it doesn't scorch the surface or create dangerous embers. On small jobs, you can even substitute a hair dryer for the heat gun; just hold it very close to the paint and don't expect it to peel off in sheets.

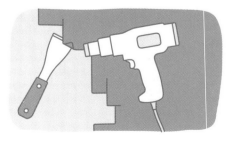

## TOOLS:

**Safety goggles** · **Chemical-resistant gloves** · **Drop cloth** · **Disposable paintbrush** · **Rags** · **Paint scraper** · **Wire brush**

## MATERIALS:

- **Paint stripper (see Chemical Warfare, opposite)**

**1 SAFETY FIRST.** Before using any corrosive chemicals like paint stripper, put on safety goggles and chemical-resistant gloves (thin latex won't do it) and make sure the work area is well-ventilated. Open windows and doors, or move the item to be stripped outside (onto a drop cloth).

**2 COAT THE SURFACE WITH PAINT** stripper. Spray or brush the paint stripper onto the surface to be stripped until thoroughly covered with an even layer. Let sit, as per the manufacturer's instructions.

**3 REMOVE THE PAINT.** With a rag, wipe away the paint stripper, gently scraping any stubborn spots. The paint should come off in sheets or globs.

# #131 HOW TO PREPARE A WOOD SURFACE FOR PAINTING

That old deck chair or thrift-store bookshelf may be weather-worn, but with a coat of paint it could be good as new. Before you go to town on it, though, you need to determine: Is the wood bare or is it coated with a non-paint finish? This is an important question, because latex paint won't stick to an oil-based varnish. If upon closer inspection the wood does in fact have a finish, consider a varnish remover or prime it with a primer matched to oil-based varnishes (see Which Primer is Prime?, below). But here's what to do if the wood really *is* bare.

## TOOLS:

**Rag** · **50-grit sandpaper**

## MATERIALS:

- **Oil soap**
- **Bleach (if needed)**
- **Primer**

**1 PREPARE THE SURFACE.** Wash the wood with oil soap, like Murphy, and water and wipe away any grime with a rag. If the wood has been outside or in a damp area, look for mildew spots. These are more than mere discolorations—they're alive! Rather than sanding or scraping or simply painting over the spots, you need to kill the spores or the mildew is likely to regrow. Scrub the affected area with a solution of one part household bleach and three parts water and let dry. Likewise, remove any rust, splinters, and obvious imperfections that may affect the paint job.

**2 SAND THE SURFACE WITH 50-GRIT** sandpaper. You want to rough up the surface and thoroughly degloss it so that the primer and paint have more to grip on to. When you're finished sanding, wipe the surface again with a damp rag to remove any sawdust. Let the surface dry.

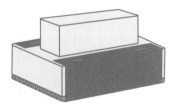

**3 APPLY PRIMER EVENLY OVER** the surface to be painted.

---

✕ ✕ ✕ ✕ ✕ ✕ ✕ ✕ ✕ ✕ ✕ ✕ ✕ ✕ ✕ ✕ ✕ ✕ ✕ ✕ ✕ ✕ ✕ ✕ ✕ ✕ ✕ ✕ ✕ ✕ ✕ ✕ ✕ ✕ ✕ ✕ ✕ ✕ ✕ ✕

# WHICH PRIMER IS PRIME?

When painting over an oil-based stain, a bonding primer will keep your paint from rolling off like water from a duck's back. Use an oil primer for unfinished or weathered wood, distressed paint, varnish, or woods like redwood that bleed tannins and so require an oil-based primer to lock the juices inside. Use a latex-based primer on non-wood surfaces like drywall, masonry, or metal, and also on softwoods like pine. Remember, before you prime, always thoroughly degloss the surface with sandpaper.

# #132
## HOW TO REFINISH FURNITURE
### (or, Giving New Life to Old Wood)

Say you just inherited the desk that was in your room as a middle schooler—complete with scars, pencil tracks, and chipped varnish. Before you can allow the desk to leave the garage, you simply have to refinish the surface. The process of refinishing wooden furniture involves removing the old finish, sanding the wood to a near-pristine state, and then protecting it with a new finish—in this case, that would be varnish, though you can see a complete list of wood finish options on page 281.

## Choosing a Varnish

Like paint, varnish comes in a variety of styles, including gloss, semi-gloss, matte, satin, and flat. It's up to you how shiny you want the finished piece, but the degree of gloss doesn't only affect shine—it also determines how smooth and how saturated with color your piece appears. A high-gloss finish accentuates a piece's lines, but also highlights its imperfections. If your piece is slightly chipped or otherwise more "rustic" than you would like, consider a flat varnish to smooth out the appearance of those rough edges.

You can also choose between natural-resin and synthetic, and oil- and water-based varnishes. It used to be that water-based varnishes were shorter-lived, but newer water-based varnishes have greatly improved on their predecessors and are now a viable, less toxic alternative to oil-based varnish. Water-based varnish doesn't yellow over time like an oil-based varnish, but it can be prone to clouding when applied in more than three layers. Also consider polyurethane varnish—a variety of synthetic. Other synthetic varnishes, like phenolics, are specifically for marine use.

Buy only as much varnish as you need for the project you have planned—once you've closed a can of varnish and let it sit in the garage for a year, dried flakes from the edges are likely to fall into the product next time you open it. A can of varnish should describe how much surface area the can will cover; if you have any leftover, properly dispose of the remainder (at a household hazardous waste collection center). Rags soaked in varnish should be hung to dry (never balled up—they can catch fire) and disposed of with other hazardous waste.

## Safety First

Varnish works by combining resin with a solvent that keeps the resin in liquid form until painted onto your wood surface. Once applied, the solvent evaporates, leaving behind the hard, translucent finish. Working with varnish necessarily releases fumes into the air—that's the solvent evaporating—so most varnish solvents are harmful to breathe. Always work outdoors or in a well-ventilated area. For a longer job, or if you plan to work with varnish frequently, consider using a respirator to protect your lungs.

## TOOLS:

**Rags • Random orbital sander (or paint stripper) • Medium to fine (80- to 100-grit) sandpaper • Putty knife • Steel wool • Disposable brush • Chemical-resistant rubber gloves • Respirator (optional) • Drop cloth (or newspapers) • Stir stick • Paint tray**

## MATERIALS:

- **Paint stripper (or random orbital sander)**
- **Grain filler (optional)**
- **Wood stain (optional)**
- **Varnish**

**1 REMOVE THE OLD FINISH.** Wipe down the piece with a damp rag to remove any accumulated dust and dirt. Follow the instructions in How to Strip Paint on page 240, and opt for a gel and not a liquid stripper (it is prone to drain off furniture before it can work properly). Use a putty knife and steel wool to remove as much paint or varnish as possible. If you don't want to use a chemical stripper, reach for the random orbital sander (or spend hours building muscle and character sanding by hand).

**2 SAND THE WOOD.** Even if you use a chemical stripper, you'll still need to sand to get a smooth finished surface. See How to Sand Wood on page 280—and remember, always sand with the grain! If your wood has a particularly high grain, consider applying grain filler before moving on to varnish. If you do, pick a filler color that either contrasts with the desired finish (to highlight the grain pattern) or matches it (to hide the grain).

**3 STAIN THE WOOD.** If you would like to add color to your piece, now's the time to stain it. It's stain that provides the color you want and varnish that protects it. Consider testing stain on scrap wood first, both to see the dried color and also to see how many coats of stain it will take to get the color you want. When applying stain, brush with the direction of the wood grain. Let the stain dry for 3 to 6 hours, then wipe with a slightly damp rag before continuing.

**4 APPLY THE VARNISH.** Once dried, varnish is extremely difficult to remove, so lay down a drop cloth or newspapers to guard the floor. Likewise, protect your hands with thick rubber gloves. The mixture of resin and solvent in a varnish means it can separate—make sure to mix the can thoroughly before applying varnish and periodically while working, Pour the varnish into a paint tray and apply it as you would a coat of paint, using light strokes to avoid streaking the finish.

**5 APPLY MULTIPLE COATS,** waiting 6 hours between each coat. Sand very lightly between coats with fine-grit sandpaper— you don't want to rub off all the varnish you just applied, but slightly roughening the finish will allow the second coat to stick better. Between coats, check the surface to ensure that there are no flies in the ointment, or accumulated dust, which can severely mar the finish. If the surface is going to see heavy, everyday use, consider applying a fourth coat of varnish.

# #133
## HOW TO CAULK A BATHTUB

Caulk has two major predators: mechanical damage like gouges and peeling, and mildew. You know the look of the first and hopefully your bathroom is ventilated enough so that you don't know the look of the second. Mildew is a generic name for any mold that grows in damp places. There are a couple of kinds of mildew, and once any one of them gets a toehold in your bathroom caulking, it can be almost impossible to kill. If your caulking is speckled black, consider replacing it.

## TOOLS:

**Caulk removal tool or putty knife and screwdriver** ▪ **Razor blade** ▪ **Vacuum cleaner** ▪ **Rags** ▪ **Caulking gun** ▪ **Utility knife or sharp scissors**

## MATERIALS:

- **Caulk softener**
- **Mineral spirits or rubbing alcohol**
- **Caulk**
- **Caulking tape**

**1 REMOVE EXISTING CAULK.** First wipe down the existing caulk and then spray, wipe, or squirt on a commercial caulk softener, letting it sit as per the manufacturer's instructions. A caulk removal tool should cost less than $10 and is a useful, but not necessary, addition to this project. Using the tool or a putty knife and screwdriver, gouge away the old caulk. If using a metal tool, be careful not to scratch the surface around the caulk, both for cosmetic reasons and because any imperfections in the finish provide footing for future mildew. Make another pass with the caulk removal tool to scrape free as much residue as possible. If needed, finish with a razor blade—you want no caulk remaining. Use a strong vacuum cleaner to suck free as many caulk pieces and other gunk as possible. Then aggressively wipe the seam with mineral spirits or rubbing alcohol.

**2 PREPARE THE TUB.** Fill the tub with water to expand it to its maximum size. (You can empty it after the caulk has dried.)

Use caulking tape along the surfaces directly above and below the seam. In addition to protecting neighboring surfaces, tape should also help you visualize, define and plan the size of the caulk bead you will draw.

**3 APPLY THE NEW CAULK.** Ideally, use a caulking gun, which allows you the best control for drawing a consistent, even bead. Most manufacturers also offer caulk in squeezable tubes, which are good for small jobs, and some caulks also come in aerosol form. Load the caulk into the caulking gun and cut off the tip of the tube at a 45-degree angle. Puncture the seal with a nail and test the bead. If the bead is too small, cut off another short section of the tip. Squeeze the trigger of the caulk gun and run a slow, consistent bead from one end of the seam to the other. If caulking a vertical seam, start at the bottom. This can take practice—if you break the bead or are unhappy with its evenness, you'll have to start over. In that case, wipe away your first attempt with a rag before it dries. Once you're happy with the bead, wet your finger and run it down the seam, pressing the caulk into the seam.

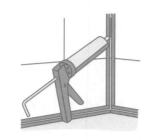

**4** **GENTLY PEEL AWAY THE TAPE** and let the caulk dry thoroughly (following the instructions on the tube) before allowing it to get wet.

× × × × × × × × × × × × × × × × × × × × × × × × × × × × × × × × × × × × × × × × × × × × × × × × × × × × × × ×

# TYPES OF CAULK

There's a caulk for every job. Here are some of the most common.

**Silicone:** This is the best caulk for bathrooms and other damp areas. It doesn't stick to wood or other porous surfaces but is ideal for ceramic and tile. Silicone caulk can't be painted, so choose a color that matches your decor.

**Latex:** Easier to apply but not as long-lasting as silicone caulk. It can be painted, however, and can also be used on porous surfaces. It's also better for gaps that don't flex—i.e., not for the space around your tub that expands slightly with the added weight of water.

**Polyurethane:** Best for window and door use, as it bonds to wood. Unlike silicone, polyurethane caulk dries hard.

**Acrylic and vinyl:** Good options for filling the gaps around windows that remain closed. These caulks adhere to wood and porous surfaces and can be painted. They also come in a variety of colors to match existing paint.

**Painter's caulk:** An inexpensive latex caulk used to fill small holes in sheetrock or plaster walls prior to painting.

**Mortar caulk:** A special formula for filling holes or cracks in brick or concrete.

In your bathroom, the most common mildew is *Cladosporium,* a speckled black or dark green mold that sometimes appears around the tub. It's different from the highly toxic "black mold" that haunts every homeowner's nightmares, but you'll still want to remove it.

# #134
## HOW TO REPLACE A CRACKED TILE

How broken is a broken ceramic tile on the floor or bathroom wall? If the answer is "Not so broken," you might be able to avoid replacing it (see A Simple Fix, opposite). But if the ceramic tile now carries a star-shaped pattern of cracks as if struck with a hammer or if sections of tile have been crushed or lost, you'll have to replace it. If you live in an older home, it may be a major challenge to find just the right replacement tile. If you don't have any leftover tiles, bring broken pieces with you to a tile store, where you should be able to find a reasonable replacement.

## TOOLS:

**Rag ▪ Hammer ▪ Chisel ▪ Putty knife ▪ Grout removal tool ▪ Craft stick or old toothbrush**

## MATERIALS:

- **Replacement tile**
- **Tile adhesive**
- **Tube of grout to match existing grout**
- **Grout sealer**

**1 REMOVE THE BROKEN TILE.** Cover the tile with a rag and smash it to bits with a hammer. (Be careful not to smash the nearby tiles.) Chisel out the bits of tile and clean out the old glue, ideally with a putty knife or chisel.

**2 EVALUATE THE GROUT.** If it's chipped or decaying, use a grout remover to scrape it free.

Wipe the edges of the hole with a rag to clear away any additional debris. Dry thoroughly.

**3 AFFIX THE REPLACEMENT TILE.** Spread tile adhesive onto the back of a new tile and push it into place.

**4 REPLACE OR REFRESH THE** grout. If you removed grout, now is the time to add new. If you didn't remove grout, now is the time to augment the existing grout so that it holds the edges of the new tile. Select a squeeze tube of grout in a color that matches the existing grout. Pack the grout around the replacement tile with a craft stick or the handle end of an old toothbrush. Once the grout is mostly dry, wipe off the tile with a damp rag.

**5** **SEAL THE GROUT.** Apply grout sealer to protect the fresh grout and its tile. Let dry completely before getting the tile wet, as per the sealer manufacturer's instructions.

× × × × × × × × × × × × × × × × × × × × × × × × × × × × × × × × × × × × × × × × × ×

## A SIMPLE FIX

**A** crack may not necessitate replacement. If the crack hasn't deformed the shape of the tile or if there aren't chunks missing, try painting over it with pigment and tile filler. Mix paint that exactly matches your tile color with tile filler, then dab it onto the crack with a cotton swab. If the crack is more than a hairline, try to push the filler into its depths. Don't worry about filler spilling over the edges. Once the mixture is tacky but not dry, wipe the area with a damp cloth. Ideally, you'll be able to pull the filler and paint down to the level of the crack, leaving a smooth repair.

**If you can't find the right tile in the tile store (and if you don't have any extras around the house), you could look into made-to-order tiles, or consider replacing multiple tiles in an "accent" pattern.**

# #135 HOW TO PATCH LINOLEUM

Repairing a damaged section of linoleum is a lot like fixing damaged tile—though perhaps even easier because there's no finicky ceramic or grout to deal with. It's a manageable fix with modest DIY skills, so there's no need to put up with ugly cracked linoleum.

## TOOLS:

**Measuring tape** ▪ **Utility knife** ▪ **Putty knife or flathead screwdriver** ▪ **Rags**

## MATERIALS:

- **Scrap linoleum**
- **Soap**
- **Linoleum adhesive**
- **Acrylic seam sealer**

**1 CUT THE PATCH.** Do you have matching scrap linoleum in the garage? If so, you're in luck. If not, consider cutting a patch from an unseen area (such as under the refrigerator or stove) or seek out matching material from a flooring specialist. Use a utility knife to cut a square patch of linoleum about an inch larger on all sides than the damaged area.

**2 MATCH THE PATCH TO THE** damage. Set the linoleum patch on top of the damaged area and use the utility knife to cut out the damaged linoleum in exactly the same dimensions as the patch.

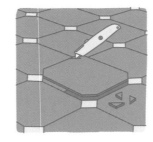

**3 REMOVE THE DAMAGED** linoleum. Use a putty knife or flathead screwdriver to pry free the damaged area. If the damaged linoleum refuses to budge, take a tip from your ceramic tile skill set and chop the damaged area into smaller, more manageable sections, which you can then pry out. You can also try heating the damaged area with a heat gun or hair dryer to loosen it. With the damaged section removed, scrub the area aggressively with soap and water and rinse with clean water. Dry the area thoroughly.

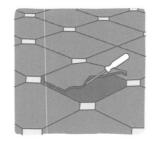

**4 DRY FIT THE PATCH.** Place the patch into the hole you cut to ensure proper sizing. If needed, trim the patch or the hole so it fits without buckling.

**5 AFFIX THE PATCH.** Apply linoleum adhesive to the back of the patch and press it into place firmly, to squeeze out any air bubbles trapped underneath.

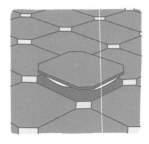

**6 SEAL IT UP.** Coat the seams with seam sealer (in a finish that matches your floor, be it high-gloss or matte) and let the area dry for at least a couple of hours before walking on it.

# #136
# HOW TO REPLACE A DAMAGED SECTION OF CARPET

There are so many ways to ruin a piece of carpet—a dropped candle, a glass of red wine, a pet with unfortunate habits. Of course, replacing wall-to-wall carpeting is an exceedingly high price to pay for one little area of damage. Fortunately, it's simple to replace just a piece of it, and no one will be the wiser—especially if the carpet is on the shaggy side, the repair is nearly invisible.

## TOOLS:

**Measuring tape • Utility knife**

## MATERIALS:

- **Carpet scrap**
- **Double-sided carpet tape or adhesive**

**1 CUT A PATCH.** Locate or purchase a piece of carpet scrap that is identical or very similar to the damaged section. (If the patch is very visible, you'll need to be especially careful about matching.) Cut a rectangle from the carpet scrap that is about an inch larger on all sides than the damaged area. In order for the patch to blend with the surrounding carpet, make sure you cut the patch so the direction of the pile (the upper layer, also called the nap) matches that of the carpet.

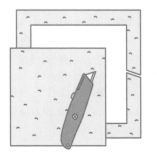

**2 MATCH THE PATCH TO THE** damage. Set the patch on top of the damaged area and use it as a guide as you cut out the damaged area with a utility knife. If possible, try not to cut into the carpet pad underneath.

**3 DRY FIT THE PATCH.** Place the patch into the hole and trim, if needed, so that it fits snugly, with no gaps.

**4 STICK THE PATCH IN PLACE.** With either double-sided carpet tape or an adhesive, press it into the hole. Allow ample time for drying before walking on it.

# #137
# HOW TO REFINISH A WOOD FLOOR

Drop a bead of water on your hardwood floor. What happens to the droplet? If it beads against the wood and then slowly soaks in, try a thorough cleaning and polishing before reaching for the drum sander. If the water fails to bead and instead soaks directly into the wood, it's time to refinish.

## TOOLS:

Drum sander (plan to rent) ▪ Extra-coarse (24-grit) sandpaper ▪ Medium (60-grit) sandpaper ▪ Fine (100-grit) sandpaper ▪ Random orbital sander ▪ Wet/dry vacuum

## MATERIALS:

- Plastic trash bags
- Masking tape
- Floor finish of your choice (consult your local home improvement store)

**1** REMOVE EVERYTHING FROM THE room. Put plastic trash bags over any light fixtures (paint during the day so you don't need to turn them on) and secure with masking tape. Tape over all electrical sockets and any other wall openings.

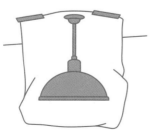

**2** PROCURE AND PREPARE THE sander. Rent a drum sander from a hardware store, and load it with extra-coarse sandpaper. If you haven't used a drum sander before, begin in an area that will be covered by a rug or furniture. Tip the drum sander back before you start it; once the sanding pad reaches speed, gently lower it onto the floor. Keep the sander moving, never letting it rest in a single spot while the sanding pad is moving.

**3** AFTER A THOROUGH PASS WITH extra-coarse sandpaper, switch to medium. Sand until the floor is level and smooth.

**4** SAND THE EDGES AND CORNERS of the room. Switch to a random orbital sander with medium sandpaper for the areas that the drum sander won't reach. Use any available means to clean the sawdust, including a wet/dry vacuum.

**5** JUST AS THERE ARE MANY ways to finish a deck (see How to Refinish a Deck, opposite), there are many ways to finish hardwood floors. Popular options include wax, water-based polyurethane, and oil-based polyurethane. Or, you can even hire a pro to acid-finish your floors (also called "Swedish finish").

# #138
# HOW TO REFINISH A DECK

So you finally got around to power washing your deck to expunge the layer of mildew and bird poop. But now the wood grain is standing high and you can't walk across your deck barefoot without risking the puncture wounds of a thousand splinters. It's time to sand and refinish the deck. Not only will it smooth down those splinters, but it will extend the life of the deck and keep your home looking spiffy. Use any power sander—a 5" random orbital sander with medium sandpaper works well.

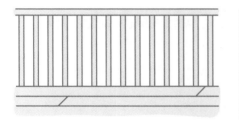

## TOOLS:

**Orbital floor sander (plan to rent)** • **Coarse to medium (20- to 50-grit) sandpaper** • **Medium to fine (80- to 100-grit) sandpaper**

## MATERIALS:

• **Deck finish of your choice (consult your local home improvement store)**

**1** **CLEAN THE DECK.** Remove all furniture, including the grill, and thoroughly sweep the deck clean of all leaves and debris. Start sanding the deck. Plan the course of your sanding so that you can cover all areas evenly (start in a corner and work your way around). Run the power sander with the grain of the wood and apply light, even pressure as you let the sander do its work. If the wood of your deck is especially weathered or warped, start with a 20-grit sandpaper. If not, start with 50-grit and then make another pass with 80-grit.

**2** **SAND THE RAILING AND** balusters by hand. Use 80-grit to 100-grit sandpaper for handrails and other surfaces that people will touch with their hands. Using a sandpaper finer than 100-grit can close the wood's pores, making staining and finishing less successful.

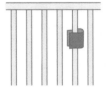

**3** **STAIN OR PAINT YOUR DECK.** There are many, many options for finishing your deck. Consider taking a picture of your deck and talking with your local home improvement store about finishing options. Your store can also offer application tips.

# #139
## HOW TO CATCH MICE
### (or, Pests Be Gone!)

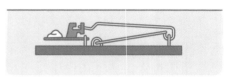

**M**ice are like teenagers: They go where there's food. So the first step toward keeping mice out of your house is to remove the incentive for their invasion. Find another place to store that birdseed in the garage, and never leave a kitchen messy overnight. Keep food in sealed glass or metal containers and clean up that food waste, and your mice *might* magically disappear. Also keep in check the clutter that hides mice—clean out the garage and be especially sure to keep a woodpile a couple of inches off the ground and away from the house.

## Keep Out!

For all their imperfections, mice are rational little creatures—make it too hard for them and they'll go elsewhere. That said, mice have soft cartilage that allows them to slip easily though openings that you swear wouldn't accommodate an ant. It's worth doing your best to plug any and all gaps and cracks in walls, ceilings, floors, foundations, and the backs of kitchen cabinets and pantries. There are a number of ways to plug these holes, including the somewhat rustic but effective strategy of cramming the hole full of steel wool and then duct taping over it. You can also try filling smaller or hard-to-reach gaps with expanding foam, though mice may eventually chew through it. If you want it done right, you will have to cover holes with metal sheeting or grating or plug them with cement. If you fail to secure their food sources, however, the little buggers may still find another way in. So remove the temptation.

## There Is No Better Mousetrap

There are seemingly dozens of so-called "mouse repellants" on the market, in spray, liquid, and even electronic form. But do any of these repellants work? Overwhelmingly, they don't. In fact, there's almost no evidence that they do any good at all. Stick with removing food sources, clearing out potential nesting spots, closing off access points, and trapping the few mice that remain. Poison can quickly wipe out a large-scale infestation but should be used as a method of last resort. That's because in addition to the danger of ingestion by children and pets, poisons allow mice to wander off and expire in places you would rather they didn't, namely in walls and other hard-to-reach places.

## Trap Types

There are two types of people in this world: Those who kill mice and those who relocate them (or make their spouse do it for them). Actually, there's a third type, too: cat people. Which are you? If you'd rather not kill the little buggers, use one of the many commercially available humane traps and then steel yourself for the job of release. If you're the killing type, there are a number of tools to choose from. Most exterminators recommend staying away from glue traps, which are less likely to catch mice than the common snap trap and less humane once they do. Snap traps can be messy but they are inexpensive and generally effective. If none of the preceding options sound spectacular, consider an electronic trap, which seems the most effective and humane way to deal with a small number of mice.

## MATERIALS:

- **Talcum powder**
- **Bait**
- **Traps**

**1 BECOME A MOUSE SLEUTH.** Look for the telltale signs of droppings and evidence of chewing. If you know mice are present but can't immediately discover their path, sprinkle a thin layer of talcum powder or flour over suspect areas—then watch for mouseprints. Mice like to follow natural contours like the edges of walls or pipes.

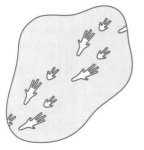

**2 BAIT THE TRAPS.** Use more traps with less bait rather than fewer traps with more bait, and position them with the catching mechanism pointing along one of these pathways. Use bait that doesn't pull free easily, like peanut butter (rather than cheese). If you have a larger infestation, try previewing the traps as feeding stations by placing food in the traps without setting them at first. Then, once the mice are habituated, bait and set the lot of them all at once.

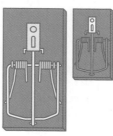

**3 CHECK THE TRAPS.** Once baited, check the traps daily. If you fail again and again, ask yourself how well you know your rodents. A mousetrap won't catch a rat and a rat trap may not be sensitive enough to catch a mouse. Consider setting a range of sizes and seeing what works.

**4 DISPOSE OF THE MOUSE.** If you're using a cheap snap-trap, you can pick whether you want to open the jaws and release the dead mouse into the trash or just ditch the whole trap, mouse and all. If you used a live trap, follow the trap instructions to release the mouse in a field or other uninhabited area (not in the driveway outside your neighbor's garage). Note that this is not a job for the squeamish. If you're overmatched or under-brave, call in the professionals.

✕ ✕ ✕ ✕ ✕ ✕ ✕ ✕ ✕ ✕ ✕ ✕ ✕ ✕ ✕

## THE REST OF THE PESTS

**M**ice are far from the only pests that like your house more than the outside world (especially in fall and winter). Additional visitors may also include cockroaches, ants, fleas, or other insects exotic and familiar (if you have termites, DIY time is over—call an exterminator). The first rule remains the same for them all: Make whatever it is they want inaccessible. Discover their food source and remove it. Beyond that there are species-specific traps. And beyond that, fumigation. So start with an aggressive campaign of prevention.

---

**Peppermint oil offers a more pleasant prevention tactic to safeguard against mice. A cotton ball soaked with a generous amount, placed near potential entry points, may deter a curious creature.**

---

# #140
## HOW TO REPAIR OR REPLACE A SCREEN

Some things seem to happen in slow motion—the first time you rode a bike without training wheels, the kiss at your wedding . . . all the way to watching a toddler smash through your screen door. Even if you don't have a blundering kid, pet, or spouse, your screen door is likely to accumulate nicks and punctures. You can patch tiny holes, and if you do so when you first see them, you might be able to stop them from getting bigger. But a screen is easy to replace, so as soon as bugs start to find passage through the holes or you're sick of unsightly rips, pull the old and install the new. Here's how to repair or replace a wire screen.

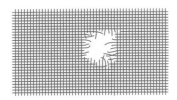

## TOOLS:

**Measuring tape ▪ Scissors ▪ Screwdriver or awl ▪ Spline installation tool ▪ Utility knife**

## MATERIALS:

- **Replacement screen**
- **Replacement spline (optional)**

### Fix Holes in Wire Screen

**1 MAKE THE PATCH.** Use scissors to cut a piece of screen a couple of inches wider on all sides than the hole from a roll of extra screen or use a patch from a repair kit.

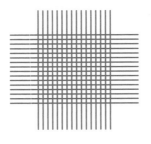

**2 BEND THE WIRES.** Screen is made of wire woven horizontally and vertically. Pull out the horizontal wires for ½" around the edges of the patch, leaving the vertical wires poking free. Bend these free wires directly backward at a 90-degree angle.

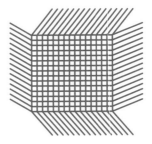

**3** **ATTACH THE PATCH.** Push the patch onto the screen so that the bent wires go through to the other side of the screen (most people choose to patch from the outside, with the bent wires pushed inside, but the choice is yours). Bend these wires down on the other side of the screen to hold the patch in place—use your fingers or needle-nose pliers. Push the wires down completely so they won't snag.

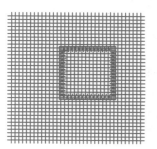

## Replace a Screen

**1** **REMOVE THE SCREEN FROM THE** window or door. Remove any hardware that intrudes on the face of the screen—most will come free easily with a screwdriver. Evaluate screen hardware for dings and discoloration and replace if damaged. If you're working on a sliding screen, check the frame's rollers while you're at it. If they are worn or tend to stick, consider replacing them. Most rollers are held in place with clips that you can pop free with a flathead screwdriver. If there is a latch, check its attachment point and replace if needed. If you are repairing a sliding door, take this opportunity to thoroughly clean the track on which it runs.

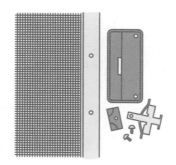

## IF YOUR SCREEN IS VINYL . . .

**V**inyl doesn't bend like wire, so you'll need to glue or sew vinyl patches. Cut a patch from material that matches the screen—unlike wire, it need only be ½" wider on all sides than the hole. Once you cut the vinyl, paint the edges with clear nail polish to keep them from fraying. Use rubber cement to hold the patch in place. For a more aesthetically appealing patch, sew the patch in place with thread that matches the color of the vinyl.

**2** **REMOVE THE SPLINE.** The screen's edges are almost certainly held in place by a thin line of rubber called the spline. This piece presses on top of the screen into a tight groove, and the friction of the spline in the groove holds the screen taught. To remove the screen, you'll have to remove the spline first. Use a thin screwdriver or awl to pick at the spline near one of the screen corners, trying to lift it free without breaking it. If possible, pull the spline free in one long strip. Repeat this procedure to remove all four sides of the spline, checking to see if there might be spline on both sides of the screen.

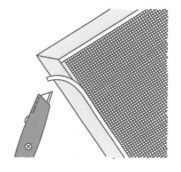

**3** **LAY THE NEW SCREEN ACROSS** the frame. Start with a piece of replacement screen at least 2" larger than the opening—later you'll trim it to size. For now, align one edge of the new screen along the corresponding edge of the frame to make sure you don't start installing the screen cockeyed.

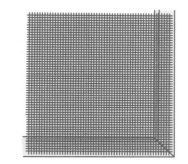

**4 INSTALL THE SCREEN.** A spline installation tool should have small, pizza-cutter-like circles on each end. One circle has a convex edge (it bulges outward), and the other circle has a concave edge (it is grooved inward). Run the convex edge of the spline installation tool on top of the screen to push it into the groove that runs along the frame edge. Press the screen firmly into the groove without ripping it.

**5 REINSTALL THE SPLINE.** Use the concave side of the spline installation tool to push old or new spline into the groove on top of the screen. Pushing too firmly can make the tool's wheel run against the screen and potentially damage it. Slightly angle the tool away from the inside of the screen so that any rips occur on the overhang rather than inside the spline. As you push the spline into the groove with the roller, use your other hand to pull the screen tight in front of the area you're seating. However, be careful not to pull so hard that you tilt the screen in the frame.

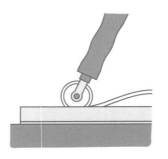

**6 USE A UTILITY KNIFE TO TRIM** the excess screen. To avoid scratching the frame, you can cut directly into the outside gap created by the spline.

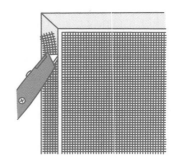

**7 REPLACE ANY NEEDED** hardware, including rollers or the handle of the door. Most rollers clip in place and most handles attach with screws. Reinstall the screen with the hardware you removed in Step 1.

By the 1950s, screen doors and windows were common in the United States, and were so useful in keeping bugs out of the house that parasitic diseases were almost eradicated.

# #141
# HOW TO WEATHER STRIP WINDOWS AND DOORS

The thermostat is set to 70 degrees, so where's the chill coming from? Think of windows and doors as holes punched in your house—improperly sealed, they are going to let cold air in. In order to keep drafts out and your heat in (and your heating bill *down*), weather strip them. The technique for weather stripping casement windows (which are hung on hinges) varies slightly from double-hung (which slide); doors have their own technique.

## On the Strip

By far the most common forms of weather stripping are adhesive foam or tubular vinyl. Foam alone is rarely appropriate for exterior weather stripping and is better used as a barrier against drafts inside the home. Tubular vinyl weather stripping resists weathering and is better for outside use. For both, the adhesive backing may or may not need to be reinforced with tack nails in order to remain in place. Other types of weather stripping include felt, which is usually nailed in place, and a variety of metal strips that can be spring-loaded or interlocking. Foam and vinyl strips are appropriate for installations where they will be compressed but nothing will slide sideways across them (the lower sill of a leaky window that opens and closes vertically, but not the lower edge of a door that swings closed). Spring-metal interlocking strips can be used in situations where they are rubbed, for example on the sides of sliding windows. Another option is V-channel strips—usually plastic, these strips can be used to insulate the sash channels on double-hung windows.

## Like a Candle in the Wind

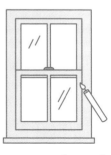

Cracks in the seal around a door or window can be nearly invisible, so you may need to do some sleuthing to find them. It's best to explore for leaks on a windy day. Carefully run a lighted candle around the edges of doors and windows, watching for the flame to flicker. If Mother Nature refuses to provide wind, make your own. Recruit a helper to blow from the outside with a handheld hair dryer while you check the integrity of the seals with a candle on the inside. Be careful with the flame, and keep a damp rag on hand to wipe away any carbon smudges (or spot fires).

## TYPES OF WEATHER STRIPPING

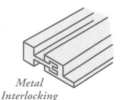

*Adhesive Foam or Vinyl*     *Tubular Vinyl*     *Felt*     *Metal Interlocking*     *V-channel*

## TOOLS:

**Measuring tape ▪ Tin snips (for double-hung windows) ▪ Utility knife ▪ Screwdriver ▪ Drill**

## MATERIALS:

- **Soap**
- **Adhesive-backed weather stripping**
- **Spring metal weather stripping (for doors and double-hung windows)**
- **Finishing nails**

## For Double-Hung Windows

These are the most common windows in modern homes—they slide rather than swing into place. Adhesive-backed weather stripping like foam is perfect for the bottom of these windows, where the base of the window may leave a leaky gap against the sash. Use weather stripping that is narrow enough to sit against the desired edge and thick enough to close the gap.

**1 CLEAN THE SURFACE.** Remove any old stripping and wash the desired edge with soap and water. Dry thoroughly.

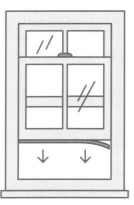

**2 SEAL THE LOWER EDGE.** Peel off the adhesive back and affix a strip cut to match the length of the lower edge. If you've prepared the surface correctly, you shouldn't need to nail or otherwise reinforce the adhesive.

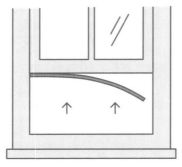

**3 SEAL THE TRACKS.** The sides of these windows slide on a track, which shouldn't but sometimes does leak air. Protect against these leaks with plastic V-channel weather stripping. Make sure you buy the correct width V-channel weather stripping for your windows and then cut the V-channel into strips about an inch longer than your sash height. Slide the weather stripping down the tracks on the sides of your windows, between the window frame and the sash (you will have to stuff it in). Use finish nails to attach the V-channel to the jamb (make sure the window doesn't get caught on the nails).

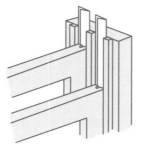

## For Casement Windows

Because casement windows swing instead of slide shut, they are much easier to insulate.

**1 CLEAN THE SURFACE.** Remove any old weather stripping or sealant, thoroughly wash the surface that forms the window's seal with soap and water, and let it dry.

**2 MEASURE THE FACES OF THE** window sash that come into contact with the window. Cut pieces of adhesive-backed foam insulation to these sizes with a utility knife. Remove a small bit from the backing and stick the end in place. Pull off the backing as you press on the strip, using additional strips as needed.

**3 IF NEEDED, TRIM THE STRIPS TO** fit. If you struggle to keep adhesive strips stuck to your window sashes, add finishing nails.

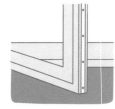

## For Doors

Unlike some kinds of windows, all four edges of a door can be fitted with weather stripping.

**1 ENSURE THAT THE DOOR IS** hung properly. Look from the outside to see if the door hangs square in the frame. If it sags, try tightening the hinge screws. After enough openings and closings, a door's hinges can pull so much against the mounting screws that they may enlarge their holes. In that case, consider replacing them with larger screws that fit the new hole size (as long as these larger screws also fit through the hinges!). You can also try filling the screw holes with toothpicks dipped liberally in wood glue and then cutting the toothpicks flush. Now evaluate the squared door. If gaps remain around the edges, it's time for weather stripping.

**2 SEAL THE SIDES.** Because the door must swing freely across the sides of the door frame, consider using "spring bronze" weather stripping instead of foam or vinyl adhesive strips here, which would quickly pull free or degrade as the door is swung across them (okay, if it's a rarely opened garage door, you might start with adhesive stripping and see how long it lasts). Measure the doorjamb and cut lengths of spring bronze to fit. Press the spring bronze in place, tight against the doorjamb. Use finishing nails about every 8 to 10 inches to hold it in place.

**3 PREPARE THE TOP AND THE** threshold. Adhesive-backed foam or vinyl weather stripping will work along the top and bottom—surfaces where the door applies direct instead of crosswise pressure. Remove any old weather stripping or sealant and thoroughly clean the surfaces with soap and water. Let dry completely.

**4 SEAL THE TOP AND THRESHOLD.** Use a utility knife to cut a length of foam weather stripping just longer than the doorstop that runs along the top of the doorframe. Peel only a bit of the backing from the weather stripping, then press the adhesive to firmly attach it to the top of the doorframe, removing the backing as you go. Do the same along the bottom.

**5 INSTALL THE DOOR SWEEP.** The door sweep hangs down from the bottom edge on the outside of the door, covering the gap at the bottom when the door is closed. Measure your door and buy the proper sweep at your home improvement store. Hold the sweep up to the bottom edge of the door so that it hangs at the desired height (it should deter drafts but not stop the door from opening). Mark through the holes on the sweep onto the door. Now use your drill and the mounting screws that came with the sweep to attach it.

# #142
## HOW TO CAULK A WINDOW

Caulking drafty windows will not only make your home more comfortable, but will cut down on heating and cooling bills and can keep out pesky insects that wiggle their way in through loose seams. If the seam isn't going to move, caulk it. If the window opens and closes onto the seam, you'll need to use weather stripping (see page 257).

## TOOLS:

**Putty knife or 5-in-1 painting tool •
Caulking gun**

## MATERIALS:

- **Candle**
- **Polyurethane caulk**
- **Craft stick (optional)**

**1 TEST FOR DRAFTS.** Following the instructions on page 257, carefully run a lit candle along window seams, watching for the flame to flicker and reveal any drafts. An interior draft may in fact be due to imperfections in the exterior

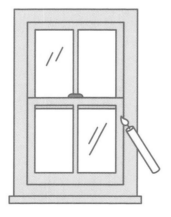

window caulk. Check outside first, as repairing a cracked or damaged outside seal should allow you to open and close the window, without inviting in a draft.

**2 REMOVE THE OLD CAULK.** Once you locate the failed seal, use a putty knife or the long, sharp edge of a 5-in-1 painting tool to remove it. Once you start removing window caulk, it's best to remove it completely and re-caulk the entire seam. Once you've removed the old caulk, wipe the surface clean with a damp rag and let dry.

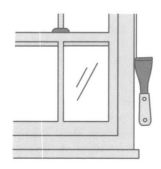

**3 APPLY NEW CAULK.** Load the caulk into the caulking gun and cut off the tip of the tube at a 45-degree angle. Puncture the seal with a nail and test the bead. If the bead is too small, cut off another short section of the tip. You needn't be as precise with polyurethane caulk as you are with silicone caulk in the bathroom. Especially with exterior use, you may need to vary the size of the bead to fill an uneven gap. In any case, squirt caulk in the gaps to fill them. Finish by running a wet finger or craft stick along the bead to smooth the seam.

# #143
## HOW TO REPLACE A WINDOWPANE

**B**e it from bird or baseball, your windows are in constant danger from flying objects. Fixing a broken pane is either fairly simple or completely impossible, depending on your windows. With older, wood-frame windows, pulling the old pane and inserting a new one requires only a bit of skill with putty and glaze. With a vinyl window, you'll most likely have to replace the entire sash.

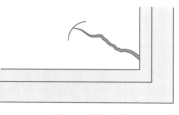

First evaluate your broken window—is it fixable, DIY or otherwise? Is the pane attached with putty or clips, or is it an integral part of the window assembly? If it looks like the pane will pop free, keep reading. If you have a new vinyl, double-paned window, get ready to shell out to replace the entire assembly.

## Temporary Fixes

You may be able to temporarily repair small cracks and holes in a windowpane until you are able to replace it. To stop a crack from spreading, try using a glass cutter to draw a shallow arc in the path of the crack. Again, this is a temporary fix, but "capping" the crack can keep it contained. Likewise, tiny holes like those from pesky pellet guns or a slingshot pebble may be patchable with clear nail polish. None of these fixes will restore a window to its previous luster, but they can keep a problem from getting worse until you find the moxie, time, and money for a real fix.

## TOOLS:

**Glass-handling gloves ▪ Safety goggles ▪ Measuring tape ▪ Screwdriver ▪ Pliers ▪ Heat gun or hair dryer ▪ 2" putty knife**

## MATERIALS:

- **Glass pane**
- **Window putty**
- **Paint**

**1 BUY A NEW PANE OF GLASS, CUT** to size. Both lumber and hardware stores should be able to provide sized glass. If in doubt about the size you need, read on to learn how to pop the sash free of the house and bring it with you when buying a new pane. If it's possible to measure the pane while it's still in the frame, measure it precisely and ensure you replace it with exact dimensions. With glass, even ⅟16" matters.

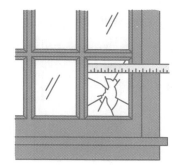

**2 GEAR UP.** When working with broken glass, wear not only protective glass-handling gloves but eye goggles as well. Especially when removing a broken pane, it is possible to fling glass shards. Unlike sawdust, a glass shard in the eye can do immediate, permanent damage.

**3** **REMOVE THE BROKEN PANE** and its sash (if possible). With an older window, this might be as easy as unscrewing the hinges that connect the sash to the casing. On newer windows, it may be easier to remove the pane from the frame than to remove the frame itself. Modern double-paned windows will need to be replaced completely, sash and all.

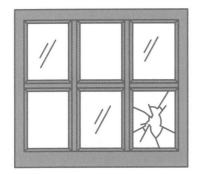

**4** **LOOSEN THE PANE.** Make sure you're wearing gloves and then use pliers to remove broken glass that may have fallen. Evaluate how the pane is attached to the frame. With older windows, it might be held fast with glazing compound. In this case, use a heat gun or hair dryer to loosen it. Work a putty knife into the loosened compound and gently pry the glass free. Scrape excess compound from the frame. With newer windows, the glass pane is likely attached to the frame with retaining clips. Use a screwdriver to press the clips and pop the pane free.

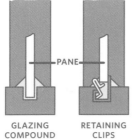

GLAZING COMPOUND     RETAINING CLIPS

**5** **CLEAN THE FRAME.** In an older, wooden window, scrape out the rabbet groove that forms the seat for the windowpane. If the wood is degraded, consider replacing the frame or chiseling away a layer to make a new, level rabbet (in that case you would need a slightly larger pane).

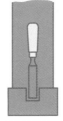

RABBET GROOVE

**6** **ATTACH THE NEW PANE.** Run a bead of window putty along the rabbet. Set the new pane in place and gently press it down into the putty. Note that at this stage, it's very easy to crack the glass. Press with care, waiting for a complete seal to form between the glass and the sash.

**7** **ADJUST THE PANE.** Move the pane in the putty until it is centered, with a $1/16$" (putty-filled) gap on all sides between the glass and the sash.

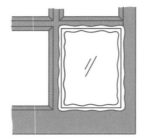

**8** **LOCK IN THE PANE.** Like most picture frames, wood-frame windows generally use small metal tabs to hold the glass in place. These tabs push into the wood, flush to the glass, about every six inches. Put a tab in place by hand, and use a flathead screwdriver to shove it into the wood. Avoid angling it into the glass, which can easily chip the pane.

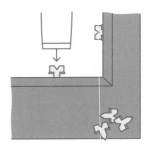

**9** **SEAL THE PANE.** Roll a $1/2$" rope of putty and press it into the back of the glass, over the tabs, to seal the edge of the pane. Free the pane of any excess putty with a putty knife or razor blade. Let dry for at least three days.

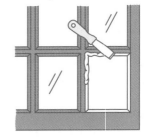

**10** **REPAINT THE FRAME WITH** paint that matches the rest of the frames. Run the paint to the very edge of the glass to hide the repair.

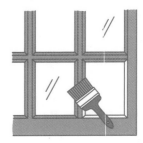

# #144
## HOW TO UNBLOCK A GUTTER

For reasons that should be obvious, it is never a good idea to climb onto the roof and lean out over the edge in order to clear leaves from your gutters. It is equally dangerous to imagine that a blocked gutter will somehow unclog itself—this mind-set can lead to corrosion or, in extreme cases, the gutters ripping free from the house. Instead, follow the steps here to clean the gutters safely.

## Proper Drainage

The purpose of a gutter is to drain water away from the foundation of the house. If your downspout is releasing water into an impromptu pond that drains back toward the house, it's not doing a very good job. If needed, add another horizontal section of downspout to eject water farther away. And make sure the ground around the foundation slopes away from instead of toward it. If it doesn't, you may need to take out a shovel and do some digging so the water has a place to go. (Some homeowners make channels and line them with gravel, bricks, or stones.)

## Before a Blockage Occurs . . .

Does a tree overhang your gutters? If so, you'll need to be diligent about cleaning the gutters at least once every

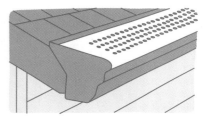

fall and then checking them again in the spring to see if the winter wind whipped any unexpected leaves or branches into the system. If the gutters seem to clog often, be proactive: Consider installing gutter guards, which are strips of steel or plastic with holes or pores for filtering water. They attach under the last course of shingles and protect the open tops of the gutters, while allowing rain from the roof to pass through. Plastic gutter guards are inexpensive and easy to install—find them at your local home improvement store.

## TOOLS:

**Rubber gloves • Bucket or heavy-duty trash bag • Freestanding ladder • Hand trowel (optional) • Garden hose with sprayer**

**1** **GET A HELPER.** You'll need someone to stabilize the base of the ladder while you work. It is best to use a freestanding ladder to avoid leaning it against the gutters, which aren't meant to support significant weight.

*(continued)*

**2 DETACH THE DOWNSPOUTS.** Before you go shoving muck around, consider detaching the downspouts so the debris doesn't make its way in and cause an even larger problem. Most downspouts will detach from the roof with a screwdriver, and then sections should come apart with a tug. That said, if the downspouts are generally clear of debris and the problem sits in the gutters, just detach the downspouts enough that muck will fall instead of washing into them.

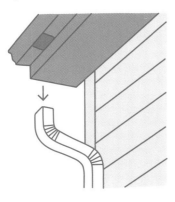

**3 SCOOP OUT THE DEBRIS.** Put on your rubber gloves and hold a sturdy trash bag or bucket in one hand. Starting at the downspout locations and working toward the middle of the gutters, scoop out all the leaves and muck. If it's been a while or if you live in a climate where significant dust washes from the roof, you may also need a hand trowel to dig into the mud that accumulates in the gutters. If muck-grabbing isn't your thing, you can blast out the gutters with a pressure washer— this is a messy job but easier than scooping them out by hand.

**4 REATTACH THE DOWNSPOUTS** and rinse the gutters. Once you've cleaned out the major debris (sticks, leaves, Frisbees) by hand, use a garden hose with a sprayer attachment to rinse the remaining dirt into the downspouts. (Watch to ensure that the water flows smoothly out with no obstructions.)

✕ ✕ ✕ ✕ ✕ ✕ ✕ ✕ ✕ ✕ ✕ ✕ ✕ ✕ ✕ ✕ ✕ ✕ ✕ ✕ ✕ ✕ ✕ ✕ ✕ ✕ ✕ ✕ ✕ ✕ ✕ ✕ ✕ ✕ ✕ ✕ ✕ ✕ ✕ ✕ ✕ ✕ ✕ ✕ ✕ ✕ ✕ ✕ ✕ ✕ ✕ ✕ ✕ ✕ ✕ ✕

# TROUBLESHOOTING A BLOCKED DOWNSPOUT

There are as many folk remedies for unblocking a downspout as there are for curing hiccups. Start by trying to blast away a clog by aiming your hose's sprayer attachment up the blocked pipe. If the water breaks the clog into pieces, clear these bits and then keep squirting until you've mined through the entire clog. If that doesn't work, haul the garden hose up a ladder (have a helper hold the base!) to the top of the clogged spout and try to blast it out from there. If the pipe is still clogged, remove the hose's sprayer attachment and feed the length of the hose down the pipe. Turn on the water and wiggle as needed until leaves, twigs, the odd squirrel and other goodies come geysering out the bottom of the pipe. If that

*still* doesn't work, you have a serious clog. At this point, weigh the difficulty of taking apart your downspout against the difficulty of feeding a plumber's snake up the spout to auger the clog. Some downspouts will

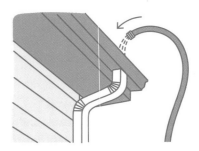

disassemble easily with the removal of a couple of screws. Others are composed of a single length of pipe, which would require cutting and sweating to fix.

# #145
# HOW TO REPAIR A CRACKED GUTTER

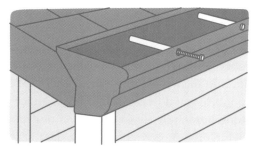

Eventually, even despite careful maintenance, gutters will corrode, crack, or take a hit from a falling branch and require repair. It's easy to repair a small hole, though more significant damage may require replacing the gutter. Another common problem is gutter sag, often a result of detached hardware. When a support pulls free, it allows the outer lip of the gutter to fall outward and can affect the slope of the gutter. There are long screws just for fixing this problem—ask for gutter screws at the hardware store and use them to pinch the gutter back into position.

## TOOLS:

**Freestanding ladder** ▪ **Tin snips** ▪ **Wire brush** ▪ **Rags**

## MATERIALS:

▪ **Metal patch or scrap**
▪ **Roofing cement**

**1 GET A HELPER.** You'll need someone to stabilize the base of the ladder while you work. Use a freestanding ladder to avoid putting extra weight on the gutters.

**2 PREPARE THE CRACK FOR** repair. Use tin snips to cut free any rust clinging to the edges of the crack or hole. Thoroughly clean the affected area by scrubbing it with a wire brush and then wiping it with a damp rag.

**3 APPLY THE PATCH.** For this repair, you need a metal patch a couple of inches larger than the crack or hole. You can buy flexible metal patching material at the hardware store or you can make your own patch by using tin snips to cut a piece from scrap metal flashing. Make sure the metal of the patch matches the metal of the gutter. Cover one side of the patch with roofing cement and stick the patch in place, centered so it completely covers the damaged area.

# #146
## HOW TO PREVENT AN ICE DAM

Keeping your home toasty as the temperature outside plummets is only one good reason to properly insulate your attic. Yes, you will save on heating costs if you aren't paying to keep your attic warm, but warm air rising through the attic to the roof can have an even more costly repercussion: a potentially catastrophic ice dam. There's a good chance your roof is peaked or otherwise slanted. Combine that with imperfect insulation and you're likely to have a hot spot at your roof's apex. In the winter, this warmer area can melt the snow, which then runs down the roof . . . until it meets a colder section of roof below and freezes solid. This is an ice dam, and it can cause serious damage (see How to Remove an Ice Dam from the Roof, opposite). The key to preventing an ice dam isn't keeping your roof warm, but rather keeping it cold enough to avoid melting the snow and creating a dam in the first place. This means not only insulating your house from the cold roof, but insulating the attic and roof from your warm house. Home improvement centers carry Styrofoam baffles specifically for this purpose. When installed, they create air channels between the attic insulation under your roof and the roof itself. Insulate the attic right, and keep ice dams at bay.

## TOOLS:

**Caulking gun** ▪ **Roof rake**

## MATERIALS:

- **Styrofoam attic baffles**
- **Fiberglass batt insulation**
- **Safety mask and gloves**
- **Window caulk**

**1 INSTALL THE BAFFLES.** Wear your mask and gloves and remove the fiberglass batt insulation by pulling it up in strips. Press the Styrofoam ventilation baffles up into the space that was insulated and reapply the insulation—while you're at it, add an extra layer.

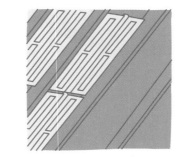

**2 INSULATE THE FLOOR.** Also focus your insulation on the floor of the attic and not just the underside of the roof. If needed, pull up old insulation and replace with new. Consider laying a second layer of insulation, rolling it down in strips perpendicular to the first layer.

**3** **ENSURE THAT YOUR ROOF IS** properly ventilated—cold air should sneak into the Styrofoam air channels from the eaves, pass through, and exit at the ridge to keep the roof properly chilled. Look for soffit vents under the eaves. If you don't have vents, consider an evaluation by a roofing expert.

**4** **INSULATE DUCTS, PIPES, AND** cables. Wrap fiberglass batt or foam pipe insulation around any ventilation or other pipes, including dryer vents or ducts connected to the kitchen or bathroom. Caulk around any cables that penetrate the attic.

**5** **KEEP THE ROOF AND GUTTERS** clear and free of debris (see How to Unblock a Gutter, page 263), which can form an anchor for a dam. If snow looks to be accumulating, use a roof rake to scrape it from the edges of the roof and around gutters.

# #147 HOW TO REMOVE AN ICE DAM FROM THE ROOF

**E**ven with proper insulation, when melting snow flows from the roof into the gutters, it's likely to refreeze and can eventually build up into a wall. Left alone, the weight of the dam will increase until it eventually rips free, creating a major safety hazard and probably taking your gutters with it as it cascades onto your parked car below. Before it does that, an ice dam can trap water behind it, pooling it on your roof where it will eventually degrade your roofing material and create leaks. Do what you can to prevent ice dams, but don't let them linger once they form. Here's how to clear an ice dam if you, unfortunately, find one attached to your roof.

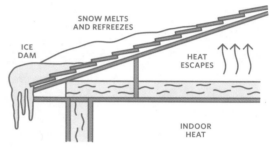

SNOW MELTS AND REFREEZES

ICE DAM

HEAT ESCAPES

INDOOR HEAT

## Danger Ahead!

Stop! *Never* walk on a snowy or icy roof. Working from below isn't safe either—as soon as you start hacking at an ice dam, you increase the likelihood of the entire thing releasing, at which point it can slide down the roof onto you and your ladder. (Not to mention the danger inherent in wielding an ax from atop a ladder resting on snowy ground.) So resist the temptation to just whale away on the dam with an ax. Likewise resist the urge to torch the dam with a propane flame in an attempt to melt it. It doesn't work. By far the safest method of dealing with an ice dam is preventing it from forming in the first place (see How to Prevent an Ice Dam, opposite). If you're past that point, here's what to do. And remember that a partially melted ice dam can break free and slide.

## TOOLS:

**Freestanding ladder** ▪ **Heat cables**

## MATERIALS:

- **Calcium chloride pellets**
- **Pantyhose**
- **De-icing salt**

**1** **TRY ICE-MELTING PELLETS.** These may or may not work, but they're relatively inexpensive, completely safe, and so easy they're worth a try. Don't use salt pellets, as they can corrode metal gutters and flashings. Instead, look for calcium chloride pellets. Hurl them onto your roof, preferably directly onto the dam itself, and then hope for the best. The pellets are likely to melt into the dam until reaching the roof, but the melt won't necessarily branch out from the holes the pellets create. However, if you have a pool of water trapped behind the dam, it may only take one small hole melted through with a calcium chloride pellet to allow the trapped water to burst forth, likely melting out the remaining dam.

**2 NEXT, TRY HEAT CABLES.** If the pellets don't work, carefully climb a freestanding ladder (have a helper hold the base) to reach the roof, where you can lay heat cables on the ice dam. Lay cables on the dam, plug in below, and then stay far away as the heat cables melt the ice. Again, if you have any question about the integrity of the dam and fear there's any chance it may break free, don't risk working below it. Call an expert.

Alternatively, some homeowners with foresight choose to leave zigzags of heat tape in place just above the gutters throughout the winter, turning them on when ice dams start to form.

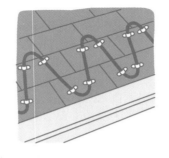

**3 FINALLY, TRY PANTYHOSE.** Heat cables or tape should solve the problem, but sometimes they are too thin to completely melt an ice dam, in which case it's time to go with pantyhose. Fill pantyhose with de-icing salt to form long, unattractive sausages. Lay these sausages on the ice dam. (And then come up with a good story to tell the neighbors.) Stay far away as the ice starts to melt the dam. Note that this isn't the best long-term strategy, as over time salt can erode gutters and other metal parts of the roof. But in a pinch, it's worth a shot.

## Is It Time for a New Roof?

When in doubt about your roof, it's tempting to call in the pros for a consultation—but the pros are more than a little biased toward replacement. Unless you know a roofer and know that said roofer already has enough work to stay busy for the next fifteen years, it's hard to trust the opinion of someone with a vested interest in the disrepair of your roof. Instead, check it out yourself before calling in a professional. It's imperative, of course, to keep your roof in tip-top shape—not only does a good roof keep the outside out, but it's a must for maintaining your home's value.

## Light (or Rain) in the Attic

The first job of a roof is to keep precipitation out. If water is coming in, blame it on the roof. Head up to the attic to look for spots where the structure of the roof deck sags inward and, on a rainy day, look for leaks. On a sunny day, check for places where light shines through. Beyond these obvious failures, look from the attic at the underside of the roof deck for dark spots and black streaks that can indicate the locations of slower leaks. Mildew can also be a sign that moisture is making its way past the roof.

✕ ✕ ✕ ✕ ✕ ✕ ✕ ✕ ✕ ✕ ✕ ✕ ✕ ✕ ✕ ✕ ✕ ✕ ✕ ✕ ✕ ✕ ✕ ✕ ✕ ✕ ✕ ✕ ✕ ✕ ✕ ✕ ✕ ✕ ✕ ✕ ✕

# KEEPING STEPS AND PATHWAYS ICE-FREE

**R**oofs are certainly not the only spot where ice likes to form in the winter—steps and walkways are prime territory for ice sheets. As with roofs, the best way to keep your walkways free of ice is to keep it from forming in the first place. As soon as it snows, shovel. This keeps the bottom layer of snow from compacting, melting against the warmer ground, and then refreezing into perilous ice patches. If you already have ice or if ice forms despite your efforts with a shovel, consider throwing down sand, gravel, or even kitty litter onto the ice to increase your grip. For tougher cases, try rock salt. Sprinkle just enough to loosen the ice and then scrape it free with a snow shovel.

## Shingled Out

From outside at ground-level, look up at the roof from below and see if you can spot any of the following problems:

**Missing shingles.** These will have to be replaced. When you notice a bare spot, check from the attic to make sure it hasn't already led to rot in the wood decking of the roof itself.

**Loose shingles.** If you notice shingle tabs flapping in the breeze, cement them down before they rip free entirely. Use roofing cement, also called flashing cement, to apply two quarter-sized dollops to the underside of each tab. Press the tabs down against the course below. Don't use too much cement or it will squeeze out when pressed.

**Damaged flashing.** Flashing is the (metal) sheeting that closes the gap between your roof and things that poke out of it, like a chimney. Damaged or punctured flashing can allow water to sneak in. In most cases, you simply replace the damaged flashing and then the surrounding shingles.

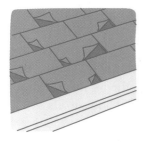

**Curling shingles.** The most common cause of curling shingles is improper fastening. Unfortunately, once the undersides have been exposed, there's a good chance the backing will crack and you'll have to replace them. Another common cause is an improperly ventilated roof (see How to Prevent an Ice Dam, page 266, for instructions on ventilation). Asphalt shingles are expert at keeping water off the roof, but they're not nearly as waterproof from below. If water is condensing from a warm house underneath the roof, it can make shingles curl upward.

**Algae.** Especially in humid climates, algae can grow on the roof (so your roof should already include algae-resistant shingles). Most often, though, an algae infestation is an eyesore and nothing more—it won't affect the integrity of the roof. Kill algae with a bleach solution in a spray bottle. Scrub vigorously, but don't pressure wash the roof, as it can shorten the life of asphalt shingles.

**Blistering.** Are there small bubbles and knobs on the shingles? They're likely the result of a defect in the shingles themselves. Sometimes moisture becomes trapped inside shingles during manufacture, which later bubbles and then bursts free. These shingles will need to be replaced. You should be able to get your money back from the manufacturer.

## The Verdict

As with an old car, it eventually stops being cost-effective to patch over the problem, and the root of the issue must be addressed. At some point, you'll need a new roof. Before making that determination, consider the problem: Is it the boards of the roof decking or the shingles that are to blame? If it's the shingles, you might get away with laying a new layer of shingles directly over the existing layer. (Some roofers will even put on a third layer of shingles, but most recommend against it.) Most often, it's the decking that will dictate when you need a new roof. Look for rot, water spots, sagging, and cracks in the wood. Then find out how long it has been since the roof was replaced—a properly installed roof should last 20 years. If you're finding problems at 10 years, turn a very careful eye on your shingles, flashing, and other roof coverings—when you find the problem, fix it. At 15 years, start getting suspicious of your decking. With harsh winters or high humidity you might be pushing into replacement territory. At 20 years, count your blessings if you can get away with spot repairs, but be ready to replace the whole thing if these repairs start to become frequent. The cardinal rule of roof replacement is to get it done before a leaky roof causes damage to the rest of the house. A typical roof replacement with asphalt shingles will cost about $100 for every 100 square feet, though this varies widely in different areas of the country. Make sure you get at least three quotes from roofers before deciding—both to explore for lower prices and for the information that an inspection can provide.

# #148
## HOW TO REPAIR A CRACK IN A CONCRETE DRIVEWAY

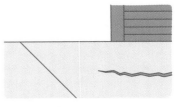

Concrete is not especially malleable, so when something pushes on it, instead of bending, it cracks. Typically, cracks in a driveway are due to tree roots burrowing underneath like attackers digging under the walls of a medieval castle. Cracks can also come from imperfect compression of the soil when the driveway was laid, resulting in uneven settling. Needless to say, when the ground falls out from beneath a driveway, it cracks. Cracks can also come from water that seeps under the driveway and expands during a winter freeze. In rare cases, you'll have to break up the slab with a jackhammer and pour a new driveway. But before you go to that extreme, try repairing the crack with concrete resurfacer.

## TOOLS:

**Pressure washer (plan to rent)** • **Masonry chisel** • **Air compressor or wet/dry vacuum (optional)** • **Bucket** • **Drill with mixing paddle** • **Flat-edge trowel** • **Concrete float** • **Rubber floor squeegee** • **Push broom (optional)**

## MATERIALS:

- **Masonry cleaning solution**
- **Concrete resurfacing powder**

**1** **CLEAN THE CONCRETE.** Add masonry cleaning solution to a pressure washer and scour the driveway, focusing on removing any dirt, debris, and mildew from in and around the crack. If loose material inside the crack proves difficult to blast loose, you'll need to chisel it free using a masonry chisel. If possible, after pressure washing and chiseling, let the crack dry and then hit it with an air compressor or vacuum out any dust with a wet/dry vacuum.

**2** **MIX CONCRETE RESURFACING** powder in a bucket, according to the package directions. Use a mixing paddle on a drill to stir the mixture until no lumps remain. The consistency of the concrete mixture should be that of a thick paste.

**3** **COAT THE CRACKS.** Pick up the bucket and pour the mixture roughly and liberally onto the cracks. Use a flat-edge trowel to aggressively pack the mixture down deep into the cracks.

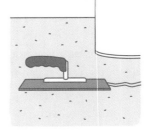

**4** **SMOOTH THE CONCRETE.** Use a concrete float, which is like a large metal paddle, to flatten the resurfacing material to the surrounding concrete. If you plan to stop after filling the cracks, feather the edges of the patch into the driveway with the concrete float and stop here. If you're up for a bit more resurfacing, you can leave the edges slightly rough and proceed to Step 5.

**5** **PREPARE TO RESURFACE.** Let the patched cracks dry overnight. Now you can resurface the rest of the driveway up to the level of the crack patch. Mix another batch of concrete resurfacer, this time much thinner than the first batch, to about the consistency of runny pancake batter. Because you'll be applying this second batch in a thin layer, wet down the driveway to keep it from drying too quickly.

**6** **COVER THE ENTIRE DRIVEWAY.** Pour the thinned resurfacer onto the driveway and spread it around with a rubber squeegee. If the driveway is especially wide, be strategic about how you pour resurfacer and then squeegee before moving on to the next section—avoid "painting yourself into a corner." The edges of the squeegee can be tricky and it takes practice to avoid leaving edge marks in the resurfacer.

**7** **SCUFF THE SURFACE.** If you like, once the resurfacer is set but not dry, use a push broom to scuff the surface so that the driveway has more traction when wet. Let the resurfaced driveway set for at least 24 hours before using.

## SEALING OUT THE SEASONS

**T**hough it is optional, sealing a driveway can help reduce cracking and will improve the overall appearance of your driveway. These instructions for sealing concrete and asphalt assume that you've already pressure washed the entire driveway surface and repaired all cracks. If that's not the case, do it now. This also assumes it's a beautiful summer weekend with no rain in the forecast for the next few days—apply sealant only if you expect at least 36 dry hours with a temperature over 60 degrees. Also be sure you completely rope off the driveway from friends and family who might unknowingly drive into the middle of your wet project with catastrophic consequences for both the project and any tires that might touch it. With the preparation handled, applying sealer is fairly straightforward: Pour what looks like a workable amount of sealant onto the driveway (about two gallons at a time works well) and spread it around with a rubber squeegee. Let it dry overnight. And cross your fingers against an unexpected summer thunderstorm.

# #149
## HOW TO PATCH CRACKED ASPHALT

Patching asphalt starts out exactly the same as patching concrete. Before you begin, pressure wash the driveway (see Step 1 of How to Repair a Crack in a Concrete Driveway, page 270), being sure to blast free any dirt and debris in the crack. If the crack is thinner than ½", patch it according to the instructions for concrete, but with asphalt patching material. If the crack is more than ½" wide, you'll need to follow a slightly different set of steps, detailed below.

## TOOLS:

**Bucket ▪ Steel tamping rod (optional)**

## MATERIALS:

- **Crushed, angular gravel**
- **4 × 4 post**
- **Asphalt repair compound**
- **Asphalt sealant**

**1 FILL THE BASE OF THE CRACK** with gravel. The best gravel to fill a large asphalt driveway crack is crushed, angular gravel. (Round gravel shifts too easily.) Fill the crack until it is only 2" deep. Use a 4 × 4 post to tamp down the gravel to a firm underlayer, adding more gravel as necessary to reach the 2" mark.

**2 MIX THE ASPHALT REPAIR** compound in a bucket, according to the manufacturer's instructions.

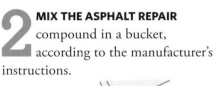

**3 POUR THE COMPOUND ON** top of the gravel underlayer. Compact the compound firmly into the crack with the 4 × 4 post (or with a steel tamping rod designed for the purpose). Add more compound as needed to bring the surface of the repair up to the level of the surrounding driveway. Tamp the compound aggressively for a durable repair.

**4 LET THE BLACKTOP ASPHALT** dry. While it will feel dry after 24 hours and you can expect it to hold weight, there's a good chance the bottom of the patch will still be slightly pliable. Wait a couple of weeks before applying asphalt sealant (see Sealing Out the Seasons, page 271), which prevents air from penetrating beneath the surface.

# WOODWORKING & METALWORKING

I still have a wooden stool I made in shop class as a teenager, with turned legs and a woven seat. It's a nice piece, and what it taught me at a tender age is that the things we make with our hands are valuable to us. It also taught me how much fun tools can be! Some items, such as hammers, planes, and saws, are great basics to have on hand for minor repair jobs, but with the addition of some (carefully used) power tools, a whole world of wood- and metalworking opens up.

# WOODWORKING TOOL KIT

## HAND TOOLS

Carpenter's square

Rulers

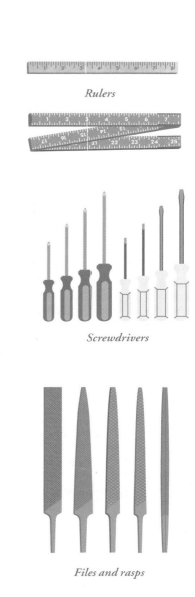

Crosscut saw

Rip saw

Level

Screwdrivers

Nails

Screws

Files and rasps

Clamps

Plane

Hammer

Ball-peen hammer

Measuring tape

Chisels

Workbench

Sharpening stone

# POWER TOOLS

Drill

Orbital sander

Router

Circular saw

Compound miter saw

Table saw

Jigsaw

*(continued)*

## Hand Tools

Watch a National Geographic film on primates and you'll see hand tools in action—chimps using thick sticks to break open nuts or long twigs to fish for ants and termites. We humans take it a few steps further. In fact, if you don't mind adding a little extra elbow grease to a project, hand tools can do anything their electric cousins can do. (Some woodworkers swear that hand tools do an even better job.) Here are the essential hand tools (see page 274 for visual reference) in any woodworking tool kit, including the trusty measuring tape, the main measuring tool you need for woodworking, along with a ruler (or two) and a carpenter's square.

**Hammer and nails.** Put a glob of metal at the end of a stick and you've got a hammer. But beyond that basic design, there is a dizzying array of hammer varieties. Eventually, you can populate your tool kit with a whole quiver of them, but to start, decide if your first hammer is going to do double duty for household fix-its or if you can justify a hammer specifically for woodworking. If you're getting just one for all uses, go with a medium-size framing hammer with a mallet face on one side and a claw on the other. If you're buying one specifically for woodworking, you'll need your hammer for more than driving and pulling nails—you'll use it to drive chisels, tap joints into place, and sink nails slightly below the surface of wood—so you'll want something with a little more finesse. Everyone has his or her favorite hammer, but consider a mid-weight mallet with a flat face opposite a ball-peen. You'll have your go-to hammer in hand more often than any other tool, so whatever you get, make sure it *feels* right. Add a set of nails in a range of sizes, and you'll be well on your way.

× × × × × × × × × × × × × × × × × × × × × × × × × × × × × × × ×

# SHOPPING FOR TOOLS

**Y**ou don't have to complete your woodworking tool kit all at once. Although you can easily spend $1,000 or more on tools, a few hundred dollars is enough to get you started with a handful of essentials. Build from there as your budget, needs, and interests evolve.

Most tool manufacturers offer three or more quality levels, and even as an amateur or hobbyist, you don't want the lowest level. (You'll likely spend more money replacing cheap tools than you will investing in quality ones.) Consider buying a few good tools, rather than a bunch of cheap tools you'll end up replacing after your first project.

**Screwdrivers and screws.** You'll want to use wood screws for projects specific to woodworking—they're thicker than drywall screws and less likely to snap in half. While you may be drilling screws most often, a screwdriver is also handy.

**Chisels and a sharpening stone.** A sharp chisel lets you change the shape of wood. You'll need the four basic sizes: ¼-, ½-, ¾-, and 1-inch. With these, you can make joints, gouge, carve, bevel, and even pry in a pinch. Whatever chisels you choose, make sure they're *sharp* (get a good sharpening stone). Even a new chisel is likely to need sharpening. Putting a fine edge on your chisel will keep slippage to a minimum and keep your thinner chisels from breaking.

**Level.** Keeping your projects aligned during construction can make the difference between a wobbly step-stool and one you can actually use. As in your domestic repair tool kit (see page 216), choose between a bubble and a laser level.

**Plane.** Basically, a plane is a sharper, heavier version of a deli cheese slicer. It makes a rough piece of wood into something nice to touch, reducing its thickness or smoothing it out before sanding and finishing. Hand planes are a quicker and less dusty way to do some of the work you might do with an electric sander. Your first plane should be a low-angle block plane, which cuts at an angle of about 37 degrees (as opposed to the standard 45 degrees). A shallower cutting angle allows you to plane all three grains of wood (face, edge, and end grain), making the shallow plane a more versatile tool.

**Files and rasps.** Rasps have sharp teeth used to aggressively shape wood. Files have parallel, diagonal rows of teeth of various sizes and are generally used as an intermediate between a rasp and sandpaper. Start with a few flat and half-round rasps and files ranging from "bastard cut" (the coarsest) to "smooth cut" (the smoothest)—you can go a long way with an 8-inch, medium cut flat file.

**Saw.** There are two basic kinds of saw: a rip saw and a crosscut saw. The rip saw has larger, more aggressive teeth for cutting quickly *with* the grain. A crosscut saw has finer teeth for cutting *across* the grain. You can also find a saw with teeth halfway between rip saw and crosscut, and still others have rip saw teeth on one side and crosscut teeth on the other. Buying a combination saw as your first saw may mean you have to do a little more sanding to get the smoothness you want from crosscutting, but it'll give you the versatility to cut things other than wood, like PVC pipe.

**Clamps and a workbench.** Even the mightiest woodworker can't hold a piece of wood and work it at the same time. Start with two 24-inch bar clamps, and then buy more as needed. Not only will clamps—and a good workbench!—keep wood from shimmying while you're hammering, chiseling, planing, and sawing, but you'll need clamps to hold pieces together while glue dries. Bar clamps are for clamping longer pieces; spring clamps (smaller, and shaped more like a clothespin) are for clamping shorter spans; and C-clamps (like bar clamps, but heavier and less adjustable) clamp within the fixed width of the "C" shape.

## Power Tools

Power tools can be intimidating, but as long as you learn to use them safely, there's nothing like the convenience of ripping an inch off the long edge of a stock board without breaking a sweat. There's no need to spend thousands of dollars on specialized woodworking power tools—basic power tools will do 95 percent of those jobs just as well.

**Drill.** If your drill will be doing double duty around the house, go cordless. But if you can justify a drill specifically for woodworking, it's worth giving up mobility for the power of a plug-in drill. You'll want a reversible drill with a variable speed trigger and adjustable clutch. The bigger the chuck—the piece that holds the rotating bit—the more torque the drill offers—a ⅜-inch chuck is enough. If you'll be drilling metal or concrete, you'll need a ½-inch chuck, while the ¼-inch chuck is only for fine projects. Keyed or keyless chuck shouldn't affect your choice, unless you're prone to losing things—in that case, go keyless.

**Circular saw.** Carpentry isn't the same as woodworking (building infrastructure as opposed to building items to populate that infrastructure), and the circular saw probably fits better in the first category. That's because a circular saw is generally used for rougher cuts. There are two basic kinds: the sidewinder, in which the motor sits next to the blade and turns it directly, and the worm-drive, in which the motor sits behind the blade and is geared for higher torque. For most woodworking projects, a high-quality sidewinder is as good as a worm-drive, but beware the underpowered sidewinder (15 amps is standard)—when a blade slows, it heats up and will dull more quickly. A slow blade can also catch on a cut and jump, meaning it won't deliver a clean line.

**Jigsaw.** You'll need a jigsaw to cut curves. As with a drill, the choice between corded or cordless comes down to the trade-off between convenience and power. If you imagine working with hardwoods (or anything besides wood), a corded jigsaw is best. If you're only working with softwoods (see page 278), a cordless jigsaw with one speed option (high) is fine. All jigsaws are *reciprocal,* meaning the blade goes up and down. Better jigsaws are *orbital* as well, meaning that the blade also goes slightly forward and backward, pulling the cutting edge away from the wood on the downstroke and putting it back against the wood on the upstroke (the cutting stroke). You'll want a range of blades to go with it—invest in a set that includes taper, wavy, and side-set teeth (for fine to rough cuts).

**Orbital sander.** The genius of a random orbital sander is a sanding belt that moves so that any single grain on the belt never travels the same path twice. The result is a much smoother finish than a belt or disc sander, but it also means you can't remove as much material as quickly. A palm sander will handle most basic needs, and whatever model you choose, make sure it has dust control—either self-contained or with a hose connection to your wet/dry vac.

**Table saw.** A table saw lets you push wood under a spinning blade. It's best for technical cuts, and it's a tool you'll likely use every day you set foot in your workshop. So if you're going to splurge on anything, splurge on a table saw. (Spend time learning about the proper use of it, too. Nothing sends hobbyists to the emergency room as often as a misused table saw.) Make sure your table saw has a blade guard (almost all do), and then look for a good rip fence and miter gauge. The rip fence is the metal bar against which you'll slide wood when cutting. A secure rip fence with quality tuning controls can help ensure a safe, straight cut. The miter gauge allows you to cut wood at an angle, though it's an accessory you can also buy separately. The table saw is a surprisingly versatile tool that you can use for many kinds of cuts, including with the grain (ripping), across the grain (crosscutting), and at an angle (for cuts like miters and bevels).

**Router.** With a single round blade sticking out below a flat baseplate, a router is used to hollow out sections in a face of wood, to round corners, and more. Make sure you buy at least a 2-horsepower router, with variable speed control and a soft start, which will keep it from bucking if you try to start it while the tooth is stuck. Most routers now come with the ability to accept ¼- or ½-inch shank router bits (smaller bits are less expensive, but the extra mass of a ½-inch bit makes for a smoother cut). You'll see both stationary routers and plunge routers—the difference is all in the base. With a stationary router, you set the base to allow a cut of defined depth, and that's where it stays. A plunge router allows the shank to dive into the wood and back out again.

**Compound miter saw.** When joining wood to wood, a couple of degrees can make a big difference. A good compound miter saw can help you ensure your angles are spot-on. With that in mind, make sure your saw has a high-quality miter gauge—the scale that shows the angle of your cut. The gauge should have accurate hard-stops at the common cutting angles of 0, 15, 22.5, 30, and 45 degrees. A 10-inch blade is enough for most projects, but, if you can afford it, a 12-inch blade will let you use your miter for slightly longer cuts.

## A Visit to the Lumberyard

If you need real wood, you can't beat the selection, quality, price, and expertise of a lumberyard. After you've found your closest lumberyards, call ahead to ask how things are done. Do they offer delivery, or might you have to rent or borrow a truck? Is there someone to show you around and help you? Can you place an order and have it show up at your house, or should you expect to go through the piles and load the wood yourself? What does the yard offer in terms of ripping boards to size? Is there a different procedure for home owners than for contractors? With a little know-how, going to a lumberyard can be like visiting with friends.

### Hard vs. Soft

Hardwoods come from deciduous trees and include maple, mahogany, cherry, oak, and teak. Softwoods come from cone-bearing trees and include types like pine, cedar, and fir. Softwoods grow faster and make up about 80 percent of the world's timber, and so tend to be significantly cheaper. Most general construction work is done with softwoods, including home construction and inexpensive furniture.

Softwoods are graded according to the American Softwood Lumber Standard. First, softwoods are divided into "select" and "common" categories. Select starts with grades A and B, which are appropriate for natural finishes and are completely or almost completely free of blemishes. Select softwood grades C and D may have significant blemishes but are still aesthetically pleasing when painted. Common lumber is rated 1 through 5. For general projects, stick with grades 1 and 2—tight-grained lumber with good structural integrity, usable in most types of building. Grade 3 common lumber is used for crates, sheathing, and subflooring. Grades 4 and 5 barely hold together—you'll have a tough time finding them in most lumberyards.

Hardwoods are graded according to the National Hardwood Lumber Association guidelines, which specify the percent of surface area that must be free of blemishes to earn each grade. The grade FAS stands for firsts and seconds, and requires a board at least 6 inches wide and 8 feet long with more than 83⅓ percent of both faces free of blemishes. Most common uses for FAS hardwoods are furniture and moldings. FAS One Face (F1F) boards must meet FAS requirements on one face. Selects is the same as FAS, but boards can be sold in smaller sizes. Number 1 Common hardwood boards must be at least 66⅔ percent free of blemishes. This is the most common grade used for cabinetry and furniture. Number 2 Common (aka Economy Grade) must be at least 50 percent blemish-free and is primarily used for smaller furniture parts, which allow you to cut around the blemishes.

### Be Choosy (or, How to Pick a Piece of Lumber)

When checking a 2 × 4, look down its length and spin it to check for curves and twists. Check for cupping, in which the board starts to take on a U shape. Check that the edges are square and that the board isn't cracked or split. With boards you plan to use in cosmetic projects, look for blemishes. Otherwise, structural integrity is the only thing that matters.

### Bring On the Preservatives

As a rule, untreated wood shouldn't see moisture—it can't touch the ground or be the outside layer of construction. Preservatives protect against fungal, microorganism, and insect decay and can be applied with or without pressure. Pressure-treated lumber lasts significantly longer (20 years or more) than wood treated with a brush-on preservative. For decking applications, you might want to consider plastic composite lumber, which lasts even longer and won't ever give you splinters.

# #150

# HOW TO MEASURE HARDWOOD BOARDS

## (or, Determining Board Feet)

**SHOP**

Hardwoods are measured and sold by the board foot, which is 1 foot long, 1 foot wide, and 1 inch thick. For your project, you may need a board of 1 × 10 of a certain length—in that case, skip to the next section and just go buy it. You can say, "I'd like an eight-foot, one-by-ten pine board." More complex projects, especially those that require widths other than the standard 1-inch thickness, may require ordering in board feet. Here's how to figure it out.

**1** **BOARD FEET IS CALCULATED BY** multiplying a board's width in inches by its length in feet by its thickness in inches and then dividing by 12. This means that a *thicker* board contains more board feet than a thinner one of equal surface area—board feet is a measure of volume, not area. So, a 16-inch-wide, 8-foot-long, 2-inch-thick board would be 16 × 8 × 2 ÷ 12 = 21.3 board feet.

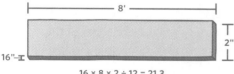

16 × 8 × 2 ÷ 12 = 21.3

**2** **FIRST, LIST THE ROUGH-CUT** sizes of the boards you need. Start by determining how thick you want the finished board, then add ⅛ or even ¼ inch to account for surface planing.

**3** **DO THE SAME THING WITH** width, again adding ¼ inch.

**4** **ADD AN INCH TO THE LENGTH OF** each finished board to determine the rough-cut length—you'll make the end cuts last, and the plane or router (see pages 276–277) has a nasty habit of chipping board ends before you get to them.

**5** **IF YOU AREN'T SURE, YOU CAN** always order your hardwood from the lumberyard S4S—"surfaced both sides"—in which case you don't need to add a cushion—just ask for what you need.

✕✕✕✕✕✕✕✕✕✕✕✕✕✕✕✕✕✕✕✕✕✕✕✕✕✕✕✕✕✕✕✕✕✕✕✕✕✕✕

## BUYING SOFTWOOD BOARDS

Softwoods are sold in standardized board sizes, not by surface area and board feet. You don't get much more standard than a "2 × 4," but a 2 × 4 actually measures 1½ × 3½ inches, the size of the board after being planed down from the rough stock. The same is true of all standard softwood boards, including the 1-by series (1 × 2, 1 × 3, 1 × 4, 1 × 6, 1 × 8, 1 × 10, and 1 × 12), the 2-by series (2 × 2, 2 × 4, 2 × 6, 2 × 8, 2 × 10, 2 × 12), and bigger wood, including 4 × 4, 4 × 6, 6 × 6, and 8 × 8. All the 1-inch dimensions are actually ¾ inch; all the dimensions from 2 to 6 inches lose exactly half an inch (e.g., a 2 × 6 is in fact 1½ × 5½). Dimensions over 6 inches lose ¾ inch. These widths and depths all come in the standard lengths of 6, 8, 10, 12, 14, 16, 18, 20, 22, and 24 feet.

# #151
## HOW TO SAND WOOD
### (or, How to Make a Sanding Block)

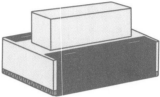

Sanding wood is an ancient art, and it is one that is crucial to all forms of woodworking. From finishing a board to flattening a deck (see page 251) to smoothing a sculpture, sanding makes your projects shine. Ancient as it is, there is a right and a wrong way of doing it. When sanding a flat surface, start with rough-grit sandpaper and continue stepping down the grit until you reach the desired smoothness. Sandpapers run from extra-coarse grits of 24-grit, 30-grit, and 36 grit (sometimes marked as P12 to P36), coarse grits of 40-grit to 50-grit (P40 to P50), medium from 60-grit to 80-grit (P60 to P80), fine from 100-grit to 120-grit (P100 to P120), and very fine from 150-grit to 180-grit and 220-grit (P150 to P220). It's rarely worth sanding with anything finer than about P180, as finishes penetrate slightly rougher woods better and the finish becomes the smooth surface of your piece anyway. Here are the Zen-like basics of sanding wood properly.

## TOOLS:

**Range of sandpaper (coarse, medium, and fine)** ▪ **Staple gun**

## MATERIALS:

- **Wood glue**
- **Felt or lightweight cardboard**
- **Scrap 2 × 4 board**

**1 MAKE A SANDING BLOCK.** Commercial sanding blocks are flat on the bottom with a nice grip and padding to spread the force of your downward pressure. Glue a layer of felt or thin cardboard to a small piece of scrap 2 × 4—anywhere from 3 to 4 inches. To get a better grip on the block, cut a second, smaller piece of 2 × 4 and glue it to the top for a handle.

**2 PREPARE THE SANDING BLOCK.** Cut a piece of sandpaper of the desired grit slightly larger than your block. Lay it on the flat part of the block (grit side out), then fold the ends over and staple them to the top of the block.

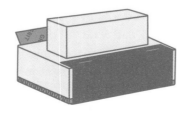

**3 START SANDING A TEST PIECE** of wood. Sand in the direction of the wood grain, applying light, even pressure. When the sandpaper gets clogged with particles or loses its grit, staple a new sheet over the old one. As you step down the coarseness of your sandpaper in stages, wipe away any accumulated sawdust from the board. Before the final sanding, wet the wood and then let it dry to raise the edges of the grain pattern. Use a fine sandpaper and light pressure to finish sanding the piece.

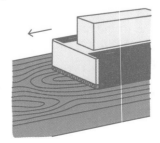

# Wood Finishes

Some modern furniture is designed to be assembled, used, and discarded. That's not the case, however, for the table with the hardwood joinery that you just spent a month slaving over, or for that heirloom antique—so you need to protect it. Finish your tabletops or other special wood surfaces with a protectant to ensure that they bring as much joy to the robot overlords of 2147 as they bring to you today.

Finishes are distinguished mostly by the solvent used as the base. You apply the finish as a liquid, but then the liquid solvent goes away, leaving the color and texture of the finish behind. Finishes lose their solvents by evaporation or reaction. In the former, the water or other emulsion liquid vaporizes, leaving just the finish itself behind. The material left after evaporation will dissolve in the original solvent, meaning that if you spill water on a water-based evaporative finish, you will lose the finish. A reactive finish, such as tung oil or varnish, changes at the chemical level while it cures. Once the finish is dry, you don't have to worry about accidental water spills. Choose based on the preferred finished look, and on your willingness to work with harsher chemicals.

**Wax.** Some consider wax a finish, while others consider it merely a polish to be used over a true finish, like lacquer or shellac. Paste waxes like carnauba and beeswax aren't necessarily waterproof and also don't create a hard shell to resist dents and dings, but they do make a piece *shine*. (Antique furniture may have remnants of an original wax finish, and it can be hard to replicate the color without applying more wax.) To apply paste wax finish, wrap a piece of cotton-based cloth around your fingers and rub on the wax as you might when polishing a pair of shoes. Rub the wax into the grain, and don't be shy about applying multiple coats.

**Oil.** Like wax, some woodworkers choose to use an oil finish as a topcoat after first applying a more durable, protective finish, like a varnish or lacquer. Also like wax, oil finishes are best applied with a cloth wrapped around your hand. Due to the long drying time of oil finishes—especially linseed oil, which can take three days—don't apply too much at once. Work the oil into the grain, and when you see the grain refuse to accept more finish, stop and let the coat dry.

**Varnish.** The durable, shiny surface of a varnish is made of resin, which is combined with drying oil and a thinner or solvent. The solvent keeps the resin in liquid form, and then evaporates to leave the hard finish. A common mistake when applying varnish is brushing it on over dust or other specks, which become permanent additions to the wood finish (until they rip free, chipping the varnish). Thoroughly clean the surface before applying varnish.

**Shellac.** Shellac is a versatile finish with a long history. It's nontoxic and can be used to seal wood before staining, or it can itself be mixed with colors. Basically, shellac is bug poop. The female lac bug of India and Thailand secretes a resin that dries on trees and can be scraped free in flakes. The flakes are dissolved in ethyl alcohol to make a liquid. After the liquid is applied to the wood, the alcohol evaporates, leaving your project covered in a thin, protective layer of lac bug secretion. Cool, huh? Shellac can be brushed or padded onto wood. Brushing is straightforward, but consider using a disposable brush, because it can be especially difficult to clean shellac from the bristles. To pad shellac, wrap cotton muslin around an old sock and then pour shellac into the sock. Gently squeeze the sock to force shellac into the muslin and then apply it to the wood with long, smooth strokes.

**Lacquer.** Lacquers come in brush-on and spray-on forms, and both dry very quickly. Lacquer is very similar to shellac, only while shellac is made from bug excrement found on lac trees, lacquer comes straight from the lac tree itself. A chemical additive cements multiple coats together, even after the first coat dries. Use a natural-bristle brush and apply a quick, thin layer first and follow with additional, thicker layers. Lacquer and polyurethane (see below) are used in much the same way, but should not be used on the same piece.

**Polyurethane.** This forgiving finish is available in water-based or oil-based formulas. Oil-based polyurethane requires fewer coats than water-based polyurethane but takes longer to dry and can hold the patterns of brush marks. Water-based finish requires at least three (and up to five) coats, and even then remains susceptible to water marks. That said, water-based stain won't smell up the room with toxic fumes. Water-based finish also self-levels, so it tends not to hold brush marks. When mixing polyurethane finish in preparation for application, go with the reverse James Bond—stir, don't shake, which would introduce thousands of tiny bubbles. Work with the grain and gently brush away any lingering bubbles. Inevitably, you will leave a few, but don't worry—the marks will disappear in a month.

# #152
## HOW TO BUILD A BIRDHOUSE
### (or, an Introduction to Measuring, Cutting, and Nailing)

A bird could probably live in just about any box that keeps it warm and dry, but if you decide to put one in your yard, why not give it a bit of charm? Here it is: the classic birdhouse. The perfect project on which to cut your woodworking teeth. Your woodworking skills will build on each other, like stacking stones for a tower. At the base of this tower are measuring, cutting, and nailing, so as you work on this project, focus on getting these essential skills just right. The first rule of woodworking is "measure twice; cut once." Take your time in preparation and assembly will be easy.

## TOOLS:

**Pencil** ▪ **Tape measure** ▪ **Ruler or carpenter's square** ▪ **2 bar clamps** ▪ **Jigsaw or handsaw** ▪ **Drill** ▪ **Spade bit** ▪ **½" bit (for optional perch)** ▪ **Hammer** ▪ **Paintbrush** ▪ **Safety goggles**

## MATERIALS:

- One 6-foot 1 × 8 cedar or pine board
- Fifty 1¼" finishing nails
- One 4" × ½" dowel (optional)
- Wood glue
- Paint, polyurethane, or varnish finish
- Galvanized wire

**1 START BY DRAWING THE SHAPES** of your largest pieces, the front and back, onto the board. Lay the 1 × 8 board on a flat surface and hook the metal end of your tape measure on a long edge of the board, near one end. The front and back of your birdhouse will be 7¼" wide, so measure exactly 7¼" on the short (8") edge and make a small tick mark with your pencil. Each piece will be 9½" tall, so use the tape measure to measure and mark 19" along the long edge of the board. At the 19" mark, line up the carpenter's square along the bottom of the board so one side of the L points exactly perpendicularly across it. Draw a line all the way across the board. Measure along this line, and make a mark at

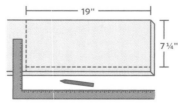

exactly 7¼". Use the long edge of the carpenter's square to draw a line connecting your two marks at 7¼". You will have a 7¼" × 19" box.

**2 USE THE TAPE MEASURE TO** make a mark in the middle of the long box, at 9½". Use the L of the carpenter's square to draw a line across the board at this point, splitting the box into two halves. To draw the triangular peaks of your birdhouse, measure 5⅞" along each of the 9½" edges. Make another mark in the exact center of the 7¼" width, at 3⅝". Now draw diagonal lines connecting the edge mark at 5⅞", with the center mark at 3⅝". You should have now drawn the front and back of the birdhouse.

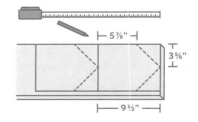

**3** **MEASURE AND DRAW TWO** pieces for the roof. One roof face will be 7" × 6½". Measure 7" from the farthest line you drew in the previous step. Then measure 6½" across the width of the board. Use the carpenter's square to draw the sides of the 7" × 6½" rectangle. The other roof face will be shorter— 6½" × 6¼". As before, measure 6½" up from the farthest pencil line. Then measure 6¼" down the board and use the carpenter's square to draw the sides of your rectangle.

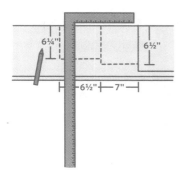

**4** **THE TWO SIDES AND THE** bottom of the birdhouse will all be 5¾" × 4" rectangles. Measure 5¾" from the last line you drew, 4" across the width of the board, and use the carpenter's square as before to draw the sides. Repeat for all three pieces.

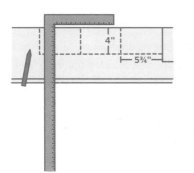

**5** **NOW IT'S TIME TO CUT.** Clamp your board to a fixed surface like a workbench, making sure that your first cutting line doesn't overlap the bench. Keep in mind that you will start by cutting the end you marked in Step 1. Put on your safety goggles and line up your jigsaw or handsaw at the end of your board, at the 7¼" line. If you like, lay the carpenter's square or a metal ruler parallel to the line to guide the saw. Keeping the face of the saw tight against the board, cut straight to the 19" line and then stop.

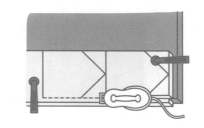

**6** **UNCLAMP, ADJUST, AND** reclamp the board to free up the lines at 9½" and 19", and then cut the front and back of your birdhouse. Clamp these cut pieces to your workbench to make the diagonal cuts, as marked.

**7** **CONTINUE ADJUSTING AND** clamping the board and making one straight cut at a time, eventually freeing all your birdhouse pieces from the board.

**8** **USE A DRILL FITTED WITH A** spade bit to cut an entrance circle in one of the identical faces. (To add a perch, drill a smaller hole right below it and add a piece of ½" dowel.)

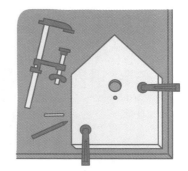

**9** **ASSEMBLE THE FOUR WALLS OF** your birdhouse. Run a thin line of wood glue along the 5¾" edges of your two side pieces and attach them to the front and back pieces. Let the glue dry until it's tacky and then use three finishing nails along each edge.

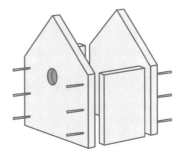

*(continued)*

**10** **ATTACH THE FLOOR.** Place the floor piece about ½" up from the base of the house walls. Glue it to hold it temporarily in place. After the glue has dried, nail it into place with three evenly spaced nails on each side. Make sure the nails from the wall hit the edge of the floor.

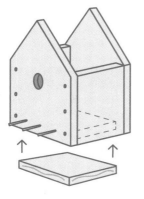

**11** **ADD THE ROOF FACES.** Glue along the top of the walls and place the 6½" × 6¼" piece in place against the glue so that it ends flush with the top of the roof angle. Use three nails to fix the roof panel permanently in place. Then use three nails to add the 7" × 6½" piece so that it overlaps and ends flush with the shorter piece.

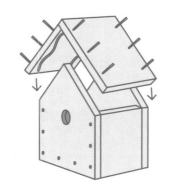

**12** **FINISH AND HANG.** Use an outdoor (oil-based) paint or clear finish to protect it from the elements. Drill two holes in the back of each of the two side walls, just below the edge of the roof and above the base. Thread a piece of wire horizontally through the two higher holes and another through the two lower ones, then tie the birdhouse securely around a tree or fencepost, preferably facing east.

## Drill Bits and How to Use Them

As with any choice you make in woodworking, material matters: You may need a different type of drill bit depending on what you're boring holes in. Steel bits work well in softwood but don't hold up as well against hardwood. Their cousin, high-speed steel bits, are so named because they can withstand higher temperatures than other types of steel—and thus will cut through materials like wood, fiberglass, PVC, and soft metals faster. Even tougher than high-speed steel is titanium-coated HSS, and moving up the spectrum, the hardest drill bits—carbide-tipped—are primarily used for tile and masonry. They stay sharp a long time! When you're inserting the bit into the drill chuck, make sure the shaft is straight and then tighten the chuck around it well.

**Twist bits.** The most common type of bit, twist bits are the kind you probably got in a starter set of bits. Twist bits are an all-purpose bit that can be used in just about any material. The spiral groove—or flute—helps to remove sawdust from the hole as you go.

**Spade bits.** These bits (they're not the kind for horses) have a pointy tip in the center of a flat edge, and they're made for ripping quick holes through soft wood. They can leave ragged edges but get the job done quickly.

**Auger bits.** Auger bits look a little bit like thinner twist bits but have a tip that starts the drill hole for you. Augers were the bit of choice when hand-powered drills were in style because they require less torque and are easy to turn. They are typically used for drilling deep holes in wood (the large flute gets chaff out of the hole easily).

**Countersink bits.** Sometimes called screw pilot bits, these are specialty bits that look like a regular bit with a sheath around the base. This type of bit is a multitasker—it drills a pilot hole, so you don't split the wood when you put in a screw—at the same time as it drills a countersink hole, a conical hole that allows you to conceal the head of the screw with sawdust or a wooden plug, lending the whole project a more refined look.

# #153
# HOW TO BUILD A PICTURE FRAME
## (or, an Introduction to Mitering and Using Moldings)

Decorative moldings give your home character—baseboards where walls meet the floor, crown molding where walls meet the ceiling—you get the idea. These are big projects, and before you jump into cutting and installing hundreds of feet of intricate molding, it's worth practicing on some smaller projects. Like a picture frame—or ten. In this project, pay special attention to the tips and tricks that will enable you to miter cut molding—that is, beveling it so it fits snugly together at an angle—without chipping it. Being able to put a perfect end angle on a piece of molding is a skill that'll serve you well down the line.

## TOOLS:

**Measuring tape** ▪ **Calculator** ▪ **Miter box and handsaw, or miter saw** ▪ **2 bar clamps** ▪ **4 corner clamps** ▪ **Hammer** ▪ **Utility knife** ▪ **Safety goggles**

## MATERIALS:

- **Picture frame molding**
- **Wood glue**
- **Backing board**
- **½" to ¾" brad nails**
- **Sandpaper and stain or paint to finish (optional)**
- **Hanging or standing hardware**

**1** **MEASURE THE MAT OR PICTURE** to determine the interior dimensions of your frame.

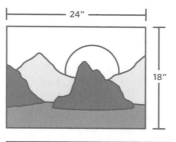

**2** **CALL AHEAD TO FRAME SHOPS** to find out if they sell picture molding in lengths. Bring along to the store your measurements, a calculator, and an idea of the style you want.

## IN THE FRAME SHOP

**1** **FIRST, ORDER A PIECE OF GLASS** and a backing board sized to the art you want to frame.

**2** **CHOOSE THE STYLE OF PICTURE** frame molding that best complements your art. Keep in mind that the more intricately a piece of molding is patterned, the more prone it is to chipping and cracking. The width of the molding should be listed on the sample. If not, the store should assist you in getting an accurate measurement.

**3** **TO DETERMINE HOW MUCH** molding to get, add twice the molding width to each length of the interior dimensions. For example, if your interior dimensions are 18" × 24" and you plan to use 2" molding, get two 22" and two

28" lengths of molding. The shop can cut the molding to length or you can add these lengths together, plus a couple of inches for scrap, and carefully transport the long length back to your shop. That said, there's a good chance a shop will have molding samples on hand, but not the actual molding. If you're in a hurry, ask to see only what's in stock. If you're not, plan on waiting to have the molding of your choice shipped to you or to the shop for pickup. The shop very well may offer to miter the molding for you. Don't let them. For the purposes of this project, that's cheating. But you can get the molding rabbeted. This will precut the inside groove that will hold your picture in place.

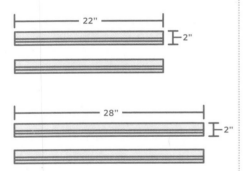

# BACK IN YOUR WOOD SHOP

**1** **CUT THE MOLDING TO LENGTH,** if necessary (see page 285, Step 3).

**2** **LAY OUT YOUR FOUR LENGTHS** of molding and double-check that each is twice the molding width longer than the interior dimensions of your frame. Miter the corners to 45-degree angles before joining them to make your frame. First, make sure that your saw blade is sharp. Use clamps (not just the pressure of your hand) to hold the molding securely to the saw. Finally, position your molding piece in the miter box or on the saw molded-side-up, so that the visible edge is pressed against the top of the box or saw table. Now line up your cuts. Put on your safety goggles, turn the blade to 45 degrees, lock it in place, load your wood, press it tight against the saw's back fence, and make the exact same cuts on one end of all four pieces of molding.

**3** **REVERSE THE 45-DEGREE ANGLE** of your miter box or saw and repeat, cutting the opposite ends of your molding. Be careful with the direction of your cuts—it's worth laying out the wood as it will eventually be assembled and drawing rough pencil lines showing the direction you want your angles. Mitering the mirror image of the angle you planned is a quick way to turn your usable molding into scrap.

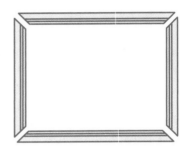

**4** **ONCE YOU'VE MITERED THE** corners, dry fit your picture frame, using the corner clamps to hold the molding in place. Remember, the picture and the glass should sit against the small ledge called the rabbet, running around the inside of the molding. If your frame pieces are slightly too big, unclamp the frame and miter again to shave the extra, being sure to cut exactly equal amounts from opposite sides of the frame. If your frame is slightly too small, cry, swear, and then start over from the beginning (or trim your art . . .). If needed, continue shaving your frame until your art fits into the rabbeted frame.

**5 GLUE THE FRAME PIECES** together at the joints and hold them in place with your corner clamps. While the joints are drying, cut your backing board to the size of your art with a utility knife.

**6 ONCE THE JOINTS ARE DRY,** reinforce them by carefully tacking them together with brad nails. This isn't the time to swing away and risk cracking your delicate project. Light taps with thin nails should do the trick.

**7 IF YOU LIKE, SAND AND STAIN** or paint your finished frame and, once it's dry, install the hanging or standing hardware on the back.

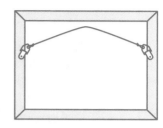

## A Few Relevant Woodworking Terms

If you're going to be making your own bookshelves, stools, and wood frames from scratch, it's also worth learning to talk the talk. Here are a few basic vocabulary terms that will help when you're shopping for materials, making the project, or asking for help along the way.

### Cross Cuts
These cuts run perpendicular to the grain of the wood.

### Rip Cuts
These cuts run parallel to the grain of the wood.

### Fence
A guide at the back of a tool (like a saw) that stops whatever you're cutting, keeping it a set distance from the blade.

### Miter Box vs. Miter Saw
A miter box is a simple tool that has slats that helps you hold the saw at an angle and clamps the wood in place. Using a miter box, you can make angled cuts on a piece of wood with a handsaw.

If you want to upgrade to a power tool, consider a power miter saw if you have the need for a crosscut chopsaw that makes it easy to shave off bits of wood with precision. Some models tilt for bevel and miter cuts. Compound miter saws can make angled cuts to the edge and face of the board (you'd want that for crown molding).

### Bevel Angle vs. Miter Angle
Although it may sound like these terms can be used interchangeably, they do have different meanings. The bevel angle is the tilt of the saw blade from vertical on the table saw, while the miter angle is the horizontal angle. Typically the maximum bevel on a miter saw is 45 degrees.

### Rabbeting
Cutting a deep groove or a notch into a wood so that you can fit and attach another piece to it. Rabbeting describes both the act of cutting the groove, and also fitting in the joining piece. A rabbet is also the name of the joint made thus. Rabbeting usually also includes gluing or fastening the grooved pieces.

# #154
# HOW TO BUILD A DOGHOUSE
## (or, an Introduction to Framing and Roofing)

Building a sturdy and comfortable doghouse splits the difference between wanting what's best for your best friend and not necessarily wanting your best friend hogging your bed. Build the house a little bigger and you've got a storage shed or small barn. A little bigger than that and you've got a garage. That's to say, the techniques you learn here are the same ones you'd use to build any framed wooden box with a top that points at the sky. Note that standard shingle size is 12" by 36", but the package size depends on the weight of the shingle, so you may want to ask for help at your home supply store.

## TOOLS:

**Measuring tape** ▪ **Pencil** ▪ **Carpenter's frame** ▪ **Circular saw or handsaw** ▪ **Jigsaw** ▪ **Drill and bit larger than your jigsaw blade** ▪ **Sandpaper or orbital sander** ▪ **Staple gun and ⅜" staples** ▪ **Utility knife** ▪ **Safety goggles** ▪ **Paint brush**

## MATERIALS:

- **One 8-foot pressure-treated 2 × 4 board**
- **One 8-foot 2 × 2 board**
- **One 4' × 8' sheet exterior-grade plywood**
- **3" galvanized deck screws**
- **1¼" galvanized deck screws**
- **Four 15-inch 1 × 1 framing strips**
- **Four 13-inch 2 × 2 framing strips**
- **15-pound tar paper**
- **½" galvanized roofing nails**
- **Asphalt shingles (to cover roof)**
- **Exterior-grade paint**

**1** **MEASURE, MARK, AND CUT AN** 8-foot, pressure-treated 2 × 4 into four pieces to make the rectangular base. You'll need to cut two lengths of 22½" and two lengths of 23". Measure, mark, and cut an 8-foot 2 × 2 into four lengths of 13" and four lengths of 15", to make the frame of the walls and roof.

**2** **USE A TAPE MEASURE,** carpenter's frame, and pencil to draw the following template onto the 4' × 8' sheet of exterior-grade plywood. Adjust the size of the opening to fit your dog—it should be about ¾ of your dog's height. (Keep in mind that the smaller the opening,

the less quickly the house will lose heat.) Either freehand the arch at the top of the entryway or use something round to stencil it—a Frisbee works well for this shape.

**3** **CUT OUT THE PIECES FROM** your plywood template. Clamp the plywood securely to sawhorses (best) or to your workbench and use a circular saw or a handsaw (more arduous) to make all of the straight cuts.

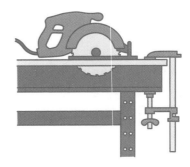

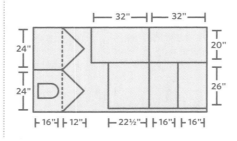

**4** **TO CUT OUT THE ENTRYWAY,** first drill a hole big enough to fit the blade of your jigsaw in the piece to be removed (the hole can go anywhere). Start your jigsaw cut in this drilled hole and follow the lines of your entryway to cut it out. Support the flap you're cutting out so that it doesn't tear free and splinter once the weight of the detached piece is too heavy.

**5** **DECIDE WHETHER YOU WANT** the roof of your doghouse to end at a mitered 45-degree angle or whether you'll overlap one roof face on top of the other. If mitering, set the blade of your circular saw to tilt 45 degrees before cutting the line that will be your roof apex on both faces. Because the roof faces are exactly the same size, you can cut both faces at the same 45-degree angle and then just flip one to join the cut sides. Sand the edges of these pieces to remove any splinters.

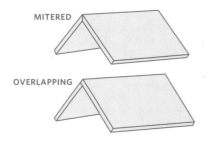

MITERED

OVERLAPPING

**6** **ASSEMBLE THE BASE FRAMING.** The pressure-treated lumber will sit against the ground, with the floor of the house sitting on top of it. Not only does this keep untreated wood from molding and rotting, and keep the treated wood away from Fido's teeth, but it also traps air underneath the house to act as insulation. The 22½" pieces are the front and back, and the 23" pieces are the sides. Laying the lumber on its edge, fit the 23" pieces inside the front and back pieces, and predrill two screw holes per joint so that you're drilling through the face of the 22½" pieces and into the ends of the 23" pieces (remember, the finished floor dimensions should be 22½" × 26"). Use 3" galvanized deck screws to hold the frame of the base together.

**7** **SCREW ON THE FLOOR.** Lay the piece of plywood that is the floor of the doghouse on top of your frame. Use 1¼" galvanized deck screws spaced about every 8" to 12" to hold the plywood floor to the frame.

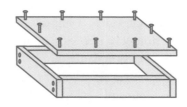

**8** **ATTACH THE FRAMING STRIPS** to the side walls, top, and back. Lay a 15" framing strip along the 26" length of one of the side pieces. Leave 1" of plywood extending past the strip at the bottom. Use 1¼" deck screws spaced about every 8" to fix the framing strip to the side wall. Repeat for the

other side wall. Lay a 15" framing strip across the bottom edge of what will be the back of the doghouse, again leaving 1" of plywood past the strip. Lay the final 15" framing strip along the bottom edge of the doghouse front, again leaving 1" extending past the strip.

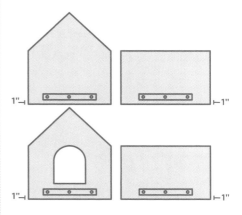

**9** **ATTACH THE SIDE WALLS** to the base. Place a side wall against the base so that the framing strip sits on the top of the base and the 1" overhang of plywood along the lower edge of the side wall extends down to the pressure-treated lumber. Use 1¼" deck screws spaced about every 5", screwed down through the framing strip and into the base to hold the pieces together. Repeat for the other side wall. Then, use 1¼" deck screws to screw through the overhanging 1" of plywood along the lower edge of each wall, into the pressure-treated lumber, spaced about every 8".

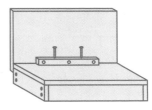

*(continued)*

**10** **ATTACH FRAMING STRIPS** along the insides of the roof angles of the front and back plywood pieces. Center one of the 13" 2 × 2 framing strips along the inside of a sloped roof edge so that the top of the strip is flush with the top of the plywood. Use three 1¼" wood screws, driven through the plywood into the framing strip, to hold the strip in place. Repeat for the remaining three 13" framing strips.

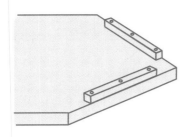

**11** **ATTACH THE BACK.** Tip the house on what will be its front and lay the back piece against the rear edges of the side walls. Seat the framing piece attached to the back down against the base. Screw it in place as you did with the side walls. Repeat to attach the front.

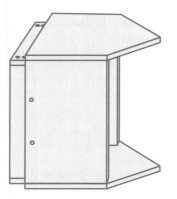

**12** **ATTACH THE ROOF PANELS.** Lay a panel flush against the framing strips you attached to the wall pieces in Step 10, making sure that if you chose to cut a 45-degree bevel to miter the top of the roof in Step 5, to place the angle appropriately at the apex. Also make sure the roof panel sits square to the walls and that the eaves hang over an equal amount on both sides. Use 1¼" wood screws spaced about every 8" to screw the roof panel to the framing pieces. Repeat with the other roof panel.

**13** **NOW SHINGLE THE ROOF.** Run 15-pound tar paper up one side of the roof and down the other, staple it in place, and use a utility knife to trim it flush with the roof panels. To install the asphalt shingles, start with an upside-down row of shingles (tab up) along both lower edges of the roof panels, using roofing nails to hold them in place. The shingles should overhang the plywood edge of the roof panel by about ¾". Then nail another layer of shingles, right-side up, directly over this first row. Install another row slightly higher, making sure it overlaps the first. Continue installing

rows until you've completely covered both roof panels. Cap the roof ridge by cutting smaller rectangles of shingles, bending them over the roof peak and nailing them in place so they overlap each other slightly, covering the nails in the previous tab.

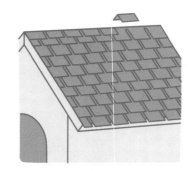

**14** **TO FINISH, PAINT THE** walls of your doghouse with an exterior-grade paint. Let dry.

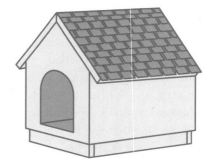

# #155
## HOW TO BUILD A SHAKER STOOL
### (or, How to Use a Template)

There are things that are unlikely, like winning the lottery, and there are things that are impossible, like cutting two identical, irregularly shaped pieces of wood without a template. A template and the skills to use it ensure that you can mass-produce complicated cuts—in this case, two identical legs for a Shaker-style step stool.

There are a couple of ways to use woodworking templates, but here we'll draw directly on a piece of ¼" plywood, trace it against our wood, and rough-cut it to shape with a jigsaw. Finally we will use what's called a "flush trim bit" mounted in a router to smooth the wood to the template. One reason cutting to a template is such a useful skill is the ubiquity and convenience of online templates. For nearly any project you can imagine, a template is but a quick search away, so you can produce professional-looking designs in your own shop. This Shaker stool is a great place to start—and the wood should set you back only about $15.

## TOOLS:

Tape measure ▪ Pencil ▪ Table saw or handsaw ▪ Jigsaw ▪ Router ▪ Clamps ▪ Flush trim bit with bearing ▪ Drill ▪ Countersink drill bit ▪ 4-foot level ▪ Safety goggles

## MATERIALS:

- One 4-foot 1 × 12 pine board
- One 1-foot 1 × 4 pine board
- Scrap ¼" plywood, at least 10" × 11"
- Double-sided tape (optional)
- Fifty 1" wood screws
- Wood glue (optional)
- Paint or finish (optional)

**1** MEASURE AND MARK 14" FROM the end of a 4-foot 1 × 12 board. Cut it off with a table saw and rip the piece down to exactly 11" wide. This will be the top of your stool. Measure, mark, and cut a 1-foot 1 × 4 into a piece 11" long and 3" wide. This will be your brace.

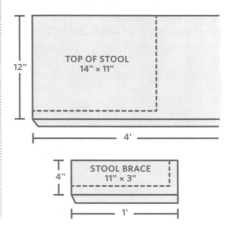

**2** CUT A 20"-LONG SECTION FROM the 1 × 12 and rip it to exactly 10¼" wide. Cut this piece in half, making two 10" × 10¼" rectangles. Once shaped, these will be the legs of your stool.

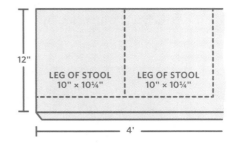

*(continued)*

**3 MAKE A TEMPLATE FOR THE** legs. Measure, mark, and cut a section of ¼" plywood into a 10" × 10¼" rectangle. Draw a shape for your stool legs onto this plywood rectangle. One common cut is to taper the legs slightly toward the top, marking ¾" in from the top sides and drawing a straight line to the bottom corners. You'll also need to cut some sort of decorative arc from the bottom center of your legs. Some ideas are shown here, but feel free to experiment with the shape of this arc. If you make an irretrievable mistake, it only costs another 10" × 10¼" scrap of plywood to start again. Use a frisbee or another rounded household object if you need something to trace.

**4 MEASURE ABOUT 3" FROM THE** top edge to find the exact center of your template. Draw a 3" × ¾" rectangle that, when cut out from each leg, will secure the brace.

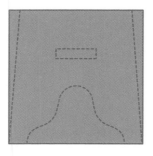

**5 CUT OUT THE PLYWOOD SHAPE** that you'll use as a template to sculpt your stool's legs. Consider using your table saw for long, straight cuts and the jigsaw for more ornate, curved cuts (and drill a hole to cut out the rectangle for the brace, as you did in Step 4 of How to Build a Doghouse). Sand or use your router to finish the template to the exact shape you want the legs.

**6 WHEN THE PLYWOOD** template is ready, lay it on top of one of the 10" × 10¼" pieces of pine that will be your stool's legs. Trace around the template with a pencil, put on your safety goggles, and then use the jigsaw to rough-cut the stool leg to shape.

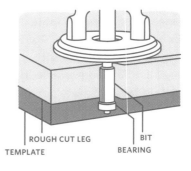

**7 PLACE THE PLYWOOD TEMPLATE** beneath the rough-cut stool leg and clamp them together to your workbench. To prevent slippage, use double-sided tape to stick the template to the wood before clamping.

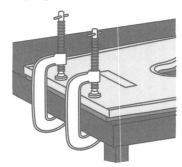

**8 MAKE SURE THE ROUTER IS** unplugged and insert the flush trim bit. Set the router on top of the clamped piece and template and look at how the bit and bearing hit the side of the stacked pieces. Adjust the bit so that when the router is flat against the piece, the bearing hits the template and the bit hits the rough-cut board.

ROUGH CUT LEG    BIT

TEMPLATE    BEARING

**9 PREPARE TO DRIVE THE ROUTER** along the rough-cut board, using the template below it as a guide. Place the router flat against the board, with the bit safely away from the edge of the wood. Plug in and turn on the router, and once the bit is up to speed, bring it into the board, stopping when you feel the bearing contact the template. Using the feel of the bearing against the template, run the router around the edge of the board, making an exact copy of the template, including the space between the legs and the brace support holes. Repeat Steps 7 to 9 with the other leg.

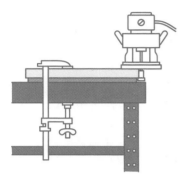

**10** **ASSEMBLE THE STOOL.** Insert the brace into the rectangular holes, connecting the two legs. Place the legs on the ground and wiggle slightly until all four feet sit flush against the ground. Lay the top of the stool across the legs and use a level to check that it lies flat. If all four feet aren't snug to the ground or if the top of your stool isn't level, use your table saw to shave your cuts accordingly. If your brace seems unsturdy, use wood glue to secure it in the hole.

**11** **ATTACH THE TOP.** Lay it atop your legs and make sure it's exactly centered and level. Countersink four evenly spaced pilot holes and use 1" wood screws to attach the top to the legs. Again, if you like, use wood glue and sawdust to camouflage the holes.

**12** **IF YOU LIKE, PAINT OR** finish your Shaker stool. Traditionally, this kind of furniture would be finished with oil and wax (talk to your local home improvement or woodworking store, or see Oil Finishes for Wood, page 301).

✗✗✗✗✗✗✗✗✗✗✗✗✗✗✗✗✗✗✗✗✗✗✗✗✗✗✗✗✗✗✗✗✗✗✗✗✗✗✗✗✗✗✗✗✗✗✗✗✗✗✗✗✗✗✗✗✗✗✗

# SANDING FURNITURE

**S**anding furniture or shaped pieces follows the same essential strategy as sanding a flat board—always go with the grain of the wood and progress from coarser to finer paper.

For flat surfaces, use a padded sanding block. For curved surfaces, use a thick sponge covered with sandpaper, which will help you exert even pressure while conforming to the shape. To sand rounded pieces like spindles or thin chair legs, cut a long strip of medium- or fine-grit sandpaper and wrap the paper around the piece so that you can hold the two ends together. Pull the

sandpaper wrap back and forth, as if using a bow and stick to start a fire.

For rounded edges, use a piece of fine-grit paper folded onto itself. For detail sanding, wrap fine-grit sandpaper around the tip of a sharpened pencil. For even finer work, use a toothpick. When sanding delicate pieces, brace both the hand doing the sanding and the hand doing the holding so that your sanding materials don't slip. Sanding can lead to chips and dings as well as scratches, especially when working with fine edges. When you're finished, blow the sawdust from the crevices or use a clean toothbrush to free it.

# #156
## HOW TO BUILD A CHESSBOARD
### (or, Learning to Veneer)

The interior decorators of King Tut's tomb used ebony and ivory veneer. So did the builders in the French Renaissance court of King Louis XIV, who used exotics and burl wood to make intricate veneer patterns called marquetry. Today Ikea continues this great tradition, as veneer is widely used in commercial furniture to stretch the use of valuable hardwoods. Done right, veneer—a thin slice of wood applied to another piece of wood as decoration—can greatly enhance a project. Here you'll apply the technique to create a chessboard.

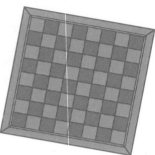

## TOOLS:

**Pencil** • **Craft or utility knife** • **Table saw, circular saw, or jigsaw (optional)** • **Carpenter's square** • **Metal straightedge** • **Miter box and handsaw, or miter saw** • **Clamps** • **Safety goggles**

## MATERIALS:

- **At least 14" × 7" sheet of dark veneer (extra preferred)**
- **At least 17" × 11" sheet of light veneer (extra preferred)**
- **At least 2" × 17" sheet of silver (or contrasting) veneer (extra preferred)**
- **Painter's tape**
- **Clear tape**
- **17" × 17" sanded plywood**
- **Wood glue**
- **Scrap wood**

**1** **THERE ARE MANY WAYS TO CUT** veneer, and each cut tends to give a different, distinctive pattern to the grain. So when you go to the home improvement store or lumberyard, explore not only the colors of veneers but also their grains. Pick 1-ply light and dark hardwood veneers that are exactly the same thickness. Then choose a third piece of contrasting 1-ply veneer—silver works well—for the trim that will go around the outside edges of your board. You may be able to use veneer scraps. Veneer comes with or without paper backing. For this project, raw (unbacked) veneer is preferable, but paper-backed will work as well.

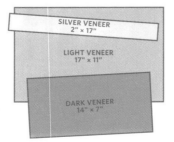

SILVER VENEER
2" × 17"

LIGHT VENEER
17" × 11"

DARK VENEER
14" × 7"

**2** **CUT THE VENEER INTO STRIPS.** Depending on your tools, use a saw or a craft or utility knife to cut your veneer to size. If you use a table saw, be sure you know how to use it safely, because you'll be making narrow cuts. Like molding, veneer tends to chip and crack when cut. Whatever saw you use, pick the blade with the smallest, most closely spaced teeth, and make sure it's sharp. To guard against splintering, put scotch tape over the lines you will cut, and then slice through the tape. Remove it carefully once you've made your cuts. Measure, mark, and cut four strips each of light and dark veneer. The standard dimension of chessboard squares is 1¾" on a side, so, for now, make eight strips that are 1¾" × 14". Measure, mark, and cut four ¼" × 17" strips of silver veneer, and another four strips of 1" × 17" light veneer for your border.

**3** **ON A FLAT SURFACE, LAY THE** 1¾" × 14" light and dark veneer strips exactly side by side with the face side down, starting with a light strip. Push the strips against a carpenter's square to ensure that they are exactly square on all sides. If squaring the strips is impossible, shave strips as necessary or replace badly cut strips with new ones. The precision of this step will determine the success of your project. Using the carpenter's square to keep them flush, use a liberal amount of clear tape on the backs of the strips to hold them all together in a square.

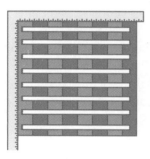

**4** **CUT YOUR STRIPS INTO SQUARES.** First, make marks every 1¾" along your first light strip and then make corresponding marks at every 1¾" along the final dark strip. Lay the metal straightedge between the corresponding marks and run your craft knife along the straightedge, being sure to hold the knife exactly vertically. It's fine if your cuts require multiple strokes with the knife. As long as you run true against the straightedge, it's better to make multiple light cuts than risk cracking the veneer. Because you backed your strips with clear tape and then cut through the tape, the cuts in this step will again make strips (held together with the tape), only this time your

strips are made of alternating light and dark squares.

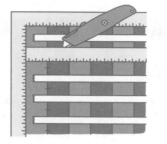

**5** **PICK UP THESE STRIPS AND, AS** before, lay the strips side by side, but this time alternate the pattern so that it looks like the standard chessboard. Square these strips against the carpenter's square and again join them together with tape into a perfect square.

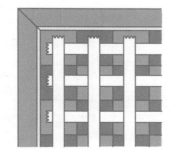

**6** **LAY THE ¼" STRIPS OF SILVER** veneer alongside your squared, chessboard-patterned strips to form a border. Use the craft knife to miter the corners at 45-degree angles (see How to Build a Picture Frame, page 285). Do the same with the 1" × 17" strips of light veneer, to complete the border.

**7** **MOUNT YOUR VENEER** chessboard surface on your 17" × 17" sanded plywood board. To do this, pick off the tape from one piece of veneer at a time, apply a dot of wood glue to the back of each piece and place it on the board. Once all pieces are in place, clamp them in place to dry. Place scrap wood against the clamp pads to spread the force of the clamp across a wider area—this will help you avoid scratching, denting, or cracking your veneer.

If you are feeling ambitious, flip to page 302 (How to Build a Storage Chest) and use the techniques there to build what is effectively a small chest to hold your chess pieces and on top of which you can mount your veneer.

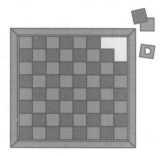

# #157
# HOW TO MAKE A BUTCHER BLOCK

## (or, Laminating 101)

A butcher block is a serious hunk of wood, used as the solid base for heavy-duty chopping and cutting. But it isn't seriously a hunk at all. Because hardwoods rarely come in the size needed for chopping blocks, they are made from many columns of wood fixed together, which is called laminate. There are two kinds of laminated chopping blocks: edge grain and end grain. Edge grain is made of long strips of wood. End grain blocks, from wood cut across the growth rings, resist nicks and chips better. And, because your knife edge goes between the wood grain instead of across it, end grain blocks tend to help your knives stay sharper longer.

Oak and maple are the most common woods used for chopping block construction, though any hardwood will work and you can find blocks made from birch, cherry, and walnut. Here you'll learn to make a stand-alone, checkerboard-patterned, end grain chopping block, using the hardwood of your choice.

## TOOLS:

**Measuring tape** ▪ **Pencil** ▪ **Table saw** ▪ **3 or more bar clamps** ▪ **Metal straightedge** ▪ **Electric sander or sandpaper and large muscles** ▪ **Rag**

## MATERIALS:

- **One 3-foot 2 × 6 light-colored hardwood board**
- **One 3-foot 2 × 6 dark-colored hardwood board**
- **Wood glue**
- **Coarse, medium, and fine sandpaper**
- **Mineral oil**

**1 BEFORE YOU START, MEASURE** the depth of your hardwood boards and make sure they are really 2". If not, let the width of your boards define the size of the cubes you will use throughout (i.e., if your board is 1¾" deep, you will make cubes of that size). Whatever the depth of the boards—let's assume it's exactly 2"—use your table saw to rip the hardwood boards into exactly square strips, the length of the board. Cut these strips in half. You should now have six 2" × 2" × 18" light strips and six 2" × 2" × 18" dark strips.

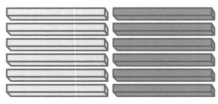

LIGHT STRIPS
2" × 2" × 18"

DARK STRIPS
2" × 2" × 18"

**2 ON A FLAT SURFACE, LAY THE** strips next to each other, alternating light and dark. Apply a thin, squiggly strip of wood glue between each wood strip, making sure they lay square to one another. Clamp the strips together with at least three bar clamps. Use a damp cloth to wipe away any excess glue that squeezes out. Let dry overnight.

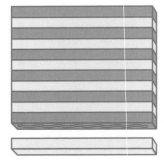

**3** **YOU JUST TURNED THE STRIPS** into a sheet, and now you'll turn the sheet back into strips. The distance between cuts will be the width of your butcher block. For this project, we'll cut the 18"-long sheet crosswise into 12 new strips each 1½" thick. Use a tape measure to make marks every 1½" along the endmost light strip and then corresponding marks every 1½" along the endmost dark strip. Use a straightedge and a pencil to draw straight lines connecting the marks opposite each other—your new strips should alternate light and dark blocks (just as in Step 4 of How to Build a Chessboard, page 295). Now use your table saw to cut these strips. Cut directly in the center of the

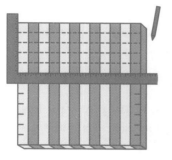

lines you drew. Because the finished thickness of your board needn't be precise, don't worry about how much wood you lose to the saw blade (this thickness is called the "kerf"). As long as you're consistent in the way you cut, your chopping block will turn out flat.

**4** **ON A FLAT SURFACE, LAY THE** alternating-block strips next to each other to create a checkerboard pattern. As before, apply a thin layer of wood glue between strips, and clamp together what should now look like a finished, checkerboard-pattern chopping block. Wipe clean any excess glue. Let dry overnight.

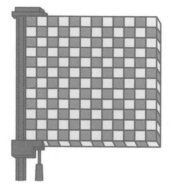

**5** **USE AN ELECTRIC SANDER OR** sandpaper and significant elbow grease to sand both faces and all corners of the block, first with coarse, then medium, and finally fine sandpaper, until smooth. Use a damp rag to wipe the block free of sawdust. Use a rag to wipe the block with mineral oil. Let the piece sit overnight, and then apply a second coat of oil. Wipe away any excess oil. Apply a new coat of oil every couple of months to keep your chopping block looking great.

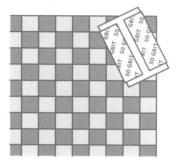

× × × × × × × × × × × × × × × × × × × × × × × × × × × × × × × × × × × × × × × × × × × × × × × × × × × × × × × × × × × × × ×

# OILING A BUTCHER BLOCK

**W**hether you make your own or have a store-bought block in need of some TLC, butcher blocks are perfect for experimenting with oil finishes (choose from the options listed on page 301). Here are some tips and tricks:

• Make sure the wood is clean—a little mild soap and a damp rag will do the trick.

• The oil works best if it's warm when you use it. You can place the bottle in a bowl of hot water for about 5 minutes to heat it.

• Use a rag or, better, an old sock, to apply the oil to the wood in multiple coats.

• Let the butcher block sit for 5 minutes or so between applications, until the block cannot absorb any more oil. (It should take 5 or 6 coats.) Wipe up any excess oil with a rag.

# #158
## HOW TO STAIN WOOD

Halfway between paint and varnish is stain, which brings its own pigment to the project but allows the look of the wood to remain dominant. Stains generally include a pigment or dye suspended in water or mineral oil as a solvent. You apply it wet, the solvent dries away, and you're left with a consistent coat of color. Oil-based stains dry slowly and don't raise the grain of the wood. Water-based stains dry more quickly, don't carry odor, and clean up with soap and water—however, they likely necessitate a final sanding. If you like the color of your wood as is, skip straight to a protective finish. If you want to darken or change the look of your wood, apply stain first, and then a protective topcoat of varnish or another finish (see How to Refinish Furniture, page 242).

## Pick a Color

The color you apply isn't always the color you end up with—stains typically change hue as they dry. And because a stain's color is influenced by the underlying wood, even the samples at the store are only best guesses. If you need to match a target color, the only way to do it right is to try a stain on a scrap or an unseen corner of your piece.

## TOOLS:

**Fine sandpaper** • **Sanding block** • **Chemical-resistant rubber gloves** • **Rags** • **Old sock or disposable paintbrush**

## MATERIALS:

• **Wood stain**

**1 PREPARE THE SURFACE.** Because stain rests in the pores of a piece, stain must be applied to bare, sanded wood. To start, unscrew any functional or decorative elements. With new wood, simply sand with fine-grit sandpaper to open the pores. With old wood, strip away any existing finish (see How to Strip Paint, page 240) and then sand.

**2 APPLY THE STAIN.** There are many ways to apply stain, but the best method depends on the size of the wood's pores. To ensure full saturation of the large pores of "open-grain" woods" (oak, ash, and mahogany), use an old sock wrapped around your gloved hand to work the stain into the wood, scrubbing across the grain in a swirling pattern. With closed-grain woods—like cherry, aspen, and birch—use a brush to apply stain in long, gentle strokes.

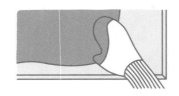

**3 WIPE THE STAIN.** The longer you leave a stain to dry before wiping, the darker the finished color. However, pools or droplets of stain left on the surface will create an uneven finish. Ideally, you would apply only as much stain as would reasonably dry to a consistent, flat color. However, wood tends to have uneven absorption, so once your piece has dried, you'll need to wipe it free of excess stain with a dry rag. Wipe in straight lines with the grain of the wood. Repeat Steps 2 and 3 for a second and even a third coat.

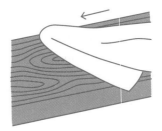

# #159

# HOW TO BUILD A BOOKCASE

## (or, How to Use Edge Banding)

**A**t some point in your woodworking career, you'll probably want to build a bookshelf. When you do, the easiest thing to build it with is plywood. But you'll have to do something about those raw plywood edges. That's where edge banding comes in. Edge banding is thin veneer with pre-applied glue that comes in rolls of various widths, most commonly ¾". In this project, you'll learn how to iron edge banding onto the exposed edges of a plywood shelf.

## TOOLS:

**Tape measure** ▪ **Straightedge** ▪ **Pencil** ▪ **Table saw, circular saw, or jigsaw** ▪ **Clamps** ▪ **Electric sander (optional)** ▪ **Utility or heavy craft knife** ▪ **Clothes iron** ▪ **Plane (optional)** ▪ **Hammer** ▪ **Drill, with a pilot bit** ▪ **Safety goggles**

## MATERIALS:

- **One 4' × 8' sheet of ¾" grade A or A/B plywood**
- **One 3' × 6' sheet of ½" grade A or A/B plywood**
- **1 roll ¾" wood veneer edge banding to match the plywood**
- **Wood glue**
- **Coarse, medium, and fine sandpaper**
- **Fifty 1⅝" wood screws or finishing nails**
- **Four 3" wood screws**
- **14" × 70" × ¼" plywood or panel backing (optional)**
- **Paintbrush**
- **Wood stain**

**1** **USE A TAPE MEASURE AND** straightedge to draw the following rectangles on the 4' × 8' sheet of ¾" plywood: two 12" × 70" strips; one 16" × 38" strip; and two 14" × 36" strips. Draw five 12" × 33½" strips and ten 1" × 12" strips on the 3' × 6' sheet of ½" plywood. Use a table saw, circular saw, or jigsaw to cut out these pieces.

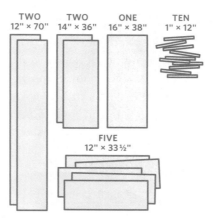

**2** **NOW YOU'LL ADD EDGE** banding to all the plywood edges that will be visible (consult the assembly instructions to determine which sides will be visible). Clamp each plywood piece to your workbench so that a visible edge points up. Sand the edge clean and wipe away any sawdust, being careful not to round the edges of the plywood. With a utility knife, roughly cut the edge banding to be slightly longer than the raw edge.

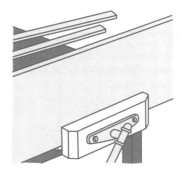

*(continued)*

**3 PREPARE THE IRON: POUR OUT** any water and set the dial to cotton/hot. When it's hot, press the edge banding to the plywood edge and run the iron along the banding slowly enough to melt the glue but quickly enough to avoid scorching. If you make a mistake, strip the edge banding and try again with a new strip. Once the banding is successfully attached, use a scrap wood block to press it firmly to the edge to secure it. Unclamp the plywood and lay it, banded-side-down, on a flat surface that is safe for cutting. Use a sharp utility knife to trim the edge banding to the exact dimensions of the plywood. Repeat for all plywood edges that will need to be covered.

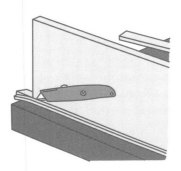

**4 MAKE THE STEPPED BASE OF** the bookcase: Lay the 16" × 38" piece on a flat surface. Center one of the 14" × 36" pieces on top of this base with a 1" margin on all sides. Glue the top piece to the bottom piece and press firmly in

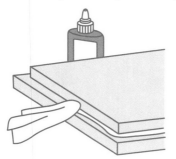

place. Let dry, preferably overnight. (Wood glue is dry to the touch in 30 minutes, but allow at least 12 hours to set completely.)

**5 THE 12" × 70" STRIPS ARE THE** sides of the bookcase. Lay them side by side to check that their lengths are exactly equal. If necessary, shave with a planer to make them even, being careful not to chip the edge banding. With the sides of the bookcase still side by side, mark the heights of the five shelves, spaced every 14". (To hold taller books or knickknacks, adjust the heights of your shelves.) Measure and mark straight lines across both boards to indicate the tops of the shelves.

**6 ATTACH 1" × 12" STRIPS JUST** under every line on what will be the insides of the bookcase sides (edge banding pointing out). Drill three evenly spaced 1⅝" wood screws from the outside to attach the strips. They will support your shelves.

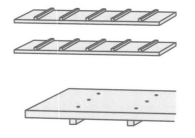

**7 ASSEMBLE THE SIDES AND TOP** of the bookcase. First, lay the sides of the shelf on their edges with the shelf supports facing each other and the edge banding pointing out, as they will appear in the finished bookcase. Because the two-sheet base is stepped by 1" and the 12" sides should be centered on the 14"-wide base, raise the sides of your shelf by 2" off the ground to match. Do this by resting the sides on stacked scraps of ¾" plywood. Position the sides of your bookcase facing each other across a 33½" gap.

**8 POSITION THE BASE ON ITS SIDE** with the edge banding pointing out and rest it against the bottom of the bookcase's sides. Center the 12" sides on the 14" base. Use two 3" wood screws per side to screw up through the bottom of the base and into the ends of the sides.

**9 LAY THE 14" × 36" BOOKCASE** top on its side with the edge banding pointing toward the front and align it with the tops of the bookcase sides so that the sides are flush and the front and back overhang by 1". Use three evenly spaced 1⅝" wood screws driven through the top and into the sides to fix the top in place.

**10** **CAREFULLY STAND UP THE** bookcase frame. Slide the 12" × 33½" shelves into place on their supports. Use finishing nails to hold the shelves securely to their supports.

**11** **IF THE BOOKCASE FEELS** as if it needs additional support, consider adding panel or ¼" plywood backing. Lay the bookcase on its face, support the shelves with plywood scraps, and use finishing nails to attach backing to the frame and shelves, being careful to drive thin nails into the center of the plywood sides so as not to split the wood. Sand the bookcase smooth and then apply stain to match the color of the edge banding.

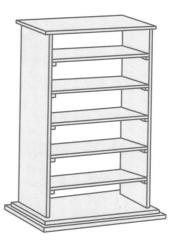

## Oil Finishes for Wood

Getting a beautiful oil finish on wood is an art as much as a science. It's also much more time-consuming than simply unleashing a can of polyurethane varnish on a project. This is partly because rather than sitting atop the wood or stain, an oil finish lives in the wood's grain itself—and it's your hard work that puts it there. The most common place to find an oil finish is on a butcher's block or cutting board in your kitchen, but oil finishes offer a rich and natural look and are easy to apply, so consider them for your woodworking projects or to revitalize vintage furniture.

**Linseed oil.** Also known as flaxseed oil, this multipurpose liquid is not only used alone as an oil finish, but also as the solvent in some varnishes (before you add it to your smoothie, note that it is processed with petroleum—it's not the same as the flaxseed oil taken as a nutritional supplement). Linseed oil isn't the clearest finish—it's likely to slightly yellow your wood, and despite its long history of use, it's not actually that protective. Consider any surface you use it on water-repellant, but not waterproof. It is the traditional finish of gun stocks, cricket bats, and the fret boards of stringed instruments like mandolins.

**Mineral oil.** As the name implies, mineral oil does not come from plant material. Instead it is distilled from petroleum. It's odorless, so you'd never know it's a cousin of gasoline. It has many uses, including in cosmetics and baby oils, as well as in an insulating fluid in electrical transformers. It is a food-safe finish that is much clearer and slightly more protective than linseed.

**Tung oil.** Tung oil, from the nut of the tung tree, dries to a golden finish somewhat similar to the look of wet wood. It is the most protective of the pure oils listed here and is arguably slightly more resistant to mildew than linseed oil. Commercial manufacturers of products labeled "tung oil" have sometimes freeloaded on the environmentally friendly cachet of the oil without including any actual tung oil in the product. When you buy any oil, and especially when you buy a tung oil finish, inspect the label closely to make sure that what you're buying is the real McCoy.

**Danish oil.** Danish oil is a somewhat imprecise term used by manufacturers to describe a few different formulas. Most oils labeling themselves "Danish" use a linseed or tung oil base and add resins that perform much like a varnish. Danish oil is likely to be more protective than other oils, but due to inconsistent labeling, test it on scrap wood before applying it to your piece. That said, the classic recipe by Watco for Danish oil has been around for many years, and many woodworkers swear by its balance of an oil finish's shine with the protection of a varnish. If you need your oil finish to hold up in a high-traffic area, consider trying Danish.

# #160
## HOW TO BUILD A STORAGE CHEST

Whether family heirloom, bench seating, or organizational unit, a storage chest is an incredibly multi-purpose piece of furniture. By hand-crafting your own, you're making a useful and timeless object to pass down to future generations. Rather than plywood sheets, this chest uses 1-by boards to make elegant walls (use the wood of your choice—pine or oak will work well). Your finished chest will be 3 feet by 2 feet, but after previewing these instructions, you could easily adjust the size as you see fit.

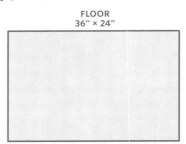

## TOOLS:

**Measuring tape ▪ Pencil ▪ Miter saw or handsaw ▪ Table saw or circular saw ▪ Bar clamps (at least three) ▪ Hammer ▪ Electric sander ▪ Drill ▪ Countersink bit ▪ Safety goggles**

## MATERIALS:

- **Nine 6-foot 1 × 4 boards**
- **Seven 39-inch 1 × 4 boards (buy larger and cut to size)**
- **36" × 24" piece of ½" plywood**
- **Fifty 1¾" wood screws**
- **Two hinges**
- **Polyurethane or tung oil (for finish)**

**1** **PUT ON YOUR SAFETY GOGGLES** and use a miter or handsaw to cut five of the 6-foot 1 × 4 boards in half to create ten 36-inch 1 × 4 strips for the front and back. Measure, mark, and cut the remaining 6-foot 1 × 4 boards into even thirds to create ten 21½-inch 1 × 4 strips for the sides. Cut seven 39-inch 1 × 4 strips for the lid.

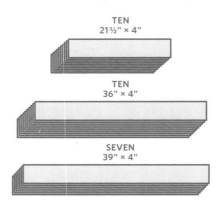

TEN
21½" × 4"

TEN
36" × 4"

SEVEN
39" × 4"

**2** **IF THE PLYWOOD IS NOT** already sized, use a table saw or circular saw to cut the ½" plywood into a 36" × 24" floor.

FLOOR
36" × 24"

**3** **ON A FLAT SURFACE, LINE UP** five 36" 1 × 4 boards—these will be the front of the chest. Make sure the boards lie flush to each other and are perfectly flat against the work surface. Apply wood glue between the boards and use three bar clamps to hold them securely together. Place a flat piece of scrap wood over the boards and use a hammer to bang any uneven seams until the face of your newly joined boards is completely smooth. Use a damp rag to wipe away any excess wood glue and allow 4 to 6 hours to dry. Repeat this step for the five 36" 1 × 4 boards that will be the back, the five 21½" 1 × 4 boards for both sides, and the seven 39" 1 × 4 strips for the lid of your chest. Once the glue is dry, remove the clamps and sand the newly made boards with an electric sander until they are smooth and the seams disappear.

**FRONT AND BACK**
**36" × 4"**

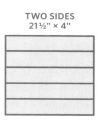

**TWO SIDES**
**21½" × 4"**

**LID**
**39" × 4"**

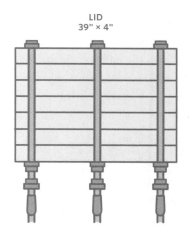

**4** MEASURE, MARK, AND USE A jigsaw to cut a notch 6" long and 1" deep in the top-center of your front panel. This will be the

handhold under the lid seen in most storage chests.

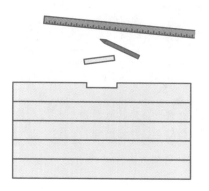

**5** ASSEMBLE THE WALLS AND base of the chest. You will be screwing through the front and back of the boards. Countersink 4 evenly spaced holes through the vertical edges of the front and back boards. Then use 1¾" wood screws to attach the front and back walls to the sides of the chest. Use wood screws or tack nails to attach the base of the chest, screwing or nailing up from the bottom.

**6** USE A TABLE SAW OR CIRCULAR saw to bevel the undersides of the front and sides of the lid to 45-degree angles. Set your saw blade to cut at a 45-degree angle and then run your lid across the blade so that it takes off a triangular strip from the undersides of these three edges. Screw hinges onto the (untouched) back underside of the lid and mount the lid to the back interior of the chest. Sand and finish as desired, with polyurethane or oil finish.

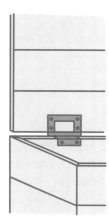

✕ ✕ ✕ ✕ ✕ ✕ ✕ ✕ ✕ ✕ ✕ ✕ ✕ ✕ ✕ ✕ ✕ ✕ ✕ ✕ ✕ ✕ ✕ ✕ ✕ ✕ ✕ ✕ ✕ ✕ ✕ ✕ ✕ ✕ ✕ ✕ ✕ ✕ ✕

# JIGSAW TIPS

**J**igsaws are commonly thought of as curve-cutting machines, but in reality, they're a versatile tool that you can use for a variety of cuts, both straight and curved. Typically used for finishing work, jigsaws can be either corded or cordless (see page 277 for the distinction), and they come as handsaws or the table-mounted variety. The saw is made to fit different blades—teeth matter, depending on the density of your wood (the teeth face the front of the saw), as do length and width, so make sure you're choosing the right blade for the material you're using.

Typically, you'll need to use a clamped straightedge guide to make straight cuts. To cut a circle (as in How to Build a Birdhouse, page 282), you should first drill a ⅜" pilot hole at one edge of the circle to drop the blade in the hole. Circle-cutting jigs will help you make a perfect circle, if you need a little artificial guidance.

When cutting, be steady with your hands, start the blade before touching the wood so it can get going, and don't pivot the blade too quickly, at the risk of chipping the wood. And remember: Practice makes perfect!

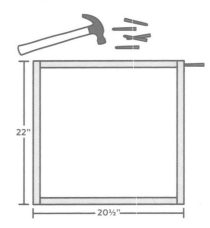

# #161
# HOW TO BUILD A TABLE

**E**ven basic woodworking can benefit from a little bling. In this project, you'll build a basic table and then choose how to decorate it—think inlay, stencils, fancy finishes. This simple design also lends itself well to stretching or squishing to fit your space. Simply consistently adjust the dimensions of all the materials to change its size.

## TOOLS:

**Measuring tape ▪ Pencil ▪ Miter saw or handsaw ▪ Bar clamps (at least 3) ▪ Hammer ▪ Tools for decorative effects (see opposite)**

## MATERIALS:

- **Three 6-foot 1 × 4 pine boards**
- **One 8-foot 1 × 4 pine board**
- **One 6-foot 1 × 1 pine board**
- **Four 2" × 2" table legs, cut to desired table height**
- **Brad nails**
- **Sandpaper**
- **Wood glue**
- **Materials for decorative effects as desired (see opposite)**

**1** **SELECT AND CUT THE THREE** 6-foot 1 × 4 pine boards in half with a saw to make six 3-foot 1 × 4 strips.

**2** **JOIN THESE BOARDS TO FORM** a 36" × 24" tabletop. Lay the six 3-foot boards side by side on a flat surface, glue between each board, adjust until flush and flat, and use at least three bar clamps to hold the boards together while they dry (at least 4 to 6 hours). Once dry, sand the tabletop until smooth.

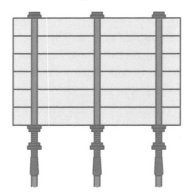

**3** **MEASURE, MARK, AND CUT** two 20½" lengths of 1 × 4 and two 22" lengths of 1 × 4. You will use these four pieces to make a boxlike frame for your tabletop to sit on. Center the four boards on their sides in a square on the underside of your tabletop, with the 22" pieces outside the 20½" pieces. With the frame perfectly square, drive two brad nails per side through the 22" pieces into the ends of the 20½" pieces to hold the frame together. Later, you'll attach this frame to the tabletop.

**4** **SAW FOUR 2 × 2s TO EQUAL** lengths for the legs. Kitchen or dining tables are usually about 29" tall, and end tables are usually about 24" tall. Place the four legs in the inside corners of the 1 × 4 frame you made in the previous step, flush to the top, and drive brad nails through the 1 × 4s to hold the legs in place.

**5** **MEASURE THE FOUR DISTANCES** along the frame between the inside faces of your 2 × 2 legs. Cut four lengths of 1 × 1 to this measurement and fix them between the legs, against the frame and flush with its top. Drive brad nails through the 1 × 1s to attach them to the frame.

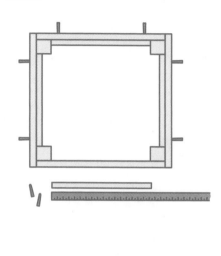

**6** **ADD THE TABLETOP.** Center it on the frame and use brad nails spaced about every 6 inches, driven up through the 1 × 1s to hold it in place.

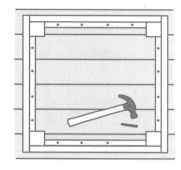

**7** **SLIGHTLY COUNTERSINK ALL** nails and cover the heads with a mixture of wood glue and sawdust (optional). Sand the table until smooth, then paint, stain, and decorate as desired (see Suggested Decorative Effects, below).

## Suggested Decorative Effects

**Inlay.** A router, some wood veneer, and a little artistic moxie can turn a table into a treasure. Draw the shapes of your inlay on carbon tracing paper, then onto thin wood veneer. Once the inlays are on the veneer, carefully cut them out with a sharp, fine-toothed jigsaw. Working with one piece at a time, use double-sided tape to hold the inlays on the table-top and trace deep lines around them with a utility knife. Remove the taped inlays and switch to your router. Use a ¹⁄₁₆" bit set to the depth of your wood veneer to carefully rout your shapes into the wood. Glue the inlays in place and clamp until dry. Sand the tabletop smooth. End with a protective finish.

**Mosaic.** Any small, tilelike pieces can be used for mosaics: bits of Venetian glass, ceramic pieces, mirrors, small stones, sea glass, marbles, and so on. Use a hammer to make small shapes and tile nippers to further sculpt them. Plan your mosaic pattern and then outline it in pencil on your table-top. Dab adhesive on the back of every piece—you'll need to match it to your mosaic materials. Try to leave less than ⅛"

between pieces, using small tiles to fill spaces. Once the tiles are in place, use a rubber squeegee to spread grout across the entire surface of the project, being sure to fill all gaps. In this case, you'll want to use fine grout. Choose a grout color that complements your mosaic and table, and consider a polymer grout if you imagine heavy use. Let the grout set until firm, at least 15 to 20 minutes, and then wipe it from the tile with a cloth or wet sponge. Scrape sticky grout with a wooden or other non-scratch tool. If you use porous material, consider finishing with a sealant.

**Distress.** In order to distress a finish, you must first put one on. Either stain and then distress or distress and then stain—both work equally well. If you'll be staining as the final step, focus on adding dents to the wood. Try one of these destructive options: Flay the table with a chain, beat it with a sock filled with nuts and bolts, or throw an old tool at your table (it works!). If you will be distressing after finishing, use extremely coarse sandpaper—50- or 60-grit—to rough up the paint or finish, adding scratches and clouds.

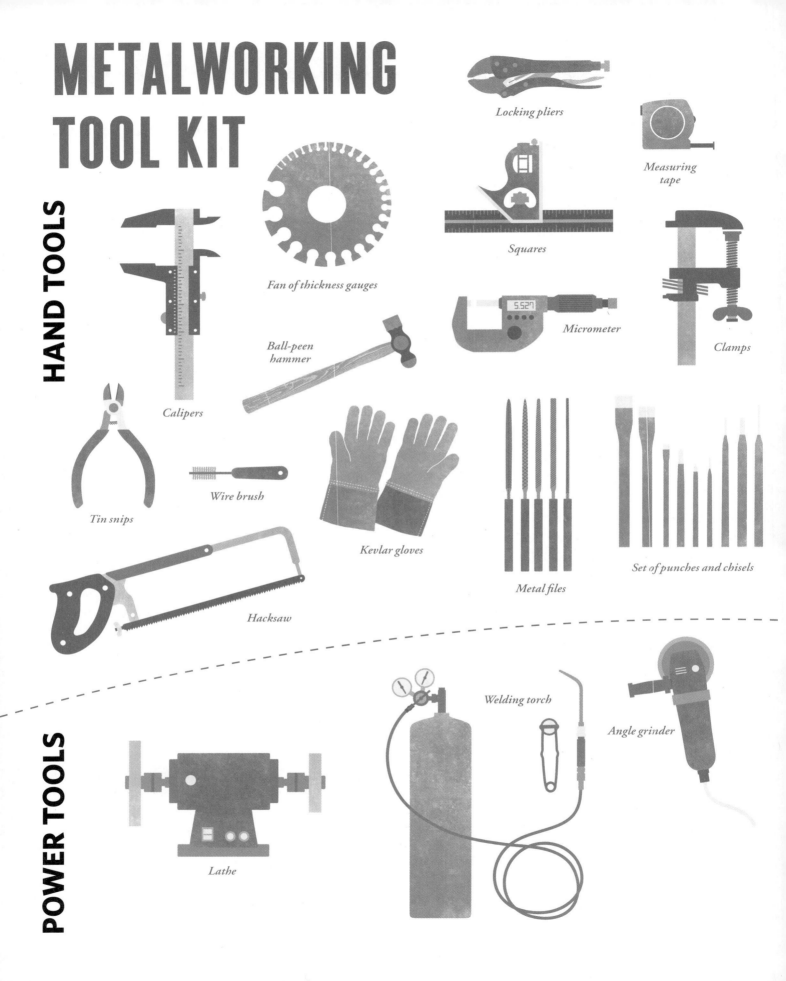

# METALWORKING TOOL KIT

## HAND TOOLS

Locking pliers

Measuring tape

Fan of thickness gauges

Squares

Micrometer

Clamps

Calipers

Ball-peen hammer

Tin snips

Wire brush

Kevlar gloves

Metal files

Set of punches and chisels

Hacksaw

## POWER TOOLS

Welding torch

Angle grinder

Lathe

## Hand Tools

Even constructing the USS *Bismarck* starts with a single box of simple tools. Start with measuring implements first. The main measuring tool for woodworking is a retractable measuring tape, but in metalworking, measuring is a new skill altogether. In addition to basic tools like a measuring tape and squares, you may need calipers, a micrometer, and a fan of thickness gauges. Another essential tool is a set of punches and chisels—make sure the set comes with pin, taper, and center punches, and with a set of cold chisels ranging from about ⅜ inch to 1 inch. You'll also need a hammer to drive these punches. Go with the basic ball-peen hammer—good for both metal- and woodworking. Rather than scissors, which are best for cutting paper, you'll need snips to cut metal—tin snips may be little more than burly scissors, whereas metal shears usually include an extra joint that increases your power and the thickness of the metal you can cut. Also get a set of metal files that includes a round and a flat rasp and a file. An adjustable wrench (or wrench set), pliers, hacksaw, clamps, and wire brush round out the necessary basics. You'll also need a very good pair of Kevlar gloves. Again, the tools for metalworking tend to be even more specific than the tools needed for woodworking, so evaluate your tool kit based on the project at hand.

## Power Tools

The term *metalworking* applies to the tiniest jewelry, the biggest ocean liners and bridges, and everything metal in between. With the huge scope of projects comes a huge scope of techniques, including welding, soldering, turning, grinding, casting, machining, and many more. And depending on whether you want to make earrings, sculpt a steel buffalo for the front yard, or trick out your truck, you'll need drastically different power tools. Shoddy metalwork makes nothing but scrap. Metal requires mettle. The following tools are good to have, but it's likely you'll need to add power tools specific to your project.

**Welding torch.** There are two common kinds of handheld torches: air and oxyacetylene. An air torch uses a bottle of gas—like propane—and burns the oxygen found in air.

An oxyacetylene torch combines gas with pure oxygen for a much hotter flame. You can weld with a torch, so if your budget is tight, get a torch before investing in a specific welder. But in an expert's shop, the torch is usually used for cutting. Expect to spend in the neighborhood of $250 for a quality unit.

**Angle grinder.** An angle grinder is the metalworking mash-up of two woodworking tools: a circular saw and a disc sander. With this handheld power tool, you can cut, grind, and polish metal, and it's a must in any metal shop. Angle grinders are driven by electricity or compressed air (pneumatic), and the latter is generally lighter and more maneuverable but less powerful. In addition to the power of your grinder, choose based on disc size, which generally runs from 4 to 7 inches or, in some cases, 12 inches. Most metalworkers start with a 4- to 4½-inch grinder and evaluate their needs from there.

**Lathe.** There are many kinds of lathes designed for many different uses, but the basic idea remains the same: a lathe spins your metal piece while stationary tools cut into it. As such, you can use a lathe for cutting, sanding, and, most important, shaping a piece of metal. Most shops will start with a lightweight bench engine lathe (a powered lathe that bolts to a workbench) and upgrade to a freestanding lathe (called a precision or gap lathe) if needed. It's important, to make sure your cutting tools are compatible with your lathe and are right for your project. Your lathe may come with a set of cutting tools, or you might need to buy them separately. Start with a basic set of carbide-tipped cutting and turning tools. Expect to spend from $600 to more than $4,000 for a quality metal lathe. Metalworking is for the detail-oriented among us—a craft that depends on fractions of millimeters. That said, there are darn good tools available that make this precision possible, and a strong finished product tends to depend more on careful work than rocket science. By starting with easy projects and slowly upping the difficulty level (it helps to have a willingness to throw out a couple of failed attempts), you can learn to bend metal to your every desire.

# #162
## HOW TO MAKE A SPOON RING
### (or, How to Cut and Bend Metal)

If you were an English servant in the seventeenth century, chances are you couldn't afford a pricey wedding band. But without a band, you couldn't wed! Many servants resorted to thievery, stealing silverware to fashion into elegant wedding bands. The practice became so common that in many places you could tell which house a servant worked for by the crest on his or her ring.

The so-called spoon ring—basically a cutlery handle bent into a circle—had a resurgence in the 1970s, when you couldn't really call yourself a hippie without a couple of lengths of sterling silver wrapped around your fingers. It's a classic that has stood the test of time; plus, this simple project is a great primer on how to cut and bend metal—skills that will serve you well in more complicated metalwork.

When you're choosing a utensil, keep in mind that you'll be using only the handle, so your spoon needn't be a spoon at all. A fork works just as well. But it's worth it to get a sterling silver rather than stainless steel utensil—stainless is much stronger and thus more difficult to work. Check thrift or antique stores, or even eBay, for sterling silver flatware—commonly stamped "sterling" or with the numbers 900 or 925. When you're buying, consider the aesthetics: Does the spoon have a decorative handle? Is the handle's width appropriate for a ring?

## TOOLS:

Measuring tape • Hacksaw • Angle grinder, half-round metal file, or emery cloth • Safety goggles • Insulating gloves • Bench vise or clamps • Butane torch (optional) • Needle-nosed pliers • Rawhide or wood mallet or a hammer covered in cloth

## MATERIALS:

- Sterling silver spoon or fork
- String or paper
- Finger-sized dowel or metal pipe, or ring mandrel
- Silver polish or polishing cloth (optional)

**1** MEASURE THE CIRCUMFERENCE of your finger. Wrap a length of paper or string around the digit on which you'll wear the ring. Mark your desired length and then straighten the paper or string to use it as your length measurement. A spoon ring can either wrap up your finger (a wrapped ring) or wrap around until one end touches the other (a closed ring). If you want a closed ring, add ¼" to your paper or string length measurement. If you want a wrapped ring, the length needn't be precise as long as it's longer than your finger circumference.

**2 CUT THE SPOON TO LENGTH.** Remove the "bowl" of the spoon, and as much of the top of the handle to make it fit as desired. A sterling silver spoon is easily cut with a hacksaw, but if you have an angle grinder, here's an excuse to use it. Grinding metal is likely to create sparks, so first, be sure to protect both yourself and your work area. Wear long clothing, safety goggles, and insulating gloves, and remove flammable items from the space. Then, install a metal cutoff wheel on your angle grinder. Secure the spoon with either a bench vise or a clamp, exposing the line on the neck of the handle where you'll make your cut. Start the angle grinder and drop it smoothly through the spoon, letting the weight of the grinder do the work.

**3 SMOOTH THE CUT END OF THE** spoon. Cutting with a hacksaw or grinder is likely to leave a viciously sharp edge. If you have an angle grinder, switch to a sanding or polishing pad, secure the metal again, and polish the spoon's cut end until smooth. If you used the center length of a spoon's handle, not the decorative end, you can also use the grinder to grind one or both ends to equalize their shape. Be careful not to remove too much—you can always take more, but adding metal back is impossible! If you don't have a grinder, you can perform the same smoothing (but not necessarily shaping) with a metal half-round file or emery cloth.

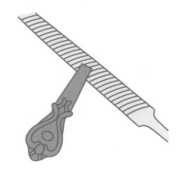

**4 SHAPE THE RING.** Because you won't be soldering the ring closed, you can always adjust the diameter of the ring once you try it on. Still, it's worth trying to get close with your first attempt. There are a couple of methods you can try to shape the spoon into a ring. First, try using finger power to bend the spoon around a finger-sized dowel. If that doesn't work, hold the metal with needle-nose pliers and tap it carefully with a mallet to curl the spoon handle around the dowel into the desired shape. You shouldn't need to heat the metal unless you're using a stainless steel spoon, but if you do, use a butane torch (and the proper safety precautions). First, grip the metal with needle-nose pliers and heat it with the butane torch until pliable (but not glowing). Then, hammer it around the dowel or mandrel with the mallet.

**5 ADJUST AS NEEDED.** Once the ring has cooled, try it on your finger. If the size is drastically wrong, reshape the spoon using a different-sized dowel or another width of ring mandrel. In most cases, though, you'll be able to shape the ring to size with just a couple of taps. Use silver polish or a polishing cloth to buff the ring until it shines.

**Paul Revere was a highly regarded silversmith—after learning the trade from his father, he spent more than 40 years in the trade, and even used it to cross over into dentistry, wiring dentures made of ivory or animal teeth into the mouths of his patients.**

# #163
## HOW TO MAKE EARRINGS
### (or, How to Beat Metal)

Ear piercing has been around since ancient times, as many of the mummies of Egypt, Europe, and the Americas can attest. Even 5,000-year-old Ötzi the Iceman, found poking out of a glacier in the Austrian Alps, had pierced ears. One of the first designs used with pierced ears was the hoop earring, first as bent metal wire and then as beaten metal. Hoops were found in the graves of Persepolis in Iran, dating to about 2500 BCE, as well as in graves of the ancient cultures of Babylonia, Assyria, Egypt, Africa, India, and Europe. One reason for the ancient ubiquity of hoop earrings is the ease of making them. Once you roll wire into a circle, you're most of the way there. This project goes a step further than a simple circle, and with that step you'll learn the skill of beating metal, which is applicable to many other metalworking projects.

## TOOLS:

Wire cutter ▪ Coarse sandpaper ▪ Rolling mill or file ▪ Round form (mandrel or appropriately sized dowel) ▪ Wooden or rawhide mallet ▪ Planishing or ball-peen hammer ▪ Needle-nose pliers

## MATERIALS:

▪ At least a 14" length of 12-gauge metal wire (copper, silver, and brass are common metals that have the advantage of being soft enough to work)

**1** **THE LENGTH OF THE WIRE** depends on what size you'd like the earrings to be—longer wire means bigger earrings. Consider buying extra wire so you can wrap a test earring and evaluate the size in the mirror. Once you have a test earring that looks about the right size, unroll it and use it as a measuring template when cutting the wire. Leave an extra ½" to be bent for the earring closures. Hoop earrings range from tiny to huge, but a 7" length of wire each is a good starting point. Cut the desired length with wire cutters and use emery cloth or coarse sandpaper to sand the cut ends until smooth.

✕ ✕ ✕ ✕ ✕ ✕ ✕ ✕ ✕ ✕ ✕ ✕ ✕ ✕ ✕ ✕

## PICKING WIRE GAUGE

Simple wire earrings in which the wire passes completely through the ear are usually 21-gauge or thinner. For this project, you'll taper the ends and beat the middle, and so a thicker gauge—which means a smaller number—works better. Approximately 12-gauge wire is ideal, though you could choose to make a thicker earring from 10-gauge wire or a slightly thinner earring from 14-gauge wire.

**2 USE A FILE TO TAPER ONE END** of each earring, 1½" per end. This tapered wire will be bent into clasps and one of these sides will pass through your ear, so file the end until you are comfortable with the result. Sand until smooth.

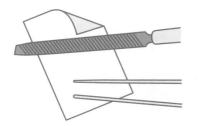

**3 HOOP EARRINGS ARE ROUND,** as their name implies, though they can be shaped like teardrops. To make a teardrop shape, simply bend the two ends together and the wire should naturally form a loop with a wide arc on the bottom coming to a point at the top. A hoop takes a little more work. Wrap the earring wire around a mandrel or a round form like a dowel, overlapping the ends by about ¼" for the clasps. Use the mallet to hammer the wire around the form until the wire holds its round shape.

**4 THERE ARE MANY STYLES OF** hoop earrings, but for this project, you'll beat the lower arc to make it flat vertically. Lay a bent earring flat on a pounding

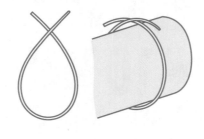

surface, preferably a metal plate or at least a flat, hardwood work surface. Use a wooden ball-peen hammer to work the earring. (If the hammer has a ridged face, consider filing and sanding the hammer until the face is smooth so that it doesn't mar the surface of the earrings.) Start with gentle taps and focus on slightly flattening the lowest point in the center of the metal wire, not the edges. Remember: You can always hit harder, but it's difficult to un-dent your work. Flip the earring frequently. Some metal jewelry intentionally has a pockmarked,

beaten look, but for this project it's worth learning how to smooth the metal, using many smaller strokes rather than a few more forceful ones. Work up the sides from the lower arc, flattening less and less as you go so that the upper widths of the earrings narrow toward the tapered ends.

**5 USE NEEDLE-NOSE PLIERS TO** form the clasp. Bend about ¼" of wire out at a right angle from one end. Grab the end and bend it back on itself to form a tiny circle. Then bend a short length (about ¼") of the other end to about 45 degrees. The bent wire hooks inside the circle to form the clasp. The earring should be wide enough that the clasp is held together by the spring of the metal. If it's not, you can slightly adjust the earring size.

# The hoop is one of the classic earring shapes—pirates wore them as a superstition, believing that the precious metals carried magical powers.

# #164
# HOW TO MAKE A DECORATIVE METAL PLATE
## (or, an Introduction to Perforating)

When working to transform sheet metal into something decorative, you'll hear the terms "blanking" and "piercing." In blanking, the shaped piece is punched from the plate; in piercing, a design is left behind when pieces are punched from the plate. In this project you'll learn about piercing, and more specifically about the piercing technique known as perforating. Basically, perforating is just what it sounds like: the process of punching holes in metal. These holes could be the result of a nail used to decorate a thin sheet of copper or of complex punch and die sets that help metalworkers mass-produce intricate designs. Here you'll use simple holes to perforate a piece of metal (think of your kitchen colander), either to let light shine through or simply for the pattern of the holes themselves.

## TOOLS:

**Pencil ▪ Paper ▪ Scissors ▪ Straightedge ▪ Drill ▪ Small cobalt or titanium bit, ⅛" to ¼" ▪ Emery cloth ▪ Hacksaw (optional) ▪ Angle grinder ▪ Bench vise**

## MATERIALS:

▪ **Any length and width "hobby" sheet of metal (0.024" or 0.048")**

**1** SEARCH, COPY, AND PRINT A stencil from the Internet, then cut it out and trace it on the piece of metal with a pencil. Or, use your creativity to draw the outline of a picture on the metal.

**2** USING A STRAIGHTEDGE, DRAW perpendicular gridlines inside the outline. For a larger picture, you might draw vertical and horizontal lines every inch. For a small, perforated design, your gridlines might be every couple of millimeters. You'll be tracing a grid that looks like graph paper inside your picture outline.

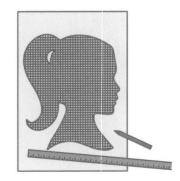

xx

# WHAT CAN YOU DO WITH DECORATIVE METAL PLATES?

The project detailed here results in, literally, a simple plate with a design on it. But as you become more experienced in the technique, there are many items on which you can use this method.

- The perforations let light shine though, making it ideal for a small metal lampshade, whether for an electric light or a candleholder or sconce.

- Use it to decorate a metal picture frame or to frame a mirror.

- Make a design on a metal garden pot, such as an ornamental copper pot in which a ceramic or terra cotta plant holder sits.

- Put a design on kitchen items or wall hangings, such as the rim of a metal serving platter, a metal spoon rest, or a wall-mounted row of hooks.

**3 USE A DRILL WITH AN** appropriately sized cobalt or titanium drill bit to make a hole at every place inside the outline where gridlines cross. For small designs with tight gridlines, you will want an equally small drill bit, such as a ⅛"; for larger pieces with more widely spaced gridlines, you could choose a larger drill bit, such as a ¼". Size your bit based on aesthetics. Smooth away excess metal shavings with an emery cloth. You should end with an organized pattern of dots that define your picture.

**4 REMOVE THE STENCILED SHAPE** from the metal surface to reveal a series of dots arranged in the shape of the image you selected.

In other materials, like paper, perforations are used to efficiently separate portions of paper (like the postcards, paper dolls, and original perforated stamps) from a larger piece, without the use of scissors.

# #165
## HOW TO MAKE WIND CHIMES

The ancient Romans hung their porticoes with bronze wind chimes to ward off evil spirits, while metal, wood, and even glass chimes have hung for centuries in temples and homes from India to Japan. Today, wind chimes are made from materials including seashells, glass, ceramic, and even flatware. Here you'll learn to make pipe chimes—drilling, hanging, and tuning a set of copper or other metal wind chimes.

Only certain combinations of musical notes are pleasing when sounded together. One of the most pleasing is the pentatonic scale, a group of five notes that can be played on a piano's black keys. It takes some fairly involved calculations to determine the pipe lengths that make the desired tones, so this project includes the required tube diameters and lengths. Deviating from these measurements may result in some odd sounds. You'll also need to choose the material of your pipes—steel or copper tubes work well.

## TOOLS:

**Measuring tape** ▪ **Pencil** ▪ **Hacksaw** ▪ **Fine sandpaper** ▪ **Bench vise** ▪ **Center punch** ▪ **Hammer** ▪ **Safety goggles** ▪ **Leather work gloves** ▪ **Drill with ⁵⁄₃₂" metal bit and small wood drill bit, such as ¹⁄₁₆"** ▪ **Cutting and tapping fluid** ▪ **Hacksaw** ▪ **Wood saw (any type)**

## MATERIALS:

- **5 feet of ¾" copper or stainless steel tubing**
- **5 no. 6 machine screws with nuts**
- **Locking nut or threadlocker compound (optional)**
- **7 small wood eyelets**
- **1 larger wood eyelet**
- **Nylon twine, string, or fishing line**
- **Scrap wood for mount, clapper, and scoop**
- **Wood glue**

**1** **WITH A HACKSAW, CUT THE** following lengths of ¾" copper or steel tubing: 11½", 10⅞", 10", 9⁷⁄₁₆", and 8⅞". These should produce the tones C-sharp, D-sharp, F-sharp, G-sharp, and A-sharp. If you have a piano (or a piano app) match the bell tones to these notes, using sandpaper to shave tube ends slightly to make higher pitches. It's impossible to add back removed material, so don't take too much!

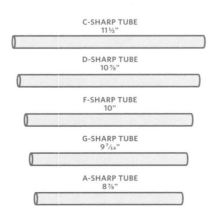

CA-SHARP TUBE
11½"

D-SHARP TUBE
10⅞"

F-SHARP TUBE
10"

G-SHARP TUBE
9⁷⁄₁₆"

A-SHARP TUBE
8⅞"

**2** **MEASURE AND MARK** mounting holes at the following distances on one end of each tube (from the longest to the shortest tube): 2⁹⁄₁₆", 2⁷⁄₁₆", 2¼", 2⅛", 2". Hanging pipes at these measurements allows for the best resonance.

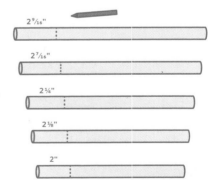

2⁹⁄₁₆"

2⁷⁄₁₆"

2¼"

2⅛"

2"

**3** **SECURE A SECTION OF TUBING** in a bench vise (tighten it enough to hold the tube, but not enough to dent the pipe). Use a center punch and a hammer to make a small depression on one side of each tube that will keep the drill bit from wandering. Carefully align the center punch with the desired mounting hole position and strike the punch once, firmly, with the hammer.

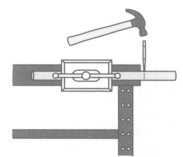

**4** **PUT ON YOUR SAFETY GLASSES** and leather work gloves. A drill press is necessary for many metal projects, but for this thin tube, you can get away with a handheld electric drill. Because you will drill directly down through the top wall

**The F-sharp major pentatonic scale is one of the most common scales used in music worldwide.**

and also through the bottom wall of the tube, be sure to turn the pipe in your vise so the center punch depression is directly on top of the tube. Secure a 5/32" metal bit in your drill and coat the bit with cutting and tapping fluid, which is a coolant and lubricant that will help to ensure clean holes. Hold the drill perfectly vertical while drilling a hole through both tube walls. When finished, use a rag to wipe away excess fluid and shavings. Repeat with the remaining tubes.

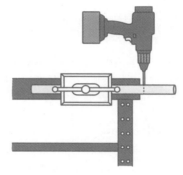

**5** **INSERT MACHINE SCREWS** through the mounting holes and secure them with nuts. Because the wind chimes will be in motion, the nuts will have a tendency to loosen. Consider using a locking nut or painting the machine screws with threadlocker compound.

**6** **MAKE THE MOUNT FROM SCRAP** lumber, using any wood saw. One successful design is a 5½" diameter circle of 1-by pine, but feel free to be creative with the shape. Draw a 4½" diameter circle on the bottom of the larger pine circle and make five equally spaced marks

around the circle, which will be the hanging locations of the five bells. Screw a small wood eyelet into each of these five marks. Screw another wood eyelet into the center of the circle, to hang the wind-powered clapper.

**7** **TIE 6 TO 8 INCHES OF TWINE,** string, or fishing line to the machine screws drilled through the bells, and tie the other ends to the five evenly spaced eyelets.

**8** **USE ANY TYPE OF WOOD SAW** to make a 2½" diameter circle of 1-by pine for the clapper— or a design of your choice. Round the edges by sanding or routing. Use a small wood drill bit to drill a small hole in the center.

*(continued)*

**9** **CUT A SMALL PADDLE OF SCRAP** wood to use as a wind scoop. Shape and smooth into an oval or the shape of your choice. Screw an eyelet into the top of the wind scoop and attach twine. Tie a knot or knots in the twine at about the midpoint of the chimes to support the clapper. Feed the twine through the hole in the clapper and then tie the top of the twine to the mount's center eyelet.

**10** **FOR AN OPTIONAL** decorative finish, stack and glue additional wood circles on top of your mount to make a pyramid-like shape. Let the glue dry for 4 to 6 hours. Mark the top-center of your mount and screw in a large wood eyelet. Use twine or chain to hang the wind chime from a secure beam or tree branch in a breezy spot.

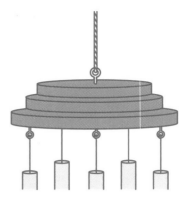

## Creating Patina

An old copper roof, like that on Chartres Cathedral, will have a pale green tint—the result of copper oxidizing over the centuries—called the patina. But you can also apply patina to your metal projects to create an aged look.

Because patina work is meant to distress metal, it generally involves chemicals you don't want on your skin or in your eyes. Always wear proper safety equipment, including chemical-resistant gloves and safety goggles, and protect your arms and legs with appropriate work clothes. Patina also requires clean metal. If you'll be using old metal, be sure to strip away any existing finish. Depending on the project, stripping may require chemical paint stripper, an orbital sander with metal paper, elbow grease—or a combination of all three. (If you're not sure which is most appropriate for your piece, ask a professional at your local hardware store.) Once the metal is clean, and even if you're working with new metal, be sure to degrease it with rubbing alcohol and a lint-free rag prior to applying the patina, and make sure no dirt or other grime remains on the surface of the piece. Once you've degreased a piece, avoid touching it with your bare hands, which can leave oil fingerprints in your patina.

**Rust patina.** Most of what you need to make a basic rust patina probably lives under your kitchen sink. Fill a spray bottle with distilled white vinegar. Spray the metal with the vinegar and then let it dry. Repeat this step a couple of times, and then mix hydrogen peroxide with a little white vinegar and salt, using the ratio 8:1:1. Put the ingredients in another spray bottle and shake vigorously to dissolve the salt. Spray the solution on the metal. It should soon start foaming. Let dry and repeat.

**Green patina.** This green patina recipe is most appropriate for copper or bronze, but will work on iron or steel as well. In a plastic spray bottle, combine white vinegar, nondetergent ammonia, and noniodized salt in the ratio 4:4:1. Shake until mixed. Put on your chemical-resistant gloves and safety goggles, then spray the solution on your prepared metal and let dry. Repeat as needed.

**Faux patinas.** Patina paints are meant to create a patina-like visual effect on metal. One useful technique is to lightly sponge turquoise paint over bronze primer. No paint will give the full effect of a real metal patina, but it's always good to have a nontoxic paint alternative.

**Finishing the patina.** Most patinas on outdoor pieces, like garden furniture or decorative metalwork, will actually help the metal resist further corrosion. However, if you find that your patina runs or streaks with moisture or stains surrounding areas, consider finishing the patina with sealant. Use an acrylic or solvent-based sealer, not urethane or polyurethane.

# PLUMBING

**C**logs, leaks, and parts-replacement are the staples of home plumbing repair. But to unplug, seal up, and troubleshoot, you'll need a fairly specialized set of tools in addition to those in your basic domestic-repair tool kit (see page 215). Not only can having these tools on hand help avoid the cost of a plumber, but (because a massive water leak waits for no one) having the ability to triage a disaster can also keep the Niagara Falls in your basement, bathroom, or kitchen from doing more damage than it has to.

# PLUMBING REPAIR TOOL KIT

Slip-joint or channel lock pliers

Adjustable wrenches

Pipe wrench

Basin wrench

Duct tape

Emery cloth

Teflon tape

Pipe solder

Hacksaw

Tube cutter

Internal and external wire brushes

Metal file

Fire-resistant cloth

Closet auger

Propane torch

Plunger

Plumber's snake

**Tongue-and-groove pliers.** Tongue-and-groove pliers will grab and twist most pipes and pipe fittings. Expect to pay about $15 for 10-inch and about $30 for 12-inch—and keep both on hand.

**Adjustable wrenches.** Adjustable wrenches (keep a 6-inch and a 10-inch in your tool kit) will help you turn the hexagonal nuts of supply lines and compression fittings. They fill the middle ground between tongue-and-groove pliers and proper pipe wrenches.

**Pipe wrench.** A pipe wrench is a serious hunk of metal. Its ingenious design allows it to lock on to round surfaces, tightening and loosening its teeth into soft iron fittings. Some repairs will require you to twist in opposite directions at once, so it's useful to have two or more pipe wrenches. A basic quiver should include one 10-inch, two 14-inch, and one 18-inch.

**Basin wrench.** The other pliers and wrenches may do double-duty on other household projects, but a basin wrench is for one use and one use only: reaching hard-to-get fasteners that you can't get a wrench on any other way. The specialized head of a basin wrench is designed to lock on to fasteners with pressure, and the very long handle allows you to get the head onto the nuts that hold faucets and other fixtures in place deep in the recesses of your sink. This is a tool that you don't need until you need it, and then there's nothing else that'll do.

**Propane torch.** "Sweating" is the process of joining copper pipe in a watertight joint, which you'll need to do if you're replacing cracked or old water pipes. To do it you'll need a small, handheld flame torch. Propane is standard for most basic home repairs, though you may also consider methylacetylene-propadiene (MAPP), which heats joints a little faster. Get a torch kit for about $50, and consider investing in a model with a self-lighting head, which is much easier than using a striker, lighter, or matches.

**Hacksaw.** A hacksaw is the go-to blade for cutting both metal and plastic pipe, as well as screws, nuts, and bolts. Ten- or 12-inch saws are standard and either will complement your kit. In addition to the saw, consider getting three blades—one with 18 teeth-per-inch (TPI), one with 24 TPI, and another with 32 TPI. The more tightly spaced the teeth, the thicker the material it will cut.

**Tube cutter.** The tube (or pipe) cutter is a specialized cousin of the hacksaw. It's not as versatile, but it does the job of cutting copper pipe so much more efficiently that it's worth adding to your kit. A tube cutter can look like a wrench with a pizza-cutter-like tooth, or it can be a clamp with the same round blade. Either way, the tube cutter fits around a pipe and you spin it, making a clean slice. Expect to pay about $20.

**Metal file.** Once you cut copper pipe, you'll want to smooth the rough edges with a metal file. It's worth having two files on hand: a half-round file, with a flat and a round side, for de-burring metal; and a rat-tail file (it's round and tapered, as its name implies) for filing concave surfaces and enlarging holes.

**Plumber's snake.** Technically called an auger and also known as an electric eel, the plumber's snake is a hand-cranked drain-cleaning tool. Twenty-five feet is a fairly standard length, and a ¼-inch cable can be used in drains up to 2 inches wide.

**Closet auger.** For any drain more than 2 inches wide—especially the toilet—you'll need the thicker version of the plumber's snake known as the closet auger. This short, hand-cranked auger usually includes a plastic stem that protects the finish on the porcelain basin and is just long enough to reach the trap under the toilet, which is home to most clogs.

**Plunger.** Before you reach for a snake, give your toilet clog the old college try with a plunger. A toilet plunger is slightly different from a sink plunger, with a second sleeve of rubber (called a "flange") that extends just below the cup and helps to form a seal with the tubular constriction at the base of most toilets. Buy one of each kind. Buying a good plunger can help you avoid other, less pleasant interventions.

**Miscellaneous supplies.** In addition to duct tape and sheer moxie, you'll also need fire-resistant cloth for guarding wood from flames while working on pipe, emery cloth for sanding metal, Teflon tape for protecting pipe threads, internal and external wire brushes, and pipe solder. Unlike the assortment of generic nails, screws, and bolts that will see you through most non-plumbing fix-its, most of your plumbing replacement parts require hardware specific to the job. Evaluate the needs of your plumbing project and then plan on going to the hardware store for the job-specific parts you need.

# #166
# HOW TO STOP A DRIP
## (or, Understanding Your Water Supply)

According to the U.S. Geological Survey, it takes 15,140 drips to make a gallon of water. If you have one faucet leaking a drip every two seconds, that's just over 1,000 gallons a year. (Never mind that a running toilet can waste up to 73,000 gallons of water in a year!) Not only does a drip waste water, but it can very easily lay waste to your sanity as well. So fix it. Usually turning off the drip is a simple fix requiring 15 minutes and only a few common tools. But this first foray into the world of plumbing can also teach you the basics of working with water—for starters, shut off the water supply before taking apart that faucet!

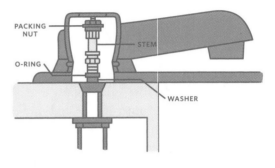

## Why a Faucet Drips

From the water treatment facility, water enters pipes that branch off into your home's water main, which in turn divert to all the taps and faucets and spigots in your house. The thing is, all of this water is pressurized—faucets don't suck water, they block it. This requires a pressure-proof seal, which is usually created by screwing a washer down tight against the top of a pipe. When the washer or its seat decays or cracks or simply comes loose, water from the pressurized pipes can leak out.

## TOOLS:

**Utility knife (if needed)** •
**Screwdriver** • **WD-40 (if needed)** •
**Slip-joint pliers**

## MATERIALS:

• **Rubber O-ring**
• **Washer**

**1 SHUT OFF THE WATER SUPPLY.** Most sinks and toilets have obvious local shutoff valves located near where the pipes enter the wall. With tubs and showers, shutoffs can be a little trickier to find. Look for a nearby access panel in the wall or check your basement or crawl space for a hidden shutoff. If all else fails, shut off the water main to the house. There should be shutoff mains on either side of your water meter, one for shutting off the supply side and one for shutting off the house side. Turn off the supply side (the pipe that comes from the street).

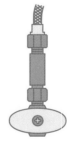

**2 MOST FAUCET HANDLES ARE** attached by one screw on the top or back, which may be hidden underneath a plastic button. Cover the drain with a stopper or towel before removing the faucet handle(s). Pop out the button with a flat blade, if necessary, and remove the screw. If it's tight, use WD-40 or another all-purpose oil to help loosen it, rather than cranking on it with the screwdriver alone and risking gouging out the screw head. Once unscrewed, remove the handle (the specifics will vary depending on your faucet).

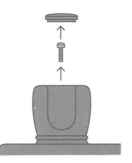

**3 UNDERNEATH THE HANDLE, A** packing nut guards the faucet's inner workings. Use slip-joint pliers to twist off the packing nut. Lubricate with WD-40 if needed.

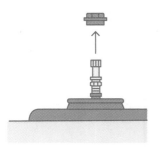

**4 THE PACKING NUT LIMITS THE** distance the faucet's stem can travel when you turn the handle. With the packing nut removed, you can use the handle itself as a wrench to remove the stem. Reseat the handle and turn it in the "on" direction to unscrew the stem.

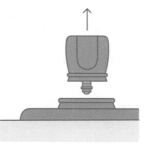

**5 ON THE BOTTOM OF THE STEM** is a small rubber washer. Remove the screw that holds the washer in place. The stem is likely to also have a rubber O-ring, which keeps water from sneaking up alongside the stem. Take the O-ring off, too. Examine the stem for any imperfections in the metal (and try to avoid making new imperfections!). If you see chips or cracks, it may be the metal and not the rubber pieces of your faucet that are causing the leak. Bring the washer and O-ring with you to the hardware store, along with the stem, if it looks damaged, so that you can match them to exact replacements. Because these pieces are cheap (and because when one fails the other can't be far behind), it's worth replacing both.

**6 ON THE STEM, REPLACE THE** washer and O-ring and reassemble everything you took apart. First insert the stem and its new parts into the faucet tube. Then replace the packing nut, the handle, the handle screw and any plastic button. Remove the rag that was blocking your drain and turn the faucet to the *off* position.

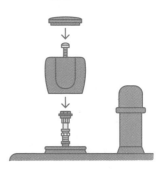

**7 TURN THE WATER BACK ON** from the wall or the main. Steps 2 to 6 should fix 99 percent of leaky faucets, but if yours continues to drip even after properly replacing the washer and O-ring, it's a good bet the stem or other metal parts are damaged. If needed, revisit these parts with a more critical eye and replace anything that looks suspect.

# #167
## HOW TO UNCLOG A DRAIN

The purpose of a drain is to get rid of things you don't want. But sometimes these things don't want to go. That's called a clog. Your job is to be stronger than the clog. It can be trickier than it sounds. Unlike the water that comes into your house, water that goes out is pressurized only by gravity and the force of the water pushing down from above. It's inevitable that at some point accumulated gunk will overpower the strength of a little bit of water. First the sink just seems a little slow. Then it takes 20 minutes to clear. Then it's an hour. And finally you wake up to find last night's toothpaste still in the basin. It's time to unclog the drain.

Unclogging a drain is a little like solving a mystery. You want to eliminate potential culprits before calling in the big guns. For instance, before taking apart your sink, try a snake; before resorting to tools, try a solvent; before using commercial solvents, try a mixture of vinegar and baking soda. You can always escalate your efforts, but it's gentler on your pipes to start small and ramp up as needed.

## TOOLS (DEPENDING ON THE CLOG):

**Sink plunger • Plumber's snake • Slip-joint pliers • Bucket • Long screwdriver or wire coat hanger**

## MATERIALS:

- **Baking soda**
- **Distilled white vinegar**

**1** **TRY A SOLVENT.** Liquid solvents that eat away at the clog can clear away some slow drains without doing too much damage to your pipes. Try baking soda and white vinegar first. Dump at least a half-cup of baking soda into the drain and then chase it with a half-cup of distilled white vinegar. The action should be immediate, bubbling out into the sink. But even once the volcanic spurt is over, the concoction continues to work. Let it sit for a few hours before rinsing with very hot water. If needed, escalate to Drano or Liquid-Plumr. (Make sure

the pipes in your home aren't old metal, since strong chemical formulas can corrode the pipes.)

**2** **TRY A PLUNGER.** A sink plunger is shaped slightly differently than a toilet plunger. Toilet plungers usually have a rubber sleeve ("flange") that extends below the base of the plunger bell to make a seal with the pipe leading from the base of a commode. Drain plungers have no skirt and instead are usually just a rubber bell on a handle.

The trick to plunging a drain is to plug any openings other than the one you're plunging; otherwise they act as pressure releasers. Start by jamming a wet rag into a sink's overflow drain. If another sink shares the same pipe (as in double basins or back-to-back bathrooms), plug all other drains and overflow openings with drain plugs and wet rags.

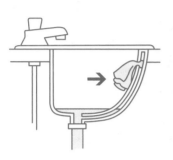

Place the plunger bell over the clogged drain. Fill the clogged basin with water to reach at least halfway up the plunger's bell.

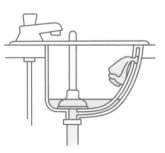

Form a seal over the drain and start working the plunger up and down—both the pushing and pulling actions help to loosen the clog.

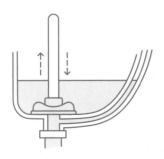

After about a dozen pushes and pulls, remove the plunger and see what happens. If water rushes out, problem solved. If not, give it a couple more tries before escalating your interventions.

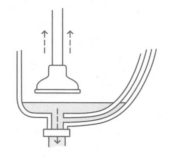

**3 TRY A SNAKE.** Plumber's snake, hand auger, sink auger—whatever you call it, it's a twisty head on a long wire that you push into a clog and crank until the clog is clear. Start the easy way, by trying to auger the clog down through the drain itself—if the clog is high enough in the pipe, a couple of cranks should clear it.

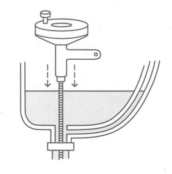

That said, many clogs will be lower in the pipe—too low to reach from the top. Instead, you'll have to auger the sink from below. If you

think you'll bump the faucet or your cat or child will delight in turning it on while you're working, turn off the water supply at the wall. Then place a bucket beneath the curved pipe under the sink, known as a P-trap.

The P-trap is held in place by friction washers and slip nuts, which may only be hand-tight. If they're too tight, give the nuts a firm crank with slip-joint pliers.

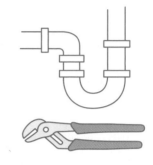

Remove the P-trap and use the bucket to catch the water that drains from the pipe ends.

Check to see if the clog is in the P-trap. If so, you should be able to clear it with a long screwdriver or with a wire coat hanger.

**4 TRY DIGGING DEEPER.** If the clog isn't high in the pipe and it's not in the P-trap, it's farther down the pipe. Feed the auger wire down the pipe. The pipe that leaves your drain eventually reaches a T-joint, at which point one pipe leads farther into the drain (possibly toward the clog) and the other pipe leads up to the outside (and away from the clog). To tell the difference, listen to the wall while you feed the auger wire. You should be able to tell if the auger head is climbing (which you don't want) or descending. Once you feel resistance, tighten the set screw at the front of the snake and turn the handle while pushing into the clog. Work the auger back and forth until the clog clears. If the clog proves difficult, try pushing the auger past the clog and then pulling it back through while cranking. Enough passes should clear the clog. Gently extract the snake, trying not to make a horrible mess. Reassemble the P-trap and run a substantial amount of hot water down the drain to wash away any material you scraped loose before it initiates a new clog.

**5 CLEAR THE HOUSE TRAP.** Hopefully one of the previous steps cleared your clogged drain. If not, the clog must be even farther down, and if it is a clear drain you seek, follow it you must. If you can follow the path of your pipes underneath the house, from either a basement or a crawl space, do it. Ideally your plumbing includes screw-off, clear-out plugs at periodic intervals, allowing you to check for clogs without removing sections of pipe. Eventually you'll reach the house trap—a U-shaped pipe probably buried in the basement floor and marked by clear-out plugs at the tops of the U. Unscrew these plugs and try the auger. If the clog remains, it's time to call a professional.

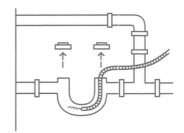

Although drains seem as though they would be fairly small and unwelcoming of larger objects, plumbers have reportedly found all kinds of living and nonliving items in them—from wedding rings to false teeth to electronic devices to . . . live badgers!

# #168
## HOW TO FIX A BURST PIPE

As water turns to ice, it expands. This expansion can be so powerful that ice pushing against pipe walls can burst the metal. Unfortunately, you're not likely to notice the problem while the water is still in its solid form. You notice a burst pipe when the ice *melts*—and the cracked pipe starts spewing water into your basement. The first step to fixing a burst pipe is actually prevention: learning to recognize the conditions likely to create it and watching like a hawk as a frigid night turns into a tepid day. The second step is being able to lay a quick hand on your house's water main, despite possible pitch-darkness and hemorrhaging plumbing. Where is your water main? Practice now. Really. Put down this book and go find your water main. Practice turning it off and then back on. The last thing you want is water rising around your ankles as you search desperately for the main. Now, with the crisis under control, it's time to think about a fix.

## Replacing a Pipe Section

If you're lucky, you're dealing with a trickling leak and preparing for a patch situation (see How to Patch a Pipe, page 327), but a more serious leak requires a more serious fix: replacing the affected section of pipe with a new section. Again, due to the combination of the desperation you're likely to feel while staring at a burst pipe and Murphy's Law, which dictates that said burst pipe be inaccessible to anyone but a contortionist, you'll likely want to practice pipe repair with scrap pipe in the comfort of your garage on some warm evening. No matter the conditions surrounding pipe replacement, however, the procedure remains the same.

## TOOLS:

Tube cutter or hacksaw ▪ Torch (propane, MAPP, or other) ▪ Measuring tape ▪ Pencil ▪ Wire brush ▪ Safety goggles ▪ Safety gloves

## MATERIALS:

- Type L copper pipe, diameter ½" or ¾" (to match the damaged pipe)
- Couplings (to fit pipe)
- Plumbing flux
- Lead-free solder

**1 GATHER YOUR MATERIALS.** Before you start cutting, make sure you have the pieces needed to replace what you remove. Modern plumbing should exclusively use type L copper pipe, diameter ½" or ¾". Keep extra lengths of both in your plumbing tool kit, along with couplings of appropriate size to cover the joints between sections of pipe.

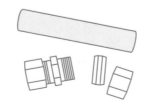

Rarely, you might need to replace a fixture, which can require a trip to the hardware store.

**2 CUT OUT THE BROKEN SECTION.** Use the tube cutter to cut the copper pipe on either side of the leak to remove the broken section. If the broken section is near a valve, joint, or coupling, you may be able to heat the section with your blowtorch, grip it with pliers, and twist it free instead of cutting it. Pulling pipe from an existing joint is slightly preferable, as it removes the need to add a new joint or coupling on that side (one fewer fitting to solder).

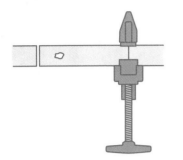

**3** **CUT NEW PIPE.** Measure the section of pipe you removed and cut a section of the same length from new, matching pipe with the tube cutter.

**4** **PREPARE THE SURFACE.** Before you slide sleeve-like couplings over the joints between the new and old pipes, clean all sections thoroughly. Use a wire brush to remove any rust from the old pipe, and do the same with the new pipe, until both sparkle. A little preparation goes a long way toward a successful repair.

**5** **ATTACH THE PIPES.** Slide two couplings onto the new section of pipe. Eventually, one coupling will cover the left seam and the other will cover the right seam. Paint plumbing flux onto the sanded ends of both the old and the new pipe. Slide the couplings to cover both joints.

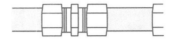

**6** **SWEAT THE PIPES.** An inexpensive propane torch—or, really, any modern blowtorch—works well to sweat copper pipe. Put on safety goggles and gloves, and then light the torch and adjust the flame until the inner cone—the hottest part of the flame—is a little more than an inch long. Hold the tip of this cone to one joint at a time, moving the flame evenly over the coupling. Plumbing can be tight work, so be careful not to bring the flame too close to ceiling joists or any other wooden or flammable material.

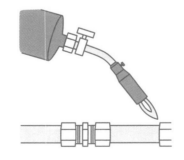

**7** **SOLDER THE PIPES.** When the flux sizzles, put down the torch and apply solder (with experience, you can torch with one hand while soldering with the other, but, for now, use caution). Lead-free plumber's solder is usually sold as silver alloy wire on rolls. There's no need to cut from the roll; just work with the roll's loose end. Touch solder to one side of the coupling, where the sleeve ends and the pipe starts. The hot joint will suck solder. As solder melts into the joint, run the loose end around the pipe until the joint looks full. Repeat this step four times—once for each side of the two couplings.

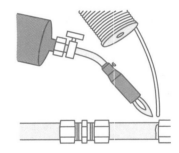

**8** **TEST THE PIPE.** Solder hardens as it cools, so after a minute or so the joint should be ready for use. Turn the water main back on and check the repaired pipe for drips. If it still drips, try again. This may include adding more solder to the joint, or heating and twisting the section free and replacing it with a new section of pipe.

# #169 HOW TO PATCH A PIPE

If the leak isn't catastrophic but instead is anywhere from a slow drip to a very moderate trickle, you may be able to patch the leaking pipe instead of replacing the section. There are many styles of plumbing patches—consider talking to employees at your local home improvement store about which kind is best for your needs. Then, in order to get most

kinds of patches to stick to smooth pipe, you'll have to rough it up a bit. Use 80- to 100-grit sandpaper to both clean and texturize the pipe surface, sanding at least an inch in every direction beyond the location of the leak. Plumbing patches are generally made to bond once wet and do so pretty quickly, so dry-fit the patch before moistening it. If needed, cut the patch to size so that it doesn't overlap itself but still covers the sanded area. If you're the gambling type, simply wet the patch, wrap it tightly over the affected area and let dry. If you're a little more careful, secure the patch with screw-together C-clamps or hose clamps. Tighten down the clamps and allow ample time to dry before testing the pipe. Due to the slightly imperfect nature of patches, check for leaks until you're confident the fix is permanent.

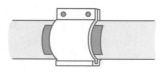

## EMERGENCY REPAIR

If under extreme duress, you can make a temporary pipe patch with a length of garden hose or a bike's inner tube. Cut a section of hose or tube longer than the split in the pipe. Slit the hose or tube lengthwise and wrap the sheath around the pipe. Hold the temporary patch in place with hose or C-clamps.

In the United States and Canada alone, there are approximately one million miles of water pipeline and aqueducts, enough to crisscross the continent about 300 times.

# #170
## HOW TO STOP YOUR PIPES FROM FREEZING

### (or, Lagging and Winterizing)

The best way to fix a pipe is to keep it from breaking in the first place, and the best way to keep it from breaking is to keep it from freezing. Because plumbing runs from the outside of your house to the inside, this can be easier said than done in climates where it gets below freezing. Plumbing also tends to run through the less insulated parts of your house, such as the basement, crawl space, and even garage. Because these pipes are a pain in the neck to access, it's worth spending a warm summer afternoon winterizing your pipes to avoid having to perform emergency repairs in the middle of some cold, dark winter night.

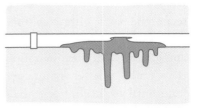

The process involves two steps. Step one is insulation, or lagging—stopping cold air from hitting the pipes so it can't freeze the water inside them. Air has a way of sneaking in through gaps, and so in order to be effective, pipe insulation has to be complete. Leave even a little gap, and inevitably that inch or two will be the part to freeze and burst. The second step is winterizing, or draining and closing vulnerable spigots.

## Before You Go on Vacation . . .

When you escape northern Minnesota for a midwinter trip to the Bahamas, your worst nightmare will be coming home to a swimming pool in your basement—or worse, an ice-skating rink. If it's just an overnight trip, and assuming your pipes are properly insulated, you should be fine with your heat set to about 40 degrees. For a longer trip, simply turn off the water main and open all your faucets (double-check them to make sure no water is sneaking past the shutoff). Opening your faucets allows water the room it needs to expand as it freezes, without pushing against the pipes. If you're expecting a solid freeze while you're away, consider also draining the water from your pipes.

## In the Cold, Cold Night

If a pipe starts to gurgle and spit on a freezing-cold night, there's a good chance it's the beginning of ice taking hold. If you can locate the exact trouble spot either by the sound of gurgling or by your considered opinion of where cold air is contacting the pipe, consider hitting it with your propane torch or, in a pinch, a hair dryer. Then, if possible, wrap the pipe with electric heating tape and leave the power on through the night. If you hit an unexpected cold snap before you've winterized your pipes, or if you know a certain line is prone to freezing despite your best efforts, you can leave a tap trickling overnight. Even a slight flow should move water through the system before it can freeze in the pipes.

## TOOLS:

**Measuring tape** ▪ **Pencil** ▪
**Flashlight (optional)** ▪ **Duct tape** ▪
**Utility knife** ▪ **Pliers** ▪ **Bucket**

## MATERIALS:

- **Fiberglass, foil, or foam pipe insulation**

**1 CHECK YOUR INSULATION.**
First, determine which areas of your home are likely to experience below-freezing temps. Pay special attention to pipes running along outside walls or underneath the house where the foundation meets the walls. In the northern hemisphere, the north side of your house is likely to see little winter sun and so may be especially prone to freezing pipes. (There should be ample fiberglass batting insulation to keep the outside from coming in. If not, fix your wall insulation after you insulate your pipes.)

**2 INSULATE THE VULNERABLE**
pipes. There are two options: sleeve-like foam insulation that sandwiches the pipe like a hot

dog bun, or tape-like fiberglass or foil insulation that wraps around the pipe. For most applications, it's easier to slip on a sleeve than wrap the tape. Measure the pipes and cut foam sleeves to length with a utility knife. Slip the sleeves over the pipe and close the slit with duct tape.

**3 SEAL AROUND BENDS IN THE**
pipe. Where a pipe turns at a 90-degree angle, use a utility knife to cut insulation ends to 45 degrees, then push the cut ends together over the pipe to make a clean right angle. Do likewise for any joint: Evaluate how to best cut the insulation to fit, and then close all open slits with duct tape.

**4 WINTERIZE THE SPIGOTS.** First, disconnect any outside garden hoses or other attachments to your outside spigots.

If you have "frost-proof" or "freeze-proof" spigots, when you turn the handle you're actually shutting off the water two or three feet down the pipe, where it's likely to be insulated anyway. (Most of these types of spigot have a plastic vacuum breaker cap on

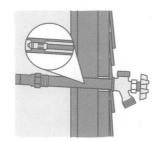

the top of the spigot—so a spigot with extra parts or bulk may be "frost-proof.") As long as the attached pipes are properly insulated and installed at a slight downward tilt that allows water to drain when the tap is off, they shouldn't require further work.

**5 SHUT OFF THE SUPPLY.**
A regular spigot requires shutoff and draining, and the procedure is similar to any pipe that's likely to freeze. First locate the shutoff valve. (All outside spigots and most pipes in general have shutoff valves far enough inside the house's insulated areas to firewall the rest of your plumbing from a burst.) Crank the valve closed, then open the spigot. Check the shutoff—there should not be any water leaking from the spigot.

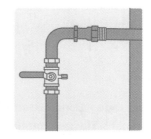

**6 DRAIN THE SPIGOT.** With the supply shut off, many homeowners make it through the winter with the spigot open. Any water remaining in the pipe has room to expand. For added security, or in especially cold climates, drain this excess water from the pipe. At the shutoff, find the drain cap and open it with locking pliers. Hold a bucket under the drain, and open the cap. Now, without water in the pipe, you can turn off the outside spigot.

# #171
# HOW TO INSTALL A SUMP PUMP

Before you find yourself pumping water out of your basement, do everything you can to keep it from coming in. That means draining water *away* from your house. Make sure that gutters are running freely and all spouts extend at least four feet past the house's foundation. Check that soil doesn't slope toward the house, which can funnel water into your basement. Still, some soils are simply wet, and if that's the case, you may need to pump water out.

## First, Try a Drain

If water is localized, and your house was built atop a layer of gravel, you may be able to drain the water into the gravel and soil below the house. In that case, simply install a drain at the lowest point in the basement floor. This will require cutting a small hole with a concrete saw, inserting a store-bought drain or grill, and then pouring a concrete patch around the drain. However, without a full gravel sub-layer, water may continue to pool up through the drain. In that case, you'll want a pit and a pump.

## TOOLS:

**Measuring tape** ▪ **Concrete saw (plan to rent)** ▪ **Sledgehammer** ▪ **Large bucket (for mixing concrete)** ▪ **Wooden float** ▪ **Trowel** ▪ **Hacksaw** ▪ **Drill with bit size matched to PVC (if needed)** ▪ **Caulking gun**

## MATERIALS:

- **Plastic sump pit liner**
- **Gravel**
- **Concrete mix**
- **Sump pump**
- **PVC pipe connectors**
- **PVC pipe**
- **One-way (check) valve**
- **Two 90-degree PVC elbows**
- **Splash plate**

**1 DIG THE SUMP PIT.** Staying at least 8 inches from foundation walls, use a concrete saw to cut a hole in the lowest section of the basement floor, where water accumulates. The shape doesn't matter as long as the section is greater than about 2 square feet. Break up the concrete in the panel to be removed by hitting it with a sledgehammer. Remove and dispose of the broken concrete. Dig a pit deep enough to accommodate the plastic sump pit liner, with the lip of the liner level with the floor.

**2 FILL THE PIT.** Insert the sump pit liner and pack gravel into the hole around the liner to hold it in place. Spread and level gravel on the dirt around the sump liner until the level of the gravel is about an inch lower than the surface of the basement floor.

**3 POUR THE CONCRETE.** Following the package instructions, mix enough concrete to fill the area around the sump pit liner. Pour the wet concrete on top of the gravel layer outside the sump pit liner. Use a wooden float to make sure the poured concrete pushes tightly against the existing basement concrete and also against the outside edge of the sump pit liner. Once the concrete is dry enough to hold its form but still wet enough to sculpt, use a trowel to finish the face of the patch in your basement floor. Let the concrete cure for a couple of days.

**4** **SINK THE SUMP PUMP.** Like toilets, sump pumps generally use a float that activates a pump once the water in the sump pit reaches a certain level. Start by screwing the appropriately sized PVC pipe connector into the sump pump discharge. With a handsaw, cut a length of PVC pipe to be just long enough to rise past the top of the pit liner with the pump in place (length of PVC will depend on the depth of your sump pump liner and how your pump sits inside the liner) and attach it. If you like, duct tape the pump's electrical cords to the vertical PVC pipe and then carefully lower the pump into the sump pit liner so that the pump float is away from the wall and able to move

without obstruction. Install the liner lid, cutting a hole in the top of the lid if necessary to accommodate the vertical PVC pipe.

**5** **ADD A CHECK VALVE.** Capping the PVC that runs to the pump, install a one-way valve, sometimes called a check valve. This keeps water from flowing back down into the pump once the pump shuts off. The check valve should come with its own plumbing connections, including couplings and clamps. Be sure the arrow on the valve points up, indicating the direction you want water to flow.

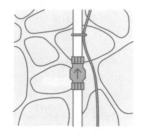

**6** **EXTEND THE PVC.** From the top of the check valve, add enough vertical PVC to bring discharged water up past the foundation to just below the ceiling joists. Attach a 90-degree PVC elbow.

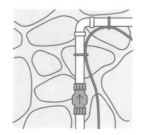

**7** **DRAIN THE DISCHARGE.** Pumped water should drain outdoors. To get the water outside, you'll need to cut a hole in the wooden rim joist that caps the house's concrete foundation. Drill a hole wide enough for the PVC to pass through. Feed PVC from the outside through the hole and connect the PVC to the elbow inside. Outside, use a handsaw to cut the PVC so that only about ½" of the tube protrudes past the joist. Attach another 90-degree PVC elbow to the outside pipe, pointing down. Use a caulking gun to run a line of caulk around the PVC on both sides of the wooden joist. If your landscaping slopes away from the foundation, you can discharge water directly from the down-pointing PVC onto a splash plate (like you would a hose spigot or gutter downspout). If discharged water has the potential to run back toward the house, forego the second 90-degree joint and use additional PVC to extend the drain away from the foundation.

# #172
## HOW TO FIX A LEAKY WASHING MACHINE

Whether you notice a slight dampening on the floor around the washing machine or a tsunami surges from the laundry room, don't delay fixing that washing machine leak. Like working on a car, working on a washing machine used to be easy—they were all roughly the same design, used roughly the same parts, and were prone to roughly the same leaks. However, with new direct-drive (as opposed to belt-driven) designs and the prevalence of computerized gadgetry, the one-size-fits-all approach to washing machine repair is no longer viable. There remain a few common leak locations, however, and thus common fixes for those leaks, but you may need to do some adapting to your specific machine. Before you start, check that repairs won't void your machine's warranty. Then, make sure the standing water near the machine isn't due to a plugged drain. It's not worth ripping apart the washing machine only to find the fix is as easy as grabbing a clump of hair.

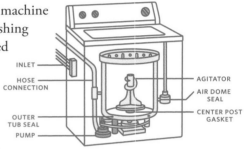

## TOOLS (DEPENDING ON THE FIX):

**Putty knife** ▪ **Adjustable pliers** ▪ **Screwdrivers** ▪ **Ratchet and socket**

## MATERIALS:

- **Hose washers**
- **Supply hoses**
- **Worm-drive clamps**
- **Pump hoses**

**1 REMOVE THE WASHING MACHINE** lid. There are holes punched in the tub, and any one of them is capable of leaking. Noting the exact location of a tub leak can help pinpoint the cause and the cure. Match the leak location to the washing machine specs. If you no longer have the paper plans that came with the washer, check online (most companies list their specs electronically). As with a car, start by looking "under the hood." Most lids are held on with a spring catch. Work a flat blade, like a putty knife, under

the front seam between the lid and the cabinet. Release the spring catch and lift the lid (some lids also require unscrewing).

**2 CHECK THE FOUR TUB SEALS.** These mount the tub to the cabinet, and each should consist of a bolt passing through a rubber washer. Bolts can rust and rubber can crack—if either is the case, replace them. If the tub itself is at fault—for example, its integrity is compromised by rust—it's time for a new washing machine. While you have the tub seals removed, it's worth lifting out the tub to check the center post gasket, which should form a seal at the base of the tub. In most washing machines, an air dome measures the internal pressure and acts as a switch, turning water on and off as needed. It can also leak. Most air domes have a slotted rubber seal. Replace it if needed.

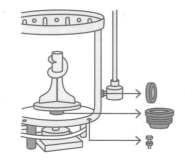

**3** **CHECK THE SUPPLY HOSES.**
Supply hoses connect your plumbing to the machine. They are almost always flexible rubber hoses tipped with metal connectors that screw onto inlets on the washing machine. After years behind the machine, these metal connectors may be corroded into what looks like little lumps of rust. Set the washing machine to the fill cycle and check here to see if water is leaking between the supply hoses and the inlet ports. If it is, turn off the machine and close the water-supply valve—it's perfectly possible to break a rusty supply hose off the inlet, which can quickly result in Niagara Falls. You can try simply tightening the supply hose connectors a good half turn with adjustable pliers and see if that fixes the problem, but a better solution is to disconnect the hoses and replace the hose washers. As these rubber circles age, they get brittle and eventually wear to the point of allowing leaks. Use a flathead screwdriver or other type of pry to pop a washer free of the supply hose

and bring it with you to the hardware store to match it. While you're at the store, if the supply hoses or their connectors are in bad enough shape, consider replacing the lot.

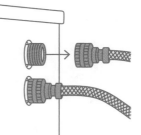

**4** **CHECK THE PUMP HOSES.** The supply hoses aren't the only water-conduits prone to leaks. There are hoses inside the machine, too, and to get at them you'll need to pull off the access panel, likely by unscrewing and/or unclipping it from the back of the machine. Once you can see underneath, start the washing machine's fill cycle and look for leaks. You should be able to trace the path from the supply hoses through a pump hose, to the pump, and then out through another pump hose. Check these pump hose joints first, looking for clues like rust and calcium deposits in addition to leaking water. Hoses should be attached to the pump with either spring clamps or worm-drive clamps. Loose or rusted clamps are a common cause of leaks. If you replace the clamps, go with worm-drive rather than spring. You may also need to replace the hoses, which is easy to do with the access panel and clamps removed.

**5** **CHECK THE PUMP.**
Unfortunately, pumps don't last forever. If you see water leaking from the pump itself, it's time for a new one. Grab a helper or two, unhook the washer, and tip it on its side to access the pump through the open bottom. Note the pump specs and buy or order a new one. Also notice the amount of wear on the drive belt—if it looks worn, this is a good time to replace it. Just slip off the old belt and replace it with a new one. Then note the location of the pump's mounting bolts. Disconnect the in and out hoses and use a ratchet and socket to remove the mounting bolts. Slide the pump away from the drive belt and slip it free. Put in the replacement pump, seating the drive wheel in the belt and reconnecting the hoses. You'll need to adjust the position of the pump to tighten the belt, so after loose-fitting the mounting bolts, pull the pump tight against the belt with one hand while tightening the rear mounting bolt with the other. If needed, tighten the belt more and tighten the front mounting bolt.

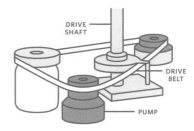

# #173
## HOW TO REPLACE A SINK FAUCET

**S**inks are easy: Open up the cabinet underneath the sink and you will find all the pipes you need to plumb a new faucet. (Bathtubs are trickier—the faucets are generally mounted flush to the wall, so just getting to the pipes is its own challenge.) Here you will learn how to replace a sink faucet, whether it's broken, leaky, or just plain unstylish.

## TOOLS:

**Rag** ▪ **Basin wrench** ▪ **Slip-joint pliers**

## MATERIALS:

- **New faucet**
- **Supply lines (if needed)**
- **Teflon tape**
- **Plumber's putty or silicone caulk**
- **Friction washer and screw (for sprayer)**

**1 TURN OFF THE WATER SUPPLY,** either at the shutoff valve in the bathroom or kitchen, at a shutoff valve farther upstream in the plumbing, or at the house's water main. Clear the area of soaps, sponges, and toiletries and make sure you have a bucket and towel on hand, just in case. Shove a rag into the drain to avoid losing hardware down the pipes.

**2 ACCESS AND REMOVE THE OLD** faucet. In most older sinks and even many newer ones, having a long-handled basin wrench greatly eases the process of loosening the nuts that hold faucets in place. If not, it's useful to have long arms and patience. Reach up behind the sink and unscrew the tailpiece nuts that lock the faucets to the sink. Remove and dispose of the old faucet.

**3 EVALUATE YOUR PLUMBING.** While under the sink, check the integrity of your water supply line and shutoff valves. If you see rust or slime in excess of what can be cleaned, you'll need to replace those parts. Replacing the shutoff valves will likely require sweating new valves to the copper pipe (see page 326). Replacing the flexible supply lines should be as easy as unscrewing them from the shutoff valves and screwing on new ones. Don't forget to wrap the threads with Teflon tape. The standard for under-sink use is braided stainless steel, which can be snaked around the myriad obstructions typical under any sink.

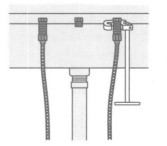

**4** **CONNECT THE TAILPIECES.**
Faucet tailpieces bring water from the supply lines to the faucet itself. Whether you attach the tailpieces to the faucet and feed them down through the mounting holes in the sink, or attach the tailpieces to the supply lines and feed them up through the holes, depends in large part on the style of faucet. The faucet manufacturer should have provided pre-assembly instructions. Follow these instructions to determine how much of the faucet you should build from the top and how much should be fed from the bottom.

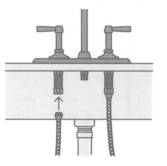

**5** **SEAL THE FAUCET PLATE.** The line where the faucet plate meets the sink is a common place for water to seep underneath the sink, where it can create mold and rot. Guard against this by running a ¼" bead of plumber's putty around the base of the faucet before mounting it on the sink (if you have a marble sink, use silicone caulk instead). Be generous with the caulk or putty and then wipe away any excess.

**6** **MOUNT THE FAUCET.** After caulking the plate, set the faucet on top of the mounting hole, making sure it's pointing in the right direction. (Don't laugh. It happens.) Press down on the mounting plate to squeeze the putty or caulk until the plate is tight to the sink. Use a basin wrench or a wrench supplied by the faucet manufacturer to tighten the mounting nut from below. To either side of a single faucet should be flange nuts that push down through open holes in the sink. Tighten these nuts now, too.

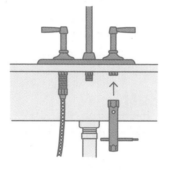

**7** **ATTACH THE SUPPLY LINES.** Under the sink, attach the braided stainless steel supply lines to the faucet tailpieces, screwing them tight with slip-joint pliers. Connect the other ends of the supply lines to the shutoff valves. Use two wrenches to tighten the lines into the valves.

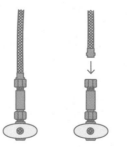

**8** **ATTACH THE SPRAYER, IF** needed. Many sinks and newer faucet systems also include a sprayer. Attaching a sprayer is very similar to attaching a faucet. Run a ¼" bead of plumber's putty along the bottom of the sprayer base. (The base should sit on top of long, screw-like threads.) Push these threads down through the appropriate hole in the sink and press the base in place. From below the sink, add a friction washer and screw on the mounting nut (which likely came with the sprayer). Tightening the nut will further pull the base of the sprayer against the sink. Wipe away any excess putty. With most sprayers, it will be easiest to feed the hose up through the hole in the base and attach it to the sprayer above the sink before setting the sprayer back into the base. Some sprayers include a length of attached hose, meant to attach to an extension hose under the sink. If that's the case, feed the hose down through the sprayer base and connect it as appropriate.

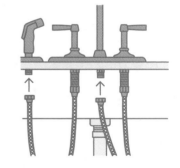

**9** **LET THE PUTTY DRY AND MAKE** sure the faucet is off before turning the water supply back on. If you have to leave the room to turn on the water, it's useful to have a second set of eyes watching for leaks so that you can immediately turn the water back off if needed. Even a tiny drip will cause problems, so watch with eagle eyes for any sign of misplaced moisture, and if it's leaking at all, scrape off the putty and start again, reapplying it carefully.

# #174
# HOW TO REPLACE A DRAIN BASKET

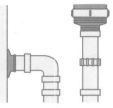

You don't want gunk in your pipes, and that's why in many sinks, there's a drain basket to guard the entrance. The basket also forms the watertight funnel that directs water from the sink down the pipes. Because it's the gunk filter, and also a heavily used funnel, the basket will almost certainly wear out before the sink itself does. When that time comes, or when you deem it simply too disgusting to remain in the household, it's time to replace the basket. Here's how:

## TOOLS:

**Slip-joint pliers** ▪ **Locknut wrench (optional)** ▪ **Pliers** ▪ **Screwdriver** ▪ **Hacksaw (if needed)** ▪ **Plastic or wooden scraper** ▪ **Rag**

## MATERIALS:

- **Plumber's putty or silicone caulk**
- **New drain basket**
- **Tailpiece washer (if needed)**

**1 CLOSE THE WATER SHUTOFF** valve. Look for it under or near your sink. Because you're working with the drain instead of the water supply, it's not technically necessary to turn off the water while completing this repair. That said, it's at least possible to loosen or unscrew something on the supply side that can quickly soak your kitchen or bathroom. Err on the side of caution.

**2 REMOVE THE TAILPIECE** washer. Under the sink, use slip-joint pliers to loosen the plastic slip nut that holds the PVC tailpipe to the base of the strainer. Spin the slip nut completely off its threads so that it falls onto the plastic pipe. There's likely a plastic washer set in the top of the tailpiece—remove it now and put it someplace you won't lose it.

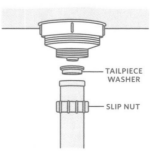

TAILPIECE WASHER

SLIP NUT

**3 EVALUATE YOUR PIPES.** If you find that you need to replace any of the PVC pipes leading from the drain basket to the wall (including the tailpiece, waste arm, trap, or any other under-sink plumbing leading from the basket), now is a good time to do it (see Step 7). Before ripping anything out, draw a diagram or take a picture of the existing plumbing so you can replicate it later. If you plan on keeping the old pipes, simply spin the tailpiece out of the way in order to complete the remaining steps of basket replacement.

**4** **LOOSEN THE DRAIN BASKET.** The locknut—the large-diameter ring that holds the bottom of the basket snug to the sink—is your number-one challenge in removing the basket. Give it a good twist with a locknut wrench or slip-joint pliers set at their widest extension. In many cases you may find that when you crank with the wrench or pliers, the entire basket spins rather than the locknut. After years of sitting in the same position under the sink, rust may be contributing to the locknut's locking power. In order to twist the locknut, you'll have to hold the basket steady. From the top of the sink, look down into the basket. At the bottom should be two or more holes. Shove the handles of a standard set of pliers into the two holes and have a helper stick a long screwdriver between the handles of the pliers and hold the screwdriver tight to resist the turn of the locknut wrench. In some cases, turning the locknut may prove impossible, in which case you'll have to cut it off with a hacksaw. Fortunately, because you're replacing the sink basket anyway, you needn't worry about cutting into it—just don't slice the sink itself. All that should be required is one cut completely through the width of the locknut, which you should be able to make (uncomfortably) with a flexible-bladed hacksaw.

**5** **REMOVE THE BASKET.** With the locknut removed, access the other under-sink parts of the basket, namely the friction ring and gasket. The friction ring is a strong cardboard circle that should make it possible to turn the locknut independently of the rest of the system. The rubber gasket presses tight to the bottom of the sink to block any water from sneaking through—both should slip free fairly easily. With these pieces pulled free, the basket should be held to the sink only by the power of the dried putty under the top rim. Pull the basket free and scrape away the old putty with a plastic or wooden tool to avoid scratching the basin.

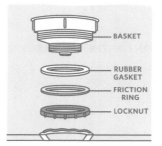

BASKET

RUBBER GASKET

FRICTION RING

LOCKNUT

**6** **INSTALL THE NEW DRAIN** basket. Run a ¼" bead of plumber's putty around the top of the drain in the sink basin. If putty won't adhere to your sink, use silicone caulk instead. Press the new basket down onto this layer of putty or caulk. Under the sink, slip the new rubber gasket and friction ring in place and then tighten the locknut

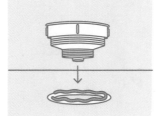

with slip-joint pliers to hold the new basket in place. Wipe away any excess putty squeezed from underneath the top lip of the basket with a damp rag.

**7** **PLUMB THE NEW BASKET.** If you kept the old PVC, spin the tailpiece back into position, reinsert the tailpiece washer (or a new one), and tighten the plastic slip nut onto the base of the basket. If you're replacing pipes, refer to the notes or picture you took in Step 3. Many home improvement stores sell outlet assembly kits that will have most everything you need to make the replacement. Installation should require cutting PVC to length, assembling with cone washers at all PVC joints, and tightening slip nuts. Between the tailpiece and the system's waste tee, make sure the PVC waste arm slopes gently downward so that wastewater flows down through the system. Sink options vary, however, sometimes including a garbage disposal, so refer to your diagram or notes to ensure that everything goes back together the same as it was.

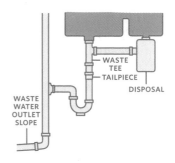

WASTE TEE

TAILPIECE

DISPOSAL

WASTE WATER OUTLET SLOPE

**8** **TURN THE WATER SUPPLY BACK** on and inspect the system thoroughly for leaks. If you see any, remove the basket, scrape out the putty and reapply carefully.

# #175
## HOW TO REPLACE A TOILET

**W**ater-efficient toilets typically use around half the water of a standard model. But that's not the only reason to replace your old commode. Maybe it's cracked. Maybe it's leaking. Maybe it's an eyesore. Whatever the reason, if it's time for a new toilet, here's how to install it. The following instructions will take you from the pipe, known as the closet bend, all the way up.

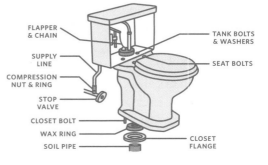

FLAPPER & CHAIN
SUPPLY LINE
COMPRESSION NUT & RING
STOP VALVE
CLOSET BOLT
WAX RING
SOIL PIPE
TANK BOLTS & WASHERS
SEAT BOLTS
CLOSET FLANGE

## TOOLS:

Bucket ▪ Tube cutter ▪ Rags ▪ Propane torch (if needed) ▪ 4-foot level ▪ Two socket or adjustable wrenches ▪ Hacksaw ▪ Screwdriver

## MATERIALS:

- Flange (if needed)
- Four 3½" closet bolts
- Shutoff valve (if needed)
- Flux and solder (if needed)
- Thread tape (if needed)
- Wax ring
- Toilet shims (if needed)
- Replacement toilet
- Braided stainless steel supply pipe that fits the space between your toilet and the water shutoff valve on the wall (if not included with toilet)

**1 TURN OFF THE WATER SUPPLY.** Make sure it's turned off! The importance of this step can't be overstated.

**2 CUT THE SUPPLY LINE.** Place a bucket beneath the supply line that runs from the wall to the toilet tank and then use a tube cutter to cut the supply line near the shutoff valve. Catch any water that drains from the line. Flush the toilet to get rid of any remaining water.

**3 REMOVE THE TOILET.** The mounting bolts are likely underneath small caps on the toilet's base. Remove the caps, use a wrench to unscrew the nuts and washers, and then, with help, lift the old toilet out of the way.

**4 EVALUATE THE PLUMBING TO** decide how much of the old material you want to keep. The flange is the circular piece that screws to the floor. If it's not in good condition, you can likely replace it without replacing the soil pipe it's connected to. Whether or not you replace the flange, plug the soil pipe with old rags to prevent sewer gas from escaping into the house and to prevent your tools and hardware from escaping into the sewer. Then, replace the 3½" closet bolts that point up from the flange.

**5** **REPLACE THE SHUTOFF VALVE.** If necessary, now is the time to swap out the shutoff valve behind the toilet. The old shutoff valve may unscrew from the wall or you may need to pull the valve slightly away from the wall and use a propane torch to heat the soldered joint until the old valve slips free. Replace with a new valve, either by screwing it in place or by sweating a new joint with flux and solder. If screwing on a new valve, use one wrench to hold the valve steady and another to tighten the nut. Wrap it with thread tape to prevent corrosion.

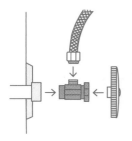

**6** **PLACE THE WAX RING.** Correctly installing the wax ring that seals the toilet base can prevent water from seeping from underneath the toilet. Be sure to purchase a wax ring correctly sized to your flange, likely 3 or 4 inches. If your toilet is too big for the flange, buy a 4-to-3 reducer. If the flange sits

below floor level, get a thicker wax ring to plug the empty space. Place the wax ring on top of the flange.

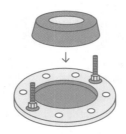

**7** **PLACE THE NEW TOILET.** Toilets are heavy, so if you're not built like an offensive lineman, get help. Slip the holes over the bolts and set the toilet down gently on top of the wax ring. Sit on the toilet to press it into the wax ring until the toilet sits flush (no pun intended) on the floor. If the toilet rocks or the floor is uneven, use toilet shims to make it level and then use a utility knife or short handsaw to trim the shims until you can't see them.

**8** **PLACE THE WASHERS AND NUTS** over the closet bolts. Make the nuts hand-tight and then use a socket or adjustable wrench to further tighten the nuts, alternating sides with every turn.

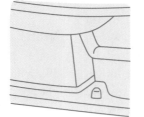

Don't over-tighten the nuts, or the porcelain toilet will crack. Once the nuts are tight, use a hacksaw to cut the closet bolts so they extend about ½" past the nut. Cover the closet bolts with the caps that came with the toilet.

**9** **NOW INSTALL THE TANK.** Push the bolts that anchor the tank to the toilet down through the included rubber washer and then down through the holes in the bottom of the tank. Line up these bolts with the mounting holes in the toilet and set the tank in position. Below the tank and toilet, place a metal washer and then a nut onto a tank anchor bolt (which should have been included with the new toilet). Hand-tighten and then use a wrench and screwdriver to tighten further.

**10** **CONNECT THE TANK'S** handle to the flapper chain inside the tank and look to be sure the float and chain aren't being held down by bands or wire.

*(continued)*

# 11

**PLUMB THE SUPPLY TUBE.**
Water flows from your plumbing through the shutoff valve, through a short length of supply pipe, and into the toilet's tank. In this step, you'll add the short length of pipe that goes between the shutoff valve and the tank. Hand-tighten the supply pipe to the tank using the provided tank nut. The supply pipe should point down toward the shutoff valve in the wall. If needed, sculpt the shape of the supply tube until it runs from the tank to the shutoff valve. When choosing the size, err on the side of leaving the pipe a little too long. The supply pipe should be able to insert easily into the shutoff valve.

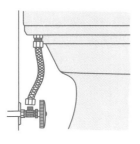

# 12

**SLIDE THE INCLUDED**
compression nut over the supply pipe end and then seat the pipe end into the shutoff valve. Use thread tape or Teflon paste to coat the screw threads. As you use a wrench to gently tighten the compression nut over the shutoff valve, the nut will squeeze the pipe to form a watertight seal. Your toilet should now be functional.

# 13

**TURN THE WATER TO THE**
toilet back on, either from the shutoff valve or from the main water supply. Flush the toilet a couple of times and inspect the unit closely for leaks. If it does leak, remove the thread tape or Teflon paste and start again, using a little more tape or paste.

**Though pitch is said to be affected by water volume and velocity, most American toilets flush in the key of E-flat.**

## Common Toilet Repairs

What other fixture bears full human weight multiple times per day and holds a reservoir of water in a tank that must be repeatedly emptied and filled? The toilet has too many moving parts, too many water transfers, and too much use to survive without problems. Here's what to do when the inevitable occurs.

**A broken seat.** The seat is meant to be sat upon. The lid is not. When you sit on the lid, it inevitably slides this way and that, stressing the hinges and their connections to the seat. And when either the hinges or the seat breaks,

there's nothing to do but replace it. Hopefully you can find a seat that matches your toilet. At the very least, make sure your replacement seat and lid set is the correct size (there are two standard sizes). Then simply unscrew the nuts and washers from below the seat mount and install the new seat. With bolts and nuts near water, the probability of rust is fairly high. If you suspect that you have a corroded nut, it's worth taking the time to fit the right size wrench socket to ensure turns without slippage.

**Water runs constantly.** Inside the toilet tank, a floating ball is attached to the switch arm. It essentially functions like a light switch: When the water reaches a certain height, the arm turns off the switch and water stops flowing into the tank. There are two common reasons why the switch might

not turn off the water. Either the switch is incorrectly gauging the amount of water in the tank, allowing water to continue flowing in through the supply pipe and straight back out through the overflow drain, or the tank is accidentally draining into the toilet bowl and the switch is correctly welcoming in new water. You may need to fiddle with fixes for both possibilities. First, work with the floating ball and the switch arm. Check the float to make sure it's not full of water. If it is, replace it. Then check that the float rod is positioned correctly to shut off the water once it reaches the desired level. You should be able to turn a screw near the anchored end of the float arm to adjust its height. If not, you can carefully bend the metal float arm to adjust it. Bend the arm and its float slightly down toward the water to make the water trip the switch earlier. If the switch isn't the problem, water is likely leaking out the bottom of the tank into the bowl. First check the length of the wire or light chain connected to the drain plug. If the chain is too short, it may be preventing the plug from forming a good seal. The chain may also simply be hooked around something—make sure it's clear of obstructions. If that doesn't work, turn off the water to the toilet, flush to drain the tank, and check the integrity of the tank drain itself. Is there corrosion? If so, thoroughly sand it away. If the plug looks torn or worn, replace it so that it forms a perfect seal with the drain. Reassemble, turn the water back on, and check that the water now flows as desired.

**Toilet won't flush.** Is the flushing mechanism not letting water into the toilet bowl or is water from the bowl failing to make its way down the pipe? If water is pooling in the bowl or even (heaven forbid!) overflowing, chances are you have a clog. First, see How to Unclog a Drain on page 322. If the flushing mechanism isn't working, check that the handle hasn't simply become detached from the tank's flushing mechanism. Another common cause of failure to flush is not enough pressure from the tank. In a toilet, pressure is created by gravity pulling water down from above—if there's not enough water, there's not enough push. Check the tank. If the water level is low, try adjusting the float ball to allow more water into the tank, either by

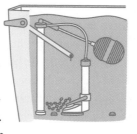

turning the adjustment screw or by gently bending the metal float arm to let the ball ride higher in the tank.

**Squealing noise when filling.** When water flow is restricted, pipes can whistle. First check that the water shutoff valve that connects the supply line to the wall is fully open. Restricted flow may also be due to pipe corrosion creating a partial blockage. Check the shutoff valve for signs of corrosion, and also check the entrance of the supply line into the tank. If you find corrosion, either use a wire brush to clear it or replace the affected part.

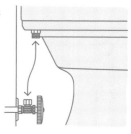

**Water leaks from the base.** By far the most common cause of a leaking toilet is a cracked wax seal. And the most common cause of a cracked wax seal is a toilet with too much wiggle. So first check the integrity of the toilet itself. If the nuts holding the toilet base to the flange have come loose, tighten them, pulling the toilet more firmly down into the wax ring. (Don't crank the nuts too tight, though, or you'll crack the porcelain!) A loose toilet can also be caused by a cracked base. If that's the case, you'll need to replace the toilet. If everything looks structurally solid, try replacing the wax ring itself. See How to Replace a Toilet, page 338 for how to trade in the old ring for a new one.

**Other leaks.** Where is the water coming from? If not the base (see above), check that a little moisture isn't due to condensation around the underside rim of the tank. Most toilet tanks include a foam ridge to block moisture from condensing—yours might need to be replaced. Also check the connection where water flows from the tank to the bowl. If needed, gently tighten the connecting nuts until you re-form a seal. Cracks can be surprisingly tricky to spot, so if everything else seems to be working properly, it's time to take a very close look at the porcelain itself. Look for hairline fractures—if you find one, it's time to replace the fixture.

# #176 HOW TO TROUBLESHOOT A SHOWERHEAD

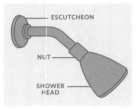

Showering lends itself to contemplation. There you are, standing in the hot water . . . fixating on the showerhead that seems stuck in time somewhere in the late 1970s, or on the trickle of water leaking out from between the head and the supply pipe. Time in the shower, in fact, is an important information-gathering period. What exactly is wrong with your showerhead?

**1 SHOWERHEAD LEAK.** It's usually easier to simply replace a head than search for the source of the leak. First try unscrewing the old showerhead by hand. Hold the supply

pipe so that it doesn't wiggle free and then give the old head a good counterclockwise crank with your other hand. If it comes off, great. Wrap the pipe threads with Teflon tape and screw on the new head. If the old head refuses to twist, it's time for wrenches. Use strap wrenches or wrap the teeth of slip-joint pliers with electrical tape to avoid scratching the finish on the supply pipe. Grab the pipe with one set of pliers and the fixture with the other and give it a forceful twist.

**2 JOINT LEAK.** If the joint where the showerhead meets the supply pipe is leaking, give the head another half a turn to tighten it. If it still leaks, unscrew the head completely (see above) and check for corrosion or other irregularities. Wrap the screw

threads with Teflon tape and reapply the head. If that still doesn't work, test the showerhead to see if water passes through it. Over a sink, pour water in the back of the head and see if it trickles out the front. The increased pressure caused by a partial obstruction could be causing the leak around the screw threads. Fixing an internal obstruction requires taking the head apart (see below).

**3 INTERIOR LEAK.** Remove the showerhead from the supply pipe (see above). All showerheads are different, but almost all swivel, and most swivels are made watertight by a rubber O-ring. If the head is leaking, the O-ring is a good place to check first. Disassemble the showerhead—if you're worried about reassembly, take notes or pictures.

On your way to the O-ring, you may find grit, grime, or other deposits. Pay special attention to the swivel ball—if there's sediment or mineral deposits, soak the ball in distilled white vinegar. Thoroughly scrub all dirty or gritty parts and look for small, embedded objects that might create channels for the passage of water. Once you reach the O-ring or a similar gasket, inspect it for grime or imperfections. Unless it looks perfectly new, replace it. There are a number of gasket types and sizes, so make sure you match the old gasket exactly. If you've replaced the O-ring, scrubbed the showerhead until it shines, used Teflon tape on the threads, screwed it as tight as you can, and the shower still leaks, admit defeat and get a new showerhead.

**4 PIPE LEAK.** In some cases, the leak might not be in the showerhead at all, and you'll need to explore farther up the pipes. Is there a visible crack in the pipe? Is the leak coming from inside the wall? If so, you'll have to go in and fix it. First check to see if the shower's supply pipe is accessible from the back, perhaps from a closet. If not, you'll have to cut a hole in the wall.

When cutting around pipes and water, consider using a hand-powered keyhole saw. The leak may be upstream, downstream, or in the middle of the elbow joint that connects the pipe running vertically up the wall to the pipe that sticks out into the shower. Once you find the leak, you'll know what section of pipe needs to be replaced. If the leak is downstream of the elbow joint, use a propane torch to heat the joint until the solder loosens and then use two pairs of pliers to pull apart the joint. Cut new copper pipe to match the removed sections and sweat the joints as described in How to Fix a Burst Pipe, page 325.

# ELECTRICAL

**A**ll electrical jobs have the potential to be dangerous if not done with care and the right tools. For obvious reasons, DIY electrical work is the most dangerous thing you're likely to do around your house. A leaky pipe can make a wet room, but a "leaky" electrical wire can cause a fire or potential for electrocution. But it's good to have a basic understanding of how your house is wired, both for emergencies, and basic repairs. Anything electrical that is not connected to the main supply is a much safer job and is well worth knowing how to do yourself if you're careful and thorough.

# ELECTRICAL REPAIR TOOL KIT

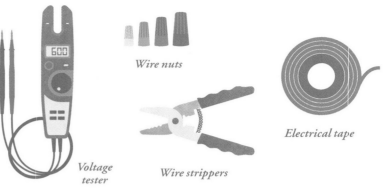

Voltage tester

Wire nuts

Wire strippers

Electrical tape

**Wire strippers.** Most wire strippers also include a wire cutter and end with tips that will do many of the jobs of a pair of needle-nose pliers.

**Electrical tape.** Insulated tape holds things together while helping the electricity stay where you want it.

**Wire nuts.** These are the screw-on "caps" that are used to hold two wires together. Get a range of sizes to keep in your tool kit.

**Voltage tester.** Even once you've turned off the electricity feeding whatever it is you're working on, you'll want to test at the source for juice. A voltage tester is a quick and easy way to confirm that what you *think* has no electricity, in fact, has no electricity.

## AC/DC: An Introduction to Electricity

The genius of modern society is that any power source that can turn a turbine (and even some that can't) can be transformed into electricity. Turbines turn loops of wire within a magnetic field. As British scientist Michael Faraday showed in the 1830s, this turning action effectively pumps electrons through the wire. It is the force of these electrons that we call electricity. Typically, electricity is generated in hydroelectric, coal-fueled, wind-turbine, and other types of power stations, after which it's concentrated for long-distance delivery in what are called step-up transformers. It then travels through transmission lines to step-down stations, which then distribute the electricity to customers. Electricity enters most neighborhoods at any level up to 34,500 volts. From there, step-down transformers (located on power poles) cut down the power to 120 or 240 volts, suitable for residential use. Here are the basics of how your residential electricity works.

**AC current.** You've probably heard of the electricity-producing piece in your car called an alternator. The reason for the name is that it produces alternating current, or AC, the same way that power stations do: by turning a metal coil within a magnetic field. In this configuration, the coil first pushes and then pulls electrons through the system, resulting in a current that travels both directions through conductive wire. Alternating current is the standard for power generation around the world. It's easy to transform AC to higher or lower voltages (using, yes, transformers), and transmission of extremely high voltages is much more efficient than transmission of lower voltages—over many miles of cable, less power is lost as heat. Early power companies realized they could concentrate AC into its efficient high-voltage form, then transmit it, then transform it back to lower voltages for use in houses and businesses.

**DC current.** DC stands for direct current, and as the name implies, electrons flow down a conductive wire in one direction. DC was Edison's great vision, but it doesn't fare well over long distances, quickly losing its punch. It's also hard to transform the voltage of a DC current, and so generally what is produced must be the same as what's used by a device. This makes DC well-suited to batteries—you can buy a battery with the exact voltage you need, and the juice needn't flow far before being used. DC is also used in some industrial applications and in some urban rail systems.

# #177
## HOW TO SLASH YOUR ELECTRICITY BILL

SHOP

**A**lmost everything we do at home relies on electricity. Turning on the lights requires power. So does heat in the winter and cool air in the summer. Want to turn on the coffeemaker or make a smoothie? Yep, it takes power. Any form of electricity costs money, and the most common sources also cause environmental damage. There are few things in this world as unambiguously good as saving power. Here are a couple of ways to do it.

**1 SWAP YOUR BULBS.** One 120-watt incandescent lightbulb left on for four hours a day costs about $50 per year in electricity. A comparable compact fluorescent bulb costs just $13 in electricity (not to mention the savings in polar bears). The United States and other countries are on the road to mandating the replacement of incandescent bulbs, but even without the power of law, there's really no reason not to. Fluorescent bulbs are a direct switch in terms of lighting quality, and with a few tweaks to your lighting design, halogen and LED lights can add layers of light with a fraction of the cost.

**2 WINTERIZE YOUR HOME.** Aggressive weather stripping and additional insulation will help keep the winter outside where it belongs. Start with insulation, which works like magic to keep the house warm in winter and cool in summer. There should be at least six inches of insulation in the attic. Older homes may not have any insulation at all in walls and floors—if that's the case in your home, add it, both for energy savings and comfort. It should be easy to roll batts of insulation into any open-topped walls. Insulating closed walls is more difficult and may require a contractor's assistance. To locate drafts where air enters your house, close all windows and the fireplace flue and then do the candle test on page 257. When you find a leak, consider insulating, caulking, weather stripping, or otherwise plugging the draft, as appropriate. (See How to Weather Strip Windows and Doors, page 257.) If you find a larger crack, use ozone-safe expanding foam sealant.

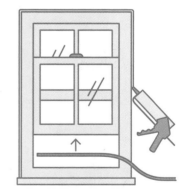

**3 PROGRAM YOUR THERMOSTAT** in winter. Set heating to automatically lower at night and during weekdays when you're gone. Also make sure the furnace is blowing freely by replacing furnace filters and clearing dust and debris from ducts. Most homes don't have insulated heat ducts—make your home an exception and you may qualify for rebates or tax incentives.

And insulate those windows! Check a window's labeled U-value to discover its efficiency. If possible, install more energy-efficient models or add drapes or heavy blinds for another layer of defense against the elements.

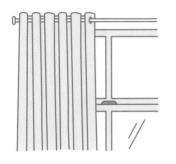

**4 REPROGRAM YOUR** thermostat in summer. Forget about setting the thermostat low as you did in Step 3—in the summer, set it as high as you can stand. And consider alternatives to running the AC, including fans and evaporative cooling. Trees can help keep homes cool, too. Planting deciduous trees on the southwest and southeast corners of your house blocks morning and evening sun in the summer, but allows the sun to warm the home in the winter.

**5 KILL VAMPIRES.** Most electronics continue to suck power even when they are switched off—hence the name "vampires." The power-suckers in your home might include TVs, game consoles, stereos, and microwaves. To kill these vampires, plug them into a power strip and then flip off the strip's power switch when not in use.

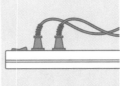

**6 AVOID KITCHEN WASTE.** Do you have a heating vent behind your refrigerator? Seems a little counterproductive, doesn't it? Likewise, keep the fridge away from that southern-facing window. If your refrigerator isn't an Energy Star model, consider replacing it (Don't forget to recycle the old one!). Also, strive to avoid oven or refrigerator overkill—a yogurt and a gallon of milk don't require a 22-cubic-foot refrigerator/freezer to keep cool, and a baked potato doesn't require an oven big enough for a Thanksgiving feast. Match your appliances to your lifestyle to avoid shelling out for unnecessary heating and cooling. Just as you mastered thermostat technology, learn to properly use the dishwasher's themed cycles to avoid overkill. You don't need to wash tea cups with the same ferocity as you wash roasting pans.

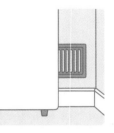

**7 BE LAUNDRY-SAVVY.** Most loads of laundry will be appropriately cleaned with cold water, especially if you use detergent designed for cold-water washing. Heating the water for a load of wash costs about 20 cents.

**"Vampire" energy costs the United States approximately $3 billion per year in energy costs. If plugged in long enough, most TVs and microwaves will have actually consumed more energy while turned off than all the times you heated up last night's leftovers and then plopped on the couch to watch your favorite TV show.**

And like the dishwasher, try to run the washing machine when it's full but not overfull, to use the most efficient amount of water. In terms of power usage, though, the washer can't compete with the dryer. A dryer can use about 5,000 watts per load, for a cost of about 30 cents. If you're going to take extra steps to save electricity somewhere in the housecleaning cycle, make it with the dryer. Who doesn't love the smell and feel of clothes dried in the sun?

**8** **WASH DISHES AT NIGHT.** Many modern dishwashers and even some clothes-washing machines have timers and delays so that you can run them long after you've gone to bed. The benefit is that energy costs are reduced at night when demand is lower, so, for example, if your dishwasher has a four-hour delay, push that button when you load your dinner dishes, and let the machine run as late at night as possible.

## If a person yelled for 8 years, 7 months, and 6 days, he or she would produce enough energy to heat one cup of coffee.

**9** **TAKE ADVANTAGE OF SMART** appliances. "Smart" or connected appliances are a major growth area in the home appliance industry. Whether or not your home system is connected to your smartphone—allowing you to cool, heat, light, or monitor your house via your phone or computer—a range of interconnected home appliances are increasingly available to give consumers far more remote control over running the home, and thus far more potential to save or conserve energy.

**10** **TAKE ADVANTAGE OF** programs and incentives. Not only are your efficiency upgrades likely to pay for themselves over time in lowered utility costs, but they may even pay for themselves up front in the form of government subsidies and other incentives. Tax credits or subsidized loans are offered for replacing windows with energy-efficient models, installing a solar water heater, and insulating exterior walls (or even for buying a hybrid car). Some state programs offer additional incentives for projects like solar panel installation, and others offer tax rebates based on meter ratings for increased electrical efficiency. Visit the Database of State Incentives for Renewables and Efficiency (dsireusa.org) for information about incentives in your state.

# #178

## HOW TO MAKE A DC CIRCUIT

### (or, the Basics of Circuit Soldering)

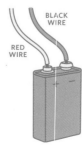

Soldering is a skill you'll use nearly anytime you do circuit work. To get started, you will first solder wires to a nine-volt battery, both demonstrating the principles of the electrical circuits that you'll be applying later when fixing lights and switches, and employing the technique of electrical soldering. You will then wire those nine volts of DC power directly into a load—it can be a small lightbulb, electric motor, buzzer, or other little electrical tchotchke. The important part is to find a tchotchke or other gizmo rated to just above nine volts—voltage should always be as close as possible to the rating without going over it.

## TOOLS:

**Soldering iron** ▪ **Safety goggles** ▪ **Wet sponge** ▪ **Wire strippers**

## MATERIALS:

- **0.025" lead-free solder**
- **9v battery**
- **2 pieces copper electrical wire (6" each, one red and one black)**
- **Small item to power**
- **Single-pull-single-throw (SPST) switch**

## SAFETY TIPS:

- **NEVER touch the heating element of the iron.**
- **Some solder contains lead. Always wash your hands after use.**
- **NEVER put the iron down on you workbench—it should remain in its stand while not in use.**

**1** **CHECK YOUR WORK AREA TO** make sure it's free of potential fire hazards. Plug in the soldering iron and let it get hot. While it's heating, cut 6" lengths of red and black copper wire and then use the wire stripper to strip about ½" of the plastic sheath from both ends of both wires. As you strip the plastic, you will see that the wire tips are made of many strands. At the end of each wire, twist each cluster of bare strands together (don't twist the two wires together!).

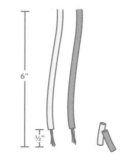

**2** **DON YOUR SAFETY GOGGLES** and wipe the tip of your hot soldering iron on a wet sponge to clean it. You should hear it sizzle. The basic idea is to use solder to connect the wire to a battery terminal and use the iron to heat the solder until it holds fast. Red wire always goes to the positive terminal on the battery and black always goes to the negative. Drip a bead of solder onto a terminal and then push the wire into it as you reheat the solder with the iron as needed. Hold the wire steady until the solder is done drying. Give the wire a gentle tug to test the joint.

**3** **USE THE BATTERY AND WIRES** you soldered to make a simple DC circuit. First, solder a small single-pull-single-throw (SPST) switch to the red wire using the same soldering technique you used to fix the wire to the battery in Step 2. Once the switch is soldered, solder another section of stripped red wire from the switch's other terminal to one terminal of the load. Finally, solder the black wire to the load's other terminal. You should now have a completed circuit: the battery's positive terminal should be connected to the first switch terminal, the second switch terminal to the first load terminal, and the second load terminal to the second battery terminal.

**4** **USE THE SWITCH TO TURN ON** the device. If it doesn't work, check your connections. If you find a loose connection, apply more solder. If it still doesn't work, try replacing the switch or load—and check that the 9v battery works!

---

## Although electricity was discovered by the ancient Greeks when they observed that rubbing fur against amber led to a mutual attraction between the two materials, Alessandro Volta produced the first steady electrical current in 1800.

---

### Always Turn Off the Power!

If you fail to properly turn off the water when making plumbing repairs, you will get soaked. Fail to turn off electricity when making electrical repairs, and you risk fire and severe injury. This isn't to scare you off—it should be simple to turn off the electricity to appropriate areas of the house while making repairs, and a wire without electricity running through it is harmless. Just make sure you do it right—and then double-check.

First, locate your home's circuit breaker box. Inside the box are voltage-controlled switches that automatically turn off the power if the fixtures and appliances plugged into the circuit overdraw the board. In other words, rather than frying the system, the breaker box turns it off. You can also use these circuit breakers to manually shut off power to different parts of the house. The breakers should be labeled according to the areas they protect. If not, think about the things that draw electricity in your house—would it be harmful to momentarily turn any of these things off? If it wouldn't, experiment: Flip the breakers until power goes off in the desired area of the house.

Like a light switch, circuit breakers are little levers that toggle between on and off, though they sometimes take a firm push to activate. If you don't have an assistant to monitor room lights for you, plug in a loud stereo or other noisy appliance in the room you are trying to power down and flip circuit breakers until you kill the sound. Next double-check that you've turned off the correct power by testing the switch or outlet you'll be working on, flipping it on and off. Absolutely nothing should happen. For added security, use a voltage tester to ensure that the outlet is no longer live—you can buy a tester or use any device that plugs in that you're absolutely certain works. If it doesn't work in this case, there's no power and you may proceed with repairs.

This should go without saying, but if you can't access the circuit breaker box, don't do the repair yourself—call in the experts.

# #179
# HOW TO INSTALL A DIMMER

## (or, Working with Switches)

A basic on-and-off light switch doesn't allow for a whole lot of *mood.* But never fear: If your mojo needs modification, it's pretty simple to install a dimmer. In fact, the procedure you'll use here to install a dimmer is the same needed to replace most common switches.

## TOOLS:

**Screwdriver** • **Wire cutter**

## MATERIALS:

- **Electrical tape**
- **Wire nuts**
- **Dimmer switch**
- **Dimmer plate**

**1** **TURN OFF THE POWER.** Make sure you've killed electricity to the fixture by flipping the switch on and off—nothing should happen.

**2** **REMOVE THE OLD SWITCH.** Most switches are covered by cosmetic switch plates. Remove the old plate; your dimmer will have its own new plate. In most light switches, wires connect at terminal screws. The terminals may be covered by a layer of electrical tape—if so, remove the tape. Loosen these screws and unhook the wires, which are most likely wrapped around the

screws themselves. You may also encounter push-in terminals in which the wires enter a hole in the switch. To loosen these wires, push a small screwdriver into the hole and then pull the wire free. If wires are permanent to the switch, it's likely the switch wires are connected to the house wires and capped with wire nuts. If needed, twist off the wire nuts and separate the wires. Because switch specifics vary, it's worth taking notes, or taking a picture of how the original switch was installed, for reference.

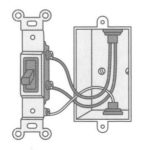

**3** **CHECK THE CONDITION OF THE** switch box. If the wires inside the box look at all suspect, replace them (or, at this point, call an electrician to do it for you). If the box is dirty, clean it. Check that the switch box is firmly mounted to a 2 × 4 stud in your wall. The box shouldn't wiggle—if it does, check that the mounting nails near the top and the bottom of the switch box are driven flush to the box wall. If needed, replace these nails, and if the nail holes have widened to the point of losing their friction, consider replacing them with screws. Finally, make sure that the ends of the house wires are pointing accessibly out of the box.

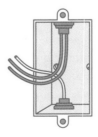

**4** PREP THE WIRES. With the old switch removed, check the condition of the wire ends, which may be weakened—look for nicks, dings, or irregular bends. Likewise, check the connections under the wire nuts, if your switch has them. You should see no copper sticking out from under the nuts, and the connection within the nut should resist a gentle tug. If in doubt, use a wire cutter to snip back the wires past the weak points and strip about ½" of the sheath from the new wire ends.

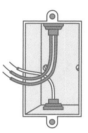

**5** INSTALL THE DIMMER. Look for the house wires—there should be two black wires and a ground, which is sometimes bare copper and sometimes wrapped in green. The dimmer should be fitted with wires of the same colors, and so your job is to attach like-colored

wires. First, if needed, strip the sheath from about ½" of the ends of the dimmer wires and wall wires, leaving exposed copper. Twist the exposed copper ends of the black-to-black, the second black-to-black, and then green-to-green (or bare) wires together. Cap the joints by screwing wire nuts over them and tightening until they won't turn anymore. Make sure the wire ends are tidy and not exposed and then cover the terminals with strips of electrical tape to insulate them.

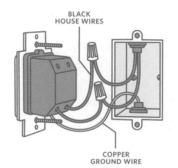

BLACK
HOUSE WIRES

COPPER
GROUND WIRE

**6** ATTACH THE DIMMER SWITCH. Gently pack the wiring back into the box, making sure all joints and connections keep their integrity as you manipulate the wires. Push the back of the dimmer into the

box on top of the wires. Use screws to attach the dimmer switch to the switch box. Replace the plate, using the new plate that came with the dimmer switch.

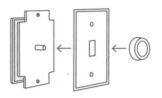

**7** AT THE CIRCUIT BREAKER BOX, flip the one breaker that is in the "off" position back to the "on" position to resend electricity to the room. Test the dimmer switch. Enjoy the newly enhanced mood.

---

Dimmers are not only used in homes. Electric lighting technicians (ELTs) in the theater industry use dimmers for more deliberate control over stage lights. The ability to subtly influence lighting helps create different moods to complement the emotions of the actors and actresses.

---

# #180
## HOW TO INSTALL A LIGHT FIXTURE
### (or Ceiling Fan)

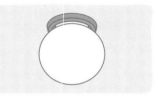

**A** bare, swinging lightbulb may be appropriate for a dramatic police interrogation, but it's probably not doing much for your living room. You'll be shocked to learn how easy it is to replace it with a chandelier. However, shocked is the last thing you want to be and so, before you go any further, make sure you turn off the electricity to the fixture (see Always Turn Off the Power!, page 349). It's tempting to simply switch off the light or fan at the wall switch, but this method could cause serious injury. Instead, go to the source: Shut off the power at the breaker box before you start and, once you can access the bare wires, use a voltage tester to double-check that they carry no power.

## Ladder Up

Replacing a light fixture or ceiling fan requires significant work at ceiling level, so it's worth taking the time to ensure a stable perch. For example, using a stepladder rather than a stepstool or chair means you have handholds throughout the project and aren't simply teetering above the ground while holding on to your new, fifty-pound fixture. It's likely that some debris may be sifting down from the hole in your ceiling, so either cover the area below the old fixture with a tarp or sheet, or expect to do some vacuuming when you're done.

## TOOLS:

**Stepladder** ▪ **Tarp or sheet** ▪ **Screwdriver**

## MATERIALS:

- **New fixture**
- **Patching plaster and paint (if needed)**

**1 EVALUATE THE OLD FIXTURE.** If it's a bare bulb on a plate, all you'll need to do is unscrew it. If it's a larger fixture or fan, support the fixture as you remove it to avoid the heavy object pulling free catastrophically, ripping down wires, likely a chunk of your ceiling, and possibly taking you with it. If needed, recruit a helper with a second ladder. Notice how the old fixture is attached to the ceiling—in the case of a ceiling fan, it will likely have a central mounting nut, and maybe other screws as well. While supporting the fixture, remove these screws. Let the fixture drop just enough to access the wires behind it. Most fixtures will be attached to your house wiring with wire-to-wire connections capped by wire nuts. Remove the wire nuts and untwist the wires before fully removing the old lighting fixture or fan.

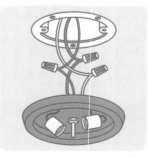

**2** **TROUBLESHOOT THE FASTENING** location. Hopefully your old fixture included a ceiling box attached firmly to a ceiling joist or support brace (if so, skip to the next step). But if not, see Mounting a Ceiling Box, below.

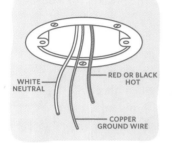

*Fixture with a ceiling box*

*Fixture without a ceiling box*

**3** **ATTACH AND WIRE THE NEW** fixture. Heavy fixtures and fans generally come with their own mounting brackets. These brackets should attach to the ceiling box—follow the manufacturer's instructions for hanging the mounting bracket and for positioning the fixture itself. The weight of a new fixture can make attaching wiring tricky. Most fixtures allow rough attachment to the ceiling to hold their weight while you attach the wires. If not, recruit a helper to hold the fixture in place while you attach the wires. Attach like-colored wires: Twist black to black and cap with a wire nut, then do the same with white and any copper or green wires. If attaching a more technologically advanced fixture—for example, a remote fan or light control—there may be additional wires. Follow the manufacturer's instructions to properly wire these components.

**4** **ASSEMBLE AND FINISH.** Many fixtures will require further assembly after wiring, perhaps adding fan blades, bulbs, or shades. Assemble these parts now. You may also need to install a fixture-specific wall switch. Double-check that the power to this switch remains off and then see How to Install a Dimmer on page 350 for detailed instructions for replacing a switch.

**5** **ONCE YOU'VE COMPLETED ALL** wiring and properly closed all junctions with wire nuts, turn the switch to the "off" position and restore power to the room and fixture by flipping the appropriate circuit breaker back to the "on" position. Switch the fixture on to test it. If needed, patch and paint the ceiling or wall.

## Mounting a Ceiling Box

Murphy's Law holds that a fixture without a ceiling box is floating on drywall. To comply with building codes, your new fixture needs to mount to a junction box (a container for electrical wires and cables), and if the fixture is more than about thirty pounds—especially with ceiling fans that tend to wobble a bit against their mount—it's best to mount to wood instead of drywall. First, take a look at the joists. Use a stud finder or other sleuthing tool (see What a Stud!, page 220) to discover the location of the ceiling joists. If a joist exists at the desired hanging location, great—use a keyhole saw or jigsaw to cut a hole in the ceiling the size of the new junction box. Discover where the wires that fed the old fixture pass nearest the joist and feed them into the box. Then screw the box into the ceiling joist (figure A).

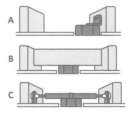

If there's no ceiling joist at the desired hanging location, you may need to add a brace between joists to which you can mount the junction box. If you can access the ceiling through an attic, do so. Nail a 2 × 4 between ceiling joists, flush to the ceiling drywall (figure B). If you can't access the joists from the top, you can feed an expandable metal brace (figure C) up through the hole left by the removed fixture. Any of these options—attaching a new junction box and fixture to a joist, wooden brace, or expandable metal brace—would be preferable to hanging a heavy light fixture or ceiling fan in drywall alone.

## Problems in the Breaker Box

Former Soviet leader Boris Yeltsin once noted that, like air, you don't notice freedom until it's gone. For the most part, the same is true of electricity. You flip a switch and you expect light. You push a button on the blender and you expect blending. You open the fridge and you expect it to be chilly. If a circuit breaker goes bad in your breaker box, however, you will have an immediate appreciation for electricity. Hopefully that appreciation isn't accompanied by absolute darkness, an unblended smoothie or spoiled food. If the problem is in fact just a bad circuit breaker or a blown fuse, and you have a replacement on hand (always keep replacements on hand!), the problem will take only a couple minutes to fix. But it might be more complicated—if so, here's how to diagnose the problem and get the electricity flowing again.

**Evaluating the breaker.** Be very careful: If a circuit breaker is tripping continuously, the breaker is likely doing its job properly and tripping in the presence of a constant problem like a short or an overload. When a breaker trips and seems unable to reset, first make sure you're resetting it properly. Force the handle firmly to the "off" position and then firmly to the "on" position. If the breaker won't stay on, observe what happens as it trips—do you hear a hum or buzz as it pops? If so, the breaker is likely good, closing the circuit in the presence of a problem. Use a screwdriver to remove a wire from the breaker and see if it now stays in the on position. Without the possibility of current, the breaker should stay on. If it doesn't, replace the breaker. If a different breaker functions where the first did not, it's a good bet the problem was a bad breaker. The opposite may also be true: A breaker may appear stuck in the "on" position, despite appliances in the relevant room remaining without power. Again, switch the breaker for a new one.

**Diagnosing a short.** If a breaker that constantly trips turns out to be functioning properly, or if you replace it and the problem continues, you'll have to look for the source of the problem. Hopefully the problem is a simple overload. Try unplugging appliances from the affected room to decrease the load. If you decrease the load and the circuit breaker stays on, experiment with the combination of appliances, electronics, fixtures, etc., to see if any particular component is drawing an overly large load. If so, move or replace that component to avoid overloading the circuit.

COPPER GROUND WIRE

FRAYED HOT WIRE

If reducing the load doesn't do the trick, you may have a more serious problem—a short circuit commonly occurs when exposed wires touch, either a hot wire to another hot, or to a neutral wire or a ground. A short circuit lets electricity bypass anything that offers resistance—an appliance or other electrical component—and allows the circuit to draw infinite amperage. This is bad—wires asked to carry an overly large load can melt through their coatings and start fires. That's the reason for a circuit breaker in the first

# TYPES OF FUSES

**B**efore you remove a broken circuit breaker ("fuse"), you'll want a replacement on hand. The most common breakers in your box take a single slot and are rated to either 15 or 20 amps—when the amperage exceeds these amounts, the breaker trips. Generally, these single breakers are 1" wide. The other common breaker in your box is a double-pole breaker, which looks like two single breakers hooked together with a bar. Single breakers typically monitor the power to a room or area of the house. Double-pole breakers typically monitor the power supply to large appliances, like clothes dryers or water heaters. When in doubt, bring a busted breaker with you to the hardware store to ensure a proper match. It's best to replace a breaker with one of identical amperage from the manufacturer of the breaker box.

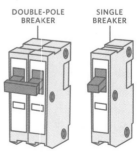

DOUBLE-POLE BREAKER

SINGLE BREAKER

place. But finding the exact location of the short can be tricky. The most important question is whether the problem is in your walls or in a device or appliance. Try unplugging appliances and flipping switches each in turn to narrow in on the source of the problem—if the short is in the interior of an appliance, it's almost certainly a goner. Next, check junction boxes, fixtures, switches, or outlets where the wires connect to other wires or terminals and look for imperfections, including bare wire or wire protruding from beneath tape or wire nuts. Consider, too, that the problem may have occurred when you smacked a big nail into the wall—it's possible to drive a nail into a bundle of wires, creating an accidental connection through the nail. Find the problem spike. If your searching has yielded no results, it is time to call an electrician.

**Replacing fuses.** If you need to replace a fuse, turn off the main power (not just a single breaker) in the circuit breaker box. This is important! Remove the faceplate from the box; typically you'll have to remove a few screws that hold the face in place. Each breaker should have two wires connected to it, one bringing electricity into the breaker and one leading out. Loosen the screws that hold these wires and bend the wires out of the way. The circuit breaker itself should now pop from its slot with finger power or with the use of a screwdriver to pry the breaker loose. Pop the new breaker into place and connect the wires to their appropriate terminals. Screw the faceplate onto the breaker box and restart the power.

## Four Rules for Safety in Electrical Repairs

Much of the safety information listed here is common sense, but it's worth repeating—when it comes to electricity, it's better to be safe than sorry. (And always keep in mind that sometimes the safest thing to do is to call a professional.)

**Turn off the mains and/or unplug the item.** Yes, the most obvious starting point, but don't get so interested in what you're doing ("Hey, I know how to fix that!") that you forget the most basic safety rule when making electrical or electronic repairs.

**Take off metal jewelry and wear rubber gloves.** Accidentally brushing a ring or watch against a metal circuit may cause an unpleasant shock while you're working.

Next time your fuse blows, thank it for its sacrifice in its sleepless quest for fire safety: A fuse blows when too much electricity passes through the circuit. The flow of electricity is interrupted by the breaker so that the sudden energy surge does not overheat the circuit and possibly cause a fire.

Slip off any jewelry, and you might consider wearing rubber work gloves if possible, since rubber is an excellent insulator against electricity.

**Be sure everything is totally dry.** Don't stand on a damp basement floor while you work. Be sure your hands are completely dry. Don't have on a damp shirt, cuffs or sleeves, either from sweat or rain or anything else. Electricity and damp combined are a serious safety hazard.

**Don't close the circuit.** If it's at all practical, work with one hand to prevent possibly making yourself part of an electrical circuit.

# #181
## HOW TO REWIRE A LAMP

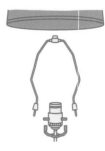

Whether it's a new-to-you lamp that's actually very old or a lamp you love whose wires have frayed, learning to rewire a lamp is an easy way to give your decor new life. First, evaluate the wiring: Check the sheathing for cracks or exposed wire. Check the switch and the plug prongs—they should be strong and free of rust. Any fails on this list and you'll need to get a new cord in addition to new wiring.

## TOOLS:

**Wire cutter** ▪ **Screwdriver**

## MATERIALS:

- **Electrical cord and two-pronged plug**
- **Two-way switch and/or socket (if needed)**

**1** **BUY NEW WIRING.** If the lamp is easy enough to transport, take it with you to the hardware store to shop for wiring, or bring along a photo that includes the lamp's old wiring. Most modern appliances use a flat electrical cord, and for a lamp, a two-pronged plug is adequate. You will need enough cord to run from the desired wall outlet up through the entire height of your lamp. You may want to add a switch along the length of the cord, or perhaps swap out the existing switch on the lamp. Evaluate the integrity of the lamp's socket, socket cap, and terminals,

too, replacing anything if it is at all in doubt.

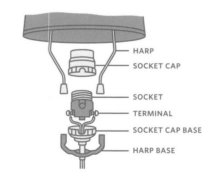

HARP
SOCKET CAP
SOCKET
TERMINAL
SOCKET CAP BASE
HARP BASE

**2** **DISASSEMBLE THE LAMP.** First, make sure it's unplugged. The base of a modern floor lamp is almost certainly held together by a nut that attaches to a tube. The cord runs inside this tube. Beyond that generality, you'll have to explore your lamp to learn its specifics. Old lamps may run the cord along the outside directly to the socket, and handmade lamps may have no base at all or run the cord in an unexpected way. In any case, note how the old cord enters the lamp and its path through or along the lamp body. Remove

the shade and, if one exists, the top of the wire harp that supports it. In one piece, unscrew the socket and its cap, and remove the wire harp base, if applicable. Use a wire cutter to cut the plug from the old wire. Use the socket still connected to the cord to pull a length of slack cord up through the system—but don't pull it completely through yet!

**3** **THREAD THE WIRE.** Once you've cut off the old plug, attach the new wire to the bottom end of the old wire with a wire cap and then pull the socket from above to thread the new wire up through the lamp. If the lamp includes a built-in switch, you'll need to run wire to the switch and then again from the switch to the socket terminals. In that case, attach new wire to the switch and run the wire along the path of the old wire so you end with new wire poking out the top of the lamp.

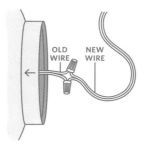

OLD WIRE  NEW WIRE

**4** **KNOT THE WIRE.** Slide the harp base (if used) and socket cap base over the new wire. Cut between the wires to separate about 3" of the end of the two-threaded wire. Strip about ½" of insulation from each end. Because you don't want the weight of the wire pulling down against the connections, tie a knot in the wires that will be supported by the socket cap—this is called an underwriter's knot. Make a loop in each wire and then pass the end of each opposite strand through each loop. You should end with a high-profile knot that won't pull through the base of the socket cap.

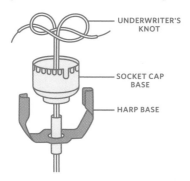

UNDERWRITER'S KNOT

SOCKET CAP BASE

HARP BASE

**5** **WIRE THE SOCKET.** The hot wire is encased in the smooth sheath, and the neutral wire is encased in ridged sheath. The socket itself will have a brass terminal for the hot wire and a silver terminal for the neutral wire. Loosen the terminal screws and wrap the stripped lengths of wire around the appropriate terminals so the insulation is fairly flush with the terminals and very little if any exposed copper wire is visible. Tighten the screws to hold the wire in place (if additional stripped wire bulges from beneath screw terminals, shorten the stripped wire and reattach it). Slip the socket down into the socket cap and screw or otherwise seat the wire sandwich down into the lamp.

**6** **ATTACH A PLUG AND SWITCH.** Most simple electrical cord switches include a removable cover that hides in and out terminals—the only tricky part is keeping track of the smooth and ridged sides of the cord, to ensure that you match the hot in with the hot out, and the neutral in with the neutral out (the kind of wire that went in should be the same as the wire that comes out). Once you have carefully matched

the wires, wrap them around the screws on the correct terminals as determined by the way the switch is made. Plugs also include a removable cover—for two-pronged plugs, try squeezing the prongs together to release the core from the cover. Inside the core are two screws; again, brass for hot and silver for neutral. Hook the appropriate wire over the appropriate screw, turn to tighten, and replace the cap.

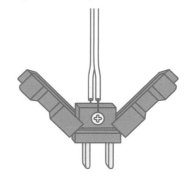

**7** **PUT THE LAMP BACK TOGETHER.** Ensure that all connections are secure and all protective caps and covers are reinstalled. Completely reassemble the lamp, including the base, bulb, and any other pieces removed during rewiring. Turn the switch to the "off" position and then plug in the lamp. Flip the switch to test.

## Lighting a Room Like a Pro

In Hollywood, a lighting director is no minor job, because good lighting can help make someone a star. And while you may not intend to star in your own personal show every time you walk in the living room, properly lighting a room takes more skill than screwing in a bulb and flipping the switch. There are many types of lights and bulbs, each with their own best use. Combine these resources to create lighting that makes you feel good when you walk in the room:

**Ambient lighting.** A room's ambient light source is the base around which you'll build additional lighting. In the daytime, ambient lighting may come from sunlight. In the absence of sunlight, a room's ambient light is typically provided by ceiling or wall-mounted fixtures like a central chandelier or track lighting.

**Task lighting.** As the name implies, task lighting is placed to aid specific activities in various areas of the house. For example, you might place a lamp near the couch for reading or over-counter lighting for preparing food. Where ambient lighting keeps you from tripping over things, task lighting highlights the things you really need to see.

**Accent lighting.** Do you want to make sure visitors notice the Picasso sketch you've placed in a glass case? Use accent lighting to call attention to it. As a rule of thumb, the lights you use to accent your home's best features should be three times as bright as the surrounding ambient and task lighting. To accomplish this ratio, use brighter bulbs, use more bulbs, or focus a bulb's light on areas to be highlighted.

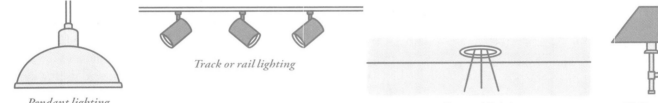

*Pendant lighting*

*Track or rail lighting*

*Recessed lighting*

*Wall sconces*

# WHICH FIXTURE WHERE?

Figure that you need 200 watts for every 50 square feet of a room, then divide those 200 watts among a few styles of lighting fixtures.

• Chandeliers are commonly used as a source of ambient light in dining rooms, but can be fitted with down-pointing sockets for task lighting or a dimmer for bedroom use.

• Pendants hang from the ceiling and—with a shade and dimmer—provide ambient light or, if more focused, provide task lighting.

• Track or rail lighting provides design flexibility and the ability to point small, individual lights as needed for accenting features or specific areas of a room.

• Recessed lighting adds brightness without being visible and is a subtle choice that can be used for ambient, accent, or task lighting.

• Wall sconces connect to our torch-lit, castle-dwelling pasts and can liven a dead wall or hallway, or even be paired with a headboard for bedtime reading.

**Types of bulbs.** Most lighting designers recommend staying away from fluorescent tubes because they cast a slightly pale glow that makes skin look sickly. That said, the best type of bulb depends on the function of a room— fluorescent tubes may be

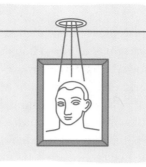

just fine for the basement or garage (as long as you can avoid hitting them with a ladder). Incandescent bulbs are the historical standby—however, these inefficient bulbs are on the outs—they're banned in some states—for environmental reasons. Halogen bulbs, compact fluorescent lightbulbs (CFLs), and light-emitting diodes (LEDs) are primarily replacing these electricity suckers.

Halogen bulbs are common and relatively inexpensive when you consider their increased efficiency and lifespan compared to incandescent bulbs. They do require that you take a couple of precautions—touching the glass during installation can leave a film of oil that shortens the life of the bulb, and because they reach temperatures of 300 degrees Fahrenheit, take care not to touch the bulb when lit or to install a halogen bulb near flammable materials. Fluorescent bulbs burn nearly without heat and are extremely efficient. CFLs are becoming the standard replacement for incandescent bulbs in fixtures that don't include a dimmer switch—fluorescent light is either on or off, there is no dimming. On the plus side, CFLs can last about 10,000 hours. Most lighting designers consider LED an up-and-coming technology—it's extremely efficient but currently doesn't pack the punch of lumens offered by other kinds of bulbs. Consider LEDs for lighting very small, defined areas, but leave the heavy lifting to halogens and CFLs.

**Room-specific lighting.** Again, your lighting design must match the function of the room. The kitchen is a functional place—light it accordingly, with task lights pointed at the various prepping and cooking areas, and of course the sink. Because the focus of a dining room is almost always the table, this is a good room for a strong centralized light source, such as a chandelier. The opposite is true of a study or home office—a strong overhead light should be replaced by task lights pointed at reading and work spaces. Bedrooms are similar to studies—install reading lights by the bed and desk, perhaps a floor lamp for dressing, and consider an overhead light with a dimmer for ambient use. For your primary bathroom, you'll likely want an especially bright light by the mirror. For guest bathrooms, consider the softer touch of sconces with dimmers.

The living room is where your creative lighting sense should shine. In the living room, more so than anywhere else in the house, lighting is part of the decor. Think of lighting in layers—rather than a single overly bright source, incorporate a range of fixtures, including table and floor lamps and recessed or track lighting. Use accent lighting to draw attention to the room's best features, be they architectural aspects or design elements, like art or plants. Consider not only the types of fixtures and bulbs and the directions in which they point, but also how you can diffuse the light with shades. A lamp can go from being a harsh eyesore to warmly glowing with the addition of an elegant shade.

## To create the first functional lightbulb, Thomas Edison used a strip of paper coated in carbon, attached it to a battery with wire, and put it inside a vacuum-sealed glass globe.

## Holiday Lights 101

At the end of the year, when the days darken early, there's nothing more festive than some holiday lights. And there are few things more frustrating than putting up a string of good, solid, expensive lights that you've used successfully the last several seasons. . . and finding that they won't turn on. Or the red ones are burnt out, or only half the string will light up.

If you're using super-cheap lights that you grabbed from a bargain bin at the front of a big-box store, well, they may not be fixable and may simply have to be replaced. But those cheapie lights that break with ease tend to be shorter strings of lights. You may have invested a fair amount in the longer strings of lights that you use to decorate the Christmas tree or hang along the eaves of your front porch, and those lights are worth a little effort. With some care and attention, you can get the festive lights back on and earn your cup of eggnog as you sit back and survey the scene.

**Change the fuses.** Longer strings of lights often have a fuse in the plug. If the plug is big, or has a box slightly up the string from it, your string most likely has fuses. With the string unplugged, slide back the plastic plate on the surface (there may be a small screw holding it in place—don't lose it!) and replace the one or two fuses you find inside. These are usually simple small fuses, and some spares may have come with your lights. Otherwise, replacement fuses are easily found where holiday lights are sold. If this doesn't get your bulbs blinking. . .

**Test all the bulbs.** This sounds like an onerous job, but the testers for holiday lights (probably sold right next to those replacement fuses) are inexpensive and easy to use. Read the packaging and try to buy the kind that only requires you to touch the bulb, not remove each bulb from its socket. As you work, tighten each bulb. Make sure none are loose or partially disconnected. You may have a loose bulb rather than a blown one, and you don't want to pass the whole string of lights through your hands a second time if you don't find one that's burnt out.

**Continue to the end.** If you do come across a blown bulb, stop and replace it, but don't lose your spot on the string. There could be additional burnt-out lights farther along, and any one of them could be blocking your holiday cheer. Continue testing to the end of the line, replacing as necessary, and including any additional strings you may have plugged together on the entire chain of lights.

**Don't let it happen next year.** If the lights came in the sort of packaging where every individual light has a slot, it's probably worth the time to pack them away with care to prevent them loosening in their sockets or breaking. If you don't have the original package, try wrapping them gently, not tightly, around a sturdy piece of cardboard to prevent them from flapping around and the bulbs banging off one another during those ten months when the lights are stored in the garage. Do not wrap your light strings in a loop around your forearm, like a rock band roadie might wrap an extension cord. That's just asking for them to break. Instead, coil them loosely and store them in a box, perhaps in a bed of all that crumpled tissue paper left over from your holiday unwrapping spree.

# MECHANICAL

Even if you think you're not a mechanic, you'll likely face an issue with one or all of your modes of transportation, whether that be bicycle, car, or motorcycle. Luckily, there are a lot of repair jobs that can be accomplished with only a few basic tools. Some auto repairs are so simple that there's absolutely no reason to take your car to a garage—other than your own!—to fix it. And anyone who rides a bike should be able to repair a flat. With these tools on hand, you can.

# GARAGE TOOL KIT

Tape

Wheel chocks

Pens

Magnetic pickup

Multimeter

Jack stands

Phillips-head screwdrivers

Flathead screwdrivers

Wire stripper

Socket wrench set

Pressure gauge

Hammer

Wire brush

Floor jack

Wrench set

Chisels

Rags

Flashlight

Funnel

Oil pan

Slip-joint or channel lock pliers

Set of punches

Pry bars

Files

Hacksaw

## Garage Tools

The crux of auto work is diagnosing the problem and having the right tool to fix it. As you'll discover, almost all car work can be done with just a handful of tool types. Here are the essential tools to keep in the garage.

**Screwdriver set.** Yes, most Phillips-head screwdrivers will fit most cross-head screws (+) and most flathead screwdrivers will fit most slot screws (–), but matching size as well as shape can help ensure a clean turn without stripping the head or dulling the driver. Because auto work might require turning screws in tough-to-reach places, make sure at least one of each type of screwdriver is magnetic so that you can work one-handed without having to hold the screw in place. In addition to a set of standard screwdrivers that includes a range of diameters and lengths, consider adding a set of hex drivers, commonly called Allen wrenches, which you'll need to turn bolts with hexagonal holes in their heads.

**Socket wrench set.** It used to be that Japanese and European cars used exclusively metric nuts and bolts, whereas American cars used inches. Now parts are sourced from everywhere and you'll need a socket wrench set for each system of measurement. It's worth making a precise match. Also look for a set with a couple of wrench extensions, which can increase your torque for pulling on an especially sticky or welded nut or improve your precision when working in tight spaces. And add a DIY cheater pipe: a length of spare, hollow pipe that you slip around a ratchet to increase your torque. A socket wrench set that comes with a spark plug socket is a bonus.

**Wrench set.** You already have a socket wrench set, but there's nothing like just the right wrench to reach tight spots. Like your sockets, you'll want wrenches from about 8 to 22 millimeters or ¼ to ⅞ inch. It's useful to buy wrenches that are open on one side and "box" on the other, allowing you to slot the box side completely over a bolt or slip the open end around a bolt if it's tough to get at. Augment with a couple of sizes of adjustable wrenches: 8- and 12-inch wrenches are a good place to start. These adjustables aren't nearly as good for aggressive tightening or loosening, but there's nothing like the ability to adjust by a millimeter or two instead of sliding all the way out from under your car to retrieve the next size fixed wrench. You'll also want a specialized oil filter wrench, a lug wrench sized to your tires (to be kept in the trunk of your cars), and maybe a torque wrench, used to tighten bolts to a specific pressure.

**Pliers.** You can never have too many pliers, and you'd be sorry to be caught without at least the basics of large and small sizes of slip-joint pliers (the kind with the sliding adjustment groove): Channellock (the eponymous tongue-and-groove slip-lock plier), needle-nose, and large and small locking wrenches, like a 7-inch Vise-Grip. You can't use Vise-Grip pliers in place of a socket or box wrench, but they're darn useful for grabbing things that don't otherwise want to be grabbed, like rounded nuts and headless screws.

**Hammer.** Most automotive work is best done with a ball-peen hammer—the one with a flat face on one side and a curved head on the other. (In the garage, use pry bars for prying, not a hammer's claw.) You'll want a couple of hammer weights, ranging from 8 ounces on the tiny side to 32 ounces on the huge side. If you're working with older cars or imagine needing to do extensive work, add a small sledge, which you can use to knock rusty bits that need extra oomph.

**Floor jack, jack stands, wheel chocks.** Much of the garage work on your car will take place underneath it, so you'll need tools to raise it safely. The basic process is to pull the emergency brake, use wheel chocks to ensure that the car can't roll forward or backward, use a floor jack to raise the car off the ground, and use jack stands to keep it up. First, the floor jack: a 2-ton floor jack might be more than your car needs, but it should run only about $10 more than a 1.5-ton jack and even with smaller cars is easier to use, requiring less power and fewer strokes to raise the car. Start with two adjustable-height floor jacks. (No matter what kind you get, make sure the jack weight capacity exceeds the weight of your car.) And wheel chocks work better than bricks—by placing these curved wheel-stoppers against tires that aren't jacked up, you can help ensure that your car doesn't slide off the jacks and on to you.

**Miscellaneous tools.** Pressure gauge, magnetic pickup tool, multimeter (to test voltage, resistance, and amperage), punches, chisels, files, pens, tape, pry bars of various sizes, wire stripper, wire brush, oil pan, funnel, hacksaw, rags, and a couple of good flashlights (because one will inevitably be broken . . .).

# TRUNK TOOL KIT

Blanket

Flares

Bungee cords

Poncho

Water

Food

Phillips-head screwdrivers

Flathead screwdrivers

Small socket wrench or nut driver set

First-aid kit

Flashlight

Knife

Replacement fuses

Jack

Tow strap

Tire pressure gauge

Tire iron

Electrical tape

Duct tape

Slip-joint or channel lock pliers

Jumper cables

Lug wrench

Spare tire

Here's what to keep in your trunk for emergency repairs on the road. As with a first-aid kit, the goal here is to be able to patch everything up just enough to get to better care.

You should carry much more than tools in your car's emergency kit, including but not limited to flares, water, food, a blanket, poncho, first-aid kit, and flashlight. These things keep you safe while you're futzing with the tools on this list in the attempt to get back on the road. Basically, you should carry a pared-down version of your garage kit and a couple of other items specific to emergency repairs. You can buy these kits ready-made or piece together your own. Here are the components of a strong roadside repair kit: large and small Phillips and flathead screwdrivers, slip-joint pliers, tire pressure gauge, electrical tape, duct tape, small (10-piece) socket wrench or nut driver set, replacement fuses, jumper cables, 2-ton tow strap, basic pocket knife, and bungee cords. Of course, you should also have tire-changing equipment in the trunk, including a jack, lug wrench (aka tire iron), and spare tire.

**Engines, gears, and moving parts.** These sound complicated, and they are. In this section, and especially when working with cars and motorcycles (as opposed to bicycles), there's a hair trigger on giving up and taking it to the experts. That said, there are absolutely things you can do at home without fancy lifts and expensive pneumatic tools. Some of these things are faster and easier than scheduling an appointment at the garage and figuring out how you're going to get around without a car for the day.

**Life-saving stuff.** Poncho, blanket, water, food (such as sealed energy bars), flares, a knife, and a first-aid kit are things that automobile drivers would really prefer never to use as they journey safely from Point A to Point B. But if you ever needed those items—and plenty of drivers have—you'd be very glad to have such a well-stocked trunk.

**Tire changing tools.** Make sure your spare always has air, and don't take the lug wrench out and forget to put it back. The jack never leaves the trunk, either, unless you're using it on the car.

**Quick-fix stuff.** A bungee cord, duct and electrical tape, pliers, socket and screwdriver sets, a tire pressure gauge, and jumper cables can all get you out of a tight spot in a hurry.

**Tow strap.** When all else fails. If you have a tow strap, someone can get your vehicle to help. Or you can tow someone else to help.

First-aid kits came into being in the late 19th century—a time when, if injury struck, a doctor would have been summoned on foot. Relying entirely upon the speed of the human body meant that precious minutes or even hours could be lost before the hurt individual received treatment.

# #182
## HOW TO WASH A CAR

It takes some elbow grease, and attention to detail, to get a gleaming, spotless car (just ask the people down at the car wash). But it's an easy car maintenance task to DIY, and on a warm summer day, it's even kind of fun. Don't use kitchen soap—it may strip your car's wax. Instead, use soap specially designed for cars.

### WAX ON, WAX OFF

**W**ax should be applied with your right hand in clockwise strokes and removed with your left hand in counterclockwise strokes—that is, if you're Ralph Macchio in *The Karate Kid.* For the rest of us, the exact strokes don't matter so much, as long as you use a clean, soft, lint-free cloth. A liquid or soft wax is fine for most washings. If it's been a while, consider a hard or paste wax, which will protect your car longer but will also be more difficult to apply and remove. For the most durable care, go with a polymer preservative. With a soft or liquid wax, apply to the whole car according to the package instructions and then use a lint-free cloth to polish the car clean. With a hard wax, apply to only a small section at a time and then polish clean before the wax sets into an impenetrable veneer.

### TOOLS:

Rags • 2 buckets • Garden hose • Large sponge or wash mitt • Long-bristled brush and short, stiff-bristled brush (optional)

### MATERIALS:

- Car wash soap
- Car wax
- Glass cleaner

**1 PARK THE CAR IN THE SHADE.** If you leave a very wet car in the sun, it will get spots similar to those on an improperly washed wineglass. You will need to be parked within reaching distance of a garden hose. And don't forget to close the windows! When your car is situated, mix the car wash soap in a bucket as instructed on the wash bottle. Fill another bucket with plain water.

**2 HOSE DOWN THE CAR.** Rinse it clean of major debris. Stay away from high-pressure jets of water, which can drive grit across the car's finish, potentially scratching it. Likewise, angle the spray down near the windows, as water pressure can blast through loose window molding and leak into the car.

**3 SOAP THE CAR.** Pull the windshield wipers up and then scrub the car with soapy water, using a large sponge or wash mitt. Start at the top and spiral your way down, soaping up one small area at a time. This is like sweeping your house from the corners first—starting at the top ensures that dirt rains down and away from cleaned areas. When the sponge or mitt looks gray, rinse it in the bucket of plain water (don't squeeze it into the soapy water). Once you've scrubbed an area of the car from top to bottom, rinse it with the hose before going on to the next section. Don't let the soap dry on any area, and periodically spray the entire car with the hose to keep it from drying (again, to prevent the spotty wineglass effect).

**4 CLEAN THE WHEELS AND** lower panels. Use an old wash mitt or sponge to scrub the lowest parts of the car last. These are the grimiest parts of the car and there's no need to sully a good sponge with the worst of the dirt. You might consider using a long-bristled brush to clean the hubcap spokes, then a short, stiff-bristled brush to clean the tires' sidewalls.

## FOR BRIGHTER HEADLIGHTS . . .

The difference between hazy and clear headlights can be the difference between seeing and not seeing the deer in the road ahead of you. If your lights are looking dim, it might be time to polish the headlight covers. After you've washed your car, cover the area around your headlights with painter's tape and use a drill-mounted polisher and plastic polish to de-haze the plastic covers. (If they're really dirty, consider removing the covers and cleaning the inside as well.) One common drill-mounted polishing tool is called Mothers PowerBall, which can be found at most auto supply stores.

**5 RINSE AGAIN.** Once more, rinse the car from the top down, spraying underneath to loosen road grime. This is especially important in the winter to make sure salt deposits from icy or snowy roads don't eat away at your undercarriage.

**6 BEFORE THE WATER HAS TIME** to evaporate, use towels to dry the car thoroughly, again from the top down. Use Windex or another glass cleaning product on the windows to avoid streaking. If you want to apply wax, now is the time. (See Wax On, Wax Off, opposite, for details.)

## No time to wash? Live in a drought zone? Using glass cleaner to wipe down windows and windshields can make a big difference in appearance and water conservation.

# #183
# HOW TO DETAIL THE INTERIOR OF A CAR

Cleaning your car is like cleaning your house—it's all about work flow. There's a certain order of doing things when detailing a car, mostly to avoid dirtying surfaces you've already cleaned. Also, as with housecleaning, standardizing the way you clean your car assures that you don't miss any hard-to-reach or hard-to-remember spots. Follow these instructions from start to finish and your car will shine inside.

## TOOLS:

**Vacuum cleaner** ▪ **Rags**

## MATERIALS:

- **Foaming car upholstery cleaner**
- **Compressed air**
- **Cotton swabs**
- **Glass cleaner**
- **Surface cleaner**

**1 CLEAN THE FLOOR MATS.** Remove all mats, front and back, and beat them free of debris. A heavy shoe works well, or a broom handle. Outside the car, coat the floor mats with a foaming cleaner designed for car upholstery. Work the cleaner into the mats with a rag and continue adding cleaner until the mats are saturated. Let them sit while you work on the rest of the interior. When they're dry, vacuum them and put them back into the floorboards.

**2 VACUUM THE INTERIOR.** Use a coin-operated car-wash vacuum, a wet-dry vacuum, or, as a last resort, your household vacuum to clean the car's upholstery. Use the smallest nozzle attachment to vacuum hard-to-reach places like the insides of door panel pockets, around the gearshift, and along the front dash and rear window ledge. Push the front seats all the way forward and then vacuum behind and underneath them. Push the seats all the way backward and vacuum underneath from the front. Don't forget the trunk and in between the backseats, where crumbs tend to accumulate.

Ray Harroun won the 1911 Indianapolis 500 after he attached a mirror to see behind his car instead of using a lookout (a crewman positioned to watch competing cars). It was thus that the rearview mirror was born.

**3 SHAMPOO THE UPHOLSTERY.** Use the foaming cleaner on the interior, this time stopping short of saturating it so you don't get mildew. If you have a vinyl or leather interior be sure to use a cleaner specific to the material (not foaming upholstery cleaner!).

**4 CLEAN THE NOOKS AND** crannies. Use a can of compressed air to blow dirt, dust, and grime from crevices and areas around buttons and dials. Use cotton swabs to clean air vents.

**5 WIPE DOWN INTERIOR** surfaces like the dashboard, parking brake, plastic interior panels, console, and steering wheel with an interior cleaner.

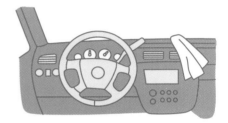

**6 CLEAN THE GLASS.** Use a glass cleaner (such as Windex) and a lint-free rag or paper towels to clean the insides of all windows, as well as the rearview and vanity mirrors.

✕ ✕ ✕ ✕ ✕ ✕ ✕ ✕ ✕ ✕ ✕ ✕ ✕ ✕ ✕ ✕ ✕ ✕ ✕ ✕ ✕ ✕ ✕ ✕ ✕ ✕ ✕ ✕ ✕ ✕ ✕ ✕ ✕ ✕ ✕ ✕ ✕

## QUICK FIX FOR UPHOLSTERY HOLES

If you have a small hole or stain in your car's upholstery, consider using a razor blade to cut a patch just bigger than the unsightly hole from an unseen area, like the underside of a seat. Then use the razor blade to clean the edges of the hole or cut around the stain. Use a small amount of epoxy or other water-resistant adhesive to carefully glue the patch in place. Holes in vinyl or leather upholstery can be patched with kits made for those materials.

# #184
## HOW TO BANG OUT A DENT

**B**odywork used to be easy—you got a dent? Just bang it out. However, banging on a plastic or fiberglass body panel is likely to do nothing but make the dent worse or even punch through the panel. So basic auto bodywork depends in large part on what your car's made of—find out the material of your panels before going any further.

If your car's panels are made of metal, which is pliable, you can bend small dents back into shape. Either an indentation will pop back to its convex form, or you can rework the shape of the metal. If you have plastic panels, duct tape your dents together as best you can and head for the nearest auto body shop. If you are feeling ambitious, consider ordering and installing your own replacement plastic panels from the dealer. Many plastic panels on modern cars simply click into place.

### TOOLS:

**Auto body or planishing hammer** ▪ **Wheel chocks** ▪ **Metal dolly**

**1** **LEVEL THE DENT.** Starting on the outside of the panel, use an auto body hammer to lightly pound the ridge of raised metal around the dent. You don't need to flatten it completely, but do your best to return this ridge to the level of the surrounding panel. Be aware that this

will likely hurt the paint, and so if you're reworking a dent, you might also have to repaint.

**2** **HAMMER THE BACK OF THE** dent. With the car on a flat surface, in gear or in park, block the tires with wheel chocks and put the parking brake on. Reach under the wheel well to access the back of the dent. You may be able to access a dent in the front fenders by raising the hood or in the back fender by opening the trunk and removing panels. If you hammer straight into the back of a dent, you will almost certainly end up punching through the metal. Instead, reach around to the front of the dent and hold a metal dolly (which looks like a metal

bar of soap) against the outside of the dent while you hammer against the inside. If your arms aren't long enough to reach both sides of the dent, you'll need a helper to hold the dolly while you hammer. Hammer the dent, from the front and back if necessary, braced against the dolly, until it smooths out.

# #185 HOW TO FILL A DING OR SCRATCH WITH PUTTY

If you have a small ding or scratch, or if you've hammered a larger dent back into a reasonable approximation of its original shape, it's time to smooth over the affected section with putty. You will end up with a somewhat unsightly patch—see How to Repaint Your Repair, page 372, to get your paint job back in tip-top shape.

## TOOLS:

**Wire brush, orbital sander, or sanding disk attached to a drill • Rags • 2-inch putty knife • Smooth-grain sandpaper**

## MATERIALS:

- **Rubbing alcohol**
- **Auto body putty (such as Bondo)**
- **Scrap cardboard**

**1 CLEAN THE SURFACE.** Start by removing any rust around the ding or scratch with a wire brush, orbital sander, or sanding disk in a drill, then clean the area with alcohol.

**2 APPLY PUTTY.** The brand name Bondo is synonymous with auto body dent repair, though other kinds of putty exist (and Bondo's parent company, 3M, sells a nice dent-repair kit that includes putty and all other needed supplies). To use Bondo, mix the putty with the bonding catalyst (following package instructions) on a piece of scrap cardboard. Make sure no leaves or dog hair have floated into your clean dent while you weren't looking, and then use a putty knife to spread Bondo over the dent. If you're repairing a rusted-out section of panel, apply the putty to the front and back of the panel until you've built an appropriate base. The more the putty overflows the dimensions of the dent, the more sanding you'll have to do later—but better too much than too little.

**3 DRY THE PATCH.** If it's a sunny day, park the car with the repair in the sun to dry. If not, consider pointing a heat lamp or hair dryer at the patch. Dry for at least 30 minutes and run your hand over the patch to check that it's not still tacky. Sand the patch with smooth-grain sandpaper until it's smooth with the body panel, then repaint as needed (see How to Repaint Your Repair, page 372).

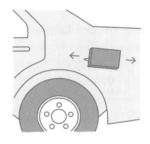

× × × × × × × × × × × × × × × × × × × × × × × × × × × × × × × × × × × × ×

## SANDING A SCRATCH

If you see a scratch in your car's paint, make sure that it isn't just something stuck to the outside of the panel—run your fingernail over the mark to see if it has depth. If your fingernail doesn't catch on the scratch, that means you have a scratch in your car's clear coat that doesn't extend down through the paint. Instead of filling the scratch, you can simply hide it by sanding down the surrounding finish to the level of the base of the scratch. Start by rubbing something into the scratch that contrasts with the car's paint color—shoe polish or Wite-Out work well. Now you'll gently sand the scratched area with very fine, 2,000-grit wet sandpaper until the shoe polish or other material disappears, at which point you'll know you've reached the base of the scratch. While sanding, pour ample water over the scratched area. Polish with rubbing compound and then finish with wax.

# #186
## HOW TO REPAINT YOUR REPAIR

Once you've repaired a ding, scratch, or dent, it's time to paint over the repair. The layers of auto body paint go from steel panel, to primer, to color, to clear coat. If you're looking to repaint a scratch, first check the depth of the scratch. What color is it? If you see the car's color, follow the sanding instructions on page 371 and then just apply a layer of clear coat. If you see primer that is different from the car's color, apply color and clear coat. If you see bare steel (or very discolored plastic), you'll have to apply all three. Unless you have an unusual car, your auto shop should have the matching paint.

## TOOLS:

**Rags** ▪ **80-grit sandpaper** ▪ **Thin paintbrush**

## MATERIALS:

- **Automotive body prep solvent**
- **Auto body primer**
- **Auto body paint**
- **Clear coat**
- **Car wash soap**
- **Car wax**

**1** USE A COLORLESS SOLVENT specific to auto painting to meticulously clean the surface to be painted.

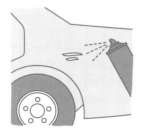

**2** APPLY PRIMER. When repainting a car completely, an auto shop will use spray primer. Ask your local auto shop for primer recommendations to use with your car and the size of your repair.

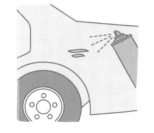

**3** IF THE AREA TO BE PAINTED IS larger than, say, a quarter, sand the primer with fine-grain sandpaper while pouring water over the area. Let dry, add a second coat, and dry according to the primer instructions.

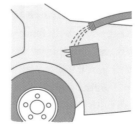

**4** USE A THIN PAINTBRUSH TO apply at least three coats of color paint, letting each coat dry thoroughly before applying the next.

**5** AFTER THE LAST COAT OF PAINT has thoroughly dried, apply the clear coat. Again, talk to your auto-parts store about which clear coat to use.

**6** FINALLY, WASH AND WAX the repaired area.

# #187
## HOW TO CHANGE A WINDSHIELD WIPER BLADE

**A** good windshield with good wiper blades goes a long way toward avoiding accidents—better visibility means lower risk. If the rubber blade is cracked or weathered, is screeching against the glass, or is leaving streaks or areas of the windshield untouched, it's time to change the blade. Even if yours seem fine, the National Highway Transportation Board recommends changing wiper blades at least every year and ideally every six months. It's much easier to install new blades on a sunny afternoon than it is to do the same on the side of the road some icy night. Take a couple of minutes to ensure your car-sight is everything that it should be.

## TOOLS:

**Screwdriver**

## MATERIALS:

- **Replacement blades**
- **Replacement clips**

**1 PULL THE OLD WIPER ASSEMBLY** away from the windshield. There are three common types of windshield wiper blade attachments: hook-slot, pin arm, and straight-end connectors. Hook-slots are the easiest to work with—look for a small tab on the underside of the wiper that holds the blade in place. Press the tab and slide the wiper clean of the blade. Pin arms are similar to hook-slots—either push the pin or remove it to free the old blade from its mount. Straight-end connectors usually require a

screwdriver to release the old blade. Once you have the blade removed, avoid letting the metal arm slam back against the glass windshield. If you need, the exposed metal arm can rest gently in the "down" position against the windshield.

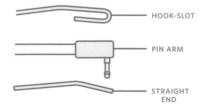

HOOK-SLOT

PIN ARM

STRAIGHT END

**2 EVALUATE THE WIPER.** Determine whether you need to replace the plastic wiper clip or just the rubber blade. If replacing the clip, examine the connection of clip to arm to discover how to free it. Commonly, wiper arms will include a U-shaped metal end that slots around the wiper clip. Discover

how to free the clip and then take notes or a picture to remember how to put it back later. If needed, remove the old wiper clips and replace with new ones, being sure to orient the new clips correctly. The new wiper clip should click into place with its mount inside the U-shaped curve at the end of the wiper arm.

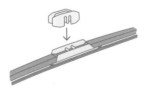

**3 INSTALL NEW RUBBER BLADES** the same way you removed the old ones. Gently lower the assembly back to the window.

# #188

# HOW TO FIX A CHIPPED WINDSHIELD

There are a number of ways to repair windshield dings, including taking the car to a repair shop, where it should take a technician five minutes to fill the nick, and your insurance company is likely to cover the repair pre-deductible (it would rather pay a little for a repair now than a lot for a replacement later). If you decide to do it yourself, buy a windshield repair kit at a car-parts store or online. Kit specifics will differ, but it should include a doughnut-shaped adhesive to surround the ding, a syringe or similar tool to pull air bubbles from the crack, and resin to fill it.

## TOOLS:

**Razor blade**

## MATERIALS:

- **Rubbing alcohol**
- **Windshield repair kit**
- **Paper towels**

**1 PREPARE THE WINDSHIELD.** Clean the affected area and a couple of inches around it with rubbing alcohol, making sure to remove all windshield gunk from the area and any small chips of glass from within the crack itself.

**2 CREATE A SEAL.** Remove the backing from the adhesive doughnut that came in your kit, and place the center directly on the chip—you want to make an airtight seal around the damage.

**3 REMOVE THE AIR FROM THE** crack. Peel the second backing off the ring to reveal the adhesive and press the syringe-like tool into the ring. Use the syringe to draw air bubbles out of the crack. If the kit allows, lock the syringe in the "up" position and leave it for about 10 minutes.

**4 FILL THE CRACK.** Now reverse the process, using the syringe to slowly add resin to the vacuum you created in the crack. Before the resin dries, have paper towels at the ready and use a razor blade to scrape free the adhesive ring. Dab the adhesive that oozes out with the paper towels.

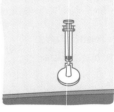

**5 FINISH THE REPAIR.** If your kit includes one, use the small plastic square to smooth adhesive. Let dry in the sun.

# #189

## HOW TO CHANGE A FLAT TIRE

Though modern tire technology makes flats less common than they used to be, there remains no skill more central to car ownership than changing a flat. At some point in your life, you'll get a flat tire, and when you do, it might be on a dirt road without cell coverage, many miles from civilization or the graces of a good Samaritan. In that case, you'll need to know how to fix the flat yourself, with naught but moxie and a couple of tools that should be stashed in your trunk (see Trunk Tool Kit, page 364).

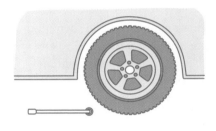

## TOOLS:

**Jack • Lug wrench • Wheel chock**

## MATERIALS:

• **Spare tire**

**1** **PUT THE CAR IN PARK AND APPLY** the parking brake. Turn the engine off, and ensure that the car is on a level surface, far enough away from traffic. If moving the car to level ground is impossible, consider calling for help. Changing a tire on a slant is not worth the risk.

**2** **IF YOU HAVE A WHEEL CHOCK** or can find a substitute, such as a heavy stone, place it behind the wheel that is diagonally opposite the one you're changing. So if you're changing the right rear tire, place a block behind the left front.

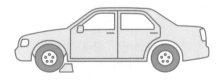

**3** **RETRIEVE YOUR SPARE TIRE** and tools. Your car's spare tire is likely hiding under the floor mat in the trunk. On an SUV, it may be held underneath the vehicle by a wire or attached to the back gate. Look for the jack and lug wrench inside trunk panels or in recessed hatches in the back. Your car may also come equipped with wheel chocks, which make changing a tire slightly safer. If your spare tire is flat, you are out of luck, so check it first.

**4** **LOOSEN THE WHEEL LUGS WITH** the lug wrench. This is the crux of the whole operation. If the lugs are rusted past the point of turning, you won't be able to get the wheel off. To maximize your chances of a successful turn, seat the wrench completely and snugly over the lug. Then crank counterclockwise with all your might. Don't remove the lugs, just loosen them each a couple of turns. If your hub cap is covering the lug nuts, remove it first. Your hubcap may have clips that pop off with a flat screwdriver, or your hubcap may have lugs of its own that screw to the lug posts of your wheel (in that case, unscrew them).

*(continued)*

**5** JACK UP THE CAR. Your owner's manual should indicate the proper jack points—the places on your car's frame strong enough to withstand the pressure of the jack. If not, look underneath the car to locate the vehicle's frame (do not jack the siding!). Generally, the proper place to set a jack is along this frame, on a seam fairly close to the tire being raised. When the car is held firmly in place by its gear, parking brake, and wheel chock, insert the provided handle into the jack and turn the handle to expand the jack itself. The jack should scissor together, pushing the head upward into the jack point. Even after the car's weight is supported by the jack, refrain from putting any part of yourself underneath the vehicle. Despite your best preparation, cars can and do roll off jacks, and you don't want any part of yourself underneath any part of your car. Keep raising the car until the wheel to be changed is completely off the ground.

**6** REMOVE THE LUG NUTS. Use the lug wrench to remove the lug nuts completely and place them in a safe place—inside the hubcap, for example.

**7** PULL OFF THE FLAT TIRE AND then seat the spare onto the wheel studs, lining up the holes in the spare with these metal posts. Expect to get dirty. Tires are heavy and it can be a surprising pain in the neck to get them lined up just right. Stick with it! Fit the spare flush against the brake hub by pushing the tire firmly onto the posts as far as it will go.

**8** HAND-TIGHTEN THE LUG NUTS. These should slip on fairly smoothly, though rust may necessitate a slightly firmer hand. Don't immediately crank them with the lug wrench or you risk cross-threading—damage to the thread that results from misaligned nuts and studs.

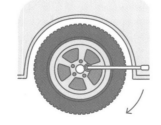

**9** TURN THE JACK HANDLE THE opposite direction to lower the jack, returning the tire to the ground. Once the jack is completely flattened, remove it and re-stow the jack (and the wheel chock, if you used one) in your car.

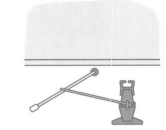

**10** USE THE LUG WRENCH TO completely tighten the lug nuts. Start by gently tightening one nut and then do the same with a nut diagonally across the circle. Continue gently tightening the nuts, each in turn, each time with a little more gusto. After driving no more than a mile, it's a good idea to double-check the tightness of the lug nuts—spinning the tire under pressure can loosen it on the posts.

**11** IF YOU HAVE A COMPACT spare, the maximum speed should be listed on the sidewall. If you have a full-size spare, you should be able to drive at full speed. Note that with the spare on your car and a flat in your trunk, you have no backup in case of another flat. Get the flat fixed quickly and reinstall it on your vehicle, or use the opportunity to get new tires. Make sure your spare is in good condition before re-stowing it.

## The Essentials of Tire Maintenance

Tires are where the rubber meets the road. And when rubber meets road, it leaves a little piece of itself behind every time. But proper maintenance will help your tires last as long as possible.

**Pressure.** Contrary to popular belief, the pressure listed on a tire's sidewall is not necessarily the best pressure for your car. In general, manufacturers list the maximum pressure allowed, not the optimal pressure for grip or efficiency. The less pressure a tire holds, the more it will deform to grip the roadway. The more it grips, the less gas mileage your car will get. The optimal PSI (pounds of air pressure per square inch) should balance performance against mileage. Check the owner's manual or the sticker inside the door frame to discern yours.

**Storage.** If you swap in snow tires seasonally, make sure you properly store your normal tires. Place them in a cool, dark, dry spot, deflate them to half their normal PSI, and, rather than stacking them, set them on their treads.

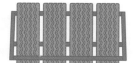

**Tread.** While the inner workings of a modern car may require computer diagnostics, your tires do not. In fact, testing your tread will cost you exactly one cent. Yes, it's the penny test. Place the top of Abe Lincoln's head between your tire's tread

and gently rest the penny against the rubber. If the tire tread comes up past the tip of the presidential hairline, the tire's good to go. Repeat the test on different areas of the tire, checking that the tread is wearing evenly along the inside and outside walls. Uneven wear on treads that pass the test signals that it's time for a tire rotation, alignment, and balancing. Uneven wear that leaves any tread below Lincoln's head means it's time to replace.

**Sidewalls.** The tread isn't the only place a tire can wear out. Check the sidewalls, too. Minor webs of cracks in the sidewall are likely not a major concern, but any crack that threatens to pull apart the rubber signals the end of a tire's life. Likewise, look for bubbles and bulges, which are also dangerous signs that the air inside your tire is close to getting out.

**Expiration date.** Over time, the essential oils in tire rubber evaporate. This is called outgassing. Enough outgassing and the tire becomes brittle. Needless to say, a brittle tire is no good. Manufacturers and oversight agencies disagree at what age a tire has expired, but you should generally be wary of any tire more than ten years old. If you're driving a car regularly, you'll wear out tires long before their expiration date, but when buying new ones, check the date stamped in the small oval on the tire's sidewall to ensure that the tire hasn't been shelved past its useful lifespan.

---

Ants, known for their disciplined pace, never get into traffic jams. Because they don't make unexpected moves, their pattern of movement is much more efficient than cars on the road.

---

# #190 HOW TO ROTATE TIRES

No matter your best efforts at balancing and alignment, your car tires will wear differently. That's especially true of front tires. As you drive, twisting and turning your steering wheel, uneven pavement grates away the rubber on your front tires. On front-wheel-drive cars, where the same tires that are steering are also providing the power, wear is particularly rapid. By rotating your tires, you can ensure that wear patterns are applied evenly, extending the life of your tires. And assuming you don't drive only in a left-hand circle, you shouldn't need to switch the sides of the tires, just swap the fronts for backs.

## TOOLS:

**Jack • 2 jack stands • Lug wrench**

**1 DETERMINE IF YOUR TIRES ARE** interchangeable. For most models, a front tire can be a back and a left can be a right, but a few models use different sizes on the front and back, and some tires change tread from the inside to the outside, making them usable on only one side of the car. If you have non-interchangeable tires, they will not be able to be rotated and will instead need to be replaced.

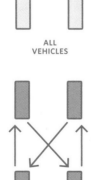

ALL VEHICLES          ALL VEHICLES

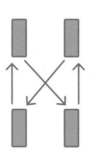

FRONT-WHEEL-DRIVE VEHICLES          REAR- AND FOUR-WHEEL-DRIVE VEHICLES

**2 PARK THE CAR ON A FLAT, LEVEL** surface and engage the parking brake. Place the jack underneath the appropriate jack point (see Step 5, How to Change a Flat Tire, page 376), lift the back tire and then rest the car onto a jack stand. Repeat the procedure in the front so that both of the wheels on one side are off the ground.

**3 SWAP THE TIRES.** Following the instructions in How to Change a Flat Tire, page 375, remove, switch, and reattach the front and back tires. Jack a wheel up off its stand, remove the stand and then lower the jack. Repeat with the second jack.

**4 REPEAT STEP 3 TO ROTATE THE** tires on the other side.

## Most manufacturers recommend rotating your car's tires every 5,000 to 10,000 miles.

# #191
## HOW TO CHECK AND TOP OFF FLUIDS
### (or, Getting Under the Hood)

There are a number of different fluids in your car, each with a way to check and fill as needed. As part of general maintenance, and especially when planning a road trip, check the oil (see page 381) and the transmission, coolant, brake, and window washing fluids. This is a great way to get familiar with what's under the hood, and is among the simplest and most satisfying ways to take your car's upkeep into your own hands.

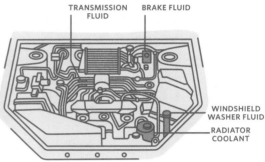

TRANSMISSION FLUID

BRAKE FLUID

WINDSHIELD WASHER FLUID

RADIATOR COOLANT

## MATERIALS:

- **Coolant**
- **Windshield washer fluid**

**1** **POP THE HOOD AND PROP IT** open. With the engine running, start by checking the transmission fluid—the cap is probably located behind the oil cap and a bit lower down. The transmission fluid should have a dipstick—pull out the dipstick, clean it, reinsert, remove, and check the fluid level. If the fluid level is low, that's a big problem—the transmission shouldn't leak. Head to your mechanic to find out what's going on.

**2** **CHECK THE COOLANT.** Make sure the engine is off and cool (not cold) before you touch the radiator. Check both the radiator cap (if your car uses a radiator) and the plastic coolant reservoir. If your car has a radiator, it's right behind the grill; the coolant reservoir should be to its side. Check that the coolant reaches the fill line on the coolant reservoir. If fluid is low, add coolant until it reaches the fill line.

**3** **CHECK THE BRAKE FLUID.** Consult your owner's manual to find the brake fluid reservoir, likely in the engine compartment. Make sure brake fluid fills the reservoir up to the fill line. It shouldn't be low—if it is, take the car to the shop.

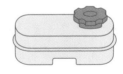

**4** **CHECK THE WASHER FLUID.** This is likely in a plastic reservoir near the dashboard. Again, ensure that fluid fills the reservoir to the fill line. If needed, top it off. Car fluids can look quite similar (think radioactive blue), so be careful not to pour washer fluid into the coolant reservoir and vice versa.

# #192
## HOW TO CHANGE THE OIL

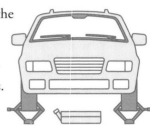

Changing a car's oil is a dirty job, but it's not hard. In fact, even the first time you change the oil, it should take you only an hour or so—half an hour once you've done it a couple of times. Consider that an oil change at the auto shop typically costs around $40. And that's only the direct savings. Consider also the role of oil: to make less friction inside your engine, which translates to less wear and tear and increased gas mileage with lower emissions. Here's how it's done.

## TOOLS:

**Jacks • Safety stands or ramp • Socket wrench • Oil pan • Work gloves • Filter wrench or ratchet**

## MATERIALS:

- **Motor oil**
- **Oil filter**

**1 BUY NEW OIL.** Consult your owner's manual to learn the type and amount of oil (typically five quarts) needed for your car. The Society of Automotive Engineers standardizes the oil labeling system (e.g., 10W-30). The first number (in the example, "10") describes the oil's viscosity at 0 degrees Fahrenheit, and the second number ("30") describes the oil's viscosity at 212 degrees Fahrenheit, or approximately an engine's operating temperature. Motor oils need to be less viscous when cold to avoid being gummy in the winter and more viscous when hot to avoid becoming thin in a hot engine. Generally, the higher the second number—meaning it's more viscous at a high temperature—the better for your engine, because the oil forms better seals and a stronger friction-reducing film. That said, engines are optimized for oil of a certain viscosity. Again, consult your owner's manual and then go to an auto-supply store or gas station to buy the right kind and amount. Note that high-performance engines may require synthetic oil.

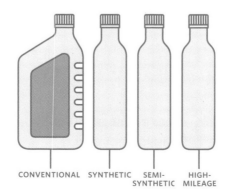

CONVENTIONAL  SYNTHETIC  SEMI-SYNTHETIC  HIGH-MILEAGE

**2 IF NEEDED, LIFT THE CAR.** To change the oil, you'll need to access the oil drain plug underneath the car. If your car doesn't naturally have enough clearance to offer access, either jack it up (see How to Change a Flat Tire, page 375) and put the car on safety stands or drive the car onto steel ramps. In either case, follow the appropriate safety precautions any time you lift a car (also see How to Change a Flat Tire, page 375). In this case, safety is doubly important, as you'll be sliding underneath the car to change the oil, and for that reason, instead of leaving the car on the jack, you will need to use safety stands. When changing oil, it's best to work with a warm but not hot car. Before you jack up the car, drive about a mile to loosen the oil and then let the car cool to a reasonable temperature while you prepare the rest of your tools. Keep in mind that driving the car will make the oil HOT.

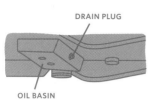

DRAIN PLUG

OIL BASIN

**3 POSITION THE OIL PAN.** Consider putting cardboard under the car, because spilled oil will stain the driveway or garage floor. Place a pan to catch the oil underneath the drain plug. A task-specific oil pan with a spout and screw-tight lid makes transporting and disposing of the used oil much easier. Notice that the plug points out at an angle and place your oil pan appropriately. Slide underneath the car in clothes that you don't mind staining (bring your work gloves).

**4 MANY NEWER CARS INCLUDE** an aerodynamic under-panel that covers the drain plug and oil filter. Before you remove it, look for a small access hatch in the panel. If an under-panel exists with no easy-access hatch, you'll have to remove the panel entirely (at this point, you might want to have your oil changed professionally). You can remove the oil filter cap at the top of the engine to vent the drain so oil flows smoothly instead of

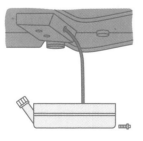

"glugging" out. Use the correct size socket wrench to loosen the drain plug. Wearing gloves, slowly unscrew the last bit by hand. Oil will start to flow. Take this opportunity to check the oil plug washer—the O-shaped gasket that helps the plug form a strong seal. Some plugs have built-in rubber washers that may be ripped or mangled and need replacing. Once all of the oil has drained out, replace the drain plug and tighten with the socket wrench. Do not overtighten or you risk stripping the threads. And don't pour old oil down the drain! Many oil change centers will accept old oil and can properly dispose of it.

**5 LOCATE THE OIL FILTER (IF** needed, check your owner's manual—it may be under the hood). Place an oil pan beneath the filter, as you will almost certainly drip. Loosen the filter with a filter wrench. Once possible, continue to work the filter loose by hand. Eventually, oil will start pouring out around the edges. Hold tight to avoid dropping the filter as you remove it. Use a rag to wipe clean any excess oil or grime and then hand-tighten a new filter in place, likely over an O-ring washer. Once the filter pulls the O-ring in contact with the sealing surface, use muscle power to turn it between three-quarters and one more full rotation. Don't overtighten.

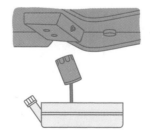

**6 ADD THE NEW OIL.** Double-check that the drain plug and filter are secure before you start to pour. Start by adding one quart less than the recommended amount. Then start the car, let it run for a minute, turn off the engine, wait a few minutes for the oil to cool, and check the oil with the dipstick. Pull out the dipstick, clean it, reinsert the stick, pull it back out and check the bottom of the stick to see how high the oil reaches. The dipstick should have two holes to indicate low and high oil levels. Continue adding oil a bit at a time until the dipstick shows you've reached the proper amount. Continue checking your car's oil on a regular (monthly) basis using this method.

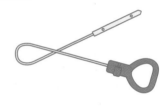

## Pro tip: When replacing an oil filter, coat it with a little bit of oil before twisting it back into place.

# #193
## HOW TO LOCATE AN OIL LEAK

Though a car has a variety of fluids that can potentially leak out (see What's That Puddle Under the Car?, opposite), oil—thick black or brown liquid—is the most common to do so. Depending on the source of the leak, dripping oil can be a quick fix or a major repair. Determining the source can help you gauge the seriousness of the problem. After exhausting the steps in this tutorial, take a car that's leaking oil to the mechanic and cross your fingers.

## TOOLS:

**Work gloves** ▪ **Rags** ▪ **Filter wrench or ratchet** ▪ **Wheel chocks**

## MATERIALS:

- **Engine cleaning solvent**
- **Talcum powder**

**1 BLOCK THE TIRES SECURELY** with wheel chocks. Put the car in park with the emergency brake on, and start the vehicle. Look underneath the car for the source of the leak, but please keep yourself safe—refrain from putting your body under a running vehicle. It's likely that an oil leak from under the car will require attention from a mechanic.

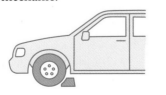

**2 CHECK THE OIL PLUG AND** filter. Because these are the spots you fidget with when changing the oil, they are also the most frequent source of a leak. If you spot a leak in one of these two places, first check that the plug or filter is attached snugly. (See How to Change the Oil, page 380, for safety precautions before diving under the car.) If that doesn't fix the leak, remove the plug and filter to check the integrity of the rubber gaskets. If needed, the gaskets are easy to replace. Note that removing either will release oil, so change into work clothes and have rags handy. (While you're at it, change the oil, if it's due!)

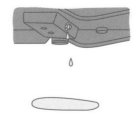

**3 CHECK THE VALVE COVERS.** Many cars with over 30,000 miles on them will develop subtle leaks from the valve cover sealing the top of the engine. Because these leaks tend to attract and trap dirt and grime, they should be obvious once you raise the hood and look around. If you find the leak here, breathe a sigh of relief—valve covers are inexpensive and easy for a pro to replace.

**4 CHECK THE PUMP.** This is a common oil leak location. It's also a leak you want to catch early, as a leaking pump can be diagnostic of a bigger problem, and if the oil pump fails, it will fail to

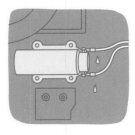

lubricate the bearings in your engine and the system can overheat and seize. Check the seals on either side of the pump to see if they are leaking oil. If you see a leak, oil pump seals are easy to replace. If the pump is leaking, but it's not the seals, you might need a whole new pump.

**5** **DEGREASE THE ENGINE WITH** aerosol cleaning solvent. If the location of a leak isn't immediately obvious, you'll likely need to do some cleaning to spot the problem—if everything's covered in oil, it's impossible to tell where a little extra is coming from. Wearing gloves, use a rag to clean around the valve covers, the engine block, and under the oil pan. If needed, you can get the engine professionally steam-cleaned, after which a leak location should be obvious. If oil appears to be seeping from solid metal, look for tiny cracks, which can be made visible by sprinkling the suspected leak location with talcum powder. Though you may be able to stop very small leaks temporarily with spray-on fluids that are like heavy paints (ask the folks at your local auto-supply store which brands to use), metal with hairline cracks can't spontaneously heal itself. You'll need to replace the parts.

## What's That Puddle Under the Car?

As the human body ages, it's increasingly prone to mysterious pains and pops and odd tweaks—if you can just ignore the discomfort for a couple of days, it generally goes away. The same is not true of your car. Unless you have a minor issue like a pebble in your tire making a clicking noise, your car's minor ailments will likely only get more severe. That's especially true of leaks. A leak won't spontaneously plug itself—you've got to do the plugging yourself. First, though, you have to figure out what's leaking. Fortunately, the fluids inside your car come in a rainbow of hues, making for fairly simple diagnostics. Park your car on top of an old, white sheet and then leave it for a couple of hours or overnight. Then match the color to the list below—and get thee to a mechanic, or an auto-parts shop, right away.

**Red.** Though some newfangled, long-life coolant is red, the rosy fluid leaking from your car is more likely power steering or automatic transmission fluid. It's time to see a mechanic.

**Clear.** A clear fluid might just be water from the condenser on the air conditioner unit, which is not a bad thing. If you've been using the AC recently and the clear fluid seems to come from near the AC, you may not need to do anything about it at all—a little condensation from the AC is perfectly normal. But it might also be power steering fluid, which is bad. Smell to determine which. If it's not water, get to a mechanic.

**Amber.** Do you smell gasoline? If so, the amber fluid is almost certainly a gas leak and it's time to visit a mechanic.

If not, consider the amber liquid yellow or brown. See below for the possible identity of the fluid.

**Green.** Bright green, slippery fluid is coolant, likely dripping from the radiator or engine. Unfortunately, antifreeze tastes good and is toxic to pets, and so the puddle of coolant under your car may be doing harm to more than just your car. Check all the connecting hoses as well as the integrity of the reservoir. If you find an obviously faulty hose or reservoir, you can consider replacing it yourself. If the source of the leak remains elusive, head to the mechanic.

**Blue.** Fluid that's blue is likely leaking from the windshield washing system, either from the reservoir itself or from a punctured or loose hose. Though blue is the most popular washing fluid color, it may also be pink or yellow. Again, if you can find the leaky part, you can evaluate replacing it yourself. If you can't find the leak, take it to a pro.

**Yellow.** Brake fluid starts out yellow and turns brown with time, so your mysterious fluid may actually be somewhere on the yellow/brown spectrum (although keep in mind that solid brown may be an oil leak). For obvious reasons, this is not a fluid leak you should take lightly. If you can test your brakes with no consequences or danger in your driveway, do so, and then drive to the nearest mechanic. If you are at all nervous, have the car towed.

# #194
## HOW TO JUMP A BATTERY

The headlights and interior lights of some cars turn off automatically when the key is removed. In other cars, the lights stay on indefinitely. Combine these mechanical tendencies with the forgetfulness of the human mind, and this means that at some time in your driving life, you'll go to start the car and find that it turns over hesitantly once, and then refuses to do anything but click at you. The battery is dead. Luckily, cars are equipped with an alternator that—as long as it's functioning properly—will recharge your battery once the car is started. Of course, to get it started, you need a power source. That's where jumper cables come in. Nothing brings people together like the need for a jump. Flag down a fellow human or recruit a neighbor, and then follow these steps to ensure that you both emerge from the experience safe and un-jolted.

## TOOLS:

**Jumper cables** ▪ **Wire brush**

**1 MOVE THE CARS INTO POSITION.** Look under the hoods to see where the battery is located in each car. Drive the car with a live battery alongside or in front of the car with the dead battery so that the batteries are close together, or at least close enough so that jumper cables will reach from one to the other.

**2 CONNECT THE TWO BATTERIES** together. It's not difficult to properly connect jumper cables between the live and the dead battery, but it's extremely important to do it right. First, turn both cars off. Locate the positive and negative battery terminals, which should be labeled with + and –. The positive terminal may also be covered by a red cap. Start with the live battery—if the battery terminals are corroded, use a wire brush to scrub free any rust. Then connect the red, positive strand of the jumper cables to the red, positive terminal on the good battery. Move to the dead battery and do the same thing, attaching only the positive jumper cable clip. Then attach the negative, black, clip to the negative terminal on the good battery. It used to be that batteries couldn't help but leak a small amount of flammable acid. It's not such a good idea to have sparks around flammable acid, so in the old days people clipped the negative side of jumper cables to the car's metal frame to ground the current. New batteries almost never leak acid and so this configuration is less important. To be safe, if your battery is more than 15 years old, clip the negative end of the jumper cable to an unpainted section of your car's metal frame (likely underneath); otherwise, clip it to the negative terminal on the dead battery.

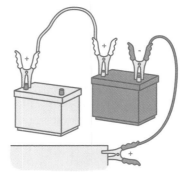

**3** **START THE CAR WITH THE** good battery and leave it running. As soon as you connect the jumper cables, the good battery will start charging the bad one. If the dead battery is really, really dead—that is, turning the key still does absolutely nothing—you may need to let the good battery in the running car feed some charge into the dead battery for a while before trying to start the dead car. Keep trying until it starts.

**4** **WITH THE CARS RUNNING,** disconnect the cables. Though it doesn't matter in what order you disconnect the cables, be sure to keep cable clips from touching each other until you've pulled the clips off at least one of each battery's terminals. If the cables remain connected to both terminals of either battery, and then you touch the other cable ends together, you'll complete a circuit and create some rather exciting fireworks. Don't make fireworks.

**5** **LEAVE THE DEAD CAR RUNNING.** Assuming a depleted battery was the only problem, with the car running, the car's alternator will recharge the battery and no additional action will be required.

## When You Need More than a Jump

**Diagnosing your battery.** After four years your car battery will start its slow fade toward the recycle bin. It might make it a few more years, but be on the lookout for signs of age and nip a fading battery in the bud before it strands you in a downpour. Unfortunately, battery testers offer imperfect diagnoses, as they are unable to tell you how long that battery is likely to *hold* a charge. So get under the hood and check the battery yourself. Remove the case and look for corrosion or leaks. Clean buildup around the terminals with a solution of baking soda and water. Keep in mind that long periods of inactivity, high gadget usage, and living in an extreme climate will all shorten battery life. And if it's been more than four years, err on the side of caution: When in doubt, replace it.

**Signs of a bad starter.** If you have a battery tester, use it to test the battery. Without a battery tester, it's hard to disentangle a dead starter from a dead battery. But if you've properly connected a dead battery to a live one with jumper cables and the car still refuses to start, it's a good bet the starter is to blame. In that case, call up the tow truck.

**It could be the alternator.** Do you notice the lights on electrical components getting dimmer while you're driving? Maybe the gauges are flickering. A warning light in your car should signal ALT or GEN when your alternator's gone south, but you can't always count on it. Instead, it might take a dead battery followed by inability to recharge to diagnose a dead alternator. That said, when you first notice  your battery failing to hold a charge, check the belt running from the alternator to the starter. If it's loose, tighten it by using a socket wrench to loosen the alternator. Push the alternator back until it tightens the belt, and then retighten the alternator bolts to hold it in place. Also check the electrical connections into and out of the alternator to ensure that there are no loose or frayed wires. If everything looks good, then the alternator itself is bad.

# #195
## HOW TO SHARPEN A LAWN MOWER BLADE

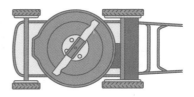

A sharp mower blade will not only help you cut longer, wetter grass, but does so with less damage to the plants. That said, you don't want your blade to be sharpened to the fine edge of a samurai sword, since a lawnmower's blade's soft metal will only dull more quickly and be prone to accumulating notches and dings. Instead, after following the safety procedures below, carefully test the blade with your finger. It should be butter-knife sharp—no more and no less. If it's feeling more like a butter knife's handle than its edge, it's time to sharpen the mower blade.

## TOOLS:

**Socket wrench** ▪ **Ratchet** ▪ **Pipe (optional)** ▪ **Bench vise** ▪ **Metal "mill bastard" file** ▪ **Rags**

## MATERIALS:

- **Newspaper**
- **Scrap 2 × 4**
- **Penetrating oil**
- **Spray paint**

**1 REMOVE THE SPARK PLUG WIRE.** The chances of your lawn mower spontaneously starting while it's tipped on its side are slim—but the penalty is severe. The motion of the engine's pistons triggers subsequent spark plug firing, which in turn powers the next piston, which drives the blade another tick in its circle. If you spin the blade while underneath the mower, you can inadvertently set off this chain of events—moving a piston, releasing a spark, and making the blade buck. Removing the spark plug wire guards against accidental starting and bucking. On most mowers, the short, rubber-coated spark plug wire is the only external wire on the mower. Pull the cap off the plug.

**2 LAY THE MOWER ON ITS SIDE.** Tip the mower onto a layer of newspaper, resting it on the side opposite the carburetor and air filter. This will prevent oil from leaking into the parts that heat up when you mow, so the mower won't belch black smoke when you start it up. Locate the carburetor by the throttle cables running into it.

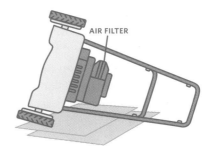

AIR FILTER

**3 LOOSEN THE MOUNTING NUT.** The blade should be held on to the mower by one central nut. And this nut is likely to be an absolute bear to loosen. Wedge a piece of scrap 2 × 4 between the blade and the mower's body to keep the blade from turning while you crank on the mounting nut with the appropriate-sized socket and your longest ratchet. To magnify the torque, slip a length of pipe over the handle of the ratchet. If needed, squirt a stubborn nut with penetrating oil and let it sit for 15 minutes.

**4** **MARK THE BLADE.** Before removing the nut and the blade completely, note which side of the blade was down. It's worth marking the blade with spray paint (or something similar) to avoid reinstalling it upside down.

SPRAY PAINT

**5** **REMOVE THE MOUNTING NUT.** Grip the blade in a bench vise so its flat sides point straight up and down. Stand behind the edge you plan to sharpen and use a metal file held at a shallow angle to sharpen the edge. A long "mill bastard" file works well, which cuts only on the push stroke and so will help you sharpen the blade in the correct direction: with strokes running from the blade's body off the sharp edge. You don't want a razor-sharp edge on the mower blade—stop when the blade could cut butter (but not bread or tomatoes).

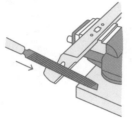

**6** **HANG THE BLADE BY ITS** center hole on a nail. Like a wet blanket in the washing machine, if your mower blade is unbalanced it will make the machine shudder. If the blade tips to one side, use your file or grinder to remove

material from that side. Work with the blade until it hangs from the nail in perfect balance.

**7** **INSPECT AND CLEAN THE** mower. Tipped on its side with the blade removed, it's a perfect time to give the underside of your mower a quick inspection and cleaning. Scrape free any caked-on grass, give it a thorough wipe-down, and consider spray-painting over any rust spots.

**8** **REINSTALL THE BLADE.** Mount the blade with the proper side pointing down and hand tighten the nut. Again, wedge the 2 × 4 against the blade. If the old mounting nut is at all suspect, with gouges in the edges or other rounding, consider replacing it. Use your ratchet and socket to tighten the nut firmly onto the mounting post.

✕ ✕ ✕ ✕ ✕ ✕ ✕ ✕ ✕ ✕ ✕ ✕ ✕ ✕ ✕ ✕ ✕ ✕ ✕ ✕ ✕ ✕ ✕ ✕ ✕ ✕ ✕ ✕ ✕ ✕ ✕ ✕ ✕ ✕ ✕ ✕ ✕ ✕

## IS IT TIME FOR A NEW BLADE?

**I**f you have a good mower, it may outlast the blade. With the blade removed, check for deep dents in the cutting edge. If you can't remove dents or other edge imperfections by filing or grinding, consider replacing the blade. Also check for bends in the blade. It's tempting to hammer a bent blade straight, but this can weaken the metal—it's best to replace it. Look also at the thickness of the metal. Over time, mower blades will simply wear thin. This will certainly happen to the cutting edge, which you'll file back into the thicker part of the blade when sharpening, but the trailing edge can also degrade. This edge has an important function—it's curved slightly upward to create suction that pulls up grass tops for cutting. If the trailing edge has gone thin, replace the blade.

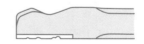

# #196
## HOW TO MAINTAIN A MOTORCYCLE

In the book *Zen and the Art of Motorcycle Maintenance*, author Robert Pirsig wrote that "the place to improve the world is first in one's own heart, head, and hands, and then work outward from there." So consider this section the first step toward a better world. Motorcycles require maintenance, just like cars, but, in the case of motorcycles, the stakes are a bit higher. Fail to maintain your car and you may end up stuck on the side of the freeway. Fail to maintain your motorcycle and you might find *yourself* on the side of the freeway.

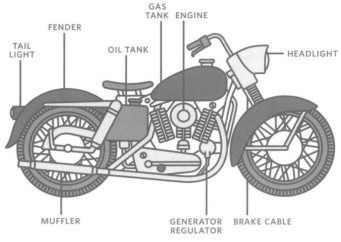

TAIL LIGHT · FENDER · OIL TANK · GAS TANK · ENGINE · HEADLIGHT · MUFFLER · GENERATOR REGULATOR · BRAKE CABLE

## Tires

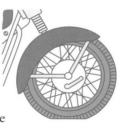

Make a habit of checking your tires before every ride. You don't have to get out the pressure gauge every morning to zip two miles to work, but a quick visual inspection can alert you of likely failures before they occur. Look for punctures like nail or screw heads and shiny shards of glass, and also for bulges or cracks that may turn into holes or slices at high speeds. Air expands as it heats, so if you do check your tire pressure, it won't be the same in your garage as it is on the road. Plan on about 5 percent increase in tire pressure once you're riding. If your tire pressure increases by more than 10 percent while you're riding (stop and check it quickly!), carry less stuff or slow down! Likewise, underinflated tires create more friction against the pavement, which in turn generates more heat, which can result in blowouts. Have a look at the treads—as with car tires (see The Essentials of Tire Maintenance, page 377), when you rest a penny with Lincoln's head down into the tread of a motorcycle tire, the top of the tread should extend past the president's hairline. Also eyeball the wheel for missing spokes and the rims for sharp cracks and dents. Even a small imperfection in a wheel can weaken the integrity of the system.

## Brakes

Braided steel brake lines last longer than plastic-sleeved brake lines and include less play in the system, leading to faster and more durable braking. If you have plastic, consider replacing with steel. Frequently check the lines for kinks, abrasions, and tears, and keep an eye on your brake pads. Letting the brake pads wear down can lead to warped rotors and a much more expensive repair. Motorcycles usually have two brake fluid reservoirs, one for the front brakes and one for the back. Look for the front reservoir in the handlebars and the back reservoir under the saddle. Check them both to ensure that fluid is up to the fill line.

## Chain

It's not difficult to lubricate the chain—just spray it with commercial lubricant. It's best to lubricate at the end of every ride, when the chain is warm. Otherwise, get in the habit of lubricating the chain when you fill up with gas. Spray additional lubricant on the side of the chain that runs against the sprockets. It seems as if the chain should be tight but that's not the case—it needs to sag ¾" to 1¼" to accommodate the movement of the suspension. Make sure the chain has this much play.

## Oil

Too little oil and your bike can seize catastrophically. Too much oil and you can go smoking down the freeway. Check your oil frequently to ensure that the level is always at its maximum—in addition to keeping your bike running smoothly, oil can be indicative of bigger problems. Basically, if you don't know your oil level, you can't be sure you're safe on the road. Always check your oil with the bike sitting level. Note that a motorcycle's oil needs to be changed much more frequently than a car's oil—adhere to the manufacturer's specifications, and when in doubt change the oil at least every 2,000 miles.

## Battery

Car batteries have reached the point of having little required maintenance. Not so with motorcycle batteries. You still need to check the fluid level in each cell, preferably every month. If the level is low, use distilled water to top it off. Also make sure the terminals remain clear of rust and grime and check the cables for loose connections.

## Inspections

Your motorcycle uses less gas than your car but requires more frequent maintenance. Call it a wash? In any case, your bike should be professionally (or very competently DIY) inspected every 3,000 miles.

## Cleaning

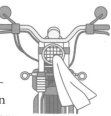

Keeping your car clean is primarily an aesthetic choice, but keeping your bike clean is a safety requirement. Clean the headlights regularly to keep them de-bugged and de-tarred—WD-40 works for this job—and try oven cleaner to remove leather boot marks from exhaust pipes (okay, that one *is* just aesthetic). Unlike on a car, do without the tire polish, as it can compromise the tires' grip (on a motorcycle you're likely to use the rounded sides of the tire more than a car might).

## Fuses and Wiring

Extra fuses should be kept clipped next to the old ones. You may notice the need for a new fuse when your horn refuses to honk . . . or your bike refuses to start. Periodically check the integrity of the fuses to nip these problems in the bud. Likewise check the integrity of your electrical wires. The wiring in your bike shouldn't give you problems—but it almost certainly will, at some point. That's doubly true if you roll down the road with loose connections or wires poking from their sheaths.

**Harley-Davidson, first conceived of in 1901 by William S. Harley, is one of just two American motorcycle companies to survive the Great Depression.**

# #197
# HOW TO FIX A FLAT TIRE ON A BICYCLE

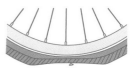

**K**eeping your bike tires properly inflated not only makes for a more efficient ride but also can help you avoid things like the dreaded pinch flat, which happens when an underinflated tire bumps against a curb or rock and squeezes the inner tube against the metal wheel rim, puncturing the tube. But, even with perfect inflation, if you're a bike rider, you'll almost certainly have to fix a flat, either in your garage after a period of disuse or on the side of the road during a ride. Luckily, if you have the right tools, repairing a flat is easy. Without the right tools, it's impossible. Whenever you ride, make sure you carry with you a flat kit including tire levers (also called spoons), a patch kit and new inner tube, and either a pump or a CO2 cartridge with a nozzle matching your valve type (either Presta or Schrader) designed for refilling bike tires.

## THE BICYCLE TOOL KIT

*Patch kit*

*Tire levers*

*Pump with Presta or Schrader nozzles*

*Inner tube*

**1** **RELEASE THE BRAKES.** The pads of most bike brakes sit close to the rim so the tire won't slip through. A small, quick-release lever allows the brake pads to expand to the sides so the tire can be removed. Flip the quick release. Some newer bikes, especially mountain bikes, may be fitted with hydraulic disc brakes. These work just like your car's brakes, and require some model-specific finagling to release when changing the tire. If you have disc brakes, make sure you know what tool you need to release them, and keep it in your kit.

**2** **REMOVE THE WHEEL.** A bike tire is held to the fork or frame by a nut or quick-release lever that clamps onto an end of the axle. If you have a front flat, removing the wheel should be as easy as loosening the lever or nut by hand and pulling off the tire (some bikes have an additional mechanism to guard against tire loss even with the lever or nut loosened). If you have a back tire flat, you'll have to pop the chain free first. Shift the bike so the chain runs along the smallest back-wheel cog. Then flip the bike over, release the axle lever or nut, and push in the bike's derailleur with one hand to make the chain go slack while you lift the wheel free with the other.

**3 DIAGNOSE THE PROBLEM.** Why did your tire go flat? If you fail to find the problem, there's a good chance that something like a thorn stuck in the tire will make a new inner tube go flat, too. Inspect the outside of the tire for punctures, tears, or excessive wear. If you find a thorn, nail, or piece of glass, remove it.

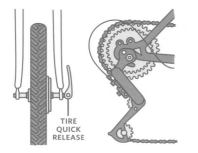

**4 REMOVE THE TIRE.** Let all remaining air out of the inner tube and attempt to slip the tire free of the rim by hand. If that doesn't work, reach for the tire levers

or spoons. Start on a section of tire opposite the valve. Use the long end of the tire lever to pry underneath the tire bead and then pop it to the outside of the wheel rim. If unseating the tire with one lever doesn't allow you to pull the tire off by hand, work in a second lever near the first and pop a longer section of tire free of the rim. Eventually, you should be able to release all of one side of the tire bead. You needn't remove the tire completely from the wheel—just one full edge of the tire so that you can access the inner tube.

**5 REMOVE THE INNER TUBE.** Slide the valve out through the hole in the rim, being careful not to damage the valve with the rim. Then pull the entire inner tube out without damaging it further.

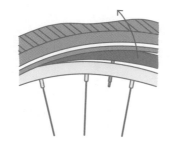

**6 INSPECT THE INNER TUBE.** If there is an obvious gash or other catastrophic tube failure, you'll need to replace the inner tube. If there's a small puncture you can simply patch it, but these

punctures can be hard to spot. If you're at home, submerge the tube in a bathtub or bucket of water and look for bubbles. If you're on the side of the road, run the tube close to your face—look, listen, and feel for escaping air. If you still can't find the puncture, you can try running water from a water bottle along the inner tube—air from the puncture will bubble in the water, making it visible. When you find the puncture, lay the tube against the wheel and explore for matched damage in the tire itself—sometimes the source of a puncture will still be embedded.

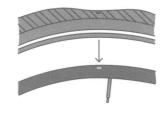

**7 PATCH THE INNER TUBE.** Inner tubes aren't that expensive, so if you have a spare, it's worth simply replacing the tube (see Step 8). If you choose to patch it, follow the patch manufacturer's instructions. Typically, after cleaning and drying the area around a puncture, you'll rough up the surface to help the glue grab, apply the glue, and then apply the patch. If you choose to replace the tube, double-check that your replacement is the right size for your wheel (match the tube specs listed on the box to the wheel specs listed on the rim).

**8** **REPLACE THE INNER TUBE.** With the new tube slightly inflated, reinsert the valve into the hole in the rim. Gently press the inner tube along the rim inside the tire, being careful not to twist the tube or otherwise compromise the path of the tire.

**9** **RESEAT THE TIRE BEAD.** This is the trickiest part, during which a mistake can result in a pinched tube and another chance to practice your tube replacement. Start near the valve and reseat the bead by hand, pressing it into the rim first in one direction and then the other. The more tire bead you seat, the harder it will get, until you're left with a short section of tire opposite the valve that (likely) requires levers to reseat. If possible, use one lever to get the remaining tire back into the rim. If your tire is especially tight, you may need two levers—one to keep the tire bead from slipping off the rim and another to pop in a further section.

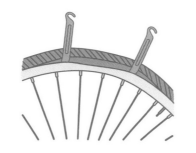

**10** **ONCE YOU'VE SEATED THE** tire bead, double-check that it doesn't pinch the tube. Then use your pump or $CO_2$ canister to inflate the tube to the proper psi (listed on the bike tire).

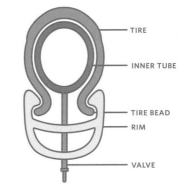

TIRE

INNER TUBE

TIRE BEAD

RIM

VALVE

The modern bicycle has taken many forms since its debut in 1817— from the Velocipede, or "Boneshaker" (the first model with pedals on the front wheel)—to the Penny Farthing, with its enormous front wheel and tiny back wheel.

# #198

## HOW TO ADJUST BICYCLE BRAKES

**B**iking is humankind's most efficient form of transportation—very little energy is lost to friction (as in a car), and unlike running, you can coast sometimes. In part, that's why more than 110 million bikes are produced every year compared to about half that number of cars. To keep bike transportation at maximum efficiency, adjust your brakes so you're not pushing against them as you pedal. Properly adjusting your brakes will also keep them from squealing and shuddering like a tortured animal every time you come to a stop. Here's how to look at and tweak the braking apparatus on your two-wheeled machine.

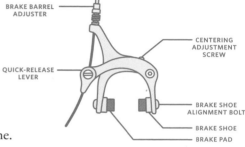

BRAKE BARREL ADJUSTER

CENTERING ADJUSTMENT SCREW

QUICK-RELEASE LEVER

BRAKE SHOE ALIGNMENT BOLT

BRAKE SHOE

BRAKE PAD

## TOOLS:

**Screwdriver ▪ Needle-nose pliers**

## MATERIALS:

▪ **Scrub pad and dish soap (or a degreaser such as WD-40)**

**1 EVALUATE THE BRAKES.** With one tire off the ground, spin it and look at the position of the brakes. In most bikes with cable-pull brakes (as opposed to hydraulic disc brakes), there should be a brake pad on either side of the wheel rims. The pads should be positioned so, when closed, they grip the rim without contacting the tire rubber or touching each other. (Rubbing against the tire can cause a catastrophic flat, and exposed pads will accumulate dirt and gunk.)

Most brakes are made of two levers connected by wire—the levers should be centered so they sit at the same angle relative to the wheel and the pads are a uniform distance from the rim—you don't want one pad in contact with the rim while the other pad sits far away. Finally, brake pads

should sit so that they are slightly "pigeon-toed" in front; with the brake applied lightly, the front of the pad should contact the rim slightly before the back. When you squeeze tighter, the pad should flatten against the rim. This keeps the brakes from squeaking.

×××××××××××××××××××××××××××××××××××××××××

## SIDE-PULL VERSUS CENTER-PULL BRAKES

**T**here are a couple of configurations of cable-pull brakes. Most common are center-pull, in which one cable reaches straight in between two calipers, at which point the cable splits into a triangle in order to pull both calipers. You may also find side-pull brakes, in which one cable extends down the side of a horseshoe-shaped piece opposite a straight arm. Neither is necessarily better than the other and both work by essentially the same mechanism, but depending on your brake type, you may have to slightly adjust the instructions in this section.

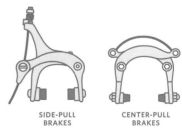

SIDE-PULL BRAKES

CENTER-PULL BRAKES

**2** **CENTER THE BRAKES.** If your brakes aren't centered, one pad may rub against the rim even when the brake is released, while the other pad sits too far away to reach the rim even when the brake is applied. First, check to see if the position of the wheel might be the problem—if the wheel is slightly tilted it will push closer to one caliper than the other. If it's not the wheel, it's the brakes. First try twisting the calipers back to the center to see if the brake pads stay appropriately centered. If that doesn't work, unhook the cable and test each arm independently to see if one side pulls more strongly than the other. Rust or grime may be restricting or affecting the movement of the levers—if so, clean them using a scrub pad and a little soapy water (or a degreaser such as WD-40). Then reassemble the brake arms and, with them centered,

tighten down the pivot bolt to hold them in place. If you remove and reinstall brakes and they still grab your tire, it's time for a trip to the bike shop.

**3** **ADJUST THE CABLES.** Lackluster braking may not be due to the pads—it could be improper cable adjustment. A cable adjustment barrel may be located at either end of the brake cable, most likely where the cable enters the handbrake. Using pliers if necessary, turn the adjustment barrel to gently adjust the length of the brake cable.

If both brake calipers are contacting the wheel rim even when you're not squeezing the brake, the cable is overall too tight—after ensuring that the cable is running along its proper path without obstruction (and without the handlebars facing straight ahead), use a screwdriver to turn the brake adjustment barrel to loosen the cable. If the brake calipers sit so far away from the rim that engaging the brake fails to make the pads grab the rim, turn the adjustment barrel in the opposite direction to shorten the cable. Note that there are also adjustment barrels for shifting cables—don't adjust the wrong ones!

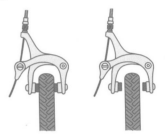

×××××××××××××××××××××××××××××××××××××××××××××

# IF THE BRAKES STILL SQUEAL . . .

**W**hile there are many things that can cause squealing brakes, the mechanics that create the squeal are the same in all cases: The brake pad grabs the rim, bending the caliper slightly forward, at which point the caliper pulls against the pad and jumps backward to continue the cycle—enough of this minor vibration at high speeds creates the sound you know and don't love. To eliminate the noise, start by cleaning the rims with rubbing alcohol or a citrus solvent. If that doesn't stop the noise, try using pliers (or your hands) to very slightly bend your brake calipers so the pads point slightly in toward the front (pigeon-toed). This keeps the brakes from contacting the rims along the length of the pad with a light squeeze, but allows them to flatten against the rims with a stronger pull. You may also be able to adjust how easily your brakes pivot open to release from the rim. Try playing with the strength of this pivot by adjusting the tightness of the nut that holds on the pivot, tightening or loosening to see if it affects the squeal. Finally, try replacing the brake pads. New pads, or even another model, may play better with your rims.

FRONT WHEEL

**4** **ADJUST THE BRAKE HANDLES.** There might be a screw in the brake handle used to adjust the position of the handle itself. If you have especially large or small hands, turn this screw to adjust the openness of the brake handle to suit your grip, and then use the cable adjustment barrel to properly position the brake cable accordingly.

# #199
# HOW TO MAINTAIN A BICYCLE CHAIN

**W**hile brakes and tires get all the attention, bicycle chains are often neglected. But in fact, chain maintenance should be at the top of your bike upkeep list. Because the chain passes through so many of the bike's other moving parts, including the gears and derailleurs, a little dirt on the chain can turn into a big problem. Over time, a dirty chain will not only deteriorate, but also impact the function of the entire drivetrain.

## TOOLS:

**Old toothbrush ▪ Bicycle chain tool ▪ Wire brush ▪ Rags ▪ Pliers ▪ Permanent marker**

## MATERIALS:

- **Chain lubricant**
- **Simple Green, citrus solvent, or bike-specific solvent**
- **WD-40**

**1 SPOT-CHECK THE CHAIN.** As part of your pre-ride checklist, eyeball the chain for problems. Listen for squeaks that can signal rusted links, and look for other dirt buildup or links that don't seem to smoothly swivel. If you find localized dirt, brush it out with an old toothbrush and apply a drop of chain lubricant.

**2 DEEP-CLEAN THE CHAIN** periodically. If you're riding regularly, clean it about every three months—more if you're riding in harsh conditions. Start by noting the path of the chain, taking a picture to help you remember how to reinstall it. Use a bicycle chain tool to break the chain at any point. Set the chain into the tool and tighten the tool's screw. This should drive a small bar into the center of the pin connecting the chain links, and drive the pin out the other side. Remove the chain from the bike and aggressively clean it with a wire brush. Soak the chain in a bike-specific solvent until most of the visible grime floats free, about 30 minutes. Dry the chain and allow the solvent to fully evaporate. Reinstall the chain, using the chain tool to reinsert the pin you removed.

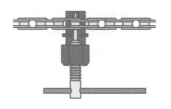

**3 LUBRICATE THE CHAIN.** Prop up the bike so that the back tire spins freely. With the chain installed on the bicycle, mark one link with a permanent marker so you know when you've cycled through all the links. Place a small drop of chain lube at each chain junction, stopping when you cycle through to the marked link. Turn the pedals for a couple of minutes to work the lube in between the links. Then hold a rag loosely around the chain and turn the pedals to drive the chain through the rag a couple of times. Any lubricant left on the surface of the chain will trap dirt and grime.

**4** **FIX FUSED OR RUSTED LINKS.** If your bike has been under a tarp out behind the garden shed for the winter or if you've kept an imperfect eye on the condition of your chain, the next time you ride, you may notice a disturbing bump every time the chain passes over one or the other gear. Most likely this is a fused link refusing to bend or straighten. You may be able to spray a fused link with some WD-40 and use pliers to wiggle it back into pliability. Also check the pins—a protruding pin can inhibit movement, and is easily fixed with a chain tool or even by laying the chain flat and using a nail to drive a loose link back into its hole. You'll eventually need to replace a fused link—do it with a chain tool. That said, if your chain is rusted to the point of fused links, consider replacing the entire chain.

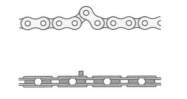

# #200 HOW TO TIGHTEN A SINGLE-SPEED CHAIN

On kids' bikes or any single-speed bike without a derailleur, adjusting the chain tension requires either resizing the chain or adjusting the position of the back wheel.

## TOOLS:

**Wrench • Chain tool**

**1** **CHECK THE TENSION.** Push down on the chain in the middle of its top length. A properly tensioned chain will bend down about an inch from its starting height.

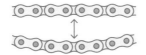

**2** **MOVE THE WHEEL.** If it bends just a bit more than an inch, use a wrench to loosen the nuts that hold the back wheel in place and slide the wheel slightly farther back along its

mounting channels. Retighten the nuts and check the chain tension again.

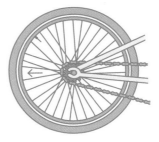

**3** **REMOVE LINKS.** If the chain pushes down 2 inches or more from its starting height, pushing back the back wheel won't be enough to pull the chain taut. In that case, remove the chain with a chain tool (see also Step 4 in How to Maintain a Bicycle Chain, left).

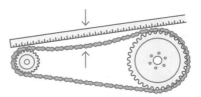

✕✕✕✕✕✕✕✕✕✕✕✕✕✕✕✕✕✕✕✕✕✕✕✕✕✕✕✕✕✕✕✕✕✕✕✕✕✕

# MANAGING CHAIN STRETCH

Chains don't actually stretch. What riders and bike mechanics call chain stretch is actually the chain metal wearing to the point that it develops play, or movement, around the pins. Enough play around enough pins can lead to a loose chain—one in which each link is a little longer than the manufacturer of the gears intended. This "stretched" chain can round the teeth of the gears, eventually necessitating that you replace the cog set. Rather than pulling a link or two to return it to its original length, replace it. A new chain costs less than new gears.

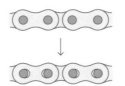

# #201
## HOW TO ALIGN BICYCLE GEARS
### (or, Advanced Bicycle Maintenance)

On older bikes, shifting is usually done with a lever that allows you to run smoothly between the gears. This old system allowed you to fine-tune the position of derailleurs to ensure that the chain ran smoothly no matter what gear you were in. Most newer bikes include twist or click shifters, in which one notch equals one gear. It's much easier to shift gears this way—but it means your notches have to be adjusted properly to ensure that one click

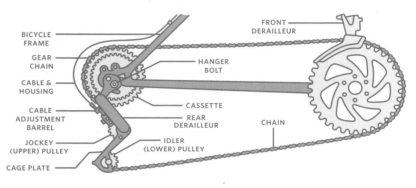

does, in fact, equal one change in gear. Whether your bike is new or old, if your chain is clicking or rattling while you ride, if shifting results in no change or slipping through multiple gears, or if the chain frequently pops off when you shift, it's time to align your gears. (Technically, this part of the bike is a cog, but as a unit, they're often called "gears.")

## ✕ ✕ ✕ ✕ ✕ ✕ ✕ ✕ ✕ ✕ ✕ ✕ ✕ ✕ ✕ ✕ ✕
## PREVENTING CHAIN RUB

Chain rub happens when your bicycle chain gets stuck between the inner ring and the chainstay. To prevent it, try these tips:

- Make sure the chain is lubricated.

- Ease up when shifting.

- Replace worn teeth as needed.

## TOOLS:

**Screwdriver • Ruler • Needle-nose pliers • Rags**

## MATERIALS:

- **Bike cable**
- **Chain lubricant**

**1 SET THE DERAILLEUR RANGE.** To adjust your gears, you must set the window in which your derailleur works—if the derailleur allows the chain to move too high it may pop off the largest gear, too low and it might pop off the smallest. First locate the limit screws. On most bikes, the front limit screws will be very near the gears, attached to a near vertical post on the bike's frame. There should be two Phillips head screws side by side (sometimes they are labeled "L" and "H"). The inner screw (away from the gears) is likely the "low" limit screw—adjust it so the inner plate of the chain guide is about 4 millimeters past the

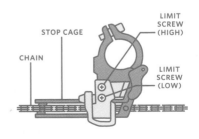

inner edge of the smallest gear. Do the same with the other limit screw, which controls how high or to the outside the chain can travel, so that the inner plate of the chain guide is about 4 millimeters past the largest gear. Do the same with the limit screws in the back.

**2 IF NEEDED, ADJUST THE GEAR** cable. A derailleur cable runs from your shifter, through a plastic sleeve, to the derailleur. If your derailleur doesn't have enough range, you may need to adjust the cable. Most cables have an anchor bolt on one end that's bigger in diameter than the cable to keep it in place. Pull the end of the cable with pliers to add tension to the cable, or loosen the anchor bolt to give it more slack.

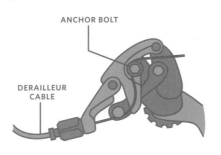

ANCHOR BOLT

DERAILLEUR CABLE

**3 CHECK THE POSITION OF THE** limit screws and derailleur cages. With the chain running on the largest gear, the cage should be 2 millimeters outside the chain. Likewise, with the chain running on the smallest gear, the opposite cage should be 2 millimeters inside the chain. If you have gears in the front and back, check the limit screws in both locations.

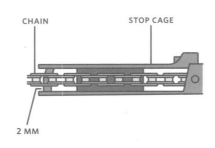

CHAIN          STOP CAGE

2 MM

**4 CHECK THE CABLE TENSION.** The indexing (the way a shifter scrolls through gears) of modern twist or click shifters may need to be fine-tuned. You can do this by adjusting the tension of the cable. Look under the shifter where the cable enters the plastic housing. There should be a twist nut, called a barrel adjuster. Turning this adjuster by hand will slightly change the

length of the plastic housing and so the tension of the wire within. Set the chain on the smallest gear. Then, with the bike's back tire off the ground, run the pedals and shift exactly one click. If the chain doesn't shift accurately to the next larger gear, turn the barrel adjuster to fine-tune the tension. The cable should be straight, no slack, and you should be able to tension it with your fingers. Do this for all gears, both front and back if needed. Once your gears are properly adjusted, the moving chain shouldn't scrape against the gears. It may take minute turns of the barrel adjusters to get the chain running perfectly.

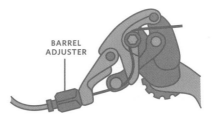

BARREL ADJUSTER

**5 LUBRICATE THE CHAIN.** Once the gears are running smoothly, spray them with chain lubricant and wipe off any excess with a rag.

# INDEX

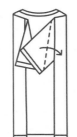

# CONVERSION TABLES

## INCHES TO CENTIMETERS

| | | | |
|---|---|---|---|
| ½ | = 1.3 | 9 | = 22.9 |
| 1 | = 2.5 | 9½ | = 24.1 |
| 1½ | = 3.8 | 10 | = 25.4 |
| 2 | = 5.1 | 11 | = 27.9 |
| 2½ | = 6.4 | 12 | = 30.5 |
| 3 | = 7.6 | 13 | = 33.0 |
| 3½ | = 8.9 | 14 | = 35.6 |
| 4 | = 10.2 | 15 | = 38.1 |
| 4½ | = 11.4 | 16 | = 40.6 |
| 5 | = 12.7 | 17 | = 43.2 |
| 5½ | = 14.0 | 18 | = 45.7 |
| 6 | = 15.2 | 19 | = 48.3 |
| 6½ | = 16.5 | 20 | = 50.8 |
| 7 | = 17.8 | 21 | = 53.3 |
| 7½ | = 19.1 | 22 | = 55.9 |
| 8 | = 20.3 | 23 | = 58.4 |
| 8½ | = 21.6 | 24 | = 61.0 |

## FEET TO METERS

| | |
|---|---|
| 1 | = .304 |
| 1½ | = .456 |
| 2 | = .608 |
| 2½ | = .760 |
| 3 | = .912 |
| 3½ | = 1.064 |
| 4 | = 1.216 |
| 4½ | = 1.368 |
| 5 | = 1.520 |

**Use these formulas for precise conversions:**

inches x 2.54 = centimeters          feet x .304 = meters

## APPROXIMATE EQUIVALENTS

1 stick butter = 8 tbs = 4 oz = ½ cup = 115 g
1 cup all-purpose, pre-sifted flour = 4.7 oz
1 cup granulated sugar = 8 oz = 220 g
1 cup (firmly packed) brown sugar = 6 oz = 220 g to 230 g
1 cup confectioners' sugar = 4½ oz = 115 g
1 cup honey or syrup = 12 oz
1 cup grated cheese = 4 oz
1 cup dried beans = 6 oz
1 large egg = about 2 oz or about 3 tbs
1 egg yolk = about 1 tbs
1 egg white = about 2 tbs

Please note that all conversions are approximate but close enough to be useful when converting from one system to another.

## OVEN TEMPERATURES

| °F | GAS MARK | °C | °F | GAS MARK | °C |
|---|---|---|---|---|---|
| 250 | ½ | 120 | 400 | 6 | 200 |
| 275 | 1 | 140 | 425 | 7 | 220 |
| 300 | 2 | 150 | 450 | 8 | 230 |
| 325 | 3 | 160 | 475 | 9 | 240 |
| 350 | 4 | 180 | 500 | 10 | 260 |
| 375 | 5 | 190 | | | |

Note: Reduce the temperature by 20°C (36°F) for fan-assisted ovens.

## LIQUID CONVERSIONS

| US | IMPERIAL | METRIC |
|---|---|---|
| 2 tbs | 1 fl oz | 30 ml |
| 3 tbs | 1½ fl oz | 45 ml |
| ¼ cup | 2 fl oz | 60 ml |
| ⅓ cup | 2½ fl oz | 75 ml |
| ⅓ cup + 1 tbs | 3 fl oz | 90 ml |
| ⅓ cup + 2 tbs | 3½ fl oz | 100 ml |
| ½ cup | 4 fl oz | 125 ml |
| ⅔ cup | 5 fl oz | 150 ml |
| ¾ cup | 6 fl oz | 175 ml |
| ¾ cup + 2 tbs | 7 fl oz | 200 ml |
| 1 cup | 8 fl oz | 250 ml |
| 1 cup + 2 tbs | 9 fl oz | 275 ml |
| 1¼ cups | 10 fl oz | 300 ml |
| 1⅓ cups | 11 fl oz | 325 ml |
| 1½ cups | 12 fl oz | 350 ml |
| 1⅔ cups | 13 fl oz | 375 ml |
| 1¾ cups | 14 fl oz | 400 ml |
| 1¾ cups + 2 tbs | 15 fl oz | 450 ml |
| 2 cups (1 pint) | 16 fl oz | 500 ml |
| 2½ cups | 20 fl oz (1 pint) | 600 ml |
| 3¾ cups | 1½ pints | 900 ml |
| 4 cups | 1¾ pints | 1 liter |

## WEIGHT CONVERSIONS

| U.S./U.K. | METRIC | U.S./U.K. | METRIC |
|---|---|---|---|
| ½ oz | 15 g | 7 oz | 200 g |
| 1 oz | 30 g | 8 oz | 250 g |
| 1½ oz | 45 g | 9 oz | 275 g |
| 2 oz | 60 g | 10 oz | 300 g |
| 2½ oz | 75 g | 11 oz | 325 g |
| 3 oz | 90 g | 12 oz | 350 g |
| 3½ oz | 100 g | 13 oz | 375 g |
| 4 oz | 125 g | 14 oz | 400 g |
| 5 oz | 150 g | 15 oz | 450 g |
| 6 oz | 175 g | 1 lb | 500 g |